Communications in Computer and Information Science 1653

More information about this series at https://link.springer.com/bookseries/7899

Costin Bădică · Jan Treur · Djamal Benslimane ·
Bogumiła Hnatkowska ·
Marek Krótkiewicz (Eds.)

Advances in Computational Collective Intelligence

14th International Conference, ICCCI 2022
Hammamet, Tunisia, September 28–30, 2022
Proceedings

 Springer

Editors
Costin Bădică 🆔
University of Craiova
Craiova, Romania

Djamal Benslimane 🆔
Claude Bernard University Lyon 1
Villeurbanne Cedex, France

Marek Krótkiewicz 🆔
Wrocław University of Science
and Technology
Wrocław, Poland

Jan Treur 🆔
Vrije Universiteit Amsterdam
Amsterdam, The Netherlands

Bogumiła Hnatkowska 🆔
Wrocław University of Science
and Technology
Wrocław, Poland

ISSN 1865-0929   ISSN 1865-0937 (electronic)
Communications in Computer and Information Science
ISBN 978-3-031-16209-1   ISBN 978-3-031-16210-7 (eBook)
https://doi.org/10.1007/978-3-031-16210-7

This Springer imprint is published by the registered company Springer Nature Switzerland AG
The registered company address is: Gewerbestrasse 11, 6330 Cham, Switzerland

Preface

This volume contains the second part of the proceedings of the 14th International Conference on Computational Collective Intelligence (ICCCI 2022), held in Hammamet, Tunisia, during 28–30 September, 2022. Due to the COVID-19 pandemic, the conference was organized in a hybrid mode which allowed for both on-site and online paper presentations. The conference was hosted by the French SIGAPP Chapter (ACM Special Interest Group on Applied Computing), France, and organized by Wrocław University of Science and Technology, Poland, in cooperation with the IEEE SMC Technical Committee on Computational Collective Intelligence, the European Research Center for Information Systems (ERCIS), the Université de Pau et des Pays de l'Adour, France, the Université de Jendouba, Tunisia, and the International University, VNU-HCM, Vietnam.

Following the successes of the previous conferences held in Wrocław, Poland (2009), Kaohsiung, Taiwan (2010), Gdynia, Poland (2011), Ho Chi Minh City, Vietnam (2012), Craiova, Romania (2013), Seoul, South Korea (2014), Madrid, Spain (2015), Halkidiki, Greece (2016), Nicosia, Cyprus (2017), Bristol, UK (2018), Hendaye, France (2019), Da Nang, Vietnam (2020), and Rhodes, Greece (2021), this conference continued to provide an internationally respected forum for scientific research in the computer-based methods of collective intelligence and their applications.

Computational collective intelligence (CCI) is most often understood as a subfield of artificial intelligence (AI) dealing with soft computing methods that facilitate group decisions or processing knowledge among autonomous units acting in distributed environments. Methodological, theoretical, and practical aspects of CCI are considered as the form of intelligence that emerges from the collaboration and competition of many individuals (artificial and/or natural). The application of multiple computational intelligence technologies such as fuzzy systems, evolutionary computation, neural systems, consensus theory, etc., can support human and other collective intelligence, and create new forms of CCI in natural and/or artificial systems. Three subfields of the application of computational intelligence technologies to support various forms of collective intelligence are of special interest but are not exclusive: the Semantic Web (as an advanced tool for increasing collective intelligence), social network analysis (as a field targeted at the emergence of new forms of CCI), and multi-agent systems (as a computational and modeling paradigm especially tailored to capture the nature of CCI emergence in populations of autonomous individuals).

The ICCCI 2022 conference featured a number of keynote talks and oral presentations, closely aligned to the theme of the conference. The conference attracted a substantial number of researchers and practitioners from all over the world, who submitted their papers for the main track and 11 special sessions.

The main track, covering the methodology and applications of CCI, included knowledge engineering and the Semantic Web, recommender systems, collective decision-making, data mining and machine learning, computer vision techniques, and natural language processing, as well as the Internet of Things (IoT) technologies and applications. The special sessions, covering some specific topics of particular interest, included cooperative strategies for decision making and optimization, optimization approaches of production systems in Industries 4.0 and 5.0, collective intelligence in medical applications, IoT, deep learning and natural language processing, computational collective intelligence, computational intelligence for multimedia understanding, machine learning for social data analytics, malware analytics in smart environment, big text mining searching, and artificial intelligence.

We received over 420 papers submitted by authors coming from 46 countries around the world. Each paper was reviewed by at least three members of the international Program Committee (PC) of either the main track or one of the special sessions. Finally, we selected 66 papers for oral presentation and publication in one volume of the Lecture Notes in Artificial Intelligence series and 58 papers for oral presentation and publication in one volume of the Communications in Computer and Information Science series.

We would like to express our thanks to the keynote speakers: Grigorios Tsoumakas from the Aristotle University of Thessaloniki, Greece; Sören Auer, Director and Head of the research group Data Science and Digital Libraries at the TIB – Leibniz Information Centre for Science and Technology and University Library, Germany; Jahna Otterbacher from the Open University of Cyprus and CYENS Centre of Excellence, Cyprus; and Grzegorz J. Nalepa from Jagiellonian University, Poland, for their world-class plenary speeches.

Many people contributed toward the success of the conference. First, we would like to recognize the work of the PC co-chairs and special sessions organizers for taking good care of the organization of the reviewing process, an essential stage in ensuring the high quality of the accepted papers. The workshop and special session chairs deserve a special mention for the evaluation of the proposals and the organization and coordination of 11 special sessions. In addition, we would like to thank the PC members, of the main track and of the special sessions, for performing their reviewing work with diligence. We thank the Local Organizing Committee chairs, publicity chair, Web chair, and technical support chair for their fantastic work before and during the conference. Finally, we cordially thank all the authors, presenters, and delegates for their valuable contributions to this successful event. The conference would not have been possible without their support.

Our special thanks are also due to Springer for publishing the proceedings and to all the other sponsors for their kind support.

It is our pleasure to announce that the ICCCI conference series continues to have a close cooperation with the Springer journal Transactions on Computational Collective Intelligence and the IEEE SMC Technical Committee on Transactions on Computational Collective Intelligence.

Finally, we hope that ICCCI 2022 contributed significantly to the academic excellence of the field and will lead to the even greater success of ICCCI events in the future.

September 2022

Ngoc Thanh Nguyen
Yannis Manolopoulos
Richard Chbeir
Adrianna Kozierkiewicz
Bogdan Trawiński

Organization

Organizing Committee

Honorary Chair

Arkadiusz Wójs   Wroclaw University of Science and Technology, Poland

General Chairs

Ngoc Thanh Nguyen   Wroclaw University of Science and Technology, Poland

Yannis Manolopoulos   Open University of Cyprus, Cyprus

Program Chairs

Richard Chbeir   University of Pau and Adour Countries, France
Costin Badica   University of Craiova, Romania
Jan Treur   Vrije Universiteit Amsterdam, The Netherlands
Djamal Benslimane   University of Lyon, France

Steering Committee

Ngoc Thanh Nguyen   Wroclaw University of Science and Technology, Poland
Piotr Jędrzejowicz   Gdynia Maritime University, Poland
Shyi-Ming Chen   National Taiwan University of Science and Technology, Taiwan
Kiem Hoang   University of Information Technology, VNU-HCM, Vietnam
Dosam Hwang   Yeungnam University, South Korea
Lakhmi C. Jain   University of South Australia, Australia
Geun-Sik Jo   Inha University, South Korea
Janusz Kacprzyk   Systems Research Institute, Polish Academy of Sciences, Poland
Ryszard Kowalczyk   Swinburne University of Technology, Australia
Yannis Manolopoulos   Open University of Cyprus, Cyprus
Toyoaki Nishida   Kyoto University, Japan
Manuel Núñez   Universidad Complutense de Madrid, Spain
Klaus Söilen   Halmstad University, Sweden
Khoa Tien Tran   International University, VNU-HCM, Vietnam

Special Session Chairs

Bogdan Trawiński   Wroclaw University of Science and Technology,
                                    Poland
Salma Sassi   Université de Jendouba, Tunisia
Bogumiła Hnatkowska   Wroclaw University of Science and Technology,
                                    Poland
Adrianna Kozierkiewicz   Wroclaw University of Science and Technology,
                                    Poland

Doctoral Track Chairs

Marek Krótkiewicz   Wroclaw University of Science and Technology,
                                    Poland
Elio Mansour   University of Pau and Adour Countries, France

Organizing Chairs

Krystian Wojtkiewicz   Wroclaw University of Science and Technology,
                                    Poland
Anis Tassaoui   Université de Jendouba, Tunisia
Abderrazek Jemai   Université de Jendouba, Tunisia
Adrianna Kozierkiewicz   Wroclaw University of Science and Technology,
                                    Poland

Publicity Chairs

Karam Bou Chaaya   University of Pau and Adour Countries, France
Farouzi Mhamdi   Université de Jendouba, Tunisia

Webmaster

Marek Kopel   Wroclaw University of Science and Technology,
                                    Poland

Local Organizing Committee

Ahmed Dridi   Université de Jendouba, Tunisia
Sami Zghal   Université de Jendouba, Tunisia
Ahmed Khemiri   Université de Jendouba, Tunisia
Amani Drissi   Université de Jendouba, Tunisia
Marcin Jodłowiec   Wroclaw University of Science and Technology,
                                    Poland
Rafal Palak   Wroclaw University of Science and Technology,
                                    Poland
Patient Zihisire Muke   Wroclaw University of Science and Technology,
                                    Poland

Keynote Speakers

Grigorios Tsoumakas	Aristotle University of Thessaloniki, Greece
Sören Auer	Leibniz University of Hannover, Germany
Jahna Otterbacher	Open University of Cyprus and CYENS Centre of Excellence, Cyprus
Grzegorz J. Nalepa	Jagiellonian University, Poland

Special Session Organizers

BDAIH 2022: Special Session on Big Data and Artificial Intelligence in Healthcare

Sami Naouali	Military Academy, Tunisia
Chihebeddine Romdhani	University of Tunis El Manar, Tunisia
Semeh Ben Salem	Military Academy, Tunisia

BigTMS&AI 2022: Special Session on Big Text Mining Searching and Artificial Intelligence

Rim Faiz	University of Carthage, Tunisia
Seifeddine Mechti	University of Sfax, Tunsia

CCINLP 2022: Special Session on Computational Collective Intelligence and Natural Language Processing

Ismail Biskri	University of Québec à Trois-Rivières, Canada
Nadia Ghazzali	University of Québec à Trois-Rivières, Canada

CSDMO 2022: Special Session on Cooperative Strategies for Decision Making and Optimization

Piotr Jędrzejowicz	Gdynia Maritime University, Poland
Dariusz Barbucha	Gdynia Maritime University, Poland
Ireneusz Czarnowski	Gdynia Maritime University, Poland

DLANLP 2022: Special Session on Deep Learning for Arabic Natural Language Processing

Mounir Zrigui	University of Monastir, Tunisia
Sadek Mansouri	University of Monastir, Tunisia

FAITSIT 2022: Special Session on Formal and Artificial Intelligence Techniques for Service and Internet of Things

Mohamed Graiet   University of Monastir, Tunisia
Mohamed Tahar Bhiri   University of Sfax, Tunisia
Lazhar Hamel   University of Monastir, Tunisia

Innov-Healthcare 2022: Special Session on Innovative use of Machine Learning and Deep Learning for Healthcare Empowerment

Yassine Ben Ayed   University of Sfax, Tunisia
Wael Ouarda   Ministry of Higher Education and Scientific
                          Research, Tunisia

IWCIM 2022: International Workshop on Computational Intelligence for Multimedia Understanding

Davide Moroni   National Research Council of Italy, Italy
Maria Trocan   Institut Supérieur d'Électronique de Paris, France
Behçet Uğur Töreyin   Istanbul Technical University, Turkey

MASE 2022: Special Session on Malware Analytics in Smart Environments

Maha Driss   University of Manouba, Tunisia
Iman Almomani   Prince Sultan University, Saudi Arabia
Wadii Boulila   Prince Sultan University, Saudi Arabia
Anis Koubaa   Prince Sultan University, Saudi Arabia

ML-SDA 2022: Special Session on Machine Learning for Social Data Analytics

Salma Jamoussi   University of Sfax, Tunisia
Hanen Ameur   University of Sfax, Tunisia
Hasna Njah   University of Gabes, Tunisia

OAPSI 2022: Special Session on Optimization Approaches of Production Systems in Industries 4.0 and 5.0

Olfa Belkahla Driss   University of Manouba, Tunisia
Houssem Eddine Nouri   University of Gabes, Tunisia
Ouajdi Korbaa   University of Sousse, Tunisia

Senior Program Committee

Plamen Angelov	Lancaster University, UK
Costin Badica	University of Craiova, Romania
Nick Bassiliades	Aristotle University of Thessaloniki, Greece
Maria Bielikova	Slovak University of Technology in Bratislava, Slovakia
Abdelhamid Bouchachia	Bournemouth University, UK
David Camacho	Universidad Autonoma de Madrid, Spain
Richard Chbeir	University of Pau and Pays de l'Adour, France
Shyi-Ming Chen	National Taiwan University of Science and Technology, Taiwan
Paul Davidsson	Malmo University, Sweden
Mohamed Gaber	Birmingham City University, UK
Daniela Godoy	ISISTAN Research Institute, Argentina
Manuel Grana	University of the Basque Country, Spain
William Grosky	University of Michigan, USA
Francisco Herrera	University of Granada, Spain
Tzung-Pei Hong	National University of Kaohsiung, Taiwan
Dosam Hwang	Yeungnam University, South Korea
Lazaros Iliadis	Democritus University of Thrace, Greece
Mirjana Ivanovic	University of Novi Sad, Serbia
Piotr Jedrzejowicz	Gdynia Maritime University, Poland
Geun-Sik Jo	Inha University, South Korea
Kang-Hyun Jo	University of Ulsan, South Korea
Janusz Kacprzyk	Systems Research Institute, Polish Academy of Sciences, Poland
Ryszard Kowalczyk	Swinburne University of Technology, Australia
Ondrej Krejcar	University of Hradec Kralove, Czech Republic
Hoai An Le Thi	University of Lorraine, France
Edwin Lughofer	Johannes Kepler University Linz, Austria
Yannis Manolopoulos	Aristotle University of Thessaloniki, Greece
Grzegorz J. Nalepa	AGH University of Science and Technology, Poland
Toyoaki Nishida	Kyoto University, Japan
Manuel Núñez	Universidad Complutense de Madrid, Spain
George A. Papadopoulos	University of Cyprus, Cyprus
Radu-Emil Precup	Politehnica University of Timisoara, Romania
Leszek Rutkowski	Częstochowa University of Technology, Poland
Tomasz M. Rutkowski	University of Tokyo, Japan
Ali Selamat	Universiti Teknologi Malaysia, Malaysia
Edward Szczerbicki	University of Newcastle, Australia

Ryszard Tadeusiewicz	AGH University of Science and Technology, Poland
Muhammad Atif Tahir	National University of Computer and Emerging Sciences, Pakistan
Jan Treur	Vrije Universiteit Amsterdam, The Netherlands
Serestina Viriri	University of KwaZulu-Natal, South Africa
Bay Vo	Ho Chi Minh City University of Technology, Vietnam
Gottfried Vossen	University of Münster, Germany
Lipo Wang	Nanyang Technological University, Singapore
Michał Woźniak	Wrocław University of Science and Technology, Poland
Farouk Yalaoui	University of Technology of Troyes, France
Slawomir Zadrozny	Systems Research Institute, Polish Academy of Sciences, Poland

Program Committee

Muhammad Abulaish	South Asian University, India
Sharat Akhoury	University of Cape Town, South Africa
Bashar Al-Shboul	University of Jordan, Jordan
Stuart Allen	Cardiff University, UK
Adel Alti	University of Setif, Algeria
Taha Arbaoui	University of Technology of Troyes, France
Mehmet Emin Aydin	University of the West of England, UK
Thierry Badard	Laval University, Canada
Amelia Badica	University of Craiova, Romania
Paulo Batista	Universidade de Évora, Portugal
Khalid Benali	University of Lorraine, France
Szymon Bobek	Jagiellonian University, Poland
Leon Bobrowski	Bialystok University of Technology, Poland
Grzegorz Bocewicz	Koszalin University of Technology, Poland
Peter Brida	University of Zilina, Slovakia
Ivana Bridova	University of Zilina, Slovakia
Krisztian Buza	Budapest University of Technology and Economics, Hungary
Aleksander Byrski	AGH University of Science and Technology, Poland
Alberto Cano	Virginia Commonwealth University, USA
Frantisek Capkovic	Institute of Informatics, Slovak Academy of Sciences, Slovakia
Amine Chohra	Paris-East Créteil University, France

Kazimierz Choroś	Wrocław University of Science and Technology, Poland
Robert Cierniak	Częstochowa University of Technology, Poland
Mihaela Colhon	University of Craiova, Romania
Antonio Corral	University of Almeria, Spain
Jose Alfredo Ferreira Costa	Universidade Federal do Rio Grande do Norte, Brazil
Rafal Cupek	Silesian University of Technology, Poland
Ireneusz Czarnowski	Gdynia Maritime University, Poland
Camelia Delcea	Bucharest University of Economic Studies, Romania
Konstantinos Demertzis	Democritus University of Thrace, Greece
Shridhar Devamane	Global Academy of Technology, India
Muthusamy Dharmalingam	Bharathiar University, India
Tien V. Do	Budapest University of Technology and Economics, Hungary
Abdellatif El Afia	Mohammed V University in Rabat, Morocco
Nadia Essoussi	University of Tunis, Tunisia
Marcin Fojcik	Western Norway University of Applied Sciences, Norway
Anna Formica	IASI-CNR, Italy
Dariusz Frejlichowski	West Pomeranian University of Technology in Szczecin, Poland
Naoki Fukuta	Shizuoka University, Japan
Faiez Gargouri	University of Sfax, Tunisia
Mauro Gaspari	University of Bologna, Italy
K. M. George	Oklahoma State University, USA
Janusz Getta	University of Wollongong, Australia
Chirine Ghedira	University of Lyon 3, France
Daniela Gifu	Romanian Academy - Iasi Branch, Romania
Barbara Gładysz	Wrocław University of Science and Technology, Poland
Arkadiusz Gola	Lublin University of Technology, Poland
Petr Hajek	University of Pardubice, Czech Republic
Kenji Hatano	Doshisha University, Japan
Marcin Hernes	Wrocław University of Economics, Poland
Huu Hanh Hoang	Hue University, Vietnam
Frédéric Hubert	Laval University, Canada
Zbigniew Huzar	Wrocław University of Science and Technology, Poland
Agnieszka Indyka-Piasecka	Wrocław University of Science and Technology, Poland
Dan Istrate	Université de Technologie de Compiègne, France

Joanna Jedrzejowicz	University of Gdańsk, Poland
Gordan Jezic	University of Zagreb, Croatia
Christophe Jouis	Université de la Sorbonne Nouvelle, France
Ireneusz Jóźwiak	Wroclaw University of Science and Technology, Poland
Przemysław Juszczuk	University of Economics in Katowice, Poland
Arkadiusz Kawa	Poznań School of Logistics, Poland
Petros Kefalas	University of Sheffield, Greece
Zaheer Khan	University of the West of England, UK
Attila Kiss	Eotvos Lorand University, Hungary
Marek Kopel	Wroclaw University of Science and Technology, Poland
Petia Koprinkova-Hristova	Bulgarian Academy of Sciences, Bulgaria
Janusz Kowalski-Stankiewicz	Pomeranian Medical University in Szczecin, Poland
Ivan Koychev	University of Sofia "St. Kliment Ohridski", Bulgaria
Jan Kozak	University of Economics in Katowice, Poland
Adrianna Kozierkiewicz	Wrocław University of Science and Technology, Poland
Dalia Kriksciuniene	Vilnius University, Lithuania
Stelios Krinidis	Centre for Research and Technology Hellas (CERTH), Greece
Dariusz Król	Wrocław University of Science and Technology, Poland
Marek Krótkiewicz	Wrocław University of Science and Technology, Poland
Jan Kubicek	VSB -Technical University of Ostrava, Czech Republic
Elzbieta Kukla	Wrocław University of Science and Technology, Poland
Marek Kulbacki	Polish-Japanese Academy of Information Technology, Poland
Piotr Kulczycki	Systems Research Institute, Polish Academy of Science, Poland
Kazuhiro Kuwabara	Ritsumeikan University, Japan
Mark Last	Ben-Gurion University of the Negev, Israel
Florin Leon	"Gheorghe Asachi" Technical University of Iasi, Romania
Doina Logofătu	Frankfurt University of Applied Sciences, Germany
Juraj Machaj	University of Žilina, Slovakia
George Magoulas	Birkbeck, University of London, UK

Bernadetta Maleszka	Wrocław University of Science and Technology, Poland
Marcin Maleszka	Wrocław University of Science and Technology, Poland
Adam Meissner	Poznań University of Technology, Poland
Héctor Menéndez	University College London, UK
Mercedes Merayo	Universidad Complutense de Madrid, Spain
Jacek Mercik	WSB University in Wrocław, Poland
Radosław Michalski	Wrocław University of Science and Technology, Poland
Peter Mikulecký	University of Hradec Králové, Czech Republic
Miroslava Mikušová	University of Žilina, Slovakia
Jean-Luc Minel	Université Paris Ouest Nanterre La Défense, France
Javier Montero	Universidad Complutense de Madrid, Spain
Anna Motylska-Kuźma	WSB University in Wrocław, Poland
Dariusz Mrozek	Silesian University of Technology, Poland
Manuel Munier	University of Pau and Pays de l'Adour, France
Phivos Mylonas	Ionian University, Greece
Laurent Nana	University of Brest, France
Anand Nayyar	Duy Tan University, Vietnam
Filippo Neri	University of Napoli Federico II, Italy
Loan T. T. Nguyen	International University, VNU-HCMC, Vietnam
Sinh Van Nguyen	International University, VNU-HCMC, Vietnam
Linh Anh Nguyen	University of Warsaw, Poland
Adam Niewiadomski	Łódź University of Technology, Poland
Adel Noureddine	University of Pau and Pays de l'Adour, France
Alberto Núñez	Universidad Complutense de Madrid, Spain
Tarkko Oksala	Aalto University, Finland
Mieczysław Owoc	Wrocław University of Economics, Poland
Marcin Paprzycki	Systems Research Institute, Polish Academy of Sciences, Poland
Marek Penhaker	VSB -Technical University of Ostrava, Czech Republic
Isidoros Perikos	University of Patras, Greece
Maciej Piasecki	Wrocław University of Science and Technology, Poland
Bartłomiej Pierański	Poznań University of Economics and Business, Poland
Marcin Pietranik	Wrocław University of Science and Technology, Poland
Nikolaos Polatidis	University of Brighton, UK
Piotr Porwik	University of Silesia, Poland

Piotr Zabawa   Wrocław University of Science and Technology, Poland

Drago Žagar   University of Osijek, Croatia

Danuta Zakrzewska   Łódź University of Technology, Poland

Constantin-Bala Zamfirescu   "Lucian Blaga" University of Sibiu, Romania

Katerina Zdravkova   Sts. Cyril and Methodius University of Skopje, Macedonia

Aleksander Zgrzywa   Wrocław University of Science and Technology, Poland

Haoxi Zhang   Chengdu University of Information Technology, China

Jianlei Zhang   Nankai University, China

Adam Ziębiński   Silesian University of Technology, Poland

Contents

Deep Learning

Computational Intelligence for Multimedia Understanding

Computational Intelligence in Medical Applications

Applications for Industry 4.0

Experience Enhanced Intelligence to IoT and Sensors

Cooperative Strategies for Decision Making and Optimization

Machine Learning Methods

Collective Intelligence and Collective Decision-Making

From Unhealthy Online Conversation to Political Violence: The Case of the January 6th Events at the Capitol

Erik-Robert Kovacs$^{(\boxtimes)}$ ⓘ, Liviu-Adrian Cotfas$^{(\boxtimes)}$ ⓘ, and Camelia Delcea$^{(\boxtimes)}$ ⓘ

Bucharest University of Economic Studies, Bucharest, Romania
{erik.kovacs,camelia.delcea}@csie.ase.ro, liviu.cotfas@ase.ro

Abstract. While social media platforms can serve as public discussion forums of great benefit to democratic debate, they can also become a source of disinformation, bullying, hate speech, and a setting for fruitless polemics. In extreme cases, discourse originating in or propagated through social media can stoke political polarization and partisanship, with potentially devastating consequences. One of the most dramatic such instances in recent years has been the January 6 2021 incident in Washington D.C., when a group of protesters contesting the results of the 2020 US Presidential election besieged the US Capitol building, resulting in a violent confrontation that claimed the lives of several protesters and police officers. The public reacted by posting messages on social media, discussing the actions of the rioters, with several competing and incompatible narratives eventually emerging. Aiming to understand the phenomenon of uncompromising partisan political discourse under the broad concept of *unhealthy* online conversation, we sample 1,300,000 Twitter posts dating from January 2021 from the #Election2020 dataset. We then train several classifiers on the Unhealthy Comment Corpus (UCC) dataset using a machine learning (ML) approach, and use the best-performing model, XLNet, to label each tweet as *healthy* or *unhealthy*, furthermore using a taxonomy of 7 attributes of unhealthy conversation: *hostile, antagonistic, dismissive, condescending, sarcastic, generalization*, and/or *unfair generalization*. We model discussion topics for each attribute using latent Dirichlet allocation (LDA) and follow their evolution over time. The results we present aim to help social media stakeholders, government regulators, and the general public better understand the dynamics of unhealthy discourse occurring on social media, and its relationship to political polarization and partisanship, and their potential to pose an internal threat to democracy.

Keywords: Social media analysis · Unhealthy online conversation · Natural language processing · Machine learning · Capitol riot

1 Introduction

The rise of social media during the past two decades presents renewed challenges to democratic societies. On one hand, social media is the public forum where a well-informed citizenry can engage in the type of dialogue and debate that is the lifeblood

C. Bădică et al. (Eds.): ICCCI 2022, CCIS 1653, pp. 3–15, 2022.
https://doi.org/10.1007/978-3-031-16210-7_1

of democracy; on the other hand, in recent years, social media proved it can also be a vector for disinformation, fake news, bullying, hate speech, and, most importantly for the present paper, increasingly polarized political discourse. Thus, discourse on social media, far from being merely a question of moderation or censorship solely of concern to social media platform administrators and stakeholders, has the potential to result in definite social effects in the real world.

One of the most dramatic such manifestations in recent years has been the Capitol riot that took place in Washington, D.C. at the seat of Congress, the American legislature. On January 6, 2021, a group of Trump supporters attending the "Save America" rally broke police lines and breached the Capitol building with the intent of interrupting the certification process of Electoral College votes [1], while displaying a mixture of pro-Trump and extremist iconography [2]. The violent incident resulted in the death of five people and significant damage to the credibility of US democratic process [1]. It must be emphasized, however, that these events must be understood in the context of the controversial results of the 2020 US Presidential Elections, dominated by bitter polarization, *ad hominem* arguments, ceaseless online polemics, and (unsubstantiated) allegations of voter fraud against the victorious Democratic party candidate Joe Biden from mass media personalities and pro-Trump factions of the Republican party [3].

In the current paper, we wish to better understand the difficulties in communication posed by such polarization and partisanship with respect to the events of January 6, 2021, in contemporary posts on Twitter, a popular social media platform [4]. We use the broad notion of "unhealthy online conversation" [5] to characterize social media discourse relevant to the events. More specifically, we are interested in answering the following questions: 1) what proportion of relevant tweets are part of unhealthy conversations; 2) how does this proportion increase over time in response to significant events; 3) do unhealthy conversations have specific markers we can identify in text data; and 4) can we identify patterns on how unhealthy conversations promote polarization or the perception of polarization. For this purpose, we retrieve 1,300,000 tweets from the #Election2020 dataset [6] dating from the month of January, 2021, and classify them with an XLNet deep learning (DL) model trained on the Unhealthy Comment Corpus (UCC) dataset annotated for attributes *healthy* and *unhealthy*, and sub-attributes *hostile, antagonistic, dismissive, condescending, sarcastic, generalization*, and/or *unfair generalization*. On this dataset, we achieve higher performance than the sample implementation presented by the authors [5]. We then proceed to discover discussion topics for each sub-attribute using latent Dirichlet allocation (LDA), and follow the trends of the attributes during the period studied.

The paper is structured as follows: in Sect. 2, we review relevant background material informing this paper. In Sect. 3, we discuss the data and methodology we used for the classifiers we used and compare their performance on the UCC dataset. In Sect. 4, we present the results of the analyses we perform and our interpretation thereof. Finally, in Sect. 5 we conclude our study, acknowledge its limitations, and give recommendations for further research.

2   From Toxicity and Incivility to Unhealthy Online Conversation

The issue of problematic online communication has only recently begun to be posed as a question of *unhealthy* (i.e. not informative) conversation, as past research focused mostly on combatting *toxicity*, or more overt abusive and destructive behavior, often with the aim of moderating or censoring it within digital common spaces. According to Yang, Wang and Wu, such automated detection still mostly relies on heuristic methods such as text matching [7], making the practical aim of such research the development of more advanced algorithmic moderation methods. Recently, interest arose in detecting less overt harmful behaviors, such as online *incivility* [8]. Studying YouTube comments, also in the context of the 2020 US Presidential election, Chen and Wang highlight the potential limits of automatic moderation, observing the fact that the YouTube recommendation algorithm and the company's advertising policies are at least partly responsible for the development toxic and incivil conversations in the comments as drivers for engagement [8]. They stress rather the regulatory aspect [8], highlighting that simple moderation is often insufficient given the contradictory market incentives.

An even broader and more nuanced approach is proposed by Price et al., who propose a novel definition of *unhealthy* as opposed to healthy conversations, defined as conversations "where posts and comments are made in good faith, are not overly hostile or destructive, and generally invite engagement" [5]. They establish a taxonomy of unhealthy attributes of conversations and release their dataset (UCC) and provide a sample BERT-based model to be used as a baseline classifier. It is their work that primarily informs the current approach.

Several authors also use the UCC dataset and the framework of unhealthy online conversation in their research. Gilda, Giovanini, Silva and Oliveira perform a survey of different classifier architectures, including a variant of long-short term memory neural network (LSTM), with the UCC dataset used as a benchmarking tool [9]. Their aim is to engineer improved algorithmic moderation techniques, and as such do not apply the classifiers to out-of-domain data as we do. Our classifiers also outperform theirs when run on the validation dataset included in UCC. On the other hand, Lashkarashvili and Tsintzadze adapt the methodology for the Georgian language [10], curating and releasing their own Georgian-language annotated dataset. They also argue that in the online forum they obtained their out-of-domain data from, the "politics" section was deemed the most probable to contain unhealthy discussions, validating our hypothesis that political polarization might be related to unhealthy online conversation. However, to the best of our knowledge, we are the first to apply the methodology at the $n > 1$ M scale, and to the topic of political polarization specifically.

3   Data and Methods

We use supervised ML models trained on public datasets for classifying unhealthy Twitter conversations and reveal latent topics in the data using unsupervised ML techniques (LDA) (Fig. 1).

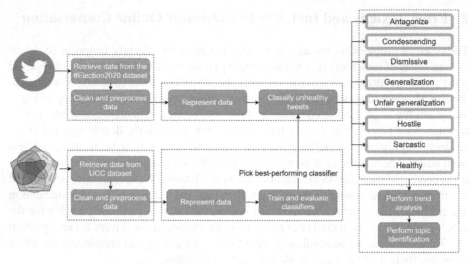

Fig. 1. The study methodology we used.

3.1 Data

As mentioned above, we have leveraged the UCC dataset for the training stage. This dataset contains 44,000 short texts in English annotated with the seven sub-attributes *hostile, antagonistic, dismissive, condescending, sarcastic, generalization,* and/or *unfair generalization* as well as the *healthy* flag. The annotations are not exclusive: each text can be part of any number of classes. Thus, classifying unhealthy comments is a multi-class classification problem rather than a multi-label one, where class membership is exclusive.

We elected to use this dataset both due to its size and to the clear definition of its attributes; earlier datasets with similar aims, such as the Google Jigsaw toxic comment dataset used by Chen and Wang [8], are in some respects inferior because there is limited information on how the data was compiled, the attributes used for annotation are only loosely-defined, and subtler forms of harmful or bad-faith comments, such as generalizations, dismissive comments or a condescending tone are not found within the set. However, the dataset size is larger (160,000) and thus attractive for a more restricted study of outright toxicity or hate speech [11].

While the authors note the sampling bias introduced by the comments being collected from the user comments section of a single Canadian newspaper [5], we feel applying it to contemporary North American texts is appropriate and should result in minimal issues due to linguistic and cultural proximity, since the out-of-domain data was obtained from the #Election2020 dataset released by Chen, Deb and Ferrara [6]. This is an enormous dataset consisting of over 1.2 billion tweets referring to the 2020 US Presidential election [6]. As mentioned above, we feel the events have to be understood in this context, so this choice of data source is appropriate. We restricted our analysis to January 2021, when the events took place, and as such we downloaded only tweets from this period. We removed tweets not in English (~12%). Even so, to make the data manageable given hardware limitations, we had to take a 3.5% stratified random sample of the tweets based on their datetime. Our final dataset numbered approximately 1,300,000 (1.3 M) tweets in total.

3.2 Representation

For the classical machine learning algorithms, we represented the data as an $n \times m$ document-term matrix M, where the columns represent the features (tokens), the rows represent the documents, and each element M_{ij} represents the TF-IDF score, a measure of the token's importance within the document [12]. We used the TF-IDF vectorizer from the scikit-learn python package. For the deep learning models, we used pre-trained tokenizers to obtain word embeddings: WordPiece encoder for BERT [13], byte-pair encoding for RoBERTa [14], and a SentencePiece-derived tokenizer for XLNet [15]. We used the tokenizer implementations from the HuggingFace provider.

3.3 Classifier Evaluation

Price et al. use the area under the receiver operating characteristic curve (ROC-AUC) performance measure to evaluate their model. The ROC curve describes the relationship between true positive rate (TPR or sensitivity, Eq. (1)) and false positive rate (FPR, Eq. (2)) as the decision threshold τ is varied in a model over the interval [0, 1] [16].

$$TPR = \frac{TP}{TP + FN} \tag{1}$$

$$FPR = \frac{FP}{FP + TN} \tag{2}$$

where TP is the number of true positives, FN the number of false negatives, TN the number of true negatives, and FP the number of false positives.

The AUC score is then the definite integral of the ROC curve, and can be calculated using the trapezoidal rule [16]:

$$AUC = \sum_{i=2}^{|T|} \frac{(FPR(T_i) - FPR(T_{i-1})) \cdot (TPR(T_i) - TPR(T_{i-1}))}{2} \tag{3}$$

where T is the set of all thresholds τ and T_i is the i-th threshold τ.

Greater value of the AUC score means better performance, with an area of value 1 corresponding to a perfect TPR (all accurate predictions and no false positives at all).

We trained six classifiers in total: three classical machine learning algorithms, adapted for multi-class problems using the one-vs.-all ensemble method: logistic regression (LR), random forest (RF), and support vector machine (SVM); and three deep learning models: BERT [13], RoBERTa [14], and XLNet [15]. To facilitate comparisons, we calculated the ROC-AUC score for each sub-attribute as well as the attribute *healthy*, then took their mean to capture the overall performance ranking of the models (see Table 1).

Contrary to our previous experience, XLNet (mean ROC-AUC score 0.8075) slightly outperformed RoBERTa (mean ROC-AUC score 0.8026), with the difference especially

Table 1. Mean ROC-AUC score of the classifiers.

Baseline [5]	LSTM [9]	LR	RF	SVM	BERT	RoBERTa	**XLNet**
0.7446	0.7121	0.7068	0.6802	0.6602	0.7745	0.8026	**0.8075**

visible at the level of the *sarcastic* class, which Price et al. note is particularly challenging to predict [5]. XLNet however obtains a 0.7410 score for this class, better than RoBERTa (0.6999) and significantly better than the baseline proposed by the authors (0.5880) [5]. The subjective quality of the predictions from XLNet is also significantly better than the other models we experimented with, and the class proportions within predictions are more consistent with Price et al.'s observations.

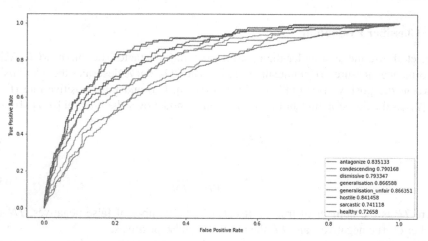

Fig. 2. ROC curves and ROC-AUC scores for each attribute, for the XLNet model we trained.

3.4 Topic Discovery

We used LDA, an unsupervised ML technique that can be used to reveal unobserved structures ("topics") in text data by treating topics as a mixture of tokens and documents as a mixture of topics [12] for each attribute. We optimized the number of topics k, as well as the hyperparameters η (the Dirichlet prior of the topic-word probability distribution) and α (the Dirichlet prior of the document-topic probability distribution) using the Cv coherence measure (which measures similarity between the sets of tokens comprising a topic, related to cosine similarity) for each attribute, excluding terms appearing in fewer than 50 tweets or more than 95% of tweets. We used the Gensim python package for this analysis.

4 Results

Useful for the interpretation of the results is the concept of meta-perception we borrow from the field of social psychology, defined as beliefs about what others believe [17]. Negative meta-perceptions are thought to be central to online political polarization, where engagement with the "other side" (the outgroup) is mediated through text-based conversations. We have detected textual markers of such expressions especially in tweets exhibiting the *dismissive, condescending* and *generalization* attributes.

4.1 Attribute Distribution and Trend Analysis

Overall, 35.30% of the tweets have been labelled as *unhealthy*. However, since the authors' methodology allows for texts to exhibit some unhealthy characteristics without being labelled as fully unhealthy, 42.39% tweets exhibit at least some unhealthy traits. Out of these tweets, overtly toxic attributes such as *antagonize, dismissive* and *hostile* were most prevalent (58.28%, 38.38% and 36.45%), followed by *condescending* (20.44%) and *sarcastic* (13.82%). The least well represented were the more subtle *generalization* and unfair *generalization attributes* (7.79% and 7.97%).

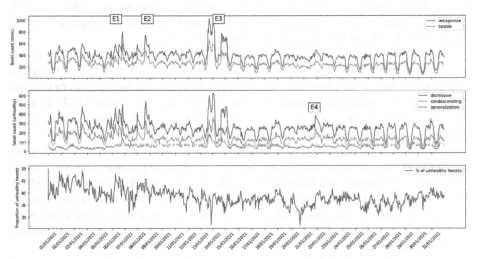

Fig. 3. Tweet trends by unhealthy attribute cluster and by proportion of unhealthy tweets relative to total number of tweets.

Even during training, some features of the seven attributes have become apparent. They cluster along distinct lines (see Fig. 2): *generalization* and *unfair generalization* cluster together and are learned very distinctly by all models, including the baseline proposed by the authors [2], despite their low proportions in the data. This poses the question whether there is any value in even making a distinction between the two, as they are clearly intrinsically related. We believe one of these classes is not informative and thus redundant; we propose for follow-up analyses to merge them during training and prediction, treating them as one, as they appear to be extremely highly correlated in our data (Pearson correlation coefficient of 0.9599).

The second cluster consists of attributes generally considered toxic rather than simply unhealthy: *hostile* and *antagonize*. The "toxic" cluster can be seen to rise rapidly and then quickly decay, while the others, especially generalization (which denotes both types of generalization in the figure) show less volatility and follow the general pattern of the tweets. The third consists of the attributes which are more subtly destructive: *dismissive* and *condescending*. *Sarcastic*, a feature difficult to identify even for humans, was difficult to learn, as mentioned above – it is possible the higher success of XLNet when learning sarcasm when compared to the other models might be because its internal structure is better suited to picking up subtle differences in word order [15]. Nevertheless, we note several characteristics of sarcasm within the observed data and the training results that suggest further improvements can be made for sarcasm detection. This is discussed at more length in Sect. 4.2.

As can be seen in the first two plots in Fig. 3, where attributes that clustered together are displayed together, there is a strong daily cyclical pattern reflecting the day-night cycle which becomes attenuated for certain periods. For instance, during the events and their immediate aftermath (6–10 January, denoted with E1 and E2), this cyclical pattern is almost flattened for all clusters, suggesting heightened engagement during all times of day. These might correspond to periods of intense discussion, or to the spread of the topic outside the US (especially in Europe) due to live news coverage and online engagement, but might also indicate the deployment of bots.

The second period of heightened unhealthy conversation happened during 13–16 January (denoted with E3), when, as a result of his role in the Capitol riots, Congress took steps towards impeaching Trump a second time [18]. The cyclical pattern prevails after 16 January, except for a significant flare-up of toxic posts during 19–23 January (denoted with E4), corresponding to Trump officially leaving office on January 20, together with the new President Biden's inauguration ceremony [19].

Finally, the third graph in Fig. 3 shows the ratio of unhealthy tweets to the overall number of tweets. Its near-stationarity suggests that unhealthy conversation makes up a relatively stable proportion (between 30%–50%) of the overall discussion throughout the entire period, being a perpetual occurrence during the normal course of social media discourse, not merely a response to dramatic events. Thus, positing a causal relationship is unwarranted; political polarization appears in this case to be a particular case of unhealthy conversation.

4.2 Topic Analysis

While discussing polarization in a similar context, Lees and Cikara stress the intergroup conflict aspect of the phenomenon [17]. This aspect is best captured by the traditionally toxic attributes *antagonize* and *hostile*, but such discussions appear to be of limited value to the study of polarization, as these topics seem uninformative, consisting of noise and vulgar abuse.

On the other hand, the attributes indicating *generalization* in a political context are especially informative as through their markers of stereotyping and labelling, they express the kind of meta-perceptions that are indicative of misperceived polarization

Table 2. Most relevant topics.

Attribute	Name	Topic
antagonize	anti_trump	gop, traitor, republican, president, party, america, american, election, loser, impeachment
antagonize, hostile	accusation_racism	white, capitol, maga, terrorist, insurrection, supporter, racist, black, woman, house, white, capitol, terrorist, maga, racist, american, black, supporter, house, crime
condescending	treason	resident, gop, traitor, election, republican, party, america, vote, country, american
generalization	anti_voting	democrat, republican, american, president, America, left, country, party, never, vote
generalization	far_right_white_supremacist	white, supporter, maga, terrorist, capitol, racist, right, supremacist, nazi, boy
generalization	proud_boys	white, black, supporter, racist, right, woman, supremacist, maga, boy, proud
generalization	right_or_republican	republican, gop, party, democrat, american, vote, dems, election, voter, left
generalization	left_or_liberal	american, democrat, america, left, hate, black, woman, country, liberal, president
hostile	trump_coward	gop, traitor, republican, party, president, election, america, vote, country, coward
sarcastic	sarcastic_keywords	yeah, lol, right, job, president, thing, make, hell, better, well, wow, gop, week, hey, rudy, maybe, twitter, big, check, riot
healthy	capitol_riot	election, republican, right, vote, capitol, president, party, even, insurrection, state
healthy	election_or_impeachment	president, first, order, house, administration, executive, covid, american, impeachment, senate
–	vulgar_abuse	f*ck, sh*t, stupid, f*cking, care, hell, dumb, shut, maga, back

[17]. They paint the outgroup with broad, possibly inaccurate strokes, using simple slur-like keywords to describe them and what they believe (see Table 2, "gop" – Republican party, "maga" – Trump's slogan "make America great again!", "proud boys" – militant extremist movement [2], "nazi"). Also important to note is the moralistic and emotional tone ("traitor", "insurrection", "terrorist") as well as the racial aspect ("white", "black", "supremacist").

It is also interesting to note how topics across attributes relate to each other. In Fig. 4 we have set up a network, with named topics as nodes and vertices representing

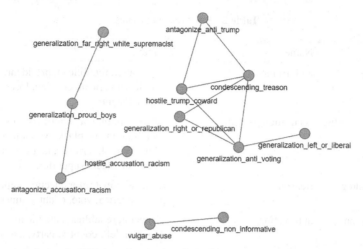

Fig. 4. Network formed of LDA topics (nodes) linked by cosine similarity scores (edges). Only scores ≥0.5 have been included.

the cosine similarity between the topics. There are two main clusters relevant to meta-perceptions, consisting of accusations against the outgroup (racists, Proud Boys, white supremacists against the Capitol rioters, etc.) and generalizations about the outgroup (equation of Democrats, liberals and leftists, and Republicans, respectively). It is also noteworthy that there existed a topic (generalization_anti_vote) that was not partisan but rather appeared to be critical of the two-party system in a very broad way, appearing to be opposed to participation in the voting process. Finally, the bottom cluster consists of uninformative topics and traditional toxic comments (vulgar_abuse), which in this context can be seen as noise.

As a final consideration, on the issue of detecting sarcasm, we have observed certain keywords (see Table 2) and syntactical structures (such as beginning a phrase with the interjections "yeah" or "well") have been deemed important by the model, but these might not generalize well to other contexts as they appear at least in part internet specific ("lol") or simply North American colloquialisms. Nevertheless, looking for such structures might become useful in retrieving sarcasm-related data from social media, similar to other cues such as the "/s" token on Reddit [20].

4.3 Discussion

Misperceived polarization refers to an unwillingness of actors to engage in a social media context due to negative meta-perceptions, the belief that "the other side" is unwilling to compromise or even present as a good faith actor [17]. Thus, toxicity appears to be a marker of avoiding dialogue due to these negative meta-perceptions and is indicative of a breakdown in communication in intergroup confrontation online. We have seen evidence of this in the fast rise and fall of toxic "storms" visible in the data (see Fig. 3).

Finally, we must note the proportions and clustering of the attributes discussed above, as well as the distinctions between topics, suggest different "layers" of toxicity and unhealthiness exhibited through polarized or adversarial online discussions, with toxicity being the most virulent, followed by bad-faith argument, trolling, dismissiveness or superiority, followed by different levels of generalization regarding the outgroup. Sarcasm appears to develop along a distinct axis and as such could be considered an unrelated characteristic that can appear at any level, but it is as of yet unclear how it affects online discussions.

5 Conclusions

We have gathered Twitter posts related to the January 6, 2021 Capitol riot in the context of the 2020 US Presidential elections and detected unhealthy attributes of posts using an ML approach. We followed the trend of each attribute in relation to the events and revealed latent topics in the data using latent Dirichlet allocation.

We found that a substantial proportion of relevant tweets are part of unhealthy conversations, but that they are aggregated along a relatively small number of topics. We also find that unhealthy conversations have specific markers for specific attributes we can identify in text data, and that we can point out patterns on how unhealthy conversations promote polarization or the perception of polarization especially in the subtler layers of online toxicity, but that traditionally toxic conversations are generally not informative with respect to political polarization. We also note that the proportion of unhealthy tweets increases over time in response to significant events, eventually decaying as conversations turn toxic and engagement declines – at the same time, we observe that overall, unhealthy conversations make up a relatively stable proportion of tweets over time, suggesting that politically polarized discourse is a particular case of unhealthy online discourse.

A possible weakness of our interpretation of the results is that, by necessity given the large volume of data and lack of underlying demographic information, we assume homogeneity and symmetry across political divides, but this was clearly not the case during the 2020 election, when unsubstantiated and sensational arguments tended to be presented in the mass media much more by certain sections of pro-Republican and specifically pro-Trump voices [3]. However, as noted above, in online conversations the proportions of stereotypical generalizations of the outgroup do appear to be consistent regardless of who is seen as the "other side". These results can help social media stakeholders and government regulators understand the magnitude of the problem of political polarization and gain better insight into the topics discussed by agents involved in politics-related unhealthy conversations online, an important first step towards addressing it via internal social media reform and/or legislative action. Similarly, they can provide guidance to the general public by highlighting certain linguistic characteristics of the confrontational inter-group dynamics leading to unproductive and unhealthy discussions online, involvement in which can be avoided or minimized by paying attention to language use and stereotyping.

Future research on the phenomenon of polarization using unhealthy comments should focus on two general directions. Firstly, markers of polarization can be detected best in the middle layers of unhealthy attributes (*dismissive, condescending, generalization*), and research can focus on studying the prevalence and nature of accurate or misperceived polarization in these layers. In addition, more data labelled with these attributes is needed. The other direction concerns studying the role of sarcasm and irony in informing unhealthy conversations, and how it relates to online political polarization.

References

1. "Capitol riots timeline: what happened on 6 Jan one year ago? BBC News. Available: https://www.bbc.com/news/world-us-canada-56004916 (2022). Accessed 26 Feb 2022
2. Simpson, M., Sidner, S.: Decoding the extremist symbols and groups at the Capitol Hill insurrection. CNN. https://www.cnn.com/2021/01/09/us/capitol-hill-insurrection-extremist-flags-soh/index.html. Accessed 26 Feb 2022
3. #StopTheSteal: Timeline of Social Media and Extremist Activities Leading to 1/6 Insurrection. Just Security. https://www.justsecurity.org/74622/stopthesteal-timeline-of-social-media-and-extremist-activities-leading-to-1-6-insurrection/ (2021). Accessed 26 Feb 2022
4. Most popular social media apps in U.S. Statista. https://www.statista.com/statistics/248074/most-popular-us-social-networking-apps-ranked-by-audience/. Accessed 26 Feb 2022
5. Price, I., et al.: Six attributes of unhealthy conversations. In: Proceedings of the Fourth Workshop on Online Abuse and Harms, pp. 114–124 (2020). https://doi.org/10.18653/v1/2020.alw-1.15
6. Chen, E., Deb, A., Ferrara, E.: #Election2020: the first public Twitter dataset on the 2020 US Presidential election. J. Comput. Soc. Sci. (2021). https://doi.org/10.1007/s42001-021-001 17-9
7. Wang, K., Yang, J., Wu, H.: A survey of toxic comment classification methods. arXiv:2112. 06412 [cs]. Available: http://arxiv.org/abs/2112.06412 (2021). Accessed 14 Mar 2022
8. Chen, Y., Wang, L.: Misleading political advertising fuels incivility online: a social network analysis of 2020 U.S. presidential election campaign video comments on YouTube. Comput. Hum. Behav. **131**, 107202 (2022). https://doi.org/10.1016/j.chb.2022.107202
9. Gilda, S., Giovanini, L., Silva, M., Oliveira, D.: Predicting different types of subtle toxicity in unhealthy online conversations. Proc. Comput. Sci. **198**, 360–366 (2022). https://doi.org/10.1016/j.procs.2021.12.254
10. Lashkarashvili, N., Tsintsadze, M.: Toxicity detection in online Georgian discussions. Int. J. Inf. Manage. Data Insights **2**(1), 100062 (2022). https://doi.org/10.1016/j.jjimei.2022.100062
11. Toxic Comment Classification Challenge. https://kaggle.com/c/jigsaw-toxic-comment-classi fication-challenge. Accessed 15 Mar 2022
12. Vajjala, S., Majumder, B., Gupta, A., Surana, H.: Practical Natural Language Processing: A Comprehensive Guide to Building Real-World NLP Systems. O'Reilly Media (2020)
13. Devlin, J., Chang, M.-W., Lee, K., Toutanova, K.: BERT: pre-training of deep bidirectional transformers for language understanding. In: Proceedings of the 2019 Conference of the North American Chapter of the Association for Computational Linguistics: Human Language Technologies, Volume 1 (Long and Short Papers), Minneapolis, Minnesota, pp. 4171–4186 (2019). https://doi.org/10.18653/v1/N19-1423
14. Liu, Y., et al.: RoBERTa: A Robustly Optimized BERT Pretraining Approach. arXiv:1907. 11692 [cs]. Available: http://arxiv.org/abs/1907.11692 (2019). Accessed 26 Feb 2022
15. Yang, Z., Dai, Z., Yang, Y., Carbonell, J., Salakhutdinov, R., Le, Q.V.: XLNet: generalized autoregressive pretraining for language understanding. In: Advances in Neural Information Processing Systems, vol. 32 (nips 2019), La Jolla (2019)
16. Kelleher, J.D., Namee, B.M., D'Arcy, A.: Fundamentals of Machine Learning for Predictive Data Analytics: Algorithms, Worked Examples, and Case Studies, 2nd edn. MIT Press (2020)

17. Lees, J., Cikara, M.: Understanding and Combating Misperceived Polarization. PsyArXiv (2020). https://doi.org/10.31234/osf.io/ncwez
18. Sheth, S.: Trump's 2nd impeachment is the most bipartisan in US history. Business Insider. https://www.businessinsider.com/trump-second-impeachment-most-bipartisan-in-us-history-2021-1. Accessed 15 Mar 2022
19. Cole, D., LeBlanc, P.: An inauguration like no other: notable moments of a momentous day. CNN. https://www.cnn.com/2021/01/20/politics/biden-inauguration-notable-moments/index.html. Accessed 15 Mar 2022
20. Khodak, M., Saunshi, N., Vodrahalli, K.: A large self-annotated corpus for sarcasm. In: Presented at the LREC 2018, Miyazaki, Japan, May 2018. Available: https://aclanthology.org/L18-1102. Accessed 15 Mar 2022

Unraveling COVID-19 Misinformation with Latent Dirichlet Allocation and CatBoost

Joy Nathalie M. Avelino$^{(\boxtimes)}$ (ID), Edgardo P. Felizmenio Jr. (ID),
and Prospero C. Naval Jr. (ID)

Department of Computer Science, University of the Philippines,
Quezon City, Philippines
{jmavelino,epfelizmenio,pcnaval}@up.edu.ph

Abstract. The COVID-19 pandemic brought upon a plethora of misinformation from fake news articles and posts on social media platforms. This necessitates the task of identifying whether a particular piece of information about COVID-19 is legitimate or not. However, with excessive misinformation spreading rapidly over the internet, manual verification of sources becomes infeasible. Several studies have already explored the use of machine learning towards automating COVID-19 misinformation detection. This paper will investigate COVID-19 misinformation detection in three parts. First, we identify the common themes found in COVID-19 misinformation data using Latent Dirichlet Allocation (LDA). Second, we use CatBoost as a classifier for detecting misinformation and compare its performance against other classifiers such as SVM, XGBoost, and LightGBM. Lastly, we highlight CatBoost's most important features and decision-making mechanism using Shapley values.

Keywords: COVID-19 · Misinformation detection · CatBoost · Latent Dirichlet Allocation · Explainable AI

1 Introduction

Infodemic refers to the influx of too much information, both true and misleading information in digital and physical environments during a disease outbreak that causes confusion and disruption of services [25]. Misinformation is a challenging problem to address in the COVID-19 pandemic as it can delay pandemic response and cause public confusion.

Since human language is ambiguous and text data is composed of hundreds and thousands of words and phrases, applying Artificial Intelligence (AI) is a popular approach in addressing misinformation detection. Natural Language Processing (NLP) is a field in AI that aims to automate the extraction of insights from textual data. Examples of NLP tasks include the identification of common themes in text documents and the classification of text documents into different categories. For COVID-19 misinformation detection, an NLP solution that classifies articles as 'information' or 'misinformation' is proposed.

In this paper, we apply CatBoost in a machine learning pipeline for COVID-19 misinformation detection. Section 2 provides a background of existing studies on COVID-19 misinformation detection and definition of terms. Section 3 details the contribution of this paper. Section 4 contains information about the dataset, data preprocessing, and implementation. Topic modeling is performed to see relevant themes present in misinformation. Performance and interpretability is discussed on Sect. 5. Finally, Sect. 6 provides the conclusion and suggestions for future work.

2 Preliminaries and Related Work

2.1 COVID-19 Misinformation Detection Literature

Several studies have already addressed the automated detection of COVID-19 misinformation in online sources, a lot of which explore the application of different classification methods.

In a study by Khan et al. [13] on fake news classification, deep learning and BERT-based models perform better than traditional models. However, there is a challenge for health-related and research-related fake news as they are the most difficult ones to detect, with a false positive rate reaching as high as 46%. In another study by Bangyal et al. [2], several machine learning and deep learning models are evaluated for COVID-19 fake news detection from Twitter posts using relevant features extracted from term frequency and inverse document frequency (TF-IDF) of preprocessed tweets. Results show that the random forest model gave the highest accuracy, recall, and F1-score, followed by the multi layer perceptron (MLP). The importance of the manner of training for COVID-19 misinformation detection is highlighted in another study [8], where it is shown that transfer learning provides significant improvements in the performance of SVM and MLP for COVID-19 misinformation detection.

2.2 Categorical Boosting (CatBoost)

CatBoost is a relatively new algorithm, created by Yandex in 2017 [9]. CatBoost employs a *gradient boosting* approach, where an ensemble of classifiers is constructed by iteratively combining weak learners with the goal of minimizing the prediction loss. CatBoost addresses several issues found in other gradient boosting techniques such as XGBoost [5] and LightGBM [12], and previous experiments have shown that CatBoost can outperform these techniques [9]. Applications for CatBoost include combined cycle power plants [10] and financial fraud detection [6]. CatBoost's performance is at par or can outperform other methods such as random forest, MLP, XGBoost, Naive-Bayes, SVM classifiers, as well as deep-learning models [27].

2.3 Term Frequency - Inverse Document Frequency (TF-IDF)

TF-IDF will be used as the word embedding technique for the ML models. The TF-IDF score can show the importance of a word, or term, to a document in a corpus [7]. Given a term t in document d, $f_{t,d}$ is denoted as the number of occurrences of t in d, and $\sum_{t' \in d} f_{t',d}$ is the sum of all the terms in d. The *Term Frequency* (tf) is the frequency of t in d.

$$tf(t,d) = \frac{f_{t,d}}{\sum_{t' \in d} f_{t',d}} \tag{1}$$

From the term frequency, the Inverse Document Frequency is computed (IDF). Given a term t and a set of documents D, the IDF is the inverse of the frequency of documents that contain term t.

$$idf(t,D) = \log\left(\frac{|D|+1}{|\{d \in D : t \in d\}|+1}\right) + 1 \tag{2}$$

A high IDF indicates that the word occurs less frequently and that it should have higher weight, with the assumption that it is biased towards a specific classification. Given the TF and the IDF, the TF-IDF is computed as:

$$tfidf(t,d,D) = tf(t,d) \times idf(t,D) \tag{3}$$

TF-IDF provides weights to each of the terms in the document, while giving importance to the terms that occur less frequently in the entire set of documents. Given a document, its features will be the $tfidf$ of each term. The `scikit-learn` [18] library is used to compute for the TF-IDF score of the tokens.

2.4 Latent Dirichlet Allocation (LDA)

Latent Dirichlet Allocation (LDA) is a technique used in NLP to identify common themes found in text documents. LDA is a generative statistical model in which each document is assumed to be a set of topics. LDA tries to identify common topics that occur in the documents as well as the words that have contributed to the occurrences of the topics [4]. The visualization is created using `gensim` [20] and `PyLDAVis` [23].

2.5 Shapley Additive Explanations (SHAP)

Interpretability is an integral part in diagnosing the results of a model since models produced by machine learning are known to be black boxes. `SHAP` is a Python library that uses Shapley values by connecting feature allocation with local explanations [17]. Shapley values originated from game theory and give interpretations generated from the input data by an ML algorithm [26].

3   Contribution

This paper aims to apply CatBoost as a tool for misinformation detection, specifically for COVID-19. With this, we developed a machine learning pipeline consisting of three parts: (1) exploratory data analysis using topic modeling using LDA, (2) classification using CatBoost, (3) and model interpretation using SHAP. To assess the viability of using CatBoost in our pipeline, we compared its performance to other classification algorithms such as Support Vector Machines (SVM), LightGBM, and XGBoost. In addition, we also highlight the application of LDA and SHAP in a misinformation detection pipeline, particularly in understanding the nature of data and the predictions of the classifier. Just as performance metrics are important, explainable AI is also a focal point.

4   Methodology

4.1   Dataset Description and Preprocessing

Three public datasets containing information about COVID-19 are used: one dataset is from Koirala [14] from *Mendeley Data*, another dataset is from *Towards Data Science* [16] by Li, and the COVID19-FNIR dataset from *IEEE* [21]. The collection period of the datasets are from December 2019 to July 2020. Li and COVID19-FNIR dataset has a 50:50 ratio distribution for true and misinformation label, while Koirala dataset has a 30:70 ratio distribution, with majority of the data as the true information.

The false information in the datasets are sourced from *Natural News* (a far-right website), and *orthomolecular[.]org* (an alternative medicine website), and fake news tagged by fact-checking organization *Poynter*. For articles that have already been removed, internet archive websites, such as *Wayback Machine*, captures a snapshot of the site, and used as part of the dataset.

Sources for the reliable articles and posts are from Harvard Health Publishing, The New York Times, Johns Hopkins Bloomberg School of Public Health, World Health Organization (WHO), Centers for Disease Control and Prevention (CDC), and other verified sources. Social media websites such as Facebook, Twitter, and WhatsApp contribute to the dataset for both true information and misinformation.

The three datasets are merged, creating a dataset that only has the 'text' field for the post/article content and 'label' field. Initially, the labels of the datasets sourced are '1' for true information, and '0' for misinformation. The focus of this study is on misinformation classification, thus the implementation will use label '1' to represent misinformation and label '0' for true information.

Preprocessing was done with the help of `Natural Language Toolkit` (NLTK) [3] to remove special characters, websites, stopwords, and numbers. For standardization, the words are converted to lowercase. Entries which have no text or labels are removed from the dataset. The final dataset comprise of 54.27% (6,435) entries for true information (label 0) and 45.73% (5,423) for misinformation (label 1) - with a total of 11,858 entries.

4.2   Topic Modeling Using LDA

Figures 1a and 2a show how the documents are clustered in a 2-dimensional plane. A sample of the most relevant terms for each topic are listed in Tables 1 and 2. The top words could be sorted by "relevance" which also takes into account word frequency in the corpus ($0 < \lambda < 1$). Based on one study, a λ value between 0.2 and 0.4 works well [22]. Each group is inspected manually to check significant themes surrounding the documents.

For the misinformation dataset, Fig. 1 shows that the frequent words in Topic 2 are 'bats' and 'laboratory' - relating to the suspected origins of COVID-19. Table 1 shows other topic groups that are identified. There are topics related with alternative medicine (Topics 5, 11, 14), false medical claims (Topics 6 and 13), and lies surrounding biopharmaceutical and biotech companies about their vaccine candidates (Topics 12, 15). Topic 20 is about vaccine conspiracies such as microchip implants in vaccines that can make people hesitant in getting vaccinated. There are also topics related to politics (Topics 1, 4, 9, 10, 16). Topic 3 is related to false information about international travel and airports. Economy is the common theme found for the words in Topics 8 and 17.

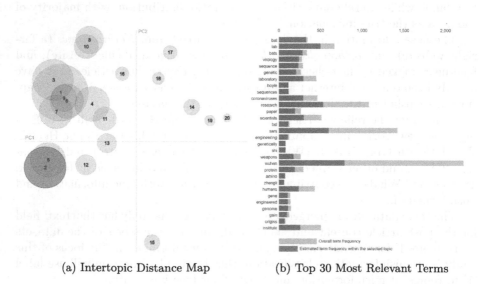

(a) Intertopic Distance Map   (b) Top 30 Most Relevant Terms

Fig. 1. LDA visualization for misinformation dataset topic 2 (Pandemic)

Table 1. Common terms and topics for misinformation dataset

Topic	Terms	Theme
1	people, world, media, war, europe	politics
2	bats, lab, genetic, sars, wuhan	pandemic
3	china, passengers, outbreak, travel, flights	travel
4	gates, bill, vaccine, foundation, covid	politics
5	vitamin, dose, intravenous, doses, selenium	medicine
6	plasma, patients, covid, hydroxychloroquine, chloroquine	medicine
7	corona, mms, paranormal, throat, water	N/A
8	futures, overnight, stocks, gains, markets	economy
9	ministry, india, minister, hospital, students	politics
10	friday, ist, kennedy, said, owners	politics
11	oils, iodine, silver, essential, heat	medicine
12	nml, xiangguo, canada, warfare, biological	healthcare
13	hius, ultrasound, cancer, chest, cure	healthcare
14	cbd, hemp, patch, cannabis, market	medicine
15	clover, antibody, ace, platform, cgmp	healthcare
16	sexual, predators, kleptocrats, institut, tip	politics
17	imp, bank, debt, colleges, financing	economy
18	galactic, divine, ufos, extraterrestrial, belt	N/A
19	beer, search, crossroads, photographer, church	N/A
20	fertility, tattoos, quantum, microchip, digital	healthcare

An LDA visualization for true news data is shown in Fig. 2. Majority of the terms in Topic 6 is related to healthcare, particularly hygiene. Aside from the visualization, notable topic groupings for true news is shown in Table 2.

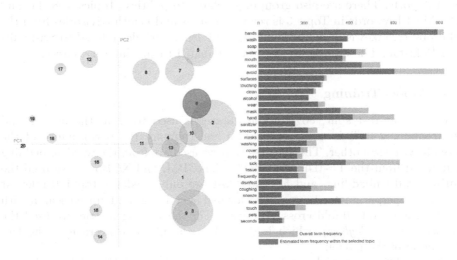

(a) Intertopic Distance Map   (b) Top 30 Most Relevant Terms

Fig. 2. LDA visualization for true information dataset topic 6 (healthcare)

Table 2. Common terms and topics for true information dataset

Topic	Words	Theme
1	impact, tourism, closed, oil, trade	economy
2	sars, humans, animals, mers, respiratory	pandemic
3	doh, hospital, philippines, manila, said	politics
4	information, elsevier, public, health, hhs	healthcare
5	covid, drugs, vitamin, immune, respiratory	medicine
6	hands, wash, sneezing, mouth, alcohol	healthcare
7	vaccine, pandemic, moderna, volunteers, fauci	medicine
8	pasteur, institut, mwc, iran, cnr	politics
9	ship, cruise, passengers, airport, port	travel
10	wellbeing, info, fitness, verified, unfold	N/A
11	liberia, donated, foundation, politics, polyu	politics
12	dna, cepi, pro, curevac, genetics	healthcare
13	beer, google, searches, trends, constellation	N/A
14	thai, pakistan, sri, lanka, ministers	politics
15	vessel, formula, fia, masters, seafarers	sports
16	malaysian, fct, cable, false, pawn	N/A
17	protein, clover, biopharmaceutical, prophylactics, mammalian	medicine
18	drones, nch, cleaner, elevator, botswana	N/A
19	nagoya, molon, pira, cordillera, nintendo	N/A
20	methioninase, methionine, anticancer, australians, oral	medicine

There are groupings related to health advisories from authorities like CDC (Topics 4 and 12), information about antibodies and blood testing (Topic 5), and vaccine development (Topics 7 and 12). Topic 9 is related to travel and flight announcements. There are travel-related keywords mixed up with keywords related to sports in Topic 15 but most keywords lean to sports so the theme is set to sports. There are also groupings related to politics (Topics 3, 8, 11, and 14). Most keywords in Topic 3 is related to news and health advisories from the Philippines. Likewise, keywords in Topic 14 denote articles related to Sri-Lanka and Pakistan. These groupings can be attributed to the dataset sources.

4.3   Model Training

For the train-test split, 80% of the dataset is used to train the models and the remaining 20% is used to evaluate and compare the performance of the models with each other. The features that we used are from the word embedding generated from the TF-IDF. For SVM, LightGBM, and XGBoost, we used the entire word embedding, and for CatBoost, we only used the top 100 relevant tokens. Hyperparameter tuning is performed by a doing randomized search with 10 iterations and 10-fold cross validation. For the scoring metric, we used the logistic loss (or *logloss*), which is defined as the negative average of the log-likelihood of the model.

Three different models are trained for CatBoost: (1) CatBoost (text data as features), (2) CatBoost + TF-IDF, and (3) CatBoost + TF-IDF (with hyper-parameter tuning). CatBoost has built-in preprocessing for text data. The unigrams/words and bigrams extracted by CatBoost will be part of its dictionary. The *feature calcers* are used to calculate new features based from the dictionary created. Two feature calcers are used: Bag of Words (which uses bigram and word dictionaries) and Naive Bayes (only word dictionary is used). The second model is used to create the third model that incorporates hyperparameter tuning.

Three parameters are checked for hyperparameter tuning: the *learning_rate*, *depth* (or *max_depth*), and the L2 regularization parameter *l2_leaf_reg* (or *reg_lambda*). The parameter space that we considered is *learning_rate* $\in$ $\{0.1, 0.01, 0.001\}$, *depth* $\in \{4, 6, 8\}$, and *reg_lambda* $\in \{1, 3, 5\}$. The number of learners is defined to a fixed value of 1000 and the training is set to stop if there is no improvement after 100 iterations. The model parameters not mentioned are set to default value.

For the SVM kernels, we used the Linear, RBF, and Sigmoid kernels. For the parameter space, we used *gamma* $\in (0.1, 6]$ and *coef0* $\in [-5, 5]$ for SVM. For LightGBM and XGBoost, we used the same parameter space from tuning the third CatBoost model.

After doing a randomized search, we identified the *best* parameters for each classifier. We define the *best* parameters as the parameters that resulted to the lowest mean logloss during randomized search. Each classifier is then retrained using the best parameters.

Finally, we evaluated each classifier using the test set. We compared the performance of the classifiers based on the *accuracy, precision, recall, F1-Score, and ROC-AUC Score* [24].

Python is used for the implementation of this study. We used `scikit-learn` [18] for the SVM model, preprocessing, and performance evaluation. For the boosting algorithms, `lightgbm` [12], `xgboost` [5], and `catboost` [9] libraries are used.

5   Results and Discussion

5.1   Performance

The accuracy, precision, recall, F1-score and ROC-AUC score is measured for the eight models. The results are shown in Table 3.

All of the CatBoost classifiers have higher Accuracy, Recall, F1-Score, and ROC-AUC. For precision, LightGBM, XGBoost, and Radial SVM outperforms all of the CatBoost classifiers, while Sigmoid SVM only outperforms the Cat-Boost models with TF-IDF.

5.2   Interpretability Using SHAP

CatBoost supports the use of SHAP values for feature importance. Figure 3 shows the SHAP plot for the model (with TF-IDF features). The features

Table 3. Comparison of CatBoost with SVM, LightGBM, and XGBoost

	Accuracy	Precision	Recall	F1-Score	ROC-AUC
CatBoost classifiers					
CatBoost	0.895	**0.905**	0.862	0.883	0.956
CatBoost + TF-IDF	0.894	0.892	**0.877**	0.885	0.960
CatBoost + TF-IDF (Tuned)	**0.897**	0.900	0.875	**0.887**	**0.961**
SVM, XGBoost, and LightGBM classifiers					
Linear SVM (Tuned)	0.874	0.890	0.838	0.863	0.943
Radial SVM (Tuned)	0.886	0.906	0.846	0.875	0.947
Sigmoid SVM (Tuned)	0.885	0.904	**0.847**	0.874	0.948
LightGBM (Tuned)	**0.888**	0.921	0.834	**0.876**	**0.9508**
XGBoost (Tuned)	**0.888**	**0.925**	0.831	0.875	0.9506

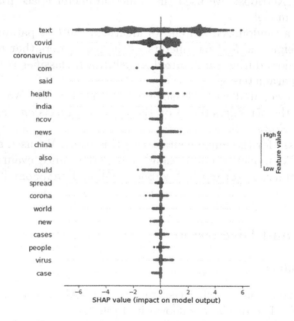

Fig. 3. SHAP values for CatBoost model

are listed in descending order of significance on CatBoost's output. CatBoost's implicit processing for text data gave the highest feature importance for determining a model's prediction.

For individual examples, Figs. 4, 5, and 6 shows the features' impact in the model's output. The *base value* is the mean prediction over the training dataset, and is the default prediction for unseen data. The prediction is affected based from the feature values.

Text: chinese student wuhan began posting godlike productions hrs ago say extremely worrisome believe telling truth chinese wu han one leave city enter city total cases dead infected cannot leave city anymore cannot allow others enter city army guarding exit entry point forms mass transit lockdowned including airport let die seen soldiers full hazmat suits hanyang second floor appartment window spraying something fluid streets via large trucks using water cannons using vpn allowed talk criticize virus jail sentence sure one fang zhong within institute people alarmed happen know personaly least two iopcas scientists put house arrest virus west thinks much dangerous mutates
Label: 1
Prediction: 1

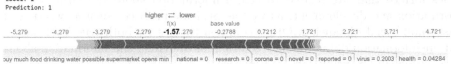

Fig. 4. Detected as misinformation (Color figure online)

Text: date specific medicine recommended prevent treat new coronavirus ncov however infected virus receive appropriate care re lieve treat symptoms severe illness receive optimized supportive care specific treatments investigation tested clinical trials helping accelerate research development efforts range partners
Label: 0
Prediction: 0

Fig. 5. Detected as true information (Color figure online)

Text: try look period social distancing opportunity get things meaning though gym right mean exercise take long walks run outside best maintain least s ix feet non family members outside yoga indoor exercise routines weather cooperating kids need exercise try get outside every day walks backyard family soccer game remember time invite neighborhood kids play avoid public playground structures cleaned regularly spread virus pull board games gathering du st shelves family movie nights catch books meaning read family read aloud every evening important stay connected even though person keep touch virtuall y phone calls skype video social media enjoy leisurely chat old friend meaning
Label: 0
Prediction: 1

Fig. 6. False positive (tagged as misinformation but is true information) (Color figure online)

The blue color on the right side are the features that have a negative impact, lowering the model's prediction while the red color on the left has the features which have a positive impact, and pushes the prediction higher.

The true positive example in Fig. 4, the tokens are the features that pushes the prediction lower while the text feature pushes the prediction higher. The text field shows the gist of the article is to spread panic. The true negative example in Fig. 5, the text feature in itself contributes to the model's lower prediction.

The last example (Fig. 6) is a false positive and this instance shows the importance of SHAP's *local interpretability*. By inspecting the features that contributed to a specific sample, the tokens are the features that contributed to the model's higher prediction.

6   Conclusion and Future Work

In this paper, we interpreted common themes on COVID-19 articles and posts about COVID-19 using LDA. Results show that majority of the themes for both types of information is related to healthcare, with misinformation topics associated with alternative treatment methods, vaccine conspiracies, and fear-mongering news regarding politics. For reliable information, there are many topics formed that are related to health information about the virus, vaccine information and development, as well as hygienic practices such as wearing of masks and social distancing. Other common themes for both true information and misinformation datasets relate to origin of the virus, and information about travel, economy, transmission, and politics.

For misinformation related to economy and the stock market - this can show that during the time the data was collected, it is too early to speculate about the market and having fake news circulating about the economy can lead to people making impulsive decisions that can subject them to scam and phish schemes.

A possible opportunity for revisiting LDA in articles related to COVID-19 is if there is a shift in topics influenced by a difference time frame from when the dataset was collected.

For the performance benchmarking of CatBoost with SVM, LightGBM, and XGBoost, results show that CatBoost variants performs better in terms of Accuracy, Recall, F1-Score, and ROC-AUC score. LightGBM and Radial SVM gave the best precision results. The Sigmoid SVM yielded better results than Cat-Boost + TF-IDF models

Lastly, it was shown that using model interpretability modules such as SHAP can help researchers diagnose model prediction and provide improvements in model training.

It is proposed in future experiments to include other features, especially categorical ones, to the dataset as they may also determine if the information is real or fake. Future implementations of this work can include hyperparameter tuning for more than three parameters as well as the full use of CatBoost's textual capabilities. Furthermore, CatBoost has many parameters, and more experiments must be performed to finetune and improve the performance of the model. It is recommended that the hyperparameters of all classifiers are further optimized to get better results.

Due to time constraints, we were unable to compare CatBoost with other classifiers found in related work, such as decision trees [11], k-Nearest Neighbors [1], and Bi-LSTM [15]. It is suggested that CatBoost is compared with the algorithms mentioned using the merged dataset. We also suggest comparing CatBoost with other power classification algorithms such as neural-based (neural networks, deep neural networks) and transformer-based approaches (pre-trained models such as BERT and RoBERTa) for a more complete performance benchmark.

Combining CatBoost with other models can greatly increase its performance. Querashi et al. [19] created an ensemble of CatBoost and recurrent neural networks for COVID-19 fake news classification with Twitter posts dataset and got an AUC score of 98%.

Aside from Bag of Words used by CatBoost and TF-IDF used by all models to represent text data, other methods such as ngram2vec, word2vec, Global Vectors

(GloVe), Bidirectional Encoder Representations from Transformers (BERT) can also be explored as word embedding techniques.

References

1. Al-Ahmad, B., Al-Zoubi, A.M., Abu Khurma, R., Aljarah, I.: An evolutionary fake news detection method for Covid-19 pandemic information. Symmetry **13**(6) (2021). https://doi.org/10.3390/sym13061091, https://www.mdpi.com/2073-8994/13/6/1091
2. Bangyal, W.H., et al.: Detection of fake news text classification on Covid-19 using deep learning approaches. Computat. Math. Methods Med. **2021** (2021)
3. Bird, S., Klein, E., Loper, E.: Natural Language Processing with Python: Analyzing Text with the Natural Language Toolkit. O'Reilly Media, Inc., Sebastopol (2009)
4. Blei, D.M., Ng, A.Y., Jordan, M.I.: Latent Dirichlet Allocation. J. Mach. Learn. Res. **3**, 993–1022 (2003)
5. Chen, T., Guestrin, C.: XGBoost: a scalable tree boosting system. In: Proceedings of the 22nd ACM SIGKDD International Conference on Knowledge Discovery and Data Mining. KDD 2016, pp. 785–794. ACM, New York (2016). https://doi.org/10.1145/2939672.2939785, http://doi.acm.org/10.1145/2939672.2939785
6. Chen, Y., Han, X.: CatBoost for fraud detection in financial transactions. In: 2021 IEEE International Conference on Consumer Electronics and Computer Engineering (ICCECE), pp. 176–179 (2021). https://doi.org/10.1109/ICCECE51280.2021.9342475
7. scikit-learn developers: 6.2. feature extraction - scikit-learn 1.1.1 documentation (2022). https://scikit-learn.org/stable/modules/feature_extraction.html. Accessed 15 Jan 2022
8. Dhankar, A., Samuel, H., Hassan, F., Farruque, N., Bolduc, F., Zaïane, O.: Analysis of Covid-19 misinformation in social media using transfer learning. In: 2021 IEEE 33rd International Conference on Tools with Artificial Intelligence (ICTAI), pp. 880–885 (2021). https://doi.org/10.1109/ICTAI52525.2021.00141
9. Dorogush, A.V., Ershov, V., Gulin, A.: CatBoost: gradient boosting with categorical features support. arXiv preprint arXiv:1810.11363 (2018)
10. Joy, R.A.: An interpretable CatBoost model to predict the power of combined cycle power plants. In: 2021 International Conference on Information Technology (ICIT), pp. 435–439 (2021). https://doi.org/10.1109/ICIT52682.2021.9491700
11. Kapusta, J., Drlik, M., Munk, M.: Using of n-grams from morphological tags for fake news classification. PeerJ Comput. Sci. **7**, e624 (2021)
12. Ke, G., et al.: LightGBM: a highly efficient gradient boosting decision tree. In: Proceedings of the 31st International Conference on Neural Information Processing Systems. NIPS 2017, pp. 3149–3157. Curran Associates Inc., Red Hook (2017)
13. Khan, J.Y., Khondaker, M.T.I., Afroz, S., Uddin, G., Iqbal, A.: A benchmark study of machine learning models for online fake news detection. Mach. Learn. Appl. **4**, 100032 (2021)
14. Koirala, A.: Covid-19 fake news dataset. https://doi.org/10.13140/RG.2.2.26509.56805. Accessed 23 Nov 2021
15. Koirala, A.: Covid-19 fake news classification with deep learning. https://doi.org/10.13140/RG.2.2.26509.56805. Accessed 20 Dec 2021
16. Li, S.: Explore Covid-19 infodemic (2020). https://towardsdatascience.com/explore-covid-19-infodemic-2d1ceaae2306. Accessed 23 Nov 2021

17. Lundberg, S.M., Lee, S.I.: A unified approach to interpreting model predictions. In: Guyon, I., et al. (eds.) Advances in Neural Information Processing Systems, vol. 30, pp. 4765–4774. Curran Associates, Inc. (2017). http://papers.nips.cc/paper/7062-a-unified-approach-to-interpreting-model-predictions.pdf. Accessed 18 Dec 2021
18. Pedregosa, F., et al.: Scikit-learn: machine learning in Python. J. Mach. Learn. Res. **12**, 2825–2830 (2011)
19. Qureshi, K.A., Malick, R.A.S., Sabih, M., Cherifi, H.: Complex network and source inspired Covid-19 fake news classification on twitter. IEEE Access **9**, 139636–139656 (2021). https://doi.org/10.1109/ACCESS.2021.3119404
20. Rehurek, R., Sojka, P.: GenSIM-Python framework for vector space modelling. NLP Centre, Faculty of Informatics, Masaryk University, Brno, Czech Republic, vol. 3, no. 2 (2011)
21. Saenz, J.A., Kalathur Gopal, S.R., Shukla, D.: Covid-19 fake news infodemic research dataset (covid19-fnir dataset) (2021). https://dx.doi.org/10.21227/b5bt-5244. Accessed 23 Nov 2021
22. Selivanov, D.: Topic modeling (2018). http://text2vec.org/topic_modeling.html. Accessed 20 Dec 2021
23. Sievert, C., Shirley, K.: Ldavis: a method for visualizing and interpreting topics. In: Proceedings of the Workshop on Interactive Language Learning, Visualization, and Interfaces, pp. 63–70 (2014)
24. Tohka, J., van Gils, M.: Evaluation of machine learning algorithms for health and wellness applications: a tutorial. Comput. Biol. Med. **132**, 104324 (2021). https://doi.org/10.1016/j.compbiomed.2021.104324, https://www.sciencedirect.com/science/article/pii/S0010482521001189
25. WHO: World health organization definition: Infodemic. https://www.who.int/health-topics/infodemic/. Accessed 28 Dec 2021
26. Winter, E.: The Shapley value. In: Handbook of Game Theory with Economic Applications **3**, 2025–2054 (2002)
27. Zhang, X., Wu, G.X.: Text classification method of Dongba classics based on Cat-Boost algorithm. In: The 8th International Symposium on Test Automation Instrumentation (ISTAI 2020), vol. 2020, pp. 133–139 (2020). https://doi.org/10.1049/icp.2021.1336

Augmentation-Based Ensemble Learning for Stance and Fake News Detection

Ilhem Salah[ID], Khaled Jouini[✉][ID], and Ouajdi Korbaa[ID]

MARS Research Lab LR17ES05, ISITCom, University of Sousse,
H. Sousse 4011, Tunisia
khaled.jouini@isitc.u-sousse.tn, ouajdi.korbaa@centraliens-lille.org

Abstract. Data augmentation is an unsupervised technique used to generate additional training data by slightly modifying already existing data. Besides preventing data scarcity, one of the main interest of data augmentation is that it increases training data diversity, and hence improves models' ability to generalize to unseen data. In this work we investigate the use of text data augmentation for the task of stance and fake news detection.

In the first part of our work, we explore the effect of various text augmentation techniques on the performance of common classification algorithms. Besides identifying the best performing (classification algorithm, augmentation technique) pairs, our study reveals that the motto *"the more, the better"* is the wrong approach regarding text augmentation and that there is no *one-size-fits-all* text augmentation technique.

The second part of our work leverages the results of our study to propose a novel augmentation-based, ensemble learning approach that can be seen as a mixture between stacking and bagging. The proposed approach leverages text augmentation to enhance base learners' diversity and accuracy, ergo the predictive performance of the ensemble. Experiments conducted on two real-world datasets show that our ensemble learning approach achieves very promising predictive performances.

Keywords: Stance and fake news detection · Text augmentation · Ensemble learning · Fake news challenge

1 Introduction

In the era of the Internet and social media, where a myriad of information of various types is instantly available and where any point of view can find an audience, access to information is no longer an issue, and the key challenges are veracity, credibility, and authenticity. The reason for this is that any user can readily gather, consume, and break news, without verification, fact-checking, or third-party filtering. As revealed by several recent studies, fake news and misinformation are prone to spread substantially faster, wider, and deeper than genuine news and real information [8, 21].

© The Author(s), under exclusive license to Springer Nature Switzerland AG 2022
C. Bădică et al. (Eds.): ICCCI 2022, CCIS 1653, pp. 29–41, 2022.
https://doi.org/10.1007/978-3-031-16210-7_3

By directly influencing public opinions, major political events, and societal debates, fake news has become the scourge of the digital era, and combating it has become a dire need. The identification of fake news is however very challenging, not only from a machine learning and Natural Language Processing (NLP) perspective, but also sometimes for the most experienced journalists [18]. That is why the scientific community approaches the task from a variety of angles and often breaks down the process into independent sub-tasks. A first practical step towards automatic fact-checking and fake news detection is to estimate the opinion or the point of view (*i.e. stance*) of different news sources regarding the same topic or claim [18]. This (sub-) task, addressed in recent research as *stance detection*, was popularized by the Fake News Challenge - Stage 1 (or FNC-1) [18], which compares article bodies to article headlines and determines if a body agrees, disagrees, discusses or is unrelated to the claim of a headline.

In this paper we propose a novel *Augmentation-based Ensemble learning* approach for stance and fake news detection. Data augmentation refers to techniques used to create new training data by slightly modifying available labelled data. Besides preventing data scarcity, one of the main interest of data augmentation is that it increases training data diversity, and hence helps to improve models' ability to generalize to unseen data [11]. Data augmentation is extensively used in Computer Vision (CV) where it is considered as one of the anchors of good predictive performance. Despite promising advances, data augmentation remains however less explored in NLP where it is still considered as the "cherry on the cake" which provides a steady but limited performance boost [23].

Ensemble learning combines the knowledge acquired by base learners to make a consensus decision which is supposed to be superior to the one attained by each base learner alone [27]. Research on ensemble learning proves that the greater are the skills and the diversity of base learners, the better are the accuracy and the generalization ability of the ensemble [27]. In this work we leverage text data augmentation to enhance both, the diversity and the skills of base learners, ergo the accuracy of the ensemble.

The main contributions of our work are therefore: (*i*) an extensive experimental study on the effect of different text data augmentation techniques on the performance of common classification algorithms in the context of stance and fake news detection. Our study provides insights for practitioners and researchers on text data augmentation and the best performing (data augmentation technique, classification algorithm) pairs; and (*ii*) a novel augmentation-based ensemble learning approach, which is a mixture of stacking and bagging.

The remainder of this paper is organized as follows. Section 2 outlines the main steps we followed to vectorize text and reduce dimensionality. Section 3 exposes the key motifs of data augmentation and the text augmentation techniques adopted in our work. Section 4 details the architecture of our novel augmentation-based ensemble learning. Section 5 briefly reviews existing work on stance and fake news detection. Section 6 presents an experimental study on two real-world fake news datasets and discusses the main results and findings. Finally, Sect. 7 concludes the paper.

2   Text as Vectors

2.1   Pre-processing and Feature Extraction

Machine Learning (ML) algorithms operate on numerical features, expecting input in the form of a matrix where rows represent instances and columns features. Raw news texts have therefore to be transformed into feature vectors before feeding into ML algorithms [9]. In our work, we first eliminated stop words and reduced words to their roots (*i.e.* base words) by stemming them using Snowball Stemmer from the NLTK library [16]. We next vectorized the corpus with a TF-IDF (*Term Frequency - Inverse Document Frequency*) weighting scheme and generated a term-document matrix.

TF-IDF is computed on a per-term basis, such that the relevance of a term to a text is measured by the scaled frequency of the appearance of the term in the text, normalized by the inverse of the scaled frequency of the term in the entire corpus. Despite its simplicity and its wide-spread use, the TF-IDF scheme has two severe limitations: (*i*) TF-IDF does not capture the co-occurrence of terms in the corpus and makes no use of semantic similarities between words. Accordingly, TF-IDF fails to capture some basic linguistic notions such as synonymy and homonymy; and (*ii*) The term-document matrix is high dimensional and is often noisy, redundant, and excessively sparse. The matrix is thus subject to the curse of dimensionality: as the number of features is large, poor generalization is to be expected.

2.2   Dimensionality Reduction

Latent Semantic Analysis (LSA) [3] is an unsupervised statistical topic modeling technique, overcoming some of the limitations of TF-IDF. As other topic modeling techniques, such as LDA (Latent Dirichlet Allocation [2]), LSA is based on the assumptions that: (*i*) each text consists of a mixture of topics; and (*ii*) each topic consists of a set of (weighted) terms that regularly co-occur together. Put differently, the basic assumption behind LSA is that words that are close in meaning, appear in similar contexts and form a "hidden topic". The basic intuition behind LSA is to represent words that form a topic not as separate dimensions, but by a single dimension. LSA represents thus texts by "semantic" or "topic" vectors, based on the words that these texts contain and the set of weighted words that form each of the topics.

To uncover the latent topics that shapes the meaning of texts, LSA performs a Singular Value Decomposition (SVD) on the document-term matrix (*i.e.* decomposes it into a separate text-topic matrix and a topic-term matrix). Formally, SVD decomposes the term-document matrix $A_{t \times n}$, with t the number terms and d the number of documents, into the product of three different matrices: orthogonal column matrix, orthogonal row matrix and one singular matrix.

$$A_{t \times n} = U_{t \times n} S_{n \times n} D_{n \times d}^{T} \tag{1}$$

where $n = min(t, d)$ is the rank of A. By restricting the matrices T, S and D to their first $k < n$ rows, we obtain the matrices $T_{t \times k}$, $S_{k \times k}$ and $D_{d \times k}$, and hence obtain k-dimensional text vectors. From a practical perspective the key ask is to determine k, which would be reasonable for the problem (*i.e.* without major loss). In our work we used the transformer TruncatedSVD from sklearn [17]. As in [12] we set the value of k to 100D. The experimental study conducted in [12] showed that using LSA (with k set to 100D) instead of TF-IDF allows a substantial performance improvement for the tasks of stance and fake news detection.

3   Text Data Augmentation

Data augmentation aims at synthesizing new training instances that have the same ground-truth labels as the instances that they originate from [30]. Data augmentation has several well-known benefits: (*i*) preventing overfitting by improving the diversity of training data; (*ii*) preventing data scarcity by providing a relatively easy and inexpensive way to collect and label data; (*iii*) helping resolve class imbalance issues; and (*iv*) increasing the generalization ability of the obtained model.

The success of data augmentation in Computer Vision has been fueled by the ease of designing semantically invariant transformations (*i.e.* label-preserving transformations), such as rotation, flipping, etc. While recent years witnessed significant advancements in the design of transformation techniques, text augmentation remains less explored and adopted in NLP than in CV. This is mainly due to the intrinsic properties of textual data (*e.g.* polysemy), which make defining label-preserving transformations much harder [23]. In the sequel we mainly focus on off-the-shelf text augmentation techniques and less on techniques that are still in the research phase, waiting for large-scale testing and adoption. For a more exhaustive survey on text augmentation techniques, we refer the reader to [1,11,28].

3.1   Masked Language Models

The main idea behind Masked Language Models (MLMs), such as BERT [4], is to mask words in sentences and let the model predict the masked words. BERT, which is a pretrained multi-layer bidirectional transformer encoder, has the ability to predict masked words based on the bidirectional context (*i.e.* based on its left and right surrounding words). In contrast with other context-free models such as GLOVE and Word2Vec, BERT alleviates the problem of ambiguity since it considers the whole context of a word.

BERT is considered as a breakthrough in the use of ML for NLP and is widely used in a variety of tasks such as classification, Question/Answering, and Named Entity Recognition [22]. Inspired by the recent work of [11,22], we use BERT as an augmentation technique. The idea is to generate new sentences by randomly masking words and replacing them by those predicted by BERT.

3.2   Back-translation (*a.k.a.* Round-Trip Translation)

Back-Translation is the process of translating a text into another language, then translating the new text back into the original language. Back-translation is one of the most popular means of paraphrasing and text data augmentation [15]. Google Cloud Translation API, used in our work to translate sentences to French and back, is considered as the most common tool for back-translation [11].

3.3   Synonym (*a.k.a.* Thesaurus-Based Augmentation)

The synonym technique, also called lexical substitution with dictionary, was until recently the most widely (and for a long time the only) augmentation technique used for textual data classification. As suggested by its name, the Synonym technique replaces randomly selected words with their respective synonyms. The types of words that are candidates for lexical substitution are: adverbs, adjectives, nouns and verbs.

The synonyms are typically taken from a lexical database (*i.e.* dictionary of synonyms). WordNet [6], used in our work for synonym replacement, is considered as the most popular open-source lexical database for the English language [11].

3.4   TF-IDF Based Insertion and Substitution

The intuition behind these two noising-based techniques is that uninformative words (*i.e.* having low TF-IDF scores) should have no or little impact on classification. Therefore, the insertion of words having low TF-IDF scores (at random positions) should preserve the label associated with a text, even if the semantics are not preserved. An alternate strategy is to replace randomly selected words with words having the same low TF-IDF scores (TF-IDF based substitution).

Section 6 presents an extensive study on the effect of the aforementioned augmentation techniques on the preredictive performance of ten common classification algorithms, namely, Decision Tree (DT), Support Vector Machine (SVM), Adaptive Boosting (AdaBoost), Random Forest (RF), eXtreme Gradient Boosting (XGBoost), Bagged Random Forests (Bagged RF), Light Gradient Boosting Machine (LightGBM), Gradient Boosting (GradBoost), Logistic Regression (LR), and Naive Bayes (NB). Moreover, in contrast with existing work, where text augmentation is considered as an auxiliary technique, our novel augmentation-based ensemble approach presented in next section, goes further and let augmentation shape the entire learning process.

4   Augmentation-Based Ensemble Learning

4.1   Diversity and Skillfulness in Ensemble Learning

Ensemble Learning finds its origins in the "Wisdom of Crowds" theory [26]. The "Wisdom of Crowds" theory states that the collective opinion of a group of individuals can be better than the opinion of a single expert, provided that the aggregated opinions are diverse (*i.e.* diversity of opinion) and that each individual in the group has a minimum level of competence (*e.g.* better than a random guess). Similarly, Ensemble Learning combines the knowledge acquired by a group of base learners to make a consensus decision which is supposed to be superior to the one reached by each of them separately [27]. Research on Ensemble Learning proves that the greater are the skills and the diversity of base models, the better is the generalization ability of the ensemble model [27]. Alternatively stated, to generate a good ensemble model, it is necessary to build base models that are, not only skillful, but also skillful in a different way from one another.

Bagging and stacking are among the main classes of parallel ensemble techniques. Bagging (*i.e.* Bootstrap aggregating) involves training multiple instances of the same classification algorithm, then combining the predictions of the obtained models through hard or soft voting. To promote diversity, base learners are trained on different subsets of the original training set. Each subset is typically obtained by drawing random samples with replacement from the original training set (*i.e.* bootstrap samples).

Stacking (*a.k.a.* stacked generalization) involves training a learning algorithm (*i.e.* meta-classifier) to combine the predictions of several heterogeneous learning algorithms, trained on the same training data. The most common approach to train the meta-model is via k-fold cross-validation. With the k-fold cross-validation, the whole training dataset is randomly split (without replacement) into independent equal-sized k-folds. $k - 1$ folds are then used to train each of the base models and the kth fold (holdout fold) is used to collect the predictions of base models on unseen data. The predictions made by base models on the holdout fold, along with the expected class labels, provide the input and the output pairs used to train the meta-model. This procedure is repeated k times. Each time a different fold acts as the holdout fold while the remaining folds are combined and used for training the base models.

4.2   Novel Augmentation Based Approach

As mentioned earlier, in conventional stacking base learners are trained on the same dataset and diversity is achieved by using heterogeneous classification algorithms. As depicted in Fig. 1, the classical approach for combining augmentation and stacking, is to: (*i*) apply one or several augmentation techniques to the original dataset, (*ii*) fuse the original dataset with data obtained through augmentation; and (*iii*) train base learners on the fused dataset.

In our work we adopt a different approach and train heterogeneous algorithms on different data to further promote diversity. More specifically, through an extensive experimental study (Sect. 6), we first identify the most accurate (augmentation technique, classification algorithm) pairs. Our meta-model is then trained on the predictions made by the most accurate pairs, using a stratified k-fold cross-validation. Figure 2 depicts the overall architecture of the proposed augmentation-based ensemble learning.

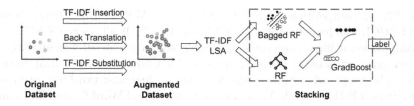

Fig. 1. Conventional approach for combining augmentation and stacking

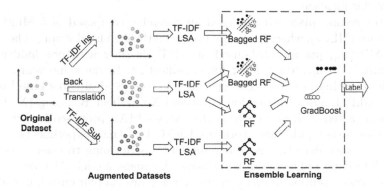

Fig. 2. Novel augmentation-based ensemble learning approach

Our augmentation-based ensemble learning approach, can be seen as a mixture between stacking and bagging. In contrast with Bagging and like Stacking, we use an ensemble of heterogeneous learning algorithms. In contrast with stacking and like Bagging, base learners are trained on different datasets, to further promote diversity. However, unlike Bagging the considered datasets are not obtained through bootstrap sampling. Instead, they are obtained by combining the original training data with the data obtained by applying one of the text augmentation techniques. Finally, like in conventional Stacking, the meta-model is trained using a stratified K-fold cross-validation.

5   Related Work

Salient stance and fake news detection approaches adopt a wide range of different features (*e.g.*, context-based, content-based), classifiers, and learning tactics (*e.g.* stacking, bagging, etc.) [5]. Due to the lack of space, we mainly focus hereafter on ensemble approaches and on approaches that rely on content-based features. We suggest readers to refer to surveys and retrospectives on recent challenges [7,10] for a more comprehensive overview of the current state of research.

The authors of the fake news challenge (FNC-1) [25], released a simple baseline model for the stance detection task. The proposed model achieves an F1-score of 79.53% and uses a gradient boosting (GradBoost) classifier on global co-occurrence, polarity and refutation features. The three best performing systems in the FNC-1 competition were "SOLAT in the SWEN" [20], "Team Athene" [7] and "UCL Machine Reading" (UCLMR) [19]. "SOLAT in the SWEN" won the competition using an ensemble approach based on a 50/50 weighted average between gradient-boosted decision trees and a Convolutional Neural Network (CNN). The proposed system is based on several features: word2vec pretrained embeddings, TF-IDF, Single Value Decomposition and Word Count. The convolutional network uses pre-trained Word2Vec embeddings passed through several convolutional layers followed by three fully-connected layers and a final softmax layer for classification.

[7], the second place winner, used an ensemble composed of 5 Multi-Layer Perceptrons (MLPs), where labels are predicted through hard voting. The system of UCLMR [19], placed third, used an MLP classifier with one hidden layer of 100 units and a softmax layer for classification. In the same vein as [7,14] uses a hard voting classifier. The ensemble is composed of three base learners, namely, MLP, Logistic Regression (LR) and X-Gradient Boosting (XGBoost). [14] experimented their approach on the dataset LIAR proposed by [29].

Recently, other published work used FNC-1 in their experiments. [5] constructed a stance detection language model by performing transfer learning on a RoBERTa deep bidirectional transformer language model. [5] leverages bidirectional cross-attention between claim-article pairs via pair encoding with self-attention. The work of [12], which is the closest to the spirit of our work, uses LSA for dimensionality reduction and a stacking-based ensemble having five base learners: GradBoost, Random Forest (RF), XGBoost, Bagging and Light Gradient Boosting Machine (Lightgbm). Besides, [12] compared LDA and LSA and found that LSA yields better accuracy. The authors in [12] experimented their approach on FNC-1 and FNN datasets.

It is worth noticing that in all the aforementioned studies, ensemble approaches yielded better results than those attained by their contributing base learners. On the other hand, despite the substantial potential improvement that text augmentation can carry out, to the best of our knowledge there exists no previous work on stance and fake news detection that compares text augmentation techniques and uses text augmentation in conjunction with ensemble learning.

6   Experimental Study

6.1   Tools and Datasets

Our system was implemented using NLTK [16] for text preprocessing, nlpaug [13] for text augmentation, SciKit-Learn (version 0.24.2) [17] for classification and Beautiful Soup for web scraping. A stratified 10-fold cross-validation was used for model fusion. The Li & al. approach was implemented as described in [12]. The experimental study was conducted without any special tuning. A large number of experiments have been performed to show the accuracy and the effectiveness of our augmentation-based ensemble learning. Due to the lack of space, only few results are presented herein.

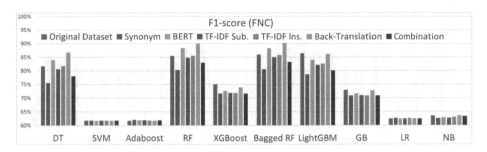

Fig. 3. F1-scores on FNC with and without text augmentation

As there are no agreed-upon benchmark datasets for stance and fake news detection [12], we used two publicly available and complementary datasets: FNC-1 [18] and FNN (*i.e.* FakeNewsNet) [24]. FNC was released to explore the task of stance detection in the context of fake news detection. Stance detection is a multinomial classification problem, where the relative stance of each headline-article pair has to be classified as either: *Agree* if the article agrees with the headline claim, *Disagree* if the article disagrees with the claim, *Discuss* if the article is related to the claim, but takes no position on the subject, and *Unrelated* if the content of the article is unrelated to the claim. The FNC-1 dataset consists of approximately 50k headline-article pairs in the training set and 25k pairs in the test set. FNN data was collected from two fact-checking websites (*i.e.* GossipCop and PolitiFact) containing news contents, along with context information. In comparison with FNN, FNC-1 provides fewer data features (4 vs. 13 features), but more data (≈75k vs. ≈997).

6.2 Results and Discussion

We ran our experiments with three objectives in mind: (*i*) identify the best performing (*Augmentation technique, Classifier*) pairs; (*ii*) quantify the actual performance improvement allowed by each text augmentation technique; and (*iii*) evaluate the effectiveness of our augmentation-based ensemble approach.

Best Performing Pairs. Figure 3 (resp. Fig. 4), reports the F1-scores obtained on FNC (resp. FNN). The results presented in these charts allow to draw important conclusions regarding text augmentation:

1. *Text augmentation does not always improve predictive performance.* This can be especially observed for SVM, LightGBM, GradBoost (Fig. 3) and AdaBoost (Fig. 4), where the F1-scores on the original dataset are higher than to those obtained on the augmented datasets;
2. *There is no one-size-fits-all augmentation technique that performs well in all situations.* As depicted in Figs. 3 and 4, an augmentation technique may perform well when combined with a classification algorithm and poorly when

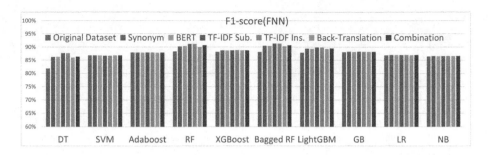

Fig. 4. F1-scores on FNN with and without text augmentation

combined with another. This is the case for example for the "Synonym" technique which yields the highest F1-score when combined with Adaboost and the lowest score when used with Naive Bayes (Fig. 3).

It is worth noting that even if BERT doesn't achieve the highest F1-scores, it provides a steady performance improvement for almost all classifiers;

3. *The motto "the more, the better" is the wrong approach regarding text augmentation and targeted approaches allow often better results.* This can be observed in Figs. 3 and 4, where in almost all cases, combining all augmentation techniques does not yield the best F1-scores.

As shown in Fig. 3, the pairs (Back-translation, Bagged RF) and (Back-translation, RF) yield the highest F1-scores on FNC and increase substantially the predictive performances ($\approx$ +4.16% in comparison with the highest F1-Score that can be achieved without text augmentation). Similarly, as shown in Fig. 4, the pairs (Substitution TF-IDF, RF) and (Insertion TF-IDF, Bagged RF) yield the best F1-scores on the dataset FNN ($\approx$ +5.87%).

Augmentation-Based Ensemble Learning. As previously stated, base learners' diversity and competency are the two key success factors of any ensemble learning approach. Our ensemble approach leverages text augmentation to enhance both. Figure 2 depicts our classification model which is a mixture of stacking and bagging. In our model, we use Bagged RF and Random Forest (RF) as base classifiers and GradBoost as meta-classifier. As depicted in Fig. 2, each of the base classifiers is trained on a dataset composed of the original dataset and the data obtained by applying one of the augmentation techniques. The choice of the (classifier, augmentation technique) pairs was driven by the experimental study conducted in Subsect. 6.2. We compare our model to a more classical stacking approach, where all base classifiers are trained on the same dataset, consisting of the original dataset and the data obtained by applying one of the augmentation techniques (Fig. 1). We also compare our model to the approach of [12], which is one of the state-of-the-art approaches that uses LSA, stacking-based ensemble learning and K-fold cross-validation. Table 1 synthesizes the predictive performances achieved by each approach.

Table 1. F1-scores achieved by conventional stacking, [12] and the proposed approach

Model	FNC	FNN
(Insertion TF-IDF, Stacking)	85,58%	**90,92%**
(Substitution TF-IDF, Stacking)	84,57%	90,43%
(Back-Translation, Stacking)	**90,31%**	89,80%
(BERT, Stacking)	87,93%	90,26%
(Synonym, Stacking)	80,71%	90,28%
(Combination, Stacking)	83,11%	90,73%
Li et al. [12]	83,72%	88,45%
Proposed approach	**90,15%**	**91,07%**

As reported in Table 1, the use of text augmentation allows better performances than those achieved by [12] in almost all situations. On the other hand, except for the Synonym technique over the FNC dataset, our model outperforms the classical approach in all situations. Overall, our stacking approach achieves an increase in F1-score of 7,72% (resp. 7,54%) over FNC (resp. FNN) when compared to [12].

7   Conclusion

Combating fake news on social media is a pressing need and a daunting task. Most of the existing approaches on fake news detection, focus on using various features to identify those allowing the best predictive performance. Such approaches tend to undermine the generalization ability of the obtained models.

In this work, we investigated the use of text augmentation in the context of stance and fake news detection. In the first part of our work, we studied the effect of text augmentation on the performance of various classification algorithms. Our experimental study quantified the actual contribution of data augmentation and identified the best performing (classifier, augmentation technique) pairs. Besides, our study revealed that the motto "the more, the better" is the wrong approach regarding text augmentation and that there is no one-size-fits-all augmentation technique. In the second part of our work, we proposed a novel augmentation-based ensemble learning approach. The proposed approach is a mixture of bagging and stacking and leverages text augmentation to enhance the diversity and the performance of base classifiers. We evaluated our approach using two real-world datasets. Experimental results show that it is more accurate than state-of-art methods.

As a part of our future work, we intend to explore the use of a multimodal data augmentation that involves linguistic and extra linguistic features. We also intend to explore the detection of fake news from streams under concept drifts.

References

1. Karnyoto, A.S., Sun, C., Liu, B., Wang, X.: Augmentation and heterogeneous graph neural network for AAAI2021-Covid-19 fake news detection. Int. J. Mach. Learn. Cybern. 13 (2022). https://doi.org/10.1007/s13042-021-01503-5
2. Blei, D.M., Ng, A.Y., Jordan, M.I.: Latent Dirichlet allocation. J. Mach. Learn. Res. **3**, 993–1022 (2003)
3. Deerwester, S., Dumais, S.T., Furnas, G.W., Landauer, T.K., Harshman, R.: Indexing by latent semantic analysis. J. Am. Soc. Inf. Sci. **41**(6), 391–407 (1990)
4. Devlin, J., Chang, M., Lee, K., Toutanova, K.: BERT: pre-training of deep bidirectional transformers for language understanding. CoRR abs/1810.04805 (2018)
5. Dulhanty, C., Deglint, J.L., Daya, I.B., Wong, A.: Taking a stance on fake news: towards automatic disinformation assessment via deep bidirectional transformer language models for stance detection. CoRR abs/1911.11951 (2019)
6. Fellbaum, C.: Wordnet and wordnets. In: Barber, A. (ed.) Encyclopedia of Language and Linguistics, pp. 2–665. Elsevier, Amsterdam (2005)
7. Hanselowski, A., et al.: A retrospective analysis of the fake news challenge stance-detection task (2018)
8. Hsu, C.C., Ajorlou, A., Jadbabaie, Ali, P.: News sharing, and cascades on social networks, December 2021. https://ssrn.com/abstract=3934010 or https://doi.org/10.2139/ssrn.3934010. Accessed 05 Jan 2022
9. Jouini, K., Maaloul, M.H., Korbaa, O.: Real-time, CNN-based assistive device for visually impaired people. In: 2021 14th International Congress on Image and Signal Processing, BioMedical Engineering and Informatics (CISP-BMEI), pp. 1–6 (2021)
10. Khan, J.Y., Khondaker, M.T.I., Afroz, S., Uddin, G., Iqbal, A.: A benchmark study of machine learning models for online fake news detection. Mach. Learn. Appl. **4**, 100032 (2021). https://doi.org/10.1016/j.mlwa.2021.100032, https://www.sciencedirect.com/science/article/pii/S266682702100013X
11. Li, B., Hou, Y., Che, W.: Data augmentation approaches in natural language processing: a survey. CoRR abs/2110.01852 (2021). https://arxiv.org/abs/2110.01852
12. Li, S., et al.: Stacking-based ensemble learning on low dimensional features for fake news detection. In: 2019 IEEE 21st International Conference on High Performance Computing and Communications; IEEE 17th International Conference on Smart City; IEEE 5th International Conference on Data Science and Systems (HPCC/SmartCity/DSS) (2019). https://doi.org/10.1109/HPCC/SmartCity/DSS.2019.00383
13. Ma, E.: NLP augmentation (2019). https://github.com/makcedward/nlpaug. Accessed 15 May 2021
14. Mahabub, A.: A robust technique of fake news detection using ensemble voting classifier and comparison with other classifiers. SN Appl. Sci. **2**(4), 1–9 (2020). https://doi.org/10.1007/s42452-020-2326-y
15. Marivate, V., Sefara, T.: Improving short text classification through global augmentation methods. CoRR abs/1907.03752 (2019). http://arxiv.org/abs/1907.03752
16. NLTK.org: Natural Language Toolkit. https://github.com/nltk/nltk. Accessed 15 May 2021
17. Pedregosa, F., et al.: Scikit-learn: machine learning in Python. J. Mach. Learn. Res. **12**, 2825–2830 (2011)
18. Pomerleau, D., Rao, D.: The fake news challenge: exploring how artificial intelligence technologies could be leveraged to combat fake news (2017). http://www.fakenewschallenge.org/. Accessed 15 Dec 2021

19. Riedel, B., Augenstein, I., Spithourakis, G.P., Riedel, S.: A simple but tough-to-beat baseline for the fake news challenge stance detection task. CoRR abs/1707.03264 (2017). http://arxiv.org/abs/1707.03264
20. Sepúlveda Torres, R., Vicente, M., Saquete, E., Lloret, E., Sanz, M.: Headlines-tancechecker: exploiting summarization to detect headline disinformation. J. Web Semant. **71**, 100660 (2021). https://doi.org/10.1016/j.websem.2021.100660
21. Serrano, E., Iglesias, C.A., Garijo, M.: A survey of Twitter rumor spreading simulations. In: Núñez, M., Nguyen, N.T., Camacho, D., Trawiński, B. (eds.) ICCCI 2015. LNCS (LNAI), vol. 9329, pp. 113–122. Springer, Cham (2015). https://doi.org/10.1007/978-3-319-24069-5_11
22. Shi, L., Liu, D., Liu, G., Meng, K.: AUG-BERT: an efficient data augmentation algorithm for text classification. In: Liang, Q., Wang, W., Liu, X., Na, Z., Jia, M., Zhang, B. (eds.) CSPS 2019. LNEE, vol. 571, pp. 2191–2198. Springer, Singapore (2020). https://doi.org/10.1007/978-981-13-9409-6_266
23. Shorten, C., Khoshgoftaar, T.M., Furht, B.: Text data augmentation for deep learning. J. Big Data **8**(1), 1–34 (2021). https://doi.org/10.1186/s40537-021-00492-0
24. Shu, K.: FakeNewsNet (2019). https://doi.org/10.7910/DVN/UEMMHS. Accessed 15 Dec 2021
25. Slovikovskaya, V.: Transfer learning from transformers to fake news challenge stance detection (FNC-1) task. In: Proceedings of the 12th Language Resources and Evaluation Conference, pp. 1211–1218. European Language Resources Association (2019). https://www.aclweb.org/anthology/2020.lrec-1.152
26. Surowiecki, J.: The Wisdom of Crowds, 1st edn. Anchor Books, New York (2005)
27. Suting, Y., Ning, Z.: Construction of structural diversity of ensemble learning based on classification coding. In: 2020 IEEE 9th Joint International Information Technology and Artificial Intelligence Conference (ITAIC), vol. 9, pp. 1205–1208 (2020). https://doi.org/10.1109/ITAIC49862.2020.9338807
28. Tesfagergish, S.G., Damaševičius, R., Kapočiūtė-Dzikienė, J.: Deep fake recognition in tweets using text augmentation, word embeddings and deep learning. In: Gervasi, O., et al. (eds.) ICCSA 2021. LNCS, vol. 12954, pp. 523–538. Springer, Cham (2021). http://doi.org/10.1007/978-3-030-86979-3_37
29. Wang, W.Y.: "liar, liar pants on fire": a new benchmark dataset for fake news detection. CoRR abs/1705.00648 (2017). http://arxiv.org/abs/1705.00648
30. Xie, Q., Dai, Z., Hovy, E.H., Luong, M., Le, Q.V.: Unsupervised data augmentation. CoRR abs/1904.12848 (2019). http://arxiv.org/abs/1904.12848

An Opinion Analysis Method Based on Disambiguation to Improve a Recommendation System

Oussama Laroussi[1](✉), Souheyl Mallat[1], Henri Nicolas[2], and Mounir Zrigui[1]

[1] RLANTIS Research Laboratory in Algebra Theory Numbers and Intelligent Systems, Faculty of Sciences, University of Monastir, Monastir, Tunisia
oussema.laroussi@gmail.com
[2] LABRI University of Bordeaux France, Talence, France

Abstract. Recommendation systems are widely used in almost all websites to help the customer to make a decision in the face of information overload problems. These systems provide users with personalized recommendations and help them to make the right decisions. Customer opinion analysis it is a vast area of research, especially in recommendation systems. This justifies the growing importance of opinion analysis. Among the great classifiers to perform this task the Wide Margin Separators classifier which gives encouraging results in the literature. Despite the results found in the classification, there is a problem of ambiguity in the meaning of words, which poses a problem in recommendation systems based on opinion analysis; an Arabic word has several meanings, so there is a probability of mis-classification of comments that contain these ambiguous words and therefore a false recommendation. We present after a comparative study between the methods proposed in the literature a method to do the disambiguation before going through the classification phase which we have done using the SVM algorithm. Our proposed system gives its best result in terms of accuracy 97.1%.

Keywords: Recommender system · Disambiguation · Collaborative filtering

1 Introduction

E-commerce appeared in the mid-90s. It refers to all commercial transactions involving the sale of goods and services online. Compared to traditional commerce, e-commerce offers various advantages in terms of convenience. In order to help a customer choose products or services online, the systems used in e-commerce often employ techniques based on information search and filtering.

Information retrieval [1, 2] is a discipline that aims to provide relevant answers to user requests. User needs are usually expressed in natural language in the form of a keyword query. Several search engines on the Web are used for this purpose (Google, Yahoo?). The query is compared with information sources stored in the system and indexed by keywords to arrive at elements (products, services, etc.) that meet the user?s or customer?s request [3, 4].

© The Author(s), under exclusive license to Springer Nature Switzerland AG 2022
C. Bădică et al. (Eds.): ICCCI 2022, CCIS 1653, pp. 42–56, 2022.
https://doi.org/10.1007/978-3-031-16210-7_4

In this work, our goal is to build a recommender system (RS) that can generate meaningful recommendations to users for items or products that might interest them. A user?s emotions are expressed explicitly through a vote or implicitly through comments written in natural language using a specific vocabulary and having a polarity score that predicts the vote associated with that comment, in order to make recommendations on items that might interest other users [5]. These comments may contain ambiguous words. In this work, we implemented SR through a sense disambiguation (SD) task which is a process by which the meaning of a word occurrence is identified; it is integrated into an opinion classification system. This implementation is important for overcoming semantic ambiguity problems and has implications for natural language processing (NLP) tasks that will help SR give more relevant recommendations.

The remainder of this paper is organized as follows. Section 2 defines the problem. Section 3 describes the different techniques of recommender systems. Section 4 explains the description of the proposed method in detail. Section 5 presents the results of the experimental analysis and evaluation.

2 Problematic

Opinion-based recommendation systems operate primarily on the decision of the rating system that processes customer reviews. These reviews may contain sarcasm or ambiguity for the customer to express their opinion. Lexical ambiguity is one of the main difficulties in automatic natural language processing, as some words may have multiple meanings. Because of these ambiguities, opinion-based recommender systems are not reliable for making recommendations.

The problem of this work is therefore how to avoid false recommendations by removing ambiguities found in the comments (See Fig. 1).

Fig. 1. Example

In this example, there are two directions of polarity: positive if we take the sentence framed by the green and negative if we take the whole sentence. But if we pass the sentence as it is in the classification phase, it returns a positive result but the real direction is negative, so when we integrate the disambiguation phase, the result becomes negative.

3 Recommender Systems

A recommender system is a specific model of information filtering that aims to present the user with data in his areas of interest, based on his behaviors.

A recommender system goes through three steps: acquiring preferences from user input, computing the recommendation using appropriate techniques, and finally presenting the recommendation results to the user [6].

3.1 Recommender System Based on Collaborative Filtering

The first recommendation system is a collaborative filter-based system developed in the mid-1990s, called Tapestry [7].

Collaborative filtering systems (CFS) work like in everyday life, for example if someone needs information he will ask his friends, who will in turn recommend him his need, so it is a collaboration that allows to improve knowledge.

Collaborative filtering is the most widely used approach in the field of recommendation, based on behavioral similarity between users [8].

3.2 Recommender System Based on Content Filtering

Content-based recommendation consists of analyzing the content of candidate articles or descriptions of these articles. Content-based recommendation methods use techniques largely inspired by the field of information retrieval. Instead, content-based approaches infer the user?s preferences and recommend articles with content similar to the content of articles that the user has previously liked [Balabanovi? and Shoham, 1997, Pazzani and Billsus, 2007].

3.3 Hybrid Recommender System

A hybrid recommender system can be seen as a combination of the two traditional methods to avoid duplication as defined by Burke in his study [9]. These methods are the most represented in the literature, especially since they are considered the most efficient.

According to the latter, the hybrid system is generally organized in two stages:

1. Filter articles independently via collaborative methods or by content (or other).
2. Combine these sets of recommendations via hybridization methods such as weights and switches [10].

3.4 Hybrid Recommender System

Table 1. Summarizes the strengths and weaknesses of the different recommendation methods.

Table 1. Comparison between types of recommendations.

Recommendation type	Advantages	Disadvantages
Recommendation based on content filtering	- Allows recommendations of new articles	- Thematic redundancy of the proposals submitted to the user (On the other hand, a user will never be proposed items that have not been judged similar to those he likes)
	- A new user can receive recommendations as soon as they start interacting with the system	- Proposing to a user unpleasant items that are not interesting to him (for example if a user is only interested in articles talking about sports, he will never receive a political article)
Recommendation based on collaborative filtering	- No need for descriptors on documents/users	- Cold start problem: no recommendations possible if there is not enough user/document interaction [13]
	- Takes into account the relationships between articles and/or between users	- In the context of explicit ratings, the average percentage of resources for which users have provided a rating is very low
Recommendation hybride	- Combines the benefits of content-based recommendation and the one based on collaborative filtering	- Problem of scaling up scale

3.5 State of the Art on Recommender Systems

This table reports several works done on collaborative filtering based recommender systems in different domains and each one chooses a specific implementation. But all these implementations are limited when we talk about recommender systems based on opinion classifications because there are always ambiguities in the comments; for this reason, we chose to make an implementation in the system by adding the classification process which is based on disambiguation to satisfy the client?s needs (Table 2).

Table 2. Related work on recommender systems

Reference	Work
SOUILAH, Saida [8] (2019)	New cold start method for recommendation systems
Dias, Charles-Emmanuel, Vincent Guigue, and Patrick Gallinari. [9] (2019)	Explicit collaborative filtering by blind sentiment analysis
Benkhouya, Badredine, and Rafik Ait Abdelmalek. (2020)	A personalized recommendation system for finding information
O. Meddeb, M. Maraoui and M. Zrigui, [10] (2021)	Deep learning-based semantic approach for Arabic text document recommendation

4 Proposed Method

The objective of our work is to build a recommendation system based on opinion analysis. Opinion analysis is concerned with the opinions and emotions expressed in comment texts. It is developing rapidly today because of the importance of the web in our society and the large number of opinions expressed daily by users. This is why a polarity detection system has been built in order to feed a recommendation system by transforming texts into a numerical evaluation to set up a collaborative filtering. In order to generate accurate recommendations and to improve the quality of these recommendations by selecting the most relevant articles.

4.1 Proposed Method Algorithm

The following algorithm shows the process details of our method (Fig. 2):

Algorithm of our method
Entry: Positive and negative labeled data; List of users. **Output:** Explicit votes ranging from 0 to 10. 1. Load the labeled data; 2. Search for similar users using the collaborative filtering algorithm ; 3. Data pre-processing; 4. Disambiguation; 5. Classification; 6. Prediction calculation ;

Fig. 2. General system algorithm

4.2 Description of the Proposed Method

Among the recommender systems, we have implemented a recommender system based on collaborative filtering and opinion analysis, as shown in Fig. 3.

As shown in Fig. 3, our model goes through four modules: filtering by using a collaborative filtering algorithm, then preprocessing, then disambiguation and classification, and finally recommendation generation by prediction calculation. In what follows, we will see the details of each module.

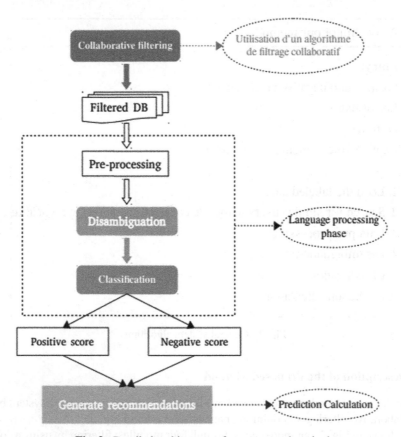

Fig. 3. Detailed architecture of our proposed method

4.3 Collaborative Filtering

In this work, we used user-based collaborative filtering algorithms [11, 12], where a set of k nearest neighbors to the target user are first identified by computing correlations or similarities between users [13]. We performed two experiments with jackard similarity and with spearman similarity, through these experiments it was noticed that the best similarity measure for our proposed recommender system is Spearman similarity [14, 15]. It is defined by:

$$Sim_{x,y} = \frac{\sum_{i=1}^{N}\left(\left(rank\left(x_i - \overline{rank}(x)\right)\right)\left(rank\left(y_i - \overline{rank}(y)\right)\right)\right)}{\sqrt{\sum_{i=1}^{N}\left(rank(x_i) - \overline{rank}(x)^2 \sum_{i=1}^{N}\left(rank(y_i) - \overline{rank}(y)^2\right)\right)}} \tag{1}$$

rank (xi) and rank (yi) are the ranks of the observation in the sample.

The similarities between users range from ?1 to 1. We chose the value 0 as a threshold to identify the nearest neighbors of a user.

When applying collaborative filtering and calculating similarity, the system selects items chosen by similar user profiles (Fig. 4).

```
Algorithm: collaborative filtering

Input: Database containing the list of users
        j : current user
        K[] : array
Begin:
        v=0
        For i from 1 to n do (with n the number of users)
            If Sim(i,j) = 0 then
                k[v] ◄——— i
                v= v+1
            End if
        End for
Return k (The list of users similar to the current user)
```

Fig. 4. Filtering algorithm

Choice of Collaborative Filtering. We chose collaborative filtering in this work because recommendation systems based on collaborative filtering rely solely on user ratings. Therefore, one of the most important criteria for deciding which recommendation technique to implement is the evaluation of the articles viewed by the user.

Collaborative Filtering Methods Used. There are two methods of collaborative filtering are: the algorithms based on the ?memory? this method is developed in 2013 by Breese (Breese, 2013) [16] is the algorithms based on the ?model? developed by Berrut in 2003 (Berrut 2003) [17]. In this work, we used the memory-based algorithms.

4.4 Automatic Language Processing

Figure 5 explains the architecture of the proposed sentiment analysis system. We first explain the disambiguation task, followed by the feature extraction task. We then give a brief overview of the selected features and explain the classification phase.

Disambiguation. After obtaining a filtered database, the disambiguation process is used to translate all ambiguous words according to their context to avoid any misclassification [18, 19].

Machine learning, which is based on a supervised approach, consists in training a classifier for each target word to predict the most relevant meaning in its context. We tested several works on disambiguation to choose the right system [20, 21].

We used the NUSPT system classifier implemented [22] which relies on three sets of features to assign a meaning to a given word:

- The parts of speech of the neighboring words (Pi), 7 lines are extracted, which correspond to the parts of speech of the labels of the three left words (P ? 3, P ? 2, P ? 1), the three right words (P1, P2, P3) and that of the target word (P0);

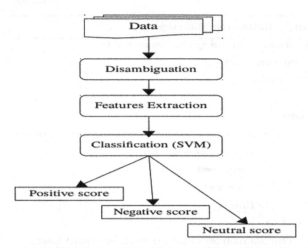

Fig. 5. Proposed model for opinion analysis

- The local collocations (Ci, j), which correspond to the ordered sequence of words between indices i and j with respect to the target word, written in lower case. 11 lines are thus extracted: C ? 1, -1, C1,1, C ? 2, -2, C2,2, C ? 2, -1, C ? 1,1, C1,2, C ? 3, ? 1, C-2,1, C-1,2 and C1,3;
- In the neighborhood context, this feature corresponds to a vector of the size of the number of different lemmas observed during the learning process. Each component of the vector corresponds to a lemma, and its value is set to 1 if the lemma of one of the words present in the same sentence as the target word corresponds to the lemma of this component. It is equal to 0 in the opposite case.

The SVM lexical disambiguation system was trained on the OntoNotes corpus. We then evaluated this system on the SensEval2 corpus.

System	Task	Accuracy	Recall	F1 Score
SVM	SensEval2	69,2	67,32	68,45
IMS+emb	SensEval2	68,3	68,3	68,3

By comparison with the results of the best supervised disambiguation system in the state of the art (Iacobacci et al., 2016) [23] (named IMS+emb). We find that the results of our system with an accuracy of 69.2 are comparable.

Features Extraction. Feature extraction is a rudimentary and essential phase of the opinion classification process. Therefore, it is important to convert the text of Arabic reviews into a feature vector, in order to process the text more efficiently. To detect polarity in our system, we used the following features:

$$\text{Number of sentences} = \sum sentences \qquad (2)$$

To calculate the number of polarity words and the average polarity scores, we used the following functions:

$$\text{Number of positive words} = \sum Positive\ Word \tag{3}$$

$$\text{Number of negative words} = \sum \text{Negative Word} \tag{4}$$

$$\text{Number of neutral words} = \sum \text{Neutral Word} \tag{5}$$

$$\sum \text{polarity words} = \sum Positive\ Word + \sum Negative\ Word + \sum Neutral\ Word \tag{6}$$

$$\text{Average of positive polarity words} = \frac{\sum \text{Positive word}}{\sum \text{polarity of words}} \tag{7}$$

$$\text{Average of negative polarity words} = \frac{\sum \text{Positive word}}{\sum \text{polarity of words}} \tag{8}$$

$$\text{Average of neutral polarity words} = \frac{\sum \text{Positive word}}{\sum \text{polarity of words}} \tag{9}$$

To calculate the number of predicates, adverbs and adjectives and the average score for each, we used the following functions:

$$\text{Number of predicates} = \sum \text{Predicates} \tag{10}$$

$$\text{Number of adjectives} = \sum \text{Adjectives} \tag{11}$$

$$\text{Number of adverbs} = \sum \text{Adverbs} \tag{12}$$

$$\text{Average of predicates} = \frac{\sum \text{Predicates}}{\sum \text{Predicates} + \sum \text{Adjectives} + \sum \text{Adverbs}} \tag{13}$$

$$\text{Average of adverbs} = \frac{\sum \text{Adverbs}}{\sum \text{Predicates} + \sum \text{Adjectives} + \sum \text{Adverbs}} \tag{14}$$

$$\text{Average of Adjectives} = \frac{\sum \text{Adjectives}}{\sum \text{Predicates} + \sum \text{Adjectives} + \sum \text{Adverbs}} \tag{15}$$

Classification of Opinions. Emotional polarity classification is a binary classification task that involves labeling opinion documents [22]. Binary classification. Some of the opinions are labeled with overall positive or negative emotions. Emotional polarity can also be called a binary decision task. The input to the emotion classifier may or may not be associated with an opinion. Sometimes it is not. When an opinion is received as input, parsing it and classifying it as good or bad news is considered a text classification task. Moreover, this information may be good or bad news, but it is not necessarily subjective (i.e., it does not express the opinion of the author) [24]. This means that this task is a multi-class classification and opinions can be positive, negative or neutral [25, 26].

We chose SVM as our classification technique after several experiments and comparisons with other learning algorithms.

Recommendation. After going through the filtering phase and computing Spearman similarity, and once we obtain neighboring users and their comments are ranked [27], we apply a weighted average to combine the ratings of neighboring items to produce a prediction value for the target user. Using the weighted sum of neighboring users? ratings on a product j and the n most similar users to that user [28, 29]. We will compute the prediction P(a, j) of the value of an item j rated by user a as follows.:

$$P_{aj} = \bar{v}_a + \frac{\sum_{i=1}^{N} s(a, i) * \left(v_{i,j} - \bar{v}_i\right)}{\sum_{i=1}^{N} |S(a, i)|} \tag{16}$$

s: Similarity;
n: number of neighbors of a, having already voted on item j;
$v_{i,j}$: the vote of user i for element j;
$\bar{v}_i$: Average user vote i;
$|s(a, i)|$: Average similarity.

The global representation of a recommendation system is represented by explicit votes varying between 0 and 5 for an uninteresting element and values between 5 and 10 for an interesting element.

The prediction value already calculated helps us to decide the relevance of the article and helps the system to generate effective recommendations for the user.

5   Experimentation, Results and Discussion

5.1   Corpus Description

After proving the effect and performance of the proposed features in the disambiguation and polarity detection process in Arabic, this experimentation allows the evaluation of the recommendation system based on opinion analysis. Since there are no recommendation evaluation databases in Arabic, we were forced to manually build a corpus containing users with their comments and votes on products. This database contains 100 users and 500 comments in Arabic collected from jumia tunisia.

5.2   Evaluation of the Referral System

This experiment allows us to evaluate the recommendation system based on the analysis and disambiguation of opinions.

We evaluated our recommender system with (?) and without (_) (filtering, classification and disambiguation) using the following three measures: Mean Absolute Error (MAE), Precision and Recall, the following table contains the results (Table 3).

Table 3. Results of the experiments conducted on the SR

Table 3. Results of the experiments conducted on the SR

	Filtering	Classification	Disambiguation	Accuracy	Recall	MAE
Exp1.a	✓	–	–	66,32	64,7	49.53
Exp1.b	–	✓	–	68.4	65.8	52
Exp1.c	–	✓	✓	73.02	71,54	58.76
Exp1.d	✓	✓	–	89.6	87.3	60.03
Exp1.e	✓	✓	✓	97.1	96	62,2

We assumed in this work that opinion analysis and disambiguation allow to improve the recommendations produced by the classical recommendation approach based on traditional collaborative filtering. The experimental protocol that we have set up has allowed us to verify through full-scale tests that our approach allows to slightly improve these recommendations.

We tested the recommendation system in different ways:

– With collaborative filtering only;
– With classification only;
– With classification and disambiguation;
– With collaborative filtering, classification but without disambiguation.
– With collaborative filtering, classification and disambiguation.

The purpose of these experiments is to show the role of each phase of our model.

We concluded that the proposed model performs well in terms of 97.1% accuracy, which guarantees the improvement of the quality of the recommender systems and the improvement of the recommendations proposed to the user.

Although this work is the first based on a combination of classification and disambiguation in a recommender system and gives good results, it still has limitations:

• Recommendation systems do not take into account document updates.
• The recommendation systems do not take into account the updates of the user classes

However, even though document filtering systems based on the user?s profile exist, they do not take into account the temporal evolution of the document classes seen by the user nor the evolution of the user?s classes [18]. Our proposal focuses on analyzing the temporal evolution of the user?s document classes and the temporal evolution of the user?s classes through incremental clustering [19]. This method becomes a central concern, it consists in processing a large volume of time-varying information [20]. Thus, a recommender system based on incremental clustering can personalize the information provided and help its users to make good choices among a large number of alternatives, even without sufficient personal experience.

To overcome these limitations, we propose to develop a recommendation system allowing the personalization of online documents: each time the user modifies his profile (consults a new document), the system recommends a collection of documents adapted to his profile.

6 Conclusion

We found that when the system recommends a product seen by other similar users, there is a high chance that this product has bad impressions among these customers. So we worked with opinion analysis and to implement our model, we removed the ambiguity found in the reviews and finally we evaluated and tested our model with different metrics and different learning algorithms.

Our experiments show the role of the disambiguation phase. The system gives a result of 89.6 without disambiguation and when we integrate this implementation, the recommendation system gives us an accuracy of 97.1%. Now with this implementation, our system is able to make relevant recommendations to users through opinion analysis.

7 Limits and Perspectives

The main limitations addressed in this study are the following.

- Recommendation systems do not take into account document updates.
- Recommender systems do not take into account updates to user classes

We propose to develop a recommendation system allowing the personalization of online documents: each time the user modifies his profile (consults a new document), the system recommends a collection of documents adapted to his profile using an incremental classification.

References

1. Belkin, N.J., Croft, W.B.: Retrieval techniques. Unknown J. **22**, 109?145 (1987)
2. Salton, G.: Automatic text processing: the transformation, analysis, and retrieval of information by computer, p. 169. Addison-Wesley, Reading (1989)
3. Mahmoud, A., Zrigui, M.: Semantic similarity analysis for corpus development and paraphrase detection in Arabic. Int. Arab J. Inf. Technol. **18**(1), 1?7 (2021)

4. Mars, M., Antoniadis, G., Zrigui, M.: Statistical part of speech tagger for Arabic language. In: ICAI 2010: Proceedings of the 2010 International Conference on Artificial Intelligence, Las Vegas, NV, 12?15 July 2010

5. Wei, W., et al.: Computer-simulated RFLP analysis of 16S rRNA genes: identification of ten new phytoplasma groups. Int. J. Syst. Evol. Microbiol. **57**(8), 1855?1867 (2007)

6. Mahmoud, A., Zrigui, A., Zrigui, M.: A text semantic similarity approach for Arabic paraphrase detection. In: International Conference on Computational Linguistics and Intelligent Text Processing. Springer, Cham (2017)

7. Goldberg, D., Nichols, D., Oki, B.M., Terry, D.: Using collaborative filtering to weave an information tapestry. Commun. ACM **35**(12), 61?70 (1992)

8. Dragut, D.V., et al.: Thermal stability and field assisted sintering of cerium-doped YSZ ceramic nanoparticles obtained via a hydrothermal process. Manuf. Rev. **4**, 11 (2017)

9. Burke, R.: Knowledge-Based Recommender Systems, vol. 69, pp. 175?186. CRC Press (2000)

10. Burke, R.: Hybrid Recommender Systems: Survey and Experiments. User Modeling and User-Adapted Interaction, vol. 12, pp. 331?370 (2002)

11. Souilah, S.: Nouvelle méthode de démarrage à froid pour les systèmes de recommandation (2019)

12. Dias, C.E., Guigue, V., Gallinari, P.: Filtrage collaboratif explicite par analyse de sentiments à l?aveugle. CAp 2019-21ème Conférence sur l?Apprentissage automatique (2019)

13. Meddeb, O., Maraoui, M., Zrigui, M.: Deep learning based semantic approach for Arabic textual documents recommendation. In: 2021 International Conference on INnovations in Intelligent SysTems and Applications (INISTA), pp. 1?6 (2021). https://doi.org/10.1109/INISTA52262.2021.9548469.

14. Herlocker, J.L., Konstan, A.J., Borchers, A., Riedl, L.: An algorithmic framework for performing collaborative filtering. In: Proceedings de la 22ème ?International ACM Conference on Researchand Development in Information Retrieval (SIGIR?99)?, États-Unis, pp. 230?237 (1999)

15. Maraoui, M., Antoniadis, G., Zrigui, M.: CALL System for Arabic Based on Natural Language Processing Tools. IICAI (2009)

16. Breese, S., Heckerman, D., Kadie, C.: Empirical analysis of predictive algorithms for collaborative filtering. In: Proceedings of the Fourteenth Conference on Wisconsin, pp. 43?52 (2013)

17. Berrut, C., Denos, N.: Filtrage collaboratif, in Assistance intelligente à la recherche d?informations. Thèse de doctorat, université de Hermes Lavoisier (2003)

18. Nakamura, A., Abe, N.: Collaborative filtering using weighted majority prediction algorithms. In: ICML ?98 Proceedings of the Fifteenth International Conference on Machine Learning, San Francisco, Morgan Kaufmann, pp. 395?403 (1998)

19. Zouaghi, A., Merhbene, L., Zrigui, M.: A hybrid approach for arabic word sense disambiguation. Int. J. Comput. Process. Orient. Lang. **24**(2), 133?152 (2012)

20. Merhben, L., Zouaghi, A., Zrigui, M.: Lexical disambiguation of Arabic language: an experimental study. Polibits **46**, 49?54 (2012)

21. Hadj Salah, M., et al.: La désambiguïsation lexicale d?une langue moins bien dotée, l?exemple de l?arabe. 25e conférence sur le Traitement Automatique des Langues Naturelles (2018)

22. Zouaghi, A., Merhbene, L., Zrigui, M.: Word sense disambiguation for Arabic language using the variants of the Lesk algorithm. WORLDCOMP **11**, 561?567 (2011)

23. Iacobacci, I., Pilehvar, M.T., Navigli, R.: Embeddings for word sense disambiguation: an evaluation study. In: Proceedings of the 54th Annual Meeting of the Association for Computational Linguistics (vol. 1: Long Papers). (2016)

24. Maraoui, M., Antoniadis, G., Zrigui, M.: SALA: Call System for Arabic Based on NLP Tools, , pp. 168?172. IC-AI (2009)

25. Haffar, N., Hkiri, E., Zrigui, M.: TimeML annotation of events and temporal expressions in Arabic texts. In: Nguyen, N.T., Chbeir, R., Exposito, E., Aniorté, P., Trawiski, B. (eds.) ICCCI 2019. LNCS (LNAI), vol. 11683, pp. 207?218. Springer, Cham (2019). https://doi.org/10.1007/978-3-030-28377-3_17
26. Zrigui, M.: Contribution au traitement automatique des langues : cas de l?arabe. (A Contribution to Automatic Processing of Languages: The Arabic Language Case). Stendhal University, Grenoble, France (2008)
27. Bouzayane, S., Saad, I.: Un système de recommandation pour la personnalisation de la recherche d?information dans les MOOCs
28. Roghayeh, M., et al.: Context-aware adaptive recommendation system for personal well-being services. In: 2020 IEEE 32nd International Conference on Tools with Artificial Intelligence (ICTAI). IEEE (2020)
29. El Guedria Sgaier, Z.: Assistance à la recherche documentaire par une approche adaptative à base d?agents et d?artefacts. Diss. Normandie (2018)

A Recommendation System for Job Providers Using a Big Data Approach

Shayma Boukari[1(✉)], Seifeddine Mechti[1], and Rim Faiz[2]

[1] LARODEC Laboratory, ISG, University of Tunis, Tunis, Tunisia
shayma.boukari@outlook.com, mechtiseif@gmail.com
[2] LARODEC Laboratory, IHEC, University of Carthage, Tunis, Tunisia
rim.faiz@ihec.ucar.tn

Abstract. In recent times, Job seekers has dramatically increased. Hence, it has become very strenuous to search for potential candidates. Recently recommendation systems have become essential in many areas and newly for human resources. As a recruiter they can identifying profiles to be recruited and this through using online professional social networks such as LinkedIn. For this reason, we present, a generic and simple recommendation system to optimize the recruitment process. In this study, To create the matching between offer made by a recruiter and profiles and to identifies the most suitable candidate we need a important dataset size. We use content based recommendation techniques and a distributed big data processing framework (Apache Spark) and machine learning (ML) libraries. We use then a data augmentation algorithm to improve our results. According to the experiment, the use of our method can result a high precision of 0.936.

Keywords: Recommendation system · LinkedIn · Machine learning · Data augmentation · Apache Spark · Spark MLlib

1 Introduction

Social networks are an excellent source of information that can be used in different areas because they are currently at the center of researchers and scientists. The amount of data transferred on social networks increases the engines of recommendation [1]. This has led to overload of data, where users are involved with knowledge and information. It is a rapid growth in data that leads to an era of data. To build more efficient, effective and innovative system these data is used.

In this new era of information, the recommendation system is one of the areas in which social data can be used to improve the reliability of recommendations. Recently, recommender engine have become the heart of several research zones and are used in different information recovery platforms, such as Facebook, LinkedIn, Amazon, Netflix and YouTube. These platforms offer users an improved experience [2]. Recommendation systems are generally categorized in three families, defined by the type of filtering used: content-based filtering (CBF), collaborative filtering

C. Bădică et al. (Eds.): ICCCI 2022, CCIS 1653, pp. 57–68, 2022.
https://doi.org/10.1007/978-3-031-16210-7_5

(CF), and hybrid filtering that combines CF and CBF. The CF focuses only on user feedback and completely ignores the knowledge related to items (most of the time provided in the form of notes attributed to the items). From the feedback provided by users and based on mathematical models, the CF aims to improve the accuracy of recommendations for a given user. These systems are applied in variety of areas research articles, music, movies, books, TV program, search queries, social tags and products in general). Also, there are applied for employer (looking for appropriate candidates) and for fresher. With the growth of professional social networks, the employment process develops. It is not just limited to job researchers but also to recruiters who are looking for suitable candidates for their offers. This development is no longer limited to social networks professionals, but also to other platforms. Indeed, recruiters also analyze the use of popular social networks (Facebook, Instagram ...) of candidates.

Recommendation systems provide users with elements adapted to their needs and to manage the large mass of information. In recent years the interest that scientists give to the Big Data has increased day by day, the number of works that have been published and which treat the Big Data is enormous. Big data can be considered a promising revolution in data processing and specially for recommendations. They have brought several advantages, they can help improve decision making, and the recruitment process, reduce computer infrastructure costs via the use of standard servers and open source software [3]. In recent years the interest that scientists give to Big Data has increased day by day, this indicates that whenever the mass of data increases the results can be improved. To analyse Big Data, several new tools and frameworks have been presented by different organizations that are competing for the ultimate tool that will fill all Big Data issues. One of this important framework is Spark. Apache Spark is a very powerful framework that treats several aspects of the big data, which is a freely available and high-performance clustering-based computing system and the important thing is openly accessible [4].

To analyze this mass of data, Spark resolves in the Different Constant, iterative or continuous algorithm memory space. Spark supports a wider scope of performance, scope and components than the function used in Hadoop in many models (that is to say Mapreduce) [5]. For programming purposes, its functions use a distributed resilient data set (RDD).

However, the execution of parallel programs is the potential force. To increase and to help at managing data scalability, Spark provides various libraries and tools such as Python, Scala and R, [6]. Recruitment is the adequacy between a person, and a job offer. Compared to any other function in the field of human resources (HR) The most important function on the growth of the margins beneficiaries of companies is the recruitment function [7]. We should find a recruitment method consisting in finding through various techniques, the right profile for a given position. This strategy requires analyzing the needs, defining a specific profile, looking for profiles of qualified people and sorting among the people targeted in order to choose the most relevant. Social networks have made this process more direct because the candidates are now visible through them. On the other hand, this increases the mass of data accessible for each candidate.

We come to determine if the candidate happens to be the right person for the given position and therefore make a selection from several filters between all the targeted people in the dataset.

In this paper we present a method using recommendation system that improve the recruitment process for recruiter and facilitates hiring and identifying candidates with the generation of matching between job offers and candidates, based on a significant amount of data. To improve the matching of candidates for jobs or specific positions, the method presented which can be used for recruiters as a decision assistance tool using Spark machine learning libraries (MLlib) [8]. This library holds multiple algorithms such as classification, clustering, Spark ML, frequent pattern matching, linear algebra, linear regression, and recommendations. We use cosine similarity as similarity measures, to discover the distance between the offer and the candidates, and it is possible to give weight to the filters chosen by the recruiter. In this study, we implemented a recommendation system using a very simple data augmentation methods (Easy Data Augmentation (EDA)) to increase the size of data. EDA consists of four simple operations (Synonym Replacement, Random Insertion, Random Swap, Random Deletion) that do a good job of helping train more robust models. This technique could improve the performance of model to produce a new data, and to create a candidate recommender system based on the ML algorithm. The paper is divided as follows: The second section details the basic concepts of the recommendation systems and their use in the field of human resources. We also synthesize the basic concepts of data augmentation as well as that its contributions to recommendation systems, through approaches to literature. The third section details the proposed approach for improving the accuracy of recommendations in the context of content-based filtering. Next, the results of the evaluation of our approach will then be discussed. Finally, we draw the main conclusions of the thesis and open new research perspectives in the areas concerned.

2   Related Work

In this section, we analyze the uses of recommendation system concept in the literature by emphasizing the field of recruitment and the use of technical of augmentation data and machine learning algorithms using spark framework. As with other concepts, recommendation systems are applied in several applications and with several techniques rigorously studied by several authors in several works. Some works use clustering techniques to find the objects in similar use in order to generate recommendations [9]. Other works use classification techniques to generate recommandations. Geng Sun et al. [10] use the algorithms of decision-making and Naive Bayes to classify the demographic characteristics of the readers to recommend learning objects. Mohammadreza Tavakoli et al. developed a Random Forest model to classify the correspondence between a competence and a learning object. This binary decision model uses several characteristics such as the length of learning objects, their levels, the number of views, and more specifically the textual similarity measurement between them.

This similarity measure is calculated using word immersion techniques with the measurement of the Cosinus [11]. In 2021, the authors implemented stock market [12] predictions using the machine learning libraries (MLlib) on Spark achieved a good running time with 90% accuracy. Jiechieu and Tsopze presents a study dedicated to the prediction of a profession from a skills profile [13].

Data volume is a very important factor in recommendation system and especially in the training phase. There are several authors who have already given great importance for big data. They have the access to nesting databases or large files. Hernandez-Nieves et al. in Their study has described that with the use of algorithms based on the exploration of data from Big Data may extract several significant information. This work has shown that the results are improving gradually with adding more data [14]. To use big data, we must prepare the infrastructure necessary to analyze it easily and rapidly. For this we have to choose a good framework that offend us this luxury. For this reason Aljunid et al. [15] proposed a significant approach in which they used machine learning libraries for a big data framework named Apache spark (Spark-ML and MLlib) to attain good results by the recommendation system. The analyse and the performance evaluation have been realised on the dataset taken from Movielens.

As we know the Big Data has a big impact in the analysis phase, but to find a large amount of data it takes a lot of time and it is not sometimes doable. For this we can sometimes use data augmentation techniques to transform their size. According to authors in [16] data augmentation In the Machine learning algorithm, is defined as the generate of artificial data samples used to improve the machine learning performance and to train the model. In computer vision data augmentation is very popular because even if the image is submit to treatment (flipping, rotation, contrast, saturation), it's meaning is not easily changed. In computer vision data augmentation is very popular because even if the image is submit to treatment (flipping, rotation, contrast, saturation) it's meaning is not easily changed. Moreover, humans can verified directly modifications on images. Study in [17] presented an example of augmentation of an image dataset. However, non-image data augmentation gives more challenges due to the high susceptible to data transformation (data meaning can be changed). In research [17], authors introduce data augmentation techniques to transform time series data by data interpolation.

In the field of human resources Diaby and Viennet [18] and Gu et al. [19] have implemented a recommender system in which they used a traditional technique for searching information (the cosine distance between offer and profiles(two documents)). Next, W. Hong et al. suggest a content-based job recommendation system based on user clustering in which they recommends a list of different jobs for different users. In this solution users are grouped in clusters [20]. In a job offer, a recruiter will mention the desired competence for a candidate. The skills thus mentioned in a profile or a job offer are linked to a well-determined sector of activity. The underlying concepts do not have intensive definitions and their extensions are often blurred. For this reason, skills have remained modeled as keywords. In the case of professional social networks such as LinkedIn or Career-Builder, users editing their profile have a section dedicated to the indication of their skills. This seizure is guided by the use of taxonomies or dictionaries of standard surface forms. In 2015 Zhao et al. collaborate with CareerBuilder to produce Skill taxonomy from the operation of 60 million professional profiles and 1.6 million job offers [21]. In 2018, Roshan G et al. proposed a RS based on collaborative filtering. They used cosine similarity. They analysed the data into the form of a matrix and they apply different matching algorithms to find the most appropriate offer for each candidate [22].

The problem of current recruiting systems can be seen from distinct perspectives: There are many Rs that select suitable job offer to a specific candidate but there are no clear systems that help to find appropriate candidates to a job offer. Other than that even if there are several solution, the precision of the results is always must be ameliorated. We try to present in our solution a method that can fill the missing needs in other solutions offered. Our solution is a content based candidates recommendation system based in the Big Data Apache Spark Framework.

3 Proposed Model

After analyzing the existing solutions, we will describe several phases of our recommender system. Our solution is constructed into various modules which are showed schematically in (Fig. 1)

- Data extraction
- Data augmentation
- Data storage
- Data processing
- Data analysis
- data transformation
- data visualization
- Modeling

Data Extraction
Nowadays, there are many data that can be easily retrieved from web and we can used in research, development and prevision. In our case, it's possible to extract information about profiles on the LinkedIn platform we used Web scraping technique to extract and collect data from LinkedIn (extract names, skills, location, experience, phone...), and then save information into a format desired by the user (csv, excel, json...). It can get complicated when we extract data manually and this process take a lot of time. For this we choose the web scraping process that will perform this tasks in a few moments [23]. For sure we collect informations only for public profiles on this network.

Data Augmentation
It is a technique used to improve automatic learning models and make them more general and efficient even in cases where large data groups are not sufficiently available. This is done by increasing the amount of original data available by adding modified copies of them or creating new artificial data depending on

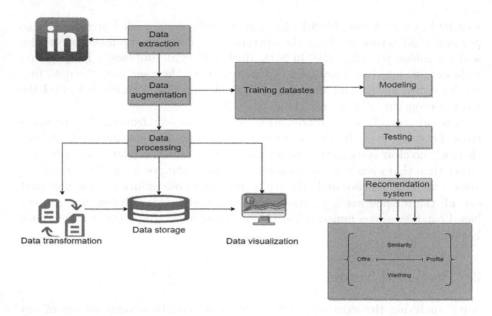

Fig. 1. Proposed-method

it. The data augmentation process also helps to avoid the problem of excessive convenience that occurs when training for models using a small-sized data set of low quality. We used easy data augmentation techniques for boosting performance on profiles classification. This technique consists of four powerful and simple operations: Synonym Replacement, Random Insertion, Random Swap, and Random Deletion [24].

Data Preprocessing

Data processing is the heart of this process. In our Method for the data processing task we use Apache Spark (Mllib) libraries. The complexity of automatic learning algorithms is often high, Spark has the ability to cache the data set in memory and this greatly helps to speed up iterative tasks. The emphasis is to be able to manage large volumes of data to synthesize a insight and usable knowledge. One of the basic steps of any data analysis problem is data pre-treatment, because it guarantees the accuracy of the model and it mainly depends on the quality of the data. After this step of preprocessing of the data we have a good quality of data which can be introduced into an automatic learning algorithm. [25]

Data Visualization

To better understand the data, data visualization is a powerful method that allows to have a better idea on the structure of the data. Visualizing big data is an important task, apache Spark comes ready for this task. With this framework we can apply off various open source visualization tools such as, Matplotlib, D3 and ggplot. This visualization has several benefits as describing data and results and shared the output of these tools with others. This does not mean that visualization should replace other approaches. In our study The Pyspark Matplotlib library was used for data visualization. The impact of data visualization in our method is to allow us to know what are the most important attributes for a profile that we can use and that according to the rate of missing data.

Data Transformation

This step makes it possible to transfer each object or objective of after taking (profile and offered) by a vector which captures the semantics of its sentences in such a way that they are close in the vector space. Then, we use the Sentence-Bert (SBERT) [26] model which represents a modification of the architect of the Bert model and was designed to accelerate the most similar search time. It is available in the Sentence Transformers library which provides a method to calculate the vector representation of the texts. It provides two main modes for semantic research, The first one symmetrical semantic research where the request and the texts of the corpus have the same length. Among the models of this category we can cite Distiluse 7. The second Mose is asymmetrical semantic research for short requests (that is to say a question or a keyword) but where the entries in the corpus are longer. Among the models in this category, we can cite MsMarco. In our recommendation approach, we are in the case of asymmetrical research (we use the fields of a form).

Data Storage

One of the primary characteristics of the Big Data is the volume, these big data must be stored above all. Several articles were interested in storage of data, the latter discussed the importance of this step and tried to explain it, among these articles, there are those who proposed new architectures and platforms for better storage of Big Data. Data Storage means distributed data Storage. Distributed data storage is a computer network where information is stored on more than one computer. Our Data is unstructured data so the storage should be on a NoSQL database. Distributed databases are NoSQL databases that quickly retrieve data over a large number of nodes. Therefore, for the experiment, HDFS is the good choice of the data storage. After the data are uploaded to the HDFS, the Spark SQL database associates the file information with the data information. After uploading the data file to the HDFS, the storage path of the file in HDFS is available, which will be written into the Spark SQL joined with the file information [27]. After these steps we can analyze our data and call our recommendation method.

Recommendation System for Job Providers

Our recommendation scenario presents itself as follows, the recruiter expressed their request (the profile sought) through the filling of a form then he is weighted according to his desire the fields, and finally a set of the most relevant candidates for this objective should be automatically suggested. In our method, we assume that a profile of Candidate is relevant for a job offer if the latter two are semantically similar. Figure 1 presents the method that we offer. We have constituted a vector of words. The vector representation of the fields of job offer and candidate profile skills, location, and education fields, experiences. Once the two lists have been created we calculated the semantic similarity between the two learning objects.

Similarity score is calculated from the aggregation between pairs of vectors representing the weighted aggregate correlation score. We use this equation:

$$\text{Finalsimilarity} = \text{Score} + \alpha \times educationranking + \beta \times SkillsRanking + \mu \times LocationRanking + \lambda \times ExperiencesRanking \tag{1}$$

$$\alpha + \beta + \kappa + \lambda = 1 \tag{2}$$

name	skills_Key_words	education_Key_words	location_Key_words	score
Hada Bechir	java jpa jee eclipse web services	diploma engineer private high school technolog...	tunisie	221.9
Hamza Atallah	angular framework sping java programmation web	ingénierie et de technologies engineer degree ...	tunisia	265.6
Haythem Bel haj youssef	javascript angularjs programmation web java	ingénierie et de technologies diplôme ingénieu...	tunisia	273.4
HAITHEM BENCHAABEN	spring web service java development	ecole nationale engineer degree ingénieurs de ...	tunisia	340.6
Fadi Idoudi	scrum spring framework java web development	ecole supérieure privée ingénierie et de techn...	tunisia	376.0
Hamza Zaafrane	javascript databases java web development	higher institute lisence student informatics m...	tunisia	402.3
habib ali	research web development java enterprise editi...	ingénierie et de technologies engineer degree ...	tunisia	405.7
Hamdi BEN KHALIFA	android development json java web services	institut supérieur ' informatique et de techni...	tunisie	417.8
Hajer Belkaid	j2ee web services jquery java méthodes agiles	information ingénieur en génie logiciels et sy...	tunisie	448.5

Fig. 2. Ranked candidates

Recruiters gives the Weighting Parameters α, β, μ and λ according to their preference. Finally the candidates are ranked in ascending order of score. Figure 2 display the list of k top suitable candidates in a brief time. In the Next section we will provides an experimental study in order to evaluate our method.

4   Experiments

We implemented our method on spark framework, which provide an open source java package for recommendation task. In this section we present the performance of our system for each parameter tested in terms of F1 score, precision and rappel.

4.1   Datasets

Firstly, we describe the different types of data we have for The dataset is made up of two main elements: job offers and candidate profiles

Candidates Dataset
In the scenario of the use of our system of recommendation, the candidate's profile is built from extracted data from LinkedIn. A profile contains fields which make it possible to know the professional and educational career (skills, location, experience, education).

Job Offer
In order to search for the right candidate an expert in human resources manually completed a form by the desired information. This offer is consist of free form text describing (title a job posting, location of a company offering a job, skills desired for the job offer selected by the recruiter, the number of years of experience desired).

4.2   Experimental Results

We perform our experiments by computing the precision, recall and F1Score of the our method. Figure 4 presents the performance of our method for each parameter tested in terms of precision, recall and F1Score. The averages of obtained results are illustrated in Figs. 4 and 5. Before applying the data augmentation technique, the evaluation results show that our method gave good training precision but produced very low validation precision, all validation values were below 0.4. We increase the size of dataset. The results obtained indicate that adding a dataset, in general, can improve validation results and overcome the overfitting.

Dataset size	Evaluation	Precision	Recall	F1_Score
	Training	0.766	0.786	0.74
Before EAD	Validation	0.222	0.344	0.269
	Training	0.949	0.968	0.958
After EAD	Validation	0.936	0.944	0.939

Fig. 3. Precision, Recall, F1score

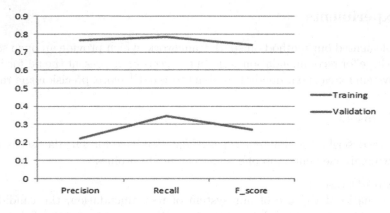

Fig. 4. Before EAD

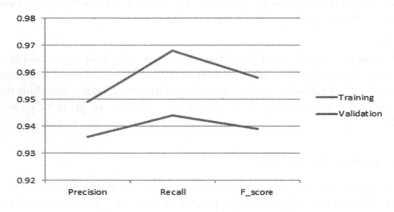

Fig. 5. After EAD

From Fig. 3, results before application of augmentation technique shows that our in terms of precision, recall and F1score in validation phase the precision of our method is equal to 0.222, the recall is equal to 0.344 and the F1score is equal 0.269, which is less than the results after data augmentation the precision value equal to 0.936 means that on average 9 of 10 recommendations are good.

Similarly, for the recall measure is largely higher than the other ones. Recall is equal 0.944 so on average about 9 of 10 are good recommendations among those top recommended. This is explained by the use of information affinity similarity measure with weighting given by the recruiter and the data augmentation has a considerable effect on the quality of the recommendation rather than the classical method. This confirms that this contribution has a great impact on recommendation results.

5 Conclusion

In this article, we have proposed a system of recommendation of candidates according to an offer proposed by the recruiter based on the calculation of their similarity distance and the score given by the recruiter and this by emphasizing the Contribution of the Spark Framework libraries and machine learning algorithms and data augmentation techniques. Our experiences show that the addition of data improves the validation results. The use of this data augmentation technique can solve the over-adjustment problem and cause great precision. According to experience, our method gives performance results with validation accuracy of 0.936.

Some improvements can be conducted in future research Implement a bidirectional recommendation system (Job Offer/candidate) and (candidate/job offer), use other data augmentation techniques and make a study on the data quality and initiate the impact of the data augmentation on the data quality.

References

1. Amato, F., Moscato, V., Picariello, A., Piccialli, F.: SOS: a multimedia recommender system for online social networks. Futur. Gener. Comput. Syst. **93**, 914–923 (2019)
2. Ko, H., Lee, S., Park, Y., Choi, A.: A survey of recommendation systems: recommendation models, techniques, and application fields. Electronics **11**(1), 141 (2022)
3. Eirinaki, M., Gao, J., Varlamis, I., Tserpes, K.: Recommender systems for large-scale social networks: a review of challenges and solutions. Futur. Gener. Comput. Syst. **78**, 413–418 (2018)
4. Xu, Y., Liu, H., Long, Z.: A distributed computing framework for wind speed big data forecasting on Apache Spark. Sustain. Energy Technol. Assess. **37**, 100582 (2020)
5. Adamov, A., et al.: Data processing in high-performance computing systems. Big Data Adv. Anal. (6-1), 33–52 (2020)
6. Morfino, V., Rampone, S.: Towards near-real-time intrusion detection for IoT devices using supervised learning and Apache Spark. Electronics **9**, 444 (2020)
7. Awan, M.J., et al.: A recommendation engine for predicting movie ratings using a big data approach. Electronics **10**(10), 1215 (2021)
8. Alfawaire, F., Atan, T.: The effect of strategic human resource and knowledge management on sustainable competitive advantages at Jordanian universities: the mediating role of organizational innovation. Sustainability **13**(15), 8445 (2021)
9. Al-Saqqa, S., Al-Naymat, G., Awajan, A.: A large-scale sentiment data classification for online reviews under Apache Spark. Procedia Comput. Sci. **141**, 183–189 (2018)
10. Mohamed, M.H., Khafagy, M.H., Ibrahim, M.H.: Recommender systems challenges and solutions survey. In: 2019 International Conference on Innovative Trends in Computer Engineering (ITCE), pp. 149–155. IEEE, February 2019
11. Sun, G., Cui, T., Xu, D., Shen, J., Chen, S.: A heuristic approach for new-item cold start problem in recommendation of micro open education resources. In: Nkambou, R., Azevedo, R., Vassileva, J. (eds.) ITS 2018. LNCS, vol. 10858, pp. 212–222. Springer, Cham (2018). https://doi.org/10.1007/978-3-319-91464-0_21

12. Tavakoli, M., Hakimov, S., Ewerth, R., Kismihok, G.: A recommender system for open educational videos based on skill requirements. In: 2020 IEEE 20th International Conference on Advanced Learning Technologies (ICALT), pp. 1–5. IEEE, July 2020

13. Ahmed, H.M., Javed Awan, M., Khan, N.S., Yasin, A., Faisal Shehzad, H.M.: Sentiment analysis of online food reviews using big data analytics. Elementary Educ. Online **20**(2), 827–836 (2021)

14. Jiechieu, K.F.F., Tsopze, N.: Skills prediction based on multi-label resume classification using CNN with model predictions explanation. Neural Comput. Appl. **33**(10), 5069–5087 (2020). https://doi.org/10.1007/s00521-020-05302-x

15. Hernandez-Nieves, E., Hernández, G., Gil-Gonzalez, A.B., Rodríguez-González, S., Corchado, J.M.: CEBRA: a CasE-based Reasoning Application to recommend banking products. Eng. Appl. Artif. Intell. **104**, 104327 (2021)

16. Aljunid, M.F., Manjaiah, D.H.: An improved ALS recommendation model based on Apache Spark. In: Zelinka, I., Senkerik, R., Panda, G., Lekshmi Kanthan, P.S. (eds.) ICSCS 2018. CCIS, vol. 837, pp. 302–311. Springer, Singapore (2018). https://doi.org/10.1007/978-981-13-1936-5_33

17. Oh, C., Han, S., Jeong, J.: Time-series data augmentation based on interpolation. Procedia Comput. Sci. **175**, 64–71 (2020)

18. Diaby, M., Viennet, E.: Developpement d'une application de ´recommandation d'offres d'emploi aux utilisateurs de Facebook et LinkedIn. In Atelier Fouille de Donnees Complexes de la 14e ´Conference Internationale Francophone sur l'Extraction et la Gestion ´des Connaissances (EGC'14), Rennes (2014)

19. Gu, Y., Zhao, B., Hardtke, D., Sun, Y.: Learning global term weights for content-based recommender systems. In: Proceedings of the 25th International Conference on World Wide Web. International World Wide Web Conferences Steering Committee, pp. 391–400 (2016)

20. Hong, W., Zheng, S., Wang, H., Shi, J.: A job recommender system based on user clustering. J. Comput. **8**(8) (2013). https://doi.org/10.4304/jcp.8.8.1960-1967

21. Zhao, Z., Cheng, Z., Hong, L., Chi, E.H.: Improving user topic interest profiles by behavior factorization. In: Proceedings of the 24th International Conference on World Wide Web, pp. 1406–1416, May 2015

22. Recommendation: Int. J. Comput. Appl. Technol. Res. **7**(6), 215–220 (2018). https://doi.org/10.7753/ijcatr0706.1003

23. Florentina, M.: Web data extraction with robot process automation, p. 1. Annals of 'Constantin Brancusi' University of Targu-Jiu. Engineering Series, Study On Linkedin Web Scraping Using Uipath Studio (2020)

24. Wei, J., Zou, K.: Eda: easy data augmentation techniques for boosting performance on text classification tasks. arXiv preprint arXiv:1901.11196 (2019)

25. Boukari, S., Fayech, S., Faiz, R.: Huntalent: a candidates recommendation system for automatic recruitment via LinkedIn. In: 2020 Seventh International Conference on Social Networks Analysis, Management and Security (SNAMS), pp. 1–7. IEEE (2020)

26. Reimers, N., Gurevych, I. : Sentence-BERT: sentence embeddings using Siamese BERT-networks. arXiv preprint arXiv:1908.10084 (2019)

27. Zheng, J., Zhao, J., Li, J., et al.: Spark-based platform for neurophysiological data storage and processing: a proof of concept. In: 2021 6th International Conference on Intelligent Informatics and Biomedical Sciences (ICIIBMS), pp. 16–19. IEEE (2021)

Natural Language Processing

Multi-module Natural Language Search Engine for Travel Offers

Karol Gawron[1][(✉)], Konrad Wojtasik[1], Bartłomiej Bojanowski[1],
Arkadiusz Janz[1], Jan Kocoń[1], Tomasz Krupa[2], Agnieszka Kukałowicz[2],
Piotr Miłkowski[1], Maciej Piasecki[1], Michał Pogoda[1], Norbert Ropiak[1],
Michał Swędrowski[1], and Wiktor Walentynowicz[1]

[1] Department of Artificial Intelligence,
Wrocław University of Science and Technology, Wrocław, Poland
karol.gawron@pwr.edu.pl
[2] Qtravel.ai, Gdansk, Poland

Abstract. In this work, we present an advanced semantic search engine dedicated to travel offers, allowing the user to create queries in the Natural Language. We started with the Polish language in focus. Search for e-commerce requires a different set of methods and algorithms than search for travel, search for corporate documents, for law documents, for medicine, etc. In travel, the complexity of data is bigger than in other domains, and the search process requires more parameters. In e-commerce, one product has 1 price, while in travel, one product (holiday package) has got tens of thousands of prices depending on time, board type, room type, number of people, children's age, etc. Providing a search for one middle-size tour operator, we need to search within hundreds of millions documents.

We present a set of methods based on natural language processing to improve the search for travel. We also present our new application for annotating travel offers, prepared in a human-in-the-loop paradigm that enables iterative system improvement. We also show a large dataset containing more than 3,000 manually constructed queries and more than 23,000 manually annotated answers, a large fraction by at least two independent experts, and a semi-automatically constructed ontology of tourism terms in OWL format containing nearly 2,000 concept classes.

Keywords: Natural language processing · Semantic search ·
Information retrieval · Travel domain

This work was supported by the European Regional Development Fund as a part of the 2014-2020 Smart Growth Operational Programme: (1) Intelligent travel search system based on natural language understanding algorithms, project no. POIR.01.01.01-00-0798/19; (2) CLARIN - Common Language Resources and Technology Infrastructure, project no. POIR.04.02.00-00C002/19.

C. Bădică et al. (Eds.): ICCCI 2022, CCIS 1653, pp. 71–83, 2022.
https://doi.org/10.1007/978-3-031-16210-7_6

1   Introduction

Search is a complex task that differs from domain to domain. Search for e-commerce requires a different set of methods and algorithms than search for travel, corporate, law or medicine documents. In travel, the complexity of data is bigger than in other domains, and the search process requires more parameters. In travel, one product (holiday package) has got tens of thousands of combinations depending on time, board type, room type, number of people, children's age, etc. Qtravel.ai research conducted on 286 users resulted in multiple conclusions regarding the needs of travellers. It has been discovered that over 89% of travellers would like to search for multiple destinations and 84% of people want to search for offers only by typing keywords. Similar findings, confirming the shortcomings of travel search, were also found in other studies published in Phocuswright [17]. According to the Eyefortravel report [5], one of the main reasons for customer dissatisfaction is the use of search engines (such as Google, Yandex, Baidu, Bing) during the purchasing process, mainly in the initial phase of the purchasing a trip. It is worth noticing that according to Millennial Travel Report [4,9] millennials and Generation Z are also more open to using conversational interfaces during contact with travel sites. What emphasises the importance of search engine quality is a finding presented by Expedia Media Solutions [23] shows that a traveller, in the 45 days before purchase, visits travel related sites at least 121 times.

These days, performing a search requires to choose from a finite number of values for each class characterizing an offer. Although it enables to find the right offer, it also requires a significant amount of time for the user to perform the search each time. For the past few years, companies like Airbnb or TripAdvisor have provided new options, interfaces and a few step processes to improve the experience of a traveller, but they have not drastically changed the overall process. We believe that the next widely used interface for search travel in the next couple of years will be natural language search. This article presents a set of methods based on natural language processing to improve the search for travel.

2   Related Work

Semantic search engines for the tourism industry has been undertaken over many years by many companies like Hopper, CheapAir, Expedia, Zaptravel, Adioso or FindMyCarrots. Most of them failed, changed their business model or have returned to classic search engines. The main reason for that is the complexity of the large volume of tourist data and users queries. Work on semantic search, is continued in the e-commerce industry, where there has been an evolution from simple product search using keywords to advanced solutions using NLP algorithms and machine learning. The best-known solutions are Open Source solutions (Apache Solr, ElasticSearch, Sphinx), as well as commercial solutions often provided as SaaS services (Algolia, Inbentu, Klevu, SearchNode, Coveo).

They are optimized for e-commerce products and transferring methods and algorithms (even with adjustments and domain-specific vocabulary) do not provide satisfactory results.

In tourism domain, a system was proposed that applies Named Entity Recognition (NER) to recognize geographic entities and resolve property names, which is combined with query intent classification [2]. In this work, system returns mapped entities and classify the intent with Long short-term memory (LSTM) recurrent neural network models. To the best of our knowledge there are no publications or benchmarks in the tourism domain for travel offer-query matching.

3 Metadata Module

This part of the processing pipeline is used to extract information from the query with which to describe the offer being sought. Examples of such data are departure dates, offer duration, destination country, city, or type of tour. All these elements can be grouped under one general type of task called information extraction from text. Sequence tagging methods are in widespread use for this type of issue, which allow a section of the text being analysed to be tagged with tags appropriate to the class of information. This extracts information about named entities, temporal expressions, or unary relations (assigned to a default entity). Using the sequence tagging technique also allows information extraction to be more based on the context in which it is embedded. This increases the coverage of finding expressions that the method has not seen during the learning process, but behave like other expressions in the class – for example, street names. Currently, models for the task of recognizing named entities are available for the Polish language, in various technologies. Packages with pretrained models that can be used right away are, for example, the spaCy [8] package and its default model for Polish, or package flair [1], which also contains models for Polish. Another approach, popular in many languages, is to fine-tune transformer architecture models to the task. One such package is the PolDeepNer2 [12] package based on the RoBERTa architecture. Because of its very good performance for PolDeepNer2, it was the package that became the basis for the models in our metadata pipeline.

3.1 Datasets

Each tool in the metadata pipeline was learned on a separate dataset in independent processes. The morphosyntactic tagger was learned on the 1 million NKJP [19] subcorpus. This dataset contains approximately 1.2 million tokens manually annotated with morphosyntactic tags. The data for the named entity recognition task was manually annotated by a team of linguists and came from the tourism domain. Moreover, the data for unary relations were manually annotated by a team of linguists. Both sets were annotated using the $2+1$ method – two independent linguists tag the sets, and then a third independent annotator unifies their annotations. These data are taken from the text of offer descriptions and tourist enquiries. The set for NER contains 112247 tokens with 6773 of named entities occurrences, and the set for unary relations contains 46093 tokens with 5051 occurrences of relations. The model for temporal expression recognition was learned on the KPWr [15] corpus, which is manually annotated. The KPWr corpus contains 6116 occurrences of temporal expressions, which fall into four categories: date, time, duration, set.

3.2 Method

The metadata processing pipeline consists of the following elements: morphosyntactic tagging, extraction of temporal expressions, recognition of named entities, determination of unary relations, exact matching of expressions from domain dictionaries, and lemmatization of multiword entities. Most of these tools are interconnected – for example, morphosyntactic tagging is required for the correct operation of the temporal expression determination module, dictionary matching, and lemmatization of all results from the pipeline. The MorphoDiTa-PL [18] package for contemporary texts was used as a morphosyntactic tagger. It is a tagger based on HMM decoding using an averaged perceptron algorithm. The module that directly uses the tagger information is the temporal expression detection module, based on the Liner2 package, which, in addition to being a tool for the CRF-based sequence tagging task, contains rules for normalizing temporal expressions [10]. In parallel, dictionary matching occurs with a tool based on searching patterns built in the WCCL language [20]. The system has dictionaries encoded with WCCL language rules that, when a condition is met, fire and verify that all conditions of the rule are met to return the found information. Models that do not need morphosyntactic tagger information are models for named entity recognition and finding unary relations based on the PolDeepNer2 package. The base of both models is the pretrained language model Polish-RoBERTa [3], which is linked to the classification head and trained for the task of tagging sequences based on a manually annotated domain dataset. These modules work in parallel with the elements associated with the tagger. The output from all tools goes to a multiword expression lemmatizer built on the Polem [11] package.

3.3 Performance

The effectiveness of the tools was measured on separate test sets that did not overlap with the training and validation sets. The effectiveness of the tagger is 92.73 using the F-Score measure. The effectiveness of NER in terms of spatial expression recognition is 66.64 using the F-Score measure. Unary relationships are recognized with an effectiveness equal to 75.28 of the F-Score measure. The temporal expression module has achieved effectiveness equal to 80.36 of F-Score measure. In selecting the final model, consideration was given to a greater focus around the measure of completeness, so that the system pays attention to as many elements as possible that can be extracted as metadata. This is important if one wants to prevent cases where there are missing matches of offers to a query.

4   Ontology-Based Text Matching Module

Ontology matching module is a module based on a taxonomy tree which contains concepts related to the tourism domain. This module matches the terms from the taxonomy with important words or phrases in travel offers and user-specified input queries. This enables *offer-to-query* matching based on common terms discovered in offers and queries. The main advantage of this module is a soft-matching mechanism facilitating inexact matching of concepts and phrases. We introduce a simple yet effective architecture of soft matching based on word and phrase embeddings. The flexibility of this mechanism allows to extend strictly supervised matching models and train the model in a weakly supervised manner avoiding labour-intensive data annotation. Pretraining on a wide range of categories is done on the generated data based on the ontology graph.

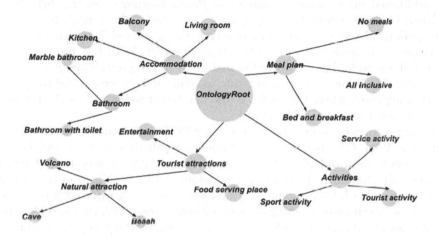

Fig. 1. Ontology taxonomy tree subgraph. The root ontology node is connected to different categories such as an accommodation node or a tourist attractions node. Then node categories have their more specific subcategories nodes. In this way we obtain travel related taxonomy tree.

4.1   Ontology and Datasets

The main issue of strictly supervised matching solutions [22] is the lack of annotated data for sequence tagging tasks. When the overall number of recognised categories is large, one has to prepare a representative training sample covering all possible categories that might appear in the input queries. On the other hand, in some domains it is very difficult to obtain such data in a short time. However, when dealing with the lack of training resources, one can use available knowledge bases and pseudodata generation methods to avoid this issue [13]. For this purpose, we build a new ontology for tourism domain Fig. 1 in a semi-automatic way. The ontology contains around 2000 nodes representing concept classes which represent the categories for text matching. It is built based on chosen categories and contains domain and hierarchical relations based on corpora analysis and linked open data. It is compliant with the OWL standard. Afterwards, the ontology is revised and manually corrected.

The ontology might be extended with new nodes at any time, which directly enforces an update of training data with additional costly annotations. To resolve this issue, we propose an approach based on pseudo-query generation based on taxonomy concepts and their properties. Let's assume every concept in an ontology has a textual label which can be used to generate training examples [14]. The procedure is as follows.

We create pseudo-queries consisting of node labels of randomly selected concepts from the ontology. These queries vary in terms of their length and content. The concatenation is done with different conjunction phrases that do not bring any additional information. Examples in Polish language are: '*i*', '*lub*', '*wraz z*' which in English would correspond to: '*and*', '*or*', '*along with*'. Some common spelling mistakes are added randomly to the generated data to increase the robustness of language models to this type of errors. With this procedure, we generated a pseudo-dataset being the main part of the pretraining model.

To prevent the model from overfitting to artificial data, we decided to apply a two-step approach where the model is also fine-tuned on a small labelled sample with true queries in natural language.

Final generated training data consist of 200k training sample queries. Every query has from 1 to 15 categories, random conjunction between and half of the sentences got random spelling mistakes. The data set was divided into a training and a test set. The training set contains 180k examples and the test set 20k examples. With this amount of training samples, each category was present in the data 720 times on average (8 categories on average with the example times the number of training examples divided by the number of categories), which is enough to train the model.

Real labelled data consist of a training set, which has 271 training samples and covers 218 categories. The test set has 23 test samples and covers 74 categories.

4.2   Method

The method consists of a transformer model with frozen weights, a 1D convolution neural network, and an ontology tree - Fig. 2. All nodes in the ontology tree are embedded with the transformer model, we used LaBSE model [6], which provided multilingual embeddings. We took the embeddings from the second layer of the transformer, as they are less contextual and serve better representation for the word matching task. To represent multiword phrases, we used max pooling over the words. The 1D convolution was trained to recognize patterns in offers and queries, and to assign an adequate category from the ontology. Each word was firstly embedded with the LaBSE model and the embeddings were passed to the 1D convolution, which is a 1D inception-like module [24] composed of kernel lengths 1, 3 and 5. In this setup, convolutions were able to detect different multiword patterns in the input. To assign the category from the ontology graph, a dot product was calculated between graph node representations and query word representations computed with convolution. This operation points to the categories with maximal activation.

There are many categories and each query only is labeled by a small subset of all categories. This leads to an imbalance between negative and positive examples during training. For this reason, focal loss is used for training as it addresses the issue of class imbalance.

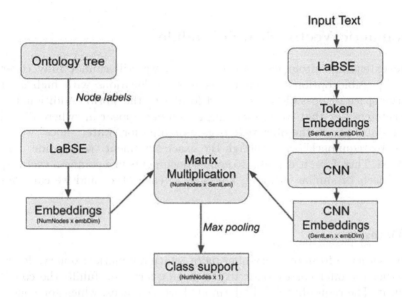

Fig. 2. Ontology module architecture schema. Language-agnostic BERT Sentence Embedding (LaBSE) was applied to node lables from the ontology tree and input texts. Convolutional Neural Network (CNN) architecture was used to find patterns in embedded input texts.

4.3   Performance

Firstly, the model was pretrained on synthetically generated data and afterwards trained on labeled real data examples with limited category sets. From the results presented in the Table 1 it is clear that the models need additional training on real texts to perform well on an actual written natural language text. After additional training on real labeled data samples, it is able to perform well on a real data sample and still keeps high performance on generated data samples, which cover a much wider category set.

Table 1. Table shows results in percent points for the model pretrained on generated data only and additionally trained on labeled real data. Metrics uses are precision, recall and F1 score, because for each sample number of positive classes is many times smaller than number of negative classes.

	Generated data only			Generated data & real labeled data		
	Precision	Recall	F1 score	Precision	Recall	F1 score
Generated data testset	93.99	99.19	96.59	92.22	70.47	81.35
Real labeled data testset	34.22	33.11	33.67	81.01	83.11	82.06

5   Semantic Vector Search Module

Despite extending ontologies, categories, etc., we still cannot fully cover the space of possible options - even just specifying locations with high accuracy is a large space of possible regions and locales in the world. Additionally, certain terms/entities that we are looking for do not appear anywhere directly in the metadata, nor in the offer text, e.g., searching for "water slides" we can be satisfied by "aquapark" even though the exact statement "water slide" was not mentioned. Therefore, it is useful to embed documents in a common vector space, where objects of similar meaning are close to each other and we can compare them.

5.1   Datasets

The dataset has a form of query-offer pairs, which are marked binary, depending on whether the offer corresponds to the given query, i.e., fulfills the conditions listed in it. The requests take the form of short sentences, which someone could type into a potential search engine for travel offers, so they take the form of complete sentences (e.g. "I am looking for a cosy hotel in Greece, near the beach, with a room for two people.") as well as written requirements/keywords (e.g. "vacation in Greece, hotel near the beach, two people"). At different stages of the project, data were collected with the help of linguists, in different ways, i.e., writing out queries to existing offers or using a specially developed application described below.

The data acquisition application (Fig. 3) was developed to simulate the environment in which the system would operate. The application allows you to type in any query and then displays results for the 10 best matchings according to cosine similarity, which are then flagged by humans in a binary fashion - whether the offer matches the requirements, including those not explicitly written in the query. The database of offers used for annotation includes tens of thousands of texts. The whole system has been developed in a user-friendly way and allows for displaying up-to-date annotation statistics, including Cohen's kappa coefficient.

The size of the total data collected, along with the size of the individual splits used to train and evaluate the biencoder models are shown in Table 2.

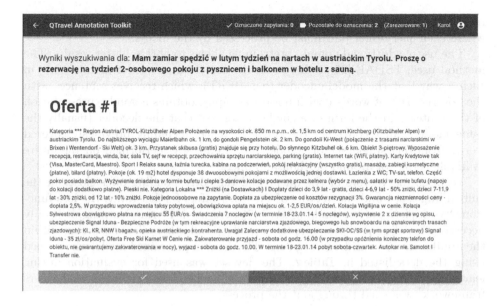

Fig. 3. The data acquisition application (Polish language interface)

The train/dev/test splits were made relative to the queries, i.e., so that queries do not repeat between subsets, however, as offers may repeat between different queries, a small fraction of offers repeats between subsets (hence do not add up to the number from the whole dataset). Other subsets may not add up to the whole due to rounding when splitting the dataset.

Table 2. Dataset: query - relevant travel offers pairs

Dataset part	Queries	Offers	All pairs	Positive pairs	Negative pairs
whole	3,156	12,146	23,605	11,904	11,701
train	2,556	10,507	19,093	9,713	9,380
dev	284	1,863	2,224	1,103	1,121
test	315	1,997	2,278	1,085	1,193

5.2   Method

The method used is called biencoder - we train one model (e.g., BERT) for vectorization so that the query embedding vector and the relevant answers are close to each other (in the embedding space). This allows us to preprocess all potential answers/offers into vectors, and at query time vectorize only the query - which we compare with all answers by cosine similarity. The limitation is trying to store all information into a single vector, however, this allows to significantly reduce the processing time in comparison to using a so-called cross-encoder [21], where each query-offer pair must be processed by the model.

The use of additional domain pretraining allows to obtain better results. The method used, TSDAE [25], is based on the use of auto-encoder architecture, in such a way that the model encoder (e.g. BERT), which receives sentences with the covered part of words ("with noise") as input, obtains a good representation of the sentence in the form of a single vector - so that the decoder (usually the same model) can reconstruct the entire sentence, including previously covered words from this single vector. Model pretraining was performed on the entire available corpus of around 80 thousand offers.

To align the vectors of the query and the corresponding offer closer in the embedding space and the vectors of the other offers further away, the loss functions "MultipleNegativesRankingLoss" [7] were used. During learning, it is only necessary to define positive pairs (query, offer) - all other offers occurring within the minibatch are considered negative. The domain pretrained model was trained using the data listed in Table 2. The dev set was used for evaluation during learning, while the test was used for final evaluation. The SentenceTrasnformers framework[1] was used throughout the process.

5.3   Performance

Evaluations of the tested models were performed using mAP@k (mean average precision at k), as this is a metric useful for evaluating rankings - in this case, travel offers that are intended to satisfy the requirements contained in the query. The ranking of offers relative to the query is based on the cosine similarity of the vector embeddings of the query-offer pair. Only positive query-offer pairs were used for evaluation, and all other offers are considered incorrect in the ranking. The mAP@k metric indicates how high in ranking generated by the model relevant offers rank relative to the entire corpus. The best biencoder model, trained using "MultipleNegativesRankingLoss" (configured: 50 epochs, batch size 20), achieved a mAP@100 of 0.399.

6   Combination of Modules

The whole system combines the previously described modules into one processing pipeline. The main goal is to use metadata and ontology tags to precisely filter out the offers that are not compliant with the query and afterwards choose the most adequate offers to the vector module.

6.1   Combination Architecture

The final system is based on the Solr search engine where offers' texts, metadata, and ontology tags are stored. In the baseline version, offers that match the

---

[1] https://github.com/UKPLab/sentence-transformers/.

query are returned only based on the text field using Tf-idf algorithm [16]. In subsequent versions, this database is extended by a column with ontology tags and a column for each metadata type (e.g., a column with detected names of countries, islands, activities, etc.). Ontology tags and metadata are extracted from offers and queries by the same processing pipeline. Then the ontology tags from a query are matched with the ontology tags extracted from an offer. The weights of each type of match were chosen empirically, taking into account expert knowledge, are as follows: country: *3.0*, equipment: *3.0*, attraction: *3.0*, activity: *3.0*, wccl attraction: *2.0*, ontology tags: *5.0*, text: *1.0*. In the production system, such weights can be fine-tuned to maximize a click rate. For performance reasons, the vector module runs separately from Solr and in the combination mode it is the postprocessing phase of the top 100 results obtained from Solr. The final score by which offers are sorted is the product of the Solr's fit score and the cosine similarity obtained from the vector model.

6.2 Performance

In the task of ranking texts from a large corpus, we do not have information about whether the results found are relevant to a given query. Therefore, for the final evaluation, the evaluation was done manually by labeling the top10 offers found by each tested module combination. A subset of 100 queries from the test part was used for evaluation, resulting in 1000 annotations per tested combination. The results presented in Table 3 show that adding more modules increases the percentage of the top 10 travel offers considered relevant to the query. Additionally, we tested the independent use of the vector module, where the entire corpus was sorted by cosine similarity - this resulted in the best mAP@10 results and the highest percentage of relevant offers in the top10.

Table 3. Individual module results based on final manual evaluation

Module	mAP@10	Relative offers @10	Non-relative offers @10
Baseline	40.12	21.92%	78.08%
+ ontology + metadata	39.57	23.43%	76.57%
+ vector score	53.02	32.16%	67.84%
Only vector score	54.76	36.87%	63.13%

7 Conclusions and Future Work

Our research shows that in terms of metrics for ranking travel offers, the independent use of the biencoder model, learned using the loss function "MultipleNegativesRankingLoss", performs best. Note, however, that this is the module that uses the largest amount of manually annotated data specifically for this task.

Additionally, due to the low explanatory power of the model, it will not necessarily work in a situation in which we want to show a search engine user factors by which offers appear at the top of the page. In this case, the ontology and metadata modules will be useful, as they will allow to indicate explicitly the categories detected in the query and offers. Therefore, in the practical application of the developed modules, a combination of modules that obtains similar results to the stand-alone use of the vector module will probably work best.

In the future work, a great improvement in real-time working application would be adding a system feedback loop after interaction with the user to fine-tune the metadata and ontology tags weights in the Solr search engine. This system might be applied in online adaptive learning or offline with gathered user data via genetics algorithms or a grid search algorithm. The application can improve with more queries coming into the system. They can be analyzed, annotated, and the models will be retrained, tested, and deployed.

More broadly, the interface using natural language to search for travel offers can, when properly tailored, be used by chat-bots and voice systems like intelligent smart speakers or other voice assistants. This will make the search for travel offers more user-friendly and may in the future look like a conversation with a travel advisor.

References

1. Akbik, A., Bergmann, T., Blythe, D., Rasul, K., Schweter, S., Vollgraf, R.: Flair: an easy-to-use framework for state-of-the-art NLP. In: NAACL 2019, 2019 Annual Conference of the North American Chapter of the Association for Computational Linguistics (Demonstrations), pp. 54–59 (2019)
2. Chandrasekaran, R., Pathak, H.N., Yano, T.: Deep neural query understanding system at eXpedia group. In: 2020 IEEE International Conference on Big Data (Big Data), pp. 1476–1484 (2020). https://doi.org/10.1109/BigData50022.2020.9378495
3. Dadas, S., Perełkiewicz, M., Poświata, R.: Pre-training Polish transformer-based language models at scale. In: Rutkowski, L., Scherer, R., Korytkowski, M., Pedrycz, W., Tadeusiewicz, R., Zurada, J.M. (eds.) ICAISC 2020. LNCS (LNAI), vol. 12416, pp. 301–314. Springer, Cham (2020). https://doi.org/10.1007/978-3-030-61534-5_27
4. expedia: Millenial travel report (2016)
5. Eyefortravel: Understanding the traveler consumer's path to purchase (2017)
6. Feng, F., Yang, Y., Cer, D., Arivazhagan, N., Wang, W.: Language-agnostic BERT sentence embedding. CoRR abs/2007.01852 (2020). https://arxiv.org/abs/2007.01852
7. Henderson, M., et al.: Efficient natural language response suggestion for smart reply. arXiv preprint arXiv:1705.00652 (2017)
8. Honnibal, M., Montani, I.: spaCy 2: Natural language understanding with Bloom embeddings, convolutional neural networks and incremental parsing (2017, to appear)
9. Inc., W.: U.S. travel trends report (2019)
10. Kocoń, J., Bernaś, T., Oleksy, M.: Recognition and normalisation of temporal expressions using conditional random fields and cascade of partial rules. Poznan Stud. Contemp. Linguist. 55(2), 271–303 (2019)

11. Marcinczuk, M.: Lemmatization of multi-word common noun phrases and named entities in polish. In: Proceedings of the International Conference Recent Advances in Natural Language Processing, RANLP 2017, Varna, Bulgaria, 2–8 September 2017, pp. 483–491 (2017)
12. Marcińczuk, M., Radom, J.: A single-run recognition of nested named entities with transformers. Procedia Comput. Sci. **192**, 291–297 (2021)
13. Meng, Y., Shen, J., Zhang, C., Han, J.: Weakly-supervised neural text classification. CoRR abs/1809.01478 (2018). http://arxiv.org/abs/1809.01478
14. Meng, Y., et al.: Text classification using label names only: a language model self-training approach (2020)
15. Oleksy, M., et al.: Polish Corpus of Wrocław University of Technology 1.3 (2019)
16. Papineni, K.: Why inverse document frequency? In: Second Meeting of the North American Chapter of the Association for Computational Linguistics (2001). https://aclanthology.org/N01-1004
17. Phocuswright: The perfect path: what travellers want -and don't want - in their digital journey (2017)
18. Piasecki, M., Walentynowicz, W.: Morphodita-based tagger adapted to the polish language technology. In: Proceedings of Human Language Technologies as a Challenge for Computer Science and Linguistics, pp. 377–381 (2017)
19. Przepiórkowski, A., Bańko, M., Górski, R.L., Lewandowska-Tomaszczyk, B., Łaziński, M., Pęzik, P.: National corpus of Polish. In: Proceedings of the 5th language & technology conference: human language technologies as a challenge for computer science and linguistics, pp. 259–263. Fundacja Uniwersytetu im. Adama Mickiewicza Poznań (2011)
20. Radziszewski, A., Wardyński, A., Śniatowski, T.: WCCL: a morpho-syntactic feature toolkit. In: Habernal, I., Matoušek, V. (eds.) TSD 2011. LNCS (LNAI), vol. 6836, pp. 434–441. Springer, Heidelberg (2011). https://doi.org/10.1007/978-3-642-23538-2_55
21. Reimers, N., Gurevych, I.: Sentence-Bert: sentence embeddings using Siamese BERT-networks. In: Proceedings of the 2019 Conference on Empirical Methods in Natural Language Processing and the 9th International Joint Conference on Natural Language Processing (EMNLP-IJCNLP), pp. 3982–3992 (2019)
22. Shen, J., Qiu, W., Meng, Y., Shang, J., Ren, X., Han, J.: TaxoClass: hierarchical multi-label text classification using only class names. In: Proceedings of the 2021 Conference of the North American Chapter of the Association for Computational Linguistics: Human Language Technologies, pp. 4239–4249. Association for Computational Linguistics, Online, June 2021. https://doi.org/10.18653/v1/2021.naacl-main.335, https://aclanthology.org/2021.naacl-main.335
23. Solutions, E.M.: The traveler's path to purchase (2016)
24. Szegedy, C., Vanhoucke, V., Ioffe, S., Shlens, J., Wojna, Z.: Rethinking the inception architecture for computer vision. CoRR abs/1512.00567 (2015). http://arxiv.org/abs/1512.00567
25. Wang, K., Reimers, N., Gurevych, I.: Tsdae: using transformer-based sequential denoising auto-encoderfor unsupervised sentence embedding learning. In: Findings of the Association for Computational Linguistics: EMNLP 2021, pp. 671–688 (2021)

Towards Automatic Detection of Inappropriate Content in Multi-dialectic Arabic Text

Nabil Badri$^{(\boxtimes)}$ ⓘ, Ferihane Kboubi ⓘ, and Anja Habacha Chaibi ⓘ

RIADI Laboratory, ENSI School, University of Manouba, La Manouba, Tunisia
{nabil.badri,anja.habacha}@ensi-uma.tn, ferihane.kboubi@fsegt.utm.tn
http://www.ensi-uma.tn/

Abstract. Nowadays, the various social networking applications give rise to millions of comments or tweets every day. This large amount of unstructured and noisy data is the subject of numerous studies on the behavior of people, their thoughts, their worries, their beliefs, etc. Currently, several research studies have focused on the detection of inappropriate content. But the number of works that have been interested in the Arabic language is very small, and the number of those that have considered multi-dialect Arabic content is even smaller. This is the context in which our work takes place. We will analyze the impact of the multi-dialectism on the performance of classifiers for the identification of inappropriate Arabic content. The key contribution of the paper is twofold. Firstly, we introduce an Arabic hate speech and abusive language dataset (Tun-EL) covering three dialects (Tunisian, Egyptian, and Lebanese). Secondly, we propose a new approach for inappropriate content detection. Our approach is based on a combination of AraVec and fastText word embedding as input features and a Convolutional Neural Network-Bidirectional Gated Recurrent Unit (CNN-BiGRU) model. The obtained results show that the proposed model is effective in detecting hateful and abusive multi-dialect Arabic content.

Keywords: Deep learning · Inappropriate content detection · AraVec · fastText · CNN · BiGRU · Arabic dialect dataset

1 Introduction

Today, Online Social Networks (OSN) are the most popular and interactive medium used to express feelings, communicate and share information around the world with the ultimate freedom. However, this freedom comes at a price, especially when it enables spreading abusive language and hate speech against individuals or groups.

Communication includes all types of data such as text, image, audio and video. Text is the most widely traded type of content on social media, through posts, tweets, comments, replies to comments, and messages. This huge amount

C. Bădică et al. (Eds.): ICCCI 2022, CCIS 1653, pp. 84–100, 2022.
https://doi.org/10.1007/978-3-031-16210-7_7

of instantly posted data causes the user's page to be inundated with posts of different topics and content. Moreover, several research works have appeared concerning the automatic analysis of large masses of unstructured and highly noisy data, extracted from comments.

Based on an Arab dataset for hate speech and abusive detection in OSN, the objective of this paper is to study the effect of multi-dialectism on classification performance and identification of inappropriate content. However, to the best of our knowledge, there was a few multi-dialect datasets targeting inappropriate Arabic texts and overall there are a few datasets of inappropriate Arabic texts, collected from other social platforms for the purpose of offensive language detection.

Therefore, in this paper, we contribute to this field by presenting a multidialect dataset of OSN comments for the three Arab countries: Tunisia, Egypt and Lebanon (**Tun-EL**), specifically designed to be used for the detection of offensive language. The proposed dataset consists of 23,033 comments annotated as Normal, hate, and Abusive.

Moreover, we will introduce our proposed models which consist of a combination of AraVec [19] and fastText [10] word embedding as input features with CNN, BiGRU and CNN-BiGRU models. We measure the performance and ability of our models in detecting inappropriate content. The organization of the paper is as follow:

In Sect. 2, we discuss related work. In Sect. 3, we talk about our approach of constructing of the Tun-EL data set. Section 4 is dedicated to inappropriate multi-dialect content detection approaches, in which we detail our adopted approaches including our proposed model. Section 5 deals with experimentation and evaluation of our model, we will describe the classification techniques used, the evaluation metrics and finally present the results of our tests. Finally, in Sect. 6 we finish with a conclusion and future work.

2 Related Work

Hate speech can occur in different language styles and through different acts, such as insult, abuse, provocation, and aggression. According to United Nations strategy and plan of action on hate speech[1], hate speech has no international legal definition, but it is hinged on incitement, which is an explicit and deliberate act aimed at discrimination, hostility and violence.

Unfortunately, this problem is difficult to deal with since it has many "faces" and exhibits complex interactions among social media users, the manual way of filtering out hateful content is not scalable, and detecting or removing such content manually from the web is a tedious task. This motivates researchers to identify automated ways, that are able to detect such toxic content on the social media. In [17], Razavi et al. detect flames (offensive/abusive rants) from text messages using a multi-level classification approach. They used a curated list

---

[1] https://www.un.org/en/genocideprevention/documents/.

of 2,700 words, phrases and expressions denoting various degrees of flames and then used them as features for a two-staged Naive Bayes classifier.

In recent years, deep learning-based approaches have become increasingly popular for this task, a variety of model designs and methods have blossomed in the context of natural language processing (NLP). Deep learning methods employ multiple processing layers to learn hierarchical representations of data, and have produced state-of-the-art results in many domains [22]. Many algorithms for modeling terms have been suggested [7,8].

In [9], Gamback and Sikdar used a deep learning models partially trained on the 6,909 English Twitter hatespeech dataset[2] created by [21], and annotated by CrowdFlower users[3], to address hate speech. They implemented a convolutional neural network (CNN) with random word vectors, word2vec word vectors and character n-grams, were considered as feature embeddings when training the CNN model, in order to classify social media text as one of four categories: "Racism", "Sexism", "Both (racism & sexism)", and "Non-hate-speech".

In [2], Aljarah et al. worked on detecting offensive language in arabic tweets using SVM, NB, DT and RF, while Safa Alsafari et al. [3] implemented a convolutional neural network (CNN) and a gated recurrent unit (GRU), a kind of recurrent neural network (RNN), to classify social media text as one of three categories: 'Clean', 'Offensive' and 'Hate'. Considering that GRUs have fewer parameters and thus may train faster, some researches [23] choose GRU as their recurrent neurons.

In [13], two datasets were proposed: a Twitter dataset of 1,100 dialectal tweets and a dataset of 32K inappropriate comments collected from a popular Arabic news site and annotated as obscene, offensive, or clean. The authors in [1] provided a dataset of 16K Egyptian, Iraqi, and Libyan comments collected from YouTube. The comments were annotated as either offensive, inoffensive, or neutral. Text classification (TC) on hate speech detection consists of assigning one or more categories from a predefined list to a document [4,5].

Previous related studies employed a variety of strategies for labelling datasets. For example, Warner and Hirschberg manually labeled user comments and a corpus of websites [20]. In [18], Reynolds et al. employed a dataset which includes 2,696 posts labelled with the use of Amazons Mechanical Turk service[4].

3   Tun-EL Dataset Construction

Our dataset[5] is a bit special in its construction compared to the creation of other datasets. Indeed, our objective is to study the effect of multi-dialectism on the performance of classifiers for the identification of inappropriate content in order to propose a system capable of handling multi-dialectical content. For this reason, we only looked for the Arabic dialect datasets which are available

---

[2] http://github.com/zeerakw/hatespeech.
[3] https://www.crowdflower.com/.
[4] www.mturk.com.
[5] Dataset available at https://github.com/NabilBADRI/Multidialect-Project.

on the internet and preferably which carry the same labeling and if this is not the case, we proceed to modify their annotations.

Table 1. List of datasets used for the study of hate speech in the Arabic language.

Ref.	Source	Classes	# Comments	M tongue
D1 [11]	F & YT	Hate, Normal, Abusive	6,040	Tunisian
D2 (*)	F	Hate, Normal, Abusive	437	Tunisian
D3 [14]	T	Hate, Normal, Abusive	5,846	Lebanese
D4 [16]	T	Abusive, hateful, Offensive, Disrespectful, Fearful, Normal	3,354	Lebanese
D5 [13]	T	Obscene, Offensive, Clean	1,101	Egyptian

Legend: 'M tongue' = Mother tongue, 'F' = Facebook, 'YT' = Youtube, 'T' = Twitter. (*): We collected and annotated this dataset.

3.1 Dataset Selection

A set of criteria is defined to select the datasets: *availability, representativeness, heterogeneity* and *balance* [15]. Those criteria ensure the quality of the study, and ensuring that it can be applied for training predictive analytics models for detecting of abusive language in arabic online communication. We considered only arabic language datasets that have been released online for free licence and related to offensive language, such as hateful, vulgar, or abusive speech. To investigate the impact of multi-dialectism on categorization and inappropriate content detection performance by using a suitable corpus, different and richer than the few ones available in the research literature, we looked at the hate speech datasets available and discovered four publically available sources in three arabic dialects: Tunisian, Egyptian, and Lebanese as shown in Table 1. We saw that combining different sorts of categories (offensive, profanity, abusive, insult etc.) was one of the initial problems. Despite the fact that these categories are connected to hate speech, they should not be confused [6]. As a result, we only use three labels: "hate", "normal" and "abusive", and we do not use any others. We included several dataset formats and most of them are composed of comments separated by commas. Table 1 lists all the datasets that were considered and used in this work, specifying for each one the number of comments, the source and the classes used for the annotation of the comments. In the following, we note the different datasets by D1, D2, D3, D4 and D5. To build our dataset, we propose to merge the five datasets together while re-annotating them if necessary. We name the resulting dataset **Tun-EL**.

3.2   Dataset Processing

To built our dataset, three main phases are followed during the investigation process. The following sections describe each of these phases in detail.

Dataset Formatting: The selected datasets are in heterogeneous formats and some of them include multiple descriptions, attributes, such as publication date, user profile or number of annotators. Thus, additional processing must be done to make them in a minimal and coherent format by keeping only the columns of the comments and their classes.

Data Set Segmentation: The two situations that can destabilize the classification system are: the length of multiple comments and the existence of words in a comment that can belong to more than one class. To solve this problem, we have opted for the segmentation of the comments, to give birth to several new comments, shorter and easier to process. This allowed us to expand the dataset and have comments that can only be classified into one class.

Dataset Annotation and Merging: We selected five different Arabic datasets with three dialects as shown in Table 1, and we concatenated them to have a single one (Tun-EL). The first (D1) dataset and the third (D3) dataset were labeled according to three labels (hate, normal, and abusive).

On the other hand, we have manually annotated the second (D2) dataset which contains 437 comments using the same labels than the previous datasets. Indeed, this dataset is collected from user comments on the official Facebook pages of Tunisian radio and TV channels.

For the fourth (D4) dataset which has been initially labeled with the following labels: "Abusive", "Hateful", "Offensive", "Disrespectful", "Fearful", and "Normal". We re-annotated this dataset as follows: the "Hateful" label is kept, the "Offensive", "Disrespectful", and "Fearful" labels are replaced by Hateful, the "Normal", and "Abusive" label are kept.

The fifth dataset is labelled by "Clean", "Obscene", and "Offensive" labels, and relabelled as follows: by changing the "Offensive" label to "Abusive", the "Obscene" label to "Hate" and the "Clean" label to "Normal". The goal is to concatenate these datasets and obtain a single dataset whose all parts are labelled with the same set of labels. We name this global dataset **Tun-EL** dataset because it concerns Arab society and more precisely their dialects.

3.3   Exploratory Data Analysis

This is an important phase of the study, the analysis phase adds value and insight to the content of the datasets. Here, we present detailed investigations of the content of Tun-EL dataset by performing statistical analyzes. Text statistics visualizations are simple but very insightful techniques that help to explore fundamental characteristics of textual data. They allow the analysis of: the frequency of words, the length of sentences, the most frequent stop words, and the most frequent significant words. For this analysis, we mainly use histograms (for continuous data) and bar charts (for categorical data). The first analysis concerns the number of words per comment. Indeed, the length of the input text for all training samples has to be specified for our neural network models. As a result, we needed to choose a suitable sentence padding length p. A reserved padding token would be used to pad any sentences with fewer than p words. Following the aforementioned data processing procedures, we used a histogram to illustrate the distribution of comments lengths in order to manipulate our decision on p. This showed that the word count in our dataset ranges up to 45 words and is typically between a few words and 30 words, as shown in Fig. 1.

4   Inappropriate Multidialect Content Detection

Certainly the Arabic language is the official language of all Arabic countries. However, in everyday life people communicate using the dialect specific to their country. Each Arabic country has its own dialect. When dealing with Arabic textual content, such as posts and comments on social networks, it is imperative to consider the multi-dialect aspect of this content. What would be the best strategy: treat each dialect separately or build a system capable of handling several dialects. In this section we begin by presenting two approaches to multi-dialect Arabic content processing. Then, we propose our classification models to detect inappropriate multi-dialect Arabic content.

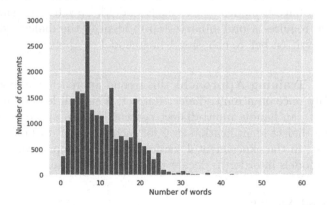

Fig. 1. Number of words per comment.

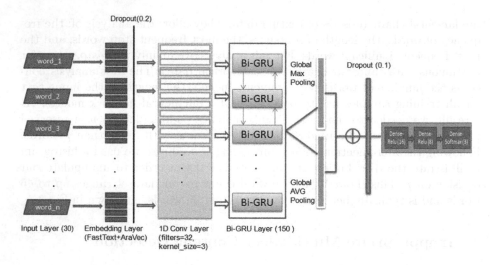

Fig. 2. Adopted architecture of the CNN-BiGRU model.

4.1 Mono-dialect vs Multi-dialect Training Approaches

To detect inappropriate content in Arabic we propose to test the two following approaches.

Mono-dialect Training Approach: this first approach consists of training n times a classifier on n mono-dialect datasets (with n number of dialects). This will allow us to have n models where each model is specific to a single dialect. This approach requires a preliminary step to identify the dialect with which a comment was written before choosing which model to apply.

Multi-dialect Training Approach: this second approach consists of training a classifier only once on a multi-dialect dataset. This will lead us to train only one model that can handle multi-dialect content. In this approach we will not need to have a dialect identification step for each comment to be processed. We propose to test, in the experimental section, these two approaches with several classification models in order to decide which one to choose.

4.2 Proposed Model

The proposed model is a combination of CNN and BiGRU neural networks as shown in Fig. 2. The input to the model were AraVec (Ara), fastText (FT) and combination of these both word embeddings. Word embeddings are ubiquitous for any NLP problem, as algorithms can not process the plain text or strings in its raw form. Word embeddings are vectors that capture the semantic and contextual information of words. AraVec provides six different word embedding models, where each text domain (Tweets, WWW and Wikipedia) has two different models; one built using CBOW technique and the other using the Skip-Gram [12] technique.

In our work we used AraVec model (aravec/full_grams_cbow_300_twitter) trained on Twitter. We believe that the AraVec Twitter-based word embeddings are adequate for our task since the used datasets are collected from several social network sources such as Facebook, Twitter and Youtube comments. On the other hand, fastText algorithm created by Facebook assumes every word to be n-grams of character. It helps to give the vector representations for out of vocabulary words. For the current work, fastText based word embedding is used for generating token vectors of dimension 300. Each vector corresponding to a tweet is generated by taking the average of token vectors. The pre-trained fastText word embeddings are one of the more practical ways of text representation since they identify the internal structure of words. In order to take advantage of both word embeddings, we used a combination that consists of computing the mean of AraVec and fastText word vector matrices for each sentence in the dataset (i.e., computing an average of vectors from the same vector space). During the training phase of the model, the weights of the embedding layer are adjusted progressively according to the training data in order to generate specific word embeddings related to the task of classification of inappropriate mono and multi-dialect content. To avoid the phenomenon of overfitting and to not let algorithm depend on all the data, we set a SpatialDropout rate of (20%) of all values. The word embeddings are fed to a one-dimensional convolutional layer. This latter is used to convolve the embedding vectors along the temporal dimension with 32 filters of width 3 using the ReLu activation function. This 1D convolutional layer is followed by a bidirectional GRU which comprises 150 units that process sequences in forward and backward directions. The combination of CNN and BiGRU approach has a number of attractive features: the 1D convolutional layer considers the local combination of words and learns effectively robust features that captures the characteristics of an inappropriate content. On the other hand, the GRU includes gating units which modulate the flow of information inside the unit without any separate memory cells and are able to process memories of sequential data by storing previous inputs in the internal state of networks and plan from the history of previous inappropriate content inputs to target output vectors. The BiGRU's output vectors are simultaneously fed to a Global Average Polling layer and a Global Max Pooling layer. The output vectors are then concatenated and followed by a Dropout layer with rate equal to 20%. Again, the output vectors are fed to a two dense layers with 16 and 8 neurons respectively. The outputs of the fully connected layer are fed to a dense layer with three output neurons and a softmax activation function. The model was trained by minimizing the categorical cross-entropy using the Adam optimizer with default learning rate. For our task, the training datasets were very unbalanced, as shown in Table 2. The class imbalance problem decreases the performance of our model. We used class weighting to solve this problem. Weight adjustments during each single run in our network would have a higher influence when training under-represented classes since the loss function was weighted by the onverse of the proportion of each class in the training set. By decreasing overfitting, this strategy helped to increase overall performance.

Table 2. Number of comments per class.

Dataset	#Abusive	#Hate	#Normal
(D1)+(D2)	1204 (18.6%)	1399 (21.7%)	3857 (59.7%)
(D3)+(D4)	1746 (19.0%)	2885 (31.4%)	4565 (49.6%)
(D5)	203 (18.5%)	444 (40.4%)	453 (41.2%)
(Tun-EL)	3850 (16.7%)	6830 (29.7%)	12353 (53.6%)

5   Experiments and Evaluation

In this section, we describe in detail the data preprocessing, our experimental setup and results while testing the performance of our models on the different datasets used.

5.1   Data Preprocessing

In order to prepare the data for use to train the classification model, preprocessing must be performed first following the idea of purging unnecessary information from documents as much as possible. This subsection outlines all the data handling and processing techniques carried out. The NLTK package[6] was used during preprocessing steps.

Data Cleaning: To perform data cleaning, we used the highly specialized regular expressions(re)[7] module that is embedded in Python. This allowed us to define a rule to eliminate any character that does not belong to the Arabic alphabet (emojis, urls, non-Arabic words and special characters).

Tokenization: A "token" is a unit defined as a sequence of characters between two separators. These separators are: blanks, punctuation marks, and some other characters like quotes or parentheses. This operation therefore makes it possible to segment a text document into word tokens.

Rooting: In vector representations, each word present in the corpus is considered as a descriptor. This process presents flaws in the overall processing of data, for example, infinitive verbs, conjugated verbs, nouns, etc., which have the same meaning can be considered as a different descriptor. Rootization comes to deal with this problem, by appealing only to the roots of the words rather than to the whole words without worrying about the grammatical analysis.

---

[6] https://www.nltk.org/.
[7] https://docs.python.org/3/library/re.html#module-re.

Removing Stop Words: Once the text documents were split into tokens, we noticed that a significant number of these tokens are present in the majority of the comments in the corpus, these tokens are empty words. Stop words in the Arabic language correspond to prepositions, conjunction letters, pronouns, etc. Since the presence of these words makes no difference either semantically or lexically, their use in the classification task is unnecessary. This is why we proceeded to remove them, our motivation being to reduce the size of our vector document, and therefore processing time and learning time.

Table 3. Machine learning model and default parameters.

Classifier	Parameters
Logistic Regression - LR	multi_class = 'multinomial', max_iter = 100
Random Forest - RF	n_estimators = 10, criterion = 'gini', random_state = 0

5.2 Experimental Setup

For our experiments, we use Keras[8] with Tensorflow[9] back-end. We run the experiments on a Google Colab environment with Graphic Processing Units (GPUs). In terms of training, a maximum of 30 epochs is allowed and we employ a separate validation set to perform early stopping: training is interrupted if the validation F1-score did not drop in eight consecutive epochs and the weights of the best epoch are restored. All the datasets were split in 60/20/20 training, validation and test respectively.

It is important to notice that the same model (with the same architecture, number of layers, units and parameters) is used for all datasets, as we want to demonstrate the performance of this architecture across mono and multi-dialect tasks. Overall, the model, including the pre-trained word embeddings, contains approximately 7,394,311 trainable parameters (i.e., weights). Finally, since there is no previous study conducted on the tested mono-dialect datasets and our Tun-EL multi-dialect dataset, we also tested a CNN and BiGRU model with fastText (FT), AraVec (Ara) and combined word embedding. We compare our results with a basic LR and RF models, using TF-IDF weights for each comment. The models' configuration are shown in Table 3.

5.3 Results and Discussion

To the best of our knowledge, this is the first work that performed this task and there is no benchmark model to compare with.

---

[8] https://keras.io/.
[9] https://www.tensorflow.org/?hl=fr.

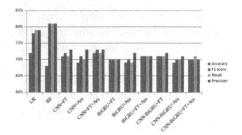

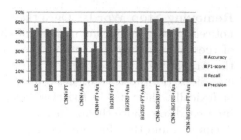

Fig. 3. Performance of the CNN, BiGRU and CNN-BiGRU models on Tunisian dataset.

Fig. 4. Performance of the CNN, BiGRU and CNN-BiGRU models on Egyptian dataset.

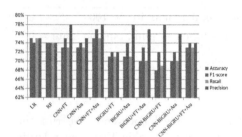

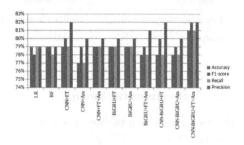

Fig. 5. Performance of the CNN, BiGRU and CNN-BiGRU models on Lebanese dataset.

Fig. 6. Performance of the CNN, BiGRU and CNN-BiGRU models on Tun-EL dataset.

For the task of identifying inappropriate content, the recall is more important to optimize than precision or other metrics. We give greater attention to identify inappropriate comments than the normal comments. As a result, we pay more attention to the Recall of abusive and hateful classes.

The results of the machine learning baselines and the neural network models trained on the test data are shown in Figs. 3, 4, 5 and 6 for the CNN, BiGRU and CNN-BiGRU models, respectively. It is apparent from these figures that the Random Forests model outperforms our models only on the Tunisian datasets however, on the Egyptian dataset, the CNN-BiGRU+FT achieved the best results, followed by CNN-BiGRU+FT+Ara and BiGRU+FT/BiGRU+Ara despite the fact that the egyptian dataset's size was too small (equal to 1,101 comments as mentioned in Table 2).

From the results shown in Fig. 3, 4, 5 and 6 we can also see that the performances of almost all models did not drop when we used them on the multi-dialect dataset (compared to the results obtained with the same models applied on mono-dialect datasets). Performance values obtained with Tun-EL dataset are even higher than the other datasets for the majority of tests. So we can retain the multi-dialect training approach instead of mono-dialect training approach.

On the Lebanese dataset, the highest results were obtained by the CNN+FT+Ara model. On the other hand, the results on the Tun-EL dataset indicate the efficiency of the CNN-BiGRU+FT+Ara model in detecting inappropriate content. Interestingly, our proposed CNN-BiGRU model which uses the proposed combination of fastText and AraVec embeddings achieved the highest values on the Tun-EL dataset. Tables 4, 5, 6, and 7 presents the classification results for each class in the Tunisian, Egyptian, Lebanese and Tun-EL datasets respectively.

What is interesting in the reported results is that the Recall values of the Abusive and Hateful classes of the machine learning models are worse than the Recall values achieved from the neural network models on the four datasets. This highlights that even if the traditional machine learning models outperformed the neural network models on the weighted metrics reported in Fig. 3, 4, 5 and 6, the former models are not as good as latter models at detecting inappropriate content.

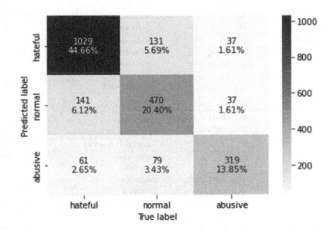

Fig. 7. Confusion matrix for the evaluated test data on the final CNN-BiGRU model.

The results in Table 7 (Tun-EL) clearly show the efficiency of the use of a combination of AraVec and fastText word embeddings for multi-dialect inappropriate content detection which can be observed from the confusion matrix highlighted in Fig. 7. From the confusion matrix in Fig. 7, we can observe that the CNN-BiGRU+FT+Ara model was able to classify 88% of the hateful content and 76% of the abusive content.

Table 4. Performance of classification models on Tunisian dataset.

Logistic regression	P	R	F1
#Abusive	82%	38%	52%
#Hateful	65%	28%	39%
#Normal	71%	98%	82%
Weighted AVG	79%	79%	78%
Random forest	P	R	F1
#Abusive	73%	50%	60%
#Hateful	40%	45%	42%
#Normal	77%	81%	79%
Weighted AVG	81%	81%	81%
CNN+FT	P	R	F1
#Abusive	64%	**57%**	60%
#Hateful	59%	**55%**	57%
#Normal	83%	81%	82%
Weighted AVG	73%	71%	72%
CNN+AraVec	P	R	F1
#Abusive	66%	**57%**	61%
#Hateful	60%	**52%**	55%
#Normal	80%	81%	81%
Weighted AVG	73%	70%	71%
CNN+FT+AraVec	P	R	F1
#Abusive	68%	**62%**	65%
#Hateful	59%	**54%**	57%
#Normal	81%	83%	82%
Weighted AVG	74%	72%	73%
BiGRU+FT	P	R	F1
#Abusive	58%	**51%**	54%
#Hateful	55%	**48%**	51%
#Normal	80%	87%	83%
Weighted AVG	70%	71%	70%
BiGRU+AraVec	P	R	F1
#Abusive	62%	**50%**	56%
#Hateful	56%	**52%**	52%
#Normal	77%	85%	81%
Weighted AVG	71%	70%	70%
BiGRU+FT+AraVec	P	R	F1
#Abusive	60%	**62%**	61%
#Hateful	53%	**50%**	51%
#Normal	82%	82%	82%
Weighted AVG	71%	71%	71%
CNN-BiGRU+FT	P	R	F1
#Abusive	60%	**62%**	61%
#Hateful	61%	**45%**	52%
#Normal	80%	85%	82%
Weighted AVG	72%	71%	71%
CNN-BiGRU+AraVec	P	R	F1
#Abusive	69%	49%	57%
#Hateful	56%	**48%**	52%
#Normal	77%	85%	81%
Weighted AVG	71%	70%	70%
CNN-BiGRU+FT+AraVec	P	R	F1
#Abusive	62%	**53%**	57%
#Hateful	59%	**48%**	53%
#Normal	77%	85%	81%
Weighted AVG	70%	71%	70%

Table 5. Performance of classification models on Egyptian dataset.

Logistic regression	P	R	F1
#Abusive	80%	21%	33%
#Hateful	58%	42%	49%
#Normal	50%	84%	63%
Weighted AVG	59%	54%	52%
Random forest	P	R	F1
#Abusive	58%	26%	36%
#Hateful	56%	48%	52%
#Normal	49%	70%	58%
Weighted AVG	54%	53%	52%
CNN+FT	P	R	F1
#Abusive	56%	**62%**	59%
#Hateful	63%	**43%**	51%
#Normal	61%	54%	57%
Weighted AVG	61%	51%	55%
CNN+AraVec	P	R	F1
#Abusive	22%	12%	16%
#Hateful	65%	30%	41%
#Normal	69%	22%	33%
Weighted AVG	60%	24%	34%
CNN+FT+AraVec	P	R	F1
#Abusive	23%	**44%**	30%
#Hateful	67%	27%	39%
#Normal	59%	34%	43%
Weighted AVG	57%	33%	39%
BiGRU+FT	P	R	F1
#Abusive	54%	**44%**	48%
#Hateful	57%	**64%**	60%
#Normal	60%	54%	57%
Weighted AVG	58%	56%	57%
BiGRU+AraVec	P	R	F1
#Abusive	55%	**69%**	61%
#Hateful	55%	**59%**	57%
#Normal	61%	50%	55%
Weighted AVG	58%	56%	57%
BiGRU+FT+AraVec	P	R	F1
#Abusive	78%	**44%**	56%
#Hateful	53%	**77%**	63%
#Normal	54%	40%	46%
Weighted AVG	57%	55%	54%
CNN-BiGRU+FT	P	R	F1
#Abusive	67%	**62%**	65%
#Hateful	64%	**68%**	66%
#Normal	63%	58%	60%
Weighted AVG	64%	63%	63%
CNN-BiGRU+AraVec	P	R	F1
#Abusive	64%	**44%**	52%
#Hateful	52%	**70%**	60%
#Normal	54%	40%	46%
Weighted AVG	54%	53%	52%
CNN-BiGRU+FT+AraVec	P	R	F1
#Abusive	67%	**62%**	65%
#Hateful	64%	**68%**	66%
#Normal	63%	58%	60%
Weighted AVG	64%	63%	63%

Table 6. Performance of classification models on Lebanese dataset.

Logistic regression	P	R	F1
#Abusive	79%	46%	58%
#Hateful	79%	69%	74%
#Normal	72%	89%	80%
Weighted AVG	75%	75%	74%
Random forest	P	R	F1
#Abusive	75%	49%	59%
#Hateful	75%	72%	74%
#Normal	74%	85%	79%
Weighted AVG	74%	74%	74%
CNN+FT	**P**	**R**	**F1**
#Abusive	76%	**76%**	76%
#Hateful	72%	**71%**	72%
#Normal	83%	71%	77%
Weighted AVG	79%	73%	75%
CNN+AraVec	**P**	**R**	**F1**
#Abusive	78%	**66%**	71%
#Hateful	68%	69%	68%
#Normal	76%	79%	78%
Weighted AVG	75%	73%	74%
CNN+FT+AraVec	**P**	**R**	**F1**
#Abusive	83%	**69%**	75%
#Hateful	71%	**72%**	71%
#Normal	79%	81%	80%
Weighted AVG	79%	75%	77%
BiGRU+FT	**P**	**R**	**F1**
#Abusive	71%	**69%**	70%
#Hateful	64%	65%	65%
#Normal	77%	75%	76%
Weighted AVG	73%	71%	72%
BiGRU+AraVec	**P**	**R**	**F1**
#Abusive	78%	**71%**	74%
#Hateful	68%	68%	68%
#Normal	83%	72%	77%
Weighted AVG	78%	71%	74%
BiGRU+FT+AraVec	**P**	**R**	**F1**
#Abusive	76%	**77%**	76%
#Hateful	70%	48%	57%
#Normal	81%	74%	77%
Weighted AVG	77%	70%	73%
CNN-BiGRU+FT	**P**	**R**	**F1**
#Abusive	74%	**81%**	77%
#Hateful	63%	69%	66%
#Normal	86%	60%	71%
Weighted AVG	78%	69%	72%
CNN-BiGRU+AraVec	**P**	**R**	**F1**
#Abusive	83%	**62%**	71%
#Hateful	62%	69%	66%
#Normal	76%	75%	76%
Weighted AVG	76%	70%	72%
CNN-BiGRU+FT+AraVec	**P**	**R**	**F1**
#Abusive	77%	**71%**	74%
#Hateful	64%	67%	66%
#Normal	77%	77%	77%
Weighted AVG	74%	73%	74%

Table 7. Performance of classification models on Tun-EL dataset.

Logistic regression	P	R	F1
#Abusive	82%	38%	52%
#Hateful	65%	28%	39%
#Normal	71%	98%	82%
Weighted AVG	79%	79%	78%
Random forest	P	R	F1
#Abusive	73%	50%	60%
#Hateful	40%	45%	42%
#Normal	77%	81%	79%
Weighted AVG	79%	78%	79%
CNN+FT	**P**	**R**	**F1**
#Abusive	76%	**83%**	80%
#Hateful	87%	**84%**	86%
#Normal	76%	68%	72%
Weighted AVG	82%	79%	80%
CNN+AraVec	**P**	**R**	**F1**
#Abusive	78%	**77%**	78%
#Hateful	86%	**82%**	84%
#Normal	72%	67%	70%
Weighted AVG	80%	77%	79%
CNN+FT+AraVec	**P**	**R**	**F1**
#Abusive	78%	**79%**	78%
#Hateful	85%	**84%**	85%
#Normal	72%	70%	71%
Weighted AVG	80%	79%	79%
BiGRU+FT	**P**	**R**	**F1**
#Abusive	78%	**78%**	78%
#Hateful	85%	**86%**	85%
#Normal	73%	66%	69%
Weighted AVG	80%	79%	79%
BiGRU+AraVec	**P**	**R**	**F1**
#Abusive	77%	**77%**	77%
#Hateful	85%	**86%**	85%
#Normal	72%	68%	70%
Weighted AVG	80%	79%	79%
BiGRU+FT+AraVec	**P**	**R**	**F1**
#Abusive	74%	**81%**	77%
#Hateful	86%	**85%**	85%
#Normal	78%	62%	69%
Weighted AVG	81%	78%	79%
CNN-BiGRU+FT	**P**	**R**	**F1**
#Abusive	78%	**77%**	78%
#Hateful	88%	**82%**	85%
#Normal	74%	71%	72%
Weighted AVG	82%	78%	80%
CNN-BiGRU+AraVec	**P**	**R**	**F1**
#Abusive	74%	**80%**	77%
#Hateful	85%	**85%**	85%
#Normal	74%	65%	69%
Weighted AVG	80%	78%	79%
CNN-BiGRU+FT+AraVec	**P**	**R**	**F1**
#Abusive	77%	**77%**	77%
#Hateful	87%	**85%**	86%
#Normal	74%	72%	73%
Weighted AVG	82%	81%	82%

6   Conclusion and Perspectives

The aim of this article is to propose a system for identifying inappropriate Arabic text content on social networks. To achieve this goal we began by proposing and building a multidialect Arabic textual dataset containing three dialects: Tunisian, Egyptian and Lebanese. Then we also proposed a new model for identifying inappropriate textual content.

Our model is based on the combination of CNN-BiGRU and fastText+AraVec word embedding. We tested our model on three mono-dialect datasets and a multi-dialect dataset. To deal with the multi-dialect aspect we wanted to check what would be the best training strategies: training n models on mono-dialect datasets (with n the number of dialects) or training a single model on a multi-dialect dataset.

The results showed that multi-dialect models did not produce worse results than those obtained by mono-dialect models. On the contrary, the results are even better. On the other hand, we also compared our neural network models with other reference models. The results showed that our models outperform others in terms of recall. Because of the complex nature of the Arabic language, more investigation is needed. Indeed, we have encountered a number of obstacles and challenges which must be taken into account in the future work. Collecting tweets that were associated with particular dialects was not an easy phase, as most people use the Arabic diglossia and switching between different Arabic dialects and Modern Standard Arabic (MSA). In addition to that, the terms used had significant similarities and the Tweepy[10] library has a limitation when the old tweets more than a week are retrieved. Therefore, a massive effort is needed to find the most single term used in each region. The similarities between the different dialects, mean that annotators had difficulty to label some tweets as being in a specific dialect. During sentiment analysis, some tweets were difficult to label as either normal, either hateful, or abusive where there is some ambiguity.

As perspectives, we will improve the results of the models by fine tuning hyper-parameters and testing several values of batch size, input length and number of epochs. We will enlarge our dataset by adding other tweets and comments, or even other dialects, we can also use the meta data of the datasets as input feature as well as the use of emojis. For the dataset imbalance problem, we will test another method for handling class imbalance, such as SMOTE method and different loss functions.

References

1. Alakrot, A., Murray, L., Nikolov, N.S.: Towards accurate detection of offensive language in online communication in Arabic. Procedia Comput. Sci. **142**, 315–320 (2018)
2. Aljarah, I., et al.: Intelligent detection of hate speech in Arabic social network: a machine learning approach. J. Inf. Sci. **47**(4), 483–501 (2021)

---

[10] https://www.tweepy.org/.

3. Alsafari, S., Sadaoui, S., Mouhoub, M.: Hate and offensive speech detection on Arabic social media. Online Soc. Netw. Media **19**, 100096 (2020)
4. Brown, E.W., Chong, H.A.: The GURU system in TREC-6. NIST SPECIAL PUBLICATION SP, pp. 535–540 (1998)
5. Chen, J., Hu, Y., Liu, J., Xiao, Y., Jiang, H.: Deep short text classification with knowledge powered attention. In: Proceedings of the AAAI Conference on Artificial Intelligence, vol. 33, pp. 6252–6259 (2019)
6. Davidson, T., Warmsley, D., Macy, M., Weber, I.: Automated hate speech detection and the problem of offensive language. In: Proceedings of the International AAAI Conference on Web and Social Media, vol. 11 (2017)
7. Duwairi, R., Hayajneh, A., Quwaider, M.: A deep learning framework for automatic detection of hate speech embedded in Arabic tweets. Arab. J. Sci. Eng. **46**(4), 4001–4014 (2021)
8. Farha, I.A., Magdy, W.: Multitask learning for Arabic offensive language and hate-speech detection. In: Proceedings of the 4th Workshop on Open-Source Arabic Corpora and Processing Tools, with a Shared Task on Offensive Language Detection, pp. 86–90 (2020)
9. Gambäck, B., Sikdar, U.K.: Using convolutional neural networks to classify hate-speech. In: Proceedings of the First Workshop on Abusive Language Online, pp. 85–90 (2017)
10. Grave, E., Bojanowski, P., Gupta, P., Joulin, A., Mikolov, T.: Learning word vectors for 157 languages. arXiv preprint arXiv:1802.06893 (2018)
11. Haddad, H., Mulki, H., Oueslati, A.: T-HSAB: a Tunisian hate speech and abusive dataset. In: Smaïli, K. (ed.) ICALP 2019. CCIS, vol. 1108, pp. 251–263. Springer, Cham (2019). https://doi.org/10.1007/978-3-030-32959-4_18
12. Mikolov, T., Sutskever, I., Chen, K., Corrado, G.S., Dean, J.: Distributed representations of words and phrases and their compositionality. In: Advances in Neural Information Processing Systems, pp. 3111–3119 (2013)
13. Mubarak, H., Darwish, K., Magdy, W.: Abusive language detection on Arabic social media. In: Proceedings of the First Workshop on Abusive Language Online, pp. 52–56 (2017)
14. Mulki, H., Haddad, H., Ali, C.B., Alshabani, H.: L-HSAB: a levantine twitter dataset for hate speech and abusive language. In: Proceedings of the Third Workshop on Abusive Language Online, pp. 111–118 (2019)
15. Nguyen, D., Demeester, T., Trieschnigg, D., Hiemstra, D.: Federated search in the wild: the combined power of over a hundred search engines. In: Proceedings of the 21st ACM International Conference on Information and Knowledge Management, pp. 1874–1878 (2012)
16. Ousidhoum, N., Lin, Z., Zhang, H., Song, Y., Yeung, D.Y.: Multilingual and multi-aspect hate speech analysis. In: Proceedings of EMNLP. Association for Computational Linguistics (2019)
17. Razavi, A.H., Inkpen, D., Uritsky, S., Matwin, S.: Offensive language detection using multi-level classification. In: Farzindar, A., Kešelj, V. (eds.) AI 2010. LNCS (LNAI), vol. 6085, pp. 16–27. Springer, Heidelberg (2010). https://doi.org/10.1007/978-3-642-13059-5_5
18. Reynolds, K., Kontostathis, A., Edwards, L.: Using machine learning to detect cyberbullying. In: 2011 10th International Conference on Machine Learning and Applications and Workshops, vol. 2, pp. 241–244. IEEE (2011)
19. Soliman, A.B., Eissa, K., El-Beltagy, S.R.: AraVec: a set of Arabic word embedding models for use in Arabic NLP. Procedia Comput. Sci. **117**, 256–265 (2017)

20. Warner, W., Hirschberg, J.: Detecting hate speech on the world wide web. In: Proceedings of the Second Workshop on Language in Social Media, pp. 19–26 (2012)
21. Waseem, Z.: Are you a racist or am i seeing things? Annotator influence on hate speech detection on twitter. In: Proceedings of the First Workshop on NLP and Computational Social Science, pp. 138–142 (2016)
22. Young, T., Hazarika, D., Poria, S., Cambria, E.: Recent trends in deep learning based natural language processing. IEEE Comput. Intell. Mag. **13**(3), 55–75 (2018)
23. Zhang, L., Zhou, Y., Duan, X., Chen, R.: A hierarchical multi-input and output Bi-GRU model for sentiment analysis on customer reviews. In: IOP Conference Series: Materials Science and Engineering. vol. 322, p. 062007. IOP Publishing (2018)

Improving Bert-Based Model for Medical Text Classification with an Optimization Algorithm

Karim Gasmi[1,2]([✉])(iD)

[1] Department of Computer Science, College of Arts and Sciences at Tabarjal,
Jouf University, Jouf, Saudi Arabia
kgasmi@ju.edu.sa
[2] ReDCAD Laboratory, University of Sfax, Sfax, Tunisia

Abstract. In the field of Natural Language Processing (NLP), automatic text classification is a classic topic that involves classifying textual material into predetermined categories based on its content. These models have been effectively applied to data containing a large number of dimensional features, some of which are inherently sparse. Machine learning and other statistical approaches, such as those used in medical text categorization, appear to be extremely successful for these tasks. However, much human work is still required to classify a large collection of training data. Recent research has shown the usefulness of pre-trained language models such as Bidirectional Encoder Representations from Transformers (BERT), all of which have demonstrated their ability to reduce the amount of work required for feature engineering. However, directly using the pre-trained BERT model in the classification task does not result in a statistically significant increase in performance. To improve the result of the BERT model, we propose an optimal deep learning model based on a BERT model and hyperparameter selection. The model consists of three steps: (1) processing medical text; (2) extracting medical text features using a BERT architecture; and (3) selecting hyperparameters for the Deep Learning model based on a Particle Swarm Optimization (PSO) algorithm. Finally, our approach uses a k-Nearest Neighbors algorithm (KNN) model to predict the matching response. Experiments conducted on the Hallmarks dataset have shown that the proposed method significantly increases the accuracy of the results.

Keywords: Medical text classification · BERT model · Optimal deep learning · PSO

1 Introduction

Over the past decade, more than 50 million academic publications have been published [12], and the number of articles produced each year continues to grow [5,15]. About half of these are medical publications indexed by MEDLINE, which is handled by the National Library of Medicine in the United States.

C. Bǎdicǎ et al. (Eds.): ICCCI 2022, CCIS 1653, pp. 101–111, 2022.
https://doi.org/10.1007/978-3-031-16210-7_8

Physicians who are well versed in the field of medicine use medical texts to accurately diagnose and classify various symptoms and disorders, according to B. Parlak [22]. Doctors and other medical professionals are already overworked, and this additional workload will only add to their burden. Therefore, the authors have remedied this by considering the lack of categorization of medical texts and the efficient use of medical records to classify diseases as beneficial.

Text categorization is one of the biggest challenges in the field of natural language processing. It is a supervised strategy where we have labeled data from which we learn a model. It consists in determining the category (or class) of a given text from a limited number of categories. It can be used for any type of text, including blogs, novels, online pages, news, and tweets. On the other hand, categorizing texts in a specific domain can lead to high dimensionality and low data volume problems, which are especially common in the medical industry.

Traditional text classification is the most common application of machine learning. Most often, machine learning is used to classify text traditionally. To classify text, a vector representation of the text is first created using feature engineering, and this vector is then fed into a machine learning algorithm. In this context, Bag-of-Words (BOW) has been the most commonly used feature creation method in the past [24].

To improve the performance of the biomedical field, Baker et al. [1] use Convolutional Neural Networks. The performance of a simple Convolutional Neural Networks (CNN) model can be compared to that of a Support Vector Machine (SVM) trained with complicated, manually generated features tailored for the task, using a recently published dataset from the field of cancer. By changing the CNN settings, it outperforms the SVM [1].

The main difficulty in using machine learning is that a well-defined representation of the text must be used, similar to manual representation. The selection of the most appropriate representation has a direct impact on the outcome of the categorization model. To solve this problem, researchers have developed deep learning models that do not require a feature extraction phase.

While Deep Learning performs well in image classification and speech recognition, it has recently been used extensively in natural language processing. Convolutional networks and recurrent neural networks (CNNs and RNNs) are the most commonly used deep Learning algorithms for text classification. Currently, research on medical text categorization focuses on medical texts, such as electronic medical records or medical literature. Huang et al. developed and evaluated bidirectional transformers (ClinicalBert). But it is research on clinical notes that reveals high-quality connections between medical ideas [10].

Several areas of natural language processing make extensive use of its superior feature extraction capabilities [6,7]. For example, recent research has demonstrated the usefulness of pre-trained language models such as Embeddings from Language Model (ELMo), OpenAI-GPT, and Bidirectional Encoder Representations from Transformers "BERT" [2,16], all of which have demonstrated their ability to reduce the feature engineering workload. In contrast, direct use of the pre-trained BERT model in the MLC task does not lead to a statistically significant increase in performance. To improve the performance of the BERT model, we propose an optimal deep learning model based on BERT and hyperparameter selection.

The rest of this paper is organized as follows: In Sect. 2, we provide an overview of current classification techniques for medical texts. Section 3 presents the architecture of our medical text classification model. Section 4 describes the experimental evaluation of our classification model and discusses the results with corresponding analysis. Concluding remarks and a discussion of future work in Sect. 5.

2   Related Work

The information contained in the clinical text is accessed by extracting structured information [21], such as the indication of diseases and their associated pathological conditions, and using automated clinical text classification to infer the information contained in the clinical text [11].

The use of symbolic approaches/statistical techniques successfully addressed the problem of categorizing medical texts. Using symbolic approaches often requires hand-crafted expert rules that are both expensive and time-consuming to develop [14]. Machine learning [9] and other statistical approaches, such as those used in medical text categorization, appear to be highly successful for these tasks. However, significant human effort is still required to classify a large collection of training data.

There are several existing systems for the classification of consecutive sentences, including Naive Bayes [10], SVMs [19], and Hidden Markov Models (HMMs) [17]. As a result, they often require the development of multiple hand-developed features based on lexical (bag-of-words), semantic (synonyms, hyponyms), structural (part-of-speech tags, headings), and sequential (sentence position, surrounding features) data. The use of artificial neural networks in natural language processing (NLP) does not require manual features because these networks are trained to automatically learn features based on word and character embeddings and other sources of information. Moreover, ANN -based models have achieved top results on a variety of natural language processing tasks.

To classify short text data, in [13], the authors used word embeddings, while most current work is based on character embeddings [26]. In the same context, the authors in [4] use word and character embeddings in their research. In their work [25], the authors introduce a new model called DRNN that incorporates the position invariance of CNN into RNN. The hidden state at each time step in RNN is restricted to represent words that are near the current position.

In the context of medical text classification, a text representation approach for clinical records of traditional Chinese medicine was proposed by Yao et al. in [27]. This technique integrates Deep Learning with the expertise of traditional Chinese medicine. Test results indicate that the strategy performs well in traditional Chinese medicine categorization. Superior feature extraction capabilities are widely used in a variety of natural language processing domains, including speech recognition and translation. In recent years, pre-trained language models such as ELMo, OpenAI-GPT [23], and BERT [3] have demonstrated their usefulness in reducing the time and effort required for feature extraction. In contrast, using the pre-trained model BERT directly in the MLC task does not lead to a statistically significant improvement.

3   Proposal Approach

In this section, we will discuss our proposed classification model for medical texts that we have developed. In the interest of full disclosure, we will also disclose the particular choices and values of hyperparameters we made to achieve the best possible performance. An overview of this procedure is given in Fig. 1, which shows the following steps: (1) medical text analysis; (2) text feature extraction; (3) parameter selection; (4) categorization.

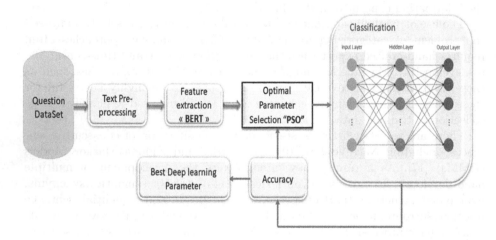

Fig. 1. Proposed model for medical text classification

3.1   Pre-processing

In text preprocessing, text data is prepared for input to a model before it is actually fed into the model. At this stage, we use the nltk package to prepare the text. First of all, text data contains noise in the form of emotions, punctuation, and text in another example. In many cases, the text data contains excess whitespace, which must be taken into account during preparation.

On the other hand, contractions, i.e., shorter versions of words, such as do not to do not and I would to I'd., must be taken into account. To examine the text data, we need to extend this contraction.

Stop words, words that do not contain meaningful information, are also among the most common text terms. Stop words include they, there, this, and where. After deleting all superfluous words, we use stemming to remove prefixes and suffixes such as "ing", "s", "it", and so on. The NLTK library stems the words. In production, stemming is not used because it is inefficient and often results in unnecessary terms. Therefore, a new method called lemmatization was developed to solve this problem.

Less like stemming, but with a different result, lemmatization reduces expanded words to their core meaning. Lemmatization, on the other hand, is the process of matching words with their lemma.

3.2 Bert-Based Model for Textual Feature Extraction

In RNNs, sequential text processing is a computational constraint. There is a cost to capturing the associations between words in a sentence, even if CNNs are less sequential than RNNs.

This problem is solved by using self-attention to compute, in parallel, an "attention score" for each word in a sentence or document, representing the effect that one word has on another. Because of this property, Transformers are able to train much larger models on huge amounts of data on GPUs more effectively than CNNs or RNNs.

As a result of this trend, large-scale Transformers-based pre-trained language models (PLMs) have emerged in 2018. Predicting words as a function of their context is a key feature of transformer-based PLMs, a type of contextualized embedding model that uses deeper network topologies (e.g., 48-layer transformers [23]) and is pre-trained on much larger text corpora.

In the PLM autocoding domain, BERT [3] is one of the most widely used solutions. While OpenGPT predicts words based on previous predictions, BERT is trained with the Masked Language Modeling (MLM) task, where some tokens in a text sequence are randomly masked before the masked tokens are independently recovered using the encoding vectors obtained by conditioning the encoding vectors obtained via a bidirectional transformer. The Bert architecture is shown in Fig. 2.

3.3 Medical Text Classification

Multilayer neural networks are structured in three layers: a first layer connected to the outside of the network, or more outside the network; one or more hidden layers connected to the input layer in sequence; and an output layer.

In this phase, we focused on the last layer to find the ideal solution. To do this, we aggregated the features collected during the process described above and used them as input to our classifier based on a softmax layer, and then computed the most correct answer.

The activation function of the output layer is different from that of the hidden layers. The task of each layer is different, as is its implementation. The last layer

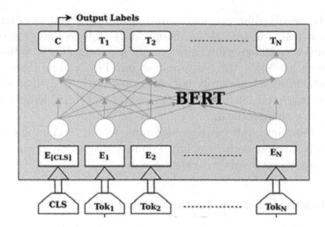

Fig. 2. Bert architecture [2]

for a classification task allows the creation of class probabilities for the input data.

$$\text{Softmax}(x_i) = \frac{\exp(x_i)}{\sum_j \exp(x_j)} \tag{1}$$

This is a vector whose members are all x_i values and which can take any real value. All output values of the function must sum to 1, so the lowest term is the normalization term, which ensures that the probability distribution is legitimate.

3.4 Hyperparameter Selection

To increase the classification accuracy, the parameters of the Deep Learning model must be selected appropriately. For this reason, we recommend using the PSO [8] algorithm to select the parameters of the Deep Learning classifier.

This algorithm was inspired by nature. It is based on a model developed by Craig Reynolds in the late 1980s that simulates the movement of a flock of birds. Sociology is also cited as a source of inspiration by James Kennedy and Russell Eberhart. It is also comparable to ant colony algorithms based on self-organization. This theory states that a group of dumb people can run a large global organization. Particles can therefore gradually converge to a global minimum using simple shift rules (in the solution space). That is, it tends to work better for continuous variables. Initially, each particle (random or not) is placed in the search space of the problem. By iteration, the particles are shifted according to 3 factors:

- Its current speed V_k,
- Its best solution P_i,
- The best solution obtained in its neighborhood P_g

This gives the following equation of motion:

$$V_{k+1} = W * V_k + b_1 (P_i - X_k) + b_2 (P_g - X_k) \tag{2}$$

$$X_{k+1} = X_k + V_{k+1} \tag{3}$$

where:

– X_k his current position
– ω inertia

The accuracy metric is used to evaluate the overall performance of this model. In the learning phase, the PSO-based method is trained to find the ideal parameter value. While improving the training error, the epoch number and batch size are controlled by the PSO algorithm, like shown in Fig. 3.

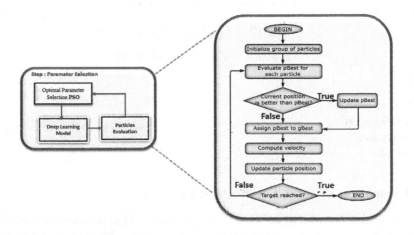

Fig. 3. Proposal model for medical text classification

The parameters that are most suitable are those that have the lowest error rate. In this way, the ideal settings are determined. Then, the updated Deep Learning parameters are used to train our classification model again with the new data. Finally, the Deep Learning classifier is now ready to be tested on more data. We conducted a series of experiments using the model described in this paper.

4   Experiment Results and Discussion

We conducted a series of experiments using the model described in this paper. Comparing the results of different Deep Learning methods is also part of our research. An Rtx 2060 graphics card and 16 GB from RAM were used to build this model in Python.

4.1 Data Description and Evaluation Metrics

To evaluate our deep learning model, we used Hallmarks dataset. Table 1 shown more information about the evaluation data set.

Table 1. Dataset description

	Size	Sentence length	Classes
Hallmarks	8474	833	3

To evaluate our classification method, we used standard metrics, such as accuracy, precision, recall and F-measure.

$$Precision = TP/(TP + FP) \tag{4}$$

$$Recall = TP/(TP + FN) \tag{5}$$

$$F1 - score = 2 * (p * R)/(P + R) \tag{6}$$

where:

- TP: true positive,
- FP: false positive,
- P: precision,
- R: recall.

4.2 Evaluation of the Classification Method

Our main goal was to build an ideal deep learning model, however in this study we decided to begin by categorizing medical text using a different model instead. So, we examined many algorithms from the classic machine learning and deep learning family in order to achieve this goal. SVM, CNN, LSTM, Random Forest [18] and Decision tree [20] were examined in this area. For word embedding, we use a simple TF/IDF for all machine learning model.

Table 2 compares the classification model based on BERT text feature extraction architecture with different machine learning and deep learning models on the Hallmark dataset. The results of the proposed deep learning model were compared with those of standard and conventional deep learning approaches. Compared to various deep learning models, the BERT model outperformed the state of the art in the literature. For example, the proposed BERT model achieved a classification accuracy of 0.71 for the Hallmark dataset.

Table 2. A comparison of the performance of the Berst-based model with various machine and deep learning models.

	Accuracy	Precision	Recall	F1-score
SVM	0.69	0.64	0.60	0.62
CNN	0.69	0.63	0.61	0.61
LSTM	0.70	0.69	0.65	0.66
BERT	**0.71**	**0.67**	**0.66**	**0.67**
Random Forest	0.66	0.63	0.62	0.63
Decision Tree	0.60	0.61	0.60	0.61

4.3   Evaluation of the Hyperparameter Selection Method

It is critical to initially find the optimal settings for the deep learning model in order to optimize the performance of this model. In order to do this, we employed an adaptive PSO approach to calculate the optimal parameter values. The primary goal of the PSO was to pick the most accurate parameters from a large range of potential values in order to achieve the best possible accuracy during the training and testing phases of the project.

Table 3. The enhancement of deep learning classifier performance based on selected parameters

Epoch number	Batch size	Accuracy	Precision	Recall	F1-score
10	64	0.71	0.67	0.66	0.67
100	128	0.74	0.70	0.68	0.69
60	32	0.70	0.64	0.65	0.65
120	**128**	**0.75**	**0.71**	**0.70**	**0.71**

Table 3 shows that the classification accuracy ranged from 0.70 to 0.75 for the Hallmarks dataset, as can be shown. All of the results were examined in light of the validation data set, which served as the standard of comparison. Changes in parameters specified by the PSO can yield a wide range of suggestions, which are shown below in order to demonstrate how accurate each class is. Accordingly, the average accuracy of the deep learning classifier attained the greatest values compared to the parameters individually chosen. The selection of hyperparameters for the deep learning classifier was used to approve it for this investigation, as discussed previously.

5   Conclusion

The majority of medical information is kept on text media. In this study, we set out to improve the analysis of textual health records. In particular, we were interested in how to categorize them better than before. In this study, we present the development of an optimal deep learning model that has been successfully verified. It was found that the proposed Bert-based model achieved a classification accuracy of 71% when applied to the Hallmarks dataset. To increase the quality of the results, we combined our model with a feature selection approach to make it even better. The PSO algorithm serves as the foundation for this selection approach. When we pick the parameters of our model automatically rather than manually, we discover that the model performs better overall.

It is intended that future research will focus on the development of more effective hybrid deep learning models for the efficient categorization of medical texts. Additionally, future study aims to investigate semantic expansion model, with the goal of combining them with extremely efficient hybrid deep learning algorithms in order to achieve high classification accuracy.

References

1. Baker, S., Korhonen, A., Pyysalo, S.: Cancer hallmark text classification using convolutional neural networks. In: Proceedings of the Fifth Workshop on Building and Evaluating Resources for Biomedical Text Mining (BioTxtM 2016), pp. 1–9 (2016)
2. Boudjellal, N., et al.: ABioNER: a BERT-based model for Arabic biomedical named-entity recognition. Complexity **2021** (2021)
3. Devlin, J., Chang, M.W., Lee, K., Toutanova, K.: BERT: pre-training of deep bidirectional transformers for language understanding. arXiv preprint arXiv:1810.04805 (2018)
4. Dos Santos, C., Gatti, M.: Deep convolutional neural networks for sentiment analysis of short texts. In: Proceedings of COLING 2014, the 25th International Conference on Computational Linguistics: Technical Papers, pp. 69–78 (2014)
5. Druss, B.G., Marcus, S.C.: Growth and decentralization of the medical literature: implications for evidence-based medicine. J. Med. Libr. Assoc. **93**(4), 499 (2005)
6. Gasmi, K.: Hybrid deep learning model for answering visual medical questions. Supercomputing (2022)
7. Gasmi, K., Ltaifa, I.B., Lejeune, G., Alshammari, H., Ammar, L.B., Mahmood, M.A.: Optimal deep neural network-based model for answering visual medical question. Cybernet. Syst. **53**, 1–22 (2021)
8. Heo, J.H., Lyu, J.K., Kim, M.K., Park, J.K.: Application of particle swarm optimization to the reliability centered maintenance method for transmission systems. J. Electr. Eng. Technol. **7**(6), 814–823 (2012)
9. Hrizi, O., et al.: Tuberculosis disease diagnosis based on an optimized machine learning model. J. Healthc. Eng. **2022** (2022)
10. Huang, K., Altosaar, J., Ranganath, R.: ClinicalBERT: modeling clinical notes and predicting hospital readmission. arXiv preprint arXiv:1904.05342 (2019)
11. Jabbar, R., Fetais, N., Krichen, M., Barkaoui, K.: Blockchain technology for healthcare: enhancing shared electronic health record interoperability and integrity. In: 2020 IEEE International Conference on Informatics, IoT, and Enabling Technologies (ICIoT), pp. 310–317. IEEE (2020)
12. Jinha, A.E.: Article 50 million: an estimate of the number of scholarly articles in existence. Learn. Publ. **23**(3), 258–263 (2010)

13. Kalchbrenner, N., Grefenstette, E., Blunsom, P.: A convolutional neural network for modelling sentences. arXiv preprint arXiv:1404.2188 (2014)
14. Krichen, M., et al.: A formal testing model for operating room control system using internet of things. Comput. Mater. Continua **66**(3), 2997–3011 (2021)
15. Larsen, P., Von Ins, M.: The rate of growth in scientific publication and the decline in coverage provided by science citation index. Scientometrics **84**(3), 575–603 (2010)
16. Lee, J., et al.: BioBERT: a pre-trained biomedical language representation model for biomedical text mining. Bioinformatics **36**(4), 1234–1240 (2020)
17. Lin, J., Karakos, D., Demner-Fushman, D., Khudanpur, S.: Generative content models for structural analysis of medical abstracts. In: Proceedings of the Workshop on Linking Natural Language Processing and Biology: Towards Deeper Biological Literature Analysis, pp. 65–72 (2006)
18. Mantas, C.J., Castellano, J.G., Moral-García, S., Abellán, J.: A comparison of random forest based algorithms: random credal random forest versus oblique random forest. Soft. Comput. **23**(21), 10739–10754 (2018). https://doi.org/10.1007/s00500-018-3628-5
19. McKnight, L., Srinivasan, P.: Categorization of sentence types in medical abstracts. In: AMIA Annual Symposium Proceedings, vol. 2003, p. 440. American Medical Informatics Association (2003)
20. Mittal, K., Khanduja, D., Tewari, P.C.: An insight into 'decision tree analysis'. World Wide J. Multidisc. Res. Dev. **3**(12), 111–115 (2017)
21. Mukhtar, H., Rubaiee, S., Krichen, M., Alroobaea, R.: An IoT framework for screening of COVID-19 using real-time data from wearable sensors. Int. J. Environ. Res. Public Health **18**(8), 4022 (2021)
22. Parlak, B., Uysal, A.K.: Classification of medical documents according to diseases. In: 2015 23nd Signal Processing and Communications Applications Conference (SIU), pp. 1635–1638. IEEE (2015)
23. Radford, A., et al.: Language models are unsupervised multitask learners. OpenAI Blog **1**(8), 9 (2019)
24. Wallach, H.M.: Topic modeling: beyond bag of words. In: Proceedings of the 23rd International Conference on Machine Learning, pp. 977–984 (2006)
25. Wang, B.: Disconnected recurrent neural networks for text categorization. In: Proceedings of the 56th Annual Meeting of the Association for Computational Linguistics (Volume 1: Long Papers), pp. 2311–2320 (2018)
26. Xiao, Y., Cho, K.: Efficient character-level document classification by combining convolution and recurrent layers. arXiv preprint arXiv:1602.00367 (2016)
27. Yao, L., Zhang, Y., Wei, B., Li, Z., Huang, X.: Traditional Chinese medicine clinical records classification using knowledge-powered document embedding. In: 2016 IEEE International Conference on Bioinformatics and Biomedicine (BIBM), pp. 1926–1928. IEEE (2016)

Reinforcement of BERT with Dependency-Parsing Based Attention Mask

Toufik Mechouma[1](✉)[ID], Ismail Biskri[2][ID], and Jean Guy Meunier[1][ID]

[1] University of Quebec in Montreal, Montreal, QC, Canada
`mechouma.toufik@courrier.uqam.ca`, `meunier.jean-guy@uqam.ca`
[2] University of Quebec in Trois Rivieres, Trois Rivieres, QC, Canada
`ismail.biskri@uqtr.ca`

Abstract. Dot-Product based attention mechanism is among recent attention mechanisms. It showed an outstanding performance with BERT. In this paper, we propose a dependency-parsing mask to reinforce the padding mask, at the multi-head attention units. Padding mask, is already used to filter padding positions. The proposed mask, aims to improve BERT attention filter. The conducted experiments, show that BERT performs better with the proposed mask.

Keywords: Bert · Transformers · Attention mechanisms · Dependency parsing

1 Introduction

Long short term memory network, was a staple in deep learning [1]. Although its impressive results, it has its downsides [3]. LSTM suffers from sequential processing, and poor information preservation [2,3]. Transformers, try to remedy to the previous LSTM inconveniences. They accomplish, a bidirectional attention learning based on an all-to-all comparison. Transformers use a Dot-Product attention mechanism [4]. They are also used in the Bidirectional Encoder Representations from Transformers (BERT) architecture [6,8]. They afford BERT, to learn words representation based on two learning strategies [9,10]. The first one is the masked language modeling (MLM) strategy. MLM, consists of masking 15% of the training dataset tokens. Next, the masked tokens are predicted by BERT. The second strategy is called Next Sentence Prediction (NSP). It differs from the first one, by learning the sentence representation. It predicts whether a sentence B comes after a sentence A or not. Thus, tokens embeddings, are learned throughout MLM and NSP learning process. BERT is built on a set of encoders. An encoder is equipped with a multi-head attention mechanism (MHAM). MHAM, performs a parallel computing of dot-product attention mechanism, to learn relationships between words. The MHAM's output, goes further throw a feed-forward (FFNN) neural network. The FFNN, provides the learned contextualized representation.

C. Bădică et al. (Eds.): ICCCI 2022, CCIS 1653, pp. 112–122, 2022.
https://doi.org/10.1007/978-3-031-16210-7_9

At MHAM and the FFNN output, designed residual connections, add previous input data to the outputs, to preserve information, and also, to avoid signal vanishing. Furthermore, a normalisation, is performed at both levels [3]. The encoders stack, achieves features extraction. The extracted features, can be used, to fine-tune BERT in order to execute downstream tasks such as text classification, summarizing and translation etc.

2 Transformers

Transformers are considered to be an alternative solution to LSTMs [9]. They are essentially composed of two main components. The first component is known as encoder. Each encoder, has two major units: a self-attention mechanism and a feed-forward neural network. The self-attention mechanism, receives input encodings from the previous encoder, and outputs its own encodings. The feed-forward neural network, compute encodings from self-attention mechanism and forward them to the next encoder, as well as to the second component of the transformers named decoder [4, 10]. Each decoder, owns three components: a self-attention mechanism, an attention mechanism that processes encodings, and a feed-forward neural network. The decoder task is similar to the encoder, however, it has an additional attention mechanism, that deal with encoders outputs.

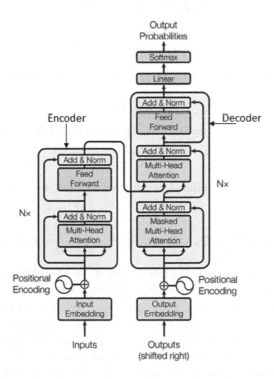

Fig. 1. Transformer (encoder-decoder)

In contrast to LSTMs, transformers use parallel computation and words positions encoding due to the multi-heads attention blocs and the positions encoding algorithm respectively (Fig. 1).

2.1 Scaled Dot-Product Attention Mechanism

Authors in [4,5] use a dot-product attention mechanism, to learn an all-to-all attention between words, by projecting the vocabulary matrix X (embedding dimension, max sentence length) into a lower dimension Q, K and V matrices (Fig. 2).

$$X = \begin{bmatrix} I \\ 0.63 \\ . \\ . \\ . \\ 0.21 \\ 0.79 \end{bmatrix} \begin{bmatrix} Love \\ 1.25 \\ 3.65 \\ . \\ . \\ 0.44 \\ 0.01 \end{bmatrix} \cdots \begin{bmatrix} Artificial \\ 5.24 \\ 3.74 \\ . \\ . \\ 0.58 \\ 1.46 \end{bmatrix} \begin{bmatrix} intelligence \\ 2.69 \\ 1.25 \\ . \\ . \\ 0.98 \\ 0.84 \end{bmatrix}$$

Fig. 2. Vocabulary matrix

$$Q = X \cdot W_q \tag{1}$$

where W_q is a randomly initialized weight matrix, and Q is the projected query matrix

$$K = X \cdot W_k \tag{2}$$

where W_k is a randomly initialized weight matrix, and K is the projected key matrix

$$V = X \cdot W_v \tag{3}$$

where W_v is a randomly initialized weight matrix, and v is the projected value matrix

$$Attention(Q, K, V) = Softmax(\frac{Q \cdot K^T}{\sqrt{d_k}}) \cdot V \tag{4}$$

where K^T is the transposed key matrix, and d_k is the embedding dimension. $Q \cdot K^T$ is divided by $\sqrt{d_k}$ and followed by softmax for normalisation purpose.

For a better understanding, $Softmax(\frac{Q \cdot K^T}{\sqrt{d_k}})$ can be considered like a filter to be applied on V, in order to compute the $Attention(Q, K, V)$. The $Attention(Q, K, V)$ is also called Scaled Dot-Product Attention. Multi-Heads attention are just a replication of h Dot-Product Attention units. Where h is a hyper-parameter that represents the number of heads per encoder, and W_q, W_k, W_v are of dimension $(d_{q,k,v}, d_{q,k,v}/h)$ (Fig. 3).

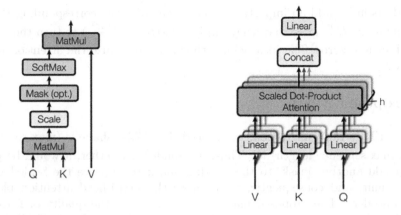

Fig. 3. (left) Scaled Dot-Product attention. (right) Multi-Head attention

Note that Mask is optional as defined by the authors in [6].

2.2 Padding Mask

Since the neural network needs to have inputs that should be in similar shape and size, padding is the operation that fulfill such a requirement (Fig. 4).

max sentence length

BERT	IS	AN	AMAZING	TOOL
I	LOVE	ARTIFICIAL	INTELLIGENCE	PAD
me	to	PAD	PAD	PAD

Fig. 4. Padding illustration.

Padding causes a problem while performing scaled Dot-Product computing. The projected Q, K and V matrices contain PADs. PADs are considered to be like a noise, and need to be cleaned out to avoid any misleading during attention computing (Fig. 5).

SoftMax

me	to	PAD	PAD	PAD
0,25	2,73	-1e9	-1e9	-1e9
.	.	-1e9	-1e9	-1e9
.	.	-1e9	-1e9	-1e9
1,74	1,46	-1e9	-1e9	-1e9

=

me	to	PAD	PAD	PAD
0,05	0,68	0	0	0
,	.	0	0	0
.	.	0	0	0
0,25	0,17	0	0	0

Fig. 5. Padding mask with SoftMax

Authors in [4] add an important negative value to the corresponding PADs positions in $Q \cdot K^T$, after that, they apply a $Softmax(\frac{Q \cdot K^T}{\sqrt{d_k}})$ to turn the negative values into zeros. The idea behind this, is to maximize the attention filter efficiency.

3   Proposed Mask

During BERT's implementation, we noticed that $\frac{Q \cdot K^T}{\sqrt{d_k}}$ shape is (max sentence length, max sentence length) [6]. Thus, we wondered whether, it would be possible to add another mask, to the padding mask to improve the Scaled Dot-Product unit, and consequently, we improve the multi-head attention blocks within encoders. The proposed mask, aims to increase the quality of features extraction, by introducing a SpaCy Dependency Parsing Mask (SDPM) [7] (Fig. 6).

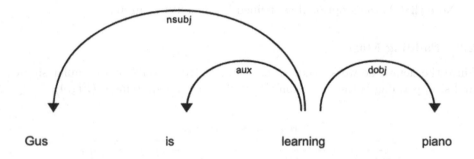

Fig. 6. SpaCy dependency parsing.

We first, build an adjacency matrix from the generated dependency graph. The adjacency matrix's shape is: (Max sentence length, Max sentence length) (Fig. 7).

	Gus	is	learning	piano
Gus	0	0	1	0
is	0	0	1	0
learning	0	0	0	1
Piano	0	0	0	0

Fig. 7. Adjacency matrix of the dependency graph.

While the one values mean, that there are direct dependencies between words, zero values mean, there are no dependencies. Note that we eliminated the cases, where words are depended to themselves. In the same way, and for the same reason as the padding mask, we add an important negative value to positions which correspond to zeros. Hence, we keep one values, and add them to attention filter.

	Gus	is	learning	piano
Gus	-1e9	-1e9	1	-1e9
is	-1e9	-1e9	1	-1e9
learning	-1e9	-1e9	-1e9	1
Piano	-1e9	-1e9	-1e9	-1e9

Fig. 8. Adjacency matrix after addition of an important negative value (Fig. 8).

The adjacency matrix quantify the semantic and syntactic relationships between words. We propose this adjacency matrix as a second mask, to be applied with the padding mask, as shown in the Eq. 5 (Fig. 9).

$$Softmax((\frac{Q \cdot K^T}{\sqrt{d_k}}) + Padding_{mask} + DepParsing_{mask}) \qquad (5)$$

	Gus	is	learning	piano	PAD	PAD
Gus	-1e9	-1e9	1	-1e9	-1e9	-1e9
is	-1e9	-1e9	1	-1e9	-1e9	-1e9
learning	-1e9	-1e9	-1e9	1	-1e9	-1e9
Piano	-1e9	-1e9	-1e9	-1e9	-1e9	-1e9
PAD	-1e9	-1e9	-1e9	-1e9	-1e9	-1e9
PAD	-1e9	-1e9	-1e9	-1e9	-1e9	-1e9

Fig. 9. Padding and Dependencies masks addition.

After addition of both masks, we apply a softmax to turn negative values into zeros, and get probability distribution. We then, compute the attention as following: $Attention(Q, K, V) = Softmax(\frac{Q \cdot K^T}{\sqrt{d_k}}) \cdot V$.

The proposed mask is integrated in all BERT's encoders, as mentioned in the Fig. 10. It takes tokens embedding vectors in input $W_1, W_2, W_3, ..., W_i$ and provide contextualized vectors $W\prime_1, W\prime_2, W\prime_3, ..., W\prime_i$

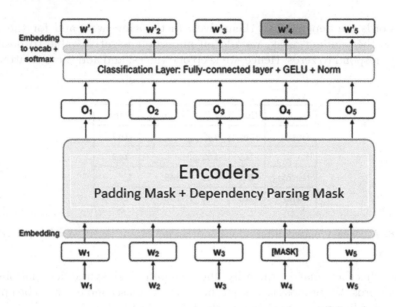

Fig. 10. BERT architecture with padding and dependency parsing mask.

4   Experimentations

To test our model, we first implemented BERT from scratch using pytorch. We used English OpenSubtitles dataset. The dataset is available on OpenSubtitles-v2016. We performed tests on three datasets with 100k, 500k,1 Million sentences. In order to evaluate the results, we use the training loss and time, with F1-Scores as performance indicators. Due to hardware limitation, we performed an embedding of 50 dimension, with 85 as maximum size of a sentence, rather than 768 and 512 respectively, as it is in BERT-base. Test are performed, on a virtual machine, with Intel(R) Xeon(R) 2.30 GHz CPU, 46080 KB cache size, 2 CPU Cores and 12 GB of RAM, with CUDA GPU. Hyper-parameters values are chosen based on hardware features and many observations. We kept the same hyper-parameters for both models, to afford comparison between them. Max sent length is the maximum size that a sentence can take. batch size is used for training performance purposes. Nbr segments is the number of sentences per input. Embedding dimension is the vocabulary vectors size. Nbr encoders is the number of the encoders that we use in the architecture of both models. Nbr heads is the number of the multi-head attention units per encoder in each model. $dim(W_q, W_k, W_v)$ is the dimension of the projecting matrices. FFNN dim is the dimension of the feed forward neural network linear layer. Learning rate is used to adjust gradient during the training. Max pred is the maximum number of tokens to be masked and predicted. Nbr epochs is the number of the needed epochs to train the models (Table 1).

Table 1. Dataset 1

	BERT	BERT (DP Mask)
Nbr of sentences	100000	100000
Hyper parameters	BERT	BERT (DP Mask)
Max sent length	85	85
batch size	10	10
nbr segments	2	2
Embedding dimension	50	50
nbr encoders	6	6
nbr heads	12	12
dim (W_q, W_k, W_v)	32	32
FFNN dim (W_o)	200	200
Learning rate	0.001	0.001
max pred	3	3
Nbr epochs	500	500
Min Loss	0.8434	**0.65**
Training time (sec)	**179.179**	185.991
F1-Score-mlm	0.5	**1**
F1-Score-nsp	0.5	**0.76**

The first test on dataset1, shows that BERT-DPM performance, overcome BERT results. We also notice, that training time for BERT, is less than BERT-DPM. We consider this as a logical result, because there are more computing steps in BERT-DPM than BERT (Fig. 11 and Table 2).

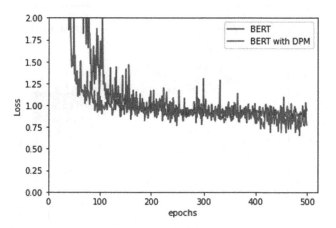

Fig. 11. Dataset 1.

Table 2. Dataset 2

	BERT	BERT (DP Mask)
Nbr of sentences	500000	500000
Hyper parameters	BERT	BERT (DP Mask)
Max sent length	85	85
batch size	10	10
nbr segments	2	2
Embedding dimension	50	50
nbr encoders	6	6
nbr heads	12	12
dim (W_q, W_k, W_v)	32	32
FFNN dim (W_o)	200	200
Learning rate	0.001	0.001
max pred	3	3
Nbr epochs	500	500
Min Loss	0.892	**0.428**
Training time (sec)	**202.286**	207.325
F1-Score-mlm	0.32	**1**
F1-Score-nsp	0.60	**0.80**

The second test on dataset2, shows that BERT-DPM performance, overcome BERT results. We also notice, that training time for BERT, is less than BERT-DPM. We consider this as a logical result, because there are more computing steps in BERT-DPM than BERT (Fig. 12 and Table 3).

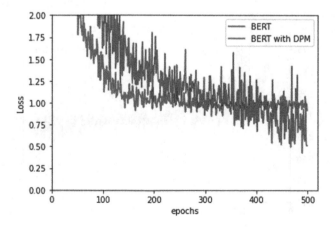

Fig. 12. Dataset 2.

Table 3. Dataset 3

	BERT	BERT (DP Mask)
Nbr of sentences	1M	1M
Hyper parameters	BERT	BERT (DP Mask)
Max sent length	85	85
batch size	10	10
nbr segments	2	2
Embedding dimension	50	50
nbr encoders	6	6
nbr heads	12	12
dim (W_q, W_k, W_v)	32	32
FFNN dim (W_o)	200	200
Learning rate	0.001	0.001
max pred	3	3
Nbr epochs	500	500
Min Loss	0.8404	**0.509**
Training time (sec)	**208.71**	218.521
F1-Score-mlm	0.43	**1**
F1-Score-nsp	0.615	**0.749**

The third test on dataset3, shows that BERT-DPM performance, overcome BERT results. We also notice, that training time for BERT, is less than BERT-DPM. We consider this as a logical result, because there are more computing steps in BERT-DPM than BERT (Fig. 13).

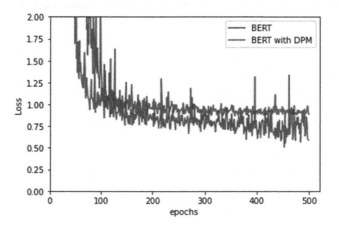

Fig. 13. Dataset 3.

5   Conclusion

The above experimentation, shows the added value of the proposed dependency parsing mask, at the Scaled Dot-Product unit level. It improved the attention filter efficiency. Thus, we wonder whether future deep learning models, can perform a dependency-parsing based attention mechanisms. The next work, will focus on how to conceive an attention mechanism that performs, in the same way as SpaCy dependency parser.

References

1. Graves, A.: Long Short Term Memory. Springer, Cham (2012). https://doi.org/10.1007/978-3-642-24797-2-4
2. Sepp H., Jürgen S.: Long short-term memory. Neural Comput. **9**(8), 1735–1780. PMID 9377276. S2CID 1915014 (1997). https://doi.org/10.1162/neco.1997.9.8.1735
3. Sak, H., Senior, A., Beaufays, F.: Long Short-Term Memory recurrent neural network architectures for large scale acoustic modeling (2014)
4. Vaswani, A., et al.: Attention Is All You Need (2017)
5. Luong, M.-T.: Effective approaches to attention-based neural machine translation (2015)
6. Devlin, J., Chang, M., Lee, K., Toutanova, K.: BERT pre-training of deep bidirectional transformers for language understanding (2018)
7. Honnibal, M., Montani, I.: spaCy 2 natural language understanding with Bloom embeddings, convolutional neural networks and incremental parsing. (2017)
8. Open Sourcing BERT: State-of-the-Art Pre-training for Natural Language Processing. Google AI Blog. Accessed 27 Nov 2019
9. Clark, K., Khandelwal, U.M, Levy, O., Manning, C.: What Does BERT Look at? An Analysis of BERT's attention. In: Proceedings of the 2019 ACL Workshop BlackboxNLP: Analyzing and Interpreting Neural Networks for NLP (2019)
10. Peters, M., et al.: Deep contextualized word representations (2018)

BERT and Word Embedding for Interest Mining of Instagram Users

Sana Hamdi[1]([⊠]), Ahmed Hamdi[2], and Sadok Ben Yahia[3]

[1] University of Tunis El-Manar, Tunis, Tunisia
sana.hamdi@fst.utm.tn
[2] L3i Laboratory, University of La Rochelle, La Rochelle, France
[3] Department of Software Science, Tallinn University of Technology, Tallinn, Estonia

Abstract. With more than one billion monthly active users and nearly 100 million photos shared on the platform daily, Instagram has become among the richest sources of information for detecting users' interests and trends. However, research works on this social network are limited compared to its competitors, e.g., Facebook and Twitter. There is no doubt that the lack of a publicly labeled dataset that summarizes the content of Instagram profiles is a prime problem bothering the researchers. To overcome this issue, here, for the first time, we present an annotated multidomain interests dataset to train and test OSNs' users and the methodology to create this dataset from Instagram profiles. In addition, through this work, we propose an automatic detection and classification of Instagram users' interests. We rely on word embedding representations of words and deep learning techniques to introduce two approaches: (i) a feature-based method and (ii) fine-tuning the BERT model. We observed that BERT fine-tuning performed much better.

Keywords: Instagram · Word embedding · Neural networks · Data analysis · Users' interests

1 Introduction

Social networks are considered a gold mine owing to the massive amount of information they collect from users. Currently, the trend is to share all the details of our lives on OSN in media content (photos and videos), comments, and posts. This wealth of information about each user helps identify the users' interests and attitudes that can be advantageous for several purposes like information retrieval, recommender systems and online advertising. Numerous research on social media analysis has been made. However, the user interests extraction task from Instagram as explicit terms was not presented in the literature. Nonetheless, since Instagram is the most powerful tool for people looking to express themselves, find interesting content, or promote their business, it becomes a rich platform with fresh visual content and pictures of different products and ads. On that account, we will put the focus on the extraction of interests from Instagram content. This work extends embedding models in two directions for implicit

© The Author(s), under exclusive license to Springer Nature Switzerland AG 2022
C. Bădică et al. (Eds.): ICCCI 2022, CCIS 1653, pp. 123–136, 2022.
https://doi.org/10.1007/978-3-031-16210-7_10

interests' extraction: (i) it jointly models interests and (ii) it directly classifies users according to their interests using a deep neural network for multi-class classification. The key contributions of our work can glance as follows:

- We model users' interests based on their shared content. In terms of the dataset, the literature is abundant with works using Twitter. We deal with using Instagram instead of Twitter despite the unavailability of Instagram public datasets in our work. To collect data, we extracted $1,000$ public profiles based on Instagram's policy explaining the right to access public accounts data through tools and third-party services, as well as the opening of Instagram's policy for academic research and innovation.
- We introduce two approaches: a feature-based approach and a Bert-based one to detect users' interests. For the **feature-based approach**, we extract features from users' content (captions and hashtags) using two powerful context word representations. Then, we compute the similarity between Users' content and interests to extract the most similar. For **the bert-based approach**, we perform a fine-tuning of the pre-trained BERT model for a multi-classification of users according to their interests.

The remainder of this paper is organized as follows. Section 2 presents literature scrutiny of the related work in this field. Section 3 describes and analyses our data. Section 4 models our task in formal terms used throughout this paper. Section 5 thoroughly presents our introduced approaches. Section 6 is dedicated to the description and analysis of experimental evaluation. Finally, Sect. 7 concludes our work and sketches some perspectives of future work.

2   Related Work

This section reviews the works that dealt with the extraction of user interests in social networks. It is worth mentioning that most of these works use Twitter as their source of information because the information that the users publish on Twitter is more publicly accessible compared to other social networks. Works in [1,2] and [3] discovered user topics of interest by running the Latent Dirichlet Allocation (LDA) topic model over the set of a user's tweets. The study in [4] modeled user interests by representing her tweets as a bag of words and by applying cosine similarity to determine alike users' profiles to infer common interests.

More recent works are modeling users' interests using semantic concepts linked to external knowledge bases and tools such as Wikipedia, the knowledge graph Freebase, DBpedia and WordNet [5,6]. Authors in [7,8] and [9] respectively used relevant and diversified keywords by proposing embedding approaches to identify users' topics of interest in Twitter temporally.

Many other works used deep learning approaches to classify users' interests [10,11] and [12]. Authors in [11], for instance, designed an effective method to provide a summary of users' interests from Twitter based on textual data. However, they settled for only 5 interests: sports, travel, fashion, food, and religion.

The mentioned works attempted to mine user interests from the tweets posted or retweeted. In contrast, some works aim to extract implicit interest that the user did not explicitly mention but might have in, such as those based on the information provided by her relations and biographies [13] and [14].

Similarly to [1,8,11] and [12], in this work we extract users' interests from their shared posts. However, in terms of the data, unlike mentioned works, we use Instagram instead of Twitter data. We believe that Twitter is more popular with journalists, politicians, and celebrities. Indeed, 74% of users turn to Twitter for trending news[1]. Nevertheless, with Instagram, users are more likely to engage and express their preferences. People go to Instagram and expect to see influencers, follow brands they like and share posts related to their interests. As we mentioned earlier, few works in the literature have used Instagram datasets for topic modeling tasks. However, most of these works do not pay heed to extract user interests from Instagram as explicit terms. In [15], authors introduced a novel method for identifying age information from user profiles extracted from Instagram. Their work presents a comparative study of teens and adults based on published content. They also found a clear difference between the two groups in terms of topic types. The work in [16] proposed a new topic model known as MultiPlatform-LDA to model topical interests of a set of common users with accounts on multiple social media platforms. They conduct experiments on three real-world datasets from Twitter, Instagram, and Tumblr. Note that their dataset construction is biased towards Twitter, conveniently used as the first social media platform to find the other linked accounts from Instagram and Tumblr. However, their dataset has only 22 common users active on all three platforms. Authors in [17] investigated, across their constructed Instagram dataset, the behavior of users labeling media with tags to determine how they devote their attention and to explore the variety of their topical interests. To determine the topical interests of each user u, they simply averaged the probabilities of each topic being exhibited by the media produced by u.

3   Dataset Overview

To the best of our knowledge, there are no publicly available datasets that sketch content from Instagram profiles. However, it goes to show that this track has had a lot of compelling challenges, and we have come out of them all.

3.1   Collecting Data

Our first thought was to use the publicly available Instagram API to get data for a predefined set of users to create our dataset. However, after the 2018 Facebook scandal, Instagram decided to strictly limit access to the API by introducing and adding quotas on the number of requests or deprecating certain endpoints. Thus, we decided to use the open-source tool InstaLoader[2] to extract content

---

[1] https://www.omnicoreagency.com/twitter-statistics/.
[2] https://instaloader.github.io/.

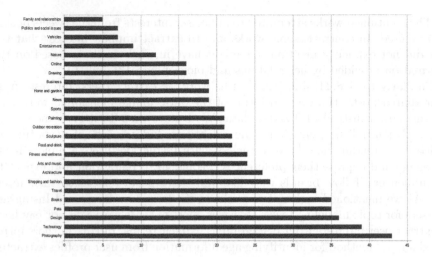

Fig. 1. Distribution of interests with respect to the number of users

from profiles. We heavily relied on it to write a custom script to raextract almost $1,000$ for public users. We relied on two articles on Instagram's policy[3] explaining the right to access public accounts data through tools and third-party services as well as the opening of Instagram's policy for academic research and innovation.

3.2   Data Description

As mentioned earlier, the data used for our experiments are collected from Instagram. Since we focused on extracting active users' interests, we cleaned up our dataset by deleting all empty profiles. We finally obtained 334 user profiles described in a JSON file. Each user profile contains between 12 and 201 posts. Each post is defined with its URL, the hashtags used, its caption (the accompanying text as well as the hashtags), the number of likes as well as the number of comments.

3.3   Labelling Data

To evaluate our models, we need a labeled dataset consisting of users already classified with their interests. However, the same does not hold for our dataset, especially that the biography element containing meaningful interests is not available for all the users. To overcome this problem, we have met a challenge to categorize users according to their interests manually. We assigned to each user 1–3 interests. To come up with a clear list of interests, we were inspired by the list used by Facebook to classify its user's[4]. This list counts nine main categories and 66 sub-categories of interests.

---

[3] https://help.instagram.com.
[4] https://interestexplorer.io/facebook-interests-list/. Last access Mar2022.

On its final status, our dataset assigns 25 interests to 334 users. Each of them has at most three interests. The distribution of interests according to the number of users is shown in Fig. 1. The most common interest is *"Photography"*, which is shared by 45 users, whereas *"Family and relationships"* is the less assigned interest to only five users. The dataset JSON file is made publicly available for download on the web[5].

3.4   Data Analysis

To understand which users' contents are likely to represent their interests, we further study Instagram captions, which are the text accompanying users' posts and hashtags exclusively. The word clouds in Fig. 2, highlights the most prominent terms used in both captions and hashtags data, before preprocessing, for the interests *"Sculpture,"* *"News"* and *"Home_and_garden"*. It is immediately apparent from the tag clouds that captions and hashtags data serve as meaningful and informative data describing interests. For example, common words like *sculpture* and its derivative words as *sculpting, sculptured, sculpt, sculptor* and *metalsculpture*, It is also clear that *returs* and *financiltimes* for instance, are related to *"News"*. Similarly, the terms *garden, plant* and *flower* can only be associated to the interest *"Home_and_garden"*. In addition, by looking at the captions data clouds for each interest, we can see that they contain more frequent words serving further for interest detection. However, many words occur many times but may not be relevant. On the one hand, captions know more relative frequency of words, where oversized words denote higher frequency. But, on the other hand, we find that they share many words in common. The scrutiny of these clouds shows that users, when writing captions' posts are more likely to use general words (unrelated to interests) than when writing hashtags. For example, all three "Sculpture", "News", and "Home_and_garden" interests contain the words *one will, see, now, link and bio* which may not be relevant to distinguish users' interests.

Nevertheless, we can see that the absolute hashtags data for each interest do not share words in common. This indicates that hashtags contain more meaningful words related to the interests in question. In this context, we explore the descriptive power of hashtags to identify users' interests in addition to captions.

4   Task Modeling

Here, we model our task in formal terms that will be of use in the remainder of this paper, and then, we formulate the task we address in this work.

---

[5] https://www.dropbox.com/sh/8rd7gppa4bt0koh/AABEAoF8DZMFVB36oCYX SIxVa?dl=0.

Fig. 2. Word clouds based on Hashtags and Captions for different interests

4.1 Instagram Model Formalization

We formally define an Instagram social network as a tuple $IG = (V, E, W)$.

(1) The vertex set has two vertices representing users and terms, respectively. Mathematically, $V = U \cup T$ where $U = \{u_1, u_2, \ldots, u_n\}$ is the set of vertices representing users and $T = \{t_1, t_2, \ldots, t_m\}$ is the set vertices representing hashtags and captions' terms shared by users; n and m are respectively the number of the user-profiles and the number of terms.

(2) The edge set $E \subset V \times V$ is the set of links between users and terms. An edge $e(t, u)$ means that the term t is used to mark the content of the user u.

(3) $W : V \times E \times V \rightarrow [0, 1]$ is the function computing a score value $w(t, u)$ for each $e \in E$ between node $u \in U$ and node $t \in T$. A weight $w(t, u)$ represents how much the term t is significant for the user u. Thus, our proposed model of Instagram social network $IG = (V, E, W)$ forms a weighted bipartite undirected graph with the vertex being divided into two independent sets (U and T), which is shown in Fig. 3.

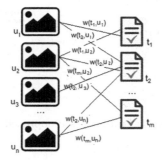

Fig. 3. Instagram illustrated by a bipartite graph

In the simplest case, word weighting methods can determine relevant users' terms to extract interests. We use the robust and popular TF-IDF method. It combines term frequency with inverse document frequency to determine the importance of terms. Thus, the high weight of TF-IDF is reached by a high term frequency in one document and a low document frequency in the whole collection of documents. In this work, where each user is regarded as a document, if the term t frequently appears with all users, then TF-IDF will return a low score. Thus, we define the weight $w(u,t)$ as follows: $w(t,u) = tf(t,u).idf(t)$ and $idf(t) = log(n/|e(t,u)|)$

4.2 Task Formulation

The task we address in this paper is the following: given a set of users and a stream of captions and hashtags generated by them on Instagram, we aim to infer a set of most k relevant interests for each user. This can be essentially formulated with a function f that satisfies: $U \xrightarrow{f} C$, where $U = \{u_i\}_{i=1}^n$ is a set of n users, and $C = \{C_{u_i}, \ldots, C_{u_n}\}$ are all users' interests results with $C_{u_i} = \{c_{u_i1}, \ldots, c_{u_ik}\}$ being the most k relevant interests for user u_i.

5 Extracting User Interests

To solve the mentioned above task, we propose to use the word representations in two ways: a feature-based approach and a Bert-based approach.

5.1 Feature-Based Variant

The feature-based approach is carried out in three stages, as shown in Fig. 4. First, we design a term-based feature generator to convert a user profile from either captions or hashtags into term vectors. Second, the target interests (Facebook categories of interests) are also converted into term vectors. Third, for each user vector, the similarities with all the vectors of Facebook interests are calculated to select the k-nearest interests and infer the user interests vector.

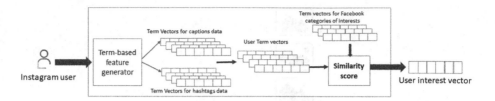

Fig. 4. Feature-based approach

Term Based-Feature Generator. The designed term-based feature generator is used to represent Instagram users into term vectors from either captions
or hashtags term vectors $\vec{t_i}$. We experiment with two pretrained models of word
embedding: the Global Vectors for Word Representation (GloVe)[6] model provided by Google and the FastText[7] model provided by Facebook. For each user u,
captions and hashtags term vectors $\vec{t_i}$ are generated by multiplying the $w(t_i, u)$
scores of each term t_i with the embedding vector of the term as defined in Eq. 1.
Afterward, each user is converted into a term vector $\vec{T_u}$ as shown in Eq. 2. It
consists of summing and normalizing the l term vectors $\vec{t_i}$ generated from her
captions and hashtags.

$$\vec{t_i} = w(t_i, u) * \overrightarrow{emb(t_i)} \tag{1}$$

$$\vec{T_u} = \frac{1}{l} \sum_{i=1}^{l} \vec{t_i} \tag{2}$$

Similarity Score Computation. The similarities can be computed by modeling the embeddings of users and interests in the same space. Thereby, we calculate the cosine similarity between each user vector with all the interest vectors.
Then, for each user, we assign the most similar interest to her term vector.

$$cosine\_sim(\vec{T_u}, \vec{T_c}) = \frac{\vec{T_u} \times \vec{T_c}}{||\vec{T_u}|| \times ||\vec{T_c}||} \tag{3}$$

where $\vec{T_u}$ and $\vec{T_c}$ are respectively the 200-dimensional vector representations of
the user and the interest category.

5.2   Bert-based Variant

Extracting users' interests according to their posts can be considered as a text
classification task. It consists of providing data to a classifier to generate a model
used for the test portion of learning. To address this issue, we used BERT (Bidirectional encoder representations from transformers) [18].

---

[6] https://nlp.stanford.edu/projects/glove/.
[7] https://fasttext.cc/docs/en/crawl-vectors.html.

BERT Model. BERT is a multi-layer bidirectional transformer encoder trained on the English Wikipedia and the Book Corpus containing $2,500M$ and 800M tokens, respectively. The BERT authors mainly present results on two model sizes including BERT-base and BERT-large [19]. BERT-base contains an encoder with 12 layers (transformer blocks), 12 self-attention heads, and 110 million parameters whereas BERT-large has 24 layers, 16 attention heads, and 340 million parameters. BERT models outperform state-of-the-art models of several Natural Language Processing (NLP) tasks by fine-tuning their pre-trained BERT models [18,20]. As an input and output, BERT takes a sequence of tokens in maximum length 512 and represents the sequence in a 768-dimensional vector. BERT inserts at most two segments to each input sequence, [CLS] and [SEP]. [CLS] embedding is the first token of the input sequence and contains the special classification embedding. The [SEP] separates the segments.

BERT Fine-Tuning. BERT is a well-known contextual language representation model, notably because the pre-trained BERT model can be fine-tuned to handle various downstream tasks. In this work, we investigate the application of BERT on the classification of Instagram users according to their interests. For our classification task, as shown in Fig. 5, we apply very few changes to the baseline model. The final hidden state of the first word ([CLS]) from BERT is input to a fully connected layer of 768 dimensions to perform the softmax activation function. So, the weights of this layer and the weights of the other layers are trained and fine-tuned accordingly using our specific data. In our case, extracting users' interests from a sequence of words might be considered as a sentence classification task as illustrated in Fig. 5. The sentence S_{ju} is either the caption or a sequence of hashtags of user u while the class label is the user interest. At the same time, we use TF-IDF to evaluate how relevant a term is to an Instagram user. The TF-IDF, based on computed $w(t_i, u)$ scores of each term t_i in the S_{ju}, is fed to our Bert model by multiplying it with the embedding vector of each term, greatly improving the predicting performance.

6 Experiments

6.1 Data Pre-processing and Implementation

Data pre-processing is an essential step in building our models. We removed the numbers, special characters and stop words to focus on the important words for both feature-based and deep-learning-based approaches. We also performed a specific pre-processing to Instagram posts. First, we removed URLs and user names (words starting with the special character '@'). Moreover, we split hashtags into multiple words. For instance, *"#Ilovetravel"* becomes *"I love travel"*. Finally, we removed all Emojis and Emoticons.

To assess our work, we consider 80% of the dataset as training data to update the weights in BERT fine-tuning approach, 10% as validation data to tune the parameters, and 10% as a test to measure the out-of-sample performance for the BERT model and the feature-based approach. Despite the fact that the

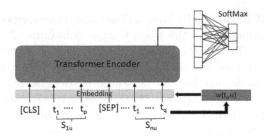

Fig. 5. Using TF-IDF in BERT for sentence classification

Table 1. Average top-k accuracies

	Feature-based				BERT fine-tuning	
	Glove		FastText			
	Hashtags	Captions	Hashtags	Captions	Hashtags	Captions
k = 3	0.5838	0.4132	0.6557	0.4431	0.8713	0.8174
k = 4	0.6707	0.4521	0.7365	0.4940	0.8802	0.8353
k = 5	0.7216	0.5240	0.7964	0.5240	0.9410	0.8623
k = 6	0.7545	0.5958	0.8443	0.5689	0.9611	0.9132

feature-based approach is not supervised, we only evaluate it on the test set for comparative reasons. Each set includes a portion of posts for each user. Using this strategy, all users take part in the train, the validation, and the test sets, so that we avoid an imbalanced distribution of users in terms of the number of posts and prevent over-fitting. Furthermore, since users' posts express actual facts, we did not perform oversampling or undersampling techniques and keep the classes' distribution in the 3 sets, as in that we supply the dataset as realistic as possible. We evaluate the performance of our approaches in terms of top-k accuracies. Accuracy is a statistical measure to analyze classification performance defined by the number of correctly predicted users out of all the users. Below, we show how to correctly compute classified users for both of the approaches.

– feature-based: a user u is considered correctly predicted when her vector representation of real interest (manually annotated by humans) $\overrightarrow{T_{label}^u}$ equals to her most similar generated category interest c_i, i.e., where the $cosine\_sim(\overrightarrow{T_u}, \overrightarrow{T_{c_j}})$ is maximized as described in Eq. 4

$$\overrightarrow{T_{label}^u} = argmax_{c_j \in C}(cosine\_sim(\overrightarrow{T_u}, \overrightarrow{T_{c_j}}))   \quad (4)$$

– BERT: a user u is correctly predicted when her vector representation of genuine interest $\overrightarrow{T_{label}^u}$ equals to generated interest c_j with the highest probability from the output of the softmax function. The latter gives a probability distribution over all predicted output classes c_j.

$$\overrightarrow{T_{label}^u} = argmax_{c_j \in C}(P(\overrightarrow{T_{c_j}}))   \quad (5)$$

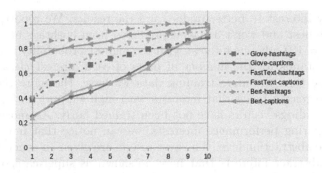

Fig. 6. Curves of top-k accuracy

Table 2. BERT-based model results

	P	R	F1	Support
Technology	0.9473	0.9231	0.9357	39
Pets	0.9118	0.8857	0.8986	35
Books	0.8649	0.9143	0.8889	35
Drawing	0.6667	0.7500	0.7059	16
Entertainment	0.6364	0.7778	0.7000	9
Nature	0.7778	0.5833	0.6667	12

6.2   Results

Additionally, we use traditional metrics (Precision, Recall, and F1-score) to evaluate the performance of each interest class.

Table 1 shows the performance of each approach using respectively the hashtags and captions data. As expected, the classification using hashtags outperforms the classification based on captions regardless of the methodology. Although posts' captions include hashtags, results show that relevant words coming from hashtags are drowned out by irrelevant words in the captions. Surprisingly, FastText shows better results than Glove despite that the latter is trained on Twitter which is supposed closely related vocabulary compared to Wikipedia data on which FastText embedding is trained. This is probably because FastText uses both characters- and subword-based word embeddings to remedy issues with out-of-vocabulary words. Finally, BERT shows better results in the classification of users using captions or hashtags. So that supervised methods are more accurate to predict the correct classes among 25 target classes. Figure 6 shows the evolution of the accuracy concerning the number of class predictions (k).

As shown, the task is the furthest from easiness to predict the genuine classes from a high number of target classes, especially when the number of predictions is low. However, the curve quickly converges when k tends to 10. For all k, the fine-tuning BERT model shows a better ability to perform users' interests classification. We compute precision, recall, and F1 scores from BERT fine-tuning for each category interest to better understand the results. We report, in Table 2, results on the best and worst 3 classes predicted from hashtags in terms of F1-score when $k = 1$ (Only one interest with the highest probability is considered). The support stands for the number of users of each interest class. Results in Table 2 denote that the more training data we have, the more the system is accurate. The reason being that interests with high support perform better is that the embeddings vectors have not been trained fairly. As another observation, by comparing performance interests, we can notice that interests do not have the same abstraction level. The best results are given on concrete interests. In contrast, abstract interests that may be shown as super-categories encompassing several specific interests have the lowest values in terms of precision and recall. To better understand the mislabeled users, we examined some posted hashtags. Considering the interests *books* and *entertainment* for instance, they share several hashtags such as #readingbooks, #newspapers and #romancenovels. Therefore, it can be understood why 2 users interested in entertainment are misclassified and predicted as interested in books. Through these errors, we investigate how interests' relatedness impacts the quality of predicted interests. We can face that by taking into account the relationships between topics. For better results, we can either use subcategories for all users or only use super-categories.

7   Conclusion and Future Work

In this work, we focused on identifying Instagram user interests. We have proposed two approaches, mapping the content of users' profiles to relevant interests. The first is a feature-based approach using FastText and Glove, while the second is a deep-learning-based approach that fine-tunes the pre-trained BERT model. We evaluated our approaches on a manually annotated dataset that includes more than 3,000 captions and defines 25 interests. This dataset is made publicly available to the community. A comparison between these two approaches shows that BERT fine-tuning is far more superior in terms of accuracy. Besides, we have also reveal that hashtags express more accurately the content of a post.

Many possible extensions can loom. In addition to textual data in Instagram, scanning users' relationship information are promising prospects. Instagram users usually follow famous users for personal interest, while they follow non-famous users because they are friends, families, etc. Therefore, we can first deduce the topical expertise of famous Instagram users based on their Instagram list features, then transitively infer the interests of the users who follow them. Moreover, since Instagram is a photo-sharing social media platform, it will be interesting and attractive to consider pictures' content. Thus, besides captions and hashtags data, we can analyze the content of the pictures posted by users.

References

1. Abbasi1, R., Rehman, G., Lee, J., Riaz, F.M., Luo, B.: Discovering temporal user interest on twitter using semantic based dynamic interest finding model. In: Proceedings of the IEEE Information Technology, Networking, Electronic and Automation Control Conference (ITNEC), Chengdu, China, December 2017
2. Weng, J., Lim, E., Jiang, J., He, Q.: Twitterrank: finding topic-sensitive influential twitterers. In: Proceedings of the 3rd International Conference on Web Search and Web Data Mining, WSDM 2010, New York, NY, USA, pp 261–270 (2010)
3. Xu, Z., Lu, R., Xiang, L., Yang, Q.: Discovering user interest on twitter with a modified author-topic model. In: 2011 IEEE/WIC/ACM International Conference on Web Intelligence and Intelligent Agent Technology, Lyon, France (2011)
4. Yang, L., Sun, T., Zhang, M., Mei, Q.: We know what @you #tag: does the dual role affect hashtag adoption? In: Proceedings of the 21st WWW Conference, Lyon (2012)
5. Piao, G., Breslin, J.G.: User modeling on twitter with wordnet Synsets and DBpedia concepts for personalized recommendations. In: Proceedings of the 25th ACM International Conference on Information and Knowledge Management CIKM 2016, IN, USA (2016)
6. Kang, J., Lee, H.: Modeling user interest in social media using news media and Wikipedia. Inf. Syst. **65**, 52–64 (2017)
7. Fani, H., Bagheri, E., Du, W.: Temporally Like-minded User Community Identification through Neural Embeddings. In: Proceedings of the 26th ACM International Conference on Information and Knowledge Management, CIK 2017, Melbourne (2017)
8. Chong, W.-H., Lim, E.-P., Cohen, W.: Collective entity linking in tweets over space and time. In: Jose, J.M., et al. (eds.) ECIR 2017. LNCS, vol. 10193, pp. 82–94. Springer, Cham (2017). https://doi.org/10.1007/978-3-319-56608-5_7
9. Liang, S., Zhang, X., Ren, Z., Kanoulas, E.: Dynamic embeddings for user profiling in twitter Shangsong. In: Proceedings of the 24th ACM SIGKDD International Conference on Knowledge Discovery & Data Mining (KDD 2018), London, UK (2018)
10. Jain, A., Gupta, A., Sharma, N., Joshi, S., Yadav, D.: Mining application on analyzing users' interests from twitter. In: Proceedings of the 3rd International Conference on Internet of Things and Connected Technologies, Jaipur, India, March 2018
11. Ombabi, A.H., Lazzez, O., Ouarda, W., Alimi, A.N.: Deep learning framework based on Word2Vec and CNN for users interests classification. In: Proceedings of the 5th Sudan Conference on Computer Science and Information Technology 2017, Sudan (2017)
12. Adjali, O., Besançon, R., Ferret, O., Le Borgne, H., Grau, B.: Multimodal entity linking for tweets. In: Jose, J.M., et al. (eds.) ECIR 2020. LNCS, vol. 12035, pp. 463–478. Springer, Cham (2020). https://doi.org/10.1007/978-3-030-45439-5_31
13. Piao, G., Breslin, J.G.: Inferring User interests for passive users on twitter by leveraging followee biographies. In: Jose, J.M., et al. (eds.) ECIR 2017. LNCS, vol. 10193, pp. 122–133. Springer, Cham (2017). https://doi.org/10.1007/978-3-319-56608-5_10
14. Arabzadeh, N., Fani, H., Zarrinkalam, F., Navivala, A., Bagheri, B.: Causal dependencies for future interest prediction on twitter. In: Proceedings of the 27th ACM International Conference on Information and Knowledge Management, CIKM 2018, Turin, Italy (2018)

15. Jang, J.Y., Han, K., Shih, P.C., Lee, D.: Generation like: comparative characteristics in Instagram. In: Proceedings of the 33rd ACM Conference on Human Factors in Computing Systems, CHI 2015, Seoul, Korea, April 2015
16. Lee, R.K.-W., Hoang, T.-A., Lim, E.-P.: On analyzing user topic-specific platform preferences across multiple social media sites. In: Proceedings of the 26th International Conference on World Wide Web, Perth, Australia, April 2017
17. Ferrara, E., Interdonato, R., Tagarelli, A.: Online popularity and topical interests through the lens of Instagram. In: Proceedings of the 25th ACM Conference on Hypertext and Social Media HT, pp 24–34, Santiago, Chile, September 2014
18. Devlin, J., Chang, M., Lee, K., Toutanova, K.: Bert: pre-training of deep bidirectional transformers for language understanding. Preprint arXiv:1810.04805 (2018)
19. Mozafari, M., Farahbakhsh, R., Crespi, N.: A BERT-based transfer learning approach for hate speech detection in online social media. In: Cherifi, H., Gaito, S., Mendes, J.F., Moro, E., Rocha, L.M. (eds.) COMPLEX NETWORKS 2019. SCI, vol. 881, pp. 928–940. Springer, Cham (2020). https://doi.org/10.1007/978-3-030-36687-2_77
20. Conneau, A., Lample, G.: Cross-lingual language model pretraining. In: Advances in Neural Information Processing Systems 32 Inc, pp. 7059–7069 (2019)

Multi-Wiki90k: Multilingual Benchmark Dataset for Paragraph Segmentation

Michał Swędrowski[(✉)] [iD], Piotr Miłkowski[iD], Bartłomiej Bojanowski[iD], and Jan Kocoń[iD]

Wrocław University of Science and Technology, 50-370 Wrocław, Poland
{michal.swedrowski,piotr.milkowski,bartlomiej.bojanowski,
jan.kocon}@pwr.edu.pl

Abstract. In this paper, we present paragraph segmentation using cross-lingual knowledge transfer models. In our solution, we investigate the quality of multilingual models, such as mBERT and XLM-RoBERTa, as well as language independent models, LASER and LaBSE. We study the quality of segmentation in 9 different European languages, both for each language separately and for all languages simultaneously. We offer high quality solutions while maintaining language independence. To achieve our goals, we introduced a new multilingual benchmark dataset called Multi-Wiki90k.

Keywords: Natural language processing · Paragraph segmentation · Multilingual

1 Introduction

Text segmentation is an interesting topic whose development will open up new possibilities for working with unstructured text. This aspect may enable development with innovative technologies based on machine learning such as Automatic Speech Recognition (ASR) or working with models with limited input size (e.g. BERT). This task can be categorised according to the complexity of the text and its language. It should be noted that text segmentation is a very broad term, which we understand as the division of text into fragments of a given granularity. One of the most popular text segmentation tasks is previously tokenization, where we divide the text into smaller fragments called tokens according to a given criterion - most often it is the occurrence of a given text fragment in the predefined dictionary. The basic types of segments in natural language processing are words (tokens), sentences and paragraphs. In the context of token and sentence partitioning, there are many advanced language libraries or frameworks that allow these operations to be performed while achieving very high performance [8,21]. However, proper segmentation into paragraphs of text is challenging [15].

Paragraph is a distinct semantically coherent section of a text thus accurately identifying paragraph range requires understanding the content of the document and making decisions based on context. When considering a single paragraph, we must take into account the fact of a coherent narrative and the topic of the statement in the following sentences, in such a way that at the end of our paragraph we do not interrupt the

C. Bădică et al. (Eds.): ICCCI 2022, CCIS 1653, pp. 137–149, 2022.
https://doi.org/10.1007/978-3-031-16210-7_11

narrative, which will result in reading content that is completely incomprehensible and illogical for the reader. A certain solution could be a dictionary approach to this problem [19], for example, by determining the beginning and ending sentences along with the punctuation marks they are characterized by. Unfortunately, even within a single language it is difficult to define such a set of features due to the different styles of speech and the length of the entire document. Additionally, the division may result from arbitrary decisions of the author. In the case of multilingual analysis, the problem becomes even more difficult due to additional syntactic and cultural differences among its users.

Popular approaches to this issue use relatively standardized text in a given language as a data source, but rarely use solutions based on transformer architecture. In this paper, we use sentence embedding solutions with our proposed classification head based on recurrent neural networks for a sequence of sentences. The developed processing pipeline allows us to take input texts, process them, and then train them to solve paragraph segmentation tasks using contextual analysis. Moreover, this approach is not limited to a single language, but to any language supported by current methods such as mBERT, LASER, LaBSE or XLM-RoBERTa. In this paper, we focus both on the use of multilingual models, allowing to work within the specific language for which the model is tuned, as well as language-agnostic solutions, allowing to work with any supported language.

As part of our work, we prepared a unique collection of texts in multiple languages that can be used as a benchmark dataset to test other solutions for segmenting text into paragraphs. This collection contains 90,000 Wikipedia articles in 9 languages in a format suitable for this task. The selection of languages was made from the most popular representatives of the Romance, Slavic and Germanic language groups. These languages are: German, English, Spanish, French, Italian, Dutch, Polish, Portuguese and Russian. The only multilingual collection we were able to find in the literature contains only 50 articles and has not been published [12], so the resource prepared and published with this paper can help develop the complex issue of language-agnostic paragraph segmentation.

2   Related Works

Subdividing text into coherent and meaningful parts of a text is a long-standing challenge. One of the first works, related to computer science, addressing this problem is made by Morris [22]. Authors were dealing with lexical coherence and algorithm for finding lexical chains.

Hearst [13] introduced *TextTiling* - an algorithm based on lexical similarity of adjacent fragments. This method assumes that two blocks of text from the same paragraph are expected to have bigger lexical similarity. Further improvements and discussions regarding this method can be found in [14] and [15]. Although this solution is a much-mentioned reference until this day, along with scientific developments the demands have also increased making the method insufficient. The need for predefined length of paragraph and being partially dependant on vocabulary are two big disadvantages of TextTiling, especially nowadays where amount and variety of processed text increased significantly.

Passonneau [23] describe works regarding usage of linguistic features to perform paragraph segmentation. The data annotation process described here is an evidence that human annotation can vary greatly. Even if the results were promising, obtaining linguistic features is not always possible.

Choi [5] generates a ranking matrix from cosine the similarity measure of word frequency in all sentence pairs and clusters small text fragments into coherent parts of text. Utiyama [28] use a probabilistic approach to interpret text as a graph and search for minimum-cost paths resulting in minimum-cost of segmentation.

Sporleder and Lapata [27] present interesting insights into paragraph segmentation in three different languages – English, German and Greek. The authors conducted a comprehensive analysis taking into account basic (e.g., sentence length), language modeling (entropy per word), and syntactic (e.g., sequence of part-of-speech tags) features of the text.

Glavaš [11] use semantic relatedness graphs. Each sentence is a graph's node. Edges exist only between two sentences if their semantic relatedness exceeds the assumed threshold value. Bron-Kerbosch algorithm [3] is applied to get the set of maximal cliques in a graph followed by a merging algorithm. Koshorek [18] use two BiLSTM networks to perform sentence embedding and paragraph prediction respectively. This method shows superiority over the others on most of the datasets studied.

One of the state-of-the-art CATS methods [12] method is based on recent discoveries such as transformer architecture, cross-lingual zero shot learning and multi-objective approach. This paper leads us to believe that using an agnostic vector representation will not cause a large decrease in the model prediction quality.

Recent work of Virameteekul [29] shows the usage of the XLNet model combined with CNN to obtain features for paragraphs combined paragraph-level attention which allows for better performance than token-level semantic features.

3   Multilingual Benchmark Dataset

During the review of literature, we did not find an adequate dataset to examine multilingual text partitioning in depth. Motivated by the shortcomings in this area, we introduced the Multi-Wiki90k dataset. The presented dataset is available on the huggingface website[1].

3.1   Existing Datasets

In the literature we have multiple English language datasets for paragraph segmentation, such as relatively small Choi [5] or CITIES and ELEMENTS [4] and much bigger one Wiki-727K and its subset Wiki-50 [18]. All datasets are available except one, proposed by Chen, and for that reason we omitted it.

After reviewing the aforementioned datasets, we decided to follow an analogous annotation - each sentence is placed in a new line and each successive piece of text is separated in the document by a line containing a multiplied "=" sign.

---

[1] https://huggingface.co/datasets/clarin-pl/multiwiki_90k.

Even though Sporleder [27] introduced and examined data sources from different languages, each was completely independent and could not be combined in the analysis. The authors highlighted differences in the division of text into paragraphs due to phonetic features specific to each language.

With this in mind, we decided to base our corpus on Wikipedia. The data made available was already broken down into high-quality chunks, which allowed us to create a new collection analogous to the approach presented in [18]. A similar approach was presented in the paper on the CATS tool [12] however, in this case a small Wiki-50 dataset was translated into only three languages. Furthermore, the dataset is not publicly available. Each Wikipedia's paragraph is a fairly unambiguous unit, which should allow us to translate the text while preserving the occurring contextual changes. Table 2 describes the quantitative analysis of each dataset.

3.2   Multi-Wiki90k

In our study, we focused on nine languages: Polish, English, Italian, Russian, German, Spanish, French, Dutch, and Portuguese. For each language, we created a corpus containing 10,000 articles from Wikimedia Dumps[2] (a complete copy of all wikis as text and metadata). Paragraphs were separated using the Wikimedia Dumps XML format structure, including information about the author segmentation of the wiki page. As part of the preprocessing, we removed all tables, images, links, HTML tags, and unnecessary template elements. Each paragraph was then split into sentences using Moses Tokenizer [17]. Finally, all headings preceding the paragraphs were removed.

Table 1. Comparison of the existing datasets. PPD: Paragraphs per document. SPD: Sentences per document.

Dataset	Wiki-727K	Choi	Multi-Wiki90k
Documents	727,746	920	90,000
Paragraphs	4,913,329	9 200	397,609
PPD	6.75	10	4.41
Sentences	38,316 080	68,113	2,810,036
SPD	7.80	6.16	4.86

We compared it with other popular collections in the literature. In addition to multilingualism, what sets Multi-Wiki90k apart is its lower average paragraph count per document and lower average sentence count per paragraph (Table 1).

Digging deeper into this problem we decided to look at the data per language (Table 2). Comparing our data for English with Wiki727K, we see that the average number of paragraphs per document is no longer significantly different. The reason for this is probably either due to the characteristics of the language that were raised in the

---

[2] https://dumps.wikimedia.org/.

paper [27] or simply because the English Wikipedia pages are better developed due to the characteristics of the society that speaks the language, such as the popularity of the language among people with internet access, the level of education in English-speaking countries, etc. What may support the second theory is the correlation of language popularity with the length of paragraphs per document, which can also be observed for languages such as German, Spanish or French in relation to Portuguese or Polish.

Table 2. Statistic of each language. PPD: Paragraphs per document.

Language	Paragraphs	PPD
Dutch	32,349	3.23
English	74,901	7.49
French	60,506	6.05
German	53,785	5.38
Italian	37,761	3.78
Polish	24,628	2.46
Portuguese	29,020	2.90
Russian	38,275	3.82
Spanish	46,384	4.64

4 Models

We consider the embedding vectors obtained from four different models. XLM-RoBERTA and mBERT are direct adaptations of the basic BERT architecture to perform multilingual tasks, while LaBSE and LASER are deliberately trained to achieve a universal language-agnostic representation of the text.

4.1 LASER

LASER (Language-Agnostic Sentence Representation) is a novel architecture introduced by Artetxe and Schwenk [1] on behalf of Facebook AI Research in 2019. In this paper, the authors described how they obtained multilingual sentence representations for 93 languages from more than 30 different language families. The main motivation behind the development of such a tool is to facilitate work in a low-resource languages by enabling the use of large corpora from other languages.

The LASER architecture is based on a sequence-to-sequence autoencoder, where its individual components are based on LSTM networks [16] and their bidirectional variants. Support for such a large number of languages is possible by byte-pair-encoding. The model was trained on 223 million parallel sentences, which were pre-processed using the Moses tool[3].

The authors created LASER to obtain universal language-agnostic sentence representation. Each sentence is encoded to a 1024 dimensional vector which is created after applying a max-pooling operation over the output of the last layer of the encoder.

---

[3] http://www.statmt.org/moses/.

4.2 LaBSE

LaBSE (Language agnostic BERT Sentence Encoder) [9] was presented in 2020 by Google AI. Just like the previously described LASER method, the main goal of the tool is to produce language-agnostic embedding vector, nevertheless this time for 109 different languages. According to the authors it is currently state-of-the-art method, especially distinguished by its improved efficiency in use with less common languages. In our work we decided to use *Sentence Transformes* implementation, described in details in [26].

The architecture of LaBSE is based on a bidirectional dual encoder architecture. The training data are 6B of monolingual and bilingual sentence pairs. The model input is given a pair of sentences with the same meaning, with the goal of creating the same vector representation. Comparison of the similarity of the obtained vectors is achieved using cosine similarity. The result of a model is a 768-dimensional vector.

4.3 mBERT

Bidirectional Encoder Representations from Transformers (or BERT as abbrevation) is different than previously mentioned language representation models [7]. It is designed to pre-train deep bidirectional representations from unlabeled text by jointly conditioning on both left and right context in all layers. As a result, the pre-trained model can be fine-tuned with just one additional output layer to create state-of-the-art models for a wide range of tasks, such as question answering and language inference, without substantial task-specific architecture modifications.

It was originally trained on unlabeled data extracted from the BooksCorpus with 800M words and English Wikipedia with 2,500M words in two variants. In later experiments it became clear that it is surprisingly good at zero-shot cross-lingual model transfer, in which task-specific annotations in one language are used to fine-tune the model for evaluation in another language [25].

Using mBERT as a source for embedding sequences is commonly done using the values from the last 4 layers of the transformer. Each layer has a 768-dimensional vector in the output, resulting in 3072-dimensional text embeddings.

4.4 XLM-RoBERTa

XLM-R (XLM-RoBERTa, Unsupervised Cross-lingual Representation Learning at Scale) is a scaled cross lingual sentence encoder [6]. It is a large multilingual model, trained on 2.5 TB of filtered CommonCrawl data based on RoBERTa [20] in 100 languages. Unlike some XLM multilingual models, it does not require *language* tensors to understand which language is used, and is able to determine the correct language from the input text.

The XLM approach uses BPE (Byte-Pair Encoding) which divides the input data into the most common sub-words in all languages. Based on this, a common vocabulary between languages is prepared. As in BERT, the goal of the model is to predict masked tokens, but XLM solutions predict tokens in other languages because different words are masked words in each language.

Analogous to other BERT-based methods, text embeddings are prepared using values from the last 4 layers, consisting of 768 values each, resulting in 3072-dimensional text embeddings.

5 Evaluation

We have adopted the P_k measure proposed by Beeferman [2] as the main measure to serve as a reference against other works [11, 12, 18].

Assuming that we sample fragments of size k (number of sentences) from the evaluated text, we interpret P_k as the probability that the starting and ending sentences **do not** belong to the same segment of a text. This implies that the higher the quality of the segmentation tool, the lower the value of this metric. Based on the previously mentioned literature, we take the hyperparameter k as half of the average paragraph length for correct text segmentation. Evaluation takes place within the labels for all sentences of a single document.

Researchers have noted that the P_k metric is flawed and have proposed improved metrics [10, 24]. Nevertheless, this metric is still most commonly used in the literature, which prompted us to follow this trend.

Therefore, we also present standard metrics for the classification task: macro F1-score, binary F1-score and accuracy. The F1-score binary metric is computed for *class 1* i.e. paragraph occurrence (see Sect. 5.1).

5.1 Configuration

We interpret text splitting as the task of identifying the sentence that ends a paragraph. Therefore, we assigned binary labels to the sentences - 0 corresponding to the sentence in the middle of the paragraph and 1 indicating the sentence ending the paragraph. To evaluate the performance of each embedding vector on the Multi-Wiki90k dataset, we created a task-specific pipeline (see Fig. 1).

We first embedded our dataset using the proposed models. Among all the BERT-based models (XLM-RoBERTa, LaBSE and mBERT) due to the possible differences in the length of tokens received as input, we decided to investigate the most efficient one. The search space was limited to 64, 128 and 256 input tokens. The P_k value for each combination is shown in Table 3.

For each configuration of BERT-based models and the LASER model, we embedded chosen texts. The vector representation was given as input to a single-layer BiLSTM network whose output was processed by the sigmoid activation function:

$$h_\theta(x) = \frac{1}{1 + e^{-x}} \tag{1}$$

A fixed BiLSTM learning configuration with 1024 hidden units was used in each run. The optimizer applied was Adam, the learning step value was $1e^{-4}$ and the batch size was 8 documents. For regularization purposes, a dropout of 0.2 was used. The training lasted 10 epochs

In turn, the results obtained are real numbers in the range 0–1. All of our research was performed with a threshold of 0.5.

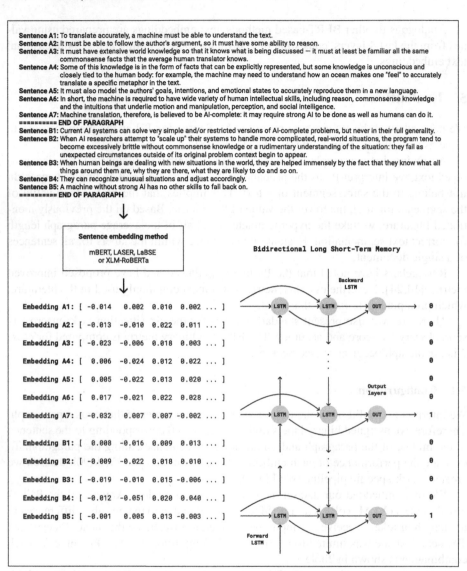

Fig. 1. Visualization of the training process. The input text is transformed into sentence-level embedding vectors to be further processed by the classifier in the form of BiLSTM.

Table 3. P_k values for each considered embedding. T64, T128 and T256 denote the first 64, 128 and 256 tokens of the embedded sentences. The best performing token lengths are marked in bold. *LASER model does not have token length constraints.

Embeddings type	T64	T128	T256
LaBSE [9]	16.45	16.40	**16.39**
mBERT [25]	**15.51**	15.52	15.63
XLM-RoBERTa [6]	**18.02**	18.90	19.28
LASER [1] *	**18.96**		

5.2 Results

Following the assumptions described in Sect. 5.1, the models for each embedding vector were trained on the full Multi-Wiki90k dataset. The dataset was divided into train, test, valid in proportions of 80%, 10%, 10%.

The study began by determining the optimal input token count for each BERT-based embedding vector and comparing the results with each other (Table 3). We chose P_k to evaluate the quality of the model.

mBERT gives by far the best results regardless of the number of sentence tokens. We suspect that the difference is due to the fact that this model was pre-trained on the task of predicting consecutive sentences, which resulted in it having more information at the sentence relation level compared to the other models. The next best model is LaBSE, where we also see a large difference between it and the last two models. This should not be surprising since LaBSE is the state-of-the-art approach for most language independent tasks. Moreover, it was trained on much more data than the other models.

Regarding the effect of the number of tokens on prediction quality, we see for BERT-based architectures that a smaller number of tokens gives better results, while for LaBSE the trend is the opposite (although the differences between configurations are small). One possibility is that BERT architectures do not perform well when the number of tokens in the input is less than the maximum supported number. LaBSE, while also a BERT-dependent architecture, creates embedding vectors on a slightly different basis due to its bidirectional dual encoder architecture.

Taking advantage of the convenient partitioning of the dataset, we decided to consider model performance both per language and collectively for the entire set.

Considering the P_k measure, results presented in Table 4 show the superiority of mBERT over the other methods.

Looking at the languages separately, we notice that for four languages it is XLM-RoBERTa that gives better results. The language that XLM-RoBERTa performs the worst with, compared to the others, is Polish. One possible reason for this large loss compared to the other models is the insufficient number of examples in Polish. In conclusion, LASER seems to be the worst model for this task, which is not surprising, having regard to the smaller amount of data used to train the model.

Unfortunately, it is difficult to refer directly to the literature with the obtained results, since no one has so far conducted an analysis of multilingual segmentation into paragraphs. By comparing our results for English with other approaches that also relied

Table 4. Metrics for each language included in Multi-Wiki90k dataset using best configurations presented in Table 3: mBERT - multilingual BERT, LaBSE - Langauge agnostic BERT Sentence Encoder, LASER - Language Agnostic Sentence Representation, XLM-R - XLM-RoBERTa.

Language	Model	Accuracy	$F1_{binary}$	$F1_{macro}$	P_k
German	LASER	0.97	0.55	0.77	20.48
	LaBSE	0.97	0.61	0.80	18.89
	XLMR	0.97	0.60	0.79	19.20
	mBERT	0.97	**0.65**	**0.82**	**17.44**
English	LASER	0.97	0.53	0.76	21.14
	LaBSE	0.97	0.59	0.79	19.52
	XLMR	0.97	0.56	0.77	20.23
	mBERT	0.97	**0.62**	**0.80**	**18.52**
Spanish	LASER	0.97	0.60	0.79	18.61
	LaBSE	0.97	0.63	0.81	18.01
	XLMR	0.97	0.63	0.81	17.37
	mBERT	0.97	**0.67**	**0.83**	**16.59**
French	LASER	0.96	0.61	0.79	18.26
	LaBSE	0.96	0.65	0.81	17.62
	XLMR	0.96	0.65	0.82	17.04
	mBERT	0.96	**0.69**	**0.84**	**16.16**
Italian	LASER	0.97	0.63	0.81	18.31
	LaBSE	0.97	0.67	0.83	17.59
	XLMR	0.97	0.68	0.83	17.41
	mBERT	0.97	**0.71**	**0.84**	**16.79**
Dutch	LASER	0.97	0.73	0.86	13.48
	LaBSE	0.97	0.75	0.87	13.05
	XLMR	0.97	0.75	0.87	13.27
	mBERT	0.98	**0.78**	**0.88**	**12.39**
Polish	LASER	0.98	0.76	**0.88**	11.71
	LaBSE	0.98	0.77	**0.88**	11.88
	XLMR	0.98	0.75	0.87	13.07
	mBERT	0.98	**0.78**	**0.88**	**11.50**
Portuguese	LASER	0.97	0.69	0.84	16.26
	LaBSE	0.97	0.72	0.85	15.81
	XLMR	0.97	0.71	0.85	16.20
	mBERT	0.98	**0.74**	**0.87**	**15.02**
Russian	LASER	0.97	0.63	0.81	16.99
	LaBSE	0.97	0.66	0.82	16.67
	XLMR	0.98	0.67	0.83	16.35
	mBERT	0.98	**0.69**	**0.84**	**16.00**
All	LASER	0.97	0.64	0.81	17.25
	LaBSE	0.97	0.67	0.83	16.56
	XLMR	0.97	0.67	0.83	16.68
	mBERT	0.97	**0.70**	**0.84**	**15.60**

on English Wikipedia, we can conclude that although we do not achieve state-of-the-art results, we do not deviate significantly from them.

In order to evaluate the results of our models, we decided to refer to the results presented in the paper [12], which is also an extension of Koshorek's work [18]. The test set for Wiki-727K was set according to the literature as 10% of the entire dataset. For the Choi dataset, the entire dataset was used to test the model.

Considering the values shown in Table 5, the slightly worse performance on the Choi and Wiki-50 datasets may be due to their small size. We can observe a similar drop in quality on the other deep network-based approaches. What distinguishes us from the other solutions is multilingualism. Undoubtedly, this is a large improvement obtained at the small cost of prediction quality. Moreover, for individual languages, e.g. Polish, we achieve lower P_k values than state-of-the-art solution in English.

Table 5. Metrics obtained on Multi-Wiki90k test part - all languages subsets combined. Model types are: Unsupervised, Supervised. *Our best model is mBERT with the maximum length of 64 tokens.

Model	Type	WIKI-727K	WIKI-50	CHOI
RANDOM	U	53.09	52.65	49.43
GRAPHSEG	U	–	63.56	07.20
[18]	S	22.13	18.24	26.26
TLT-TS	S	19.41	17.47	23.26
CATS	S	15.95	16.53	18.50
mBERT T64*	S	20.77	–	24.91

6   Conclusions and Future Work

In summary, in the work done so far we can clearly observe the lack of suitable datasets for text segmentation, especially for multilingual solutions. With the exception of Wiki-727K, all data sources are extremely small, making it difficult to work with deep models. The Multi-Wiki90k dataset we introduced is the first multilingual dataset for paragraph segmentation, which can be used as a reference for further development of segmentation methods. We believe that such a benchmark collection allows for even better results in the future, especially in the context of multilingual approaches.

The P_k measure, which is the main reference point, is flawed. Researchers mainly refer to this outdated metric although there are better options such as WinDiff [24], Boundary Similarity [10] or the F1-score we used. Nevertheless, following the current trend we also refer P_k, but keeping in mind the low reliability of the method we also consider other standard classification metrics.

Incorporating our dataset into the currently available resources, we note that the only larger datasets were based on Wikipedia. While the use of Wikipedia allows us to be confident in the high quality of the text partitioning, it causes the solutions produced to be biased towards the structure of Wikipedia articles. In the future, we would like to address this problem by exploring other data sources as well.

While our model does not achieve state-of-the-art results, it also does not deviate significantly from them while maintaining support for a large number of languages. It is not clear to us whether this is significant for all languages on which the vector embedding model was trained, which makes this another area for further exploration. In the context of the research conducted, we see further scope for development in the aspect of investigating the effect of the classifier used on the quality of text segmentation.

Acknowledgements. This work was financed by (1) the National Science Centre, Poland, project no. 2019/33 /B/HS2/02814; (2) the Polish Ministry of Education and Science, CLARIN-PL; (3) the European Regional Development Fund as a part of the 2014–2020 Smart Growth Operational Programme, CLARIN – Common Language Resources and Technology Infrastructure, project no. POIR.04.02.00-00C002/19; (4) the statutory funds of the Department of Artificial Intelligence, Wrocław University of Science and Technology.

References

1. Artetxe, M., Schwenk, H.: Massively multilingual sentence embeddings for zero-shot cross-lingual transfer and beyond. Trans. Assoc. Comput. Linguist. **7**, 597–610 (2019)
2. Beeferman, D., Berger, A., Lafferty, J.: Statistical models for text segmentation. Mach. Learn. **34**(1), 177–210 (1999)
3. Bron, C., Kerbosch, J.: Algorithm 457: finding all cliques of an undirected graph. Commun. ACM **16**(9), 575–577 (1973)
4. Chen, H., Branavan, S., Barzilay, R., Karger, D.R.: Global models of document structure using latent permutations. Association for Computational Linguistics (2009)
5. Choi, F.Y.: Advances in domain independent linear text segmentation. In: Proceedings of the 1st North American chapter of the Association for Computational Linguistics Conference, pp. 26–33 (2000)
6. Conneau, A., et al.: Unsupervised cross-lingual representation learning at scale. arXiv preprint arXiv:1911.02116 (2019)
7. Devlin, J., Chang, M.W., Lee, K., Toutanova, K.: Bert: pre-training of deep bidirectional transformers for language understanding. In: Proceedings of the 2019 Conference of the North American Chapter of the Association for Computational Linguistics: Human Language Technologies, Volume 1 (Long and Short Papers), pp. 4171–4186 (2019)
8. Fabricius-Hansen, C.: Information packaging and translation: aspects of translational sentence splitting (German-English/Norwegian). Sprachspezifische Aspekte der Informationsverteilung pp. 175–214 (1999)
9. Feng, F., Yang, Y., Cer, D., Arivazhagan, N., Wang, W.: Language-agnostic Bert sentence embedding. arXiv preprint arXiv:2007.01852 (2020)
10. Fournier, C.: Evaluating text segmentation using boundary edit distance. In: Proceedings of the 51st Annual Meeting of the Association for Computational Linguistics (Volume 1: Long Papers), pp. 1702–1712 (2013)
11. Glavaš, G., Nanni, F., Ponzetto, S.P.: Unsupervised text segmentation using semantic relatedness graphs. In: Proceedings of the Fifth Joint Conference on Lexical and Computational Semantics, pp. 125–130 (2016)
12. Glavaš, G., Somasundaran, S.: Two-level transformer and auxiliary coherence modeling for improved text segmentation. In: Proceedings of the AAAI Conference on Artificial Intelligence, vol. 34, pp. 7797–7804 (2020)
13. Hearst, M.A.: Texttiling: a quantitative approach to discourse. Technical report USA (1993)

14. Hearst, M.A.: Multi-paragraph segmentation of expository text. In: 32nd Annual Meeting of the Association for Computational Linguistics, pp. 9–16 (1994)
15. Hearst, M.A.: Text tiling: segmenting text into multi-paragraph subtopic passages. Comput. Linguist. **23**(1), 33–64 (1997)
16. Hochreiter, S., Schmidhuber, J.: Long short-term memory. Neural Comput. **9**(8), 1735–1780 (1997)
17. Koehn, P., et al.: Moses: open source toolkit for statistical machine translation. In: Proceedings of the 45th Annual Meeting of the Association for Computational Linguistics Companion Volume Proceedings of the Demo and Poster Sessions, pp. 177–180 (2007)
18. Koshorek, O., Cohen, A., Mor, N., Rotman, M., Berant, J.: Text segmentation as a supervised learning task. In: Proceedings of the 2018 Conference of the North American Chapter of the Association for Computational Linguistics: Human Language Technologies, Volume 2 (Short Papers), pp. 469–473. Association for Computational Linguistics, New Orleans, Louisiana, June 2018. https://doi.org/10.18653/v1/N18-2075, https://www.aclweb.org/anthology/N18-2075
19. Kozima, H.: Text segmentation based on similarity between words. In: 31st Annual Meeting of the Association for Computational Linguistics, pp. 286–288 (1993)
20. Liu, Y., et al.: Roberta: a robustly optimized Bert pretraining approach. arXiv preprint arXiv:1907.11692 (2019)
21. McNamee, P., Mayfield, J.: Character n-gram tokenization for European language text retrieval. Inf. Retrieval **7**(1), 73–97 (2004)
22. Morris, J., Hirst, G.: Lexical cohesion computed by thesaural relations as an indicator of the structure of text. Comput. Linguist. **17**(1), 21–48 (1991)
23. Passonneau, R.J., Litman, D.J.: Discourse segmentation by human and automated means. Comput. Linguist. **23**(1), 103–139 (1997)
24. Pevzner, L., Hearst, M.A.: A critique and improvement of an evaluation metric for text segmentation. Comput. Linguist. **28**(1), 19–36 (2002)
25. Pires, T., Schlinger, E., Garrette, D.: How multilingual is multilingual Bert? arXiv preprint arXiv:1906.01502 (2019)
26. Reimers, N., Gurevych, I.: Making monolingual sentence embeddings multilingual using knowledge distillation. In: Proceedings of the 2020 Conference on Empirical Methods in Natural Language Processing. Association for Computational Linguistics, November 2020. https://arxiv.org/abs/2004.09813
27. Sporleder, C., Lapata, M.: Broad coverage paragraph segmentation across languages and domains. ACM Trans. Speech Language Process. (TSLP) **3**(2), 1–35 (2006)
28. Utiyama, M., Isahara, H.: A statistical model for domain-independent text segmentation. In: Proceedings of the 39th Annual Meeting of the Association for Computational Linguistics, pp. 499–506 (2001)
29. Virameteekul, P.: Paragraph-level attention based deep model for chapter segmentation. PeerJ Comput. Sci. **8**, e1003 (2022)

CAE: Mechanism to Diminish the Class Imbalanced in SLU Slot Filling Task

Nguyen Minh Phuong[1] , Tung Le[2,3] , and Nguyen Le Minh[1]([⊠])

[1] Japan Advanced Institute of Science and Technology, Nomi, Japan
{phuongnm,nguyenml}@jaist.ac.jp
[2] Faculty of Information Technology, University of Science, Ho Chi Minh, Vietnam
lttung@fit.hcmus.edu.vn
[3] Vietnam National University, Ho Chi Minh city, Vietnam

Abstract. Spoken Language Understanding (SLU) task is a wide application task in Natural Language Processing. In the success of the pretrained BERT model, NLU is addressed by Intent Classification and Slot Filling task with significant improvement performance. However, classed imbalance problem in NLU has not been carefully investigated, while this problem in Semantic Parsing datasets is frequent. Therefore, this work focuses on diminishing this problem. We proposed a BERT-based architecture named JointBERT Classify Anonymous Entity (JointBERT-CAE) that improves the performance of the system on three Semantic Parsing datasets ATIS, Snips, ATIS Vietnamese, and a well-known Named Entity Recognize (NER) dataset CoNLL2003. In JointBERT-CAE architecture, we use multitask joint-learning to split conventional Slot Filling task into two sub-task, detect *Anonymous Entity* by Sequence tagging and *Classify* recognized anonymous entities tasks. The experimental results show the solid improvement of JointBERT-CAE when compared with BERT on all datasets, as well as the wide applicable capacity to other NLP tasks using the Sequence Tagging technique.

Keywords: SLU · Slot filling · Semantic parsing · Class imbalanced · NER

1 Introduction

Nowadays, with the rapid development of virtual assistants (e.g. Google Home) and dialog systems, numerous researches investigate the SLU task which is the core component of smart speakers. The SLU task is typically addressed by two essential sub-tasks that include Intent Prediction (ID) and Slot Filling (SF) tasks [25]. Recently, the impressive improvements [1,2] are largely based on the success of pre-trained language models such as BERT [5] with little fine-tuning.

However, most previous works have not considered the class imbalance problem in the Slot Filling task. Based on our primary analysis about the distribution of entity types in two well-known SLU datasets: ATIS [10] and Snips [3] (Fig. 1),

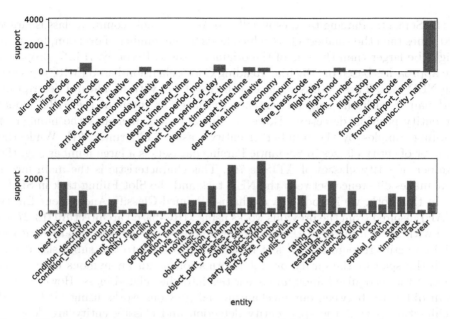

Fig. 1. Distribution of Slot classes in ATIS (top) and Snips (bottom) datasets. Some Slot classes in ATIS are ignored due to the space limitation of the paper. In the graph, x, y denotes the Slot class name and the number of instances.

we found that the class imbalance problem in these datasets is highly critical, especial on ATIS.

Indeed, the target of the SF task is to extract slot information that usually is the text span in the input sentence. Similar to the Named Entity Recognition (NER) task in Natural Language Processing (NLP), this task is solved by sequence labeling technique with BIO schema [1,2,16,21,28,29]. In the NER area, the class imbalance problem is also investigated by many previous works [7,27]. In the SLU task, given a sentence, the required output is the intent and slots information of the sentence. With each kind of intent, the type of slot information may differ, therefore, the number of slot information types is ordinarily high. For example, there are 79 different Slot types in ATIS. Besides, not only the imbalance among classes of entities but also the imbalance between positive and negative words is also important. In detail, there is a small number is positive words that are inside entity names, while there is a large number of negative words which are outside entity span. Both kinds of imbalance affect the performance of the SF task as well as the overall system [7].

The previous works [7,13,27] related to the class imbalance almost show the solutions on the NER task. [7] proposed a re-sampling data method to diminish this problem by duplicating the samples of less occurrence class. This method is proven to work well on Stockholm EPR PHI Corpus [7] which has the most common class larger 24 times than the smallest class. However, the authors choose the threshold of oversampling size manually without explanation. Besides, in the Semantic Parsing task, especially on Atis, the most common class is larger 400 times than the smallest class, which leads to the number of oversampling that might be larger than the size of the original dataset. Recently, [13,27] proposed the approaches based on Machine Reading Comprehension-based (MRC) to solve the NER task. These works replace each class label with its natural description and pair it with the original sentence to make the input of the MRC model for entity position detection. However, this approach increases the number of training samples by the number of entity classes ($|C|$) times [27]. While the number of entity classes in Semantic Parsing datasets is a large number (e.g. the number of entity classes of ATIS is 79). This characteristic is the main factor that makes difference between the NER task and the Slot Filling task in SLU.

In this work, we introduce a mechanism named Classify Anonymous Entity (CAE) inspired from the previous works using MRC-based architecture [13,27] to deal with Slot Filling in SLU task. In our proposed mechanism, we also split the original entity recognition (or slot detection) process into two sub-tasks: determine the span of the entity or slot information as an anonymous entity, and classify the recognized anonymous entities into the related class. However, the main difference between our mechanism and previous works using MRC-based architecture is that the span entity detection and classify entity are done by sequence tagging architecture. In this way, it is unnecessary to increase the number of artificial samples in the training process. Besides, the proposed mechanism diminishes the class imbalance between entity classes with the outside entity (0) class. More detail, we design a new entity class called Object for span entity recognition and replace all original entity classes labels by new entity Object label (Fig. 2). For example, B-PER, B-ORG labels are replaced by B-Object label, and apply by similar way to the I-* labels. After that, each anonymous entity is classified into the related entity class in the second step. Briefly, our contributions are summarized as follows.

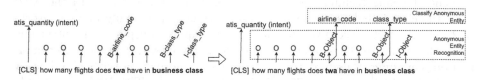

Fig. 2. Comparison of SLU task using Joint ID and SF task between original approach (left) and our proposed approach using CAE mechanism (right).

- We propose a simple yet effective mechanism, CAE, to handle the class imbalance problem in the Slot Filling task of SLU as well as the NER task.
- Our experimental results show that our proposed model improves the performance of the Slot Filling task using the F1 score leads to improve performance of the overall system on two Semantic Parsing datasets Snips, ATIS, and CoNLL 2003 NER dataset, compared with the original approach.
- The proposed model achieves new SOTA performance on ATIS Vietnamese dataset [4] with a 1.4 F1 score improvement.

2   Related Work

2.1   SLU Task

The SLU task using the Deep learning model has been attracted by numerous works for a long time [1,2,9,20–22,28,30]. In the first development period of this task, two sub-tasks ID and SF are typically addressed by Convolutions Neural Network (CNN) [30] and Long Short-Term Memory (LSTM) Network [23,28]. In the success of pre-trained language using the Self-Attentive model [5,26] and two-stage training fashion in the last few years, the performance of the SLU system is substantially improved in many recent works [1,2]. Together with the strength of pre-trained language models, many approaches put much more effort into improving the overall systems. In particular, [9] focuses on incorporating external knowledge (e.g. WordNet) to enhance the performance of SF sub-task, especially boosting out-of-vocab words recognition. [6,8,12,19,22] introduces architectures targeted to intent-slot interaction, and [22] shows the advancement on the SLU multi-intent task. Besides, [20] also focuses on co-interaction between intent and slot information. This work is inspired by vanilla Transformer with intent while slot information is considered as a query and key component in the self-attention mechanism. Difference from the previous works, our work focus on the class imbalance of the Slot Filling task. To our best knowledge, we are the first to investigate this problem in the SLU task.

2.2   Class Imbalance in Sequence Labeling

Based on the primary analysis shown in the introduction section, we found that the imbalance class in the Slot Filling of SLU is quite critical. To deal with this problem, there are lots of approaches in previous works, especially in the NER task [7,13,14]. [14] introduces a dynamic adjusted-weight loss function that reflects the importance of easy-negative examples in training data. [7] proposes methods for re-sampling training data based on the distribution of entity classes, especially oversampling approach. The works [13,27] focus on adapting MRC architecture to deal with the NER task. By this approach, the model can ignore the imbalance between positive (inside entity) and negative (outside entity) words, however, it is a bias into imbalance among entity classes and increases the number of training examples. In our proposed model using the CAE mechanism, the imbalance among positive and negative words is diminished by combining all original entity classes into a special object entity class (`Object`). Besides, this mechanism in technical also abates the imbalance among entity classes by removing meta labels (`B-*`, `I-*`) in each entity class. Therefore, the number of training samples has remained and the imbalance problem is partly addressed by our delicate consideration.

3   Methodology

In this section, we describe the detail of the baselines, the oversampling mechanism [7] and our CAE mechanism incorporating with CRF layer [24].

3.1 Baseline Model

BERT Model. The architecture of this model is the combination of multiple Transformer Encoders [26] layers. In each Encoder layer, the major component to extract and digest linguistic features is the Self-Attention layer that learns the long-range dependencies between the pairs of words in the sentence. Given the input is the natural sentence ($s = \{w_i\}_1^{|s|}$ where $|s|$ is the number of words[1]), by using BERT model, we get the hidden vector representation of each word (h_i). For the classification task, the authors [5] introduce a simple method adding a special token ($[CLS]$) into the input sentence and using the hidden vector of this token for sentence representation.

$$h^{[CLS]}, h_i^{word} = \text{BERT}(s) \tag{1}$$

JointBERT Model. We follow the previous work [2] to handle sub-tasks Intent Detection (ID) and Slot Filling (SF) by joint learning all sub-tasks together. For ID task, hidden vector of [CLS] token ($h^{[CLS]}$) is forwarded to Dense layer to reduce dimension and processed by a *softmax* function to get intent probabilities.

$$y^{ID} = \text{softmax}(W^{ID} h^{[CLS]} + b^{ID}) \tag{2}$$

where W^{ID}, b^{ID} is learnable parameters. For SF task, after we get the hidden vector of words (h_i^{word}) encoded by BERT model, these vectors are also forwarded to Dense and *softmax* layers.

$$y_i^{SF} = \text{softmax}(W^{SF} h_i^{word} + b^{SF}) \tag{3}$$

where W^{SF}, b^{SF} is learnable parameters. Besides, if a word in the sentence is split into sub-words by the BERT Tokenizer module, only the first sub-word will be used for the whole original word representation. Finally, for the joint training process, the objective loss function is computed by the weighted sum of the Cross-Entropy losses of SF and ID sub-tasks.

$$\mathcal{L} = \text{CrossEntropy}(y^{ID}, y^{gID}) + \lambda \times \sum_{i=1}^{|s|} \text{CrossEntropy}(y_i^{SF}, y_i^{gSF}) \tag{4}$$

where λ is the hyper-parameters to adjust the strength of SF loss; y^{g*} is the gold labels from SLU datasets.

---

[1] We use "word" to simplify, in practice, it should be sub-word split by BER Tokenizer.

3.2 Oversampled Data

The result from the previous work [7] shows that oversampling technique on NER tasks can improve the performance of the overall system for imbalanced datasets. The target of this mechanism is to duplicate the samples of minority classes and endeavor the balance among entity classes in training data. To this end, we construct a threshold r is the ratio of samples in minority entity classes $(0 < r < 1)$ that need to be reached when comparing with the largest entity class. After that, the sentences that contained labels of minority classes are randomly selected until the ratio of all these entity classes reaches the threshold r.

3.3 Proposed Model

JointBERT-CAE Model. In this architecture, we use two different classifiers for the SF task (Fig. 3). The first one is used for anonymous entity span recognition while the second is for related entity (slot) classification. Especially, the second classifier only considers positive words which are in the recognized anonymous entity span. To this end, the second classifier does not face the imbalance problem between positive (inside entity) and negative (outside entity) words. For the ID task, we follow the baseline model architecture. Mathematically, Eq. 3 is replaced by the following formulas:

$$\mathbf{y}_i^{SF1} = \mathrm{softmax}(\mathbf{W}^{SF1}\mathbf{h}_i^{word} + \mathbf{b}^{SF1}) \tag{5}$$

$$\mathbf{y}_i^{SF2} = \mathrm{softmax}(\mathbf{W}^{SF2}\mathbf{h}_i^{wordEntity} + \mathbf{b}^{SF2}) \tag{6}$$

where $\mathbf{W}^*, \mathbf{b}^*$ is learnable parameters; $\mathbf{h}^{wordEntity}$ is the hidden states of positive words at begin of the entity (the bold words in the example of Fig. 3). Finally, the objective loss function is also computed by the weighted sum of the Cross-Entropy losses of SF and ID sub-tasks for the joint training process.

$$\mathcal{L} = \mathrm{CrossEntropy}(\mathbf{y}^{ID}, \mathbf{y}^{gID}) + \lambda \times \sum_{i=1}^{|s|} \Big(\mathrm{CrossEntropy}(\mathbf{y}_i^{SF1}, \mathbf{y}_i^{gSF1})$$
$$+ f_i \times \mathrm{CrossEntropy}(\mathbf{y}_i^{SF2}, \mathbf{y}_i^{gSF2}) \Big) \tag{7}$$

where $\mathbf{y}^{g*}$ is the gold labels from SLU datasets; f_i is the flag storing positive $(f_i = 1)$ or negative $(f_i = 0)$ word information.

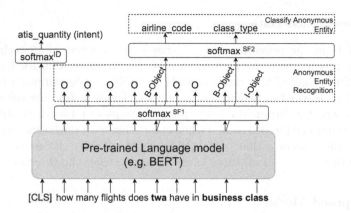

Fig. 3. JoinBERT-CAE model architecture using joint ID and SF sub-tasks incorporating our proposed mechanism (CAE).

Conditional Random Field. Many previous works show the use of CRF layer on the top of neural network architecture to support sequence label tagging [2,11,17]. We aim to utilize the strong relation between Intent and Slot types, so our CRF layer is constructed to process Intent and the Slots (or entities) without considering outside entity words. In detail, we treated Intent as a Slot class of special token *[CLS]*. Difference from [2,4], CRF layer in these works only considers relations between Slot types without Intent information.

$$\text{score}(\mathbf{s}, \mathbf{y}) = \sum_{i=1}^{|s|}(\mathbf{W}^e\mathbf{h}_i^{wordEntity} + \mathbf{b}^e)[\mathbf{y}_i] + \sum_{i=0}^{|s|}(\mathbf{W}^t[\mathbf{y}_i, \mathbf{y}_{i+1}]) \tag{8}$$

$$p(\mathbf{y}|\mathbf{s}) = \frac{\exp(\text{score}(\mathbf{s}, \mathbf{y}))}{\sum_{\mathbf{y}'}\exp(\text{score}(\mathbf{s}, \mathbf{y}'))} \tag{9}$$

where $\mathbf{y}_0, \mathbf{y}_{|s|+1}$ is additional start and end of Slot label; $\mathbf{W}^e, \mathbf{b}^e, \mathbf{W}^t$ are the learnable parameters for emission and transmission scores. By using CRF layer, the model is trained to maximize the log-probability of gold Slot sequence labels.

4   Experiments and Analysis

We conducted experiments on three public benchmark SLU datasets, Snips [3], ATIS [10], Vietnamese ATIS [4]. Besides, to prove the generalization of our proposed model, we also evaluate our model on CoNLL 2003 dataset for NER task. Snips dataset contains 13,084 training samples, 700 testing samples, and 700 development samples. English ATIS and Vietnamese ATIS datasets are the same sizes with 4,478 training samples, 893 testing samples, and 500 development samples. With the Vietnamese ATIS dataset, we use a *word* version having data is segmented [10]. CoNLL2003 dataset contains 14,041 training samples, 3,453 testing samples, and 3,250 development samples. Based on our analysis (Sect. 1), the SLU datasets have more entity (Slot) classes than NER datasets, and the imbalanced class problem is more critical.

4.1 Experimental Settings

With our aim to evaluate the performance of our proposed model, we conducted experiments using JointBERT-CAE, JointBERT-CAE using CRF layer on top, and baseline JointBERT (re-implemented) models on all datasets. Similar to previous work [2] on ATIS and Snips datasets, with pre-trained model, we used the BERT-based setting[2] [5] with 12 layers, 12 heads, 768 hidden size. On ATIS Vietnamese dataset, we also used the pre-trained Vietnamese model PhoBERT[3] [18] with base setting. On CoNLL 2003 dataset, we used pre-trained BERT-based setting version case sensitive[4] and pre-trained RoBERTa-Large [15] model[5]. For fine-tuning hyper-parameters process, all experiments are conducted on the dev set of each dataset which the number of epochs is selected in $\{5, 10, 20, 30\}$, the weight of SF loss (λ) is selected in $\{0.2, 0.3, 0.4, 1.0\}$, init learning rate is selected in $\{2e^{-5}, 5e^{-5}\}$. Besides, to compare with the previous approach using Oversampled training data [7] for imbalance entity class problem, we conducted experiments on ATIS dataset by duplicating samples minority class with ratio threshold (r) is selected in $\{0.01, 0.02, 0.03, 0.04, 0.05\}$. In these experiments, only training data is re-sampled while the test and dev set is original data. For comparison with the previous works, we use three metrics to evaluate our experiments: Intent accuracy, Slot F1, and Sentence Frame accuracy.

4.2 Experimental Results

Main Results. We show the experimental results of our proposed models on three SLU datasets in Table 1, and NER CoNLL 2003 dataset in Table 2. To overcome the limits related to the experimental environments and libraries, we re-implemented the JointBERT as our baseline system. Firstly, we found that the Slot F1 scores of our proposed model JointBERT-CAE on three datasets achieve state-of-the-art (SOTA) performance. Through comparison with our baseline, it increases 0.4 points on Snips, 0.3 points on ATIS, and 0.6 points on Vietnamese ATIS. These results proved that our proposed model using the CAE mechanism works effectively while the model size almost does not change. Therefore, it boosts the performance of the overall system in Sentence Frame Accuracy score, especially on ATIS, and Vietnamese ATIS datasets. In the comparison with the previous works on the Sentence accuracy metric, the JointBERT-CAE model improves 0.1 points on ATIS, 1.6 points on ATIS Vietnamese, and promising results on Snips. By using the CRF layer on the top of the pre-trained model, the results are slightly decreased, which is similar to the result shown in previous

---

[2] Downloaded from https://huggingface.co/bert-base-uncased.
[3] Downloaded from https://huggingface.co/vinai/phobert-base.
[4] Downloaded from https://huggingface.co/bert-base-cased.
[5] Downloaded from https://huggingface.co/roberta-large.

works [2,4]. We argue that joint learning using the pre-trained model is powerful enough in learning the relation between Intent and Slot information. Therefore, the CRF layer does not show a clear improvement.

Table 1. Result of our proposed models on the test set of three SLU datasets: Snips, ATIS, and ATIS Vietnamese. The bottom part of the table presents the results of experiments conducted in this work.

Model	Snips			ATIS			ATIS (vi)		
	Intent	Slot	Sent	Intent	Slot	Sent	Intent	Slot	Sent
BERT-Joint [1]	**99.0**	96.2	91.6	**97.8**	95.7	88.2	–	–	–
JointBERT [2]	98.6	**97.0**	92.8	97.5	**96.1**	88.2	–	–	–
JointIDSF [4]	–	–	–	–	–	–	97.6	95.0	86.3
Stack-propagation [19]	99.0	**97.0**	**92.9**	97.5	**96.1**	88.6	–	–	–
JointBERT (ours)	98.6	96.6	92.0	97.4	95.8	87.6	97.7	94.9	86.5
JointBERT-CAE +CRF	98.3	96.9	92.7	97.5	96.0	88.4	**97.8**	95.4	87.6
JointBERT-CAE	98.3	**97.0**	92.6	97.5	**96.1**	**88.7**	97.7	**95.5**	**87.9**

Besides, we conducted extensive experiments in the NER task to inspect the generalize of our proposed model. We show the results of BERT architecture using our proposed mechanism, CAE, on dev set (Fig. 4) and test set (Table 2) of CoNLL 2003 dataset. In these experiments, we constructed BERT-CAE architecture by removing the components to learn Intent information in JointBERT-CAE architecture (Eq. 2), and the loss of intent detection in Eq. 7. The results on the dev set show that our CAE mechanism clearly improves the original BERT in the same setting and works effectively when incorporated with the CRF layer. The results on test set also show that our proposed mechanism improves the performance of baseline system BERT with 0.6 F1 scores, and 0.8 F1 scores when incorporating with CRF layer. Compared with the public result on this dataset, although we used the same setting described in [5], our baseline is lower, we argue that the reason relates to the pre-processing data and experimental libraries. Besides, we also conducted experiments using a pre-trained model RoBERTa-Large [15] for this task (Table 2). By using this pre-trained model, our proposed mechanism CAE increases 0.2 F1 scores when compared with the baseline model using RoBERTa large and boosts 0.3 F1 scores when incorporating with CRF layer. These results proved the solid improvement of our CAE mechanism on the different pre-trained models.

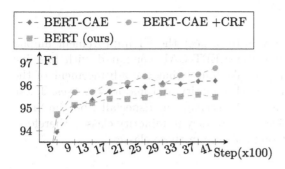

Fig. 4. Performance comparison between our proposed mechanism (CAE) using BERT-Base model and baseline models (ours re-implemented) on dev set of CoNLL 2003 data.

Table 2. Performance comparison of our proposed model with the baseline models on the CoNLL 2003 test set.

Model	F1 score
BERT-Base [5]	92.4
BERT-Large [5]	92.8
BERT-Base (ours)	91.4
BERT-Base-CAE+CRF	92.2
BERT-Base-CAE	92.0
RoBERTa-Large (ours)	92.6
RoBERTa-Large-CAE+CRF	**92.9**
RoBERTa-Large-CAE	92.8

Oversampled Data. To evaluate our proposed approach with the previous approach [7] relating to the Imbalanced Entity Class problem, we re-implemented the method using oversampling training data for comparison. Figure 5 shows the Sentence Frame Accuracy of our proposed models compared with the baseline model (JointBERT) trained on oversampling training data with different ratio thresholds (r) on both dev set and test set of ATIS dataset. These results show that the re-sampling method can improve the baseline model in the small margin, however, the improvement is not solid, especially on the dev set. By using threshold $r = 0.01$, the rate of duplicated samples is 18.8%, and increase to 54.3% with $r = 0.02$. Therefore, the distribution in original data is hugely different when applying this approach, especially in strong imbalanced data like ATIS. Meanwhile, our proposed models using the CAE mechanism do not increase the size of the training dataset and still beat the re-sampling method.

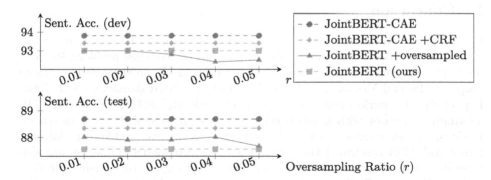

Fig. 5. Performance comparison on the dev set (above) and test set (bellow) of ATIS dataset, among our proposed models (BERT-CAE), baseline model (JointBERT), and baseline model using Oversampling data with respect to oversampling ratio threshold.

4.3 Analysis

We conducted statistical data analysis to inspect the F1 improvement among
Slot classes of our proposed model JointBERT-CAE compared with baseline
model JointBERT, as shown in Fig. 6. We found that the advancement of the
JointBERT-CAE model is shown in both minority and majority classes. These
results proved the generalize of the CAE mechanism. Especially, on the Snips
dataset, the baseline model is typically inaccuracy in minority classes, therefore,
the JointBERT-CAE showed a strong advance in these classes.

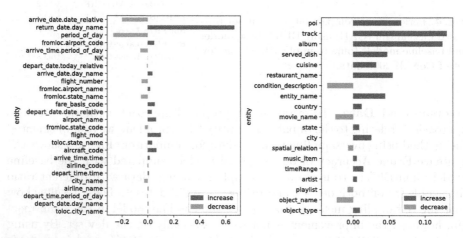

Fig. 6. Distribution of Slot F1 improvement between JointBERT-CAE compared with
JointBERT in the test set of ATIS (left) and Snips (right) datasets. The order of Slot
classes is sorted from minority to majority class.

5 Conclusion

In this paper, we introduced a novel architecture JointBERT-CAE that work
effectively on SLU datasets having highly imbalanced Slot class problem. We con-
ducted the experiments and showed solid improvements on three SLU datasets
Snips, ATIS, and Vietnamese ATIS as well as on a NER dataset CoNLL 2003.
Especially, the performance of our model leads the SOTA result on ATIS
Vietnamese dataset with a substantial margin compared with previous works.
Besides, the analyses statistical the output data on two well-known datasets
Snips and ATIS confirmed the generalization of our model. These results also
proved that the CAE mechanism is the potential to apply to sequence labeling
tasks in NLP (e.g. POS task). In future works, we would like to incorporate the
CAE mechanism into various Neural Network architectures to increase the per-
formance of the SLU model as well as the models using the Sequence Labeling
technique. We believe that our proposed model can be widely applied in the
NLP community and real-world applications.

Acknowledgment. This work was supported by JSPS Kakenhi Grant Number 20H04295, 20K20406, and 20K20625.

References

1. Castellucci, G., Bellomaria, V., Favalli, A., Romagnoli, R.: Multi-lingual intent detection and slot filling in a joint Bert-based model. CoRR, abs/1907.02884 (2019)
2. Chen, Q., Zhuo, Z., Wang, W.: Bert for joint intent classification and slot filling. arXiv preprint arXiv:1902.10909 (2019)
3. Coucke, A., et al.: Snips voice platform: an embedded spoken language understanding system for private-by-design voice interfaces. CoRR, abs/1805.10190 (2018)
4. Dao, M.H., Truong, T.H., Nguyen, D.Q.: Intent detection and slot filling for Vietnamese. In: Proceedings of the 22nd Annual Conference of the International Speech Communication Association (INTERSPEECH) (2021)
5. Devlin, J., Chang, M.-W., Lee, K., Toutanova, K.: BERT: pre-training of deep bidirectional transformers for language understanding. In: Proceedings of the 2019 Conference of the North American Chapter of the Association for Computational Linguistics: Human Language Technologies, Volume 1 (Long and Short Papers), Minneapolis, Minnesota, June 2019, pp. 4171–4186. Association for Computational Linguistics (2019)
6. Goo, C.-W., et al.: Slot-gated modeling for joint slot filling and intent prediction. In: Proceedings of the 2018 Conference of the North American Chapter of the Association for Computational Linguistics: Human Language Technologies, Volume 2 (Short Papers), pp. 753–757, New Orleans, Louisiana, June 2018. Association for Computational Linguistics (2018)
7. Grancharova, M., Berg, H., Dalianis, H.: Improving named entity recognition and classification in class imbalanced swedish electronic patient records through resampling. In: Eighth Swedish Language Technology Conference (SLTC). Förlag Göteborgs Universitet (2020)
8. Hardalov, M., Koychev, I., Nakov, P.: Enriched pre-trained transformers for joint slot filling and intent detection. CoRR, abs/2004.14848 (2020)
9. He, K., Yan, Y., Xu, W.: From context-aware to knowledge-aware: boosting OOV tokens recognition in slot tagging with background knowledge. Neurocomputing **445**, 267–275 (2021)
10. Hemphill, C.T., Godfrey, J.J., Doddington, G.R.: The ATIS spoken language systems pilot corpus. In: Speech and Natural Language: Proceedings of a Workshop Held at Hidden Valley, Pennsylvania, 24–27 June 1990 (1990)
11. Lafferty, J.D., McCallum, A., Pereira, F.C.N.: Conditional random fields: Probabilistic models for segmenting and labeling sequence data. In: Proceedings of the Eighteenth International Conference on Machine Learning, ICML 2001, San Francisco, CA, USA, 2001, pp. 282–289. Morgan Kaufmann Publishers Inc (2001)
12. Li, C., Li, L., Qi, J.: A self-attentive model with gate mechanism for spoken language understanding. In: Proceedings of the 2018 Conference on Empirical Methods in Natural Language Processing, Brussels, Belgium, October-November 2018, pp. 3824–3833. Association for Computational Linguistics (2018)
13. Li, X., Feng, J., Meng, Y., Han, Q., Wu, F., Li, J.: A unified MRC framework for named entity recognition. In: Proceedings of the 58th Annual Meeting of the Association for Computational Linguistics, pp. 5849–5859, Online, July 2020. Association for Computational Linguistics (2020)

14. Li, X., Sun, X., Meng, Y., Liang, J., Wu, F., Li, J.: Dice loss for data-imbalanced NLP tasks. In: Proceedings of the 58th Annual Meeting of the Association for Computational Linguistics, pp. 465–476, Online, July 2020. Association for Computational Linguistics (2020)
15. Liu, Y., et al.: Roberta: a robustly optimized Bert pretraining approach. arXiv preprint arXiv:1907.11692 (2019)
16. Louvan, S., Magnini, B.: Recent neural methods on slot filling and intent classification for task-oriented dialogue systems: a survey. In: Proceedings of the 28th International Conference on Computational Linguistics, pages 480–496, Barcelona, Spain (Online), December 2020. International Committee on Computational Linguistics (2020)
17. Ma, X., Hovy, E.: End-to-end sequence labeling via bi-directional LSTM-CNNs-CRF. In: Proceedings of the 54th Annual Meeting of the Association for Computational Linguistics (Volume 1: Long Papers), pages 1064–1074, Berlin, Germany, August 2016. Association for Computational Linguistics (2016)
18. Nguyen, D.Q., Nguyen, A.T.: PhoBERT: pre-trained language models for Vietnamese. In: Findings of the Association for Computational Linguistics: EMNLP 2020, pp. 1037–1042 (2020)
19. Qin, L., Che, W., Li, Y., Wen, H., Liu, T.: A stack-propagation framework with token-level intent detection for spoken language understanding. In: Proceedings of the 2019 Conference on Empirical Methods in Natural Language Processing and the 9th International Joint Conference on Natural Language Processing (EMNLP-IJCNLP), pp. 2078–2087, Hong Kong, China, November 2019. Association for Computational Linguistics (2019)
20. Qin, L., Liu, T., Che, W., Kang, B., Zhao, S., Liu, T.: A co-interactive transformer for joint slot filling and intent detection. In: ICASSP 2021–2021 IEEE International Conference on Acoustics, Speech and Signal Processing (ICASSP), pp. 8193–8197 (2021)
21. Qin, L., Xie, T., Che, W., Liu, T.: A survey on spoken language understanding: recent advances and new frontiers. In: Zhou, Z.-H. (ed.) Proceedings of the Thirtieth International Joint Conference on Artificial Intelligence, IJCAI-21, pp. 4577–4584. International Joint Conferences on Artificial Intelligence Organization, 8 2021. Survey Track (2021)
22. Qin, L., Xu, X., Che, W., Liu, T.: AGIF: an adaptive graph-interactive framework for joint multiple intent detection and slot filling. In: Findings of the Association for Computational Linguistics: EMNLP 2020, pp. 1807–1816, Online, November 2020. Association for Computational Linguistics (2020)
23. Ravuri, S., Stolcke, A.: Recurrent neural network and LSTM models for lexical utterance classification. In: Proceedings Interspeech, pp. 135–139. ISCA - International Speech Communication Association, September 2015
24. Souza, F., Nogueira, R., de Alencar Lotufo, R.: Portuguese named entity recognition using BERT-CRF. arXiv:abs/1909.10649 (2019)
25. Tur, G., De Mori, R.: Spoken language understanding: systems for extracting semantic information from speech. In: Spoken Language Understanding: Systems for Extracting Semantic Information from Speech, March 2011
26. Vaswani, A., et al:. Attention is all you need. In: Guyon, I., et al. (eds.), Advances in Neural Information Processing Systems, volume 30. Curran Associates Inc (2017)

27. Wang, Y., Chu, H., Zhang, C., Gao, J.: Learning from language description: low-shot named entity recognition via decomposed framework. In: Findings of the Association for Computational Linguistics: EMNLP 2021, pp. 1618–1630, Punta Cana, Dominican Republic, November 2021. Association for Computational Linguistics (2021)
28. Wang, Y., Shen, Y., Jin, H.: A bi-model based RNN semantic frame parsing model for intent detection and slot filling. In: Proceedings of the 2018 Conference of the North American Chapter of the Association for Computational Linguistics: Human Language Technologies, Volume 2 (Short Papers), pp. 309–314, New Orleans, Louisiana, June 2018. Association for Computational Linguistics (2018)
29. Weld, H., Huang, X., Long, S., Poon, J., Han, S.C.: A survey of joint intent detection and slot-filling models in natural language understanding. arXiv preprint arXiv:2101.08091 (2021)
30. Xu, P., Sarikaya, R.: Convolutional neural network based triangular CRF for joint intent detection and slot filling. In: 2013 IEEE Workshop on Automatic Speech Recognition and Understanding, pp. 78–83 (2013)

Deep Learning

An Image Retrieval System Using Deep Learning to Extract High-Level Features

Jihed Jabnoun[1($\boxtimes$)], Nafaa Haffar[1], Ahmed Zrigui[2], Sirine Nsir[3], Henri Nicolas[2], and Aymen Trigui[1]

[1] Research Laboratory in Algebra, Numbers Theory and Intelligent Systems, University of Monastir, Monastir, Tunisia
`jihed.jabnoun@gmail.com, nafaa.haffar.5@gmail.com, trigui.aymen@gmail.com`
[2] LaBRI Laboratory, University of Bordeaux, Talence, France
`ahmedzrigui01@gmail.com, henri.nicolas@u-bordeaux.fr`
[3] DB CONSULTING, 4 rue Simone de Beauvoir, 94140 Alfortville, France
`contact@db.consulting-group.com`

Abstract. The usual procedure used in Content Based Image retrieval (CBIR), is to extract some useful low-level features such as color, texture and shape from the query image and retrieve images that have a similar set of features. However, the problem with using low-level features is the semantic gap between image feature representation and human visual understanding. That is why many researchers are devoted for improving content-based image retrieval methods with a particular focus on reducing the semantic gap between low-level features and human visual perceptions. Those researchers are mainly focused on combining low-level features together to have a better representation of the content of an image, which make it closer to the human visual perception but still not close enough to reduce the semantic gap. In this paper we'll start by a comprehensive review on the recent researches in the field of Image Retrieval, then we propose a CBIR system based on convolutional neural network and transfer learning to extract high-level features, as an initiative part of a larger project that aims to retrieve and collect images containing the Arabic language for natural language processing tasks.

Keywords: Image retrieval · CNNs · Features extraction · Transfer learning

1 Introduction

The amount of shared and stored multimedia data is growing, and searching or retrieving a relevant image from an archive is a difficult search problem. Most search engines retrieve images based on captions as input. The user submits a query by entering text or keywords that match with the metadata placed in the archive. The output is generated based on the match between the query and the metadata, but the problem with this process is that it can retrieve images that are not relative to the query. The fundamental need of any image retrieval model

C. Bădică et al. (Eds.): ICCCI 2022, CCIS 1653, pp. 167–179, 2022.
https://doi.org/10.1007/978-3-031-16210-7_13

is to search for and organize images that are in a visual semantic relationship with the query given by the user. The difference between several potential human visual perception and manual labeling/annotation is the main reason why the output is not relevant. Moreover, it is almost impossible to apply the concept of manual labeling to large image archives containing millions of images. The second approach for image retrieval and analysis is to apply an automatic image indexing system that can label images based on their content. The efficiency of approaches based on automatic image indexing, depend on how accurately a system detects color, edges, texture, spatial arrangement and shape information. Significant research is being done in this area to improve the performance of automatic image indexing [1,2], but the difference in human/machine visual perception can induce an error in the retrieval process, this is the problem of the semantic gap. The semantic gap is the lack of coincidence between the information that can be extracted from visual data and the interpretation that the same data has for a user in a given situation [3]. In Saint Exupery words, the semantic gap is the difference between the perception of an image with the eyes - objectively, as a representation of objects, shapes, textures, and the perception of an image with the heart, subjectively, including knowledge of the world and emotions, reading and writing. Knowledge of the world and emotions, reading "between the pixels" [4].

Depending on the methods used for the CBIR, we can classify the features into low-level features and high-level features. Low-level features are used to eliminate the sensory gap between the object in the world and the information in a description derived from a recording of this scene. High-level features are used to eliminate the semantic gap between the information that can be extracted from visual data and the interpretation that the same data has for a user in a given situation [5].

Color Feature: In image retrieval, color is the commonly used feature because of its robustness, efficiency and simplicity of implementation. Color-based image retrieval is the most basic and important method for CBIR and image processing in general [6]. Compared to other image features such as texture and shape, etc., color features are very stable and robust. It is invariant to rotation, translation and scale change [7]. Various methods are used for image color feature extraction such as *Color space*, they are more related to human perception and widely used in CBIR like RGB, LUV, HSV, YCrCb and LAB. *Color histogram* to calculate the frequency of appearance of different colors in a certain color space[2]. Also there are *Color moments* that are used to estimate the brightness and intensity of images [8].

Texture Feature: Textural images are those images in which a specific pattern of texture distribution is repeated sequentially throughout the image. Many features in an image could be differentiated simply by texture, without any additional data. It defines the complete information about the structural organization of a region and the association of adjacent regions. For texture extraction, the RGB color image is converted into 256 gray level images. In order to obtain the features of the texture, the gray image is transformed into a binary image using a threshold.

Shape Feature: Shape is also considered an important low-level feature, as it is useful for identifying real-world shapes and objects. Without shape, the visual content of the object cannot be recognized correctly. Shape-based methods are grouped into region-based techniques and contour-based techniques. Methods such as Fourier descriptors and geometric moments are often used. Local descriptors such as scale invariant feature transform (SIFT), accelerated robust features (SURF), histograms of oriented gradient (HOG), basic scene descriptors, the Hough transform [9] etc. are also available for image retrieval. These descriptors are mostly invariant to geometric transformations but have high computational complexity.

Features Fusion: Obtaining the search result using a single feature may return an irrelevant result. It may either retrieve images that are not similar to the query image, or fail to retrieve images that are similar to the query image. Therefore, to produce efficient results, we can use a combination of several features instead of using a single feature [10, 11]. Retrieve images using similarity matching on images that are similar to the input image either by color, texture or shape by considering all features simultaneously. Combine all the features to obtain a single feature vector for the input image and for each image in the database as shown in Fig. 1. As each feature has a different value, they are combined using variable weights according to the following formula:

$$S = \frac{W_C.D_C + W_T.D_T + W_S.D_S}{W_C + W_T + W_S} \tag{1}$$

W_C, W_T et W_S contribution factors assigned to distance values D_C for   color, D_T for texture and D_S for shape [10].

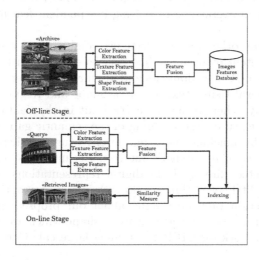

Fig. 1. CBIR system based on color, texture and Shape fusion.

2 Related Work

The exponential growth of multimedia content makes image retrieval a challenging research field. Thus a lot of work has been done to make information retrieval systems [12,13] in general and CBIR systems in particular more efficient. In this section we'll be reviewing some of the works conducted in the field of content image retrieval recently. Jun et al. [5] Proposed a Content-based image retrieval using color and texture fused features. Based on their works, a CBIR system is designed using color and texture fused features by constructing weights of feature vectors. The relevant retrieval experiments show that the fused features retrieval brings better visual sensitivity than the single feature retrieval, which means better retrieval results. Kavitha et al. [14] proposed an efficient image retrieval technique which uses local color and texture features. They're method consist of partitioning an image into sub-blocks of equal size as a first step, then they extract the HSV[1] color and GLCM[2] texture features of each sub-block. As a result the proposed method by Kavitha et al. based on color and texture features of image sub-blocks has better retrieval performance compared with the Image retrieval system using only HSV color, only GLCM texture and combined HSV color and GLCM texture. Kiran et al. [1] implemented An Improved CBIR System Using Low-Level Image Features Extraction and Representation. In this work the lower-level Features like color, texture and shape are extracted and stored in feature vector representation format that are fused to generate a unique feature vector. The suggested approach has shown better precision-recall rates and efficiency compared to some other approaches. Also Reshma et patil. [7] proposed an algorithm which incorporates the advantages of various other algorithms to improve the accuracy and performance of retrieval using a combination of color and shape Features. The proposed methodology had increased the average precision from an average of 44% using independent features to an average of 72%.

Along with many other research that use combination of low-level features to represent the content of an image like Anusha et al. [8] with a Content Based Image Retrieval Using Color Moments and Texture, Shirazi et al. [15] a Content-Based Image Retrieval Using Texture Color Shape and Region.

In spite of many other researches carried out in the field of CBIR systems based on low-level features, the bridging of the semantic gap between low-level features captured by machines and high-level features anticipated by humans remains a vivid area of researcher's interest. Because most of these low-level features are extracted directly from digital representations of objects in the database and have little or nothing to do with human perception.

In the next section we'll be talking about our propsed method that uses more advanced features than color, texture or shape which are extracted using a deep learning framework for CBIR by training largescale Convolutional Neural Networks (CNN).

---

[1] HSV: Hue, Saturation, Value.
[2] GLCM: Gray-Level Co-occurrence Matrix.

3 Proposed Method

In order to reduce the "semantic gap" between the features captured by machines and humans' perception, we propose to use features derived from a pre-trained deep convolutional neural network by transfering knowlage gained from certain tasks like for example recognizing triangles and applying it to solve the problem in the associated target task, recognizing rectangles as shown in Fig. 2. This knowledge transfer technique is called transfer learning or self-taught learning [16]. While most machine learning are designed to address a single task, the development of algorithms that facilitate transfer learning is a topic of ongoing interest in the machine learning community.

3.1 Transfer Learning

There are several models that are already trained on some large-scale datasets, but they can be used for other more specific tasks like in our case the content-based image retrieval, three of these models are frequently used:

- VGG (e.g., VGG16 or VGG19). VGG16 is a simple CNN Architecture trained on ImageNet, used in visual object recognition it achieved 71.3% top-1 test accuracy in ImageNet [17].
- GoogLeNet (e.g., Inception V3). Inception v3 is a commonly used image recognition model that has been shown, on the ImageNet dataset, to have an accuracy greater than 78.1% [17].
- Residual Network (e.g., ResNet 50). Is also a commonly used image recognition model that has been shown, on the ImageNet dataset, to have an accuracy greater than 74.9% [17].

Keras (python library) provides access to a number of the most powerful pre-trained models that have been developed for image recognition tasks. They are available via the Applications API and include functions to load a model with or without the pre-trained weights.

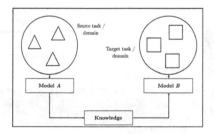

Fig. 2. Transfer learning model (SEBASTIAN RUDER) [19].

3.2   Convolutional Neural Networks

Convolutional neural network, also known as a CNN or convNet, is an artificial neural network that is most often applied to image processing problems [18,20]. What differentiates it from just a standard multi-layer perceptron or MLP is that CNN has hidden layers called convolutional layers, and these layers are the reason why a CNN able to detect and identify objects in an image, but it can be also be used in natural language processing [21–23] and speech recognition projects too [24–28].

In this work we used CNN as an image feature extractor, on both query (On-line stage) and database images (Off-line stage) before applying a similarity measure. For the database we used CNN to extract 4096 embedding vector that represent the distinctive features of each image and store theme in an index as shows in Fig. 3. The same for the query we used the pre-trained CNN model to extract a feature vector, then compare it to each feature vector in the index using similarity mesure. There are various distance metrics that can be used such as Euclidean distances, Manhattan distances and Chi-squared distances, but we but we chose Chi-squared because it is more suited for image retrieval [29].

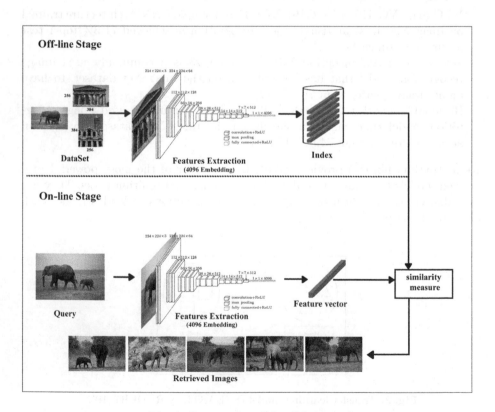

Fig. 3. Proposed model architecture

4   Experiments

This section describes our experiment for the propsed method. For the CNN model we use VGG16 because it has a smaller network architecture and easy to implement compared to other. The VGG-16 model was developed by the Visual Graphics Group (VGG) at Oxford and was described in [30]. And The proposed image descriptor is evaluated on the Corel-1000 dataset.

4.1   Dataset

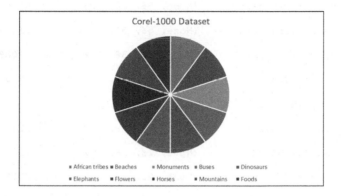

Fig. 4. Images distribution per class in corel-1000 dataset.

Corel-1000 includes ten concept groups of (African tribes, Beaches, Monuments, Buses, Dinosaurs, Elephants, Flowers, Horses, Mountains, and Foods). For each concept group the images are divided into 90 images for training and 10 images for test with size of 384×256 or 256×384, Fig. 4 shows the distribution of images per class.

4.2   Image Descriptor

The first step to build a CBIR system is to choose an image descriptor to specify the type of features that we're going to extract from the image. In our experiment we used VGG-16 model without the top layer (classification layer) which allows us to represent the image as a feature vector. The input shape for all images is (224, 224, 3) and we get the output weights from the fully connected layer 'FC1' (4096 neurones) before the classification layer as shown in Fig. 5.

4.3   Indexing

After defining our image descriptor, the next step is to extract features from each image in our dataset and save it as an ".npy" file. NPY files contains an

Layer (type)	Output Shape	Param #
input_2 (InputLayer)	[(None, 224, 224, 3)]	0
block1_conv1 (Conv2D)	(None, 224, 224, 64)	1792
block1_conv2 (Conv2D)	(None, 224, 224, 64)	36928
block1_pool (MaxPooling2D)	(None, 112, 112, 64)	0
block2_conv1 (Conv2D)	(None, 112, 112, 128)	73856
block2_conv2 (Conv2D)	(None, 112, 112, 128)	147584
block2_pool (MaxPooling2D)	(None, 56, 56, 128)	0
block3_conv1 (Conv2D)	(None, 56, 56, 256)	295168
block3_conv2 (Conv2D)	(None, 56, 56, 256)	590080
block3_conv3 (Conv2D)	(None, 56, 56, 256)	590080
block3_pool (MaxPooling2D)	(None, 28, 28, 256)	0
block4_conv1 (Conv2D)	(None, 28, 28, 512)	1180160
block4_conv2 (Conv2D)	(None, 28, 28, 512)	2359808
block4_conv3 (Conv2D)	(None, 28, 28, 512)	2359808
block4_pool (MaxPooling2D)	(None, 14, 14, 512)	0
block5_conv1 (Conv2D)	(None, 14, 14, 512)	2359808
block5_conv2 (Conv2D)	(None, 14, 14, 512)	2359808
block5_conv3 (Conv2D)	(None, 14, 14, 512)	2359808
block5_pool (MaxPooling2D)	(None, 7, 7, 512)	0
flatten (Flatten)	(None, 25088)	0
fc1 (Dense)	(None, 4096)	102764544

Fig. 5. Model summary.

array saved in the NumPy (NPY) file format. NPY files store all the information required to reconstruct an array on any computer, which includes dtype and shape information. This process of extracting the features and storing them is called "indexing", so now we have a database that contain all images' informations.

4.4 Similarity Measure

For a given query image, we extract features from that image and then calculate the distance to all feature vectors in our index database. Images that have a distance of 0 are considered identical to each other. While if the similarity value increases, the images are considered less similar to each other. To calculate the similarity, we used the chi-squared distance illustrated in the Eq. (2) below. The chi-square distance calculation is a statistical method that usually measures the similarity between two feature matrices. Such a distance is generally used in many applications such as similar image retrieval, image texture, feature extraction, etc.

$$\chi^2 = \sum_{i=1}^{n} \frac{(x_i - y_i)^2}{(x_i + y_i)} \tag{2}$$

Chi-square distance of two arrays 'x' and 'y' with 'n' dimension [31].

Finally, it is sufficient to sort the result dictionary according to the similarity value in ascending order Fig. 6.

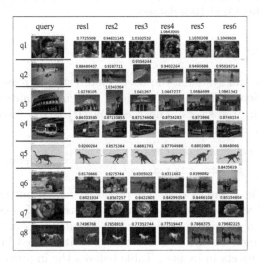

Fig. 6. Illustration of the search results of the system based on VGG-16.

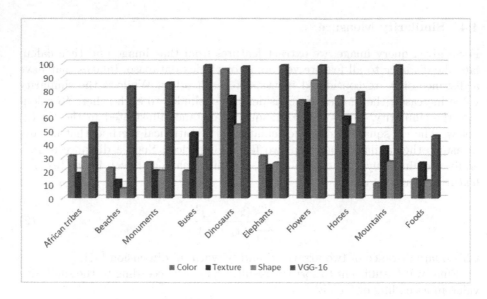

Fig. 7. Precision comparison between the proposed method and other standard retrieval systems using Corel-1000 dataset.

5   Perfomance Measure

In information retrieval systems, the user is interested in relevant answers from the system. Therefore, information retrieval systems require the evaluation of precision and recall of answers. The precision (P) is the fraction of recovered documents that are relevant.

$$Precision = \frac{\#(\ relevant\ elements\ retrieved)}{\#(elements\ retrieved)} = P(relevant|retrieved) \quad (3)$$

The chart in Fig. 7 shows that our proposed model outperforms the other standard low-level features models with average retrieval precision of 83.10%, The improvement in average precision is seen in all classes of the dataset, since VGG-16 is pre-trained on the ImageNet dataset it learned how to distinguish between different objects in images. Table 1 shows the improvement in the average retrieval precision obtained by the propsed method compered to other methods based on low-level features. We also compered the precision results with the work using color and shape features fusion in [11]. The average precision attained by low-level features independently is fluctuating between 34.8% and 39.7%, and for the fused features the average precision reached 81.5% witch is still 1.6% less than the average precision attained by our proposed method.

In our model we have set the lastFourTrainable layer to false, then just the last fully connected layer of the model will be trainable. But if we set this parameter to true, then the last four layers of the model, which have parameters will be trainable, and instead of just extracting the features from images, the model will learn more about the dataset and that may improve the precision.

Table 1. Precision improvement rate compering to the proposed model.

Model	Color feature	Texture feature	Shape feature	Fusion features
Precision	39.7%	39.2%	34.8%	81.5%
Improvement	43.4%	43.9%	48.3%	1.6%

6 Conclusion

In this paper, we conducted a search on the recent development in the field of CBIR and tested some of the retrieval systems based on Low-level features, then we presented a CBIR system based deep convolutional networks [32] to extract high-level features in order to reduce the semantic gap between images content represented by low-level features and visual human perception, for the CNN we choose the VGG16 pre-trained model on ImageNet dataset, and used the transfer learning technique to adapt the weights of the pre-trained model to our dataset. As for the similarity metric, we used the chi-square distance to match between the query feature vector and the target feature vector in the image dataset. The experimental result for the suggested approach is carried out on Corel-1K and experimented on Python tools. The performance of the suggested approach showed that it has better performance and higher precision rate compared to other standard CBIR approaches.

References

1. Kiran, D., Suresh Babu, C.H., Venu Gopal, T.: An Improved CBIR system using low-level image features extraction and representation. Int. J. Appl. Eng. Res. **12**(19), 9032–9037 (2017). ISSN 0973–4562
2. Nagaraja, S., Prabhakar, C.J.: Low-level features for image retrieval based on extraction of directional binary patterns and its oriented gradients histogram. Comput. Appl. Int. J. (CAIJ) **2**(1) (2015)
3. Arnold, W.M., Marcel, W., Amarnath, G., Ramesh, J.: Content-based image retrieval at the end of the early years. IEEE Trans. Pattern Anal. Mach. Intell. **22**(12), 1349–1380 (2000)
4. Barz, B., Denzler, J.: Content-based image retrieval and the semantic gap in the deep learning era. In: International Workshop on Content-Based Image Retrieval: Where Have We Been, and Where are We Going (CBIR 2020) (2020)
5. Jun, Y., Zhenbo, L., Lu, L., Zetian, F.: Content-based image retrieval using color and texture fused features. Math. Comput. Model. **54**(3–4), 1121–1127 (2011)
6. Farhani, N., Terbeh, N., Zrigui, M.: Object recognition approach based on generalized Hough transform and color distribution serving in generating Arabic sentences. Int. J. Comput. Inf. Eng. **13**, 339–344 (2019)
7. Reshma Chaudhari, A.M.: Patil: content based image retrieval using color and shape features. Int. J. Adv. Res. Electr. Electron. Instrum. Eng. **1**(5), 386–392 (2012)

8. Anusha, V., Reddy, V.U., Ramashri, T.: Content Based Image Retrieval Using Color Moments and Texture. Int. J. Eng. Res. Technol. (IJERT) **3**(2), 2812–2815 (2014). ISSN: 2278–0181

9. Farhani, N., Terbeh, N., Zrigui, M.: Image to text conversion: state of the art and extended work. In: 2017 IEEE/ACS 14th International Conference on Computer Systems and Applications (AICCSA), November 2017. ISSN: 2161–5330

10. Nigam, A., Garg, A.K., Tripathi, R.C.: Content based trademark retrieval by integrating shape with colour and texture. Inf. Int. J. Comput. Appl. (0975–8887) **22**(7), 40–45 (2011)

11. Nazir, A., Nazir, K.: An efficient image retrieval based on fusion of low-level visual features. Comput. Res. Repository (CoRR) (2018)

12. Mallat, S., Zouaghi, A., Hkiri, E., Zrigui, M.: Method of lexical enrichment in information retrieval system in Arabic. Proc. Int. J. Inf. Retrieval Res. (IJIRR) **3**(4), 35–51 (2013)

13. Zrigui, M., Charhad, M., Zouaghi, A.: A framework of indexation and document video retrieval based on the conceptual graphs. J. Comput. Inf. Technol. **18**(3), 245–256 (2010)

14. Kavitha, Ch., Prabhakara Rao, B., Govardhan, A.: Image retrieval based on color and texture features of the image sub-blocks. Int. J. Comput. Appl. (0975–8887) **15**(7), 33–37 (2011)

15. Shirazi, S.H., Arif, U., Saeeda, N., Noor, K., Muhammad, R., Bandar, A.: Content-based image retrieval using texture color shape and region. (IJACSA) Int. J. Adv. Comput. Sci. Appl. **7**(1), 418–426 (2016)

16. Raina, R., Battle, A., Lee, H., Packer, B., et al.: Self-taught learning: transfer learning from unlabeled data. In: Proceedings of the 24th International Conference on Machine Learning, pp. 759–766 (2007)

17. Keras Applications. https://keras.io/api/applications/

18. Mounir, A.J., Souheyl, M., Zrigui, M.: Analyzing satellite images by apply deep learning instance segmentation of agricultural fields. Periodicals Eng. Natural Sci. **9**(4), 1056–1069 (2021)

19. Sebastian ruder. The State of Transfer Learning in NLP. https://ruder.io/state-of-transfer-learning-in-nlp/

20. Cheikh, M., Zrigui, M.: Active learning based framework for image captioning corpus creation. In: Kotsireas, I.S., Pardalos, P.M. (eds.) LION 2020. LNCS, vol. 12096, pp. 128–142. Springer, Cham (2020). https://doi.org/10.1007/978-3-030-53552-0_14

21. Maraoui, M., Antoniadis, G., Zrigui, M.: CALL system for Arabic based on natural language processing tools. In: IICAI 2009, pp. 2249–2258 (2009)

22. Merhbene, L., Zouaghi, A., Zrigui, M.: Lexical disambiguation of Arabic language: an experimental study. Polibits **46**, 49–54 (2012)

23. Haffar, N., Ayadi, R., Hkiri, E., Zrigui, M.: Temporal ordering of events via deep neural networks. In: Lladós, J., Lopresti, D., Uchida, S. (eds.) ICDAR 2021. LNCS, vol. 12822, pp. 762–777. Springer, Cham (2021). https://doi.org/10.1007/978-3-030-86331-9_49

24. Haffar, N., Hkiri, E., Zrigui, M.: Using bidirectional LSTM and shortest dependency path for classifying Arabic temporal relations. Procedia Comput. Sci. **176**, 370–379 (2020)

25. Zouaghi, A., Zrigui, M., Antoniadis, G.: Compréhension automatique de la parole arabe spontanée : Une modélisation numérique". Revue TAL Varia. No. 1, Janvier 2008, Vol. 49 (2008)

26. Terbeh, N., Labidi, M., Zrigui, M.: Automatic speech correction: A step to speech recognition for people with disabilities. In: ICTA 2013, Hammamet, Tunisia, 23–26 October (2013)
27. Slimi, A., Hamroun, M., Zrigui, M., Nicolas, H.: Emotion recognition from speech using spectrograms and shallow neural networks. In: Proceedings of the 18th International Conference on Advance Mobile Computing Multimedia, pp. 35–39, November 2020
28. Maraoui, M., Terbeh, N., Zrigui, M.: Arabic discourse analysis based on acoustic, prosodic and phonetic modeling: elocution evaluation, speech classification and pathological speech correction. Int. J. Speech Technol. **21**(4), 1071–1090 (2018). https://doi.org/10.1007/s10772-018-09566-6
29. Patil, S., Talbar, S.: Content based image retrieval using various distance metrics. In: Kannan, R., Andres, F. (eds.) ICDEM 2010. LNCS, vol. 6411, pp. 154–161. Springer, Heidelberg (2012). https://doi.org/10.1007/978-3-642-27872-3_23
30. Karen, S., Andrew, Z.: Very Deep Convolutional Networks for Large-Scale Image Recognition, Published as a conference paper at ICLR 2015 (2015)
31. https://www.geeksforgeeks.org/chi-square-distance-in-python/
32. Mahmoud, A., Zrigui, M.: Deep neural network models for paraphrased text classification in the Arabic language NLDB, pp. 3–16 (2019)

An Effective Detection and Classification Approach for DoS Attacks in Wireless Sensor Networks Using Deep Transfer Learning Models and Majority Voting

Safa Ben Atitallah[1]([envelope]) [iD], Maha Driss[1,2] [iD], Wadii Boulila[1,3] [iD], and Iman Almomani[2,4] [iD]

[1] RIADI Laboratory, University of Manouba, 2010 Manouba, Tunisia
safa.benatitallah@ensi-uma.tn
[2] Security Engineering Lab, CCIS, Prince Sultan University, Riyadh 12435, Saudi Arabia
[3] Robotics and Internet-of-Things Lab, Prince Sultan University, Riyadh 12435, Saudi Arabia
[4] CS Department, King Abdullah II School of Information Technology, The University of Jordan, Amman 11942, Jordan

Abstract. The Internet of Things (IoT) has been used in various critical fields, including healthcare, elderly surveillance, autonomous transportation, and energy management. As a result of its emergence, several IoT-based smart applications have been established in various domains. Wireless Sensor Networks (WSNs) are the most common infrastructure for these applications. A WSN is a network that includes many diverse sensor nodes. These nodes are scattered across large areas, collecting data and transmitting it wirelessly. These networks are subjected to a variety of security threats. Protecting WSNs against incoming threats is both necessary and challenging. This paper presents a deep transfer learning-based approach for intrusion detection and classification in WSNs. To identify and categorize Denial-of-Service (DoS) attacks, we deployed several pre-trained Convolutional Neural Networks (CNNs). To improve the classification performance, the final outputs of the CNN models are combined using ensemble learning, precisely the majority voting method. We used the recent and rich WSN-DS dataset for the experiments, which includes four types of DoS attacks as well as benign samples. The experimental findings confirm the effectiveness of the suggested method, which provides an accuracy of 100%.

Keywords: Wireless sensor networks · DoS attacks · Intrusion detection and classification · Convolutional neural networks · Transfer learning · Ensemble learning

This work is supported by Prince Sultan University in Saudi Arabia.

1   Introduction

IoT is a new technology that has enabled the collecting, processing, and sharing data in smart environments. Because the IoT provides advanced big data analytics assets at the network edge, it has attracted scientists, researchers, and industrials from diverse fields [11, 18, 22]. IoT applications are undergoing a phenomenal evolution and emergence. According to Statista [3], the total installed base of IoT-linked devices globally is estimated to reach 30.9 billion units by 2025, representing a significant rise from the 16.4 billion units projected by the end of 2022. The IoT's basic building blocks are WSNs. WSNs are made up of geographically distributed autonomous sensors that operate together to monitor the physical environment and transmit data to a central station [26]. Both the IoT and WSNs technologies have contributed to the development of broad variety of essential and critical applications that touch practically every aspect of modern life, such as healthcare, energy, agriculture, and transportation. However, these networks are vulnerable to a variety of security flaws, and this is due to their dispersed and wireless nature [4, 10, 16, 21]. Indeed, because sensors have limited battery capacity, fewer calculations can be done to extend the network's lifetime, limiting the deployment of common security procedures and rendering the network vulnerable. Attackers may easily exploit such insecure networks to get network access, which is a significant security concern in WSNs.

WSNs are particularly vulnerable to DoS attacks when deployed in a hostile environment where sensor nodes are physically seized, and controlled [23]. DoS attacks [14] reduce or severely damage internet bandwidth and can trigger conventional connections' termination by flooding the network with massive volumes of useless data. Several types of DoS attacks have been identified by the taxonomic analysis of WSN's jamming threats [24], the most prominent of which are Blackhole, Grayhole, Flooding, and Scheduling. When compared to conventional wired and wireless networks, DoS attacks in WSNs are generally prominent. WSNs and IoT architectures present several vulnerabilities at practically every layer, making them a potential target of DoS attacks that can be implemented by employing various attack techniques. Data-driven techniques are mainly employed to build effective defensive strategies and solutions against security assaults, typically DoS attacks, in IoT and WSNs environments. These techniques rely on Deep Learning (DL) and Machine Learning (ML)-based approaches. Recently, the Transfer Learning (TL) of deep CNNs has gained popularity in many industries and applications. Its purpose is to reuse DL models that have already been trained as the basis for new missions.

In this study, we aim to detect and classify DoS attacks by deploying a variety of pre-trained CNNs. The proposed approach adopts the TL methodology to fine-tune the core models' higher-order feature representations and make them more task-relevant. To improve the performance of the considered models, we opted for ensemble learning, precisely the majority voting method, to combine decisions from the considered CNN models that had been independently calibrated. The main contributions of this paper are highlighted in the following points:

- Propose a deep TL approach for DoS detection and classification in WSNs;
- Adopt a visualized approach allowing to transform the tabular data of DoS attacks into images to be used as inputs for the pre-trained CNNs;
- Use five pre-trained CNN models for DoS detection and classification, which eliminates the need for features engineering;
- Conduct the experiments using a recent, massive, and highly imbalanced dataset, which is the WSN-DS dataset, including more than 374000 records with 19 features. WSN-DS is constituted by Blackhole, Grayhole, Flooding, and Scheduling attacks, as well as normal (i.e., benign) records;
- Apply majority voting technique to ensure high detection and classification performance measures for each DoS attack type;
- Compare the obtained performance results with the recent related ML and DL-based approaches that have carried out their experiments on the same dataset.

The present article is divided into six sections. Section 2 examines recent relevant works about DL/ML-based DoS detection and classification in IoT and WSNs ecosystems. In Sect. 3, the used dataset for the paper experiments is described. The proposed approach is presented in depth in Sect. 4. Section 5 summarizes the experiments and analyzes the findings. Finally, Sect. 6 highlights the major contributions made by this study and suggests future research directions.

2 Related Work

WSNs and IoT infrastructures present several vulnerabilities at almost every layer, making them a potential subject of DoS attacks that can be carried out via the use of various attack techniques and strategies. As a result, efficient IoT security solutions research remains a top concern in such highly distributed and heterogeneous ecosystems. Various analytical approaches have been used in many DoS detection and classification studies. ML, DL, and vision-based algorithms have recently been used to conduct extensive research on DoS detection and classification in IoT and WSNs. This section summarizes recent and pertinent DoS detection and classification approaches that employ these techniques.

For instance, Almomani et al. [8] designed an Artificial Neural Network (ANN) for detecting and classifying different DoS attack types. They developed and employed the WSN-DS dataset in this work. The data were collected using the NS-2 simulator. The collected records contained the signatures of the different classes of attacks. Their ANN achieved an acceptable classification accuracy rate with 92.8%, 99.4%, 92.2%, 75.6%, and 99.8% for Blackhole, Flooding, Scheduling, Grayhole, and benign samples, respectively.

For DoS attacks detction, Park et al. [24] designed a Random Forest (RF) model. Using the WSN-DS dataset, the proposed model obtains good performance results with an F1-score of 99%, 96%, 98%, 96%, and 100% for Blackhole, Flooding, Grayhole, Scheduling attacks, and Normal samples, respectively.

Alqahtani et al. [9] proposed a new model to identify distinct forms of DoS assaults by using the WSN-DS dataset. The proposed GXGBoost model was built on the genetic algorithm and an extreme gradient boosting classifier to enhance the detection of minority classes of assaults in highly unbalanced WSN datasets.

The SLGBM intrusion detection method for WSN DoS attacks was developed by Jiang et al. [19]. This method started by using the sequence backward selection (SBS) technique to minimize the dimensionality of data, hence lowering the computing cost. After that, the LightGBM method was employed to identify and classify the DoS attacks. Based on the WSN-DS dataset, the experimental findings revealed good results with a recall of 99.57%, 98.95%, 98.10%, and 93.07% for Blackhole, Grayhole, Flooding, and Scheduling attacks, respectively.

Almashlukh [7] proposed an end-to-end ANN architecture based on entity embedding. Instead of hand-crafted feature engineering, the proposed architecture used entity embedding to convert raw characteristics into more rigorous representations to obtain more accurate detection and classification results. After that, these representations were directly learned through a multi-layer perception (MLP) ANN classifier.

Different contemporary methodologies, such as artificial neural network-based methods and statistical and ML-based techniques, are clearly being utilized to develop effective defensive tactics and solutions against DoS attacks in WSNs. However, no previous study has used the DL and TL approaches with the rich and highly imbalanced WSN-DS dataset to build more robust and effective DoS attack applications. DL techniques have demonstrated their effectiveness in several and different applications and domains, especially in cybersecurity field [5,20] since they have improved capabilities for extracting, identifying, and classifying higher-order features from raw and massive datasets. Recently, the TL of deep CNNs has gained popularity in a wide range of industrial and research applications [6,12,13]. Its goal is to utilize previously trained DL models as the foundation for future missions. This enhances performance on related difficulties while also increasing the effectiveness of training [27]. The goal of this study is to use a variety of pre-trained CNNs to identify and categorize DoS assaults. The suggested method uses the TL methodology to fine-tune the higher-order feature representations of the core models such that they are more task-relevant.

3   Dataset

In this study, the WSN-DS dataset [8] is employed to assess the effectiveness of the suggested approach. The collection of the WSN-DS dataset considered the use of the Low Energy Aware Cluster Hierarchy (LEACH) protocol [17], which is one of the most prominent hierarchical routing protocols in WSNs. To collect the necessary data and features, NS-2 [1] was utilized. WSN-DS contains 374661 records with 19 features representing four types of DoS, including Blackhole, Grayhole, Flooding, Scheduling attacks, and benign samples. An explanation of each attack type and its distribution are presented in Table 1.

Table 1. Distribution of the WSN-DS dataset.

Attack type	Description	No. of records
Blackhole	A DoS attack disrupts the LEACH protocol by posing as a CH at the beginning of the round. Then it starts dropping all received packets and does not forward them	10048
Grayhole	A DoS attack disrupts the LEACH protocol by posing as a CH for other nodes. Then it starts selectively or randomly dropping the received packets and not forwarding them	14596
Flooding	A DoS attack disrupts the LEACH protocol in different ways. For example, the attacker can send large number of control messages with high transmission power to consume the network resources	3312
Scheduling	A DoS attack occurs during the LEACH protocol's setup. The attacker poisons the schedule by setting the same time slot for all nodes to transmit data. Consequently, causing packets collision that introduces data loss.	6638
Normal	Normal records with no attack	340066
Total	Totat number of instances in the WSN-DS dataset	**374662**

4 Proposed Approach

This study aims to provide a vision-based DoS attacks detection and classification solution that addresses the shortcomings of existing attack detection systems. To improve detection and classification performance results, the suggested approach uses the advantages of pre-trained CNN architectures and ensemble learning methods.

The proposed approach is divided into four steps, as depicted in Fig. 1, which are: 1) data preprocessing, 2) data transformation, 3) transfer learning, and 4) ensemble learning-based on majority voting. The dataset is first cleaned, filtered, and normalized. Then, the tabular data samples of the WSN-DS dataset are transformed into grayscale images. After that, five pre-trained CNN architectures are loaded with their pre-learned weights, fine-tuned, and trained on the transformed WSN-DS dataset. ResNet18, DenseNet161, VGG16, SqueezeNet, and EfficientNetB3 are the five models utilized for TL in our proposed approach. Finally, the outputs of the models are combined, and ensemble learning, precisely the majority voting method, is used to offer more accurate classification results.

4.1 Data Preprocessing

To eliminate the influence of the attack label letters on the deployed CNNs, these labels need to be converted to numeric values. Blackhole, Flooding, Grayhole, Normal, and, Scheduling are the existent types in the WSN-DS dataset. For the conducted experiments, these types are transformed to be represented using numbers 0, 1, 2, 3, and 4 and used as data labels, as it is depicted in Table 2.

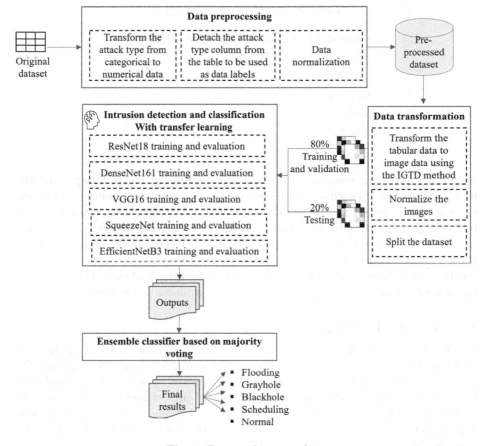

Fig. 1. Proposed approach.

Normalization is an essential technique in data preparation for various ML/DL applications. Normalization's primary purpose is to turn data into dimensionless and similar distributions. After removing the id and time features from the dataset and focusing on the remaining 16 features, the values of these features are normalized between 0.0 and 1.0 using Eq. 1.

$$x' = \frac{(x - x_{min})}{(x_{max} - x_{min})} \tag{1}$$

where x presents the raw feature value, x_{max} is the highest feature value, and x_{min} is the lowest.

4.2   Data Transformation

In this step, the data is transformed from a table to grayscale images using the image generator for tabular data (IGTD) algorithm proposed by Zhu et al. in

Table 2. Transformed attack types.

Original attack type	Transformed attack type
Blackhole	0
Flooding	1
Grayhole	2
Normal	3
Scheduling	4

[28]. Each feature is matched to a pixel in the resulting image by applying the IGTD algorithm. According to this matching, for each data sample, an image is created with pixel intensity indicating the sample's related feature value. The IGTD algorithm aims to minimize the difference between scores of paired distances among features and scores of paired distances among the allocated image pixels. IGTD permits the creation of concise picture representations while preserving and enhancing the organization of feature neighborhood. The generated images will be utilized as input for the CNNs' training in the next step.

4.3 Transfer Learning

This step aims to address this new DoS attacks detection and classification problem by using existing knowledge. Instead of developing and training DL models from scratch, that requires a lot of time as well as needs a large number of computing resources and data, the application of pre-trained CNN architectures by reusing their layers' weights will facilitate and enhance the learning process. This paper uses five pre-trained CNNs, namely ResNet18, DenseNet161, VGG16, SqueezeNet, and EfficientNetB3 for TL.

4.4 Ensemble Classifier Based on Majority Voting

The last step is to create a majority voting-based ensemble classifier. The majority voting technique [25] aims to count the votes for all classes and returns the class with the most n votes. This technique's fundamental concept is to choose the final output class from the most commonly anticipated one. Each model predicts a classification. The classification results are recorded in a vector: $[\mathcal{R}1(x), \mathcal{R}2(x), ..., \mathcal{R}n(x)]$, where n represents the total number of used classifiers. The voting procedure is then applied to determine the output class $\mathcal{Y}$ of a test sample based on the most often predicted class in the vector by computing Eq. 2.

$$\mathcal{Y} = mode[\mathcal{R}_1(x), \mathcal{R}_2(x), ..., \mathcal{R}_n(x)] \tag{2}$$

5 Experiments

In this section, we begin by discussing the implementation details. Then, performance metrics are described. Finally, results and comparisons with existing approaches are detailed.

5.1   Implementation Details

The experiments in this research are conducted out on a PC with the following setting properties: a CPU based on x64; an Intel Core i9-11900H (11th Gen); a 32 GB RAM; and a NVIDIA GeForce RTX 3080 (8G) graphics card. Jupyter notebook with Python 3.8 programming language are used to program the whole process. We have employed the PyTorch library [2]. PyTorch is an open-source, adaptable, and extensible framework built on the Torch library. It supports distributed training, computer vision, and natural language processing. Different libraries and tools are provided by PyTorch to accelerate the development of DL models, optimize production, and enable easy scaling.

5.2   Performance Metrics

To evaluate the performance of the suggested approach, we compute the recall, precision, F1-score, and accuracy metrics. These metrics are computed according to the following equations:

$$Precision = \frac{TP}{TP + FP} \tag{3}$$

$$Recall = \frac{TP}{TP + FN} \tag{4}$$

$$F1 - score = \frac{2 * Precision * Recall}{Precision + Recall} \tag{5}$$

$$Accuracy = \frac{TP + TN}{TP + TN + FP + FN} \tag{6}$$

where:

- The number of samples correctly categorized as attacks is referred as True Positive (TP).
- The number of samples incorrectly categorized as attacks is referred as False Positive (FP).
- The number of samples correctly categorized as normal samples is referred as True Negative (TN).
- The number of samples incorrectly categorized as normal samples while they are attacks is referred as False Negative (FN).

5.3   Results

After data preprocessing, the IGTD algorithm is used to convert the WSN-DS dataset into image representations. Examples of the generated images are illustrated in Fig. 2. The suggested approach's main purpose is to appropriately identify and categorize DoS attacks in WSNs. ResNet18, DenseNet161, VGG16, SqueezeNet, and EfficientNetB3 were used to achieve this goal. The five CNN architectures are trained over 25 epochs. For the models' configuration, the Adam

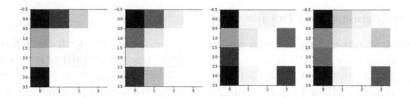

Fig. 2. Examples of images generated using the IGTD algorithm (16 features are used).

Table 3. The used parameters for models' training.

Models training parameters	Values
Batch size	64
Epochs	25
Images size	150, 150
Optimizer	Adam
Loss function	Cross-entropy

optimizer, the cross-entropy loss function, and the SoftMax activation function have been used. Table 3 illustrates the parameters setting of the models' training.

Precision, recall, F1-score, accuracy, and training time measures are used to evaluate the CNN models fine-tuned and trained on the processed dataset. Dataset is split as 60%, 20%, and 20% for training, validation, and testing, respectively. The overall models' effectiveness was assessed through the test images. As shown in Table 4, it is clear that the DenseNet161 model performed the best with an accuracy of 99.995%, while the VGG16 model obtained the lowest performance. The performance of all the CNNs is excellent and accurate, and there is not a significant difference in results. ResNet18, SqueezeNet, and EfficientNetB3 had very similar performances with an accuracy of about 99.9%.

The approach's next step is to apply ensemble learning, which integrates the output of all the pre-trained CNNs through the majority voting technique. The performance of this classifier is assessed using the testing dataset. Table 4 presents a comparison of performance results of the used TL-based DL classifiers. It is obvious that the proposed classifier produces higher classification results and exceeds the performance of individual CNNs. It achieved 100% of precision, recall, F1-score, and accuracy. The ensemble classifier with TL demonstrated an excellent performance for the DoS attacks detection. The confusion matrix of the proposed approach for detecting and classifying the DoS attacks is depicted in Fig. 3.

The results prove the role of both, TL and ensemble learning, for the correct and robust DoS attacks detection and classification.

5.4   Comparison with Existing ML/DL-based Approaches

We compare the findings of the proposed approach to the previously published studies, which used the same dataset, to verify its performance. The comparison

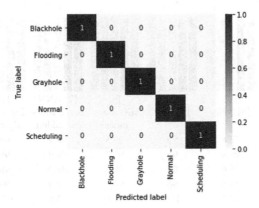

Fig. 3. Normalized confusion matrix for the Dos attacks detection and classification using the proposed approach.

Table 4. Comparison of performance results of different TL-based DL classifiers.

Model	Class	Precision	Recall	F1-score	Accuracy	Training time
ResNet18	Blackhole	99.90	99.95	99.92	99.983	219 m 50 s
	Flooding	98.95	100	100		
	Grayhole	100	99.96	99.98		
	Normal	100	99.95	99.97		
	Scheduling	99.77	99.84	99.81		
DenseNet161	Blackhole	100	100	100	99.995	1043 m 56 s
	Flooding	100	99.84	99.92		
	Grayhole	100	100	100		
	Normal	99.99	100	99.99		
	Scheduling	100	100	100		
VGG16	Blackhole	99.90	99.95	99.92	99.951	744 m 46 s
	Flooding	98.95	100	100		
	Grayhole	100	99.96	99.98		
	Normal	100	99.95	99.97		
	Scheduling	99.77	99.84	99.81		
SqueezeNet	Blackhole	99.95	100	99.97	99.959	98 m 13 s
	Flooding	99.39	99.54	100		
	Grayhole	99.93	100	99.65		
	Normal	99.98	99.97	99.98		
	Scheduling	100	99.77	99.88		
EfficientNetB3	Blackhole	100	100	100	99.991	555 m 21 s
	Flooding	100	99.69	99.84		
	Grayhole	100	100	100		
	Normal	99.98	100	99.99		
	Scheduling	100	100	100		
Proposed approach	Blackhole	100	100	100	100	–
	Flooding	100	100	100		
	Grayhole	100	100	100		
	Normal	100	100	100		
	Scheduling	100	100	100		

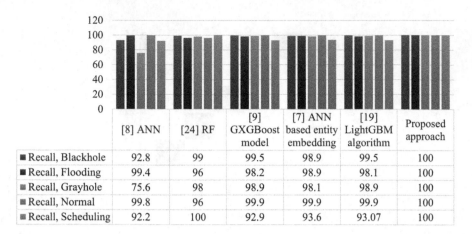

	[8] ANN	[24] RF	[9] GXGBoost model	[7] ANN based entity embedding	[19] LightGBM algorithm	Proposed approach
■ Recall, Blackhole	92.8	99	99.5	98.9	99.5	100
■ Recall, Flooding	99.4	96	98.2	98.9	98.1	100
■ Recall, Grayhole	75.6	98	98.9	98.1	98.9	100
■ Recall, Normal	99.8	96	99.9	99.9	99.9	100
■ Recall, Scheduling	92.2	100	92.9	93.6	93.07	100

Fig. 4. Performance comparison of the proposed approach with related studies.

is made among papers that worked with the same problem and utilized the same dataset, the WSN-DS dataset. As shown by the performance results in Fig. 4, our model achieved the greatest recall percent among the evaluated studies that are mainly based on ML methods and ANNs. This is justified by the fact of adopting the DL, TL, and ensemble learning techniques in our approach. The effectiveness of this methodology is proved in our case study, dealing with DoS attacks in WSNs, by increasing the detection accuracy and ensuring the correct classification. In fact, the transformation of tabular data into images has allowed the use of TL through different pre-trained CNN architectures, which efficiently coped with the dataset's massively imbalanced distribution of classes. This is evident from Fig. 4, where it is noticed that works [7,9,19] obtained high recall, between 98.1% and 99.9%, for Blackhole, Flooding, Grayhole, and Normal classes. However, the Scheduling class had less accuracy compared to the other classes. The obtained results reveal that using the TL and ensemble learning techniques on the transformed WSN-DS dataset images has a considerable influence on the performance of the deployed CNN models and has dealt well with the severe imbalance of the WSN-DS dataset, where we acheived high precision, recall, F1-score, and accuracy for all DoS classes.

6   Conclusion

This paper proposes an efficient DoS attacks detection and classification approach in WSNs. The proposed methodology is based on TL and ensemble learning to detect the attack then classify it into one of four classes: Blackhole, Flooding, Grayhole, and Scheduling. A set of pre-trained CNN architectures is used to ensure high DoS attacks detection and classification performance, including ResNet18, DenseNet161, VGG16, SqueezeNet, and EfficientNetB3. In addition an ensemble classifier based on majority voting is adopted to combine the results of these CNNs and provide more accurate results. Extensive experiments were conducted on the WSN-DS dataset. For evaluation, the performance of the suggested approach was assessed with different performance metrics, including precision, recall, F1-score and accuracy. The experiments' results demonstrated that the suggested approach detects and classifies DoS attacks in WSNs in an accurate and efficient manner.

In future work, we plan to evaluate the performance of the suggested approach on other public, huge, and highly imbalanced datasets. Furthermore, we plan to examine the potential field of federated learning, which is an exciting technique that has found tremendous success in bringing intelligence to various distributed systems and applications by enabling participating devices to train a global model initialized from a central authority independently [15].

References

1. The network simulator - ns-2. http://nsnam.sourceforge.net/wiki/index.php/User_Information. Accessed 30 Mar 2022
2. Pytorch - from research to production. https://pytorch.org/, Accessed 30 Mar 2022
3. Statista-internet of things (IoT) and non-IoT active device connections worldwide from 2010 to 2025. https://www.statista.com/statistics/1101442/iot-number-of-connected-devices-worldwide, Accessed 22 Feb 2022
4. Ghaleb, F.A., et al.: Misbehavior-aware on-demand collaborative intrusion detection system using distributed ensemble learning for vanet. Electronics 9(9), 1411 (2020)
5. Al-Garadi, M.A., Mohamed, A., Al-Ali, A.K., Du, X., Ali, I., Guizani, M.: A survey of machine and deep learning methods for internet of things (IoT) security. IEEE Commun. Surv. Tutor. 22(3), 1646–1685 (2020)
6. Alkhelaiwi, M., Boulila, W., Ahmad, J., Koubaa, A., Driss, M.: An efficient approach based on privacy-preserving deep learning for satellite image classification. Rem. Sens. 13(11), 2221 (2021)
7. Almaslukh, B.: Deep learning and entity embedding-based intrusion detection model for wireless sensor networks. CMC Comput. Mater. Contin 69, 1343–1360 (2021)
8. Almomani, I., Al-Kasasbeh, B., Al-Akhras, M.: WSN-DS: a dataset for intrusion detection systems in wireless sensor networks. J. Sens. 2016 (2016)
9. Alqahtani, M., Gumaei, A., Mathkour, H., Ismail, M.M.B.: A genetic-based extreme gradient boosting model for detecting intrusions in wireless sensor networks. Sensors 19(20), 4383 (2019)
10. Ben Atitallah, S., Driss, M., Almomani, I.: A novel detection and multi-classification approach for IoT-malware using random forest voting of fine-tuning convolutional neural networks. Sensors 22(11), 4302 (2022)
11. Ben Atitallah, S., Driss, M., Boulila, W., Ben Ghézala, H.: Leveraging deep learning and IoT big data analytics to support the smart cities development: review and future directions. Comput. Sci. Rev. 38, 100303 (2020)
12. Ben Atitallah, S., Driss, M., Boulila, W., Ben Ghezala, H.: Randomly initialized convolutional neural network for the recognition of covid-19 using x-ray images. Int. J. Imaging Syst. Technol. 32(1), 55–73 (2022)

13. Ben Atitallah, S., Driss, M., Boulila, W., Koubaa, A., Ben Ghezala, H.: Fusion of convolutional neural networks based on dempster-shafer theory for automatic pneumonia detection from chest x-ray images. Int. J. Imaging Syst. Technol. **32**(2), 658–672 (2022)
14. Bhatt, S., Ragiri, P.R., et al.: Security trends in internet of things: a survey. SN Appl. Sci. **3**(1), 1–14 (2021)
15. Driss, M., Almomani, I., Ahmad, J., et al.: A federated learning framework for cyberattack detection in vehicular sensor networks. Complex Intell. Syst., 1–15 (2022)
16. Hassan, W.H., et al.: Current research on Internet of Things (IoT) security: a survey. Comput. Netw. **148**, 283–294 (2019)
17. Heinzelman, W.R., Chandrakasan, A., Balakrishnan, H.: Energy-efficient communication protocol for wireless microsensor networks. In: Proceedings of the 33rd Annual Hawaii International Conference on System Sciences, p. 10. IEEE (2000)
18. Jemmali, M.: Intelligent algorithms and complex system for a smart parking for vaccine delivery center of Covid-19. Complex Intell. Syst., 1–13 (2021)
19. Jiang, S., Zhao, J., Xu, X.: SLGBM: an intrusion detection mechanism for wireless sensor networks in smart environments. IEEE Access **8**, 169548–169558 (2020)
20. Kumar, P., Kumar, A.A., Sahayakingsly, C., Udayakumar, A.: Analysis of intrusion detection in cyber attacks using deep learning neural networks. Peer-to-Peer Netw. Appl. **14**(4), 2565–2584 (2021)
21. Lata, S., Mehfuz, S., Urooj, S.: Secure and reliable WSN for Internet of Things: challenges and enabling technologies. IEEE Access **9**, 161103–161128 (2021)
22. Latif, S., Driss, M., Boulila, W., Huma, Z.e., Jamal, S.S., Idrees, Z., Ahmad, J.: Deep learning for the industrial internet of things (iiot): a comprehensive survey of techniques, implementation frameworks, potential applications, and future directions. Sensors **21**(22), 7518 (2021)
23. Mittal, M., Kumar, K., Behal, S.: Deep learning approaches for detecting ddos attacks: a systematic review. Soft Comput., 1–37 (2022)
24. Park, T., Cho, D., Kim, H., et al.: An effective classification for dos attacks in wireless sensor networks. In: 2018 Tenth International Conference on Ubiquitous and Future Networks (ICUFN), pp. 689–692. IEEE (2018)
25. Rehman, M.U., Shafique, A., Khalid, S., Driss, M., Rubaiee, S.: Future forecasting of Covid-19: a supervised learning approach. Sensors **21**(10), 3322 (2021)
26. Shahraki, A., Taherkordi, A., Haugen, Ø., Eliassen, F.: A survey and future directions on clustering: from WSNs to IoT and modern networking paradigms. IEEE Trans. Netw. Serv. Manag. **18**(2), 2242–2274 (2020)
27. Tan, C., Sun, F., Kong, T., Zhang, W., Yang, C., Liu, C.: A survey on deep transfer learning. In: Kůrková, V., Manolopoulos, Y., Hammer, B., Iliadis, L., Maglogiannis, I. (eds.) ICANN 2018. LNCS, vol. 11141, pp. 270–279. Springer, Cham (2018). https://doi.org/10.1007/978-3-030-01424-7_27
28. Zhu, Y., et al.: Converting tabular data into images for deep learning with convolutional neural networks. Sci. Rep. **11**(1), 1–11 (2021)

SSTop3: Sole-Top-Three and Sum-Top-Three Class Prediction Ensemble Method Using Deep Learning Classification Models

Abdulaziz Anorboev[1] , Javokhir Musaev[1] , Jeongkyu Hong[1(✉)] ,
Ngoc Thanh Nguyen[2] , and Dosam Hwang[1(✉)]

[1] Yeungnam University, Daegu, Republic of Korea
jhong@yu.ac.kr, dosamhwang@gmail.com
[2] Wroclaw University of Science and Technology, Wroclaw, Poland
Ngoc-Thanh.Nguyen@pwr.edu.pl

Abstract. Computer Vision (CV) has been employed in several different industries, with remarkable success in image classification applications, such as medicine, production quality control, transportation systems, etc. CV models rely on excessive images to train prospective models. Usually, the process of acquiring images is expensive and time-consuming. In this study, we propose a method that consists of multiple steps to increase image classification accuracy with a small amount of data. In the initial step, we set up multiple datasets from an existing dataset. Because an image carries pixel values between 0 and 255, we divided the images into pixel intervals depending on dataset type. If the dataset is grayscale, the pixel interval is divided into two parts, whereas it is divided into five intervals when the dataset consists of RGB images. In the next step, we trained the model using the original dataset and each created datasets separately. In the training process, each image illustrates a non-identical prediction space where we propose a top-three prediction probability ensemble method. Top-three predictions of newly generated images are ensemble to the corresponding probabilities of the original image. Results demonstrate that learning patterns from each pixel interval and ensemble the top three prediction vastly improves the performance and accuracy and the method can be applied to any model.

Keywords: Deep learning ensemble method · Classification task · Image pixel interval

1 Introduction

In this work, we focus mainly on two key issues for knowledge transferring and ensemble: what to transfer and when to ensemble. We propose Image Pixel Interval Power (IPIP) that is divided into subsection according to the data type: Image Pixels' Double Representation (IPDR) and Image Pixels' Multiple Representation (IPMR). Detailed explanation of IPDR and IPMR was given in Sect. 3. The second method is Top Three

© The Author(s), under exclusive license to Springer Nature Switzerland AG 2022
C. Bădică et al. (Eds.): ICCCI 2022, CCIS 1653, pp. 193–199, 2022.
https://doi.org/10.1007/978-3-031-16210-7_15

Prediction that is ensemble prediction probabilities from multiple CNN model to target high accuracy classification.

In our current work, we applied IPDR and IPMR sub methods combined with configuration changes in the Top Three Prediction Probability method. Because our current method consists of multitasks, it begins with dividing the dataset into sub methods, depending on the type of dataset. If the dataset consists of single color images, the IPDR sub method is applied. If the dataset is colorful that is the RGB type, the IPMR sub method is applied. After dividing the image pixels interval, each dataset is trained using the custom-made model. At the next stage of the method, we ensemble top-three or three maximum prediction probabilities of each trained image into the corresponding position within the prediction probabilities of the main model.

The key point to mention in the paper is the increase in accuracy. In deep learning ensemble models, it is challenging to achieve better results with few data samples. The prediction scope of an ensemble is usually located in the prediction scope of the main model and does not allow increasing the accuracy. However, with our method, we partially solved this problem and obtained better results for our models. Also the method does not affect the training of the main model because it is trained separately and includes nearly all knowledge of the main model.

The rest of this work is organized as follows. Section 2 presents previous research works that is related to our method. Section 3 explains the methodology of our work. The experiments and results are reported in Sect. 4. Section 5 presents a summary of this work and discussion for the future work.

2   Related Works

Several authors addressed in the past the issues of what, how and when to ensemble and several image preprocessing methods to increase the amount of the data. We review below the most prominent approaches.

Ensemble learning of image pixel values and prediction probabilities-based methods have shown their advantages in numerous research areas, such as image classification, natural language processing, speech recognition, and remote sensing. In recent years, many machine learning [1, 2] and deep learning models [3], including the convolutional neural network [4] and recurrent neural network have been evaluated for image classification tasks. To tackle the shortcomings of conventional classification approaches, [5] proposed a novel ensemble learning paradigm for medical diagnosis with imbalanced data, which consists of three phases: data pre-processing, training base classifier, and final ensemble. CNNs or deep residual networks are used as individual classifiers and random subspaces; to diversify the ensemble system in a simple yet effective manner to further improve the classification accuracy, ensemble and transfer learning is evaluated in [6] to transfer the learnt weights from one individual classifier to another (i.e., CNNs). The generalization of the existing semi-supervised ensembles can be strongly affected by incorrect label estimates produced by ensemble algorithms to train the supervised base learners. [7] proposed cluster-based boosting (Cboost), a multiclass classification algorithm with cluster regularization. In contrast to existing algorithms, Cboost and its base learners jointly perform a cluster-based semi-supervised optimization.

In computer vision, visual information is captured as pixel arrays. These pixel arrays are then processed by convolutions, the de-facto deep learning operator for computer vision. Convolutions treat all image pixels equally regardless of importance, explicitly model all concepts across all images, regardless of content, and struggle to relate spatially distant concepts. Majority of the above reviewed papers skipped the image pixel interval variance knowledge and ensemble of their top three prediction outcomes, which could be an effective tool to increase the classification accuracy of CNN models.

[11] proposed the Image Pixel Interval Power (IPIP) Ensemble method for DL classification tasks. Two sub methods (IPDR and IPMR), which describes IPIP to make other datasets out of original dataset that is used for a DL classification task. In this research, we studied the effect of above-mentioned method and applied ensemble of prediction outcomes in both separate and assemble methods to fulfill the gap in DL.

3 Proposed Methodology

Data Pre-processing: In the data-processing, we applied the IPIP method, that studies image pixel variance and includes two sub methods: IPDR and IPMR. IPIP is described using IPDR and IPMR. The main contribution of IPIP is the use of datasets copied from the original dataset, leaving certain interval pixel values. The difference in the number of intervals encouraged us to make an initially double representation of the main dataset and multiple representation of the main dataset.

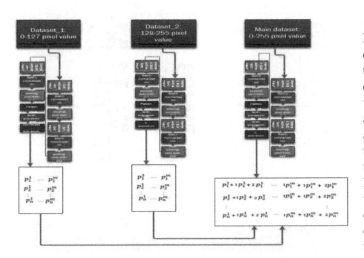

Fig. 1. Sole-Top3 ensemble method for MNIST dataset.

IPDR is a simple double representation of the main dataset. With IPDR, we create two zero arrays (dataset_1 and dataset_2) with the same size as the main dataset. In our experiments, we used the MNIST dataset. For this dataset we created two arrays with a size of 60000 × 32 × 32 × 1 all filled with zeros. For dataset_1, we took only pixel values from the main dataset that belongs to the [0:127] interval and copied and pasted them at the same position in dataset_1 and all other image pixels in the dataset changed to zeros. Dataset_2 was also built using the same method as dataset_1, except the pixel value interval for dataset_2 was [128:255]. All values higher than 127 were copied and pasted at the appropriate position in dataset_2 and all other image pixels in the dataset changed to zeros.

With the IPMR method, we applied the same method as previously described, although instead of two intervals, we used multiple intervals of 50 (i.e., [0:50], [51:100], [101:150], [151:200], and [201:255]) for the Cifar10 dataset. The number of intervals depends on the type of dataset. During our experiments, we found out that to achieve high accuracy in training the RGB channel image, they should be divided into five parts.

Training the Pre-processed Data with the Model: In the pre-processed data training, we used two different model architectures with different numbers of parameters. The main model includes 226,122 trainable parameters and is designated for the main dataset. A model of the other created datasets has 160,330 trainable parameters. We chose a smaller model for the created datasets to avoid an overuse of time and power during the IPIP implementation. Generally, the larger the model is, the higher the results achieved. The architecture for the main model consists of three convolutional layers with 32, 64, and 128 filters, and four dense layers with 256, 256, 128, and the number of class nodes for each dataset, respectively. Additionally, we used max pooling with a 2 × 2 filter and batch normalization layers in both model architectures. The filter used for the convolutional layers in both models had a size of 3 × 3. The architecture of the model includes three convolutional layers with 32, 64, and 128 filters, and three dense layers, which have following numbers of nodes: 256, 128, and the number of classes in each dataset.

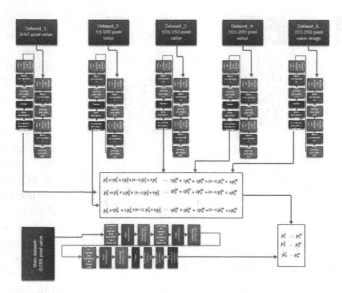

Fig. 2. Sum-Top3 ensemble method for Cifar-10 dataset.

Prediction Probability Ensemble: In this part of our method, we propose the Top-Three Prediction Probability Ensemble. Each trained dataset, in our case three datasets for MNIST dataset and six datasets for Cifar10 dataset, represents different prediction spaces. We used the top three prediction probabilities of each image that is trained in the sub model and ensemble them into main models corresponding to the prediction probabilities. The ensemble process was experimented in two distinct ways; Sole-Ensemble and Sum-Ensemble. The workflow of the sole-ensemble is shown in Fig. 1; each sub model's top three prediction probabilities merged to the main model's corresponding prediction probability. In sum-ensemble as shown in Fig. 2, the aggregate top three prediction probabilities of all sub models were ensemble into the main model's corresponding prediction probabilities.

4 Experiments and Results

4.1 Evaluation Metrics

In this work, we proposed a method that mainly focuses on the accuracy of the model. In many other studies including different metrics like the F1 score, Recall, IoU, ROC, etc. For our research, we chose two metrics that meaningfully explains the method's achievements in different datasets. The accuracy is the ratio of the true predictions to the total number of cases that are used to evaluate the model. Equation 1 shows the calculation of the accuracy.

$$Accuracy = \frac{TP + TN}{TP + TN + FP + FN} \tag{1}$$

TP-true predicted positive results
TN-true predicted negative results
FP-false predicted positive results
FN-false predicted negative results

$$UTP(X, Y) = X - X \cap Y \tag{2}$$

UTP-Unique True Prediction
X-Prediction Scope of a model X
Y-Prediction Scope of a model Y.

The next evaluation metric is UTP, which identifies the percentage of unique predictions for each model with respect to another one. In Eq. 2, UTP(X, Y) finds unique true predictions of model X with respect to model Y. This metrics explain why our proposed model achieved better results than the main model where we trained only the main dataset. The indexes of the true predicted images are different in each model and even have the same accuracy. This leads the ensemble to achieve better results. The main motivation of this work was to utilize the knowledge from the pixel level variance by changing the data representation and to achieve better accuracy metrics for the classification task of the work. After changing the data representation, we proposed the ensemble of each sub dataset's outcomes top three prediction to the main model's corresponding three predictions. We used classic training as the baseline method for the experimental evaluations. Classic training was chosen because of the difficulty of finding alternative similar methods that can be used to compare the results. Most of the DL ensemble models focused on model architectures and data representations by image level preprocessing not researching the pixel level variances. The main objective of this method is to apply it in various combinations and with many other DL ensembles simultaneously.

Our work began from preparing the dataset for training by dividing into different parts, depending on the image. Cifar-10 was divided into six types. By applying the best epoch to the test prediction, we chose the top three predictions from each sub model and ensemble into the main model's corresponding class. In the Sole-Top3 ensemble method, we achieved 73,45% accuracy, presented in Table 1. With the help of the Sole-Top3 method we successfully increased the prediction knowledge of the model compared to the IPIP method with 73,38% accuracy. Additionally, we applied the Sum-Top3 method for the trained model. The main difference between the Sum-Top3 method from the Sole-Top3 method is in the ensemble of the prediction probabilities. In the Sole-Top3 method, each sub model's top three predictions were merged to the main model's corresponding prediction class. In the Sum-Top3, the sum of the sub models' top three predictions were ensemble to the main model. Consequently, we achieved 73,58% accuracy much better than in previous methods. The same experiments were conducted with the MNIST dataset, although the data preprocessing was different. The main model was trained using the original MNIST dataset with all pixel values. In the Sole-Top3 method, we achieved 99.01% where the accuracy of the IPIP methods was 98.90%. By applying Sum-Top3 method, prediction metrics figure the accuracy was increased up to 99.07%. The comparison between our previous work's method and the Sole-Top3 and Sum-Top3 is presented in Table 1.

Table 1. Test set accuracy for MNIST and CIFAR-10 datasets and proposed methods.

Dataset	Methods	PA
MNIST	IPIP	0.9890
	Sole-Top3	0.9901
	Sum-Top3	0.9907
CIFAR-10	IPIP	0.7338
	Sole-Top3	0.7345
	Sum-Top3	0.7358

5 Conclusion

This short work proposed a method for improving the performance of classification tasks based on image pixel interval power and top-three-prediction ensembles in CNN models. The feature ensemble model was built by splitting a database into image intervals and gathering the top three predictions individually and in-group as well. We achieved better results using both the Sole-Top3 and Sum-Top3 ensembles, by merging the probabilities of sub models to the main model. It is worth noting that the use of any knowledge to improve the metrics of the CNN model will help with the development of Computer Vision in all studies. Selecting the top three prediction rather than whole class prediction probabilities adds more knowledge to the model. We attempted to solve the generalization problem of deep learning using an ensemble of prediction probabilities. There is still a huge gap in this work that needs to be addressed in this field. In the future work we plan to use ontology structures for building a knowledge base for the metadata about the images, which should be an additional sources for the classification tasks [8–10].

Acknowledgements. This work was supported by the National Research Foundation of Korea (NRF) grant funded by the Korea government (MSIT) (No.2022R1F1A1074641).

References

1. Gaikwad, D.P., Thool, R.C.: Intrusion detection system using bagging ensemble method of machine learning. In: Proceedings – 1st International Conference on Computing, Communication, Control and Automation, ICCUBEA 2015, Jul 2015, pp. 291–295. https://doi.org/10.1109/ICCUBEA.2015.61

2. Tolstikhin, I., et al.: MLP-Mixer: an all-MLP architecture for vision, May 2021 [Online]. Available: http://arxiv.org/abs/2105.01601

3. Chollet, F.: Xception: deep learning with depthwise separable convolutions, Oct 2016 [Online]. Available: http://arxiv.org/abs/1610.02357

4. Krogh, A.: Neural network ensembles, cross validation, and active learning

5. Liu, N., Li, X., Qi, E., Xu, M., Li, L., Gao, B.: A novel ensemble learning paradigm for medical diagnosis with imbalanced data. IEEE Access **8**, 171263–171280 (2020). https://doi.org/10.1109/ACCESS.2020.3014362

6. Chen, Y., Wang, Y., Gu, Y., He, X., Ghamisi, P., Jia, X.: Deep learning ensemble for hyperspectral image classification. IEEE J. Sel. Top. Appl. Earth Observ. Remote Sens. **12**(6), 1882–1897 (2019). https://doi.org/10.1109/JSTARS.2019.2915259

7. Soares, R.G.F., Chen, H., Yao, X.: A cluster-based semisupervised ensemble for multiclass classification. IEEE Trans. Emerg. Top. Comput. Intell. **1**(6), 408–420 (2017). https://doi.org/10.1109/TETCI.2017.2743219

8. Nguyen, N.T., Sobecki, J.: Using consensus methods to construct adaptive interfaces in multimodal web-based systems. J. Univ. Access Inf. Soc. **2**(4), 342–358 (2003)

9. Nguyen, N.T.: Conflicts of ontologies – classification and consensus-based methods for resolving. In: Gabrys, B., Howlett, R.J., Jain, L.C. (eds.) KES 2006. LNCS (LNAI), vol. 4252, pp. 267–274. Springer, Heidelberg (2006). https://doi.org/10.1007/11893004_34

10. Pietranik, M., Nguyen, N.T.: A multi-atrribute based framework for ontology aligning. Neurocomputing **146**, 276–290 (2014)

11. Anorboev, A., Musaev, J.: An image pixel interval power (IPIP) method using deep learning classification models. Accepted to the proceeding of ACIIDS 2022 Conference

Hyperparameter Optimization of Deep Learning Models for EEG-Based Vigilance Detection

Souhir Khessiba[1,2]([✉])[ID], Ahmed Ghazi Blaiech[1,3][ID], Antoine Manzanera[5][ID],
Khaled Ben Khalifa[1,3][ID], Asma Ben Abdallah[1,4],
and Mohamed Hédi Bedoui[1][ID]

[1] Laboratoire de Technologie et Imagerie Médicale, Faculté de Médecine de Monastir,
Université de Monastir, 5019 Monastir, Tunisie
souhirkhessiba75@gmail.com
[2] Institut Supérieur d'Informatique et des Technologies de Communication
de Hammam Sousse, Université de Sousse, 4011 Sousse, Tunisie
[3] Institut Supérieur des Sciences Appliquées et de Technologie de Sousse,
Université de Sousse, 4003 Sousse, Tunisie
[4] Institut supérieur d'informatique et de Mathématiques, Université de Monastir,
5019 Monastir, Tunisie
[5] U2IS, ENSTA Paris, Institut Polytechnique de Paris, 91120 Palaiseau, France

Abstract. ElectroEncephaloGraphy (EEG) signals have a nonlinear and complex nature and require the design of sophisticated methods for their analysis. Thus, Deep Learning (DL) models, which have enabled the automatic extraction of complex data features at high levels of abstraction, play a growing role in the field of medical science to help diagnose various diseases, and have been successfully used to predict the vigilance states of individuals. However, the performance of these models is highly sensitive to the choice of the hyper-parameters that define the structure of the network and the learning process. When targeting an application, tuning the hyper-parameters of deep neural networks is a tedious and time-consuming process. This explains the necessity of automating the calibration of these hyper-parameters. In this paper, we perform hyper-parameters optimization using two popular methods: Tree Parzen Estimator (TPE) and Bayesian optimisation (BO) to predict vigilance states of individuals based on their EEG signal. The performance of the methods is evaluated on the vigilance states classification. Compared with empirical optimization, the accuracy is improved from 0.84 to 0.93 with TPE and from 0.84 to 0.97 with Bayesian optimization using the 1D-UNet-LSTM deep learning model. Obtained results show that the combination of the 1D-UNet encoder and LSTM offers an excellent compromise between the performance and network size (thus training duration), which allows a more efficient hyper-parameter optimization.

Keywords: Deep learning models · Hyperparameter optimization · EEG · Vigilance

© The Author(s), under exclusive license to Springer Nature Switzerland AG 2022
C. Bădică et al. (Eds.): ICCCI 2022, CCIS 1653, pp. 200–210, 2022.
https://doi.org/10.1007/978-3-031-16210-7_16

1 Introduction

ElectroEncephaloGraphy (EEG) is the main modality for studying the electrical activity of the brain. However, the classification of these states from this signal requires sophisticated approaches in order to achieve the best performance. Deep Learning (DL) approaches have shown a good performance in learning the high-level features of signals [7,18], particularly for EEG. They are characterized by their large number of hidden layers that provide the most effective solutions thanks to massive calculations.

One of the most powerful models in DL approaches is the Convolution Neural Network (CNN). Thus, many studies have suggested CNN models for analyzing the EEG signal. In [2], the authors utilized the concept of DL on EEG signals to predict the driver's cognitive workload. A CNN model was used to extract features and accurately classify the cognitive workload. The experimental results showed that the proposed system could provide an accurate classification of high and low cognitive workload sessions. In [12], three types of deep covariance learning models were suggested to predict drivers' drowsy and alert states using EEG signals: the CNN, the Symmetric Positive Definite Network (SPDNet), and the Deep Neural Network (DNN). The experimental results indicated that all the three models of deep covariance-learning reported a very good classification performance compared with shallow learning methods. In [14], the authors proposed two DL models to predict individuals' vigilance states based on the study of one derivation of EEG signals: a 1D-UNet model and 1D-UNet-Long Short-Term Memory (1D-UNet-LSTM). Experimental results showed that the suggested models can stabilize the training process and well recognize the subject vigilance. Specifically, the per-class average of precision and recall could be respectively up to 86% with 1D-UNet and 85% with 1D-UNet-LSTM. All these studies have used several DL approaches to analyze EEG signals [2,12,14], but the choice of the architecture has been done empirically by the human expert through a slow trial and error process, guided mainly by intuition.

The success of the CNNs is highly dependent on the selection of the hyper-parameters. Determining which hyper-parameters to tune and defining value domains for those hyper-parameters, and then selecting the best set of values require meticulous design and experiment processes which can only be conducted by the participation of an expert from the domain. The need for the automatic design of CNNs is especially important for complex CNN architectures where the parameter space is so large that trying all possible combinations is computationally infeasible. Much research has been done in the field of Hyperparameter Optimization (HPO), such as grid search, random search, Bayesian optimization, and gradient-based optimization [4,9]. Grid search and manual search are the most widely used strategies for HPO [9,11]. These approaches make reproducibility harder and are impractical when there are a large number of hyper-parameters. Thus, many authors have focused on further automating the calibration of hyper-parameters. Particle Swarm Optimization (PSO) is among the metaheuristics that has been successfully applied for the optimization of CNN hyper-parameters. In [8], a parallel version of PSO algorithm was proposed for the hyper-parameter optimization of DL models to overcome two problems: (i) the search space which is usually high dimensional, and (ii) the high runtime. The experiments have revealed that the PSO would largely take advantage of the rapidity offered by computational parallelization. Another PSO-based approach used to configure the CNN architecture was introduced in [15]. The parameters to be tuned are kernel size, padding, number of feature maps, and pooling patterns. By using the PSO adaptation, authors achieved better results than those found by AlexNet and got a high accuracy. In [10] an OLPSO (orthogonal Learning Particle Swarm Optimization) approach was presented in which hyperparameters values were optimized for both VGG16 and VGG19 networks for plant disease diagnosis. Batch size and dropout rate are employed as hyperparameters. Through practical experiments, the authors proved that their approach achieves higher performance and accuracy compared to other methods tested for the same data. The authors in [15] investigated lung nodule classification by proposing a multi-level CNN whose hyperparameter configuration was optimized by using a proposed Gaussian process with stationary kernels. The experiments demonstrated that the algorithm outperformed manual tuning. TPE algorithm in [17], has been proposed through Hyperas tool in order to optimize CNN hyperparameters to classify pulmonary nodules at an early stage. It was shown that the smallest, more basic CNN architecture, just one convolutional layer following of one max-pooling layer obtained the best results. The hyperas tool with the TPE algorithm allowed to explore all the hyperparameters in the experiments and it was important to achieve excellent results. Therefore, in this paper, we describe the use of two popular methods: TPE and BO for automatically designing and training DL models to predict individuals' vigilance states from an EEG signal. Those algorithms are applied on the 1D-UNet and 1D-UNet-LSTM models proposed in [14] to improve the classification performance.

This paper is structured as follows: Sect. 2 presents the materials and methods and introduces the DL models successfully implemented for vigilance state classification. It also defines TPE and BO optimization algorithm. Section 3 presents the data and the experimentation setup. Moreover, this section describes the results of the optimized suggested model and elaborates the discussion based on the obtained results. The last section concludes the paper and gives some future perspectives.

2   Materials and Methods

One of the most important strategies used to estimate vigilance consists in using physiological measures to give more precise data about the state of an individual. The sequential steps of the development of the automated vigilance state detection system are: EEG data collection, pre-processing and classification by DL, using hyperparameter optimization (see Fig. 1).

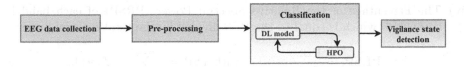

Fig. 1. EEG signal processing steps with HPO of DL models for vigilance state classification

2.1   EEG Signal Acquisition and Pre-processing

In this paper EEG signal is used to predict the vigilance states. This nonlinear and non-stationary signal characterizes the brain activity through a weakly invasive acquisition process, with electrodes placed along the scalp. To prepare the dataset, we use the same two subjects (S1, S2) as those collected in the experimentation of the previous work of our team [5,14]. The EEG data are directly recorded from 28 active electrodes from the scalp at the Department of Functional Explorations of the Nervous System at Sahloul University Hospital, Tunisia. This signal is recorded during three 24h periods with a 15 days interval, and it involves two healthy male subjects aged between 18 and 23. For each subject, the signal is recorded for two states: vigilance state (VS) and drowsiness state (DS). The EEG recordings are done, reviewed and approved by an expert, in order to label the different levels of alertness. In this work, we focus on analyzing a single EEG signal from the right parieto-occipital (Pz-Oz) electrode used to characterize analyzed vigilance states. This choice is justified by the fact that experts agree that this signal is the most appropriate to reflect a state of vigilance and to enable the system portability [5,6,14]. In the first step of pre-processing, we split the signal into time periods of four seconds (recommended by an expert), in order to reduce the computation complexity. Then, we filter this signal to eliminate artifacts using a high-pass filter to remove low frequencies less than 0.1 Hz, and a low-pass filter to filter out frequencies 21 Hz, in order to focus on frequencies most related to the state of alertness. Experts agree that this range is one of the most relevant ranges for vigilance. The next step of pre-processing is the spectral analysis of the signal which was proposed in [5,14]:

(i) The 512-point Fast Fourier Transform (FFT) is used to map the acquired time-series EEG data $f(t)$ to the frequency domain $F(u)$.

(ii) The frequency range [0.1 Hz, 21 Hz], which is specific to the range of physiological waves, is split into k elementary frequency bands to characterize this electrical activity.

(iii) In each band $[u_i, u_{i+1}]$, the Spectral Band Power (PBS), which corresponds to the sum of the spectral amplitudes belonging to the frequency band, is calculated:

$$\mathrm{PBS}_i = \sum_{u \in [u_i, u_{i+1}]} ||F(u)||; \quad \begin{cases} u_i = 0.1 + (i-1) * \Delta u; i \in [1..k] \\ \Delta u = \frac{(21-0.1)}{k} \end{cases}$$

(iv) The Percentage of the Relative Spectral Power (PRSP) of each band is
computed, which is equal to the PBS divided by the total spectral power:

$$\mathrm{PRSP}_i = \frac{\mathrm{PBS}_i}{\mathrm{TSP}} \times 100 \text{ , with TSP} = \sum_{u \in [0.1,21]} ||F(u)||$$

where Δu is the length of the frequency band (Hz), k is the number of bands,
and TSP represents the total spectral power. Thereby, the PRSP will be the
input to the classification tool for vigilance state detection, for each four second
time sample.

2.2 DL Models Hyperparameters

DL models are widely applied to various areas like computer vision, classification
and segmentation, since they have had great success solving many types of highly
complex problems. Among the most powerful models in DL approaches are the
CNN, in particular the 1D-CNN which has been well adopted in the literature for
processing EEG signals [16]. Its architecture is usually composed by a series of 1D
convolutional, pooling, normalization and fully connected layers. In this paper,
we use the 1D-UNet-LSTM DL model recently proposed in [14] and successfully
implemented for vigilance state classification.

1D-UNet-LSTM: The model presented in (Fig. 2) is a combination between
1D-UNet and LSTM.

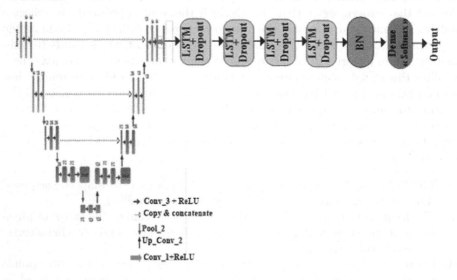

Fig. 2. 1D-UNet-LSTM architecture

The 1D-UNet-LSTM architecture takes the output of 1D-UNet (last layer) to
feed in as the input of the LSTM network. This latter is made up of five hidden

cells, where each cell is followed by a dropout layer to prevent overfitting. At the end, the 1D-UNet-LSTM architecture integrates a batch normalization layer, a fully connected (dense) layer and Softmax layers to accomplish the classification task.

Hyperparameters: The DL neural network have many hyperparameters, including those that specify the structure of the network itself and those that determine how the network is trained. As the training of these networks is slow, it is difficult to adjust the hyperparameters. When training a network, the result of the model will depend not only on the chosen structure but also on the training method, which itself has several hyperparameters such as the learning rate, the loss function, the mini-batch size, and the number of training iterations. Furthermore, the structure of the neural network itself involves numerous hyperparameters in its design, including the size of each layer, the number of hidden layers, the number of convolution layers, the kernel size, the filter size, the activation function, the weight initialization, etc. Table 1 summarizes the hyperparameters responsible for defining the structure of the network and those related to the optimization and training process. Tuning the hyperparameters of DL neural network is a critical and time-consuming process that has been mainly done relying on the knowledge of the experts. This explains the necessity of automating the calibration of these hyperparameters.

Table 1. Hyperparameters defining architectures (top) and training process (bottom) of the neural network.

Hyperparameters	Types	Scope
Number of convolution layers	Integer	0,1,..,25
Number of LSTM layers	Integer	0,1,..,25
Number of dense layers	Integer	0,1,..,25
LSTM units	Integer	32,,..,512
Optimizer	Categorical/Integer	Adam, Rmsprop, Adadelta
Filter size	Integer	64,128,..,1024
Kernel Size	Integer	0,.....,10
Batch size	Integer	10, 32, 64,128
Learning rate	Float	0;1
Dropout rate	Float	0;1
Activation function	Categorical	Relu, Sigmoid, Tanh

2.3 HPO Algorithms

Deep model design requires strong knowledge of algorithms and appropriate hyperparameter optimization techniques. Several methods have been proposed for HPO such as grid search [9], random search, simulated annealing [?], BO

[19] and TPE [3]. The TPE and BO success in expensive optimization problems indicates that they may outperform existing methods.

TPE algorithm is a Sequential Model-Based Optimization (SMBO) approach. SMBO methods sequentially construct models to approximate the performance of hyperparameters based on historical measurements, and then choose new hyperparameters to be tested based on this model. Consequently, the TPE is an iterative process that uses the history of evaluated hyperparameters to create a probabilistic model, which is used to suggest the next set of hyperparameters to evaluate. Let assume a set of observations $\{(x^{(1)}, y^{(1)}), \dots (x^{(k)}, y^{(k)})\}$, To apply the TPE, the observation results are divided into good and poor results by a pre-defined percentile y^*. The TPE defines p(x | y) using the following two probability density functions given by the equation:

$$P(x \mid y) = \begin{cases} l(x) & \text{if } y < y^* \\ g(x) & \text{if } y \geq y^* \end{cases}$$

where $l(x)$ is the probability density function formed using the observed variables $\{x^{(i)}\}$ such that $y^* > y^{(i)} (= f(x^{(i)}))$, and $g(x)$ is the probability density function using the remaining observations. Value y^* is selected to be a quantile γ of the observed y values satisfying $p(y^* > y) = \gamma$ After that, the expected improvement in the acquisition function is reflected by the ratio between the two density functions, which is used to determine the new configurations for evaluation.

BO algorithm tries to minimize a scalar objective function $f(x)$ for x. Depending on whether the function is deterministic or stochastic, the output will be different for the same input x. The minimization process comprises three main components: a Gaussian process model for the objective function $f(x)$, a Bayesian update process that modifies the Gaussian model after each new evaluation of the objective function, and an acquisition function $a(x)$. This acquisition function is maximized in order to identify the next evaluation point. The role of this function is to measure the expected improvement in the objective function while discarding values that would increase it. Hence, the expected improvement (EI) is calculated as:

$$EI(x, Q) = \mathbb{E}_Q \left[\max(0, \mu_Q(x_{\text{best}}) - f(x)) \right]$$

where Q is the posterior distribution function , x_{best} is the location of the lowest posterior mean and $\mu_Q(x_{\text{best}})$ is the lowest value of the posterior mean.

Compared to a grid search or manual tuning, BO allows us to jointly tune more parameters with fewer experiments and find better values [13].

3   Experiments and Results

The implementation has been done to show the effectiveness of the HPO algorithm used to improve the performance of vigilance state classification.

3.1   Experiment Setting

We evaluate the hyperparameter optimization algorithms on the 1D-UNet-LSTM architecture. This architecture is developed using Keras whose libraries are written in Python. The experiments are achieved with an experimental implementation on a Pop Gaming laptop PC with an Intel 9th-generation Core i5-9300H processor, a NVIDIA GeForce GTX 1650 Graphics card and 8 GB Memory. To tackle HPO problems, we use Optuna framework [1], which provides many HPO algorithms including the TPE and Sherpa [20] framework which provides BO algorithm.

3.2   Results and Discussion

This section describes the results obtained. We focus on two subjects [5,14] with the same size of observations in order to detect the vigilance states. The within-subject vigilance state classification is applied to evaluate the performance by different models, where each subject is taken separately and divided into 80% and 20% of observations for training and testing, respectively. Table 2 presents the hyper-parameter values obtained by the implemented DL models for the two subjects. This table shows that Adam function is more often selected as an optimizer, which justifies the effectiveness of this function. Furthermore, the ReLU activation is selected for all implementations. We note that the hyper-parameter values change between the models for the same subject. This proves that the hyperparameters are specific to the utilized architecture. Furthermore, the hyperparameter values vary between the subjects within the same DL model. This proves also that the hyperparameters depend on the input data, even if we work in the same context.

Table 2. Best hyperparameters configurations using TPE and BO algorithms

	1D UNET-LSTM			
	TPE		BO	
	S1	S2	S1	S2
Number of convolution layers	10	10	9	13
Number of LSTM layers	4	5	5	7
LSTM Units	100	64	150	125
Optimiser	Adam	Adam	Adam	Adam
Filter size	64	32	128	64
Kernel size	1	1	1	1
Batch size	10	10	64	10
Learning rate	0.002	0.003	0.002	0.001
Dropout rate	0.4	0.3	0.3	0.5
Activation function	Relu	Relu	Relu	Relu

Table 3 exposes the accuracy results obtained using HPO algorithms and compared with the results before the optimization process for the 1D-UNet-LSTM model. We note that the classification performance in terms of accuracy is good using TPE and BO algorithms. Accuracy for subject S1 using TPE can be up to 0.93 with 1D-UNet-LSTM.and with BO, Accuracy can be up to 0.97. The accuracy gain with TPE can reach 12.5% and with BO can reach 15.51% for subject S2 using 1D-UNet-LSTM compared to an implementation without optimization.

Table 3. Subject vigilance state classification Accuracy

	S1					S2				
	Without HPO [2]	HPO-TPE	HPO-BO	Gain-TPE (%)	Gain-BO(%)	Without HPO [2]	HPO-TPE	HPO-BO	Gain-TPE (%)	Gain-BO(%)
1D Unet-LSTM	0.840	0.932	0.973	9.8	13.6	0.735	0.840	0.870	12.5	15.51

Table 4 describes the classification performance in terms of recall, precision and F1-score using UNet-LSTM architecture for subject S1, which has the best classification accuracy, as depicted in Table 2 (the per-model average is 0.956 using BO). This table shows that the precision can achieve 0.92 using 1D-UNet-LSTM with HPO. The Precision gain is 13.41% using 1D-UNet-LSTM with HPO (BO algorithm) compared to the same model without optimization.

Table 4. Performance measures of proposed models for subject 1

	Recall					Précision					F1-Score				
	Without HPO [2]	HPO-TPE	HPO-BO	Gain-TPE (%)	Gain-BO(%)	Without HPO [2]	HPO-TPE	HPO-BO	Gain-TPE (%)	Gain-BO(%)	Without HPO [2]	HPO-TPE	HPO-BO	Gain-TPE (%)	Gain-BO(%)
1D Unet-LSTM	0.85	0.89	0.902	4.4	5.7	0.80	0.90	0.924	11.1	13.41	0.81	0.894	0.912	9.3	11.18

Given Table 3 and Table 4, we note that including an optimization phase of hyperparameters allows to significantly improve the classification performance for all subjects and for all implemented DL model. Indeed, these results show that the iterative process of BO and TPE are suitable for our application.

4   Conclusion and Perspectives

In this paper, we have introduced and explored the potential of HPO algorithms in order to give the best configurations of hyperparameters and to improve the performance of vigilance state classification EEG signals. The HPO TPE and BO have been applied to the 1D-UNet-LSTM model, and the optimal hyperparameter configuration has been generated. The experimental results in the study have revealed that the performance of vigilance state classification has been improved using the HPO BO method and the accuracy gain can reach 15.51% for subject S2 using 1D-UNet-LSTM compared to an implementation without an optimization process. In the future, we will add more subjects for further validation of the DL architecture with hyperparameter optimization. In addition, we will evaluate more HPO algorithms in order to improve the system performance.

References

1. Akiba, T., Sano, S., Yanase, T., Ohta, T., Koyama, M.: Optuna: a next-generation hyperparameter optimization framework. In: Proceedings of the 25th ACM SIGKDD International Conference on Knowledge Discovery Data Mining, pp. 2623–2631 (2019)
2. Almogbel, M.A., Dang, A.H., Kameyama, W.: EEG-signals based cognitive workload detection of vehicle driver using deep learning. In: 2018 20th International Conference on Advanced Communication Technology (ICACT), pp. 256–259. IEEE (2018)
3. Bergstra, J., Bardenet, R., Bengio, Y., Kégl, B.: Algorithms for hyper-parameter optimization. Adv. Neural Inf. Process. Syst. **24** (2011)
4. Bergstra, J., Bengio, Y.: Random search for hyper-parameter optimization. J. Mach. Learn. Res. **13**(2) (2012)
5. Blaiech, A.G., Ben Khalifa, K., Boubaker, M., Bedoui, M.H.: LVQ neural network optimized implementation on FPGA devices with multiple-word length operations for real-time systems. Neural Comput. Appl. **29**(2), 509–528 (2018)
6. Blaiech, A.G., Khalifa, K.B., Boubaker, M., Bedoui, M.H.: Multi-width fixed-point coding based on reprogrammable hardware implementation of a multi-layer perceptron neural network for alertness classification. In: 2010 10th International Conference on Intelligent Systems Design and Applications, pp. 610–614. IEEE (2010)
7. Boudegga, H., Elloumi, Y., Akil, M., Bedoui, M.H., Kachouri, R., Abdallah, A.B.: Fast and efficient retinal blood vessel segmentation method based on deep learning network. Comput. Med. Imaging Graph. **90**, 101902 (2021)
8. Brito, R., Fong, S., Zhuang, Y., Wu, Y.: Generating neural networks with optimal features through particle swarm optimization. In: Proceedings of the International Conference on Big Data and Internet of Thing, pp. 96–101 (2017)
9. Claesen, M., De Moor, B.: Hyperparameter search in machine learning. arXiv preprint arXiv:1502.02127 (2015)
10. Darwish, A., Ezzat, D., Hassanien, A.E.: An optimized model based on convolutional neural networks and orthogonal learning particle swarm optimization algorithm for plant diseases diagnosis. Swarm Evol. Comput. **52**, 100616 (2020)
11. Firdaus, F.F., Nugroho, H.A., Soesanti, I.: Deep neural network with hyperparameter tuning for detection of heart disease. In: 2021 IEEE Asia Pacific Conference on Wireless and Mobile (APWiMob), pp. 59–65. IEEE (2021)
12. Hajinoroozi, M., Zhang, J.M., Huang, Y.: Driver's fatigue prediction by deep covariance learning from EEG. In: 2017 IEEE International Conference on Systems, Man, and Cybernetics (SMC), pp. 240–245. IEEE (2017)
13. Injadat, M., Salo, F., Nassif, A.B., Essex, A., Shami, A.: Bayesian optimization with machine learning algorithms towards anomaly detection. In: 2018 IEEE Global Communications Conference (GLOBECOM), pp. 1–6. IEEE (2018)

14. Khessiba, S., Blaiech, A.G., Ben Khalifa, K., Ben Abdallah, A., Bedoui, M.H.:
    Innovative deep learning models for EEG-based vigilance detection. Neural Comput. Appl. **33**(12), 6921–6937 (2021)
15. Khoong, W.H.: A heuristic for efficient reduction in hidden layer combinations for
    feedforward neural networks. In: Science and Information Conference, pp. 208–218.
    Springer (2020). https://doi.org/10.1007/978-3-030-52249-0_14
16. Kiranyaz, S., Avci, O., Abdeljaber, O., Ince, T., Gabbouj, M., Inman, D.J.: 1d convolutional neural networks and applications: a survey. Mech. Syst. Signal Process.
    151, 107398 (2021)
17. Konar, J., Khandelwal, P., Tripathi, R.: Comparison of various learning rate
    scheduling techniques on convolutional neural network. In: 2020 IEEE International
    Students' Conference on Electrical, Electronics and Computer Science (SCEECS),
    pp. 1–5. IEEE (2020)
18. LeCun, Y., Bengio, Y., Hinton, G.: Deep learning. Nature **521**(7553), 436–444
    (2015)
19. Snoek, J., Larochelle, H., Adams, R.P.: Practical bayesian optimization of machine
    learning algorithms. Adv. Neural Inf. Process. Syst. **25** (2012)
20. Wu, J., Chen, X.Y., Zhang, H., Xiong, L.D., Lei, H., Deng, S.H.: Hyperparameter optimization for machine learning models based on Bayesian optimization. J.
    Electron. Sci. Technol. **17**(1), 26–40 (2019)

A Hybrid Face Recognition Approach Using Local Appearance and Deep Models

Mert Arı[1,2]([✉]) [iD] and Hazım Kemal Ekenel[2] [iD]

[1] Microelectronic Guidance and Electro-Optical Group, Aselsan, Ankara, Turkey
mertari@aselsan.com.tr
[2] Department of Computer Engineering, Istanbul Technical University,
Istanbul, Turkey
ekenel@itu.edu.tr

Abstract. Visible and thermal face recognition are highly important topics in computer vision. Existing face recognition models generally focus on facial images in the visible domain. However, they fail in the lack of the light and become non-functional at night. In addition, the performance of the models decreases in the case of occlusion. This work aims to build a hybrid two-branch pipeline that detects, aligns, represents, and recognizes a face from either thermal or visible domains using both a local appearance-based and a deep learning-based method. In addition, we present a fusion scheme to combine the outputs of these methods in the final stage. The recent state-of-the-art deep learning-based face recognition approaches mainly focus on eye region for identification. This leads to a performance drop when these models are confronted with occluded faces. On the other hand, local appearance-based approaches have been shown to be robust to occlusion as they extract features from all parts of the face. Therefore, in order to enable a high-accuracy face recognition pipeline, we combine deep learning and local appearance based models. We have conducted extensive experiments on the EURECOM and ROF datasets to assess the performance of the proposed approach. Experimental results show that in both domains there are significant improvements in classification accuracies under various facial appearances variations due to the factors, such as facial expressions, illumination conditions, and occlusion.

Keywords: Visible and thermal face recognition · Occlusion · Illumination · Deep neural network · Discrete cosine transform

1 Introduction

Face recognition is among the prominent topics in the field of biometrics. Recent studies on face recognition achieved highly successful results using deep neural network architectures on visible images [17,19,22]. On the other hand, infrared (IR) imaging is frequently encountered as well as visible light imaging in surveillance systems, especially in public security and military applications. IR imaging

C. Bădică et al. (Eds.): ICCCI 2022, CCIS 1653, pp. 211–222, 2022.
https://doi.org/10.1007/978-3-031-16210-7_17

systems detect how heat energy is distributed throughout an environment. The energy is then converted into an image over thermal detectors. Thus, IR and visible images have different properties and there is a domain gap between these modalities.

Although most of the previous works have focused only on visible images, thermal face recognition has received considerable attention in recent studies. For instance, a deep structure was established with three convolutional layers followed by pooling layers [25]. They showed that their approach achieved better results than traditional methods under extreme conditions on thermal subset of RGB-D-T face database [20]. In addition to the thermal face recognition, there is an interest in cross-domain face matching using generative adversarial networks (GANs). One of the most successful approaches to thermal to visible domain transformation is Thermal-to-Visible Generative Adversarial Network (TV-GAN) method [27]. It is based on Pix2Pix network [12] and adds an identity loss, inspired from Disentangled-Representation GAN (DR-GAN) [21]. On the other hand, Dong et al. [2] investigated the effects of visible and thermal image fusion. They suggested feature-level and score-level image fusion strategies in order to handle the drawbacks of visible images under poor illumination conditions. It was reported that both approaches provide complementary information and improve the accuracy of the face recognition task.

In our study, a two-branch hybrid face recognition approach is proposed, which takes either a visible or thermal image as an input. To detect the faces in the input images max-margin object detection (MMOD) [16] in Dlib library [15] and multitask cascaded convolutional neural networks (MTCNN) [26] are used. Inspired from [5], detected images are aligned and augmented using eye center locations. In the feature extraction phase, even though the deep neural networks are known to be highly successful, Erakin et al. [7] show that they focus on the eye region for identification. This leads to a decrease in the performance of the model in the case of upper-face occlusion. On the other hand, local appearance-based approaches are shown to be more robust to occlusion [5,6]. Therefore, we combine deep learning and local appearance-based methods into a hybrid face recognition pipeline. As a result, features are extracted from both discrete cosine transform (DCT) [3,4] and deep Arcface model [1]. The extracted features from these branches are compared to the ones extracted from gallery images. The outputs of these comparisons are then combined using the proposed fusion scheme. The contributions of the study can be summarized as follows:

– A two-branch face recognition pipeline is proposed, which combines a local appearance and a deep learning based approach.
– We propose a fusion scheme to combine the outputs of these approaches efficiently.
– The proposed approach improves the face recognition performance significantly both in the visible and thermal domains.
– It is shown that the proposed approach is robust to the facial appearance variations due to factors, such as illumination, expression, and occlusion.

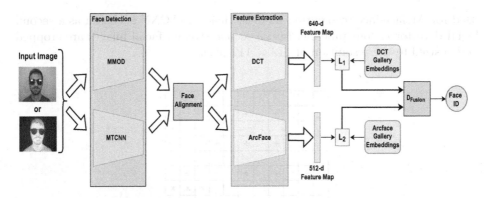

Fig. 1. The illustration of our hybrid face recognition pipeline. Our approach has two-stream structure with different approaches. It takes either a visible or a thermal image as an input. Face detection is performed by Dlib's CNN detector [15,16] in the first branch, and by MTCNN [26] in the second. Then, facial images are augmented and aligned with the face alignment stage for both branches. Features are extracted by using both DCT and Arcface approaches. The extracted features are compared with the corresponding gallery embeddings using different distance metrics. Finally, the outputs of the metrics are combined with a fused distance scheme to obtain face identity.

The remainder of the paper is organized as follows. Section 2 explains the structure of the proposed two-branch pipeline and its components in detail. Then, Sect. 3 provides a description of the datasets, gives implementation details and shows the experimental results. Finally, Sect. 4 concludes the paper.

2   Methodology

In this study, we develop a hybrid face recognition pipeline. Figure 1 depicts the overview of the proposed method. Either a visible or thermal image is given to the pipeline as an input. The faces in the image are then detected and aligned. Facial features are extracted from two different branches. Then, these feature maps are separately compared with the corresponding gallery embeddings. In the final stage, distance fusion is applied to obtain the identity. The steps of the proposed pipeline are detailed in the following subsections.

2.1   Face Detection

We use a two-stream face detection structure carried out by two different CNN-based detectors, which takes either visible or thermal images as input. Firstly, MMOD CNN face detector [16], implemented in Dlib library [15], is used to detect faces since in our experiments it is observed that it achieves better face detection results than the other face detector MTCNN [26]. Detected faces are cropped and set to the resolution of 64×64 pixels in the first detector. In the other branch, MTCNN architecture [26] has been applied, as MTCNN is widely used for Arcface face recognition models. Hence, MTCNN is chosen as a second facial detector for our pipeline. In the second stream, facial images are cropped and resized to the resolution of 112 × 112 pixels.

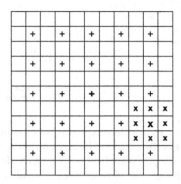

Fig. 2. The illustration of the search scheme in a window size of 11 × 11 pixels. The red "+" shows the manually labelled eye center position while the others indicate the search locations at the first step. In the second step, the finer search is conducted, for example, around the location denoted as green "x". (Color figure online)

2.2   Face Alignment

We are inspired from [5], which deals with misalignment problem, especially in the case of upper face occlusion. They train their method on multiple samples of facial images obtained by modifying eye center location combinations within a fixed size window. In this manner, we use manually labelled eye center points from [13] for our pipeline. In addition to the annotations, we manually label eye center points of occluded images in our test set. The hierarchical search scheme is used to generate the eye center locations of facial images as described in [5] and as illustrated in Fig. 2. In this way, in the first step, new eye center positions are obtained by searching ±2 pixels in a window size of 11 × 11 pixels around the manually labelled eye coordinates. In total, 625 combinations of eye coordinates are produced in this step. Then, the combination that leads to the minimum classification distance is determined among them. New 81 combinations are produced by searching ±1 pixel around the determined eye center point from the first step. However, this generates 80 additional eye center coordinates because the combination with the minimum classification distance is already considered in the first step. Finally, in total, 705 (= 625 + 80) eye center location combinations are obtained for each facial image. New images are generated by performing face alignment with respect to these eye center combinations for the data augmentation purpose.

2.3   Feature Extraction

In the feature extraction phase, both local appearance based and deep neural network methods are used. Deep neural networks have nearly reached to human performance on face recognition tasks [23]. However, they focus on the eye region, which leads to a decrease in the face recognition performance in the case of upper-face occlusion. On the other hand, block/local appearance based approaches are known to be more robust to this problem. For example, in [5,6], it is shown that the degradation of the performance is mainly due to misalignment that is caused by imperfect eye center localization in the case of upper-face occlusion. They have also shown that using a local appearance based method, which obtains the local representation of the detected facial image by preserving the spatial information, is robust to occlusion. On account of these reasons, deep learning and local appearance based approaches are combined into a single hybrid pipeline to benefit from their advantages.

In the first branch of the feature extraction, the local appearance based face recognition method is used. As suggested in [3], block-based DCT produces the local features by preserving spatial information from facial images. Besides, in [6], inaccurate facial feature localization problem in case of occlusion is handled. In our implementation, it takes a 64×64 pixel resolution aligned gray-scale facial image obtained from MMOD face detector. The images are divided into 64 blocks with the size of 8×8 pixel resolution. Coefficients are calculated by performing DCT on each block and they are ordered using zig-zag scanning. The first coefficient is removed from each local representation. Then, the following ten coefficients are extracted and normalized with the unit normalization. As a result, this method produces a 640-dimensional feature vector.

Deng et al. [1] proposed an additive angular margin loss for deep face recognition (Arcface) in order to obtain discriminative facial features. They achieved very high correct verification rates on LFW [11] and YTF [24] datasets. Therefore, we preferred this deep model to produce the deep feature embeddings on the facial images in the second branch. It takes 112×112 pixel resolution aligned faces obtained from MTCNN [26] as input and generates 512-dimensional feature maps. We use ResNet-50 [10] as the backbone network for the Arcface model which is pre-trained on MS1MV2 dataset [1]. For visible face recognition, we used the pre-trained Arcface model [1]. In the case of thermal face recognition, this deep model is fine-tuned on the Carl thermal face dataset [8,9] in order to close the domain gap due to spectrum differences between visible and thermal images.

2.4   Distance Metric Fusion

Outputs from two different branches are fused in order to produce face identity prediction. We perform fusion by combining the distance outputs of these branches. Euclidean distance metric is widely used for Arcface while DCT reaches better recognition results with Manhattan distance metric. On account of these reasons, we propose a scheme to combine the distances arising from different

Table 1. Number of images in the datasets. G, E, I, HP, O, and UO refer to Gallery, Expression, Illumination, Head Pose, Occlusion, and Upper Occlusion images, respectively.

Dataset	Test domain	Image classes					
		G	E	I	HP	O	UO
EURECOM [18]	Visible	50	300	250	200	250	50
EURECOM [18]	Thermal	50	300	250	200	250	100
Carl [8,9]	Thermal	–	2460	–	–	–	–
ROF [7]	Visible	483	–	–	–	–	4627

metrics. The corresponding formula is given in Eq. (1). Euclidean distance is used to calculate the distance between gallery and probe images for Arcface feature vectors, denoted as $L_2{}^{\text{Arcface}}$. On the other hand, $L_1{}^{\text{DCT}}$ indicates Manhattan distance between the DCT feature maps of probe and gallery images. Feature vectors from two different branches have different sizes; therefore, the distance measurements are divided by the dimension of the feature vectors in order to normalize the scale differences between them. In this manner, $L_1{}^{\text{DCT}}$ is normalized by the dimension of the DCT feature vector, denoted as d^{DCT} while $L_2{}^{\text{Arcface}}$ is divided by the square root of the dimension of the Arcface feature vector, denoted as d^{Arcface}. The scaled individual distance measurements $L_2{}^{\text{Arcface}}$ and $L_1{}^{\text{DCT}}$ are then weighted by the parameters α and β, respectively. The optimal parameters based on the validation results are $\alpha = 0.87$ and $\beta = 0.13$, which are described in the Experiments section.

$$D_{Fusion} = \alpha * \frac{L_2^{Arcface}}{\sqrt{d^{Arcface}}} + \beta * \frac{L_1^{DCT}}{d^{DCT}} \tag{1}$$

3   Experiments

We use three publicly available datasets, namely, Carl [8,9], ROF [7], and EURECOM [18]. The number of images used in our experiments is presented in Table 1. Figure 3 depicts several sample images under different variations from the datasets.

3.1   Dataset Description

The Carl dataset [8,9] is a multi-modal dataset with the domains of visible, near and long-wave infrared. However, fine-tuning process is performed only on long-wave infrared, also known as thermal, face images with a resolution of 160×120 to adapt Arcface model to the thermal domain. The Carl dataset [8,9] has 41 subjects captured with thermographic camera TESTO 880-3. Each of them is obtained in four different acquisition sessions performed in different dates. In

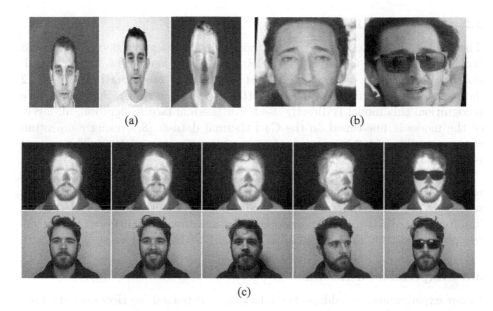

Fig. 3. Sample face images from (a) Carl dataset [8,9], (b) ROF dataset [7] and (c) EURECOM visible and thermal paired face dataset [18]. Images in (a) are samples of visible, near infrared, and long-wave infrared images, respectively. Images in (b) are examples of gallery and upper occlusion image classes. In (c), images in the first row are captured in thermal domain and the ones in the second row are captured in visible domain with neutral, expression, illumination, head pose, and occlusion.

each session, thermal images are taken under three different illumination conditions with the combination of five different facial expressions for each subject.

The Real World Occluded Faces (ROF) dataset [7] consists of 161 identities and each subject contains three gallery images with a resolution of 112×112 pixels. ROF [7] contains 4627 images captured with upper face occlusion, of which randomly chosen 1000 samples are used to validate the weighting parameters and the rest for testing the performance of the pipeline, denoted as *ROF UO*, where *UO* stands for upper occlusion.

EURECOM visible and thermal paired face dataset [18] contains 50 subjects with a total of 2100 image pairs captured with a dual sensor camera FLIR Duo R by FLIR System under various conditions, which includes neutral, expression, illumination, head pose, and occlusion variations. In addition, we create a subset of occlusion image pairs to form a set of upper face occlusion. Thus, the subset is comprised of visible images with sunglasses and thermal images with sunglasses and eyeglasses, denoted as *UO*.

3.2 Implementation Details

The models are implemented with Python script language version of 3.6.8[1] and trained on NVIDIA GeForce GTX 1050 Ti. MXNet version of Arcface, available in InsightFace[2], is used. This Arcface model is pre-trained on MS1MV2 dataset [1]. It uses ResNet-50 [10] as the backbone network. For visible face recognition, this model is directly used. For thermal face recognition, all layers of the model is fine-tuned on the Carl thermal dataset [8,9] using momentum optimizer value of 0.9, batch size of 16, and learning rate of 10^{-5}. The process is terminated after 150 epochs.

Unlike visible domain, face detection methods could not achieve successful results in the thermal domain. In order to handle this issue, inspired from [14], when the face in the thermal image could not be detected, the detected facial landmark coordinates from the visible image are directly transferred to the corresponding position of its thermal pair in the EURECOM dataset [18].

3.3 Experimental Results

In our experiments, we address the following four points: (a) How does the fine-tuning process affect the thermal face recognition performance? (b) How do the distance metrics and alignment affect the DCT performance? (c) How can we determine the optimal weighting parameters? (d) How well can our proposed hybrid pipeline improve visible and thermal face recognition results?

Impact of Domain Adaptation. We observe the contribution of domain adaptation on the pre-trained Arcface model. For this reason, Arcface model is fine-tuned on the Carl thermal dataset [8,9]. Then, the pre-trained and fine-tuned models are evaluated on the EURECOM thermal test dataset [18] captured under various expressions, illumination conditions, head pose variations, and occlusion types. The results are presented in Table 2. It can be clearly seen that fine-tuning process improves the results significantly on all four test sets. Even though fine-tuning was performed on a different thermal dataset, the results indicate that the deep model has been successfully adapted to the thermal domain.

Table 2. Impact of thermal domain adaptation on Arcface model. E, I, HP, and O refer to Expression, Illumination, Head Pose, and Occlusion cases from EURECOM Dataset [18], respectively.

Arcface	Domain adaptation	Test domain	Results(%)			
			E	I	HP	O
Pre-trained	–	Thermal	77.67	64.40	23.50	38.80
Fine-tuned	Carl #150	Thermal	**93.00**	**88.40**	**41.50**	**59.20**

---

[1] https://www.python.org/downloads/release/python-368/.
[2] https://github.com/deepinsight/insightface.

Effect of Distance Metrics and Alignment on Local Appearance-based Face Recognition. Distance metrics are compared in Table 3. The table demonstrates that DCT achieves the best recognition results with Manhattan (L_1) distance metric for EURECOM multi-spectral test setups [18]. To observe the contribution of the alignment module, we evaluate DCT performance with and without it. The alignment step significantly increases the recognition performance.

Table 3. Effect of distance metrics with and without the alignment on DCT results. E, I, O, and UO refer to Expression, Illumination, Occlusion, and Upper Occlusion images from EURECOM Dataset [18], respectively.

Distance metric	Alignment	Test domain	DCT Results(%)			
			E	I	O	UO
Euclidean (L_2)	×	Thermal	56.00	50.80	26.40	23.00
Manhattan (L_1)	×	Thermal	59.33	53.60	32.00	32.00
Manhattan (L_1)	✓	Thermal	**85.33**	**75.60**	**58.40**	**58.00**
Euclidean (L_2)	×	Visible	54.67	42.00	27.20	22.00
Manhattan (L_1)	×	Visible	60.00	43.20	34.00	30.00
Manhattan (L_1)	✓	Visible	**91.00**	**79.60**	**90.80**	**90.00**

Optimization of the Distance Weighting Parameters. We obtain the optimized values of the distance weighting parameters through the experiments. To generate a validation set, we randomly choose 50 samples from our Upper Occlusion subset of EURECOM dataset [18] for thermal images and 1000 samples from the ROF sunglasses dataset [7] for visible images. In Fig. 4, we plot the validation results to analyze the recognition performance of different values of the distance weighting parameters. It is observed that α at 0.87 and β at 0.13 achieved better results during the validation. Therefore, these values are used in the experiments.

Analysis of the Proposed Approach. We compare our hybrid pipeline with different approaches. Carl dataset [8,9] is only used for the fine-tuning process while the models are tested on EURECOM [18] and ROF [7] datasets. The evaluation results are shown in Table 4, which contains nine different approaches: (i, ii, iii and iv) Arcface-34, Arcface-100, MobileFaceNet, and VGGFace2 from [7]: The results of these deep learning models are taken from [7] for visible domain; (v) DCT with Alignment: We use DCT approach with our face detection and alignment steps; (vi) Pre-trained Arcface: Arcface model is pre-trained on MS1MV2 dataset with ResNet-50 backbone network; (vii) Fine-tuned Arcface: Same model as (vi) but additionally fine-tuned on the Carl dataset; (viii) Ours with L_2: Our hybrid pipeline except D_{Fusion} uses only L_2 distance metrics for both DCT

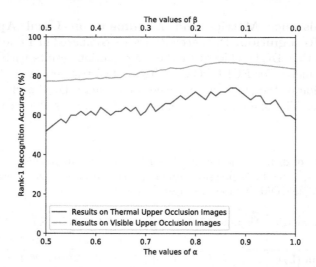

Fig. 4. Recognition performance of the proposed approach with respect to varying weighting parameters on the validation subset of upper occlusion images.

and Arcface feature maps; (ix) Ours with D_{Fusion}: Our final hybrid pipeline. Although our proposed approach with D_{Fusion} has less parameters than Arcface-100 [7], which is based on ResNet-100 architecture, it achieves the best recognition results for both image domains on all test sets. Besides, the table validates the effectiveness of the distance metric fusion and confirms that the proposed pipeline produces more reliable results on both domains.

Table 4. Comparison of our method with different approaches. E, I, and UO refer to Expression, Illumination, and Upper Occlusion Images from EURECOM Dataset [18]. ROF UO refers to Upper Occlusion images from ROF Dataset [7], respectively.

Method	Distance metric	Test domain	Results(%)			
			E	I	UO	ROF UO
DCT with alignment	Manhattan (L_1)	Thermal	85.33	75.60	58.00	–
Pre-trained arcface	Euclidean (L_2)	Thermal	77.67	64.40	42.00	–
Fine-tuned arcface	Euclidean (L_2)	Thermal	93.00	88.40	58.00	–
Ours	Euclidean (L_2)	Thermal	96.00	92.80	70.00	–
Ours	D_{Fusion}	Thermal	**96.67**	**93.60**	**76.00**	–
Arcface-34 from [7]	Euclidean (L_2)	Visible	–	–	–	83.51
Arcface-100 from [7]	Euclidean (L_2)	Visible	–	–	–	86.60
MobileFaceNet from [7]	Euclidean (L_2)	Visible	–	–	–	77.16
VGGFace2 from [7]	Cosine similarity	Visible	–	–	–	76.83
DCT with alignment	Manhattan (L_1)	Visible	91.00	79.60	90.00	70.37
Pre-trained arcface	Euclidean (L_2)	Visible	99.67	83.20	**98.00**	84.18
Ours	Euclidean (L_2)	Visible	99.67	89.60	**98.00**	85.00
Ours	D_{Fusion}	Visible	**100.0**	**91.20**	**98.00**	**86.90**

4   Conclusion

In this paper, we presented a two-branch hybrid pipeline for face recognition task. The proposed pipeline consists of four main stages. Firstly, facial images are obtained from both MMOD [16] in Dlib library [15] and MTCNN [26]. Then, they are aligned and augmented in the face alignment step. Feature representations are extracted using both DCT and Arcface methods. Feature vectors of the probe images are compared to the ones from the gallery face images using different distance metrics. Finally, the outputs of the metrics are combined with a fused distance scheme in order to predict face identity.

Experimental results demonstrated that fine-tuned Arcface model is successfully adapted to the thermal domain. We also show that utilizing the optimized parameters in the fused distance scheme remarkably increase the robustness of our hybrid pipeline against various conditions in both visible and thermal domains. Finally, the proposed pipeline outperforms different approaches on the EURECOM [18] and ROF [7] datasets in terms of Rank-1 identification accuracy.

References

1. Deng, J., Guo, J., Xue, N., Zafeiriou, S.: ArcFace: additive angular margin loss for deep face recognition. In: Proceedings of the IEEE/CVF Conference on Computer Vision and Pattern Recognition, pp. 4690–4699 (2019)
2. Dong, X., Wong, K., Jin, Z., Dugelay, J.L.: A secure visual-thermal fused face recognition system based on non-linear hashing. In: 2019 IEEE 21st International Workshop on Multimedia Signal Processing (MMSP), pp. 1–6. IEEE (2019)
3. Ekenel, H.K., Stiefelhagen, R.: Local appearance based face recognition using discrete cosine transform. In: 2005 13th European Signal Processing Conference, pp. 1–5. IEEE (2005)
4. Ekenel, H.K., Stiefelhagen, R.: Analysis of local appearance-based face recognition: effects of feature selection and feature normalization. In: 2006 Conference on Computer Vision and Pattern Recognition Workshop (CVPRW 2006), pp. 34–34. IEEE (2006)
5. Ekenel, H.K., Stiefelhagen, R.: Face alignment by minimizing the closest classification distance. In: 2009 IEEE 3rd International Conference on Biometrics: Theory, Applications, and Systems, pp. 1–6. IEEE (2009)
6. Ekenel, H.K., Stiefelhagen, R.: Why is facial occlusion a challenging problem? In: Tistarelli, Massimo, Nixon, Mark S.. (eds.) ICB 2009. LNCS, vol. 5558, pp. 299–308. Springer, Heidelberg (2009). https://doi.org/10.1007/978-3-642-01793-3_31
7. Erakın, M.E., Demir, U., Ekenel, H.K.: On recognizing occluded faces in the wild. In: 2021 International Conference of the Biometrics Special Interest Group (BIOSIG), pp. 1–5. IEEE (2021)
8. Espinosa-Duró, V., Faundez-Zanuy, M., Mekyska, J.: A new face database simultaneously acquired in visible, near-infrared and thermal spectrums. Cogn. Comput. 5(1), 119–135 (2013)
9. Espinosa-Duró, V., Faundez-Zanuy, M., Mekyska, J., Monte-Moreno, E.: A criterion for analysis of different sensor combinations with an application to face biometrics. Cogn. Comput. 2(3), 135–141 (2010)

10. He, K., Zhang, X., Ren, S., Sun, J.: Deep residual learning for image recognition. In: Proceedings of the IEEE Conference on Computer Vision and Pattern Recognition, pp. 770–778 (2016)
11. Huang, G.B., Mattar, M., Berg, T., Learned-Miller, E.: Labeled faces in the wild: a database for studying face recognition in unconstrained environments. In: Workshop on Faces in 'Real-Life' Images: Detection, Alignment, and Recognition (2008)
12. Isola, P., Zhu, J.Y., Zhou, T., Efros, A.A.: Image-to-image translation with conditional adversarial networks. In: Proceedings of the IEEE Conference on Computer Vision and Pattern Recognition, pp. 1125–1134 (2017)
13. Kantarcı, A., Ekenel, H.K.: Thermal to visible face recognition using deep autoencoders. In: 2019 International Conference of the Biometrics Special Interest Group (BIOSIG), pp. 1–5. IEEE (2019)
14. Keong, J., Dong, X., Jin, Z., Mallat, K., Dugelay, J.L.: Multi-spectral facial landmark detection. In: 2020 IEEE International Workshop on Information Forensics and Security (WIFS), pp. 1–6. IEEE (2020)
15. King, D.E.: Dlib-ml: a machine learning toolkit. J. Mach. Learn. Res. **10**, 1755–1758 (2009)
16. King, D.E.: Max-margin object detection. arXiv preprint arXiv:1502.00046 (2015)
17. Liu, W., Wen, Y., Yu, Z., Li, M., Raj, B., Song, L.: SphereFace: deep hypersphere embedding for face recognition. In: Proceedings of the IEEE Conference on Computer Vision and Pattern Recognition, pp. 212–220 (2017)
18. Mallat, K., Dugelay, J.L.: A benchmark database of visible and thermal paired face images across multiple variations. In: 2018 International Conference of the Biometrics Special Interest Group (BIOSIG), pp. 1–5. IEEE (2018)
19. Meng, Q., Zhao, S., Huang, Z., Zhou, F.: MagFace: a universal representation for face recognition and quality assessment. In: Proceedings of the IEEE/CVF Conference on Computer Vision and Pattern Recognition, pp. 14225–14234 (2021)
20. Simón, M.O., et al.: Improved RGB-D-T based face recognition. IET Biomet. **5**(4), 297–303 (2016)
21. Tran, L., Yin, X., Liu, X.: Disentangled representation learning GAN for pose-invariant face recognition. In: Proceedings of the IEEE Conference on Computer Vision and Pattern Recognition, pp. 1415–1424 (2017)
22. Wang, H., et al.: CosFace: large margin cosine loss for deep face recognition. In: Proceedings of the IEEE Conference on Computer Vision and Pattern Recognition, pp. 5265–5274 (2018)
23. Wang, M., Deng, W.: Deep face recognition: a survey. Neurocomputing **429**, 215–244 (2021)
24. Wolf, L., Hassner, T., Maoz, I.: Face recognition in unconstrained videos with matched background similarity. In: CVPR 2011, pp. 529–534. IEEE (2011)
25. Wu, Z., Peng, M., Chen, T.: Thermal face recognition using convolutional neural network. In: 2016 International Conference on Optoelectronics and Image Processing (ICOIP), pp. 6–9. IEEE (2016)
26. Zhang, K., Zhang, Z., Li, Z., Qiao, Y.: Joint face detection and alignment using multitask cascaded convolutional networks. IEEE Signal Process. Lett. **23**(10), 1499–1503 (2016)
27. Zhang, T., Wiliem, A., Yang, S., Lovell, B.: TV-GAN: generative adversarial network based thermal to visible face recognition. In: 2018 International Conference on Biometrics (ICB), pp. 174–181. IEEE (2018)

Deep Learning-Based Text Recognition of Agricultural Regulatory Document

Fwa Hua Leong[1]([✉])(iD) and Chan Farn Haur[2](iD)

[1] Singapore Management University, 81 Victoria St, Singapore 188065, Singapore
hlfwa@smu.edu.sg
[2] Syngenta Asia Pacific Pte Ltd, 1 Harbourfront Ave, Keppel Bay Tower,
Singapore 098632, Singapore

Abstract. In this study, an OCR system based on deep learning techniques was deployed to digitize scanned agricultural regulatory documents comprising of certificates and labels. Recognition of the certificates and labels is challenging as they are scanned images of the hard copy form and the layout and size of the text as well as the languages vary between the various countries (due to diverse regulatory requirements). We evaluated and compared between various state-of-the-art deep learning-based text detection and recognition model as well as a packaged OCR library - Tesseract. We then adopted a two-stage approach comprising of text detection using Character Region Awareness For Text (CRAFT) followed by recognition using OCR branch of a multi-lingual text recognition algorithm E2E-MLT. A sliding windows text matcher is used to enhance the extraction of the required information such as trade names, active ingredients and crops. Initial evaluation revealed that the system performs well with a high accuracy of 91.9% for the recognition of trade names in certificates and labels and the system is currently deployed for use in Philippines, one of our collaborator's sites.

Keywords: Deep learning · Text detection · Optical character recognition · Regulatory document

1 Introduction

In many industries, the conversion of company assets from non-machine readable into machine readable form is a prerequisite of their journey towards digitalization – the use of digital technologies to transform their business model and provide new opportunities for optimizing their business operations and/or discovering new revenue streams. Optical Character Recognition (OCR) is frequently employed to convert scanned documents in images and pdf formats into machine-readable form for further data processing.

Our collaborator is a leading provider of agricultural science and technology who specializes in the development and provision of seeds and crop protection products to farmers. Rampant use of pesticides as a convenient way of eradicating

© The Author(s), under exclusive license to Springer Nature Switzerland AG 2022
C. Bădică et al. (Eds.): ICCCI 2022, CCIS 1653, pp. 223–234, 2022.
https://doi.org/10.1007/978-3-031-16210-7_18

pests found on crops and reports of possible impact of human health in the early years have prompted the government of various crop producing nations to regulate and control the use of seed and crop protection products such as pesticides and herbicides [6]. These regulatory measures include the submission of an application to register for pesticide or herbicide use accompanied by the relevant test data. A draft of the product label which lists the composition of the product, application and use of the product must also be filed with the regulatory authority.

Upon the approval of the registration, the regulatory authority will then issue a signed certificate which validates the product to be ready for sale and use in the relevant markets for a specified duration. These labels and certificates contain important information such as the active ingredient, the crops and pests which the product is targeted to be use on and the mode and rate of application of the product e.t.c. The labels and certificates can be in soft copy but non-textual format e.g. graphical formats or can be scanned images of the actual hard copy, thus necessitating the use of OCR techniques to extract the textual information within the certificates and labels. In addition, the layout and size of the text and language within the certificates and labels varies between the different countries due to diverse languages and regulatory requirements. This issue of differing regulatory standards and languages is especially pervasive among the countries within Asia where this research is targeted for.

The early optical character recognition efforts involve the use of hand-crafted low-level features e.g. stroke width, gradient, texture e.t.c. [4,7,13]. In most contexts, tedious image pre-processing and post-processing are also required to improve the accuracy of text detection and recognition. This reduces the robustness in the use of such techniques for diverse images e.g. images with diverse fonts, layouts and orientations, multilingual texts and complex backgrounds. These attributes are prevalent in scene text or text that occurs in our natural environment. As opposed to text recognition of type-written or well-formatted documents with high document image quality, achieving high recognition accuracy for scene text is a challenging endeavor as it is characterized by more variability and noise [25].

In recent years, deep learning techniques hold great promise for both image as well as text detection and recognition. The advent of deep learning techniques has contributed to state-of-the-art results on challenging computer vision problems such as object detection and classification [9,14,21,22]. The deep learning models for object detection and classification are similarly adapted for use in text detection and recognition e.g. the use of Convolutional Neural Network model LeNet [15] for handwritten digit recognition. Several deep learning architectures involving the use of Convolutional Neural Networks (CNNs) have evolved along the years with deeper layers and enhanced accuracy for scene text detection and recognition - localizing and recognizing text that occurs in natural images. In contrast to the use of traditional image processing techniques, deep learning techniques eliminate the need for laborious creation and testing of low-level hand-crafted features which thus lead to better model generalizability.

The main contributions of this work are as follows:

- We evaluated state-of-the-art deep learning models for text detection and recognition for use in a real-life industrial application.
- We detailed the techniques that we used for enhancing the accuracy of capturing the essential information from regulatory documents i.e. certificates and labels.
- Lastly, we presented a real-life implementation of regulatory information capturing system with a high level of accuracy.

2   Related Studies

2.1   Text Detection and Recognition

OCR comprises of first distinguishing the text from non-text region within an image (text region detection) and then recognizing the text content (text recognition). Some studies on text detection and recognition adopted a two-stage approach where text region detection is first performed for prediction of the bounding boxes before passing the image cropped using the predicted bounding box to a separate text recognition model. There were also studies which adopted a single stage approach where both text detection and recognition were trained in a single end-to-end pass. A single stage approach models a joint loss function for both localization and recognition and this is postulated to result in a higher accuracy of recognizing the text. More studies are however required to justify this [11]. In our study, we selected a dual stage model for our implementation.

Text detection using deep learning techniques can be divided into Regression-based, Segmentation/link-based and Character-level detectors. In regression-based methods, horizontal/quadrangular boxes are first placed over text instances [18,19]. Iterative regression of the bounding boxes is then applied to generate coordinates of bounding boxes that enclosed the text. A structural limitation of regression-based methods is with their inability to capture all possible text bounding shapes that occur in the wild. Segmentation/link-based methods overcome this limitation by breaking text instances into multiple parts and then linking these parts using some features to detect the final text [23]. The Efficient And Accurate Scene Text detection (EAST) [24] is a segmentation based method that generates multi-oriented text predictions by feeding image pixels directly into a Fully Convolutional Neural Network (FCN) architecture. The model then outputs multiple channels of score map (representing the confidence of the predicted geometry shape) and the geometry shape coordinates. Character level detectors detect text with characters as its unit instead of words. The Character Region Awareness For Text (CRAFT) [1] is one such model which used a FCN to output character region score and affinity score for localizing individual character and linking the detected characters to text respectively. From the published results, CRAFT demonstrated robustness in detecting text with varying sizes including curved or deformed text.

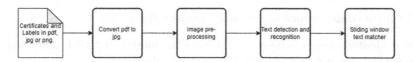

Fig. 1. Overall processing workflow for recognizing and extract essential text information

Methods for text recognition usually consist of a feature extractor that maps the text instance image into a representation with attributes that are relevant for text recognition. Convolutional Neural Networks (CNNs) are widely used in this feature representation stage [5]. After extraction of the text features, the prediction stage then estimates the target string sequence from the extracted features. The two major techniques that are applied here are the Connectionist Temporal Classification (CTC) [8] and the Attention mechanism [2]. CTC converts the features made by CNNs into a target string sequence by calculating the conditional probability. In CTC, the maximum likelihood of the output sequence is computed by summing over the probabilities of all possible input-output sequence alignments. With the insertion of a blank symbol to denote repeated occurrence of a character in CTC, there is no need for prior alignment between the input and target output sequences. Attention on the other hand, learns the alignment between the input and target output sequences from the history of the target characters and the encoded features. Both CTC and Attention are widely used in scene text recognition deep learning architectures.

Industrial Applications of OCR. The study by Kim et al. [12] proposes a method of symbols and text in Piping and Instrumentation Diagrams (P&ID) within the process industry. The need for digitizing P&IDs arises as many P&IDs especially for older plants exist in image form. The authors first constructed a P&ID dataset consisting of 386 symbols relating to piping and instrumentation before passing the dataset to a deep learning model for symbol recognition. For the text portion, the authors used easyOCR for text region detection and Tesseract [20] for text recognition. They justified that this combination provided better performance. The proposed system achieved a precision of 0.9718 and recall of 0.9827 for symbol recognition. The precision and recall for text recognition are 0.9386 and 0.9175. The authors acknowledged that text recognition in P&IDs is less challenging than that in natural images as P&IDs are properly formatted document with no complex background.

A system for the detection and recognition of embossed codes printed on tyre sidewalls for automated tyre condition monitoring was proposed by Kazmi et al. [10]. The authors first applied circular Hough transformation to unwarp text arches into rectangular shaped text. A two-stage approach was adopted where a histogram of gradient features formulated from the tyre images, was passed into a CNN cascade for localizing the text codes before passing the cropped image into another cascade of CNNs for text recognition. In this study, an average accuracy of 86% was attained with the proposed system as opposed to close to zero recognition when using Tesseract. The authors thus postulated that the use of packaged OCR library may not be adequate for all OCR contexts.

3   Methodology

Figure 1 shows the overall processing workflow for recognizing and extracting the essential information from product certificates and labels.

3.1   Image Pre-processing

We pre-processed the documents by first converting them from pdf into image files. To achieve higher accuracy of detection, we converted the images to greyscale and applied adaptive thresholding. The quality of the document scans varies and some of these scanned document may be slanted or oriented in the wrong direction e.g. rotated 90° either clockwise or anti-clockwise. Automatic correction of the document orientation is necessary to ensure that the subsequent text detection and recognition is as accurate as possible. We applied Canny edge detection and Hough transform to calculate the correction angle for proper orientation of the document. Finally, we also resized the document image to constraint it to a maximum of 1280 pixels in either the horizontal (for width larger than height) or vertical dimension (for height larger than width) while maintaining the original aspect ratio.

3.2   Evaluation of Text Detection and Recognition Models

We employed CRAFT as the text detection method for this study. From our initial evaluation comparing CRAFT to EAST, we found that CRAFT performed better with more text detected and lesser overlaps in the predicted bounding boxes. We used a pre-trained CRAFT model for the text detection phase in this project.

For text recognition, we experimented with 3 methods. For the first method, we used the text recognition branch of E2E-MLT [3] which is made up of deep convolutional layers. For the second method, we used Show, Attend and Read model (SAR) [17] which makes use of ResNet [9] and attention-based LSTM encoder-decoder architecture. For the last model, we used Tesseract, an open-source text recognition library from Google. For E2E-MLT and SAR models, we used the pre-trained weights provided by their respective authors. In E2E-MLT, the original model is an end-to-end single stage model which optimized both text localization and text recognition with a joint loss function. The original E2E-MLT generates and filters text proposals for detecting and locating text within an image. We replaced the text localization branch of E2E-MLT with CRAFT and used only the text recognition branch of the model. Our rationale is since it has not been proven conclusively that an end-to-end text detection and recognition model works better than a dual stage one, this dual stage design

Table 1. Character error rates (CER) of models

Model	CER
E2E-MLT	0.12
SAR	0.32
Tesseract	0.10

allows us the flexibility of evaluating and selecting the best of breed models separately for the text detection and recognition phases.

To evaluate the performance of the 3 text recognition models, we randomly selected 5 certificates and 5 labels from our dataset. For E2E-MLT and SAR, we passed the certificates and label images through CRAFT model for prediction of the bounding boxes which is then used for cropping out the detected text. The cropped text images were further passed to both E2E-MLT and SAR for text recognition. For Tesseract, we passed the certificates and label images directly into the library for both text detection and recognition. We compared the character error rate for the first 30 detected words with their ground truth for each label and certificate. The character error rate is a metric that is used to evaluate OCR output quality. The results are shown in Table 1.

As can be seen in Table 1, the CER for Tesseract is the best at 10% while the CER for E2E-MLT is comparable to that of Tesseract at 12%. SAR's CER is rather high at 32%. In addition, we also calculated the percentage of instances of non-text regions detected as a percentage of the total detection instances for both CRAFT and Tesseract. We noted that Tesseract detected a higher number of instances of non-text regions at 26.8% while that for CRAFT is just 6.9%. A higher incidence of false positives in the detection of text region would result in higher inaccuracies in subsequent text recognition on top of the cost of additional processing time. Thus, considering both model CER and false positives of text detection, we selected E2E-MLT (with CRAFT for text detection) as the final model for our implementation.

4 Models

4.1 Character Region Awareness for Text (CRAFT)

CRAFT is a fully convolutional network architecture which uses VGG-16 as its backbone. VGG-16 is a feature extraction architecture that encodes an image input into a certain feature representation. The decoding segment of CRAFT also uses skip connections to aggregate lower-level features. CRAFT predicts two scores for each character - region score which localizes the character and affinity score, a measure of association of one character with another. The affinity score is used for combining the characters together into words. The combination of these two scores then defines the bounding boxes that enclose the detected text.

FIRST

DIRECTIONS

Alika

USE:

247

ZC

RE-ENTRY

PERIOD:

ALD:

suspected

Fig. 2. Sample OCR text output

4.2 E2E-MLT OCR Branch

The OCR branch of the E2E-MLT is a FCN module for multi-language text recognition. The bounding boxes predicted by CRAFT are used to crop out the word level image segments and the cropped images are then passed into the FCN module for recognition of the specific text. The cropped image passed into the FCN module are scaled to a $\bar{W} \times 40 \times C$ where height (h) of the cropped image is fixed at 40 pixels and $\bar{W} = \mathrm{w}\frac{H'}{h}$. The FCN module then outputs a matrix of size $\frac{\bar{W}}{4} \times \left|\hat{A}\right|$, where $\hat{A}$ is the union of characters in all languages. The loss for text recognition is computed using CTC. E2E-MLT OCR supports 8 different languages – Arabic, Bangla, Chinese, Japanese, Korean and Latin.

Algorithm 1. Sliding window text matcher algorithm

1: **procedure** WINDOWEDTEXTMATCHER($wordlist, cutoffscore$)
2:     $w \leftarrow 1$ ▷ w is the window width
3:     **while** not end of list **do**
4:        **while** $w <= 5$ **do**   ▷ Loop for window size 1 to 5
5:           Combine k words to form new word separated by space
6:           **while** not end of global dictionary **do**
7:              Calculate Levenshtein ratio (lr) between new word(s) and the word(s) in global dictionary
8:              **if** $lr \geq cutoffscore$ **then**
9:                 **return** $word$
10:     **return** $null$

4.3 Sliding Windows Text Matcher

The outputs from CRAFT and E2E-MLT models comprises of a list of words detected from the individual certificate or label. From the list of words, it is still not possible to identify the trade name, active ingredient, crops and pests. One technique to extract the required information e.g. trade name is to annotate a few possible locations where the trade name is found on the certificates or labels. However, this limits both the generalizability and reliability of the system as a change in the document format or layout would result in non-extraction. Most of the useful text that we need to extract for feeding into our collaborator's knowledge management system relate to the trade name, active ingredient and crops and pests. Some trade names, crops and pests also consist of multiple words joined together e.g. Alika 247 ZC. In addition, the terms or words that make up the trade name may not be in consecutive locations due to diverse font sizes and orientations. A sample of a part of the output from the text recognition model is shown in Fig. 2.

From the sample OCR text output, it would not be possible to pick out the trade name "Alika 247 ZC" as it is split into 3 different words and at non-consecutive locations. To resolve this, we first extracted a global dictionary of trade names, active ingredients, crops and pests from both the company's internal sources as well as from the company's subscriptions of external databases. A sliding windows text matcher (Algorithm 1) is then applied to match the global dictionary against the detected text.

The formula to calculate Levenshtein Ratio (LR) is given below.

$$LR = (len(S) + len(D) - LD)/(len(S) + len(D)) \qquad (1)$$

where LD is the Levenshtein Distance. LR is used as it normalizes for different word length, giving a score between 0 and 100 where 100 denotes a perfect match between the source (S) and destination (D) word. Levenshtein Distance(LD) [16] computes the number of edits (inserts, deletes or subsitutes) required to transform the source word to the destination word and is given by

$$lev_{a,b}(i,j) = \begin{cases} max(i,j) & \text{if } min(i,j) = 0 \\ min \begin{cases} lev_{a,b}(i-1,j) + 1 \\ lev_{a,b}(i,j-1) + 1 \\ lev_{a,b}(i-1,j-1) + 1 \end{cases} & \text{otherwise} \end{cases} \qquad (2)$$

The use of LD and LR allows us to compute a measure for the comparison of the global dictionary against the recognized text (trade name, active ingredient, crop or pest). We have set the LR cutoff for recognition of trade name, active ingredient, crop and pest at 0.96 currently.

Table 2. Recognition accuracy of trade name, active ingredients and crops

Document	Trade name	Active ingredients	Crops
Certs	94.90%	82.00%	75.80%
Labels	88.90%	64.30%	95.20%
Overall	91.90%	73.15%	85.50%

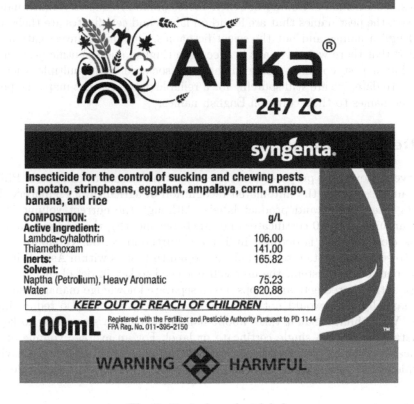

Fig. 3. Typical product label

5 Results

With the proposed sliding windows text matcher, we refined the extraction of trade names, active ingredients and crops from a total of 39 certificates and 9 labels. These certificates and labels are provided by our collaborator in Philippines (where our proposed solution has been deployed).

As seen in Table 2, the recognition of trade name from certificates is high at 94.9% accuracy. For labels, the accuracy for recognition of trade name is lower at 88.9% accuracy. A typical product label is shown in Fig. 3. With closer examination, we surmise that the diverse font styles and text sizes for the text found in product labels made it more challenging to accurately detect the text bounding boxes and this thus lowered the accuracy of text recognition of labels.

Aggregating across certificates and label, the overall recognition accuracy for trade name is the highest at 91.9% followed by that for crops at 85.5% and lastly for active ingredients at 73.15%. For overall recognition accuracy, we averaged the accuracy for certificates and labels as our collaborator reflected that the number of certificates and labels should be quite balanced. We did not measure the recognition accuracy of pests as the global database currently only contains the pests' scientific names and not their more commonly known English names. However, the pest names that are found on labels and certificates are their common English names and not the scientific names. Our initial investigation also revealed that there were overlaps between the English and scientific pest names such that a pest common name might be associated with multiple scientific names. To date, we are still sourcing for a reliable database that maps the pests' scientific names to their common English names.

6   Real World Deployment

We have deployed the proposed system in one of our collaborator's site in Philippines and used it for the automated recognition of agricultural regulatory documents - certificates and product labels. Although the current volume is not huge (around 10 to 20 certificates and labels per month), the recognition accuracy is close to what is detailed in Table 2. Furthermore, our collaborator has plans to scale this system to be deployed to multiple sites within Asia. With the deployment of this system, the user will not need to key in detail such as trade names, active ingredients and crops into a separate knowledge management system manually. This would not only conserve man effort but also reduce input errors. We estimate that it takes about half an hour for a single user to key in the details listed in a single certificate or label. For an average volume of 100 certificates or labels per month, our system can achieve 50 man hours savings and this will be more significant when the use of the system is further scaled up.

7   Conclusion

In this study, we have detailed the design of an OCR system based on deep learning techniques that is used for the recognition of agricultural regulatory document. We have also evaluated the use of state-of-the-art deep learning based text detection and recognition algorithms as well as a packaged OCR library, Tesseract for the recognition of the regulatory certificates and labels. With the use of CRAFT for text detection and E2E-MLT OCR for text recognition, we managed to achieve an accuracy of 91.9%, 73.15% and 85.5% for the recognition of trade name, active ingredients and crops. To avert the need to annotate possible locations where the required term is located within the regulatory document and to achieve a high generalizability and reliability of extraction, we used a sliding window text matcher to match against a global dictionary of the required terms. The proposed system is currently deployed for use in a client site in Philippines and the user has plans to scale up the use of the system.

In order to scale the use of the system in other sites within Asia, an important future task is the detection and recognition of multi-lingual text. E2E-MLT can currently support 8 languages but we intend to explore other multi-lingual OCR techniques and apply fine-tuning to enhance the recognition accuracy.

References

1. Baek, Y., Lee, B., Han, D., Yun, S., Lee, H.: Character region awareness for text detection. arXiv:1904.01941 [cs], April 2019. http://arxiv.org/abs/1904.01941
2. Bahdanau, D., Cho, K., Bengio, Y.: Neural machine translation by jointly learning to align and translate. arXiv preprint arXiv:1409.0473 (2014)
3. Bušta, Michal, Patel, Yash, Matas, Jiri: E2E-MLT - an unconstrained end-to-end method for multi-language scene text. In: Carneiro, Gustavo, You, Shaodi (eds.) ACCV 2018. LNCS, vol. 11367, pp. 127–143. Springer, Cham (2019). https://doi.org/10.1007/978-3-030-21074-8_11
4. Chen, X., Yuille, A.L.: Detecting and reading text in natural scenes. In: Proceedings of the 2004 IEEE Computer Society Conference on Computer Vision and Pattern Recognition, 2004. CVPR 2004, vol. 2, p. II. IEEE (2004)
5. Chen, X., Jin, L., Zhu, Y., Luo, C., Wang, T.: Text recognition in the wild: a survey. arXiv:2005.03492 [cs], December 2020. http://arxiv.org/abs/2005.03492
6. Gaston, C.P.: Pesticide Regulatory Policies of Selected Countries in Asia, p. 35
7. Gllavata, J., Ewerth, R., Freisleben, B.: Text detection in images based on unsupervised classification of high-frequency wavelet coefficients. In: Proceedings of the 17th International Conference on Pattern Recognition, 2004. ICPR 2004, vol. 1, pp. 425–428. IEEE (2004)
8. Graves, A., Fernandez, S., Gomez, F., Schmidhuber, J.: Connectionist Temporal Classification: Labelling Unsegmented Sequence Data with Recurrent Neural Networks, p. 8
9. He, K., Zhang, X., Ren, S., Sun, J.: Deep residual learning for image recognition. In: Proceedings of the IEEE Conference on Computer Vision and Pattern Recognition, pp. 770–778 (2016)
10. Kazmi, W., Nabney, I., Vogiatzis, G., Rose, P., Codd, A.: An efficient industrial system for vehicle Tyre (Tire) detection and text recognition using deep learning. IEEE Trans. Intell. Transp. Syst. 22(2), 1264–1275 (2021). https://doi.org/10.1109/TITS.2020.2967316, https://ieeexplore.ieee.org/document/8968735/
11. Khan, T., Sarkar, R., Mollah, A.F.: Deep learning approaches to scene text detection: a comprehensive review. Artif. Intell. Rev. 54(5), 3239–3298 (2021). https://doi.org/10.1007/s10462-020-09930-6, https://link.springer.com/10.1007/s10462-020-09930-6
12. Kim, H., et al.: Deep-learning-based recognition of symbols and texts at an industrially applicable level from images of high-density piping and instrumentation diagrams. Expert Syst. Appl. 183, 115337 (2021). https://doi.org/10.1016/j.eswa.2021.115337, https://linkinghub.elsevier.com/retrieve/pii/S0957417421007661
13. Kim, K.I., Jung, K., Kim, J.H.: Texture-based approach for text detection in images using support vector machines and continuously adaptive mean shift algorithm. IEEE Trans. Pattern Anal. Mach. Intell. 25(12), 1631–1639 (2003)
14. Krizhevsky, A., Sutskever, I., Hinton, G.E.: ImageNet classification with deep convolutional neural networks. Adv. Neural Inf. Process. Syst. 25 (2012)
15. Lecun, Y., Bottou, L., Bengio, Y., Haffner, P.: Gradient-based learning applied to document recognition. Proc. IEEE 86(11), 2278–2324 (1998). https://doi.org/10.1109/5.726791, http://ieeexplore.ieee.org/document/726791/
16. Levenshtein, V.I., et al.: Binary codes capable of correcting deletions, insertions, and reversals. In: Soviet Physics Doklady, vol. 10, pp. 707–710. Soviet Union (1966)
17. Li, H., Wang, P., Shen, C., Zhang, G.: Show, attend and read: a simple and strong baseline for irregular text recognition. arXiv:1811.00751 [cs] (March 2019), http://arxiv.org/abs/1811.00751

18. Liao, M., Shi, B., Bai, X.: Textboxes++: a single-shot oriented scene text detector. IEEE Trans. Image Process. **27**(8), 3676–3690 (2018)

19. Liao, M., Shi, B., Bai, X., Wang, X., Liu, W.: Textboxes: a fast text detector with a single deep neural network. In: Thirty-First AAAI Conference on Artificial Intelligence (2017)

20. Patel, C., Patel, A., Patel, D.: Optical character recognition by open source OCR tool tesseract: a case study. Int. J. Comput. Appl. **55**(10), 50–56 (2012)

21. Simonyan, K., Zisserman, A.: Very deep convolutional networks for large-scale image recognition. arXiv preprint arXiv:1409.1556 (2014)

22. Szegedy, C., et al.: Going deeper with convolutions. In: Proceedings of the IEEE Conference on Computer Vision and Pattern Recognition, pp. 1–9 (2015)

23. Tian, S., et al.: Multilingual scene character recognition with co-occurrence of histogram of oriented gradients. Patt. Recogn. **51**, 125–134 (2016). https://doi. org/10.1016/j.patcog.2015.07.009, https://linkinghub.elsevier.com/retrieve/pii/ S0031320315002691

24. Zhou, X., et al.: East: an efficient and accurate scene text detector. In: Proceedings of the IEEE Conference on Computer Vision and Pattern Recognition, pp. 5551–5560 (2017)

25. Zhu, Y., Yao, C., Bai, X.: Scene text detection and recognition: recent advances and future trends. Front. Comput. Sci. **10**(1), 19–36 (2016). https://doi.org/10. 1007/s11704-015-4488-0, http://link.springer.com/10.1007/s11704-015-4488-0

Computational Intelligence
for Multimedia Understanding

Textural Features Sensitivity to Scale and Illumination Variations

Pavel Vácha[1] and Michal Haindl[1,2(✉)]

[1] The Institute of Information Theory and Automation of the ASCR,
Prague, Czechia
{vacha,haindl}@utia.cas.cz
[2] Faculty of Management, University of Economics, Jindřichuv Hradec, Czechia
http://www.utia.cas.cz

Abstract. Visual scene recognition is predominantly based on visual textures representing an object's material properties. However, the single material texture varies in scale and illumination angles due to mapping an object's shape. We present a comparative study of the color histogram, Gabor, opponent Gabor, Local Binary Pattern (LBP), and wide-sense Markovian textural features concerning their sensitivity to simultaneous scale and illumination variations. Due to their application dominance, these textural features are selected from more than 50 published textural features. Markovian features are information preserving, and we demonstrate their superior performance for scale and illumination variable observation conditions over the standard alternative textural features. We bound the scale variation by double size, and illumination variation includes illumination spectra, acquisition devices, and 35 illumination directions spanned above a sample.

Keywords: Markovian textural features · LBP · Gabor features · Scale sensitivity · Illumination sensitivity

1 Introduction

A human observer recognizes a visual scene using shape and material attributes. Unfortunately, the surface material's appearance vastly changes under variable observation conditions, negatively affecting its automatic and reliable recognition in numerous artificial intelligence applications. As a consequence, most material recognition attempts apply unnaturally restricted observation conditions [2,6,37]. Modeled Scale Invariant Feature Transform (SIFT) features using Johnson distribution [18] allow features invariant in rotation, scale, and illumination. Authors [29] proposed fractal dimension calculated in the Gaussian scale-space texture representation. Fractal images combined with LBP images using an indexing function to obtain scale-invariant features. Galois field-based features in [31] were used for rotation and scale invariant texture classification.

The Czech Science Foundation project GAČR 19-12340S supported this research.

Rotation, scale, and illumination invariant features [39] use LBP and log-polar energy-based descriptors in the dual-tree complex wavelet transform domain. Another rotation, illumination, and scale invariance variant of LBP (IRSLBP) was published in [38], where partial scale invariance authors achieved using three different neighborhood radii. Although over 50 various textural features were published [23,33], we restricted our comparison to the most effective and thus dominant textural features. An ideal model for representing and classifying materials should be capable of capturing fundamental perceptual materials properties. A multi-dimensional visual texture is an appropriate paradigm for such a surface reflectance function model. The best measurable representation is the seven-dimensional Bidirectional Texture Function (BTF) [10]. BTF can be simultaneously measured, even if it is not a trivial task, modeled using state-of-the-art measurement devices and computers and the most advanced visual data mathematical models. Features derived from such multi-dimensional data models are information preserving because they can synthesize data spaces resembling the original measurement data space. The authors have introduced a family of fast multi-resolution Markov random field-based models. They have shown that these models excel in robustness to illumination conditions [14].

This paper's contribution is a joint test of scale and illumination variations to simulate realistic visual scene recognition conditions and we present a comparative analysis with several most common alternative textural features representing four alternatives most commonly used textural features. For this analysis, we take advantage of the unique UTIA BTF visual material measurements [13].

2   Markovian Textural Features

The texture is factorized into K levels of the Gaussian down-sampled pyramid and subsequently each pyramid level is modeled by a wide-sense Markovian type of model - the Causal Auto-regressive Random (CAR) model. Let us assume that each multispectral (color) texture is composed of C spectral planes (usually $C = 3$), $Y_r = [Y_{r,1}, \ldots, Y_{r,C}]^T$ is the multispectral pixel at location r. The multiindex $r = (r_1, r_2)$ is composed of row index r_1 and column index r_2. The spectral planes are mutually decorrelated by the Karhunen-Loéve transformation. The two-dimensional models assume that the j-th spectral plane of the pixel at position r can be modeled as:

$$Y_{r,j} = \gamma_j Z_{r,j} + \epsilon_r , \tag{1}$$

where $Z_{r,j} = [Y_{r-s,j} : \forall s \in I_r]^T$ is the $\eta \times 1$ data vector, ϵ_r is Gaussian white noise with constant but unknown variance, $\gamma_j = [a_{1,j}, \ldots, a_{\eta,j}]$ is the $1 \times \eta$ unknown parameter vector. Some selected contextual causal or unilateral neighbor index shift set is denoted I_r and $\eta = cardinality(I_r)$, see Fig. 1. The texture is analyzed in a chosen direction, where multi-index t changes according to the movement on the image lattice I. Given the known CAR process history $Y^{(t-1),j} = \{Y_{t-1,j}, Y_{t-2,j}, \ldots, Y_{1,j}, Z_{t,j}, Z_{t-1,j}, \ldots, Z_{1,j}\}$, $\hat{\gamma}_j$ can be estimated using fast, numerically robust recursive statistics [9]:

$$V_{t-1,j} = \begin{pmatrix} \sum_{u=1}^{t-1} Y_{u,j} Y_{u,j}^T & \sum_{u=1}^{t-1} Y_{u,j} Z_{u,j}^T \\ \sum_{u=1}^{t-1} Z_{u,j} Y_{u,j}^T & \sum_{u=1}^{t-1} Z_{u,j} Z_{u,j}^T \end{pmatrix} + V_0 = \begin{pmatrix} V_{y,j(t-1)} & V_{zy,j(t-1)}^T \\ V_{zy,j(t-1)} & V_{z,j(t-1)} \end{pmatrix} \quad (2)$$

$$\hat{\gamma}_{t-1,j}^T = V_{z,j(t-1)}^{-1} V_{zy,j(t-1)} , \qquad (3)$$

$$\lambda_{t-1,j} = V_{y,j(t-1)} - V_{zy,j(t-1)}^T V_{z,j(t-1)}^{-1} V_{zy,j(t-1)} , \qquad (4)$$

where the positive definite matrix V_0 represents prior knowledge. Our textural features are $a_{s,j} \, \forall s \in I_r, j = 1, \ldots, C$ which are color invariants and additional color invariant features derived from this model in [15]. The spectral index is excluded for simplification in (10)–(20) for all statistics in these invariants.

$$\alpha_3 = \sqrt{\sum_{\forall r \in I} (Y_r - \hat{\gamma}_t Z_r)^T \lambda_t^{-1} (Y_r - \hat{\gamma}_t Z_r)} , \qquad (5)$$

$$\alpha_4 = \sqrt{\sum_{\forall r \in I} (Y_r - \mu)^T \lambda_t^{-1} (Y_r - \mu)} \} , \qquad (6)$$

$$\beta_6 = \ln \left(\sum_{\forall r \in I} \frac{1}{|I|} \, p\left(Y_r | Y^{(r-1)}\right) |V_{y(t)}|^{\frac{1}{2}} \right) , \qquad (7)$$

$$\beta_7 = \ln \left(\ln p\left(Y^{(t)} | M\right) + (\psi(t+1) + 2) \ln |V_{y(t)}| \right) , \qquad (8)$$

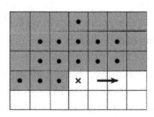

Fig. 1. Unilateral contextual neighborhood I_r of sixth-order used for CAR model. X marks the current pixel, the bullets are pixels in the neighborhood, the arrow shows movement direction, and the grey area indicates acceptable neighborhood pixels. (Color figure online)

Fig. 2. The appearance of patterns from the UEA database with varying illumination spectra, acquisition devices (top row), and scale (bottom row).

$$\alpha_1 = \sum_{j=1}^{C} a_{i,j} \ \forall i \ , \tag{9}$$

$$\alpha_2 = 1 + Z_t^T V_{z(t)}^{-1} Z_t \ , \tag{10}$$

$$\beta_1 = \ln\left(\frac{\psi(r)}{\psi(t)} |\lambda_t| |\lambda_r|^{-1}\right) \ , \tag{11}$$

$$\beta_2 = \ln\left(\frac{\psi(r)}{\psi(t)} \left|V_{z(t)}\right| \left|V_{z(r)}\right|^{-1}\right) \tag{12}$$

$$\beta_3 = \ln\left(\left|V_{z(t)}\right| |\lambda_t|^{-\eta}\right) \ , \tag{13}$$

$$\beta_4 = \ln\left(\left|V_{z(t)}\right| \left|V_{y(t)}\right|^{-\eta}\right) \ , \tag{14}$$

$$\beta_5 = \mathrm{tr}\left\{V_{y(t)} \ \lambda_t^{-1}\right\} \ , \tag{15}$$

$$\beta_8 = \left(\frac{\psi(r)}{\psi(t)} |\lambda_t| |\lambda_r|^{-1}\right)^{\frac{1}{2}} \ , \tag{16}$$

$$\beta_9 = \left(\frac{\psi(r)}{\psi(t)} \left|V_{z(t)}\right| \left|V_{z(r)}\right|^{-1}\right)^{\frac{1}{2\eta}} \tag{17}$$

$$\beta_{10} = \left(\left|V_{z(t)}\right| |\lambda_t|^{-\eta}\right)^{\frac{1}{2}} \ , \tag{18}$$

$$\beta_{11} = \left(\left|V_{z(t)}\right| \left|V_{y(t)}\right|^{-\eta}\right)^{\frac{1}{2}} \ , \tag{19}$$

$$\beta_{12} = \sqrt{\left|V_{y(t)}\right| |\lambda_t|^{-1}} \ , \tag{20}$$

where μ is the mean value of Y_r and $\psi(t)$ is a number of the pixel from the beginning. $p\left(Y^{(t)}|M\right)$ is the posterior probability of the model (1), and $p\left(Y_r|Y^{(r-1)}\right)$ is prediction probability, both defined in [9]. We used neigborhood I_r of sixth order (see Fig. 1), where $\eta = 14$, $r = 0$ coresponding to prior, and t equals to the last pixel in the image. All invariants (10)–(20) were computed on all spectral planes and concatenated into the feature vector. The CAR model and color invariant feature vector were computed on $K = 5$ Gaussian pyramid levels and in 3 directions, and the features were again concatenated. Finally, the feature vectors were compared with fuzzy contrast FC_3 [30]. Downscaling on the Gaussian pyramid is possible as the image provides sufficient resolution. It may be needed for lower resolution images to use $K = 4$ levels of the Gaussian pyramid, which was also tested. When the Karhunen-Loéve transformation preceded CAR features computation, they were denoted by the '-KL' suffix. The feature vector size is 1515 for $K = 5$ and 1212 for $K = 4$ pyramid levels.

3   Frequented Alternative Features

Hundreds of various textural features were published and to test all these features on the extensive UTIA BTF wood database (426 465 wood images, 260 TB of data) is infeasible. Hence, we compare the CAR features with the following most frequented four alternatives, each compared with their author's suggested distance:

- Color histogram features computed as cumulative histogram [34] on each spectral plane separately and concatenated, compared with L1 distance (384 features).
- Gabor features [7,16,21,25] computed on each spectral plane separately and concatenated, compared with L1 distance normalized to standard deviation of features (144 features).
- Opponent Gabor features [19] compared with L2 distance normalized to standard deviation of features (252 features).
- Local Binary Patterns $LBP_{8,1+8,3}$ and $LBP^u_{16,2}$ [27] computed either on grayscale images or each spectral plane separately and concatenated, compared with the Kullback Leibler divergence (1536 and 243 features). LBP features exist in various modifications [1,5,17,20,22,26,40], but they have similar behavior; hence we chose two of their variants as representatives of the whole group as any comparison cannot be considered an exhaustive investigation without the LBP strategy.

The setup of listed features is described in more detail in [15]. The other tested parameters were under-performing, namely histogram and Gabor features on gray images. We excluded fashionable neural net features due to their uncompetitiveness on often restricted test data in practical applications. They are little understood, wasteful, dependent on the net topology, and thus cannot be regarded as well-defined textural features. Moreover, we use only between one to six training images which are insufficient for neural net robust learning. The MRF features outperformed deep CNN in the bark recognition problem even on extensive training data, as demonstrated in [28]. This result is understandable because MRF features are descriptive while neural net features are discriminative. Similar results were presented in the extensive comparison of the multilayer NN marble textures classification with 17 variants of the LBP feature and three types of key-point texture descriptors in [32]. In their results, the CNN features never outperform all these alternatives. Another comparison where NN - ScatNet, PCANet, FV-AlexNet, and RandNet do not outperform LBP features on Outex, CUReT, ALOT, and KTHTIPS data can be consulted in [24]. However, it would be interesting to include tests with a low number of training samples which would reveal the robustness of features to various conditions as in [3,36].

4   Experiments

We tested the scale sensitivity of the selected textural features on two databases:

Fig. 3. The appearance of two veneers from the Wood UTIA BTF database in varying illumination direction (upper two rows) and different scale (bottom row).

(i) University of East Anglia (UEA) Uncalibrated Image Database [4] consisting of patterns under different illumination spectra and
(ii) wooden BTF measurements from the extensive UTIA BTF database [13] composed of material images under varying illumination directions.

4.1   University of East Anglia Uncalibrated Image Database

The UEA dataset contains 28 textile designs, captured with six different devices (4 color cameras and two color scanners), and images for cameras were illuminated with three different illumination spectra, which sums up to 394 images in total (see examples in Fig. 2). UEA images are supposed to include even non-linear relations of images caused by different processing in acquisition devices (gamma correction) [4], no light calibration was performed. Since the UEA database images include some scale variations, we have corrected this and rescaled the images to have the same scale and resolution.

4.2   Wood UTIA BTF Database

This study's Wood UTIA BTF database contains veneers from sixty-five varied European, African, and American wood species. The UTIA BTF database[1] was measured using the high precision robotic gonioreflectometer [11], which consists of independently controlled arms with a camera and light. Its parameters, such as angular precision of 0.03°, the spatial resolution of 1000 DPI, or selective spatial measurement, classify this gonioreflectometer as a state-of-the-art device. They

---

[1] http://btf.utia.cas.cz/.

measured each wood sample in 81 viewing positions times 81 illumination positions resulting in 6561 images per sample, 4 TB of data. Because of substantial storage requirements, we took only images for one camera position (top view), and we selected 35 from 81 illumination directions (1 image with the tilt of $0°$, 12 images with $30°$, ten images with $60°$, and 12 images with $75°$). The images uniformly represent the space of possible illumination directions (examples in Fig. 3).

4.3 Setup

In both experiments, all images were scaled down to $95\%, 90\%, 85\%, \ldots, 50\%$ of their original size, and regions with the same resolution were cropped. Consequently, the image of scale 50% covers double the size of the original texture image, but with half of the details than scale 100%. The training set contains only images with original scales, and the classification accuracy was tested for all scales separately. Training images per each material were randomly selected from the training set, and the remaining images were classified using the Nearest Neighbor (1-NN) classifier. The number of training images went from 1 to 6, and the results averaged over 10^3 of random selections of training images. Even single training samples were randomly selected, so they could have different illumination conditions for each material, making recognition more challenging. In total, we used 4 312 images with 332×275 resolution for UEA and 25 025 images with 816×802 resolution for Wood UTIA BTF.

Table 1. Classification accuracy [%] averaged over all scales and illumination angles on the UEA/Wood UTIA BTF datasets. Columns display results for the increasing number of training samples per class.

	UEA			Wood UTIA BTF		
No. of training samples	1	3	6	1	3	6
Color histogram	15.3	23.2	32.6	10.6	19.7	28.6
Gabor	33.9	46.2	59.7	18.0	28.6	36.8
Opponent Gabor	44.0	61.0	70.1	24.0	36.4	44.3
$LBP^u_{16,2}$, gray	18.4	35.0	45.8	7.2	11.0	13.3
$LBP_{8,1+8,3}$, color	14.1	28.2	38.1	13.3	21.0	25.6
2D CAR-KL ($K = 4$)	43.1	58.2	67.0	39.9	55.7	64.3
2D CAR-KL	48.4	62.8	70.2	**45.4**	**61.4**	**69.4**
2D CAR	**52.1**	**66.2**	**73.0**	32.8	47.1	55.7

4.4 Results

Table 1 summarizes recognition accuracy for the best parameters of compared features. The 2D CAR features are superior for all test numbers of random training images per material. The classification of the accuracy of 2D CAR-KL averaged over all scale variations goes from 48.4%/45.4% (UEA/Wood UTIA BTF) for one training sample to 70.2%/69.4% for six training samples per class. The standard deviation is less than 4 for one training sample, less than 3 for six training samples for UEA, and less the 2 for Wood UTIA BTF for all features. The 2D CAR model achieved slightly better results without the Karhunen-Loève transformation for UEA. However, we include 2D CAR-KL for more detailed analysis since it has better classification accuracy for other experiments [14]. Also, the 2D CAR-KL model on $K = 4$, levels of the Gaussian pyramid achieved lower accuracy than the standard $K = 5$ levels if the images have sufficient resolution (Wood UTIA BTF). The only comparable features for UEA are opponent Gabor features that achieved similar performance as 2D CAR-KL with slightly lower accuracy for one training sample. Gabor features are also the best alternative in Wood UTIA BTF, but their accuracy is more than 20% points lower than 2D CAR-KL. Color histograms suffer from their sensitivity to color changes, which results in their low performance. Even though the color histograms are robust to scale variation (because they do not describe spatial relations) they are unable to recognize materials under different illumination spectra. LBP and histogram features did not perform satisfactorily. The reason is that binarized LBP micropatterns are sensitive to illumination direction [35]. They are also very sensitive to even slight scale variations, as confirmed by [15].

Table 2. Classification accuracy [%] shown for different illumination tilt (declination angle from the surface normal) without any scale variation (Wood UTIA BTF). The training sample is illuminated from the surface normal direction.

Illumination tilt [deg]	30	60	75	Avg.
Opponent Gabor	50.1	26.1	14.9	30.8
LBP$_{8,1+8,3}$, color	55.8	25.2	13.6	31.5
2D CAR-KL	83.3	62.9	42.1	**62.8**

University of East Anglia. Detailed comparison for UEA scale variation is displayed in Fig. 4, where we can see classification accuracy significantly increases if scales of training and test samples are closer to each other. The only exception is color histogram features, which cannot recognize the same materials on the same scale due to insufficient robustness to the illumination spectra changes. These conclusions hold for one training sample and six random training samples per class. The 2D CAR-KL features again achieved the best results, where classification accuracy for one training sample starts on 23.1% for half scale factor and goes to 64.9% for the same scale (15% better than alternative features). Opponent Gabor features were slightly better for the highest difference in the scale factor. A similar situation holds for six training samples, where classification accuracy goes from 36.9% to 90.0% for 2D CAR-KL features. However, opponent Gabor features performed better with a significant difference in scale factor (0.5 - 0.7).

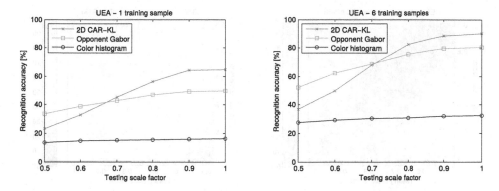

Fig. 4. The illustration of the classification accuracy [%] progresses with decreasing scale differences among training and test sets (UEA). On the left for one training sample and on the right for six training samples per class.

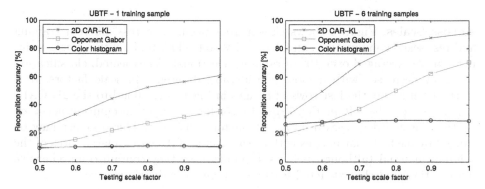

Fig. 5. Classification accuracy [%] progresses with decreasing scale differences among training and test sets (Wood UTIA BTF). On the left for one training sample and on the right for six training samples per class.

Wood UTIA BTF. The detailed comparison of scale variation on Wood UTIA BTF is displayed in Fig. 5. The classification accuracy increases as scales of training and test samples are closer (except for histogram features). The best results were again achieved by 2D CAR-KL features, where classification accuracy for one training sample starts at 22.7% for half scale and goes to 60.9% for the same scale. This improvement is more than 10% better than the opponent Gabor features for all scale factors. A similar situation holds for six training samples, where classification accuracy goes from 31.5% to 91.0% for 2D CAR-KL features, again more than 10% better than opponent Gabor features.

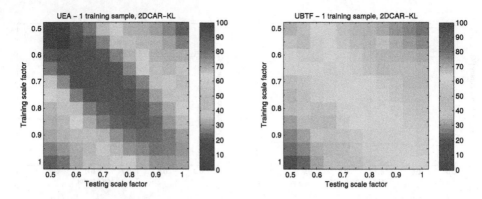

Fig. 6. The classification accuracy [%] for all combinations of scales among training and test sets UEA (left)/Wood UTIA BTF (right), one training sample per class was used.

Across Scales. Figure 6 shows classification accuracy across different training and test scales combinations on UEA and Wood UTIA BTF, with a single training sample (averaged over 10^3 of random selections). As expected, classification accuracy decreases with a more considerable difference in scale factors. It is worth noting that the last rows of images in Fig. 6 correspond to the 2D CAR-KL graphs on the left in Fig. 4 and Fig. 5. Interestingly, recognition accuracy on the diagonal decreases from a scale factor of 0.5 to 1. This decrease may be caused by the fact that images with a scale factor of 0.5 cover a larger area of the original material (although being subsampled), so they contain comprehensive information, and the extracted features can be more discriminative.

Illumination Tilt. The additional experiment utilizes different illumination angles in Wood UTIA BTF and splits classification accuracy for different illumination tilts. The single training sample was fixed to the illumination from a normal surface direction (0-° tilt), and the remaining images were classified. The classification accuracy is averaged for each illumination tilt: 30, 60, and 75° (12, 10, and 12 images). Training and test sets have the same scaling factor 1. The results are displayed in Table 2, where classification accuracy decreases as illumination direction moves further from training sample illumination. The last column's average results roughly correspond to the left graph in Fig. 5 for test scale factor 1. As the scale variation is not present, the results of LBP and opponent Gabor features are comparable.

5   Conclusion

The results indicate that Markovian illumination invariant texture features (2D CAR), based on the Markovian descriptive model, are the most robust textural features for realistic texture classification under the natural conditions when learning and classifying textures differ in scale and illumination properties. The 2D CAR features outperformed alternative tested textural features, i.e., the Gabor, opponent Gabor, variants of LBP, or color histogram texture features. 2D CAR statistical features are analytically derived from the underlying descriptive textural model and can be efficiently, recursively, and adaptively learned. Their additional advantage is their numerically robust estimation. The method's correct recognition accuracy improvements are between 27% and 44%, compared to the LBP features and up to 25% compared to the opponent Gabor features (the second-best alternative). The worst are color histograms with an accuracy decrease between 35% and 43%. The color Markovian textural features were also successfully applied elsewhere in recognition of wood veneers using a smartphone camera [14], or tree taxonomy categorization based on bark or coniferous tree needles [28]. The presented results apply for recognition with bounded scale variation. The full scale-invariant textural features should be considered for extreme expected scale variation. However, fully invariant features usually lose some discriminability. Thus, each application needs carefully balance invariance to expected variability and discriminability.

References

1. Ahonen, T., Matas, J., He, C., Pietikainen, M.: Rotation invariant image description with local binary pattern histogram Fourier features. In: SCIA, pp. 61–70 (2009). https://doi.org/10.1007/978-3-642-02230-2_7
2. Bell, S., Upchurch, P., Snavely, N., Bala, K.: Material recognition in the wild with the materials in context database. In: Proceedings of the IEEE Conference on Computer Vision and Pattern Recognition, pp. 3479–3487 (2015)
3. Burghouts, G.J., Geusebroek, J.M.: Material-specific adaptation of color invariant features. Patt. Recogn. Lett. **30**, 306–313 (2009). https://doi.org/10.1016/j.patrec.2008.10.005
4. Finlayson, G., Schaefer, G., Tian, G.: The UEA uncalibrated colour image database. Technical Report SYS-C00, School of Information System, University of East Anglia, Norwich, UK (2000)
5. Fu, X., Wei, W.: Centralized binary patterns embedded with image Euclidean distance for facial expression recognition. In: ICNC 2008. Fourth International Conference on Natural Computation 2008, vol. 4, pp. 115–119, October 2008. https://doi.org/10.1109/ICNC.2008.94
6. Gibert, X., Patel, V.M., Chellappa, R.: Material classification and semantic segmentation of railway track images with deep convolutional neural networks. In: 2015 IEEE International Conference on Image Processing (ICIP), pp. 621–625. IEEE (2015)
7. Grigorescu, S.E., Petkov, N., Kruizinga, P.: Comparison of texture features based on Gabor filters. IEEE Trans. Image Process. **11**(10), 1160–1167 (2002)
8. Haindl, M., Havlíček, V.: A multiscale colour texture model. In: Kasturi, R., Laurendeau, D., Suen, C. (eds.) Proceedings of the 16th International Conference on Pattern Recognition, pp. 255–258. IEEE Computer Society, Los Alamitos, August 2002. https://doi.org/10.1109/ICPR.2002.1044676
9. Haindl, M.: Visual data recognition and modeling based on local Markovian models. In: Florack, L., Duits, R., Jongbloed, G., Lieshout, M.C., Davies, L. (eds.) Mathematical Methods for Signal and Image Analysis and Representation, Computational Imaging and Vision, vol. 41, chap. 14, pp. 241–259. Springer, London (2012), https://doi.org/10.1007/978-1-4471-2353-8_14

10. Haindl, M., Filip, J.: Visual Texture. Advances in Computer Vision and Pattern Recognition, Springer-Verlag, London, London, January 2013. https://doi.org/10.1007/978-1-4471-4902-6
11. Haindl, M., Filip, J., Vávra, R.: Digital material appearance: the curse of terabytes. ERCIM News (90), 49–50 (2012). http://ercim-news.ercim.eu/en90/ri/digital-material-appearance-the-curse-of-tera-bytes
12. Haindl, M., Havlíček, V.: A multiresolution causal colour texture model. Lecture Notes in Computer Science, vol. 1876, pp. 114–122 (2000)
13. Haindl, M., Mikeš, S., Kudo, M.: Unsupervised surface reflectance field multisegmenter. In: Azzopardi, G., Petkov, N. (eds.) Computer Analysis of Images and Patterns. Lecture Notes in Computer Science, vol. 9256, pp. 261–273. Springer International Publishing, September 2015. https://doi.org/10.1007/978-3-319-23192-1_22
14. Haindl, M., Vacha, P.: Wood veneer species recognition using Markovian textural features. In: Azzopardi, G., Petkov, N. (eds.) Computer Analysis of Images and Patterns. Lecture Notes in Computer Science, vol. 9256, pp. 300–311. Springer International Publishing, September 2015. https://doi.org/10.1007/978-3-319-23192-1_25
15. Haindl, M., Vácha, P.: Scale sensitivity of textural features. In: Beltrán-Castañón, C. et al. (eds.) Progress in Pattern Recognition, Image Analysis, Computer Vision, and Applications: 21st Iberoamerican Congress, CIARP 2016, Lima, Peru, 2016, Proceedings. LNCS, vol. 10125, pp. 84–92. Springer International Publishing AG, Gewerbestrasse 11, Cham, CH-6330, Switzerland, November 2017. https://doi.org/10.1007/978-3-319-52277-7_11
16. Han, J., Ma, K.K.: Rotation-invariant and scale-invariant Gabor features for texture image retrieval. Image Vis. Comput. **25**(9), 1474–1481 (2007)
17. Heikkilä, M., Pietikäinen, M., Schmid, C.: Description of interest regions with local binary patterns. Pattern Recogn. **42**(3), 425–436 (2009). https://doi.org/10.1016/j.patcog.2008.08.014
18. Hlaing, C.S., Zaw, S.M.M.: Tomato plant diseases classification using statistical texture feature and color feature. In: 2018 IEEE/ACIS 17th International Conference on Computer and Information Science (ICIS), pp. 439–444. IEEE (2018)
19. Jain, A.K., Healey, G.: A multiscale representation including opponent color features for texture recognition. IEEE Trans. Image Process. **7**(1), 124–128 (1998)
20. Khellah, F.: Texture classification using dominant neighborhood structure. IEEE Trans. Image Process. **20**(11), 3270–3279 (2011). https://doi.org/10.1109/TIP.2011.2143422
21. Li, Z., Liu, G., Jiang, H., Qian, X.: Image copy detection using a robust Gabor texture descriptor. In: Proceedings of the First ACM Workshop on Large-scale Multimedia Retrieval and Mining, pp. 65–72. LS-MMRM 2009. ACM, New York, NY, USA (2009). https://doi.org/10.1145/1631058.1631072
22. Liao, S., Law, M.W.K., Chung, A.C.S.: Dominant local binary patterns for texture classification. IEEE Trans. Image Process. **18**(5), 1107–1118 (2009). https://doi.org/10.1109/TIP.2009.2015682
23. Liu, L., Chen, J., Fieguth, P., Zhao, G., Chellappa, R., Pietikainen, M.: A survey of recent advances in texture representation. arXiv preprint arXiv:1801.10324 (2018)
24. Liu, L., Fieguth, P., Wang, X., Pietikäinen, M., Hu, D.: Evaluation of LBP and deep texture descriptors with a new robustness benchmark. In: European Conference on Computer Vision, pp. 69–86. Springer (2016). https://doi.org/10.1007/978-3-319-46487-9_5

25. Manjunath, B.S., Ma, W.Y.: Texture features for browsing and retrieval of image data. IEEE Trans. Pattern Anal. Mach. Intell. **18**(8), 837–842 (1996). https://doi.org/10.1109/34.531803
26. Nanni, L., Lumini, A., Brahnam, S.: Survey on LBP based texture descriptors for image classification. Expert Syst. Appl. **39**(3), 3634–3641 (2012). https://doi.org/10.1016/j.eswa.2011.09.054
27. Ojala, T., Pietikäinen, M., Mäenpää, T.: Multiresolution gray-scale and rotation invariant texture classification with local binary patterns. IEEE Trans. Pattern Anal. Mach. Intell. **24**(7), 971–987 (2002)
28. Remeš, V., Haindl, M.: Bark recognition using novel rotationally invariant multispectral textural features. Pattern Recogn. Lett. **125**, 612–617 (2019). https://doi.org/10.1016/j.patrec.2019.06.027
29. Roy, S.K., Bhattacharya, N., Chanda, B., Chaudhuri, B.B., Ghosh, D.K.: FWLBP: a scale invariant descriptor for texture classification. arXiv preprint arXiv:1801.03228 (2018)
30. Santini, S., Jain, R.: Similarity measures. IEEE Trans. Patt. Anal. Mach. Intell. **21**(9), 871–883 (1999)
31. Shivashankar, S., Kudari, M., Hiremath, P.S.: Galois field-based approach for rotation and scale invariant texture classification. Int. J. Image, Graph. Signal Process. (IJIGSP) **10**(9), 56–64 (2018)
32. Sidiropoulos, G.K., Ouzounis, A.G., Papakostas, G.A., Sarafis, I.T., Stamkos, A., Solakis, G.: Texture analysis for machine learning based marble tiles sorting. In: 2021 IEEE 11th Annual Computing and Communication Workshop and Conference (CCWC), pp. 0045–0051. IEEE (2021)
33. Simon, P., Uma, V.: Review of texture descriptors for texture classification. In: Data Engineering and Intelligent Computing, pp. 159–176. Springer (2018). https://doi.org/10.1007/978-981-10-3223-3_15
34. Stricker, M.A., Orengo, M.: Similarity of color images, vol. 2420, pp. 381–392. SPIE (1995). https://doi.org/10.1117/12.205308
35. Vácha, P., Haindl, M.: Texture recognition using robust Markovian features. In: Salerno, E. et al. (eds.) Computational Intelligence for Multimedia Understanding, Lecture Notes in Computer Science, vol. 7252, pp. 126–137. Springer, Berlin/Heidelberg (2012). https://doi.org/10.1007/978-3-642-32436-9_11
36. Vácha, P., Haindl, M., Suk, T.: Colour and rotation invariant textural features based on Markov random fields. Pattern Recogn. Lett. **32**(6), 771–779 (2011). https://doi.org/10.1016/j.patrec.2011.01.002
37. Varma, M., Zisserman, A.: A statistical approach to material classification using image patch exemplars. IEEE Trans. Pattern Anal. Mach. Intell. **31**(11), 2032–2047 (2009). https://doi.org/10.1109/TPAMI.2008.182
38. Veerashetty, S., Patil, N.B.: Novel LBP based texture descriptor for rotation, illumination and scale invariance for image texture analysis and classification using multi-Kernel SVM. Multimedia Tools Appl. **79**(15), 9935–9955 (2020)
39. Yang, P., Zhang, F., Yang, G.: Fusing DTCWT and LBP based features for rotation, illumination and scale invariant texture classification. IEEE Access **6**, 13336–13349 (2018)
40. Zhang, B., Gao, Y., Zhao, S., Liu, J.: Local derivative pattern versus local binary pattern: face recognition with high-order local pattern descriptor. IEEE Trans. Image Process. **19**(2), 533–544 (2010)

Recognizing Handwritten Text Lines in Ancient Document Images Based on a Gated Residual Recurrent Neural Network

Olfa Mechi$^{(\boxtimes)}$ ⓘ, Maroua Mehri ⓘ, and Najoua Essoukri Ben Amara ⓘ

LATIS-Laboratory of Advanced Technology and Intelligent Systems,
Université de Sousse, Ecole Nationale d'Ingénieurs de Sousse, 4023 Sousse, Tunisie
olfamechi@yahoo.fr, maroua.mehri@eniso.u-sousse.tn,
najoua.benamara@eniso.rnu.tn

Abstract. Over several decades, many archives and libraries have high-lighted the growing need to assist them in the preservation and enrich-ment of the huge mass of digitized documentary heritage by using effi-cient handwritten text recognition (HTR) frameworks. To address this issue, we propose in this paper a deep learning based framework for recognizing handwritten text lines in historical document images. The proposed framework is based on a gated residual recurrent neural net-work, called G2R2N. G2R2N is composed of two modules: encoder and decoder. The encoder module is based on merging the gated and skip connection layers, while the decoder module is composed of the bidirec-tional long short-term memory (BLSTM), followed by the connectionist temporal classification (CTC) architectures. The proposed framework is evaluated using the same evaluation metrics computed in the context of the *ICDAR2017* competition. Numerical and qualitative observations are reported on different benchmark datasets used in the most well-known HTR contests.

Keywords: Text line recognition · Historical handwritten documents · Gated mechanism · Skip connection · BLSTM · CTC

1 Introduction

Since the early 1990s, many scientist working on document image analysis (DIA) have focused their research works on proposing more efficient engines dedicated to the offline optical character recognition (OCR) task. An offline OCR engine focuses on generating the character sequences corresponding to the text present in digitized documents or captured images of words, text lines or paragraphs (i.e., text recognition). The state-of-the-art engines have often achieved satisfy-ing results for printed material, but not for historical handwritten documents. Indeed, handwritten text recognition (HTR) remains a tricky task due to the

C. Bădică et al. (Eds.): ICCCI 2022, CCIS 1653, pp. 250–263, 2022.
https://doi.org/10.1007/978-3-031-16210-7_20

still outstanding issues related to the idiosyncrasies of this kind of document images [2, 31]. Among the main issues encountered when dealing with the HTR task are: *i)* the different levels and format definitions of ground truths (e.g. character, word, line paragraph), *ii)* the ground truth preparation, *iii)* the large variety of handwriting styles, *iv)* the presence of significant degradation levels and different kinds of noise, *v)* the presence of connected characters, *vi)* the digitization quality and background of the input image and *vii)* the irregularity and diversity of text shapes [12]. Figures 1(a), 1(b) and 1(c) illustrate few examples of historical handwritten document images of the IAM^1, $Rimes^2$ and $Bentham^3$ datasets, respectively.

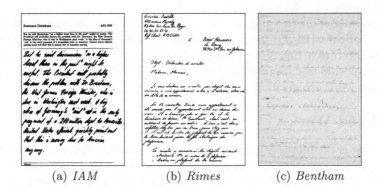

(a) *IAM*   (b) *Rimes*   (c) *Bentham*

Fig. 1. Examples of historical handwritten document images of the *IAM* (a), *Rimes* (b) and *Bentham* (c) datasets.

In the literature, the main research works dedicated to the HTR task are mainly based on using the paragraph, line or/and sub-word segmentation tasks as preliminary steps before handling the recognition process [4, 10]. In the early 2010s, the offline HTR has really taken off thanks to the deep learning (DL) based models, particularly the cell based neural network architecture called long-short term memory (LSTM). Recently, a large variety of deep architectures has been successfully applied for both the text line segmentation and text recognition tasks, outperforming many state-of-the-art results [10]. Most recent HTR systems are based on deep architectures to extract features from the input document images and recognize text without using preliminary word or character segmentation tasks [14].

To address the different challenges related to the HTR task whilst also benefiting the recent advances in DL for object detection and recognition, we propose a DL based HTR framework that processes the whole text line image as input.

---

[1] https://fki.tic.heia-fr.ch/databases/iam-handwriting-database.

[2] http://www.a2ialab.com/doku.php?id=rimes_database:data:icdar2011:line: icdar2011competitionline.

[3] http://transcriptorium.eu/datasets/bentham-collection/.

Specifically, we tackle in this paper the text line recognition task in ancient Latin handwritten document images (French and English). The proposed HTR architecture, called in our work the gated residual recurrent neural network (G2R2N), has the particularity to merge the skip connection and gated convolution techniques in the encoder part. G2R2N combines the gated layers with skip connection ones in order to prevent loss of significant information thorough the network on the one hand, and to improve the selection process of pertinent features characterizing text lines on the other hand. This leads to both guarantee a reduction of the complexity of the network and a gain of the network performance. We have experimentally shown that the proposed framework is able to deal with different HTR challenges after conducting a set of experiments on many benchmark datasets.

The remainder of this paper is structured as follows. Section 2 reviews the main state-of-the-art HTR methods. Section 3 describes the proposed framework for handwritten text line recognition. In Sect. 4, we detail the experimental corpora, the experimental protocol and the obtained results. Finally, our conclusions and further work are given in Sect. 5.

2   Related Work

The existing HTR methods can be categorized into two classes: the traditional and DL based approaches. The traditional methods are based on applying different classical classifier algorithms, such as the random forest or the support vector machine, on the extracted character features in order to recognize the characters in text images. For instance, Touj et al. [33] applied the planar hidden Markov models (HMM) for offline Arabic handwritten word recognition. Plötz et al. [28] presented a survey focused on using the HMM for the offline handwritten recognition task. Both Krevat et al. [22] and Marti et al. [25] used the HMM, followed by a language model to improve the HTR performance. Ben Halima et al. [1] proposed a fuzzy technique to recognize Arabic text in video sequences. The main drawback of this category of HTR approaches, particularly the HMM based solutions, consists of their inability to handle the context information in the case of long input text sequences [30].

Recently, the effectiveness of the DL architectures has been shown for numerous image segmentation, detection, recognition and classification tasks, etc. Particularly for the HTR task, DL based solutions have become an interesting alternative to the traditional ones thanks to their high accuracy rates on the one hand, and to their ability to deal with long input text sequences on the other hand [13]. For instance, Coquenet et al. [12] proposed an encoder-decoder model based on using a gated convolutional neural network (GCNN) to address the unconstrained handwritten text recognition task. They presented a thorough comparison of the convolutional models and the classical recurrent architectures in terms of the training time, complexity and performance. Yousef et al. [38] applied a FCN based architecture with the gated mechanism. They used data augmentation and heavy normalization techniques, such as layer and normalizations. They showed that their method achieved competitive results compared with many state-of-the-art solutions. Dutta *et al.* [15] proposed a CNN-RNN architecture to recognize Devanagari script. Their architecture is composed of the spatial transform layer (STN) preceded by a CNN model, and then followed by two BLSTM layers and the connectionist temporal classification (CTC). Dutta *et al.* [15] stated that a CNN-RNN architecture is well-adapted for document images having varying hand movements and handwriting styles, but it requires extensive data in the training phase. Ingle *et al.* [20] proposed a FCN based model associated with a gated mechanism to tackle the text line recognition task. They demonstrated that their results outperformed the state-of-the-art ones when using external data (they converted online *IAM* samples into offline samples for generating more samples of the handwritten text lines). Coquenet *et al.* [11] applied a gated fully convolutional network (GFCN) to recognize unconstrained handwritten text, without introducing a post-preocessing step. Their method achieved competitive results compared with a recurrent architecture. Moysset *et al.* [26] proposed to combine the convolutional layers with the multi-dimensional LSTM ones for the feature extraction step. Their results were compared with those obtained after adding a statistical model on many multi-languages datasets in order to assess the impact of the language model for improving the performance. Their method showed competitive results in terms of performance and prediction time. To the best of our knowledge, Bluche *et al.* [4,5] presented the first works using the attention mechanism to tackle the multi-lines text recognition task. They applied an encoder-decoder model based on the attention mechanism. Bluche *et al.* [4,5] used a pre-trained model at the line level without considering the line breaks into the transcription labels. Yousef *et al.* [37] addressed the issue of multi-line recognition (i.e., feed a full page as input). They combined a FCN encoder with a bi-linear interpolation layer. Their method did not require text line level annotations, since their model used the whole page as a single text line image. Yousef *et al.* [37] demonstrated that their method achieved satisfactory results and outperformed many state-of-the-art methods in terms of the character error rate on the *ICDAR2017* and *IAM* datasets. However, their architecture has a huge number of trainable parameters. De Sousa Neto *et al.* [13] proposed a method based on a gated CNN architecture, followed by the bi-directional gated recurrent unit (BGRU) architecture combined with language models to recognize text lines. Their method achieved a high-performance recognition rate using few trainable parameters and fewer computational resources in the training phase. Puigcerver [29] proposed a classical CRNN model which achieved satisfactory results at the cost of high number of parameters. Unlike to Puigcerver [29], Bluche *et al.* [6] presented a gated-CNN model which achieved satisfactory recognition rate with very few numbers of parameters. Cojocaru *et al.* [9] proposed a deep architecture based mainly on the deformable convolution layers for the feature extraction step. Zayene *et al.* [39] recognized Arabic text in news video frames using the MDLSTM architecture coupled with the CTC layer.

Although the DL based solutions used for the HTR task outperform the traditional ones, they have the drawbacks of requiring large masses of precise ground truthed data and having high computational complexity. Hence, scientists are continuing to propose deep architectures that have the best trade-offs between maximizing the accuracy, and reducing the complexity (i.e., less hyperparameters in the network architecture) [15].

3 Proposed Framework

Recently, it has been shown in the literature that a more advantageous way of ensuring an efficient and effective text recognition system consists in combining different deep structures [6]. Hence, we propose in this work a deep framework based on combining gated convolution and skip connection, followed by the BLSTM network [19] and the CTC layer [17] for recognizing handwritten text lines. Figure 2 illustrates the architecture of the proposed framework. The architecture of the proposed framework is composed of two main parts, the encoder and decoder. The encoder part is based on using the convolutional blocks, while the decoder part is composed of the recurrent blocks. A detailed description of the proposed framework is given in what follows.

The encoder part should be modular enough to deal with different handwritten scripts. It is considered a rather important block that focuses on extracting text line features. It is dedicated to extracting features from the analyzed text line images. By increasing the number of the convolutional layers, the depth of the neural network will be also increased, and hence an output image having enriched data from the previous layers will be generated, and afterward better prediction results will be ensured. Nevertheless, increasing the depth of the neural network in inappropriate ways could generate a significant alteration of the network performance. Indeed, this issue can be explained by the fact that the network accuracy is saturated due to the vanishing gradient issues. Hence, to overcome these issues, many researchers propose to use the residual learning approach by means of the skip/shortcut connections [18]. Furthermore, a skip connection has the advantage of preventing loss of information in the network that gets deeper by adding a connection between one of the previous layers to a later one. More specifically, the skip connection technique consists in aggregating convolutional activation from one of the previous layers to those of a later layer (i.e., the activation of a particular layer is added or concatenated to another action layer). It is widely applied for image transformation tasks, such as image denoising [7] and image super-resolution [36].

More recently, convolutional models with gated mechanism have been proposed in the literature [20,38]. These models provide higher performance compared to the classical ones. The main role of the gated mechanism is to extract the most relevant features that ensure faster convergence and better results. Indeed, the idea behind the gated mechanism is to control the process of feature propagation to the subsequent layers. More specifically, the gated mechanism computes a generic feature across the whole input image and selects the most relevant features. The feature selection is firstly processed based on analyzing each feature value at a given position and according to its neighboring values,

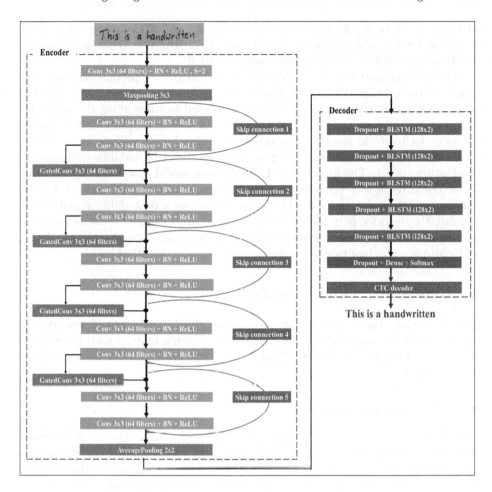

Fig. 2. Architecture of the proposed framework.

and then deciding whether that feature should be removed or retained. The main advantage of using the gated convolution compared to the classical ones consists in having an efficient and effective architecture with few trainable parameters thanks to the selection process of the most relevant information representing the input image.

Hence, we propose in the encoder part a novel network architecture, called the gated residual recurrent neural network (G2R2N) that combines the convolutional gated and the skip connection layers. This combination allows the network to both better learn and faster converge. The base network used in the encoder part of the proposed framework to perform the feature extraction phase is the ResNet-12 model. Then, we use the gated mechanism that was introduced in [6], in the convolutional block. The convolutional block is composed of 3 × 3 traditional and gated convolutional layers that have a kernel size of 3 × 3 pixels and

64 features. Only the first layer is followed by a 3×3 Maxpooling layer. Each traditional convolutional layer is composed of the ReLU activation operation, batch normalization and L2 regularization of 10^{-3}.

The decoder part focuses on determining the character probabilities for each frame of the extracted text line features. It is firstly composed of 5 BLSTM layers that ensure the propagation of the extracted features along the sequence. The 5 BLSTM layers have 128 hidden units and a dropout probability equal to 0.5 in order to avoid the over-fitting issues. These layers analyze at each time step a feature vector, and afterward generate the label probabilities assigned to the feature vector. The final layer of the decoder model is a dense layer having a size equal to $M + 1$ (i.e., M denotes the size of the charlist and $+1$ for the blank symbol), and is preceded by a dropout having a probability equal to 0.5. Finally, the decoder part includes a CTC layer that generates the transcribed text by selecting at each time step the most probable character on the one hand, and removing the blanks and duplicate character on the other hand.

4   Experiments and Results

In this section, the experimental corpora are firstly presented. Secondly, the experimental protocol and the performance evaluation metrics used to evaluate the proposed framework are described. Finally, the obtained results are discussed and analyzed.

4.1   Experimental Corpora

The different publicly-available datasets used for evaluating the state-of-the-art HTR systems were released in the context of many *ICDAR* and *ICFHR* contests. In order to assess the performance of the proposed framework, three public benchmark datasets written in the Latin script have used in our experiments.

- **IAM**(See footnote 1): is a publicly-available multi-writer dataset which was released in the context of *ICDAR1999* competition. It contains $8,922$ images of text lines written in English. Its ground truth at the text line level is provided (cf. Fig. 1(a)).
- **Rimes**(See footnote 2): is composed of $12,104$ gray-level scaled images of text lines written in French. It was provided in the context of *ICDAR2011* competition. It was approximately written by $1,300$ people. The ground truths at word, line and page levels are available (cf. Fig. 1(b)).
- **Bentham**(See footnote 3): is a publicly-available multi-writer dataset that was written between 1748 and 1832. It contains $11,470$ images of text lines written in English. It was released in the context of *ICFHR2014* competition on HTR on Transcriptorium datasets (HTRtS). The segmented text lines with their corresponding transcriptions are available (cf. Fig. 1(c)).

Table 1 details the data partition (train, validation and test) in terms of the number of lines of the three datasets used in our experiments.

4.2   Experimental Protocol

First, few pre-processing steps have been applied on the input images of the segmented text lines by means of the illumination compensation [8] and the deslanting [34] in order to alleviate the shadow issues and correct the non-uniform slant of the cursive text lines.

Table 1. Data partition (train, validation and test) in terms of the number of lines of the three datasets used in our experiments.

	#lines	Data partition [#lines & rate (%)]		
		Train	Validation	Test
IAM	8,922	6,161 69.05%	900 10.08%	1,861 20.85%
Rimes	12,104	10,193 84.21%	1,133 09.36%	778 06.42%
Bentham	11,470	9,195 80.16%	1,415 12.33%	860 07.49%

Then, a data augmentation strategy is carried out in order to reduce the over-fitting issues on the one hand, and to make the proposed network architecture more robust and efficient on the other hand. Indeed, we have applied the following data augmentation techniques only on the train sets: rotation (1.5% degrees), horizontal shift (5% of image size), and vertical shift (2.5% of image size), dilation (3×3 kernel), erosion (5×5 kernel) and resizing (5%). The total numbers of text line images used in the training phase after using the aforementioned data augmentation strategy are $36,966$, $61,158$ and $55,170$ for the *IAM*, *Rimes* and *Bentham* datasets, respectively. Furthermore, we have resized all the text line images to 1024×128.

Afterward, we have set the following parameters to train the proposed network architecture: *RMSprop* optimizer with a learning rate equal to 10^{-3} and a mini-batch size of 16 images. Besides, an early stopping mechanism has been used after 100 epochs when no improvement of the validation loss value is reached. Finally, the vanilla beam search decoding and a common charset for all the used datasets have been adopted. In our experiments, neither a post-processing step nor a language model have been introduced.

4.3   Evaluation Metrics

To evaluate the performance of the G2R2N framework, two following evaluation metrics are computed: the word error rate (*WER*, cf. Eq. 1) and the character error rate (*CER*, cf. Eq. 2). The two following evaluation metrics are computed using the Levenshtein distance which determines the number of substitution

(S), deletion (D) and insertion (I) errors at the character level by comparing the predicted result $\widehat{X}$ and the ground truth X.

$$WER = \frac{\sum Words\_not\_correctly\_recognized}{\sum_{i=1}^{N} Word_i} \tag{1}$$

$$CER = \frac{\sum_{i=1}^{N} edit(\widehat{X_i}, X_i)}{\sum_{i=1}^{N} length(X_i)} \tag{2}$$

4.4   Results

In this section, we first present the quantitative and qualitative assessments of the proposed G2R2N framework. Then, the achieved results are compared with those of the participating methods in the *ICFHR2014* competition on HTR on Transcriptorium datasets. In what follows, we compare the obtained results with the main recent state-of-the-art methods which do not use neither language models nor lexicon constraints (i.e., dictionaries).

First, we compute the performance of the G2R2N framework in terms of the *CER* and *WER* metrics on the test set of the *IAM* dataset, and then the achieved results are compared with those of the main recent state-of-the-art methods (cf. Table 2). The proposed framework achieves a *CER* value of 5.87% and a *WER* value of 21.50%. We show that G2R2N has ranked within the top three according

Table 2. Performance comparison of the proposed G2R2N framework with recent state-of-the-art methods on the *IAM* dataset.

Method	CER (%)	WER (%)
Coquenet *et al.* [11]	4.32	16.24
Gao *et al.* [16]	5.80	17.80
G2R2N (proposed framework)	5.87	21.50
Markou *et al.* [24]	6.14	20.04
Wang *et al.* [35]	6.40	19.60
Ly *et al.* [23]	6.76	20.89
Bluche *et al.* [3]	7.30	24.70
Kang *et al.* [21]	7.62	24.54
Bluche *et al.* [4]	7.90	24.6
Coquenet *et al.* [10]	7.99	28.61
Puigcerver *et al.* [29]	8.20	25.4
Zhang *et al.* [40]	8.50	22.20
Sueiras *et al.* [32]	8.80	23.80
Moysset *et al.* [26]	8.86	29.31
Pham *et al.* [27]	10.80	35.10

to both the computed *CER* and *WER* metrics. The performance of the proposed framework on the *IAM* dataset are competitive and can be improved either by using a language model as a post-processing step, or by using more data in the training phase.

Second, we compute the performance of the G2R2N framework in terms of the *CER* and *WER* metrics on the test set of the *Rimes* dataset, and then the achieved results are compared with those of the main recent state-of-the-art methods (cf. Table 3). We note that the Bluche *et al.* [4]' method achieves the best performance (i.e., *CER* and *WER* are equal to 2.9% and 12.6%, respectively). However, the G2R2N framework achieves *CER* of 3.66% and *WER* of 11.31%. The obtained results are competitive compared to the five following state-of-the-art methods [4, 10, 13, 23, 29] that have higher computational complexities (i.e., important number of trainable parameters). Furthermore, we state that the proposed framework outperforms considerably many recent state-of-the-art methods [3, 9, 11, 26, 27, 32], in terms of both the computed *CER* and *WER* metrics.

Table 3. Performance comparison of the proposed G2R2N framework with few recent state-of-the-art methods on the *Rimes* dataset.

Method	CER (%)	WER (%)
Bluche *et al.* [4]	2.90	12.60
Coquenet *et al.* [10]	3.19	10.25
Puigcerver *et al.* [29]	3.30	12.80
Ly *et al.* [23]	3.43	11.92
G2R2N (proposed framework)	3.66	11.31
Coquenet *et al.* [11]	4.35	18.01
Suciras *et al.* [32]	4.80	15.90
Moysset *et al.* [26]	4.80	16.42
Cojocaru *et al.* [9]	5.50	17.50
Bluche *et al.* [3]	5.60	20.90
Pham *et al.* [27]	6.80	28.50

Third, we assess the G2R2N performance on the *Bentham* dataset in terms of *CER* and *WER*. We also compare the obtained performances with those of the *CITlab* method which participated in the restricted track of the *ICFHR2014* competition. As reported in Fig. 3, the proposed framework achieves a *CER* of 7.61% and *WER* of 13.36%. Although the *CER* rate of the proposed framework is higher than that of the *CITlab* method, the proposed framework outperforms the *CITlab* method in terms of the *WER* metric (overall performance gains of 1.24%). The fact that G2R2N has a lower *WER* and a higher *CER* compared with the *CITlab* method can be justified by the mis-recognition of many characters in the same word.

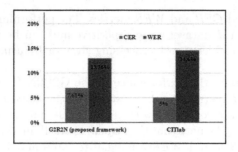

Fig. 3. Performance comparison of the proposed G2R2N framework with the *CITlab* method on the *Bentham* dataset.

Figure 4 illustrates three different prediction errors (which are highlighted in red color) occurred on three text line image examples of the *IAM* test set. These errors can be justified by a higher character similarity (e.g. substitution error) on the one hand, and the insufficient number of the samples of symbols, digits, and punctuation marks used in the training phase on the other hand. Moreover, we note that the G2R2N performance remains satisfactory even in the case of variable spaces between words in a text line. Finally, we conclude that the proposed G2R2N achieves competitive performance with a reduced computational complexity. It is worth noting that by integrating a post-processing step based on using lexicon constraints or language models, the mis-recognition errors will be reduced and the G2R2N performance will be improved.

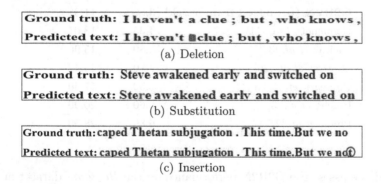

(a) Deletion

(b) Substitution

(c) Insertion

Fig. 4. Prediction errors on three text line image examples of the *IAM* dataset.

5   Conclusions and Further Work

In this paper, we propose a handwritten text line recognition framework based on using in the encoder part a novel network architecture, called the gated residual recurrent neural network (G2R2N). G2R2N combines the gated layers with skip connection ones in order to prevent loss of significant information thorough the network on the one hand, and to select the most relevant features on the other hand, thus allowing to have both a reduced model complexity and an efficient network. To evaluate the performance of the proposed framework, a set of experiments have been conducted on different benchmark datasets of handwritten document images. We have experimentally demonstrated the G2R2N effectiveness on many datasets having different scripts. Furthermore, the proposed framework has shown competitive performance compared to many recent state-of-the-art methods which do not use neither language nor lexicon constraints.

Our further work will focus on evaluating the proposed HTR framework on other publicly-available datasets of historical document images written in scripts other than Latin (e.g. Arabic). Moreover, we will integrate standard character or word language model to further improve the results. Furthermore, based on the recognized text lines, we plan to propose a novel indexing system of historical Arabic and Latin document images.

References

1. Ben Halima, M., Alimi, A., Vila, A.F., et al.: NF-SAVO: neuro-fuzzy system for Arabic video OCR. arXiv:1211.2150 (2012)
2. Bezerra, B.L.D., Zanchettin, C., Toselli, A.H., Pirlo, G.: Handwriting: recognition, development and analysis (2017)
3. Bluche, T.: Deep neural networks for large vocabulary handwritten text recognition. Ph.D. thesis, Université Paris-Sud (2015)
4. Bluche, T.: Joint line segmentation and transcription for end-to-end handwritten paragraph recognition. arXiv:1604.08352 (2016)
5. Bluche, T., Louradour, J., Messina, R.: Scan, attend and read: end-to-end handwritten paragraph recognition with MDLSTM attention. In: ICDAR, pp. 1050–1055 (2017)
6. Bluche, T., Messina, R.: Gated convolutional recurrent neural networks for multilingual handwriting recognition. In: ICDAR, pp. 646–651 (2017)
7. Chang, Y., Yan, L., Chen, M., Fang, H., Zhong, S.: Two-stage convolutional neural network for medical noise removal via image decomposition. IM, pp. 2707–2721 (2019)
8. Chen, K.N., Chen, C.H., Chang, C.C.: Efficient illumination compensation techniques for text images. DSP, pp. 726–733 (2012)
9. Cojocaru, I., Cascianelli, S., Baraldi, L., Corsini, M., Cucchiara, R.: Watch your strokes: improving handwritten text recognition with deformable convolutions. In: ICPR, pp. 6096–6103 (2021)
10. Coquenet, D., Chatelain, C., Paquet, T.: End-to-end handwritten paragraph text recognition using a vertical attention network. arXiv:2012.03868 (2020)
11. Coquenet, D., Chatelain, C., Paquet, T.: Recurrence-free unconstrained handwritten text recognition using gated fully convolutional network. In: ICFHR, pp. 19–24 (2020)
12. Coquenet, D., Soullard, Y., Chatelain, C., Paquet, T.: Have convolutions already made recurrence obsolete for unconstrained handwritten text recognition? In: ICDAR, pp. 65–70 (2019)

13. De Sousa Neto, A.F., Bezerra, B.L.D., Toselli, A.H., Lima, E.B.: HTR-Flor: a deep learning system for offline handwritten text recognition. In: SIBGRAPI, pp. 54–61 (2020)
14. Diem, M., Fiel, S., Kleber, F.: Handwritten digit and digit string recognition. In: Document Analysis And Text Recognition: Benchmarking State-of-the-Art Systems, p. 67 (2018)
15. Dutta, K., Krishnan, P., Mathew, M., Jawahar, C.: Offline handwriting recognition on Devanagari using a new benchmark dataset. In: DAS, pp. 25–30 (2018)
16. Gao, L., Zhang, H., Liu, C.L.: Handwritten text recognition with convolutional prototype network and most aligned frame based CTC training. In: ICDAR, pp. 205–220 (2021)
17. Graves, A.: Supervised sequence labelling with recurrent neural networks (2012)
18. He, K., Zhang, X., Ren, S., Sun, J.: Deep residual learning for image recognition. In: CVPR, pp. 770–778 (2016)
19. Hochreiter, S., Schmidhuber, J.: Long short-term memory. Neural Comput. **9**, 1735–1780 (1997)
20. Ingle, R.R., Fujii, Y., Deselaers, T., Baccash, J., Popat, A.C.: A scalable handwritten text recognition system. In: ICDAR, pp. 17–24 (2019)
21. Kang, L., Riba, P., Rusiñol, M., Fornés, A., Villegas, M.: Pay attention to what you read: non-recurrent handwritten text-line recognition. arXiv:2005.13044 (2020)
22. Krevat, E., Cuzzillo, E.: Improving off-line handwritten character recognition with hidden Markov models. PAMI (2006)
23. Ly, N.T., Nguyen, H.T., Nakagawa, M.: 2D self-attention convolutional recurrent network for offline handwritten text recognition. In: ICDAR, pp. 191–204 (2021)
24. Markou, K., et al.: A convolutional recurrent neural network for the handwritten text recognition of historical Greek manuscripts. In: ICPR, pp. 249–262 (2021)
25. Marti, U.V., Bunke, H.: Handwritten sentence recognition. In: ICPR, pp. 463–466 (2000)
26. Moysset, B., Messina, R.: Are 2D-LSTM really dead for offline text recognition? IJDAR, pp. 193–208 (2019)
27. Pham, V., Bluche, T., Kermorvant, C., Louradour, J.: Dropout improves recurrent neural networks for handwriting recognition. In: ICFHR, pp. 285–290 (2014)
28. Plötz, T., Fink, G.A.: Markov models for offline handwriting recognition: a survey. IJDAR, p. 269 (2009)
29. Puigcerver, J.: Are multidimensional recurrent layers really necessary for handwritten text recognition? In: ICDAR, pp. 67–72 (2017)
30. Sadaf, F., Raju, S.T.U., Muntakim, A.: Offline bangla handwritten text recognition: a comprehensive study of various deep learning approaches. In: International Conference on Electrical & Electronic Engineering, pp. 153–156 (2021)
31. Sajedi, H.: Handwriting recognition of digits, signs, and numerical strings in Persian. Comput. Electr. Eng. **49**, 52–65 (2016)
32. Sueiras, J., Ruiz, V., Sanchez, A., Velez, J.F.: Offline continuous handwriting recognition using sequence to sequence neural networks. Neurocomputing **289**, 119–128 (2018)
33. Touj, S.M., Amara, N.E.B., Amiri, H.: A hybrid approach for off-line Arabic handwriting recognition based on a planar hidden Markov modeling. In: ICDAR, pp. 964–968 (2007)
34. Vinciarelli, A., Luettin, J.: A new normalization technique for cursive handwritten words. PRL, pp. 1043–1050 (2001)
35. Wang, T., et al.: Decoupled attention network for text recognition. In: AAI, pp. 12216–12224 (2020)

36. Wang, X., Gu, Y., Gao, X., Hui, Z.: Dual residual attention module network for single image super resolution. Neurocomputing **364**, 269–279 (2019)
37. Yousef, M., Bishop, T.E.: OrigamiNet: weakly-supervised, segmentation-free, one-step, full page text recognition by learning to unfold. In: CVPR, pp. 14710–14719 (2020)
38. Yousef, M., Hussain, K.F., Mohammed, U.S.: Accurate, data-efficient, unconstrained text recognition with convolutional neural networks. PR, p. 107482 (2020)
39. Zayene, O., Touj, S.M., Hennebert, J., Ingold, R., Ben Amara, N.E.: Multi-dimensional long short-term memory networks for artificial Arabic text recognition in news video. IETCV, pp. 710–719 (2018)
40. Zhang, Y., Nie, S., Liu, W., Xu, X., Zhang, D., Shen, H.T.: Sequence-to-sequence domain adaptation network for robust text image recognition. In: CVPR, pp. 2740–2749 (2019)

Damage Detection of Coated Milling Tools Using Images Captured by Cylindrical Shaped Enclosure Measurement Setup

Mühenad Bilal[1]($\boxtimes$) (iD), Christian Mayer[1], Sunil Kancharana[1] (iD),
Markus Bregulla[1], Rafal Cupek[2] (iD), and Adam Ziebinski[2] (iD)

[1] Technische Hochschule Ingolstadt, Esplanade 10, 85049 Ingolstadt, Germany
{muehenad.bilal,christian.mayer,sunil.kancharana,markus.bregulla}@thi.de
[2] Silesian University of Technology, Gliwice, Poland
{rafal.cupek,adam.ziebinski}@polsl.pl
https://www.thi.de

Abstract. Currently, only two direct automatic tool damage detection systems are available in the tool resharpening industries of German market. Both systems work on the principle of laser-optical 3D detection. By means of non-contact laser scanning, 3D models of the scan object are created which are then compared with digitally stored original model of the tools through a software. Damage images are created based on detected deviations. However, these systems have the major decisive disadvantage that they require about 15 to 20 min for a complete detection of a tool and are quite expensive, ranging between 100,000–400,000 Euros. Therefore, there is a scope of technically and economically optimized tool quality inspection system. The main goal of this work is to develop a new method by which the damages of different coated tools are identified with reduced cost and without compromising the accuracy of the damage.

Keywords: Quality inspection · Damage detection · Image processing · Tool regrinding · Measurement setup

1 Introduction

Industry data suggests that by 2026, the global CNC machine market is expected to reach \$128.86 billion in value, registering an annual growth rate of 5.5% from 2019 to 2026 [1]. In an automated machining environment tooling accounts for 25% to 30% of both fixed costs and variable costs of production [2]. One of the major challenges in CNC machining is tool wear [3]. Especially in machining process like milling, the tool is kept continuously in contact with the work piece so there is usually a high tool wear rate that leads to low tool life and low productivity which further increases the tooling cost. To decrease the tool wear rate,

C. Bădică et al. (Eds.): ICCCI 2022, CCIS 1653, pp. 264–272, 2022.
https://doi.org/10.1007/978-3-031-16210-7_21

variety of coating techniques have been adopted in the industries. Coated tools are tools with thin hard protective surface films which exhibit high mechanical strength and hardness, chemical inertness, and low thermal conductivity [4]. Even though coated tools are widely used in industries the problem with the tool wear is still prevalent. Studies shows that it is possible to recover more than 60% of the original tool life using regrinding process at a cost of 9% the original purchase price [5].

The regrinding of tools helps to decrease the tooling cost and increase the production rate. For this reason, there is a good demand for regrinding process in the market. The production value on the precision tooling market exceeded the mark of 11.2 billion euros in 2018. Although there is only a small decrement from 2018 to 2021 due to covid global pandemic the growth from the past decade shouldn't be ignored. With approximately 57,000 employees, the precision tooling industry represents one of the largest specialized branches of mechanical engineering. The regrinding market shares about 4% of the whole market which consists of machine tools, cutting tools, clamping tools and Regrinding/Tool repairing [6].

The first and foremost criteria for regrinding a tool is to identify the damage location or tool wear. The methods to measure tool wear can be divided into two types which are direct and the indirect measuring method [7,8]. Despite the fact that both direct and indirect approaches have their own pros and cons, this paper concentrates on the direct method of damage detection on coated milling tools.

This paper aims to contribute a novel approach for detecting damages of different coated milling tools by inspecting them under a customized measurement setup. The current paper is structured as follows: Sect. 2 gives an overview of the coated milling tools and specifications of the tools that are used in this paper. Section 3 describes the measurement setup which was developed by the first and second author of this paper. Section 4 briefs about the algorithm which has been used for damage detection. Section 5 and 6 describes the results and conclusion.

2   Coated Milling Tools

Coatings produced by chemical vapor deposition (CVD) were already commercialized for carbide inserts in the 1960s [9,10]. Physical vapor deposition (PVD) was developed almost 20 years later, and today both CVD and PVD are sharing the coating market of cutting tools.

2.1   Tool Specifications

Both CVD and PVD have their own pros and cons, it is dependent upon the use case a tool is determined to undergo CVD or PVD coating process. PVD coatings can be deposited at temperatures lying-in the range of 450–550 °C, which allows the film deposition on high-speed steel tools [11,12]. Typical deposition temperatures for CVD process range from 800 to 1200 °C. The possibility to produce thick layers by CVD at increased deposition rates renders the CVD coated tools suitable for high material removal operations, whereas the PVD ones are selected in medium-finish and finish operations. PVD films can be produced without any chemical interaction with the substrate [4] Table 1.

Table 1. Specifications of the tools which are used in this study.

Tool ID number	W1	W2	W3
Coating process	PVD	PVD	PVD
Coating	TiAlN	TiN	ZrN
No of images	23	23	23
Color	Rose	Gold	Yellow
Camera brand	Nikon	Nikon	Nikon
Model	D800E	D800E	D800E
No of flutes	4	4	4
Overall length (in mm)	93	71.6	82
Cutting length (in mm)	37	24	28
Tool diameter (in mm)	16	10	12
Shaft diameter (in mm)	16	10	12

3 Measurement Setup

The proposed measurement setup (see Fig. 1) has been filed for an (EU) European patent. It consists of a Cylindrical Shaped Enclosure (CSE) whose inner walls are coated with Barium Sulfate (BaSO4) to enhance multi-light scattering. This idea was inspired by a conventional integrating sphere, which is used as a light source with a uniform luminance field at the exit port and also as a uniform illumination field at various distances for photo-metric and radiometric applications [13]. For uniform distribution of light 14 multi-spectral Light Emitting Diodes (LED) are distributed uniformly around the circumference of CSE. Diffusion disks in front of the LED are mounted. The measurement setup also consists of a camera system which has a commercial camera along with a slider. The slider helps in adjusting the focal length of the lens according to the tool length. This unique and innovative light source can be used for various computer vision tasks such as object detection and semantic segmentation. A rotation plate is located below CSE to ensure that images are captured in a sequence of 15° so that, the entire 360° view of the tool is obtained. To understand the importance of the proposed measurement setup, a TiN coated milling tool has been captured under two different lighting conditions see Fig. 2. The tool image captured under normal lighting conditions tend to show huge reflections and too much scattering of light whereas, the tool image captured with the proposed measurement setup has uniform distribution of the light and gives a clear image.

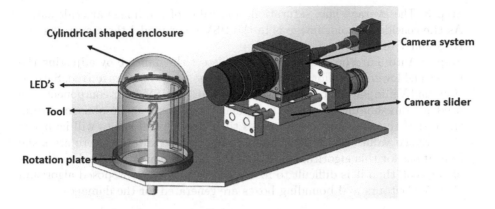

Fig. 1. Proposed measurement setup.

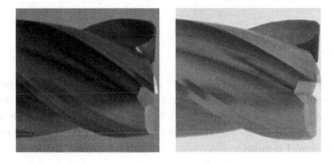

Fig. 2. TiN coated milling tool captured under two different lightning conditions. In the left the tool image was captured using normal lightning conditions, the right image represents the tool captured with the proposed measurement setup.

4 Algorithm for Damage Detection

Each tool is inserted inside CSE of the proposed measurement setup on the top of rotation plate. A total of 23 pictures of each tool are captured for every 15° rotation interval. For 3 tools combined 69 pictures are captured from different rotation angles. After this step, all the images were inspected by an industry professional to mark the damages from the images. These damages which are marked by the professional were considered as Ground Truth (GT). In the next step all the images were processed into an algorithm where damages are detected automatically by applying thresholding. The entire process of the algorithm is described in the following steps

- Step 1: The images of the tool are taken with a white background. The background is separated from the foreground using global thresholding
- Step 2: The RGB image is converted to an HSV image

- Step 3: The average hue, saturation, and value of the image are calculated. As the considered color image is in the HSV color model three averages i.e., H, S and V are expected
- Step 4: Auto Thresholding is defined to detect the damage by adjusting the upper and lower limits for the mask within the range of average Hue, Saturation, and Value parameters. The average values of HSV color components are used for thresholding because the damage areas tend to be abnormal from the rest of the tool and in most cases the damage pixel values will lie below the average values of the HSV color components. However, there are some limitations for this algorithm such as if the damaged area has a color same as of the tool, then it is difficult to make use of the current proposed algorithm
- Step 5: Contours and bounding boxes are generated for the damages

For each image the True Positive (TP), False Positive (FP) and False Negative (FN) are counted and at the end precision and recall are calculated (Fig. 3).

5   Results

The main focus of the paper is to identify the damages of the coated milling tools. For a given tool the aim is to identify the damaged area so that the location of the damage/wear can be forwarded to the regrinding machine which then regrinds the damaged area. The 3 coated tools which were used for examination have provided good results.

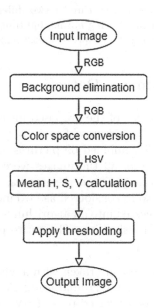

Fig. 3. Proposed automatic thresholding algorithm.

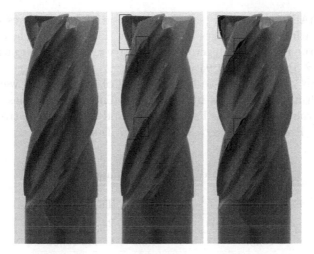

Fig. 4. TiN coated milling tool original image captured with proposed CSE setup (left) and ground truth image whose damages are marked by the expert (center) and result image which is obtained by processing through the proposed algorithm (right).

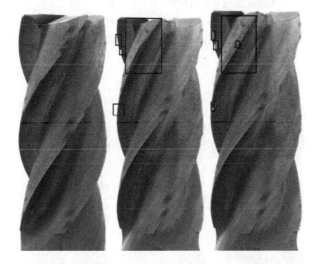

Fig. 5. TiAlN coated milling tool original image captured with proposed CSE setup (left) and ground truth image whose damages are marked by the expert (center) and result image which is obtained by processing through the proposed algorithm (right).

For the TiN coated tool (see Fig. 4) a total of 138 damages were marked as Ground Truth from 23 images by the expert. The algorithm has detected all of the 138 damages as True Positive with zero False Negative and zero False Positive achieving a total of 100% Precision and 100% Recall.

For the TiAlN coated tool (see Fig. 5) a total of 119 damages were marked as Ground Truth from 23 images by the expert. The algorithm has detected 112 damages as True Positive with zero False Positive and 7 False Negative achieving a total of 100% Precision and 94% Recall.

For the ZrN coated tool (see Fig. 6) a total of 155 damages were marked as Ground Truth from 23 images by the expert. The algorithm has detected 138 damages as True Positive, 9 as False Positive and 17 False Negative achieving a total of 93.8% Precision and 89% Recall Fig. 7 Table 2.

Table 2. Results summary.

Coating	TiAlN	TiN	ZrN
No of images	23	23	23
Color	Rose	Gold	Yellow
Ground Truth (GT)	138	119	155
True Positive (TP)	138	112	138
False Positive (FP)	0	0	9
False Negative (FN)	0	7	17
Precision (in %)	100	100	93.8
Recall (in %)	100	94	89

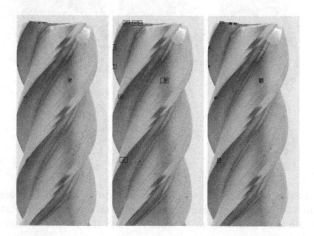

Fig. 6. ZrN coated milling tool original image captured with proposed CSE setup (left) and ground truth image whose damages are marked by the expert (center) and result image which is obtained by processing through the proposed algorithm (right).

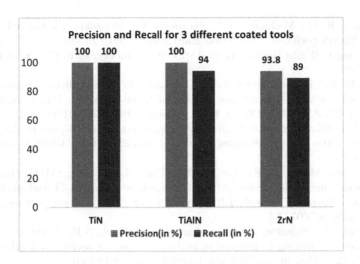

Fig. 7. Precision and Recall values for TiN, TiAlN and ZrN coated milling tool images that were captured through the proposed measurement setup.

6 Conclusion

A new measurement system along with an algorithm was proposed to identify the damages of the coated milling tools. The proposed setup has the potential to replace the current existing solutions which are often quite expensive or time consuming. Although satisfactory results have been achieved with TiN, TiAlN and ZrN coated milling tools, there is still a need to study some other coatings such as AlCrN, AlTiCrN, TiAlN, AlTiN, CrCN and AlTiSi. There is a high possibility that the current measurement setup could face difficulties when it is operated to perform damage detection for some of the above-mentioned coatings due to their reflective properties. The proposed measurement system can provide an aid for tool regrinding industries however, there is a need to improve the current existing algorithm. As a next step of the study, deep learning algorithm would be developed which works on the input images provided by the current measurement setup.

References

1. Thomas Insights, CNC Machining Projected to Become $129 Billion Industry by 2026 [Online]. https://www.thomasnet.com/insights/cnc-machining-projected-to-be-100b-industry-by-2025/. Accessed 19 Jan 2022
2. Gray, A.E., Seidmann, A., Stecke, K.E.: A synthesis of decision models for tool management in automated manufacturing. Manage. Sci. **39**, 549–567 (1993). https://doi.org/10.1287/mnsc.39.5.549
3. Smith, S., Tlusty, J.: Current trends in high-speed machining. J. Manuf. Sci. Eng. **119**, 664–666 (1997). https://doi.org/10.1115/1.2836806

4. Bouzakis, K.-D., Michailidis, N., Skordaris, G., Bouzakis, E.: Coated tools. In: 'Cirp Encyclopedia of Production Engineering' (ed.: Produ T. I. A. f.), pp. 1–13. Springer, Berlin Heidelberg (2018). https://doi.org/10.1007/978-3-642-35950-7_6395-4

5. Conradie, P.J.T., Oosthuizen, G.A., Dimitrov, D.: On the effect of regrinding cutting tools for high performance milling of titanium alloys. Int. J. Adv. Manuf. Technol. **90**, 2283–2292 (2017). https://doi.org/10.1007/s00170-016-9550-z

6. VDMA: Precision tools 2020: positive expectations after 23 percent drop in sales [Online]. https://www.vdma.org/viewer/-/v2article/render/4765841. Accessed 20 Jan 2021

7. Kim, J.-H., Moon, D.-K., Lee, D.-W., Kim, J.-S., Kang, M.-C., Kim, K.H.: Tool wear measuring technique on the machine using CCD and exclusive jig. J. Mater. Process. Technol. **130–131**, 668–674 (2002). https://doi.org/10.1016/S0924-0136(02)00733-1

8. Mohanraj, T., Shankar, S., Rajasekar, R., Sakthivel, N.R., Pramanik, A.: Tool condition monitoring techniques in milling process - a review. J. Market. Res. **9**, 1032–1042 (2020). https://doi.org/10.1016/j.jmrt.2019.10.031

9. Madhuri, K.V.: Thermal protection coatings of metal oxide powders. In: 'Metal Oxide Powder Technologies' Elsevier, pp. 209–231 (2020)

10. Tahir, M.B., Rafique, M., Rafique, M.S., Nawaz, T., Rizwan, M., Tanveer, M.: Photocatalytic nanomaterials for degradation of organic pollutants and heavy metals. In: 'Nanotechnology and Photocatalysis for Environmental Applications' Elsevier, pp. 119–138 (2020)

11. Faraji, G., Kim, H.S., Kashi, H.T.: Introduction. In: 'Severe Plastic Deformation', pp. 1–17. Elsevier(2018)

12. Makhlouf, A.S.H.: Current and advanced coating technologies for industrial applications. In: 'Nanocoatings and Ultra-Thin Films', pp. 3–23. Elsevier (2011)

13. Liu, L., et al.: Luminance uniformity of integrating sphere light source. In: Proceeding of the 2015 International Conference on Optoelectronics and Microelectronics (ICOM), Changchun, China, pp. 265–268 (2015)

Efficient Machine-Learning Based 3D Face Identification System Under Large Pose Variation

Souhir Sghaier[1] , Moez Krichen[2,3]([⊠]) , Abir Othman Elfaki[1] ,
and Qasem Abu Al-Haija[4]

[1] University College of Ranyah, Taif University, Taif, Kingdom of Saudi Arabia
{sdsghaier,aoelfaki}@tu.edu.sa
[2] FCSIT, Al-Baha University, Al-Baha, Saudi Arabia
[3] ReDCAD Laboratory, University of Sfax, Sfax, Tunisia
moez.krichen@redcad.org, mkreishan@bu.edu.sa
[4] Department of Computer Science/Cybersecurity, Princess Sumaya University
for Technology (PSUT), Amman 11941, Jordan
q.abualhaija@psut.edu.jo

Abstract. Large pose variation is considered a major research concern due to its significant impact on the performance of face recognition systems. In this paper, we present a new efficient Machine-Learning Based System that identifies a person's face in 3D under Large pose variation. The proposed system can automatically detect and recognize people under translations and rotation by leveraging the anthropometric methodology and geometric descriptors. We evaluated our system on three well-known 3D face databases: 3DFPE, GAVAB, and 3DFRAV. These databases have a considerable change in the position of the face, even for the same individual. Additionally, we use the ICP algorithm to align the face to the front view. Our experimental simulation results show that the proposed system posed great robustness for significant changes in the pose and proved its advantages over state-of-the-art systems in terms of identification accuracy, specificity, and sensitivity.

Keywords: 3D face identification · Machine Learning · ICP · Alignment · Pose · Geometric · Rotation · Translation

1 Introduction

With modern smart technological advancements [9–11] in the simulation methods of identification and authentication, it becomes necessary to search for new and more accurate methods to determine the identity of people. Face recognition [8,14] is detachable, and all biometrics have been widely used in control systems, video conferencing control, weapon control systems, network security, others. Consequently, the detection and recognition are supervised learning techniques [1] that consist of a group of technologies for a human-computer interface, database management system, video monitoring, and a human behavior monitoring system [19]. This, in turn, highlights face detection and recognition that will integrate with advanced technology.

The automatic biometric system of identification and authentication for individuals by their faces has become an important research field in computer vision. This technology is used in many fields such as biometrics, robotics, control of the human-machine interface, photography, indexing images and videos, and the security applications used in many places such as airports supermarkets. The research studies conducted on 2D faces [12] have reported that the algorithms used suffer from the high sensitivity to changes in lighting, pose variations, and changes in facial expressions. However, 3D facial recognition systems have emerged to address such problems that 2D facial recognition systems face. The 3D facial recognition systems are more robust against pose changes and can better overcome the variation in illumination. These are used in video applications, autonomous robotics, face recognition, and academic and industrial applications. 3D image acquisition technology has become simpler and cheaper. The main advantage of using 3D data is that it retains all the geometric information of the object, which is close to the representation of reality [17].

Therefore, we propose an intuitive, robust, fast, and reliable Machine-Learning based 3D face recognition approach to address the problems of facial expression variation and substantial change of pose and translation. Indeed, we correct the variation of the pose of the faces to obtain front faces by using the ICP algorithm. Specifically, the proposed automatic system has six main phases: data acquisition, a region of interest detection process in phase, data characterization, learning and classification, and the recognition and decision phase.

The paper is organized as follows: in Sect. 2, we review some recent works of the state-of-the-art related to 3D face recognition. Section 3 explains the technique used to align the ace with large pose variation. In Sect. 4, a description of the proposed system is provided. In Sect. 5, we present the performance evaluation of this system along with a comparative study with other biometric systems. The conclusion and the perspectives are presented in Sect. 6.

2   Related Works

Recently, the 3D facial recognition system has been thoroughly investigated and researched. Large numbers of approaches have been conducted and proposed in the literature. For instance, authors of [13] proposed a unified 3D face authentication system. They first presented a method for creating a facial depth map from stereoscopic films using a facial depth recovery method. Then, they developed a new feature descriptor for detecting intrinsic scale features on 3D facial mesh regions for interesting places. The proposed technique was evaluated using publicly available databases and self-collected scene databases. In the same context, the authors of [5] provided a framework for statistical shape analysis of facial surfaces. They also suggested a local representation that uses a curve representation of a 3D face and a quality filter to select curves to handle pose variation and missing data. Furthermore, the authors developed an elastic form analysis of 3D faces to manage fluctuations in facial emotions.

Also, in [6], a local feature-based shape matching approach for expression-invariant 3D face identification was proposed. Each 3D face is first automatically recognized from raw 3D data and normalized to accomplish position invariance. A set of key points and their associated local feature descriptors are then used to depict the 3D face. A probing face is matched to each gallery face using local feature matching and 3D point cloud registration during face recognition. Whereas contributors of [7] suggested a 3D face recognition approach based on covariance descriptors. The latter allows for the fusion and encoding of several characteristics and modalities into a single compact representation. The authors considered the geodesic distance on the manifold, t. The proposed method's performance was evaluated using the FRGCv2 and GAVAB databases.

Moreover, in [16], a novel intrinsic coordinate system alignment-based pose and expression invariant 3D face recognition technique was proposed. A two-tier region ensemble-based classification strategy was used, with three parallel face recognition algorithms. An exponential rank reordering strategy is used to integrate the results of the parallel algorithms. Several experiments were conducted using the FRGCv2 3D database to validate the proposed method. Similarly, a pose invariant deeply learned multiview 3D face recognition system was proposed in [15] to address two issues: face alignment and recognition. Extensive trials on four databases: FRGCv2, Bosphorus, GavabDB, and UMB-DB, demonstrated the performance of the suggested methodology.

In addition, the researchers of [4] proposed a 3D face recognition method that allows face matching even in the event of probe scans with missing sections. The suggested method captures distinctive features of the face by first extracting 3D key points from the scan and then utilizing local shape descriptors to measure how the face surface changes in the keypoints' neighborhood. On the other hand, using numerous keypoint descriptors and sparse representation-based classification, the authors of [20] developed a novel generic strategy to cope with the 3D face recognition challenge. The suggested method avoids the need for pre-alignment between two face scans and is resistant to data loss, occlusions, and expressions.

Another noticeable research is the landmark localization strategy presented in [18]. The method is divided into two steps based on local coordinate coding. The authors perform nose detection in the first step. Next, the authors find a 3D affine transformation that aligns the input face to a reference face using the iterative closest points approach. The authors use resampling in the second step to creating correspondences between the input 3D face and the training faces.

3   Pose Normalization

Changing the pose of the faces is a significant concern attracting a large number of researchers due to its substantial role in various areas such as the authentication system. Indeed, the pose variation in the images, especially with a significant variation of rotation and translation, affects the performance of face recognition systems. Suppose the rotation of the face is greater than 30°, then, in this case, it remains difficult to detect all facial features and significant challenge to detect a region of interest and identify the concerned individual. Moreover, if the face has a rotation of ± 90°, for example, it doesn't remain easy to detect all the face features and even for the translation down or up since it appears only half of the face.

To tackle this problem, we propose working on several faces clouds in different positions (rotation, translation) then combining them into a single cloud. To do this, the image registration technique can be used. Recalibrate a cloud of points concerning another cloud (reference cloud) is finding the transformation matrix. This matrix modifies the geometrical position in the space of the points of the cloud. However, it coincides as much as possible with the points of the cloud reference. In this paper, the transformations are called "rigid" and consist of a single rotation and translation for all points in the cloud. The size of the matrix of transformation is (4×4). It consists of the rotation matrix (3×3) and the translation vector (3×1). This homogeneous coordinate is added to this matrix to make the square matrix with size (4×4) as is shown in Fig. 1.

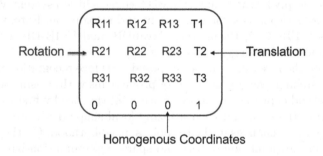

Fig. 1. Transformation matrix.

In the state-of-the-art, to perform the image registration, several algorithms are proposed, such as SIFT (Scale Invariant Feature Transform), PCA (Main Component Analysis), and ICP (Iterative Closest Points). This paper is interested in the Iterative Closest Points (ICP) algorithm, a famous registration algorithm in the field of computer vision that aligns two clouds points. There are mainly two versions of this algorithm: the static version (rigid) and the dynamic version (non-rigid). In our approach, the static ICP is used.

- **Input: Left face N1, right face N2, face looking down N3, face looking up**
- **Output: Face in front view**
- **Algorithm:**
    - **Step 1: Search for matches between the points of the first cloud and those of the second cloud.**

/ Matches are found using the nearest Character criterion. This criterion finds a point p in a cloud N1, the point q in the closest cloud N2 in the 3D space. A Euclidean distance was calculated between the points. When two points are corresponding, the algorithm associates them. */*

- **Step 2: Estimation of the transformation using the correspondences found in the previous step.**
  / The transformation is estimated using the least-squares method, which Characters the error between all the points and their correspondent.*/*
- **Step 3: Estimation of the transformation using the correspondences found in the previous step.**
  / The transformation is estimated using the least-squares method, which Characters the error between all the points and their correspondent.*/*
- **Step 4: The estimated transformation applied to all points.**
- **Step 5: The algorithm repeats the previous three steps until an end criterion is reached.**
  / The end criterion can be the number of iterations or the value of the maximum error to be reached. As long as the value of the error is not below the set threshold or the maximum number of iterations is not reached, the algorithm continues the three steps. */*

The ICP algorithm under the PCL library requires as input two point clouds, the target point cloud, and the source point cloud to be shifted. However, to get a frontal face, it is needed to enter four points clouds (N1, N2, N3, and N4) in different positions (up, down, right, and left). First, recalibrate the second cloud (N2) on the first cloud (N1). A second recalibrated cloud (N2') was obtained. Then, we recalibrate the third cloud (N3) on the fourth cloud (N4) to obtain a third recalibrated cloud (N4'). Finally, a final adjustment is made between (N2') and (N4') to obtain the frontal face (Fig. 2).

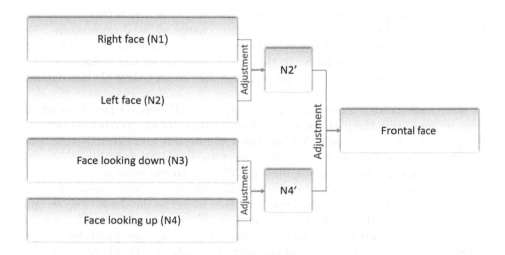

Fig. 2. Cloud setting to obtain a frontal face.

The following matrix represents the final transform matrix after a left face adjustment on a straight face:

$$\begin{bmatrix} 1 & 8.3819e-009 & 3.1665e-008 & 3.05176e-005 \\ -1.34576e-007 & 1 & -5.96046e-008 & 3.05176e-005 \\ -5.79748e-008 & -5.96046e-008 & 1 & -6.10352e-005 \\ 0 & 0 & 0 & 1 \end{bmatrix}$$

The matrix below represents the final transformation matrix after a high face adjustment on a face looking down:

$$\begin{bmatrix} 1 & 5.96046e-008 & -3.63216e-008 & 0 \\ -2.23517e-008 & 1 & -5.96046e-008 & 0 \\ -6.42613e-008 & -8.9407e-008 & 1 & 0 \\ 0 & 0 & 0 & 1 \end{bmatrix}$$

The matrix below represents the final transformation matrix after the last adjustment between (N2') and (N4') to obtain the frontal face:

$$\begin{bmatrix} 1 & 3.8743e-007 & 1.80677e-007 & 0 \\ -2.45869e-007 & 1 & -1.78814e-007 & 0.000183105 \\ -1.33179e-007 & 2.68221e-007 & 1 & 0.00311279 \\ 0 & 0 & 0 & 1 \end{bmatrix}$$

Figure 3 shows the different positions and the result of the last adjustment after the 3D mesh.

4   Description of the Proposed System

The idea of the proposed project comes from the problems encountered in 2D face recognition biometric systems such as the change of facial expressions, illuminations, and especially changes of the pose, etc. To solve these problems, we propose to work with 3D faces. In this paper, we base on the variation of the position of the face. To deal with this problem they created their 3D face dataset named 3D FPE.

The methodology followed in Fig. 4 returns a 3D meshed face in front of view to ameliorate the performance and the accuracy of the recognition system. We propose a new approach that automatically detects and extracts regions of interest from the face as well as its characteristic points. It is based on real anthropometric measurements applied on 3D faces to recognize it.

The proposed approach consists primarily of six necessary steps (Fig. 5). Beginning first, by reading the entire 3D face from the database. The second phase is the detection of regions of interest. We focus on the static area of the face that is hard against facial expressions. So they are interested in the detection and extraction of the upper part of the 3D face (forehead, eyes, and

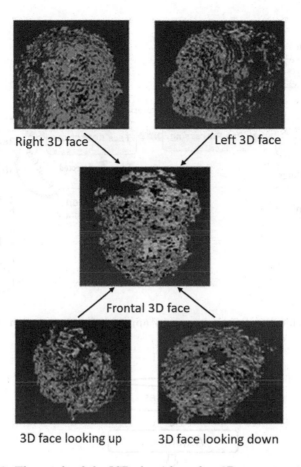

Right 3D face   Left 3D face

Frontal 3D face

3D face looking up   3D face looking down

Fig. 3. The result of the ICP algorithm after 3D reconstruction.

nose). This is achieved by applying the anthropometric proportions and a filter for the segmentation. This step is considered as a first contribution.

Also, we added a preprocessing [2] step of the region of interest extracted to obtain more reliable results and increase the algorithm's performance. At the same time, we used the Delaunay triangulation to fill the holes. We used the median and Laplacian filters to eliminate the maximum unwanted noise for the 3D face. Once we obtain well-treated specific areas, we can detect the points of interest, which are the ends of the eyes in the concave part and the tip of the nose in the convex part of the face. This step is considered as a second contribution.

The next phase is the determination of the relevant and discriminating primitives that lead to characterizing the person's face. We calculated the entropy of the region of interest the width of the front. Then they extracted the Euclidean distances between the points of interest determined and calculated the trigonometric angles between them. These characteristics are merged to determine a resulting characteristic vector needed for the next learning and classification

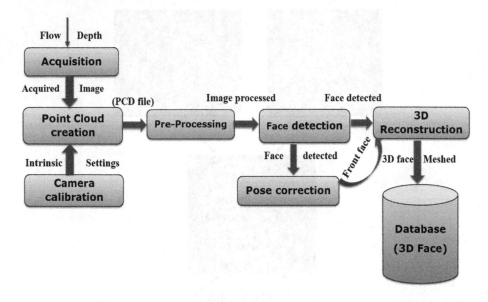

Fig. 4. The architecture of the proposed approach for the creation of the 3D FPE dataset.

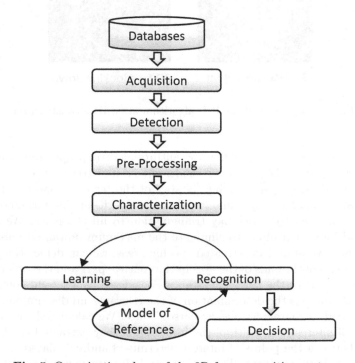

Fig. 5. Organization chart of the 3D face recognition system.

phase. It is based on SVM (Support Vector Machine) with an RBF (Radial Basis Function) type kernel. This step is considered as a third contribution.

At the data learning and classification phase level, we use the SVM method. This method is used for people recognition. The decision on the results of the performance of the proposed system requires a clear and well-defined knowledge of extracted primitives. This phase is used to evaluate system performance and determine the recognition rate (RR) of the 3D face recognition system.

5   Performance of the Proposed System

To measure the effectiveness of the proposed model, we conducted our evaluation experimental tests on three real databases GAVAB, 3DFPE, and FRAV3D. Figure 6 shows the receiver operating characteristic (ROC) curve. This curve measures the performance of the proposed 3D face system graphically. It shows the false rejection rate (FRR) for different thresholds based on the false acceptance rate (FAR). According to the ROC curve, if the FAR decreases, the FRR increases and vice versa. The Equal Error Rate (EER) shows the FAR's percentage equal to FRR. For This system, it is 2.4%.

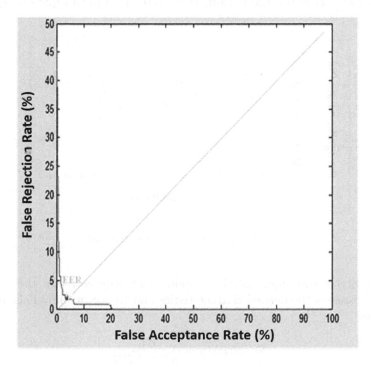

Fig. 6. ROC curve.

According to Fig. 7, the experimental evaluation reported an outstanding recognition rate approaching 100% for the majority of individuals. For example, the individual number 3, the individual number 9, the individual number 40, the individual number 49, and the individual number 45 have recorded a recognition rate of 99.9%. Another example, the individual number 2, the individual number 29, the individual number 9, the individual number 45, and the individual number 47 have recorded a recognition rate of 99.8%. Except for a few individuals, such as the individual 30 and the individual 48 of the GAVAB database. The low impact on these people can be explained by the fact that the images of these individuals present not only much noise but also a large intra-personal variation. Moreover, the image scans of those people contain a large portion of the face with some areas of interest on the face that are missing. Additionally, to measure the performance of the proposed 3D face recognition system, we have used the three standard evaluation metrics [3] that are commonly used to evaluate the recognition systems: specificity, sensitivity, and accuracy. Specificity is the system's capability to correctly determine the people who do not possess the characteristics and reject them. This metric is defined as:

$$Specificity = \frac{TRR}{TRR + FAR} \tag{1}$$

With TRR (True Rate Rejection) is the rate of people adequately rejected.

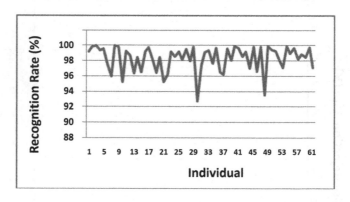

Fig. 7. Recognition rate per individual.

Sensitivity is the ability of the system to identify correctly the true person who possesses the desired characteristics and to accept him. This metric is defined as:

$$Sensitivity = \frac{RR}{RR + FRR} \tag{2}$$

The accuracy is the ability of the system to distinguish between the real people who have the desired characteristics and to accept him and to reject the person who does not have the required signatures. This metric is defined as:

$$Accuracy = \frac{RR}{RR + FAR} \qquad (3)$$

As shown in Fig. 8, our recognition system recorded 91%, 98%, and 99% for specificity, sensitivity, and accuracy respectively.

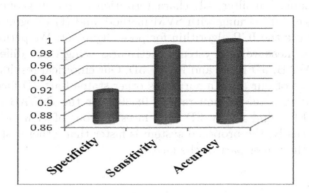

Fig. 8. Specificity, sensitivity, and accuracy performance of the recognition phase.

Finally, Table 1 provides a comparison between our proposed approach with other existing 3D face recognition approaches.

Table 1. Comparison of our approach with other state-of-the-art approaches.

Reference	Year of Publication	Used Databases	Obtained Results
[13]	2016	Bosphorus	RR = 95.03%
		GAVAB	RR = 92.62%
		FRGC v2	RR = 89.20%
[5]	2013	FRGC v2	RR = 98.02%
[6]	2016	Bosphorus	RR = 96.85%
		FRGC v2	RR = 97%
[7]	2016	FRGC v2	RR = 98.5%
		GAVAB	RR = 97.81%
[16]	2016	FRGC v2	RR = 94.64%
[15]	2019	GAVAB	RR = 83.60%
[4]	2013	FRGC v2	RR = 96%
		CASIA	RR = 95.4%
[20]	2014	Bosphorus	RR = 93.40%
		GAVAB	RR = 95.10%
		FRGC v2	RR = 77.10%
[18]	2014	BU-3DFE	RR = 93.70%
		GAVAB	RR = 86.60%
		FRGC v2	RR = 92.30%
Our approach	2022	GAVAB	RR = 98.30%

6   Conclusion

This paper presents an efficient 3D face recognition system with a wide variation of rotation and translation. The proposed system is composed of six essential steps: (a) acquisition of scan from 3D databases, (b) detection of the region of interest based on anthropometric proportion, (c) preprocessing step based on median and Laplacian filter, (d) characterization based on geometric descriptors for 3D face, (e) learning with SVM method, and (f) recognition of the 3D face. Also, we use the ICP algorithm for pose alignment. We performed several experiments to measure the system effectiveness using three different 3D face databases: GAVAB, 3D FPE, and FRAV 3D. Our empirical results showed that the performance of our system surpasses other state-of-art 3D face recognition systems recording a recognition rate of 98.30% for the GAVAB database and 100% for 3D FPE and FRAV 3D with faces in front of view (after pose correction). Eventually, the proposed system is faster than other systems since we focus only on the upper part of the face.

References

1. Al-Haija, Q.A., Nasr, K.A.: Supervised regression study for electron microscopy data. In: 2019 IEEE International Conference on Bioinformatics and Biomedicine (BIBM), pp. 1–6 (2019)
2. Abu Al-Haija, Q., Krichen, M., Abu Elhaija, W.: Machine-learning-based darknet traffic detection system for IoT applications. Electronics 11(4), 1–19 (2022)
3. Al-Haija, Q.A., Smadi, M., Al-Bataineh, O.M.: Identifying phasic dopamine releases using darknet-19 convolutional neural network. In: 2021 IEEE International IOT, Electronics and Mechatronics Conference (IEMTRONICS), pp. 1–6 (2021)
4. Berretti, S., Werghi, N., Del Bimbo, A., Pala, P.: Matching 3D face scans using interest points and local histogram descriptors. Comput. Graph. 37(5), 509–525 (2013)
5. Drira, H., Amor, B.B., Srivastava, A., Daoudi, M., Slama, R.: 3D face recognition under expressions, occlusions, and pose variations. IEEE Trans. Pattern Anal. Mach. Intell. 35(9), 2270–2283 (2013)
6. Guo, Y., Lei, Y., Liu, L., Wang, Y., Bennamoun, M., Sohel, F.: EI3D: Expression-invariant 3D face recognition based on feature and shape matching. Pattern Recogn. Lett. 83, 403–412 (2016)
7. Hariri, W., Tabia, H., Farah, N., Benouareth, A., Declercq, D.: 3D face recognition using covariance based descriptors. Pattern Recogn. Lett. 78, 1–7 (2016)
8. Jabbar, R., Shinoy, M., Kharbeche, M., Al-Khalifa, K., Krichen, M., Barkaoui, K.: Driver drowsiness detection model using convolutional neural networks techniques for android application. In: 2020 IEEE International Conference on Informatics, IoT, and Enabling Technologies (ICIoT), pp. 237–242. IEEE (2020)
9. Krichen, M.: Anomalies detection through smartphone sensors: a review. IEEE Sens. J. 21(6), pp. 7207–7217 (2021)
10. Krichen, M., Alroobaea, R.: A new model-based framework for testing security of IoT systems in smart cities using attack trees and price timed automata. In: 14th International Conference on Evaluation of Novel Approaches to Software Engineering - ENASE 2019 (2019)

11. Krichen, M., Cheikhrouhou, O., Lahami, M., Alroobaea, R., Jmal Maâlej, A.: Towards a model-based testing framework for the security of internet of things for smart city applications. In: Mehmood, R., Bhaduri, B., Katib, I., Chlamtac, I. (eds.) SCITA 2017. LNICST, vol. 224, pp. 360–365. Springer, Cham (2018). https://doi.org/10.1007/978-3-319-94180-6_34

12. Liu, S., Wang, Y., Peng, Y., Hou, S., Zhang, K., Wu, X.: Singular value decomposition-based virtual representation for face recognition. Mach. Vis. Appl. **31**(3), 1–9 (2020). https://doi.org/10.1007/s00138-020-01067-4

13. Ming, Y., Hong, X.: A unified 3D face authentication framework based on robust local mesh sift feature. Neurocomputing **184**, 117–130 (2016)

14. Ndong, P.S.B., et al.: A face-mask detection system based on deep learning convolutional neural networks. In: Saeed, F., Al-Hadhrami, T., Mohammed, E., Al-Sarem, M. (eds.) Advances on Smart and Soft Computing. AISC, vol. 1399, pp. 273–283. Springer, Singapore (2022). https://doi.org/10.1007/978-981-16-5559-3_23

15. Ratyal, N., et al.: Deeply learned pose invariant image analysis with applications in 3D face recognition. Math. Probl. Eng. **2019**, 1–21 (2019)

16. Ratyal, N.I., Taj, I.A., Bajwa, U.I., Sajid, M., Baig, M.J.A., Butt, F.M.: 3D face recognition based on region ensemble and hybrid features. In: 2016 International Conference on Computing, Electronic and Electrical Engineering (ICE Cube), pp. 294–300. IEEE (2016)

17. Sghaier, S., Farhat, W., Souani, C.: Novel technique for 3D face recognition using anthropometric methodology. Int. J. Ambient Comput. Intell. (IJACI) **9**(1), 60–77 (2018)

18. Song, M., Tao, D., Sun, S., Chen, C., Maybank, S.J.: Robust 3D face landmark localization based on local coordinate coding. IEEE Trans. Image Process. **23**(12), 5108–5122 (2014)

19. Zeng, X., Peng, X., Wang, Y., Qiao, Y.: Finding hard faces with better proposals and classifier. Mach. Vis. Appl. **31**(7), 1–15 (2020)

20. Zhang, L., Ding, Z., Li, H., Shen, Y., Lu, J.: 3D face recognition based on multiple keypoint descriptors and sparse representation. PLoS ONE **9**(6), e100120 (2014)

Arabic Handwritten Character Recognition Based on Convolution Neural Networks

Lamia Bouchriha[1]([✉]), Ahmed Zrigui[2], Sadek Mansouri[1], Salma Berchech[3], and Syrine Omrani[3]

[1] Research Laboratory in Algebra, Numbers Theory and Intelligent Systems RLANTIS, Monastir University, Monastir, Tunisia
`lamia.bouchriha@gmail.com`
[2] Paul Sabatier University, Toulouse, France
[3] DB CONSULTING, 4 Rue Simone de Beauvoir, 94140 Alfortville, France

Abstract. Automatic handwriting recognition is a useful task for many applications. The main Research has focused on the Latin languages. However, few approaches have been proposed for the Arabic language due to the specific and complex features of handwritten Arabic text. In this paper, we propose a Deep Learning (DL) approach for Arabic character recognition using proposed model of convolutional neural networks (CNN). In our work, we dealt with the specific features of Arabic text, in particular the variation of the shape of characters according to its position in the word based a new model of CNN network. In the experimental evaluation, we use hijja dataset in train and test steps. Obtained results prove the efficiency of our model, achieving accuracy of 95% on the Hijja dataset.

Keywords: Arabic handwriting recognition · CNN · Hijja

1 Introduction

Until today, writing is considered a more important means of communication between human beings. On the other hand, there is handwriting which is more complex than printed writing due to its style, inclination, fluctuations, variability of forms and the variability of spacing between words and characters, consequently, it attracts the attention of several researchers in several fields thanks to its major services (postal or bank checks, postal sorting, forms (invoices, declarations taxes,etc.), administrative files,etc.) [1,2].

Indeed, automatic handwriting recognition is an intelligent computer system that comes closest to the human being whose role is to digitize handwritten data and then find its meaning [3]. There are two ways of recognizing handwriting: online and offline. The online mode is performed in real time using the graphic tablet with an electronic pen, the touch screen, etc. On the other hand, the other mode presents a static recognition of images of handwritten texts from

© The Author(s), under exclusive license to Springer Nature Switzerland AG 2022
C. Bădică et al. (Eds.): ICCCI 2022, CCIS 1653, pp. 286–293, 2022.
https://doi.org/10.1007/978-3-031-16210-7_23

previously written documents, obtained by a scanner or a camera, this leads to characterize it as a more complex mode than the first because of the presence of noise during image acquisition. As well as, its recognition rate is lower due to lack of contextual information compared to online handwriting recognition rate which is higher due to the presence of information on position, direction of movement, start points, end points and line order. Therefore, only the offline mode will be considered in our work.

The Arabic handwriting is complex [4,5] due to the overlap of the characters, the variability of the styles of writing of its diacritical points and some vowels as well as the positions of four forms (beginning, middle, end and isolated) of certain characters in a word. Yet little progress has been made in research for automatic Arabic handwriting recognition due to the lack of datasets and adequate funding support unlike Latin handwriting [6,7].

DL is a field in machine learning that uses artificial neural networks made up of thousands of units (neurons), each performing small, simple operations. Thus, the outputs of a first layer of neurons serve as an input for calculations of a second layer, and so on [8]. It is the adaptation of these networks that mimics the structure of the human brain. Indeed, the strength of deep learning lies in the fact that the machine learns characteristics directly without the need to extract them manually [9]. There are a large number of DL algorithms, the most efficient for classifying images are models of convolutional neural networks.

Convolutional Neural Network is a type of feed-forward artificial neural network referred to by the acronym CNN. CNNs are derived from multi-layered perceptron. Indeed, they are based on convolution operations, each of them functions as an extractor of characteristics of images. Additionally, there are many applications of CNNs, including image classification, image semantic segmentation [10–12], object detection in image [13,14], etc.

The rest of the paper is organized as follows: In Sect. 2, we are particularly interested in stating the existing works of the different classification approaches of the Arabic handwriting recognition system. Section 3 details the architecture of proposed CNN model. Section 4 describes the experiment task including the dataset used and the results obtained. Finally, we end this paper with a conclusion and perspectives in Sect. 5.

2 Related Work

Automatic recognition of Arabic Handwritten text is a challenging task in the field of computer vision. Same works have been proposed in these last years.

Among them we find the work of El-Sawy et al.(2017) [15] consists in presenting a classification approach based on a convolutional neural network (CNN) made up of two convolutional layers, two Max Pooling layers and two Dense layers using a base of Arabic handwritten characters called AHCD. This is divided into two sets of 28 classes: a 13440 character learning set (480 images per class) and a 3360 character test set (120 images per class). Indeed, this proposed CNN gives an average classification error of 5.1%, i.e. the recognition rate reached 94.9% on the test set.

The work of Maalej et al.(2018) [16] describes an offline handwritten Arabic word recognition system using a hybrid classifier. The latter is composed of two convolutional neural networks: the first is CNN to automatically extract the characteristics of the raw images and the second is BLSTM followed by a connectionist temporal classification (CTC) layer for sequence labeling. Furthermore, this two-level hybrid classifier achieved an average recognition accuracy of 92.21% based on the Arabic handwritten words IFN/ENIT.

The proposed work of Altwaijry et al.(2021) [17] is a CNN model for automatic recognition of handwritten characters. This model is formed on Hijja containing 47434 characters written by 591 participants in different forms. Results show that the model's achieving accuracy of 88% on the Hijja dataset.

3   Proposed CNN Model

In this section, we describe the details of the proposed model of CNN for Arabic handwritten character recognition. The main aims is to recognize special handwritten Arabic character according to its positions in the word. The following figure (Fig. 1) shows the architecture of our proposed CNN model.

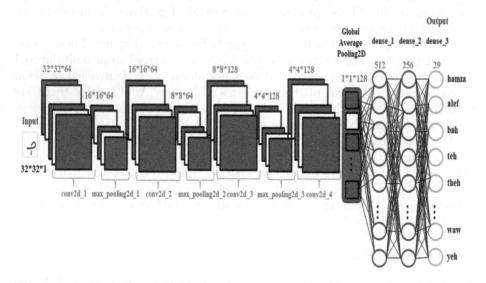

Fig. 1. Architecture of our CNN model.

3.1   Input Layer

The input layer is a width*height*channels. When, the images are in gray levels so the number of channels c per pixel is equal to 1. The sizes of the images are 32 * 32 pixels in size and grayscale (number of channels is 1), i.e. our model has a 32 * 32 * 1 image as input.

3.2 Hidden Layers

In our CNN model, we used two convolution layers of 64 filters of size 3 * 3 and two convolution layers of 128 filters of size 3 * 3. These four layers are taken from the pre-trained VGG-16 [18] network provided by Keras. In this convolution layers, the convolution step is equal to 1 (by default strides = 1) and the border mode is equal to the size of the previous image (padding = 'same'). Additionally, each of our convolutional layers is followed by a ReLU activation function (activation = 'relu') which forces neurons to return positive values. It is a non-linear real activation function which returns 0 if the input z is less than 0 and returns z itself if it is greater than 0 [19]. Acronym for Rectified Linear Unit defined by:

$$ReLU(x) = max(0, x) \tag{1}$$

After each first three convolution layers, we used a pooling layer [20]with the parameter pool_size (size of pool) is equal to 2 * 2 pixels so the size of the image in this each pooling layer will be divided by 2 [21]. Then, after the four convolution layers used and three Max Pooling2D layers used, we used a Global Average Pooling 2D layer [20] which gives an average output of each 128 feature map of size 4 * 4 obtained a priory from the previous layer. When applying this pooling layer, the pool_size is always defined by the size of the input of the layer, but, instead the average of the pool_size is taken. That is the output is 128 features maps of size 1 * 1. Indeed, we used a Fully-Connected layer (dense_1) which has 512 neurons whose activation function used is ReLU and a Fully-Connected layer (dense_2) of 256 neurons followed by a ReLU activation function.

3.3 Output Layer

The third fully connected layer (dense_3) is a Softmax [21] which allows calculating the probability distribution of the 29 classes (number of classes in the Hijja dataset). The Softmax non-linear activation function assigns decimal probabilities to each class of a multiple class problem. This activation function is calculated using the following formula:

$$Softmax(Z)_j = \frac{e^{Z_j}}{\sum_{k=1}^{K} e^{Z_k}} \ , \ j\varepsilon\{1, ..., K\} \tag{2}$$

With j is the index of a class and K is the number of classes and Z equal to:

$$Z = W * X + b \tag{3}$$

Moreover, it suffices to use the function argmax [21] on the output of the function Softmax to obtain the predicted class denoted by $\hat{y}$, as described in the equation below:

$$\hat{y} = argmax(Softmax(Z)) \tag{4}$$

4   Experimental Results

4.1   Hijja Dataset

Hijja[1] is a free and publicly accessible set of unique letters collected from Arabic speaking schoolchildren aged 7 to 12. These letters were collected in Riyadh, Saudi Arabia, from January 2019 to April 2019. This represents a total of 47434 characters written by 591 participants in different forms. The characters are labeled from hamza to yeh that is to say the number of classes is equal to 29 and each image is 32 by 32 in size and in grayscale. Furthermore, each folder contains subfolders of different letter shapes for each letter. Each subfolder contains the images of each particular letter shape [17].

4.2   4.2. Results and Discussion

We choose the mini-batch gradient descent [22] method to train our model and the categorical cross-entropy loss which is the default loss function for multi-class classification. Then, we compiled our model using the Adam optimization algorithm [23]which has the advantages such as simplicity of implementation, computational efficiency, little memory required, well suited to large problems in terms of data and/or parameters, etc. Our model is better since it obtained a recognition rate of 95% after 20 epochs whereas the CNN model of Altwaijry et al. [17] reached 88% after 30 epochs (see Table 1).

Table 1. Comparison of experimental results on the Hijja dataset between our model and the model of Altwaijry et al. [17]

Characters	Models					
	Altwaijry et al. [17]			Our model		
Class. Character	P	R	F1	P	R	F1
1. Alef	0.99	0.98	0.98	1.00	0.99	0.99
2. Bah	0.92	0.97	0.94	1.00	0.89	0.94
3. Teh	0.89	0.89	0.89	0.93	0.94	0.93
4. Theh	0.90	0.87	0.88	0.95	0.94	0.95
5. Jeem	0.89	0.92	0.91	0.99	0.95	0.97
Accuracy			**0.88**			**0.95**
Macro avg	0.87	0.87	0.87	0.95	0.94	0.95
Weighted avg	0.88	0.88	0.88	0.95	0.95	0.95

The figure Fig. 2 shows some examples of classification and character forms lam in a word. For example, number 56 is correctly classified with its beginning

---

[1] Hijja is available at https://github.com/israksu/Hijja2.

form, image numbered 95 is well classified with its end form, image 249 is well classified with its isolated form and also image numbered 293 is well classified with its middle form. On the other hand, images 57 and 93 are misclassified.

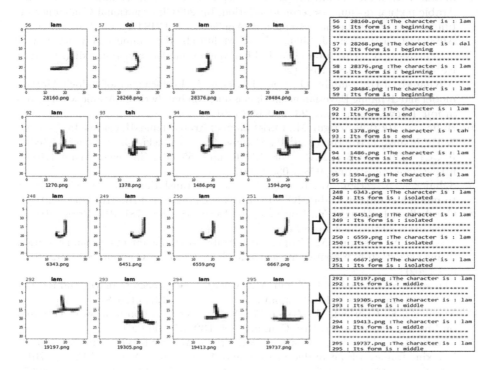

Fig. 2. Examples of lam character classification and forms

5 Conclusion

The main goals of all research are to gain good results and to accomplish an effective recognition approach. Indeed, we made an automatic recognition of the handwritten Arabic characters carried out on the Hijja base which is composed of the handwritten Arabic characters in different forms by applying our CNN model (composed of four convolution layers, three Max Pooling layers, a Global Average layer Pooling and three Dense layers). This work obtained a recognition rate of 95% which is better than that of Altwaijry et al. [17] for each character position (beginning, middle, end and isolated). Finally, as perspective, we plan to enrich our work with the combination of two convolutional neural networks.

References

1. Bellagha, M.L., Zrigui, M.: Using the MGB-2 challenge data for creating a new multimodal Dataset for speaker role recognition in Arabic TV broadcasts. KES Procedia Comput. Sci. **192**, 59–68 (2021)

2. Mahmoud, A., Zrigui, M.: Distributional semantic model based on convolutional neural network for Arabic textual similarity. Int. J. Cogn. Inform. Nat. Intell. **14**(1), 35–50 (2020)
3. Meddeb, O., Maraoui, M., Zrigui, M.: Deep learning based semantic approach for Arabic textual documents recommendation. In: 2021 International Conference on Innovations in Intelligent Systems and Applications (INISTA), pp. 1–6 (2021)
4. AlKhateeb, J.H., Ren, J., Jiang, J., Al-Muhtaseb, H.: Offline handwritten Arabic cursive text recognition using hidden Markov models and re-ranking. Pattern Recogn. Lett. **32**, 1081–1088 (2011)
5. AlKhateeb, J.H., Pauplin, O., Ren, J., Jiang, J.: Performance of hidden Markov model and dynamic Bayesian network classifiers on handwritten Arabic word recognition. Knowl.-Based Syst. **24**, 680–688 (2011)
6. Haffar, N., Hkiri, E., Zrigui, M.: Enrichment of Arabic TimeML corpus. In: Nguyen, N.T., Hoang, B.H., Huynh, C.P., Hwang, D., Trawiński, B., Vossen, G. (eds.) ICCCI 2020. LNCS (LNAI), vol. 12496, pp. 655–667. Springer, Cham (2020). https://doi.org/10.1007/978-3-030-63007-2_51
7. Sghaier, M.A., Zrigui, M.: Rule-based machine translation from Tunisian dialect to modern standard Arabic. KES Procedia Comput. Sci. **176**, 310–319 (2020)
8. Goodfellow, I., Bengio, Y., Courville, A.: Deep Learning, 781.MIT Press. http://www.deeplearningbook.org (2016)
9. Meddeb, O., Maraoui, M., Zrigui, M.: Arabic text documents recommendation using joint deep representations learning. KES Procedia Comput. Sci. **192**, 812–821 (2021)
10. Mansouri, S., Charhad, M., Zrigui, M.: A heuristic approach to detect and localize text on Arabic news video. Computación y Sistemas **22**(1) (2018)
11. Mansouri, S., Charhad, M., Zrigui, M.: Arabic text detection in news video based on line segment detector. Res. Comput. Sci. **132**, 97–106 (2017)
12. Mansouri, S., Lhioui, C., Charhad, M., Zrigui, M.: Text-to-concept: a semantic indexing framework for arabic news videos. In: Gelbukh, A. (ed.) CICLing 2017. LNCS, vol. 10762, pp. 575–584. Springer, Cham (2018). https://doi.org/10.1007/978-3-319-77116-8_43
13. Mansouri, S., Zrigui, S., Zrigui, M., Berchech, D.: Text detection in Arabic news video based on MSER and RetinaNet. In: 2021 IEEE/ACS 18th International Conference on Computer Systems and Applications (AICCSA), pp. 1–7 (2021)
14. Manita, S., Mansouri, S., Zrigui, M., Berchech, S.: Arabic text detection in news video using RetinaNet. KES Procedia Comput. Sci. **192**, 796–803 (2021)
15. El-Sawy, A., Loey, M., El-Bakry, H.: Arabic handwritten characters recognition using convolutional neural network. WSEAS Trans. Comput. Res. **5**, 11–19 (2017)
16. Maalej, R., Kherallah, M.: Convolutional neural network and BLSTM for offline Arabic handwriting recognition. In: International Arab Conference on Information Technology (ACIT), Werdanye, Lebanon, pp. 1–6 (2018)
17. Altwaijry, N., Al-Turaiki, I.: Arabic handwriting recognition system using convolutional neural network. Neural Comput. Appl. **33**(7), 2249–2261 (2020). https://doi.org/10.1007/s00521-020-05070-8
18. https://towardsdatascience.com. Accessed 24 May 2021
19. Buduma, N.: Fundamentals of Deep Learning Designing Next-Generation Machine Intelligence Algorithms. O'Reilly Media, Inc. (2017)
20. https://github.com/christianversloot/machine-learning-articles/. Accessed 24 May 2021
21. Wu, J.: Introduction to Convolutional Neural Networks. National Key Lab for Novel Software Technology Nanjing University, China (2017)

22. Li, M., Zhang, T., Chen, Y., Smola, A.J.: Efficient mini-batch training for stochastic optimization. In: Proceedings of the 20th ACM SIGKDD International Conference on Knowledge Discovery and Data Mining, KDD 14, New York, NY, USA, pp. 661–670 (2014)
23. Kingma, D., Ba, J.: Adam: a method for stochastic optimization. arXiv preprint arXiv:1412.6980 (2014)

An End to End Bilingual TTS System for Fongbe and Yoruba

Charbel Arnaud Cedrique Y. Boco$^{(\boxtimes)}$ (ID) and Théophile K. Dagba

University of Abomey Calavi, Cotonou, Benin
bococharbel@gmail.com, theophile.dagba@eneam.uac.bj

Abstract. This paper aims to present an end to end bilingual TTS system for Yoruba and Fongbe based on Fastspeech 2, a non-autoregressive model. From this baseline, a simple concatenation of speaker, language and phoneme embeddings was used as input for the encoder and the decoder. The training was done on a multi-speaker dataset collected for both languages. Two types of input were used: a shared representation of phoneme between both languages and a language specific representation of phonemes. Then some experimentations were made to test both input representations showing that results are smoother for the shared representation of phoneme. But with all input sets, the proposed model was able to synthesize speech in each language with voice cloning ability. The model produces good speech quality waveform with great fidelity and naturalness and shows its ability to generate speech waveforms for both languages. A comparison was also made between the proposed bilingual system and the same model trained on monolingual dataset to show that the bilingual dataset allows more accurate result.

Keywords: Bilingual text-to-speech · African language · Tonal language

1 Introduction

End to end neural network-based model is a quantum leap on the design of high quality text to speech (TTS) systems. Autoregressive systems such as Tacotron 2 [1] or non-autoregression such as FastSpeech 2 [2] provided reliable results with high fidelity and quality speech waveform generation [3].

The autoregressive neural network models are made of layers which transform input symbols (phone, char, byte, etc.) to Mel spectrogram and then use a vocoder (often neural network based) to transform Mel to speech waveform. Autoregressive models can learn to synthesize speech from massive pairs (text and audio) of data with few human annotation and without the need of previous phoneme-level alignment information (e.g.: speech duration information) [3]. But they present many shortcomings such as slow training and inference speed, phone skipping and phone repeating [2]. Non-autoregressive TTS models differ from the previous ones in a more fast inference speed but need labeled duration information.

Those neural network systems really enhance the performance of speech synthesis. They allowed the modeling of great quality speech synthesis system with for instance

C. Bădică et al. (Eds.): ICCCI 2022, CCIS 1653, pp. 294–304, 2022.
https://doi.org/10.1007/978-3-031-16210-7_24

a Mean Opinion Score (MOS)[1] of 4.53 for Tacotron 2 and 3.77 for Fastspeech 2 for English. Based on that performance, they were extended to multilingual and polyglot speech synthesis with great result [4, 5]. Some works were realized to prove that high resource languages can be used to improve the quality of under-resourced language in neural TTS due to the massive need of data of neural network end to end TTS Systems [6, 7]. In fact, the problem of limited data of under resourced languages can be handled by adding data of high resource languages in a bilingual or multilingual system.

In this work, we propose a bilingual TTS System for Fongbe and Yoruba based on Fastspeech 2.

Multilingual speech synthesis system is of great interest for African countries with several under-resourced languages. Instead of having one system for each language, it provides a single system capable of speaking several languages. It also solves the problem of collecting a large amount of data required by neural network models by combining small amounts of data obtained for several languages.

2 Objectives

The main objective is to build an end to end neural network TTS System for two tonal languages (Yoruba and Fongbe) in a context of low available data and unbalanced dataset. To our knowledge, there is no speech synthesis system based on neural networks for Fongbe. The only published work for Fongbe TTS System is [8] and is based on a unit selection approach. The current work is the first attempt to build a bilingual Yoruba and Fongbe TTS system that will be able to synthesis speech fluently in both language with good voice cloning ability (see Fig. 1). From the input text written in one of the target language, the neural network architecture will be able to produce Mel spectrogram as input for a vocoder which will generate the output speech waveform.

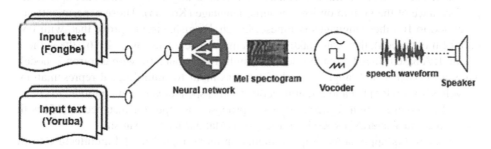

Fig. 1. Global system architecture

3 Related Work

End-to-end neural TTS aims at unifying the main components of TTS Systems like G2P (grapheme to phone) or phonemizer, acoustic and prosody modeling, duration modeling

---

[1] MOS (Mean Opinion Score) is a subjective test where some evaluators give a score between 1 (Low) and 5 (Excellent) to the generated waveforms of a TTS system.

and speech synthesizer to provide a fast, reliable and accurate system. Those components, in previous older systems, are implemented in different modules combined in a multiple step process. Recent end-to-end neural network-based TTS systems have shown promising results with great naturalness and quality quite close to human speech. One of the main examples are Tacotron [9] and Tacotron 2 [1] which achieve respectively a MOS of 3.82 and 4.53 for English. Tacotron is a sequence to sequence model with attention mechanism which is able to synthesize speech directly from text without a previous phoneme level alignment. It is composed of convolutional layers, GRU (Gated recurrent units), LSTM (Long Short Term Memory) and fully connected layers organized in an Encoder-Decoder architecture and use Griffin Lim Vocoder [10]. It uses an autoregressive alignment method to predict speech duration without previous duration labeled data. Tacotron 2 improves the architecture of the latter by replacing GRU with LSTM and using location sensitive attention mechanism [11] with WaveNet Vocoder [12]. Other examples are Fastspeech [13] and Fastspeech 2 which are non-autoregressive feed-forward Transformer networks. They use a mechanism of feature length regulation to predict the number of frames generated by acoustic feature. They achieved respectively a MOS of 3.84 and 3.77 for English. Fastspeech uses a teacher model with a knowledge distillation method to train the duration prediction (using a previously pretrained phoneme duration model). This is replaced in Fastspeech 2 by components whose roles are to predict duration, pitch and energy with the need of accurate duration label. Those models have faster inference speed than Tacotron 2 and needs less data for training.

Based on the results obtained for monolingual systems, models like Tacotron2 have been widely used in several works intended for the design of multilingual and polyglot systems. Some works mainly focus on input data. For instance, in [5], a bilingual English and Korean TTS system based on Tacotron proposes as input a language specific phoneme representation based on IPA (International Phonetic Alphabet) and Griffin-Lim Vocoder. The model is pretrained with a high resource language (English) to improve the performance of the system on low resource language (Korean). Those experiments are extended to 10 other languages (Chinese, Dutch, Finnish, etc.) to prove that, with few data (2 h of speech), they can make the system learn new languages. In [6], the authors use an IPA based shared phoneme sets for English and Mandarin with tacotron 2 model. They add speaker and language embeddings as input for multilingual representation, WaveRNN vocoder [14] and integrate a pre-trained speaker verification model to create a speaker representation. Unicode bytes is proposed as input for instance in [15] with Tacoton 2 and WaveRNN vocoder for English, Mandarin and Spanish.

Other works apply some improvements on monolingual model architecture to fit multilingual synthesis framework. For instance, in [16] the authors work on Tacotron 2 architecture modification for Mandarin and English with alphabetic characters as input and Griffin-Lim Vocoder. They propose two models: a shared multilingual encoder by incorporating language embedding into encoder through fully-connected layers and a separate encoder framework (one for each language).

In [17], an adversarially-trained speaker classifier using adversarial loss is added to Tacotron 2 with WaveRNN vocoder for English, Spanish and Chinese cross-lingual TTS system. They also add speaker and language embeddings to the decoder's input. Experiments have been carried out for phonemes, characters and UTF-8 encoded bytes.

Authors achieve more reliable result for phonemes because the same character (or UTF-8 byte) may correspond to different phonemes in two given languages. The adversarially-trained speaker classifier is also used in [4] to create a multilingual TTS that supports 10 languages including German, Spanish, French, Chinese and English with cross-lingual and code-switching capabilities (alternate languages within sentences). The Tacotron 2 model has been modified using a parameter generator network where a language embedding is used to produce parameters for the encoder's convolutional layers.

In [18], the authors build a cross-lingual multi-speaker neural end-to-end TTS for Chinese and English languages based on Tacotron 2 with Griffin-Lim Vocoder and a separate neural speaker encoder network based on RESCNN (used to create a speaker embedding from groundtruth Mel spectrogram). The input is IPA phoneme annotation.

In [19], the authors build a multilingual TTS system for 50 languages based on Transformer TTS [20] and WaveNet vocoder with a highly unbalanced dataset. The input is an unshared language dependent phoneme representation. They add a speaker and language encoding networks based on a lookup table. This model has been modified in [7] to handle high unbalanced datasets and to improve low resource languages synthesis. The authors use the byte input strategy of [15] for almost 40 languages and propose a tier-wise progressive training steps and a strategy to train an unbalanced dataset.

Especially for the target languages (Fongbe and Yoruba), there are some works which focus on building monolingual TTS systems with methods like concatenation or unit selection. In [8], the authors use unit selection to build a TTS System for Fongbe with a MOS score of 2.79. In [21] and [22] authors use unit selection method for Yoruba with respectively a score of 2.9 and 3.6 for MOS test. For multilingual neural network TTS, a yoruba dataset designed in [23] has been used in [7] in combination with the datasets of many other languages but the results have been given for some sample datasets like English or chinese (not especially for Yoruba). To our knowledge, presently there is no multilingual TTS system for Fongbe.

4 Model Architecture

In the context of the current work, we choose a non-autoregressive model to avoid the problem of phoneme skipping and ensure a faster inference and training speed. In fact, the proposed architecture is based on Fastspeech 2. Phonemes are used as input to allow a better estimation of the duration of each phonetic unit which will impact the quality of speech generation. The base model of Fastspeech 2 is multi-speaker but not multilingual. Then we need to add new components to ensure multilingual speech synthesis. Fastspeech 2 is composed of (see Fig. 2):

- an encoder which includes a set of self-attention modules, batch normalization, convolutional and fully connected layers
- duration, F0 and energy predictors (denoted variance adaptor) which are modules built with linear and convolutional layers
- a decoder whose composition is the same as that of the encoder (a set of attention layers, batch normalization, convolutional and fully connected layers).

From the baseline model, we concatenate phoneme embedding with language embedding as input for the encoder. The speaker embedding is added to the expected input of the decoder (the decoder takes as input the outputs of the encoder and the variance adapter which is composed of f0, duration and energy predictors outputs). By concatenating language with phoneme, we assume that the encoder will learn a suitable phoneme + language representation. By the same way, incorporating speaker embedding in the decoder input can improve multi-speaker Mel spectrogram generation [4, 17].

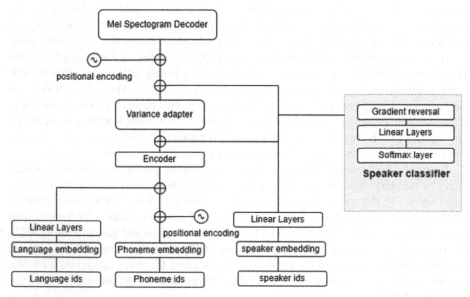

Fig. 2. Multilingual Fastspeech 2 architecture following baseline Fastspeech 2 model with added language and speaker embeddings.

The adversarial speaker classifier is used for Tacotron 2 in [4, 5] to create a speaker independent representation for the Encoder's output. It is built with two linear layers, a softmax layer and a gradient reversal layer. The gradient reversal layer is placed on top of the speaker classifier to clip the gradient flowing to the encoder and scale it by a factor of $-\lambda$.

We apply this classifier in Fastspeech 2 to improve voice cloning. The model uses Melgan Vocoder [24] for speech waveforms generation. Our implementations of Fastspeech 2 and Melgan are based on a publicly available library [25] written with TensorFlow.

5   Datasets

5.1   Fongbe Language

Fongbe is a West African tonal language which belongs to the Niger-Congolese language family mainly spoken in Benin by about 2 million people [26]. It has 22 consonants and

12 vowels with 4 tones (high, low, mid and low-high). Then we consider 70 (22 + 12 × 4) phonemes unique representation.

5.2 Yoruba Language

Yoruba is also a tonal language belonging to the Niger-Congolese language family and is spoken mainly in Nigeria and Benin by more than 40 million people [26]. It has 11 vowels with 3 tones, 18 consonants and 3 syllabic nasal sound. Then we use 54 phonemes.

5.3 Characteristics of the Datasets

The Fongbe dataset is collected from:

- a dataset of 513 sentences (1 speaker) used in [8] with 3000 other sentences from the bible;
- a second dataset of 10400 sentences (27 speakers) used in [27] designed for speech recognition.

This corpus was not recorded under the appropriate conditions with professional speakers. It contains errors of pronunciation, several repeated sentences and noises on some samples.

For Yoruba, we use the dataset of [23] composed of 3583 sentences recorded in a professional studio by male and female speakers.

Before training, we apply cleaning and filtering to the fongbe dataset. It consists in text normalizing and removing the following:

- speakers with less than 50 registered recordings;
- poor quality audio;
- samples whose durations are under 1 s or exceed 30 s.

Table 1 shows durations and numbers of speakers per language.

Table 1. Total data size per language after processing.

Language	Duration in hour	Number of speakers
Fongbe	14	28
Yoruba	4	36

Yoruba shares 17 consonants and 11 vowels with Fongbe; then there is just 1 yoruba consonant not used in Fongbe. However, Fongbe has 7 consonants and one vowel not used in Yoruba.

We experiment two phoneme representations:

- **unshared phoneme set**: all phonemes of Fongbe and Yoruba are considered different and represented without mapping shared phonemes
- **shared phoneme set**: IPA is used to create a shared phoneme representations by mapping closed phonemes between both languages.

MFA (Montreal Forced Aligner) [28] is used for phoneme level alignment and automatic duration estimation. For Fongbe and Yoruba, we first generate a dictionary of transcription and use it to train a G2P (Grapheme to phoneme) model. Then, we find the phonetic transcription and estimate the duration of each phoneme of the whole dataset.

6 Experiments

The training is done on a Tesla V100 GPU with a batch size of 16. Adam Optimizer [2] is used with a learning rate between 10^{-3} and 10^{-5}, with a decay steps of 120 K.

The model is pretrained with the publicly available LJSpeech dataset [29] composed of a monolingual (male speaker) set of 13 k English sentences. Then we train the models with various configurations. We also train the MelGAN vocoder with pairs of 16 kHz audio groundtruth and corresponding spectrogram on the whole dataset.

6.1 Monolingual Training

We train Fastspeech 2 with monolingual dataset. We evaluate the TTS System with the MOS metric. We choose 5 native (or fluent) Fongbe and Yoruba speakers. They evaluate the similarity, naturalness and intelligibility of the generated speech of 10 sentences for each language.

The results stored in Table 2 show the ability of the system to synthesize fluent speech, but the MOS is still low due to the need of massive data.

Table 2. Results of monolingual MOS tests with 95% confidence intervals

Language	MOS
Fongbe	3.4 ± 0.31
Yoruba	3.1 ± 0.41

6.2 Multilingual Training

The model is used to synthesize 100 sentences of both languages. We compute MCD [30] between groundtruth and generated speech using Griffin Lim. The results are given in Table 3. From the analysis, we find that, with shared phoneme set as input, we get mainly the best value for MCD.

Table 3. Results of multilingual MCD tests

Input type	Fongbe	Yoruba
Shared phoneme set	25	34
Unshared phoneme set	26	36

We evaluate the TTS System with the same metric and the same evaluators for 10 sentences for each language and each input type.

As illustrated in Table 4, the MOS metric is in the range 3.36 to 3.68 which is characterized as more than good. We have the best score for fongbe with the shared phoneme set and lowest score for Yoruba with the unshared phoneme set.

In comparison with the monolingual training test results (Table 2), the system performs better with a bilingual dataset due to the great amount of available data.

Table 4. Results of multilingual MOS tests with 95% confidence intervals

Input type	Fongbe	Yoruba
Shared phoneme set	3.68 ± 0.31	3.62 ± 0.25
Unshared phoneme set	3.53 ± 0.27	3.36 ± 0.3

In Table 5 we make a comparison between the current system and other TTS Systems of Yoruba and Fongbe. Our system outperforms those monolingual systems.

Table 5. Comparison with other Yoruba and Fongbe TTS systems

TTS Systems	Fongbe	Yoruba
Our bilingual TTS system	3.68	3.62
Yoruba monolingual TTS system [22]		3.6
Yoruba monolingual TTS system [21]		2.9
Fongbe monolingual TTS system [8]	2.79	

6.3 Voice Cloning

Voice cloning consists in using the same speaker to produce speech in many languages. For instance, the system will use the Fongbe speaker to pronounce Yoruba sentences. The speaker similarity (MOS) test results are reported in Table 6. It is done on 5 sentences of each language for one male Fongbe speaker and one female Yoruba speaker with only shared phoneme set. We use the same 5 evaluators as for the previous tests. The speaker similarity is scored with 3.35 for Fongbe speaker with Yoruba sentences and 3.25 for Yoruba speaker pronouncing Fongbe sentences. It shows the system ability to synthesize fluent Yoruba speech with a Fongbe speaker and the same for Yoruba female speaker. The model also shows good learning capabilities in speaker characteristic preservations across language mainly in the case of shared phoneme set. It is able to transfer voices across languages. We notice some pronunciation errors which occur in unshared phonemes between both languages and accents.

Table 6. Speaker similarity MOS (with 95% confidence intervals) for voice cloning (model trained with speaker classifier)

Speaker Language	Target language	
	Fongbe	Yoruba
Fongbe		3.35 ± 0.5
Yoruba	3.25 ± 0.5	

We test the model without the adversarial speaker classifier to prove the impact of this component on voice cloning ability of the model. Table 7 presents the speaker similarity results. The decreasing similarity score is noticeable in the case of Fongbe speaker used to pronounce Yoruba sentences when we compare the score on Table 7 with the same score on Table 6.

Table 7. Speaker similarity MOS (with 95% confidence intervals) for voice cloning (model trained without speaker classifier)

Speaker language	Target language	
	Fongbe	Yoruba
Fongbe		3.05 ± 0.6
Yoruba	3.2 ± 0.52	

7   Conclusion

This paper presents a bilingual TTS System for Fongbe and Yoruba built on Fastspeech 2 model with phoneme, language and speaker embeddings. The system shows an ability to synthesize speech in both languages with good fidelity and accuracy. It also shows good speaker characteristic cloning between languages and the improvement on voice cloning with the adversarial speaker classifier. As a contribution, the current system is the first attempt to our knowledge to build a bilingual TTS system for Yoruba and Fongbe. The modification applied to Fastspeech 2 for multilingual synthesis is also important to notice.

In future work, we plan to extend the system to other languages with unbalanced data problem and then to study unseen speaker and language extension with few available data.

References

1. Shen, J., et al.: Natural TTS synthesis by conditioning WaveNet on mel spectrogram predictions. In: 2018 IEEE International Conference on Acoustics, Speech and Signal Processing (ICASSP), pp. 4779–4783. IEEE (2018)
2. Ren, Y., Hu, C., Tan, X., Qin, T., Zhao, S., Zhao, Z., Liu, T.-Y.: Fastspeech 2: fast and high-quality end-to-end text to speech. ArXiv Prepr. ArXiv:200604558 (2020)
3. Mu, Z., Yang, X., Dong, Y.: Review of end-to-end speech synthesis technology based on deep learning. ArXiv Prepr. ArXiv210409995 (2021)
4. Nekvinda, T., Dušek, O.: One model, many languages: meta-learning for multilingual text-to-speech. ArXiv Prepr. ArXiv200800768 (2020)
5. Lee, Y., Shon, S., Kim, T.: Learning pronunciation from a foreign language in speech synthesis networks. ArXiv Prepr. ArXiv181109364 (2018)
6. Cai, Z., Yang, Y., Li, M.: Cross-lingual multispeaker text-to-speech under limited-data scenario. ArXiv Prepr. ArXiv200510441 (2020)
7. He, M., Yang, J., He, L., Soong, F.K.: Multilingual Byte2Speech models for scalable low-resource speech synthesis. ArXiv Prepr. ArXiv210303541 (2021)
8. Dagba, T.K., Boco, C.: A text to speech system for fon language using multisyn algorithm. Procedia Comput. Sci. **35**, 447–455 (2014)
9. Wang, Y., et al.: Tacotron: towards end-to-end speech synthesis. ArXiv Prepr. ArXiv1703 10135 (2017)
10. Griffin, D., Lim, J.: Signal estimation from modified short-time fourier transform. IEEE Trans. Acoust. Speech Signal Process. **32**, 236–243 (1984)
11. Battenberg, E., Skerry-Ryan, R., Mariooryad, S., Stanton, D., Kao, D., Shannon, M., Bagby, T.: Location-relative attention mechanisms for robust long-form speech synthesis. In: ICASSP 2020–2020 IEEE International Conference on Acoustics, Speech and Signal Processing (ICASSP), pp. 6194–6198. IEEE (2020)
12. Oord, A. van den, et al.: Wavenet: A generative model for raw audio. ArXiv Prepr. ArXiv1 60903499 (2016)
13. Ren, Y., et al.: Fastspeech: Fast, robust and controllable text to speech. ArXiv Prepr. ArXiv1 90509263 (2019)
14. Kalchbrenner, N., et al.: Efficient neural audio synthesis. In: International Conference on Machine Learning, pp. 2410–2419. PMLR (2018)
15. Li, B., Zhang, Y., Sainath, T., Wu, Y., Chan, W.: Bytes are all you need: end-to-end multilingual speech recognition and synthesis with bytes. In: ICASSP 2019–2019 IEEE International Conference on Acoustics, Speech and Signal Processing (ICASSP), pp. 5621–5625. IEEE (2019)
16. Cao, Y., et al.: End-to-end code-switched TTS with mix of monolingual recordings. In: ICASSP 2019–2019 IEEE International Conference on Acoustics, Speech and Signal Processing (ICASSP), pp. 6935–6939. IEEE (2019)
17. Zhang, Y., et al.: Learning to speak fluently in a foreign language: multilingual speech synthesis and cross-language voice cloning. ArXiv Prepr. ArXiv190704448 (2019)
18. Chen, M., et al.: Cross-lingual, multi-speaker text-to-speech synthesis using neural speaker embedding. In: Interspeech, pp. 2105–2109 (2019)
19. Yang, J., He, L.: Towards universal text-to-speech. In: INTERSPEECH, pp. 3171–3175 (2020)

20. Li, N., Liu, S., Liu, Y., Zhao, S., Liu, M.: Neural speech synthesis with transformer network. In: Proceedings of the AAAI Conference on Artificial Intelligence, pp. 6706–6713 (2019)
21. Aoga, J.O.R., Dagba, T.K., Fanou, C.C.: Integration of Yoruba language into MaryTTS. Int. J. Speech Technol. **19**, 151–158 (2016)
22. Akinwonm, A.E.: Development of a prosodic read speech syllabic corpus of the Yoruba language. Commun. Appl. Electron. CAE Found. Comput. Sci. FCS **7**(36), 13–32 (2021). https://doi.org/10.5120/cae2021652884
23. Gutkin, A., Demirşahin, I., Kjartansson, O., Rivera, C., Túbdòsún, K.: Developing an open-source corpus of Yoruba speech. In: Proceedings of Interspeech 2020, pp. 404–408. International Speech and Communication Association (ISCA), Shanghai, China (2020)
24. Kumar, K., et al.: Melgan: Generative adversarial networks for conditional waveform synthesis. ArXiv Prepr. ArXiv191006711 (2019)
25. TensorFlowTTS: https://github.com/tensorspeech/TensorFlowTTS. Last accessed 1 June 2022
26. Eberhard, D.M., Simons, G.F., Fennig, C.D.: Ethnologue: Languages of the World. Twenty-fifth edition. Dallas, Texas: SIL International. Online version: http://www.ethnologue.com (2022). Last accessed 1 June 2022
27. Laleye, F.A., Besacier, L., Ezin, E.C., Motamed, C.: First automatic fongbe continuous speech recognition system: development of acoustic models and language models. In: 2016 Federated Conference on Computer Science and Information Systems (FedCSIS), pp. 477–482. IEEE (2016)
28. McAuliffe, M., Socolof, M., Mihuc, S., Wagner, M., Sonderegger, M.: Montreal forced aligner: trainable text-speech alignment using Kaldi. In: Interspeech, pp. 498–502 (2017)
29. Ito, K., Johnson, L.: The LJ Speech Dataset. 2017. https://keithito.com/LJ-Speech-Dataset (2017). Last accessed 1 June 2022
30. Kubichek, R.: Mel-cepstral distance measure for objective speech quality assessment. In: Proceedings of IEEE Pacific Rim Conference on Communications Computers and Signal Processing, pp. 125–128. IEEE (1993)

Application of the Laplacian Smoothing on 3D Static Models and Their Evaluation by the New Objective Quality Metric 3DrwPSNR

Nessrine Elloumi[1]($\boxtimes$) , Habiba Loukil[2] , and Mohamed Salim Bouhlel[1]

[1] SETIT, ISBS, University of Sfax, 3000 Sfax, Tunisia
ellouminessrine@gmail.com, medsalim.bouhlel@isbs.usf.tn
[2] ISGI Sfax, University of Sfax, 3000 Sfax, Tunisia
habiba.loukil@isgis.usf.tn

Abstract. Interest in 3D modeling has increased in recent years. However, efforts to improve compression and transmission quality are severely hampered by a lack of effective quality assessment measures. This is a particularly serious problem for researchers trying to improve the robustness of lost packet transmission. Subjective measures are generally used to assess the robustness of applied treatments such as compression, watermarking and smoothing. These measures present enormous demands in terms of time and resources. To solve this problem, the researchers developed the objective metrics which are developed and executed by a computer. These metrics are integrated into many applications that require rendering or exchanging 2D images or 3D models. This article presents a new objective metric for evaluating the visual quality of static 3D models. The proposed full-reference metric is based on the relativity of the Human visual system. The performance of the presented approach are evaluated using a dataset of static model smoothed by the 3D Mesh Processing Platform (MEPP). The obtained results show that the proposed metric outperforms the MSDM metric value.

Keywords: Visual quality assessment · 3D static models · HVS objective metric

1 Introduction

Technological advances in the fields of telecommunications and computer graphics over the past two decades have contributed to the development of a new type of multimedia data: three-dimensional (3D) data. These objects are present due to their massive use in various fields through the development of computer graphics applications. 3D data are generally represented by a 3D mesh. This mesh has different properties and requires a large amount of information to be stored in order to obtain an accurate representation. This requires processing to enable the storage, transmission and visualization of the three-dimensional models. These models are used in various applications such as augmented/virtual reality, video games, telemedicine and cinema. 3D model is a digital representation of an object made by a Computer Aided Design software or an acquisition via a 3D scanner. Different representations are possible for a 3D model after its

C. Bădică et al. (Eds.): ICCCI 2022, CCIS 1653, pp. 305–314, 2022.
https://doi.org/10.1007/978-3-031-16210-7_25

acquisition such as mesh or point cloud data. The use of the 3D models necessities the application of an optimization processing which generate a specific deformation on the geometry of the shape. For example, to protect the 3D content a watermarking method is needed. Also, to send 3D data over the network a compression schema is always applied to reduce the size of the 3D file and guarantee a reception without any percent of lost data [1]. Various processing which are specific to 3D meshes can be used in other situation such as simplification, smoothing, remeshing and subdivision.

Distortions are a critical factor in the development process of an objective metrics in order to evaluate the quality of 3D models. However, conventional measures based on geometric differences such as RMS and Hausdorff distance, used in many software programs do not match well with human visual perception. This perceptual shortcoming has been the subject of the most research in the development of perceptual objective metrics for 3D deformed models.

2   State of the Art

Several method have been developed in order to process the 2D images and 3D data of static or animated 3D models such as the remeshing, watermarking, simplification, smoothing and compression algorithms. These methods are done to optimize the rendering process and data transmission through different types of network [2]. These treatments introduce various modifications on the content of the data (2D images or 3D models). Therefore, they will be misinterpreted during their visualization by the human observer. In this regard, it is essential to study the perceptual quality of 3D data to evaluate the new processing algorithms (compression, watermarking, smoothing, etc.) or transmission techniques [3]. To measure 2D or 3D quality, there are two methods: the first method consists of measurements made by observers (subjective measurements), the second is done through algorithmic processes (objective measurements).

Subjective measurements are rarely used because for each observer the quality may have a different definition according to personal criteria [4]. Also, subjective measures require a precise environment to evaluate correctly the perceptual quality (light, screen,…) and need time and material resources. While, objective metrics allow to integrate the behavior of the Human Visual System [5] to evaluate the quality of the 3D data, as human observers perceive it.

There are two approaches to measure 2D or 3D visual quality. The top-down approach which considers the SVH as a black box and tries to imitate the behavior of the human visual system. The bottom-up approach, which is based on the simulation and imitation of each component of the human visual system. The majority of existing metrics follow the Top-Down approach to studying the human visual system [6].

In the field of 2D image processing, the objective measures are very developed; among the most known metrics of 2D visual quality are SSIM, SNR and PSNR. These metrics do not adapt to the dynamic characteristics of the image. Indeed, the most visible distortion is found in regions with little texture. The first works on this subject is proposed by Dally with the visible Difference Predictor and Lubin with the Sarnoff Visual discrimination model [7]. These metrics predict the visibility of an artifact in a degraded image by trying to model and reproduce the low-level mechanisms of the human visual system. In 2012, Loukil et al. [8] develop the relative weighted PSNR (rwPSNR) which is based on the relative weighted difference of the 2D image information. The rwPSNR metric incorporates two important properties of the human visual system: the contrast sensitivity and the visual relativity modeled by the Contrast Sensitivity Function (CSF function) and weber's law respectively. The rwPSNR gives excellent results in terms of correlation with the human visual system.

In the field of 3D metrics, researchers can use two alternatives: either they use an existing 2D perceptual quality metric (2D image-based metrics) or they develop a 3D model-based metrics that exploit the geometry of 3D models to assess quality [9]. To measure the quality of a 3D model two types of metrics can be used: geometric metrics or HVS metrics.

Geometric metrics are based on the calculation of the Euclidean distances between the vertices of the reference mesh and the mesh to be compared (deformed mesh). The well-known metrics are the RMS that measure a distance between two surfaces in 3D space [10] and the Hausdorff distance (Hd) that measure the geometric distance between two surfaces [11]. Hd distance is defined using the minimum Euclidean distance of a point p between a continuous surface S and another surface S'.

These geometric metrics are based on the mathematical Euclidean distances. However, they do not reflect the correct quality perceived by humans [12]. However, the HVS metrics are based on the calculation of the deformation quantities in 3D deformed model by incorporating the visual properties of the HVS. Among the SVH metrics, we cite the 3DWPM, GL, MSDM, FMPD and DAME.

In 2007 Corsini et al. developed the 3DWPM (3D Watermarking Perception Metric) metric based on the calculation of the distance between two meshes relying on the surface roughness [13]. This approach measures the distance between two meshes $M1$ and $M2$. Karni and Gotsman propose a metric called Geometric Laplacian (GL) based on the roughness of the model. The limitation of this metric is that the compared models must have the same connectivity. To overcame this limitation Sorkine et al. proposed a different version of GL1 called GL2 that proposes a small change in the value of α ($\alpha = 0.15$) [14].

In 2009 Lavoué et al. proposed a structural mesh distortion measure (MSDM) [15] that was inspired from the 2D image quality measure SSIM (the Structural Similarity Index) developed by Wang and Al [16]. MSDM is based on the difference of the average curvature amplitudes to measure the perceptual quality between two 3D meshes. In 2011, Lavoué et al. improved the MSDM metric by incorporating a multiscale analysis MSDM2 [17]. MSDM and MSDM2 are based only on the curvature magnitude statistics since they take into account the structure of the 3D model.

Wang et al. proposed a reduced reference metric named Fast Mesh Perceptual Distance (FMPD) [18]. It is based on the calculation of global roughness between two 3D models. This approach uses a roughness descriptor derived from the Gaussian curvature. The FMPD metric incorporates a power function to capture the spatial masking effect on the surfaces of the 3D deformed mesh.

Váša and Rus developed a metric named Dihedral Angle Mesh Error (DAME) that measures the perceptual quality of a deformed 3D model [19]. This approach is based on the calculation of the dihedral angle on each pair of neighboring triangles in the processed mesh.

In this paper, a new 3D HVS quality metrics for measuring the degradation of the three-dimensional geometric model is presented. The proposed approach is tested on a corpus, which contain seven 3D models having different geometric properties. The obtained results are summarized and compared with another state of the art metric in the experiments section.

3 Proposed Approach

In order to measure the quantity of a distortion of a 3D deformed model acquired by different means (modeled by a CAD tool or given from 3D scanners). The developed approach represent a full reference metric which measure the quantity of deformation in a 3D deformed model based on its reference version. The proposed approach is largely inspired from the 2D rwPSNR image metric proposed by Loukil et al. [8], which considers that the human visual system is highly sensitive to visual relativity between two pixels. The 2D rwPSNR metric, incorporate the relative difference between the original pixels and the distorted version weighted by the variance of the image gray levels. This approach have a good correlation with the subjective scores [20]. This research work aims to extending this metric in order to evaluate the Laplacian smoothing processing applied on 3D models. In 3D representation, the distortion of a 3D model depends on the visual relativity of the affected area with respect to its original version. In this context, this metric is based on the calculation of the relative weighted differences between the information content of two 3D models in order to measure the perceptual quality of the processed 3D model compared to its reference version. The 3DrwPSNR integrates the visual properties of the HVS to detect the distortions in a 3D deformed model [21]. The main idea of the proposed metric is based on the fact that a distance between two vertices is judged from the relative difference of these positions in the 3D space. To compute the final 3DrwPSNR value, the calculation of the 3D weighted relative root mean square error (3DrwRMSE) between the vertices within the original model and its distorted version is needed. The 3DrwMSE is defined by Eq. (1):

$$3DrwMSE = \frac{1}{M} \sum_{j=0}^{M-1} \left(\frac{2 * \left| \frac{x_j - y_j}{(x_j + y_j)} \right|}{1 + var(y_j)} \right)^2 \tag{1}$$

M represent the number of 3D point. x and y are respectively the point cloud within the 3D original model and the 3D deformed model. The variance $var(y_j)$ represent the variance of the distance between all the vertices of the deformed model. The quotient $2 * \left| \frac{x_j - y_j}{(x_j + y_j)} \right|$ measure the relative difference between the position of a point in the original model and the distorted version. The 3DrwPSNR value is calculated as follows:

$$3DrwPSNR = 10 * log_{10} \frac{dx_{max}^2}{3DrwMSE} \tag{2}$$

The 3DrwPSNR measures the weighted relative error between an original model x and a degraded model y where dx_{max}^2 is the maximum distance of all vertices within the original model.

4 Experiments

In order to test the effectiveness of the proposed metrics a Laplacian smoothing processing is applied with three different strength on a corpus containing seven 3D models "Bunny, Hand, Head, Skull, Duck, Beethoven, Brain" acquired from different tool. The selected models of the used corpus are chosen considering different properties: mesh topology, number and points, number of faces. The first model "Bunny of Stanford" is composed of 2503 points and 4968 faces with unstructured mesh topology. The second model "Hand" is composed of 41122 points and 41120 faces with structured mesh topology. The third model "Head" is composed of 475 points and 442 faces with semi-structured mesh topology. The fourth model "Skull" is composed of 40062 points and 39288 faces with structured mesh topology. The fifth model "Duck" is composed of 8590 points and 8588 faces with structured mesh topology. The sixth model "Beethoven" is composed of 2655 points and 8588 faces with semi-structured mesh topology. The seventh model "Brain" is composed of 18844 points and 36752 faces with semi-structured mesh topology. The Laplacian smoothing processing is applied on the original version of the corpus models with different Laplacian smoothing strength using the 3D Mesh Processing Platform tool (MEPP).

Fig. 1. Laplacian smoothing processing applied on the Bunny

Figure (Fig.1) present the "Bunny" model respectively, (a) Reference "Bunny" model, (b) "Bunny" model distorted by smoothing strength = 0.10, (c) "Bunny" model distorted by smoothing strength = 0.15, (d) "Bunny" model distorted by smoothing strength = 0.25.

Table 1. The evaluation of the Laplacian smoothing processing on Bunny model.

Model	Metrics	Strength = 0.10	Strength = 0.15	Strength = 0.25
Bunny	3DrwPSNR	6.16	8.80	12.94
	MSDM	0,33	0,54	0,60

Figure (Fig. 2) present the "Hand" model respectively, (a) Reference "Hand" model, (b) "Hand" model distorted by smoothing strength = 0.10, (c) "Hand" model distorted by smoothing strength = 0.30, (d) "Hand" model distorted by smoothing strength = 0.50.

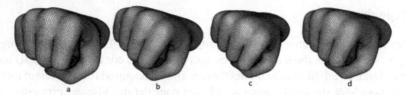

Fig. 2. Laplacian smoothing processing applied on the Hand

Table 2. The evaluation of the Laplacian smoothing processing on Hand model.

Model	Metrics	Strength = 0.10	Strength = 0.30	Strength = 0.50
Hand	3DrwPSNR	118,23	108,85	104,56
	MSDM	0,08	0,12	0,15

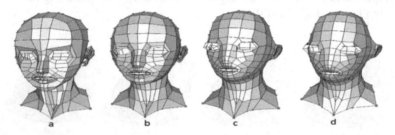

Fig. 3. Laplacian smoothing processing applied on the Head

Figure (Fig. 3) present the "Head" model respectively, (a) Reference "Head" model, (b) "Head" model distorted by smoothing strength = 0.15, (c) "Head" model distorted by smoothing strength = 0.35, (d) "Head" model distorted by smoothing strength = 0.50.

Table 3. The evaluation of the Laplacian smoothing processing on Head model.

Model	Metrics	Strength = 0.15	Strength = 0.35	Strength = 0.50
Head	3DrwPSNR	21.69	21.46	19,29
	MSDM	0,49	0,66	0,68

Figure (Fig. 4) present the "Skull" model respectively, (a) Reference "Skull" model, (b) "Skull" model distorted by smoothing strength = 0.10, (c) "Skull" model distorted by smoothing strength = 0.30, (d) "Skull" model distorted by smoothing strength = 0.50.

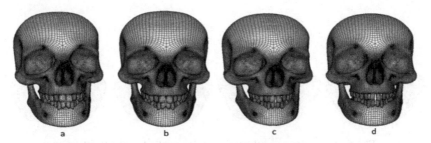

Fig. 4. Laplacian smoothing processing applied on the Skull

Table 4. The evaluation of the Laplacian smoothing processing on Skull model.

Model	Metrics	Strength = 0.10	Strength = 0.30	Strength = 0.50
Skull	3DrwPSNR	70,56	69,75	54,21
	MSDM	0,14	0,26	0,34

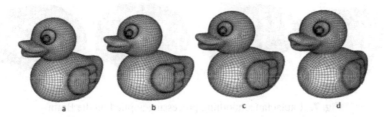

Fig. 5. Laplacian smoothing processing applied on the Duck

Figure (Fig. 5) present the "Duck" model respectively, (a) Reference "Duck" model, (b) "Duck" model distorted by smoothing strength = 0.15, (c) "Duck" model distorted by smoothing strength = 0.20, (d) "Duck" model distorted by smoothing strength = 0.30.

Table 5. The evaluation of the Laplacian smoothing processing on Duck model.

Model	Metrics	Strength = 0.15	Strength = 0.20	Strength = 0.30
Duck	3DrwPSNR	41.06	39.21	35.55
	MSDM	0,17	0,32	0,41

Figure (Fig. 6) present the "Beethoven" model respectively, (a) Reference " Beethoven" model, (b) "Beethoven" model distorted by smoothing strength = 0.20, (c) " Beethoven" model distorted by smoothing strength = 0.25, (d) "Beethoven" model distorted by smoothing strength = 0.30.

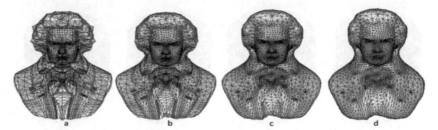

Fig. 6. Laplacian smoothing processing applied on the Beethoven

Table 6. The evaluation of the Laplacian smoothing processing on Beethoven model.

Model	Metrics	Strength = 0.20	Strength = 0.25	Strength = 0.30
Beethoven	3DrwPSNR	34.75	30.55	25.34
	MSDM	0,47	0,67	0,73

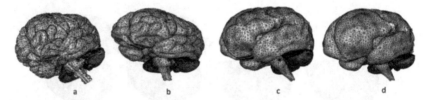

Fig. 7. Laplacian smoothing processing applied on the Brain

Figure (Fig. 7) present the "Brain " model respectively, (a) Reference " Brain" model, (b) "Brain" model distorted by smoothing strength = 0.15, (c) "Brain" model distorted by smoothing strength = 0.25, (d) "Brain" model distorted by smoothing strength = 0.35.

Table 7. The evaluation of the Laplacian smoothing processing on Brain model.

Model	Metrics	Strength = 0.15	Strength = 0.25	Strength = 0.35
Brain	3DrwPSNR	28.79	17.56	13.55
	MSDM	0,59	0,74	0,77

The above Tables (1, 2, 3, 4, 5, 6 and 7) highlights the results of the proposed metrics "3DrwPSNR" on a heterogeneous corpus that contain seven 3D reference model with different properties. In this paper, we have applied the Laplacian smoothing processing with different strength on the whole of the reference model. These results are compared with the value of the HVS metric MSDM, which is, consider as the best metric in the field of the quality assessment metrics. The value of the MSDM metric are normalized in the range of [0,1]. When the smoothing strength increase the quality of the model degrades relatively to the amount of the deformation. Regarding the Brain model with a strength = 0.15, MSDM = 0.59 and with strength = 0.35, MSDM = 0.77. We conclude that more we apply a high strength of Laplacian smoothing processing on a 3D model the quality of the model decrease. In this case the quality of the model with strength = 0.15 is good comparing to the quality of the model with strength = 0.35. Regarding the 3DrwPSNR metric, values decrease proportionally as the quality degrades. More the deformation is visible the value of the proposed metric decreases. The obtained results prove that the 3DrwPSNR metric is very efficient to evaluate the visual quality of 3D models after the application of the Laplacian smoothing processing. This is validated where we compare the 3DrwPSNR values with the MSDM values. Regarding the mesh topology of the tested models, the 3DrwPSNR give a good result with the structural or semi-structured mesh such as Hand, Skull, Duck, Beethoven and Brain.

5 Conclusion

Several methods for estimating the visual quality of 3D static models are used by the 3D Processing platform in order to evaluate the 3D processing method. There are two families of 3D metrics: geometric methods and methods that incorporate properties of the human visual system (HVS metrics). These methods are classified into three categories: metrics with reference (full reference), metrics without reference (no reference) and metrics with reduced reference (reduced reference). This paper focuses on a study of some methods for the perceptual quality of 2D images and 3D static models and the evaluation of the Laplacian smoothing processing using proposed perceptual quality metric (3DrwPSNR) which measure the quality of a deformed model taking into account the limitations of the human visual system. In order to evaluate the efficiency of the developed approach, a database which contain seven models with different geometric properties is used. The obtained results are compared with the MSDM metric. The highlighted results prove that the 3DrwPSNR is very efficient to measure the quantity of distortion of a 3D deformed model. In the future work, we will apply other type of processing on this database such as Uniform Noise and Gaussian Noise.

References

1. Amri, H., Khalfallah, A., Lapayre, J.C., Bouhlel, M.S.: REPro. JPEG: a new image compression approach based on reduction/expansion image and JPEG compression for dermatological medical images. The Imaging Sci. J. 65(2), 98–107 (2017)
2. Ahmad, F.A., Kumar, P., Shrivastava, G., Bouhlel, M.S.: Bitcoin: digital decentralized cryptocurrency. In: Shrivastava, G., Prabhat Kumar, B.B., Gupta, S.B., Dey, Nilanjan (eds.) Handbook of Research on Network Forensics and Analysis Techniques, pp. 395–415. IGI Global (2018). https://doi.org/10.4018/978-1-5225-4100-4.ch021
3. Chemak, C., Lapayre, J.C., Bouhlel, M.S.: A new scheme of image watermarking based on 5/3 wavelet decomposition and turbo-code. WSEAS Trans. Biol. Biomed. 4(4), 45–52 (2007)

4. Elloumi, N., Kacem, H.L.H., Bouhlel, M.S.: A comparative study of the 3D quality metrics: application to masking database. In: Abraham, A., Cherukuri, A.K., Melin, P., Gandhi, N. (eds.) Intelligent Systems Design and Applications: 18th International Conference on Intelligent Systems Design and Applications (ISDA 2018) held in Vellore, India, December 6–8, 2018, Volume 2, pp. 740–748. Springer International Publishing, Cham (2020). https://doi.org/10.1007/978-3-030-16660-1_72

5. Pan, Y., Cheng, I., Basu, A.: Quality metric for approximating subjective evaluation of 3-D objects. IEEE Trans. Multimedia 7(2), 269–279 (2005)

6. Moon, G., Chang, J.Y., Lee, K.M.: Camera distance-aware top-down approach for 3D multi-person pose estimation from a single RGB image. In: Proceedings of the IEEE/CVF international conference on computer vision, pp. 10133–10142 (2019)

7. Daly, S.J.: Visible differences predictor: an algorithm for the assessment of image fidelity. In: Human Vision, Visual Processing, and Digital Display III, vol. 1666, pp. 2–15 (1992)

8. Loukil, H., Kacem, M.H., Bouhlel, M.S.: A new image quality metric using system visual human characteristics. Int. J. Comput. Appl. 60(6), 32–36 (2012). https://doi.org/10.5120/9697-4138

9. Bulbul, A., Capin, T., Lavoué, G., Preda, M.: Assessing visual quality of 3-D polygonal models. IEEE Signal Process. Mag. 28(6), 80–90 (2011)

10. Bhuiyan, M.A.A., Khan, A.R.: Image quality assessment employing RMS contrast and histogram similarity. Int. Arab J. Inf. Technol. 15(6), 983–989 (2018)

11. Alexiou, E., Ebrahimi, T.: Point cloud quality assessment metric based on angular similarity. In: 2018 IEEE International Conference on Multimedia and Expo (ICME), pp. 1–6. IEEE (2018)

12. Elloumi, N., Kacem, H.L.H., Dey, N., Ashour, A.S., Bouhlel, M.S.: Perceptual metrics quality: comparative study for 3D static meshes. Int. J. Serv. Sci., Manag., Eng., Technol. 8(1), 63–80 (2017)

13. Corsini, M., Gelasca, E.D., Ebrahimi, T., Barni, M.: Watermarked 3-D mesh quality assessment. IEEE Trans. Multimedia 9(2), 247–256 (2007)

14. Lavoué, G., Corsini, M.: A comparison of perceptually-based metrics for objective evaluation of geometry processing. IEEE Trans. Multimedia 12(7), 636–649 (2010)

15. Lavoué, G.: A local roughness measure for 3D meshes and its application to visual masking. ACM Trans. Appl. Percept. 5(4), 1–23 (2009)

16. Sung, T.L., Lee, H.J.: Image translation: verifiable image transformation networks for face sketch-photo and photo-sketch. In: Proceedings of the Korea Information Processing Society Conference, pp. 451–454. Korea Information Processing Society (2019)

17. Lavoué, G.: A multiscale metric for 3D mesh visual quality assessment. Comput. Graph. Forum 30, 1427–1437 (2011)

18. Wang, K., Torkhani, F., Montanvert, A.: A fast roughness-based approach to the assessment of 3D mesh visual quality. Comput. Graph. 36(7), 808–818 (2012)

19. Vasa, L., Skala, V.: A perception correlated comparison method for dynamic meshes. IEEE Trans. Visual Comput. Graphics 17(2), 220–230 (2010)

20. Rahali, M., Loukil, H., Bouhlel, M.S.: The improvement of an image compression approach using Weber-Fechner law. In: Madureira, A.M., Abraham, A., Gamboa, D., Novais, P. (eds.) Intelligent Systems Design and Applications, pp. 239–249. Springer International Publishing, Cham (2017). https://doi.org/10.1007/978-3-319-53480-0_24

21. Elloumi, N., Kacem, H.L.H., Bouhlel, M.S.: Quality metric of 3D models using Weber's Law. In: Eleventh International Conference on Machine Vision (ICMV 2018), vol. 11041, pp. 77–84. SPIE (2019)

Computational Intelligence in Medical Applications

Brain Tumors Detection on MRI Images with K-means Clustering and Residual Networks

Hai Thanh Nguyen[1]([✉]) [iD], Huong Hoang Luong[2] [iD], Tan Ha Ngoc Kien[2] [iD],
Nghia Trong Le Phan[2] [iD], Thuan Minh Dang[2] [iD], Tin Tri Duong[2] [iD],
Tong Duc Nguyen[2] [iD], and Toai Cong Dinh[2] [iD]

[1] Can Tho University, Can Tho, Vietnam
nthai.cit@ctu.edu.vn
[2] FPT University, Can Tho, Vietnam

Abstract. Many perspectives have been grown and extended instanta-
neously due to the evolution of the Fourth Industrial Revolution. Brain
tumor detection is one of the most crucial mechanisms for standardization and care for injured patients. Early diagnosis from the beginning state lets the medical team develop comprehensive recovery protocols that help enhance patients' survival rates. We have deployed the
k-means clustering algorithm to stratify samples into three different view
angles of MRI images (transverse, coronal, and sagittal) and combined
a modified Residual Network (ResNet) architecture to diagnose three
brain tumor types: glioma and meningioma pituitary tumor and recognize MRI images without tumor. The approach is evaluated on the
dataset from Nanfang Hospital and General Hospital, Tianjin Medical
University, China, with MRI images. Our result achieved 96% in brain
tumor classification accuracy, the best among considered famous pre-
trained networks.

Keywords: Brain tumors detection · Convolutional neural networks ·
Clustering · Pre-trained networks

1 Introduction

In recent years, so many diseases negatively influenced everybody's health. Some
of them are related to brain tumors. It is not an adversity disease but is a
deserving remark. It involves some circumstances that may likely induce fatal
infections. Brain tumors occur when brain cells form and turn abnormally and
become uncontrollable. There are two primary types of brain tumors: malignant
and benign brain tumors [1]. When researching related information about the
human brain in our body, it is a hard mass and accounts for about 2% of the
entire body's weight. However, its energy consumption is high, maybe up to 30%
of the body's energy. Many complex neuron systems structure this complicated
organ, which plays a vital role in the nervous system of the human body [2].

© The Author(s), under exclusive license to Springer Nature Switzerland AG 2022
C. Bădică et al. (Eds.): ICCCI 2022, CCIS 1653, pp. 317–329, 2022.
https://doi.org/10.1007/978-3-031-16210-7_26

Therefore, any abnormal growth of tissues in this organ contributes to numerous symptoms and affects other body parts.

Furthermore, the nerve tissue controls the functioning of other organs in the body. So whenever patients have different clinical symptoms, it would be hard to detect brain tumors and is likely to confuse with clinical syndromes of similar diseases. Another crucial factor that needs mentioning is that the human brain is surrounded by a hard skull, which makes up a mass and the entire complex neural system, making applying surgery to detect brain tumors highly troublesome [3].

Besides machine learning, deep learning is one of the components of machine learning, producing an extensive artificial neural network with performed learning behavior. Deep learning consists of three formats: supervised, semi-supervised, and unsupervised. Convolutional Neural Network (CNN) is in the initial step of these formats. CNN uses neurons network in serial and continuous windows. So at the top of the dataset, the symbols can extract. CNN applies to image analysis and image recognition problems. The first time that CNN estimated the algorithm used with target documents was in 1998 [4].

Our purpose when doing this research is to propose a new method approaching the usage of K-means Clustering, Data Augmentation, and 5-fold Cross-Validation and propose a CNN architecture to enhance the accuracy when predicting the diseases related to brain tumors. Applying K-means clustering, the dataset can be clustered so that each cluster is expected to have the same shooting angle based on the brain tumor types. The shooting angles can be divided into three view angles of MRI images: transverse, coronal, and sagittal. This work helps classify the dataset into folders in the pre-processing data stage. We have classified the dataset into three brain tumor diseases: glioma, meningioma, pituitary, and no tumor. Then applying the data augmentation is expected to enhance the number of MRI images in the training set to avoid overfitting and use 5-fold Cross-Validation to give reliable results when training and testing the model. This project aims to give a promising result by creating a brain tumor predicting system for classifying MRI images based on the given classification.

Our research article consists of five main sections. In the next sect. 2, we point out some of the related research we used for references. After the related research section is the methodology sect. 3, this section describes all the methods used in the article. After that, sect. 4 mentions how we perform and measure the accuracy of the deep learning model. Finally, in the last sect. 5, we conclude our article and review the necessary domains correlated to the study.

2   Related Work

A brain tumor is the uncontrolled growth of brain cells in brain cancer if not detected from the beginning. Detecting a brain tumor is complex because of its shape, size, and appearance variations. There have been many studies related to brain tumor segmentation and detection. For example, Selvapandian A. [5] applied the method of detecting brain tumors that is Glioma on Brain Tumor Segmentation (BRATS) Image. At the same time, Rajan PG (2019) has also investigated the use of MR images combined with K-means clustering integrated with Fuzzy C-Means (KMFCM) as a powerful tool to help detect abnormal tissues in the brain easily [6], and both achieve stable accuracy. TKhan MA (2019) applies segmentation of brain tumors performed using a marker-based watershed algorithm on three datasets Harvard, BRATS 2013, MR images, and tumor classification using Support Vector Machine (SVM) also gives expected results [7]. Using MR images, Toğaçar M (2019) detected brain tumors using a Convolutional Neural Network (CNN) model called BrainMRNet [8] and segmented the tumors through Unet with ResNet50 on the Figshare dataset by the author Sadad T (2021) that has satisfactory results [9].

Numerous researchers and experts have studied and researched medical image analysis implementing machine learning. The learning data must be sufficient and high-quality to achieve high-grade achievements. However, having adequate data for research is greatly difficult. Therefore, data augmentation is an effective and efficient method to solve incorrect accuracy problems when training data. Based on the patient's MR images, Kim S (2021) synthesized brain tumor images from ordinary images using tumor masks transformed from concentric circles through deep neural networks [10]. To improve discriminator and generator learning in GAN training, A (2021) used an abbreviated framework named Data Augmentation Optimized to minimize the Jensen-Shannon (JS) divergence between the model distribution and original distribution [11]. Both of these methods have better results than other GAN-based methods. Moreover, Luo Y (2020) applied the data augmentation method sWGAN in emotion recognition based on EEG dataset[8] and WGAN in brain-computer interface (BCI) on the Functional near-infrared spectroscopy (fNIRS) dataset of Nagasawa T (2020) [12] that has significantly improved the performance of support vector machines and neural networks.

3   Methodology

3.1   The Research Implementation Procedure

The implementation process of our research is divided into eleven main steps, which are illustrated in Fig. 1 and explained in detail below.

The steps to implement the research are described as follows.

1. The dataset is collected at Nanfang Hospital and General Hospital, Tianjin Medical University, China. Three types of brain tumors are provided: 822 images of meningioma tumor, 826 images of glioma tumor, 827 images of pituitary tumor, and 395 images of none tumor in the dataset, and all of them are MRI images. The dataset is gathered from 233 patients.
2. Dividing the dataset into training and testing set: After collecting all the MRI images in the dataset, the images are randomly chosen for the training and testing process. In detail, there were 2870 images used for training and 394 images used for testing the model's accuracy.

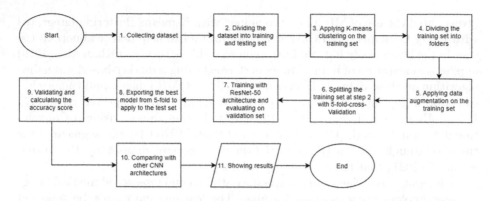

Fig. 1. The implementing procedure flowchart

3. Applying K-means clustering on the training set: Shooting angles provide similar characteristics based on the specific features. Therefore, we apply the K-means clustering technique to determine the three angles synthesized from the collected dataset. This can perform in the pre-processing data stage. The training set can be clustered and classified into folders. Each cluster represents the shooting angle of the MRI images. Then based on that cluster, each MRI image is put into a separate folder based on the shooting angle and the brain tumor types.

4. Dividing the training set into folders: After applying K-means clustering on the training set, we can recognize the three angles of the MRI images, namely coronal, transverse, and sagittal. Therefore, from the four initial directories consisting of three types of brain tumors (glioma tumor, meningioma tumor, and pituitary tumor) and without brain tumor images, the samples in the training set can be stratified into twelve folders containing brain tumor types and their shooting angles as mentioned above. All of these folders are glioma - coronal, glioma - transverse, glioma - sagittal, meningioma - coronal, meningioma - transverse, meningioma - sagittal, pituitary - coronal, pituitary - transverse, pituitary - sagittal, no tumor - coronal, no tumor - transverse, and no tumor - sagittal.

5. Applying data augmentation on the training set: Because the small quantity of the training set may lead the trained model to overfit, we use data augmentation techniques such as rotating, flipping, sharpening, and shearing to enhance the number of images in the training set.

6. Splitting the training set at step 2 with 5-fold-cross-Validation: We divide the training set with 5-fold-cross-validation. Thus, we have new training sets and validation sets (generated from the 5-fold-cross-validation process) to train with convolutional neural networks and evaluate the validation set to choose the best model among the five models learned in the 5-fold-cross-Validation.

7. Training with ResNet-50 architecture and evaluating on validation set: We implement the ResNet-50 architecture for training, and based on 5-fold

Cross-Validation, the splitting data is then used to train the model. Each fold is trained and replaced with other folds until all of the folds have finished training. After finishing training, the model performance is evaluated on the validation set. Moreover, the training accuracy can be given out after finishing validation.

8. Exporting the best model from 5-fold to apply to the test set: After training the model, we will figure out the fold with the highest accuracy score. Then using that model, we apply the test set separated from the dataset to get the test accuracy of the model.

9. Validating and calculating accuracy score: When we finish training the model, based on the proposed model prediction, we calculate its precision after the training process. The results given out are the training accuracy. After that, using the testing set separated in the initial stage, the results give out the accuracy of the test set. The test set is independent of the training set.

10. Comparing with other CNN architectures: After finishing the validation, we compare the training accuracy and the accuracy of the test set of the proposed model with some common CNN architectures, VGG16, ResNet-50, ResNet-101, InceptionV3, InceptionResNetV2, and DenseNet121. The test set applying compared to the architectures above is the same.

11. Showing results: After comparing, the results will be illustrated in tables and graphs to make relevant comparisons.

3.2   K-means Clustering

We discovered that all three angles had been synthesized after analyzing the input dataset, including transverse (shot from the top down), sagittal (shot from one side of the brain), and coronal (shot from the front of the brain). The processing is then carried out using the K-means clustering technique. Closely aligned shooting angles provide similar characteristics based on the specific features. The approach is based on a mathematical formula in which we observe a simple vector set of length L to divide n observation points into f clusters. To reduce the set variance, we have 1 cluster $P = \{P_1, P_2, P_3....P_n\}$. The equation for applying K-means clustering is calculated as shown in Eq. 1.

$$arg_P min = \sum_{j=1}^{f} \sum_{a \in P_j}^{f} |a - U_j|^2 = arg_P \sum_{j=1}^{f} |P_j| Var P_j \qquad (1)$$

It means that U is the average of the points in the set P_j. This implementation minimizes the variance of the cluster's point pairs. Since this overall variance does not change considerably, this corresponds to maximizing the sum of squared deviations across points in various clusters and finding clusters of points in the original set that share similar characteristics to the original set. It is also a characteristic that must be examined to classify MRI tumor images into distinct clusters. We use the K-means technique to classify the MRI tumor pictures into clusters with the same angle. K-means is the most basic unsupervised learning algorithm, with unlabeled data as its input. This approach aims to divide the data into f clusters with n objects, each having q qualities, so each element in the group must have the same properties [13].

There are several steps in the K-means algorithm. The initial step is to decide how many clusters (K) to separate from the dataset; for example, we will extract three. The second step is to choose three distinct data points from the data at random to be the centroid. The third step is to calculate the distance between one data point and the three centroids that were chosen and then assist that data point to the cluster closest to it. Finally, the fourth step is to calculate the mean of each cluster and identify it at the new centroid, then repeat the third step based on the new centroid rather than the three before until all points have been assisted to the nearest centroid and no change to the position of the centroid.

3.3   Data Augmentation

While training the model, we realize the dataset is relatively small. Therefore, it can lead the model to overfit. To reduce overfitting, we use data augmentation to increase the size of the training dataset. In this research, we apply some data augmentation techniques to increase the size of the dataset [14]. The list of all techniques we applied to perform data augmentation to our dataset is illustrated in Table 1.

Table 1. List of all techniques used to perform the data augmentation to the dataset

No.	1	2	3	4
Types of technique	Image rotating (degree)	Image flipping (axis)	Image sharpening (lightness value)	Image shearing (axis and degree)
Parameters	±45°	X-axis	0.5	X-axis ±10°
	±90°	Y-axis	1.0	Y-axis ±10°
	±15°		1.5	X-axis ±5°
	±20°		2.0	Y-axis ±5°
	±40°			X-axis -15°
	±75°			Y-axis -15°
	±60°			
	±80°			

One of the most typical augmentation techniques is image rotation. It can help our model be resilient to changes in the object's orientation. Figure 2 shows an example of the result after performing the rotation image.

Besides image rotating and flipping, image sharpening is a set of techniques that improve the image's edge lightness and detail without introducing noise or artifacts. Any group of unique pixels will be highlighted using a high-pass filter,

Image shearing is a technique that tilts an image along with one of its sides. The two most widely utilized methods are vertical shear and horizontal shear. After applying data augmentation with all of the image transformations discussed in this section, we extended the dataset based on the initial one. After applying data augmentation on the dataset that has been applied, K-means clustering will be shown in Table 2.

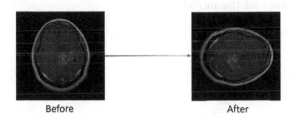

Before   After

Fig. 2. An example of image generated after performing rotating technique

Table 2. Result of data augmentation

The order of diseases	Type of view angles	Quantity (image)
1. Glioma tumor	Transverse	5220
	Coronal	5640
	Sagittal	5640
2. Meningioma tumor	Transverse	8896
	Coronal	3084
	Sagittal	3300
3. Pituitary tumor	Transverse	3096
	Coronal	3372
	Sagittal	3456
4. No tumor	Transverse	3132
	Coronal	1344
	Sagittal	2816
TOTAL		**48.996**

3.4 The Proposed CNN Architecture

The image's most profound features and characteristics are extracted from the output as the last convolution block in the 50-layer network (ResNet-50). Figure 3 represents the overall proposed architecture of the ResNet-50, which is composed of 5 convolutional blocks stacked on top of each other. ResNet-50 has alternative connections between the input and output of each block that traditional CNN architectures do not have, allowing users to utilize the ResNet network more deeply, optimally [15]. Additionally, it also reduces the complexity and computational cost during training. The overall shapes of the object located in the region of interest (ROI) will be extracted from the fully connected layers of the pre-trained model by using the weights from ImageNet, and the CNN architecture applied is ResNet-50. Next, we will turn off all the last dense with *include_top = False*. The steps above will make it easier to manage the input and output accuracy of the model.

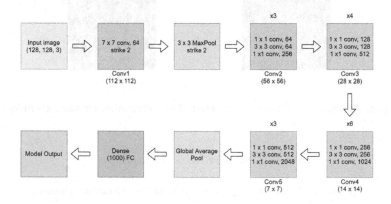

Fig. 3. ResNet-50 architecture

We already have many parameters from all layers applied in the ResNet-50 model. We need to notice the remarkable thing that we can only modify the weight and "freeze" as many layers as we want without changing its value. In this process, we have saved plenty of time and computational costs. Especially, avoiding overfitting during training is necessary. In this research, we have turned off all layers except the last convolution block of the ResNet-50 model (Conv5). Then we used a "Flatten" layer to join the previous layers in the pre-trained model with our new layers. Combining a "Dense" layer with "softmax" can connect the model and begin the classification process. Throughout the experiments, we also found many factors that could affect the accuracy of the training model. By adjusting those factors, we have reduced overfitting and optimized our results based on some opinions below: Using a batch size that is the powers of 2 (Examples: 8, 16, 32, etc.) because it fits with the computer memory.

- Figuring out the learning rate is low because we do not want the transfer learning process to be different from the previous one.
- Figuring out the number of layers will depend on the degree of transition from the layers of the pre-trained model.

- Adding the optimization method called "Adam". It replaces stochastic gradient descent while training deep learning models by combining the most suitable characteristics of the AdaGrad and RMSProp algorithms.
- Using "Batch normalization" and "Dropout" to extract dense layers is also one of the methods to avoid overfitting.

4   Experiments

4.1   Dataset

We used a single dataset for both training and testing in this research. The data was taken between 2005 and 2010 at Nanfang Hospital and General Hospital, Tianjin Medical University, China. This dataset contains the MRI images of 233 patients. In addition, we are using a version of the dataset published in BraTS 2015, including meningioma tumor, glioma tumor, pituitary tumor, and a set image of none tumor image in the dataset with 826 images of Glimoma tumor, 822 images of Meningioma tumor, 827 images of Pituitary tumor, and 395 cases of no findings of the tumor. Figure 4 gives out an example of the images in the dataset, which has three different view angles: transverse (above), coronal (front), and sagittal (side). The data supporting this study's findings are openly available at [16].

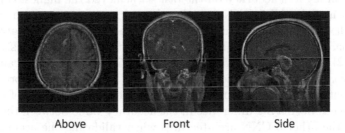

Above   Front   Side

Fig. 4. Example MRI images of the three angles included in the dataset

4.2   Comparison with Some Well-Known CNN Architectures

To check the accuracy of the proposed model that our article has just given out in the previous section, we compare the accuracy score of the proposed model with other CNN architectures, VGG16, ResNet-50, ResNet-101, InceptionV3, InceptionResNetV2, and DenseNet121.

When training, we divided the dataset into the neural network into 80 epochs. The purpose why we chose 80 epochs was that we needed to utilize the algorithm with the given dataset, so we need to put all the data into the neural network several times to find the most desirable result. If the epoch was too inadequate, the model is easily underfitting. Moreover, when we enhance the repetition of data into the neural network, the model can be changed from optimal to overfitting. Therefore, determining the number of appropriate epochs is essential when training the model. Based on the training accuracy and test set, we divide the repetition of data into the neural network into five stages, corresponding with figuring out the results at the fifth, tenth, twentieth, fortieth, and eightieth epoch. We chose these epochs because they helped us evaluate the training and validate the process from the initial stage till the end. Checking the performance based on accuracy is a crucial thing to remark when suggesting a new model. Furthermore, these results are made comparisons with other common CNN architectures. Finally, the result of getting the value of training and accuracy on the test set is illustrated as shown in Table 3.

The results are based on the best fold of the compared pre-trained networks and the proposed model, as illustrated in Table 3. For all of the five pre-trained CNN architectures, we perform pure running, which means we do not apply any algorithms for the training and testing process, and those results are used to compare with our proposed model, which applied K-means clustering and data augmentation. At the pre-processing data stage, the K-means clustering help cluster the dataset so that the dataset can be separated into folders, and each folder can be stored the MRI images with the same shooting angle, based on the brain tumor types. Then applying data augmentation helps the model avoid overfitting. These important algorithms help the model train more efficiently and with reliable results. As we can see from the table, the proposed model's training accuracy and accuracy on the test set achieved the highest compared to other CNN models. All 5 CNN models achieved great accuracy when training. However, the accuracy of the test set of these models was not desirable enough. At the initial stage of training, ResNet-50, ResNet-101, InceptionResNetV2, and DenseNet121 achieved an accuracy of more than 50%, while others can get lower performance. After finishing the training process, all models got more than 84% accuracy, but the proposed model achieved the highest accuracy of more than 98%. There has been a big difference in the accuracy value between the proposed model and the other 5 CNN architectures when validating the accuracy on the test set. Although the training accuracy of these CNN architectures was high, they did not achieve the same as the test set validation process. After finishing

Table 3. Accuracy comparisons between the proposed model and other CNN architectures

Method	Epoch	Training accuracy					Accuracy on test set				
		5	10	20	40	80	5	10	20	40	80
VGG16		0.446	0.527	0.583	0.787	0.846	0.282	0.269	0.291	0.324	0.513
ResNet-50		0.741	0.795	0.862	0.908	0.967	0.322	0.418	0.391	0.628	0.704
ResNet-101		0.577	0.743	0.797	0.868	0.923	0.278	0.395	0.295	0.484	0.602
InceptionV3		0.483	0.619	0.792	0.845	0.942	0.285	0.251	0.289	0.495	0.675
InceptionResNetV2		0.851	0.895	0.931	0.951	0.981	0.467	0.505	0.715	0.658	0.665
DenseNet121		0.823	0.883	0.924	0.959	0.978	0.549	0.507	0.635	0.687	0.588
Proposed approach		**0.487**	**0.659**	**0.821**	**0.923**	**0.985**	**0.746**	**0.867**	**0.912**	**0.932**	**0.961**

training and getting the accuracy based on the test set, the 5 CNN architectures only achieved the accuracy in a range of 50 to 70%, while the proposed model had a high accuracy on the test set, achieving 96%. The difference between the proposed model and the VGG16 model, which was the model that had the lowest accuracy on the test set, was more than 40%. It can be concluded that when finishing training and testing the model based on cross-validation, at the eightieth epoch, the training accuracy and the accuracy on the test set of the proposed model achieved 0.985 and 0.961, respectively. These accuracy values prove that this proposed model has greater precision than other CNN models. Furthermore, after applying all of the techniques mentioned in the methodology section, we obtained the best results for fold three, 96%. Based on results validated in 5 folds, we had the highest accuracy for prediction is 96% in fold 3. Furthermore, all five folds have an accuracy greater than 94%. The mean accuracy is 95.55%, with the standard deviation of the mean only 0.56%. These results prove that the proposed model achieved a promising result, with all folds, training and testing got a high accuracy, and the standard deviation when comparing the accuracy value with all folds was low, proving that the proposed model is optimal and can be used with great accuracy and low difference.

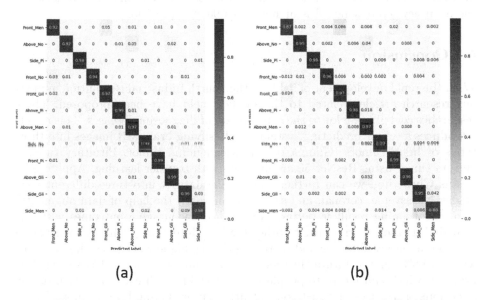

(a)   (b)

Fig. 5. Confusion matrix - (a) of the best fold, (b) average of all folds

We illustrate the confusion matrix based on the testing results of the best fold, which was the third fold, as shown in (a) of Fig. 5. The entries on the confusion matrix's diagonal based on the best graph's test results, as shown in (a) of Fig. 5 have incredibly high precision. The correct classification scores of each data class have an accuracy of over 88% (the maximum is up to 99% for Above-Pituitary, Front-Pituitary, and Above-Glioma). This result is significantly larger than the rest (the surrounding cells represent results based on incorrect guesses, and the results are as low as 0.01 to 0.09). In addition, we also calculated the average confusion matrix by using all results in each confusion matrix of 5 folds, as illustrated in (b) of Fig. 5.

According to (b) of Fig. 5, the average matrix has promising results with exceptionally high accuracy for all values on the diagonal. Those values ranged from the lowest 0.87 in Front Man to the highest 0.99 in Side-No tumor and Front-Pituitary. However, the outcome is based on incorrect predictions for shallow values, the highest of which is 0.0086, which has no significant effect on the accuracy of the results in the matrix. The author in [17] used K-Nearest Neighbor (Knn) and Artificial Neural Networks (ANN) to classify the MRI images into Glioma, Meningioma, and Pituitary brain tumors. The highest success rate in brain tumor classification was 95.56% when applying the feature extraction method and the K-NN model. Waghmare VK's research (2021) also used this dataset for evaluating brain tumor classification. Applying data augmentation and VGG16 neural network for the designed model, the accuracy that can detect tumors is 95.71% [18]. Compared to our proposed model, it can be concluded that when performing K-means clustering and data augmentation in the preprocessing data stage, then using the ResNet-50 convolutional neural network, the accuracy score achieved is higher (with 96.08% precision)

5   Conclusion

With the rapid development of fields in the Fourth Industrial Revolution, numerous research articles related to the medical field have been proposed. These researches contribute a lot to the convenience of diagnosing diseases. This article introduces a tumor predicting system for classifying brain MR images into three types of brain tumors (Glioma tumor, Meningioma tumor, Pituitary tumor), and no tumor using ResNet-50 architecture with transfer learning. Applying K-means Clustering, we can further classify the dataset into three different view angles (transverse, coronal, and sagittal), and with the help of data augmentation, the training result is better. We reached encouraging outcomes with the provided dataset. Correlating to other CNN architectures, it has demonstrated that the accuracy is higher and more stable. The highest accuracy shown in our work is 96%. In the future, further research can be performed based on this premise, which can motivate people to a better life with early detection of any infections or diseases, not just concentrating on predicting brain tumors.

References

1. Kathawala, F., Shah, A., Shah, J., Vora, S., Patil, S.: Brain tumor detection and classification. In: Sharma, H., Govindan, K., Poonia, R.C., Kumar, S., El-Medany, W.M. (eds.) Advances in Computing and Intelligent Systems. AIS, pp. 547–556. Springer, Singapore (2020). https://doi.org/10.1007/978-981-15-0222-4_52

2. Das, J., Ghosh, S., Chakraborty, R., Pramanik, A.: Deep learning based classification of brain tumor types from MRI scans. In: Nayak, J., Favorskaya, M.N., Jain, S., Naik, B., Mishra, M. (eds.) Advanced Machine Learning Approaches in Cancer Prognosis. ISRL, vol. 204, pp. 425–454. Springer, Cham (2021). https://doi.org/10.1007/978-3-030-71975-3_16
3. Valentino, D.J., Mazziotta, J.C., Huang, H.K.: Visualization of human brain structure-function relationships. In: Images of the Twenty-First Century. Proceedings of the Annual International Engineering in Medicine and Biology Society, vol. 6, pp. 1737–1738 (1989)
4. Lecun, Y., Bottou, L., Bengio, Y., Haffner, P.: Gradient-based learning applied to document recognition. In: Proceedings of the IEEE, vol. 86, pp. 2278–2324 (1998)
5. Selvapandian, A., Manivannan, K.: Fusion based glioma brain tumor detection and segmentation using ANFIS classification. Comput. Methods Programs Biomed. **166**, 33–38 (2018)
6. Rajan, P.G., Sundar, C.: Brain tumor detection and segmentation by intensity adjustment. J. Med. Syst. **43**(8), 1–13 (2019). https://doi.org/10.1007/s10916-019-1368-4
7. Khan, M.A., et al.: Brain tumor detection and classification: a framework of marker-based watershed algorithm and multilevel priority features selection. Microsc. Res. Tech. **82**, 909–922 (2019)
8. Toğaçar, M., Ergen, B., Cömert, Z.: BrainMRNet: brain tumor detection using magnetic resonance images with a novel convolutional neural network model. Med. Hypotheses **134**, 109531 (2020)
9. Sadad, T., Rehman, A., Munir, A., Saba, T., Tariq, U., Ayesha, N., Abbasi, R.: Brain tumor detection and multi-classification using advanced deep learning techniques. Microsc. Res. Tech. **84**, 1296–1308 (2021)
10. Kim, S., Kim, B., Park, H.: Synthesis of brain tumor multicontrast MR images for improved data augmentation. Med. Phys. **48**(5), 2185–2198 (2021). https://doi.org/10.1002/mp.14701
11. Tran, N.T., Tran, V.H., Nguyen, N.B., Nguyen, T.K., Cheung, N.M.: On data augmentation for GAN training. IEEE Trans. Image Process. **30**, 1882–1897 (2021). https://doi.org/10.1109/TIP.2021.3049346
12. Luo, Y., Zhu, L.Z., Wan, Z.Y., Lu, B.L.: Data augmentation for enhancing EEG-based emotion recognition with deep generative models. J. Neural Eng. **17**, 056021 (2020)
13. Sinaga, K.P., Yang, M.S.: Unsupervised k-means clustering algorithm. IEEE Access **8**, 80716–80727 (2020). https://doi.org/10.1109/ACCESS.2020.2988796
14. Ke, X., Zou, J., Niu, Y.: End-to-end automatic image annotation based on deep CNN and multi-label data augmentation. IEEE Trans. Multimedia **21**(8), 2093–2106 (2019). https://doi.org/10.1109/TMM.2019.2895511
15. Sai Sundar, K.V., Bonta, L.R., Reddy, A.K., Baruah, P.K., Sankara, S.S.: Evaluating training time of inception-v3 and Resnet-50, 101 models using tensorflow across CPU and GPU. In: 2018 Second International Conference on Electronics, Communication and Aerospace Technology (ICECA), pp. 1964–1968 (2018)
16. Cheng, J.: Brain tumor dataset. Figshare (2017)
17. Kaplan, K., Kaya, Y., Kuncan, M., Ertunç, H.M.: Brain tumor classification using modified local binary patterns (LBP) feature extraction methods. Med. Hypotheses **139**, 109696 (2020)
18. Waghmare, V.K., Kolekar, M.H.: Brain tumor classification using deep learning, pp. 155–175 (2021)

Approximating Sparse Semi-nonnegative Matrix Factorization for X-Ray Covid-19 Image Classification

Manel Sekma[1]([✉]), Amel Mhamdi[2], and Wady Naanaa[3]

[1] Higher Institute of Computer Sciences and Mathematics of Monastir,
University of Monastir, 5000 Monastir, Tunisia
`manel.sekma@isimm.rnu.tn`
[2] Aivancity School for Technology, Business and Society, Paris-Cachan, France
`mhamdi@aivancity.ai`
[3] University of Tunis El Manar, 1000 Tunis, Tunisia
`wady.naanaa@enit.utm.tn`

Abstract. Medical imaging has been intensively used to help the radiologists do the correct diagnosis for the COVID-19 disease. In particular, *chest X-ray imaging* is one of the prevalent information sources for COVID-19 diagnosis. The obtained images can be viewed as numerical data and processed by non-negative matrix factorization (NMF) algorithms, one of the available numerical data analysis tools.

In this work, we propose a new sparse semi-NMF algorithm that can classify the patients into COVID-19 and normal patients, based on chest X-ray images. We show that the huge volume of data resulting from X-ray images can be significantly reduced without significant loss of classification accuracy. Then, we evaluate our algorithm by carrying out an experiment on a publicly available dataset, having a known chest X-ray image bi-partition.

Experimental results demonstrate that the proposed sparse semi-NMF algorithm can predict COVID-19 patients with high accuracy,compared to state-of-the-art algorithms.

Keywords: Non-negative matrix factorization · Sparse semi-NMF · Classification · K-means · Medical images · COVID-19

1 Introduction

Non-negative matrix factorization (NMF) is one of the most effective unsupervised technique in the field of numerical data analysis. It consists in approximating a given non-negative matrix $\mathbf{M}$ by a matrix product $\mathbf{WS}^T$, where both $\mathbf{W}$ and $\mathbf{S}$ are required to be non-negative. The goal of such an approximation is to reduce the dimensionality of the data, since the number of components comprised in both of the two factors is typically much less than the number of components of the input matrix. In counter part, it is unlikely to obtain a

C. Bădică et al. (Eds.): ICCCI 2022, CCIS 1653, pp. 330–336, 2022.
https://doi.org/10.1007/978-3-031-16210-7_27

perfect equality between the input matrix and its approximation. The quality of the approximation, $\mathbf{M} \approx \mathbf{WS}^T$, is therefore evaluated using some matrix norm or divergence [4]. In addition to providing low-rank approximation for non negative data, NMF algorithms have an inherent clustering property. Indeed, a r-clustering, where r is the factorization rank, of the columns of the input matrix can be easily deduced, once we have obtained the two factors [3].

Standard NMF can be formulated as follows:

$$\underset{\mathbf{W},\mathbf{S}}{\text{Minimize}} \ \|\mathbf{M} - \mathbf{WS}^T\|_F^2 \ \text{subject to} \ \mathbf{W} \succeq \mathbf{0}, \quad \mathbf{S} \succeq \mathbf{0} \tag{1}$$

where the matrix norm employed is given by $\|\mathbf{X}\|_F = \sqrt{\operatorname{tr} \mathbf{X}^T \mathbf{X}}$.

However, NMF has many variations for different contexts. In this paper, we focus on a variation that relaxes the non-negativity constraint on one of the factors, namely $\mathbf{W}$, resulting in the *Semi-NMF* variant. Moreover, in order to guide the factorization to the relevant factors, we resort to an optimisation criterion that favours sparse matrices for one of the factors, namely $\mathbf{S}$. The motivation behind favouring sparse factors has been widely discussed [6], and simplifying the data interpretation is one of the most mentioned arguments.

Nonetheless, even if we consider the more constrained settings of standard NMF, a unique identification of $\mathbf{W}$ and $\mathbf{S}$ is not possible, because any one of the two factors might be permuted and scaled provided that the other factor is transformed accordingly. Indeed, if $\mathbf{P}$ is a permutation matrix and $\mathbf{\Lambda}$ a non-singular positive diagonal matrix then we have $\mathbf{WS}^T = (\mathbf{WP\Lambda})(\mathbf{\Lambda}^{-1}\mathbf{P}^{-1}\mathbf{S}^T)$. The matrix pairs $(\mathbf{W}, \mathbf{S})$ and $(\mathbf{WP\Lambda}, \mathbf{SP}^{-T}\mathbf{\Lambda}^{-1})$ are, therefore, regarded as equivalent solutions in the context of NMF.

Since the work by Paatero and Tapper [10], many other were developed [7]. The block principle pivoting algorithm is a fairly simple NMF algorithm which has, however, proved to be very efficient [7]. Since then, it forms the core of many state-of-the-art algorithms. Yet another track explored for the purpose of performing NMF is the one relying on convex geometry. NMF algorithms adopting this approach are referred to as *geometric algorithms* [8]. One of these algorithms is EDA, for Extreme Direction Analysis, [9], which proceeds by identifying relevant facets of the *data cone*. These facets are identified by solving a number of linear programs using the simplex algorithm.

In the present paper, we focus on the sparse semi-NMF context, which can be met in various real world situations such as hyper-spectral pictures taken by a satellite [13].

The proposed sparse semi-NMF algorithm, REDA (for Rectangular EDA), is built up on EDA. Recall that this latter algorithm applies only when one of the factors is a square matrix. However, in the general context of sparse semi-NMF, each of the two factors may be a rectangular matrix. Hence, the main theoretical contribution of this article, which consists in transforming sparse semi-NMF into a particular sparse semi-NMF where one of the factors is a square matrix. REDA is, therefore, used to help in COVID-19 diagnosis via chest X-Ray images. We chosen to apply our algorithm to the analysis of these particular images because existing works concern mainly supervised algorithms [11,12]. The paper is structured as follows: In Sect. 2, we present the theoretical background of our algorithm. The proposed sparse semi-NMF algorithm, REDA, is detailed in Sect. 3. In Sect. 4, we report the details of an experiment that demonstrates the efficiency of REDA in classifying chest X-ray images into COVID-19 and non COVID-19 images.

2   Sparse Semi-NMF as a Linear Optimisation Problem

This work concerns sparse semi-NMF (SSNMF). This is about finding a pair of matrices $\mathbf{W}, \mathbf{S}$ whose product $\mathbf{WS}^T$ is close to an input matrix $\mathbf{M}$, while also favouring a sparse matrix for $\mathbf{S}$. As in a lot of research, the quality of the approximation is measured by the Frobenius norm of the difference between the input matrix and its approximation. In turn, the sparseness of $\mathbf{S}$ may be evaluated via the multichannel sparseness criterion, which is defined as follows $\mu(\mathbf{S}) = (\sqrt{\det \mathbf{S}^T \mathbf{S}})/(\Pi_{j=1}^n \|\mathbf{s}_j\|_1)$, where $\mathbf{s}_j$ denotes the jth column of $\mathbf{S}$. It has been shown, in [9], that $0 \le \mu(\mathbf{S}) \le 1$ and $\mu(\mathbf{S}) = 1$ if and only if $\mathbf{S}$ is a column orthonormal matrix. Moreover, since $\mathbf{S}$ is a non negative matrix, $\mu(\mathbf{S}) = 1$ implies that $\mathbf{S}$ contains, at least, $n(r - 1)$ zeros, which corresponds to a rather sparse matrix.

In order to simplify the expression of $\mu(\mathbf{S})$, we enforce the columns of $\mathbf{S}$ to sum to 1. By the equivalence between NMF solutions, this additional constraint does not entail any loss of generality. Using matrix notation, the latter constraint can be written as $\mathbf{S}^T \mathbf{1} = \mathbf{1}$, where $\mathbf{1}$ denotes an all-one vector that has the appropriate size. It follows that $\mu(\mathbf{S})^2 = \det \mathbf{S}^T \mathbf{S}$.

The studied NMF variation is therefore specified as follows

$$\underset{\mathbf{W},\mathbf{S}}{\text{Minimize}} \ \|\mathbf{M} - \mathbf{WS}^T\|_F^2 \ + \ \gamma \det \mathbf{S}^T \mathbf{S}, \text{ subject to } \mathbf{S} \succeq \mathbf{0}, \ \mathbf{S}^T \mathbf{1} = \mathbf{1} \quad (2)$$

where $\gamma \le 0$. As it can be seen from (2), the objective is a weighted sum of two terms: an *approximation* term and a *sparseness* term. We note that minimizing the sparseness term is a rather difficult task, because this is neither a concave nor a convex function of $\mathbf{S}$. The objective could, however, be approximated by considering the two terms of the objective separately. Consider therefore the following Semi-NMF sub-problem, which is obtained from (2) by setting $\gamma = 0$:

$$\underset{\mathbf{W},\mathbf{S}}{\text{Minimize}} \ \|\mathbf{M} - \mathbf{WS}^T\|_F^2 \text{ subject to } \mathbf{S} \succeq \mathbf{0}, \quad \mathbf{S}^T \mathbf{1} = \mathbf{1} \quad (3)$$

The following theorem[1] is the main theoretical contribution of this paper.

Theorem 1. *Let* $(\mathbf{M}, r)$ *be a Semi-NMF instance and let* $\mathbf{S}$ *be a non negative matrix whose columns sum to 1. Then* $\mathbf{S}$ *is an optimal solution for* $(\mathbf{M}, r)$ *if and only if it is a full column rank matrix whose columns are in the range of* $\mathbf{V}_{:,1:r}$, *where* $\mathbf{V}$ *is the right singular factor of* $\mathbf{M}$.

---

[1] The proof the this theorem is omitted in this short version of the paper.

From the above theorem, we can evaluate the quality of the proposed rank r approximation. beginAmel

Corollary 1. *The error of approximating an m-by-n matrix* $\mathbf{M}$ *by a rank* r *SNMF* $\mathbf{M} \approx \mathbf{WS}^T$ *is given by* $\|\mathbf{M} - \mathbf{WS}^T\|_F^2 = \sum_{i=r+1}^m \sigma_{i,i}^2$, *where* $\sigma_{i,i}, i : r+1, \ldots, m$ *are the smallest* $m - r$ *singular values of* $\mathbf{M}$.

In what follows $\bar{\mathbf{V}}$ will designate $\mathbf{V}_{:,1:r}$.

Let $\mathbf{c} = \bar{\mathbf{V}}^T \mathbf{1}$. Theorem 1 suggests that any n-by-r matrix $\mathbf{S}$ that verifies $\mathbf{S} = \bar{\mathbf{V}}\mathbf{X} \succeq 0$ and $\mathbf{S}^T \mathbf{1} = \mathbf{X}^T \mathbf{c} = \mathbf{1}$, for some non singular matrix $\mathbf{X}$, yields an optimal solution for Problem (3). Then solving Problem (3) reduces to solving the following problem:

$$\underset{\mathbf{X}}{\text{Minimize}}\ 1 \ \text{subject to}\ \bar{\mathbf{V}}\mathbf{X} \succeq 0,\ \mathbf{X}^T \mathbf{c} = \mathbf{1} \tag{4}$$

Problem (4) presents many advantages, with regard to Problem (3). First, the matrix to be computed, that is $\mathbf{X}$, is r-by-r, which is a relatively small matrix compared to $\mathbf{S}$ in a context where $r \ll n$. Moreover, Problem (4) is a satisfiability problem, that is, it has no objective. Thus, Problem (4) should be much more easier to solved. This simplified problem will be used as the starting point to cope with the main problem, namely Problem (2).

Thanks to Theorem 1, we obtain $\mathbf{S}^T\mathbf{S} = \mathbf{X}^T\mathbf{X}$. And since $\mathbf{X}$ is a square matrix, this implies that $\det \mathbf{S}^T\mathbf{S} = (\det \mathbf{X})^2$. Hence the following mathematical program

$$\underset{\mathbf{X}}{\text{Maximize}}\ |\det \mathbf{X}| \ \text{subject to}\ \bar{\mathbf{V}}\mathbf{X} \succeq 0,\ \mathbf{X}^T \mathbf{c} = \mathbf{1} \tag{5}$$

3 The Algorithm

Thanks to Theorem 1, a suboptimal solution for Problem (2) can be obtained via EDA, the sparse semi-NMF algorithm described in [9]. Roughly speaking EDA proceeds by replacing the columns of matrix $\mathbf{X}$, one at a time, by other feasible vectors, in order to increase the objective $|\det \mathbf{X}|$. Thus, EDA can be used to find an approximate solution for Problem (2) at the expense of minor changes. These changes consist in the singular value decomposition and the choice of the r first right singular vectors of $\mathbf{M}$, performed at lines 2 and 3 of Algorithm 1. The resulting algorithm will be referred to by REDA (for rectangular EDA).

Next, we show how REDA can be employed to perform a classification tack. More precisely, we assume that the goal is classify the columns of the data matrix, $\mathbf{M}$, into r classes. To this end, we apply REDA to the SSNMF instance defined by $(\mathbf{M}, r)$ Once we have obtained an approximate solution, say $(\mathbf{W}, \mathbf{S})$, this latter is used to dispatch the columns of $\mathbf{M}$ into the r classes as follows. The class of each column is determined by measuring the similarity between each column of the approximate matrix $\mathbf{WS}^T$, on the one hand, and each column of $\mathbf{W}$ on the other hand. The similarity between each pair of column vectors is evaluated by the cosine of the angle formed by the two vectors. The resulting cosine matrix, which has size n-by-r, is used to determine the class of each of the n columns of $\mathbf{M}$. This is done by simply determining the position of the maximum in each row of the cosine matrix.

Algorithm 1: REDA

    Data: $\mathbf{M}, r$
    Result: $\mathbf{W}, \mathbf{S}$
    // r must not exceed the rank of $\mathbf{M}$
1 $r \leftarrow \min(r, \mathrm{rank}(\mathbf{M}))$
2 $[\mathbf{U}, \mathbf{\Sigma}, \mathbf{V}] \leftarrow \mathrm{svd}(\mathbf{M})$
    // $\bar{\mathbf{V}}$ is composed of the first r right singular vectors of $\mathbf{M}$
3 $\bar{\mathbf{V}} \leftarrow \mathbf{V}(:, 1 : r)$
    // Initializing matrix $\mathbf{X}$ to a non singular matrix
4 $\mathbf{f} \leftarrow 1$
5 **for** $j \leftarrow 1$ **to** r **do**
6     $\mathbf{X}(:, j) \leftarrow \arg\max_{\mathbf{x}} |\mathbf{f}^T \mathbf{x}|$ subject to $\bar{\mathbf{V}} \mathbf{x} \succeq 0$, $\mathbf{c}^T \mathbf{x} = 1$
7     $\mathbf{N} \leftarrow \mathrm{nullspace}(\mathbf{X})$
8     $\mathbf{f} \leftarrow \mathbf{N}^T \mathbf{1}$
9 **end**
10 stop $\leftarrow$ **false**
11 **while not** stop **do**
12   stop $\leftarrow$ **true**
13   max $\leftarrow 1$
14    $\mathbf{Y} \leftarrow \mathbf{X}^{-1}$
15   **for** $j \leftarrow 1$ **to** r **do**
16      $\mathbf{f} \leftarrow \mathbf{Y}(:, j)$
17      $\mathbf{x}^* \leftarrow \arg\max_{\mathbf{x}} |\mathbf{f}^T \mathbf{x}|$ subject to $\bar{\mathbf{V}} \mathbf{x} \succeq 0$, $\mathbf{c}^T \mathbf{x} = 1$
18   **if** $(|\mathbf{f}^T \mathbf{x}^*| \geq max)$ **then**
19        $max \leftarrow |\mathbf{f}^T \mathbf{x}^*|$
20        $j_{max} \leftarrow j$
21        $\mathbf{x}_{max} \leftarrow \mathbf{x}^*$
22   stop $\leftarrow$ **false**
23   **end**
24   **end**
25   **if not** stop **then** $\mathbf{X}(:, j_{max}) \leftarrow \mathbf{x}_{max}$
26 **end**
27 $\mathbf{S} \leftarrow \bar{\mathbf{V}} \mathbf{X}$
28 $\mathbf{W} \leftarrow \mathbf{M} \mathbf{S}^{T\dagger}$

---

4   Experimental Results

We experimentally evaluate the performances of our algorithm by attempting to partition a dataset of X-ray images into a COVID-19 and a non COVID-19 subsets. The dataset used for the experiments is obtained from the Kaggle

Table 1. Comparison between clustering algorithms. Performance values are reported in the form of accuracy percentages.

Classes	Kmeans	NMF	REDA
NORMAL	94.69	93.24	96,34
COVID-19	84.89	92.18	87,15

Table 2. Average classification accuracy. (Performance values are reported in the form of Accuracy percentages

Methods	Classification Accuracy
K-means	92.08
NMF	92.96
REDA	93,88

repository COVID-19 Radiography Database [2]. It contains 576 X-ray images of COVID-19 patients and 1583 images for normal people. All the results quoted in this work were performed using the original dataset.

In a first step, we applied an image preprocessing, which consists in resizing the X-ray radio images in order to obtain 180-by-150 images. This substantially reduce the input matrix size and boosts computational speed. The obtained images were subsequently converted into grayscale images, since the luminance is more important than the colours, for this kind of image.

The second step consists in building the input matrix. Then, the rows of each preprocessed image are concatenated to form a single column of the input matrix M. Thus, the number of columns in M correspond to the number of images in the dataset, and the number of rows correspond to the number of pixels in each image.

REDA is compared with two existing non supervised clustering algorithms, namely the NMF algorithm described in [1], which was parametrized for clustering tasks, and the K-means algorithm [5]. This latter algorithm is a distance-based algorithm that assigns a points into clusters based on the notion of cluster centres, and it is known as one of the most competitive unsupervised clustering algorithms.

The results of our experiment is shown in Table 1. We used the COVID-19 label to designate the row containing the accuracy obtained for the class of COVID-19 infected patients, and the NORMAL label for the row containing the accuracy for the not infected patients.

As it can be noticed from Table 1, for all algorithms, the NORMAL class is identified with more accuracy than the COVID-19 class. And the highest accuracy is obtained by REDA (96,34%). In contrast, for the COVID-19 class, the state-of-the-art NMF obtained the highest accuracy. Finally, the overall accuracy (see Table 2) gave the advantage to REDA, which obtained highest global accuracy, with 93,88%.

5   Conclusion

In this paper, we have proposed a sparse semi-NMF algorithm, REDA, which has been built upon an existing geometric sparse semi-NMF algorithm. When applied to chest X-ray images, REDA significantly reduces the huge volume of data, issued from these images, without loss of classification accuracy.

The experimental results showed that the classification accuracy of the proposed algorithm is very competitive with dedicated state-of-the-art algorithms.

References

1. Cichocki, A., Phan, A.H.: Fast local algorithms for large scale nonnegative matrix and tensor factorizations. IEICE Trans. Fundam. Electron. Commun. Comput. Sci. **92**(3), 708–721 (2009)
2. Cohen, J.P., Morrison, P., Dao, L., Roth, K., Duong, T.Q., Ghassemi, M.: Covid-19 image data collection: Prospective predictions are the future. arXiv preprint arXiv:2006.11988 (2020)
3. Ding, C., He, X., Simon, H.D.: On the equivalence of nonnegative matrix factorization and spectral clustering. In: SIAM International Conference on Data Mining, pp. 606–610 (2005)
4. Gillis, N.: The why and how of nonnegative matrix factorization. CoRR **abs/1401.5226** http://arxiv.org/abs/1401.5226 (2014)
5. Hartigan, J., Wong, M.: Algorithm AS 136: a K-means clustering algorithm. Appl. Stat. **28**(1), 100–108 (1979)
6. Kim, H., Park, H.: Sparse non-negative matrix factorizations via alternating non-negativity-constrained least squares for microarray data analysis. Bioinformatics **23**(12), 1495–1502 (2007)
7. Kim, H., Park, H.: Nonnegative matrix factorization based on alternating nonnegativity constrained least squares and active set method. SIAM J. Matrix Anal. Appl. **30**(2), 713–730 (2008)
8. Laurberg, H., Christensen, M.G., Plumbley, M.D., Hansen, L.K., Jensen, S.H.: Theorems on positive data: On the uniqueness of NMF. Comput. Intell. Neurosci. **2008**, 764206 (2008)
9. Naanaa, W., Nuzillard, J.: Extreme direction analysis for blind separation of nonnegative signals. Signal Process. **130**, 254–267 (2017)
10. Pentti, P.: Tapper unto: positive matrix factorization: a nonnegative factor model with optimal utilization of error estimates of data values. Environmetrics **5**(2), 111–126 (1994)
11. Ucara, F., Korkmaz, D.: COVIDiagnosis-Net: deep Bayes-SqueezeNet based diagnosis of the coronavirus disease 2019 (COVID-19) from X-ray images. Med. Hypotheses **140**, 109761 (2020)
12. Waheed, A., Goyal, M., Gupta, D., Khanna, A., Al-Turjman, F., Pinheiro, P.: CovidGAN: data augmentation using auxiliary classifier GAN for improved Covid-19 detection. IEEE Access **99**, 1–1 (2020)
13. Wang, Z., He, M., Wang, L., Xu, K., Xiao, J., Nian, Y.: Semi-NMF-based reconstruction for hyperspectral compressed sensing. IEEE J. Sel. Top. Appl. Earth Obs. Remote Sens. **13**, 4352–4368 (2020). https://doi.org/10.1109/JSTARS.2020.3010332

Hybrid Architecture for 3D Brain Tumor Image Segmentation Based on Graph Neural Network Pooling

Islem Gammoudi[1]($\boxtimes$) (ID), Raja Ghozi[2] (ID), and Mohamed Ali Mahjoub[3] (ID)

[1] Université de Sousse, Ecole Nationale d'Ingénieurs de Sousse, LATIS-Laboratory of Advanced Technology and Intelligent Systems, Université de Tunis El Manar, Faculté des Sciences Mathématiques Physiques et Naturelles de Tunis, 2092 Tunis, Tunisia
islemislem65@gmail.com
[2] Université Américaine de Bahreïn, Collège d'ingénierie, P.O. Box 38884, Riffa, Bahrain
raja.ghozi@aubh.edu.bh
[3] Université de Sousse, Ecole Nationale d'Ingénieurs de Sousse, LATIS-Laboratory of Advanced Technology and Intelligent Systems, 4023 Sousse, Tunisia

Abstract. The Brain tumor image segmentation process is a delicate and a challenging task in medical image analysis. Gliomas are the dominant type of brain tumor, the reason behind which brain image segmentation research has been focusing on. Manual segmentation of Glioma for this type of cancer diagnosis is a difficult and time-consuming task. In this work, we develop an automatic segmentation method to segment 3D MRI brain tumor images. Graph-based Neural Networks (GNNs) is used to exploit the structural information present in graph data by aggregating information over connected nodes, allowing them to effectively capture information relation between data elements. By considering GNN to model the content information of the image, the medical image segmentation problem is transformed into a graph-based energy minimization problem. Aiming at segmenting 3D MRI images, we develop a Deep Learning segmentation method called SCGNN-3DBUNet for 3D brain tumor task segmentation. For that, we have adopted a variation of GNNs for the automatic segmentation of brain tumors from MRI scans by combining an extension of U-Net with GNNs. We evaluated this hybrid approach performance using the online BraTS 2020 dataset. The obtained results are promising compared with the state-of-the-art approaches with a Dice score of 0.89 for the whole tumor.

Keywords: Brain tumor segmentation · Deep learning · 3DBUNet · GNN · BraTS'2020 dataset

1 Introduction

Machine learning has proved to be one of the most successful to integrate, analyze and make predictions based on large, heterogeneous data sets [1]. Traditionally, machine learning models are trained to perform manually designed features, extracted from features learned by other simple machine learning models, from the raw data. In deep

C. Bădică et al. (Eds.): ICCCI 2022, CCIS 1653, pp. 337–351, 2022.
https://doi.org/10.1007/978-3-031-16210-7_28

learning, the computers learn useful features and their representations automatically, directly from the raw data, thus bypassing this manual and challenging step.

Deep neural networks have been at the heart of machine learning models in use across a variety of fields and have been widely deployed in academia applications [1]. These developments bring a new promising potential for medical data analysis, medical imaging technology, medical diagnostics, and healthcare in general. In fact, healthcare applications of deep learning include the prediction of sudden incidents such as cardiac arrests [2], computer-aided health incident detection [3], diagnosis supporting patient survival analysis, drug discovery aid therapy selection, and best operational surgery.

Due to the soft tissue contrast and its wide availability, an MRI image is considered the standard technique to evaluate brain tumor diagnosis and treatment planning [4]. MRI image segmentation into different and coherent regions has benefited from the use of deep learning approaches in the medical imaging field. Furthermore, an efficient segmentation is an essential step for brain tumor analysis via MRI images. The brain tumor segmentation process has for long been a challenging and delicate task in medical image processing and analysis, given the high health stakes.

Since manual segmentation is a very time-consuming procedure, current brain tumor segmentation research is mainly focused on fully automatic methods, especially for the segmentation of a large amount of multimodal MRI images. The development of a robust automatic segmentation method to provide efficient and objective brain MRI image segmentation, has been emerging as a promising research area. At the same time, Deep learning algorithms have evolved to be a powerful tool for both 2D and 3D medical image segmentation [5].

In his work, we consider automatic MRI brain image segmentation based on deep learning algorithms. It is important to recall that multi-channel segmentation has been a challenge in the field of computer vision. Graph-based Neural Networks (GNNs) have been widely applied as a graph analysis method [6]. It provides an expanded framework with novel structures and has been introduced in several applications.

In this work, we also introduce a new spectral clustering method using the GNN architecture as an extension of the U-Net [7] with batch normalization [8] (3DBUNet). This new hybrid model is called SCGNN-3DBUNet is designed to provide an accurate segmentation in medical images with a special emphasis on 3D tumor MRI image segmentation. Specifically, we present a deep learning segmentation method by combining a 3DBUNet architecture with a graph neural network model. This strategy relies on the use of a GNN algorithm in order to cluster pixels to the same informatic group.

The remaining of the paper is structured as follows: In Sect. 2, we present a brief overview of the relevant literature to the proposed hybrid model used in this work. In Sect. 3, we detail the proposed image segmentation method. The experimental results are reported in Sect. 4, along with discussion. A summary of the present work along with perspectives are given in Sect. 5.

2 Related Work

There is a rich literature, focusing on traditional and deep learning methods for MRI-based brain tumor image segmentation. In this section, we provide a review of the state-of-the-art methods based on deep learning, which will be preceded by a brief overview of classical techniques used in medical image segmentation.

2.1 Classical Segmentation Methods

Traditional tumor segmentation algorithms relied mainly on threshold-based segmentation methods, region-based segmentation methods, and edge-based segmentation methods [9, 10].

Thresholding is used for segmentation in various images processing applications. There are different types of thresholding techniques: global thresholding, adaptive thresholding, histogram equalization, and otsu thresholding. For instance, an extended Sobel operator to perform 2D spatial gradient measurement on a mammography image was used in enhancing the tumor area in mammography images [10].

In line with these traditional methods, there are various advanced approaches, including graph-based methods, that were used in medical image segmentation. Graph-based segmentation approaches played a crucial role in medical image segmentation. In these approaches, an image is modeled as a graph in which vertices represent individual pixels and weighted edges describe the similarity of neighboring pixels. Typical graph-based segmentation algorithms include minimum spanning tree-based methods, shortest-paths-based methods, graph-cuts [11–13] approaches, among others. In the Normalized Cut, the generalized eigenvectors problem of the linear system was used for the image segmentation [11]. The k-means clustering algorithm for MR breast image segmentation was used in image segmentation [12].

Recently, the use of complex networks analysis domain has been considered in segmenting images achieving great results. In this regard, the work in [13] attempted to apply community detection problems in complex networks to solve image segmentation problems and investigate a new graph-based image segmentation. The well-known learning algorithms are the support vector machine (SVM) and the random forest (RF).

2.2 Deep Learning Segmentation Methods

The Neural network (NN) have been considered the more recent variant of the learning algorithm that employs the concepts of deep learning [5] in order to address the problem of medical image segmentation. Deep learning techniques have strongly influenced progress in several fields, especially in medical image analysis wide applications. In this regard, they were found to be top-performing methods in segmenting brain tumors images, liver tumors, or stroke lesions.

Therefore, the integration of a learning scheme at some stage of the processing pipeline is key step in attaining good segmentation outcome. With such high performances, deep learning methods are currently considered as the state of the art for Glioma segmentation (the most common brain tumor).

The new generation of deep learning techniques called convolutional neural networks (CNNs) has successfully been applied to image recognition tasks. CNN was proved successful in automatically classifying the normal and pathological brain MRI scans in the past few BraTS challenges [14]. One of the first deep networks applied to image segmentation can be found in FCN [15]. One of the early uses of CNN to segment medical images was reported in [7], where an encoder-decoder structure of Convolutional Neural Networks called U-Net for medical image segmentation, was proposed. This architecture was originally suggested for cell images. It uses skip connection to include the high-resolution feature maps in the encoding path to include more fine-grained information. Another class of neural networks architectures is known as recurrent neural networks (RNNs) [16].

Closely related to CNN one finds the Graph Neural Networks (GNNs) [6]. This latter has shown an outstanding performance in numerous graph related application. Recently, learning representations of entire graphs have attracted a lot of attention in the fields of bioinformatics. The success of (GNNs) in many domains is related to their ability to extract meaningful representations from graph-structured data. The combination of deep learning and another method is proving to be a new powerful technique that is achieving high performance in any aspects.

In this work, we seek to segment 3D MRI images in multi-modalities. Specifically, an image segmentation strategy seeded in the neural networks, providing an automatic deep learning segmentation method by combining a 3DBUNet architecture with the graph neural network (GNN) model.

3 Proposed Method

In the field of computer vision, multi-modal segmentation has always been challenging. In this work, we seek to segment 3D MRI glioma brain tumor images containing multi-modalities. To satisfactory segmentation performance, a carefully designed network-based method is often needed. For this reason and to address the need for more accurate medical image segmentation, we propose an automatic architecture for multi-modal 3D MRI using Graph-based Neural Networks (GNNs), and an extension of U-Net. In what follows, we detail the suggested framework called SCGNN-3DBUNet for 3D medical image segmentation developed in our work. The hybrid network structure of SCGNN-3DBUNet is shown in Fig. 1.

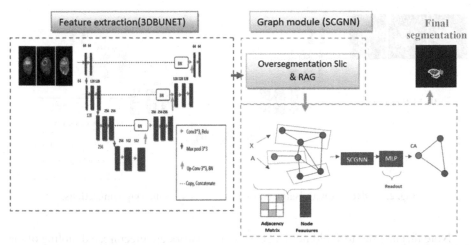

Fig. 1. The Workflow of the proposed deep segmentation framework (SCGNN-3DBUNet), which includes the 3DBUNet, the graph module(SCGNN). First, the 3DBUNet extracts the deep features for the semantic initialization of the graph nodes. Then the graph module is used to construct the graph with weighted RAG. Finally, the GNN module combines the features and the spatial relationships in the graph to perform the image segmentation

This network structure is named SCGNN-3DBUNet, whose main workings consists of two phases. In the first phase, a modified U-Net architecture is set up so it can effectively process the multi-modal MRI images as input. A 3DBUNet is then presented as an extension of U-Net with batch normalization for biomedical image segmentation. During the second phase, a Graph pooling GNN is used to combine the spatial relationships and features between nodes to divide an image into regions and perform the segmentation. The SCGNN model is used to learn, combine features, and divide an image into homogenous regions, as shown in Fig. 1.

3.1 Feature Extraction via 3DBUNet

In contrast to traditional segmentation methods, where hand crafted features are fed into the segmentation algorithm, a U-Net automatically learns representative complex features directly from the data itself. We recall that U-Net is a widely used method for biomedical 2D image segmentation, which has an encoder-decoder architecture with skip connections. It uses skip connection to include the high-resolution feature maps in the encoding path to include more fine-grained information.

While the standard U-Net is an entirely 2D architecture, 3DBUNet extends this architecture to process 3D MRI volumes. The 3DUNet proposed in this work takes 3D volumes as input and processes them with corresponding 3D operations: 3D convolutions, 3D max pooling, and 3D up-convolutional layers (See Fig. 2). Because different tumor subregions are more visible in MRI Images of different modalities, three different-modal MRI images are jointly used in our proposed pipeline, including T1CE, T2, and FLAIR.

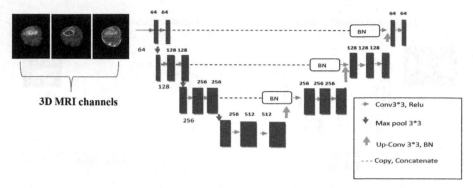

Fig. 2. 3DBUNet with Batch Normalization(BN) in the skip connections.

Note that in order to avoid bottlenecks in the network architecture, a doubling of the number of channels before maximum pooling and using batch normalization [8] before each ReLU are performed. The 3DBUNet can be divided into an encoder-decoder path or contracting-expansive path equivalently. Figure 2 shows an overview of the proposed 3DBUNet. These steps are further explained next.

Encoder Path: In the encoder path, each layer contains two 3×3 convolutions, where each followed by a rectified linear unit (ReLu) and a batch normalization. Then a 3×3 max pooling operation is applied to reduce the spatial dimensions. At each downsampling step, we double the number of feature channels, while we cut in half the spatial dimensions.

Decoder Path: In the decoder path every step consists of an upsampling of the feature map followed by a 3×3 transpose convolution, which halves the number of feature channels. Each transpose convolution is followed by a ReLU and batch normalization. A concatenation with the corresponding feature map from the contracting path, and usually a 3×3 convolutional is used.

Batch Normalization (BN): The BN is a fundamental unit in modern deep networks. The BN layer is typically placed after the activation layer, producing normalized activation maps by subtracting the mean and dividing by the standard deviation for each training batch. Including these batch normalization layers as a regulator for the network, speeds up the training process [8].

The extension of U-Net (3DBUNet) is transformed to a feature extraction network and then used to provide the initial shape boundary to build a segmentation graph. The 3DBUNet is trained to extract the high-level features to initialize the graph nodes, then the SCGNN combines the extracted features and spatial relationships between nodes to perform the ultimate segmentation stage.

3.2 Graph Module

Combined with the extension of U-Net (3DBUNet), the spectral clustering via GNN (SCGNN) framework allows the reformulation of the segmentation problem in the form of a graph-based minimization problem. The GNN captures the dependence of graphs via message passing (MP) between the nodes of the graphs and therefore would have high level performance in the segmentation tasks.

Initial Segmentation and Weighted RAG. Once the feature extraction procedure is completed, a region adjacency graph (RAG) [17], using as nodes the regions generated by an initial segmentation, is activated. The input images are transformed into region adjacency graphs (RAGs) in which regions are superpixels and edges connect neighboring superpixels [17]. Superpixels group similar pixels to create meaningful regions while reducing the number of primitives for subsequent algorithms and processing steps [18]. These properties have made superpixel algorithms highly attracted since their appearance in 2003[18].

In our work, we use the SLIC algorithm [19], to reduce the number of nodes in the graph. In fact, each superpixel is treated as a graph node instead of the pixel in the input image; therefore, the amount of graph nodes can be significantly reduced, and the computational efficiency can be improved. The connectivity of pixel neighborhoods is represented by an adjacency matrix describing the connectivity between pixels. This pixel connectivity of an image in a graph is an important step in our segmentation process.

The GNN Module (SCGNN). Once the conversion of images into graph structures is completed, the GNN is used to classify the nodes of these graphs and produce the required segmentation image.

We recall that a graph G is defined by its adjacency matrix $A \in R^{N \times N}$ and the node features $X \in R^{N \times N}$ where $|V| = N$..

One of the main feature concepts of CNNs is pooling, which is a form of non-linear down-sampling. Pooling helps GNNs to keeps model complexity under control by limiting the size of the intermediate features and discarding information that is superfluous. In fact, obtaining an accurate representation for a graph requires a pooling function that maps a set of node representations into a compact form.

GNNs are used in this work to consolidate the graph structure and feature details to pursue better presentations of graphs with integration and feature distribution. Due to its persuading execution and high interpretation, GNN have been adopted in this model. GNNs are particularly essential since there is so much information that can be expressed also as graphs. Graph pooling is a crucial operation that allows a GNN to generate more coarser representations of the input graphs, by discard redundant information and summarizing local components.

Spectral Clustering with GNN(SCGNN). Spectral clustering (SC) is a well-established technique used to find strongly connected "communities" on a graph. However, the eigen decomposition of the Laplacian is long, computationally expensive. Therefore, pooling methods based on SC must perform a new optimization for each new sample. The SC method is used in GNNs to implement pooling operations that aggregate nodes belonging to the same cluster [6]. There are several pooling strategies for GNNs, however, they lagged the design of newer and more effective MP operations [20], such as graph convolutions [21].

The GNN-based implementation we adopted, is termed as SCGNN, is differentiable and does not require the costly spectral decomposition of the Laplacian. For each node, our method learns a soft cluster assignment (CA) vector that depends on the node features and on the connectivity structure of the graph.

We base our SCGNN architecture on a smooth and simple MP operation commonly used for all GNNs that fuses the features of each node with its first-order neighbors. We adopted the implementation of MP which does not need modifying the graph by adding self-loops [21] yet accounting for the initial node features through a skip connection. The output of this MP layer is defined as follow:

$$\tilde{X} = \mathrm{MP}\left(X, \tilde{A}\right) = \mathrm{RELU}\left(\tilde{A}\, X\Theta_m + X\Theta_s\right) \tag{1}$$

where Θ_m and Θ_s are trainable parameters

Moreover, the SCGNN was further generalized to the MP scheme where the models are distinguished by choice of the aggregate and combined functions. Nodes send their messages, state, and features to the neighboring nodes along with the edges. The SCGNN is based on computing the cluster assignments between node features strongly connected which have similar features. This later reduces the issue and risk of finding a degenerate solution.

The layer of the SCGNN algorithm is given by:

$$m_i^{(k)} = aggregate^{(k)}(\{h_j^{(k-1)} : j \in N(i)\}) \tag{2}$$

$$h_i^{(k)} = combine^{(k)}(h_i^{(k-1)}, m_i^{(k)}) \tag{3}$$

where $m_i^{(k)}$ and $h_i^{(k)}$ represents respectively the vector of (N(i)) and (i) at the kth layer, and (N(i) indicates the i-th neighbor.

At the core of SCGNN, the cluster assignments (CA) $\in R^{N \times k}$ computed by means of a multi-layer perceptron (MLP) [22], which maps each node feature x_i into the i-th row of CA; In fact, nodes with similar features will likely belong to the same cluster because they will be "classified" similarly by the MLP (see in Fig. 3):

$$CA = \mathrm{MLP}(\mathrm{SCGNN}(\tilde{A}), X) \in R^{N \times k} \tag{4}$$

Finally, we sought in this study to explicitly account for the connectivity of the graph to pool it. For that, we use a loss called **orthogonality loss** to train the MLP. In practice, this loss encourages the MLP to "make a decision" about which nodes belong to which clusters.

Orthogonality Loss: it is used to find clusters that are orthogonal between each other.

$$\text{The Orthogonality loss}: L_{or} = \left\| \frac{S^T S}{\|S^T S\|_F} - \frac{I^K}{\sqrt{K}} \right\|_F \tag{5}$$

where $\|\cdot\|_F$ represents the Frobenius norm.

The SCGNN algorithm has been fitting to perform pooling operations in GNNs which learns feature representation for various nodes employing neighborhood aggregation schemes.

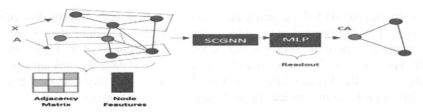

Fig. 3. A SCGNN layer followed by one single layer MLP to calculate the cluster assignments (CA). First, the layer computes the cluster assignment matrix CA by applying a softmax MLP to the node features. The actual pooling step is simply implemented as a simple multiplication of CA with A and X.

4 Pre-processing and Image Segmentation Results

In this section, we present the main results of image segmentation using the described approach. We first address datasets pre-processing then followed by the various results attained in our study.

4.1 Datasets Pre-processing: BraTS Annotations and Structures

Multimodal Brain Tumor Segmentation Challenge (BraTS) is the largest and publicly available dataset, which focuses on segmenting the brain tumors, namely Gliomas, from multi-MRI modalities. All the imaging datasets have been segmented manually, by one to four raters, following the same annotation protocol, and their ground truth annotations were approved by experienced neuroradiologists. The tumor sub-regions considered for evaluation are:

- the "active tumor" (AT),
- the gross tumor, also known as the "tumor core" (TC), and
- the complete tumor extent also referred to as the "whole tumor" (WT)

The BraTS 2012–2016 dataset defined four tumor subregions, delineating the NCR, ED, AT, and NET [23].

Label 1: NCR. Label 2: ED. Label 3: NET. Label 4: AT.

We state that the NET ('Label 3') can be overestimated by some annotators on one hand, and sometimes there is insufficient evidence in the image data for this sub-region on the other hand. Moreover, this region presents numerous artifacts, which could result in substantially various annotations labels generated by the annotators in multiple institutions.

BraTS 2017-Present dataset contains three tumor sub-regions in order to handle the problem introduced in BraTS 2016 by eliminating the NET label ("Label 3") [23].

WT: Segmenting the whole tumor extent (present in T2-FLAIR: Union of all labels).

TC: Segmenting the core tumor outline (visible in T2: Union of labels 1 and 4).

AT: Segmenting the active tumor regions.

In our study, we utilized the BraTS 2020 dataset, which contains a total of 369 training cases and there are 125 cases in the validation dataset [24]. In fact, BraTS

2020 contains four 3D MRI sequence modalities for each patient. It can be divided into subsets of manual segmentation including tumor sub-regions. Example of each sequence and tumor sub-regions are shown in Fig. 4. We used 3 channels: Flair, T1CE, and T2, which represent a single volume. In addition, we combined three-channel input images employing FLAIR, T2, and T1CE into a single volume. This step could increase the visibility of the brain tumors leading to extract more robust features.

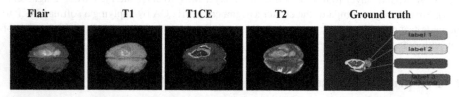

Fig. 4. From left to right: sequence slices from a patient: FLAIR, T1, T1CE, T2 and the ground truth. Images are generated using BraTS 2020 data [24].

We first train our model on the training set, and then we use the testing set to evaluate the accuracy of the resulting model. Many studies show that the best results are obtained if we use 20–30% of the data for testing, and the remaining 70–80% of the data for training. In this work, for data training and testing, we have randomly split the images into 80% training and 20% for validation. For the evaluation, we had three classes used: AT, TC and WT.

Since the MRI data has multi-modalities, the image contrast in these modalities are not the same, which may result in gradient disappearance presented in the training phase. The Standardization technique can reduce the generation of gradient disappearance; therefore, we use the mix-max method to normalize the images of each modality.

After standardization, images were cropped to a variable size employing the smallest bounding box that contains the whole brain sub image. Afterward, each image is randomly re-cropped to a fixed patch having a size of $128 \times 128 \times 128$. This technique allowed to remove the useless background that was introduced in the original volume and have the complete focus the brain tumor.

4.2 Experimental Results

We present in this section the segmentation results obtained by our SCGNN-3DBUNet architecture using a qualitative and a quantitative evaluation. The main performance metrics used in evaluating the performance of SCGNN-3DBUNet on the datasets are next explained. We evaluate the quality of the assignments of the CA found by the proposed tumor segmentation architecture. We consider the Dice as a qualitative evaluation, which is the measurement of overlap between automatic and ground-truth segmentation. The specificity and sensitivity are used for quantitative evaluation to examine the behavior and generalizability of data to fit the model.

$$\text{Dice} = \frac{2TP}{FN + FP + TP}; \quad \text{Sensitivity} := \frac{TP}{TP + FN}; \quad \text{Specificity} = \frac{TN}{TN + FP} \quad (6)$$

where TP, FP, FN, and TN are the number of true positive, false positive, false negative, and true negatives respectively.

Experimental Setup. The experimental environment is on Tensorflow with GPU, NVIDIA TITAN RTX, 64-bit Windows 10. The approximate time for training 200 epochs is about 9 h. The Adam optimization algorithm was used to train the network with a learning rate of 0.0001 on the BraTS data set [25].

We tested the effectiveness of our proposed method on the BraTS 2020 corpus and compared it with the state-of-the-arts methods [26]. Some segmentation and comparison results between our method and the standard U-Net on the BraTS 2020 datasets are shown in Fig. 5.

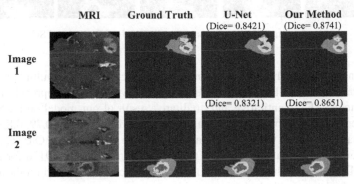

Fig. 5. Sample segmentation results on 2 images from our test split. We note that 3DBUNet significantly performs better than U-Net.

Given an MRI image, a feature extraction procedure using 3DBUNet is performed, followed the transformation of a region adjacency graph using as nodes the regions generated by an over-segmentation (Slic) procedure then cluster the nodes of the RAG graph with the SCGNN module. Predictions of SCGNN-3DBUNet have been shown in Fig. 6.

The spectral clustering technique (SC) applied in this example is the normalized cut based on [11]. For SCGNN-3DBUNet, node features represent total and average color in each over-segmented area. We assign the number of determined clusters to K = 4. The results in Fig. 6 show that SCGNN-3DBUNet yields precise segmentation results.

Moreover, The SC aggregates the wrong regions and find too many segments. While the SC technique requires computing the spectral decomposition for every new sample, here the cluster assignments are computed by a neural network that learns a mapping from the nodes features space to the clusters assignment space. By minimizing the orthogonality loss, the SCGNN learns to find optimum clusters on any given graph and aggregates the clusters to reduce the graph's size. This allows our pooling results to be aggregated as the final pooled graph.

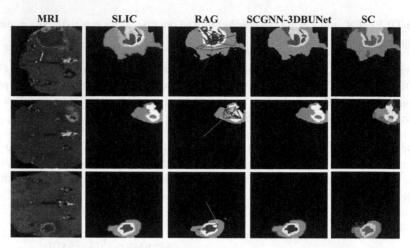

Fig. 6. Image segmentation using SCGNN-3DBUNet and SC

To quantitatively analyze the segmentation accuracy, we apply multiple metrics. As a part of BraTS 2020 challenge, we implemented and evaluated our approach with online validation tools. The quantitative and qualitative result of our model on the validation dataset is provided in Table 1. Our solution has achieved a Dice of 0.79, 0.89 and 0.84 for the enhancing tumor, whole tumor, and tumor core, respectively. Our segmentation result has also obtained a specificity of 0.9927 and sensitivity of 0.9178 for the whole tumor in MRI images. The average results of the indicators obtained on the validation dataset set are shown in Table 1.

Table 1. The average results of the indicators obtained on the validation set

Datasets	Dice (ET)	Dice (WT)	Dice (TC)	Sensitivity (WT)	Specificity (WT)
BraTS 2020	0.79	0.89	0.78	0.91	0.99

To demonstrate the performance of our approach, we compare the experimental results with other participating methods in the BraTS 2020 Challenge. We maintain the index results of other participated on the website of the challenge [26].

Table 2 illustrates the comparison results, from which we can observe comparable results compared to other state-of-the-art methods. The best performance is indicated in bold text in Table 2.

We also evaluate the performance of our network using two different learning rates, as shown in Fig. 7. Our architecture achieves the best performance where the learning rate equal to 0.0001.

Table 2. The comparison of teams participating in the BraTS 2020 challenge

Team	Datasets	Dice (ET)	Dice (WT)	Dice (TC)
Proposed	BraTS 2020	**0.79**	**0.89**	**0.78**
Unet3d	BraTS 2020	0.70	0.84	0.72
LMB	BraTS 2020	0.72	0.82	0.76
MARS	BraTS 2020	0.76	0.87	0.75

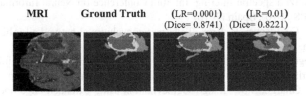

MRI   **Ground Truth**   (LR=0.0001)   (LR=0.01)
(Dice= 0.8741) (Dice= 0.8221)

Fig. 7. Image segmentation using CSGNN-3DUNet with different learning rate

The experimental results demonstrate that the developed architecture in this study has good robustness. We observe that the proposed architecture has also a better segmentation impact on the WT area of brain tumors. In addition, the Dice score of the ET, WT and TC region validation set of our method is significantly better than the results found by other team in the BraTS 2020. Our method surpasses the Unet3d, the LBM and MARS in multimodal MRI for the same datasets.

5   Conclusion

A new automatic architecture has been proposed in this paper for 3D MRI brain tumor segmentation. The performance of the proposed hybrid algorithm (SCGNN-3DBUNet) was evaluated employing an online verification check-tool on the BraTS 2020 challenge website Data base. The obtained results demonstrate high-quality segmentation results of our SCGNN-3DBUNet architecture, where the average Dice is as high as 89.2%. The experimental results illustrate the robustness and effectiveness of our proposed model as well. SCGNN3DBUNet's robustness is demonstrated during test results to perform significantly better than the original U-Net architecture and among other methods on brain tumor segmentation. Overall, the developed deep learning architecture was relatively effective in segmenting Gliomas in multimodal images. Additionally, SCGNN-3DBUNet has a faster inference speed on test sub-dataset. The developed hybrid method can be applicable to other medical image processing such as skin lesions detection, lung cancer detection, and other numerous biomedical applications.

References

1. Ravi, D., et al.: Deep learning for health informatics. IEEE J. Biomed. Health Inform. **21**, 4–21 (2017)

2. Kwon, J.M., Lee, Y., Lee, Y., Lee, S., Park, J.: An algorithm based on deep learning for predicting in-hospital cardiac arrest. J. Am. Heart Assoc. **7**(13), e008678 (2018)
3. Shin, H.C., et al.: Deep convolutional neural networks for computer-aided detection: CNN architectures, dataset characteristics and transfer learning. IEEE TMI **35**, 1285–1298 (2016)
4. Zhang, L., Ren, Z.: Comparison of CT and MRI images for the prediction of soft-tissue sarcoma grading and lung metastasis via a convolutional neural networks model. J. Clin. Radiol. **75**, 64–69 (2020)
5. Liu, X., Song, L., Liu, S., Zhang, Y.: A review of deep-learning-based medical image segmentation methods. J. Sustain. **2021**(13), 1–21 (2021)
6. Defferrard, M., Bresson, X., Vandergheynst, P. Convolutional neural networks on graphs with fast localized spectral filtering. In: 30th Conference on Neural Information Processing Systems (NIPS 2016), Spain (2016)
7. Ronneberger, O., Fischer, P., Brox, T.: U-net: convolutional networks for biomedical image segmentation. Int. Conf. MICCA **I**, 234–241 (2015)
8. Ioffe, S., Szegedy, C.: Batch normalization: accelerating deep network training by reducing internal covariate shift. In: International conference on machine learning, pp. 448–456 (2015)
9. Kekre, H.B., Gharge, S.M.: Image segmevntation using extended edge operator for mammography images. IJCSE **2**, 1086–1091 (2010)
10. Falcao, A.X., Udupa, J.K.: A 3D generalization of user-steered live-wire segmentation. J. Med. Image Anal. **4**, 389–402 (2000)
11. Jianbo, S., Malik, J.: Normalized cuts and image segmentation. IEEE Trans. Pattern Anal. Mach. Intell. **22**(8), 888–905 (2000)
12. Moftah, H., Azar, A., Al-Shammari, E., Ghali, N., Hassanien, A., Shoman, M.: Adaptive k-means clustering algorithm for MR breast image segmentation. Neural Comput. Appl. **24**(7–8), 1917–1928 (2013)
13. Gammoudi, I., Mahjoub, M.A.: Brain tumor segmentation using community detection algorithm. In: International Conference on Cyberworlds (CW), pp. 1–7 (2021)
14. Kamnitsas, K., et al.: Efficient multi-scale 3D CNN with fully connected CRF for accurate brain lesion segmentation. J. Med. Image Anal. **36**, 61–78 (2017)
15. Long, J., Shelhamer, E., Darrell, T.: Fully convolutional networks for semantic segmentation. In: IEEE Conference on Computer Vision and Pattern Recognition, pp. 3431–3440 (2015)
16. Alom, M.Z., Hasan, M., Yakopcic, C., Taha, T.M., Asari, V.K.: Recurrent residual convolutional neural network based on u-net (r2u-net) for medical image segmentation. J. Med. Imaging 1–12 (2018)
17. Tremeau, A., Colantoni, P.: Regions adjacency graph applied to color image segmentation. IEEE Trans. Image Process. **9**, 1–10 (2000)
18. Stutz, D., Hermans, A., Leibe, B.: Superpixels: an evaluation of the state-of-the-art. J. Comput. Vision Image Underst. **166**, 1–27 (2018)
19. Radhakrishna, A., Appu, S., Kevin, S., Aurelien, L., Pascal, F., Sabine, S.: SLIC superpixels compared to stateof-the-art superpixel methods. IEEE Trans. Pattern Anal. Mach. Intell. **34**, 2274–2282 (2012)
20. Gilmer, J., Schoenholz, S.S., Riley, P.F., Vinyals, O., Dahl, G.E.: Neural message passing for quantum chemistry, pp. 1–14 (2017)
21. Kipf, T.N., Welling, M.: Semi-supervised classification with graph convolutional networks. Int. Conf. Learn. Represent. 1–14 (2017)
22. Kurt, H.: Approximation capabilities of multilayer feedforward networks. J. Neural Networks **2**, 251–257 (1991)
23. Bakas, S., et al.: Identifying the best machine learning algorithms for brain tumor segmentation, progression assessment, and overall survival prediction in the BRATS challenge (2018)

24. https://www.med.upenn.edu/cbica/brats2020/data.html
25. Kingma, D.P., Ba, J.: Adam: a method for stochastic optimization. In: ICLR, pp. 1–15 (2017)
26. https://www.cbica.upenn.edu/BraTS20/lboardValidation.html

Right Ventricle Segmentation in Cardiac MR Images Using Convolutional Neural Network Architecture

Sana Slama[1]($\boxtimes$), Ramzi Mahmoudi[1], Badii Hmida[2], Mézri Maatouk[2], and Mohamed Hedi Bedoui[1]

[1] Faculty of Medicine of Monastir, Laboratory TIM-LR12ES06, University of Monastir, 5019 Monastir, Tunisia
sanaslama95@gmail.com

[2] Radiology Service- UR12SP40, CHU Fattouma Bourguiba, 5019 Monastir, Tunisia

Abstract. Artificial intelligence approaches have vastly improved the health care field in several tasks such as image processing and information extraction. These techniques assist experts to predict and diagnose the risk of certain diseases earlier and more efficiently, such as cardiovascular disease through the evaluation of cardiac function. This paper presents a segmented private dataset for Right Ventricle, as well as associated the manual annotation method. In addition, we propose an adapted U-Net architecture for automatic RV contours segmentation. This approach ensures high accuracy while minimizing the manual evaluation time for this cavity.

Keywords: RV segmentation · cMRI short-axis · U-Net · DenseNet

1 Introduction

The heart is a small organ. It represents a sign of life for humans. Its dysfunction represents the first cause of death according to the "World Health Organization". Previously, the right ventricular (RV) was considered the in-essential cardiac chamber. Although, in recent years, the significance of the right ventricle is increasingly recognized for pulmonary circulation and cardiac function [1]. Therefore, RV segmentation is an essential step for cardiovascular disease diagnosis. As well manual segmentation is time-consuming and depends on the expert's observation due to its complex and variable shape. In contrast, the results provided by fully convolutional encoder-decoder architecture are highly encouraging [2]. Several imaging modalities are available for the evaluation of cardiac function [3]. Magnetic resonance imaging (MRI) is a gold standard technique for the visualization and diagnosis of RV disease using a short-axis view. An important advantage of MRI is that the patient is not exposed to radiation through the use of a magnetic field produced by a magnet and radiofrequency waves.

In this paper, we propose a right ventricular segmentation algorithm using a private base of MRI scans. Our model presents a modified U-Net architecture to obtain fewer parameters while ensuring more accuracy.

C. Bădică et al. (Eds.): ICCCI 2022, CCIS 1653, pp. 352–359, 2022.
https://doi.org/10.1007/978-3-031-16210-7_29

In the following: Sect. 2 proposes a brief overview of the existing study. The architecture and dataset adopted are detailed in the next section. Section 4 includes the experimental results provided. Finally, Sect. 5 presents the conclusion and future work.

2 State of the Art

Recently, the work on RV segmentation has become more and more varied and developed. A number of researchers have chosen to use traditional segmentation algorithms.

In 2014, the use of the ML Random Forest algorithm for the segmentation of the right ventricle was introduced [4]. A right ventricle segmentation approach based on a five-layer deep convolutional neural network (CNN) is developed by Luo et al. [5]. For proper segmentation and better extraction of the pixel mask, a region of interest (ROI) localization task is performed. This approach is trained and evaluated using the basis offered by the MICCAI 2012 challenge. 16 patients were used for training and 32 patients for the resulting evaluation. Using DM and HD, including clinical parameters, we notice a low correlation obtained for systolic volume versus epicardium. Therefore, it can be concluded that the segmentation method presented in this article shows that the segmentation process of the endocardium is more efficient than in the epicardium.

"Ronneberger et al." developed an alternative architecture to the FCN architecture called "U-Net" which is mainly developed for segmentation in biomedical imaging [6]. It is composed of two main branches "encoder" or "contraction path" and "decoder" or "expansion path". This U-Net is characterized by a large number of filters. A modified U-Net approach is proposed by Nagaraj V. et al. in 2021 for automatic RV segmentation. The dataset used for training the model is proposed by the MICCAI'12 challenge. It consists of 48 patients (16 for training, 16 for the first test set, and 16 for the second test set). 243 slices of size 216×256 pixels are retrieved after manual segmentation by the doctor of the treatment set. The test sets are unlabeled and consist of 514 images. The architecture of this model is slightly rectified compared to the U-Net architecture. This approach uses only 3 layers for each branch and one layer at the bottom. Dice Metric and Jaccardindex are the two metrics used for the evaluation of this network. The proposed model gives an important accuracy compared to the manual segmenta-tion performed by the expert.

A new challenge "Multi-Disease, Multi-View & Multi-Center Right Ventricular Segmentation in Cardiac MRI (M&Ms-2)" is launched by "MICCAI2021" for the segmentation of the various cardiac chambers, specifically for the RV [7]. The proposed dataset contains 160 annotated subjects for model training, 40 unannotated patients for the validation set, and 160 subjects for testing.

Using these data, M. Saber et al. applied the modified U-Net model. The original resolution of the images is kept. The proposed preprocessing is 15° spatial rotation, normalization, and cropping to make the images square. The model learning time is about 8h using a GTX 1080 TI GPU. DC and HD are applied to evaluate this approach. The results provided are very encouraging.

In 2016, "Huang et al." developed the DenseNet approach [9]. This architecture is defined by dense blocks. Each layer in a dense block receives feature maps from all previous layers and passes its output to all subsequent layers. The feature maps received from other layers are merged by concatenation. Due to the dense connections, the model requires fewer layers because it doesn't need to learn from duplicate maps, allowing the reuse of collective knowledge. The feature dimensions remain the same in a dense block. To prevent the network to become too large, a 1x1 convolutional bottleneck layer to reduce the number of feature maps before the costly 3x3 convolution is used.

Zhao et al. proposed a Dilated-DenseNet architecture for VR segmentation. This method combines the DenseNet architecture with dilated convolution. An increase to the receiver field of the convolution kernel is guaranteed by the dilated convolution while keeping the number of parameters unchanged. For the test set, the DC metric gives a value of 0.90. Therefore, the suggested method is an important efficiency for VR segmentation [8].

3   Methodology

3.1   DataSet

Until now, the ground truth of public RV sets is still poorly available to assist us in solving variable shape problems. During RV segmentation learning, we need large labeled images, while the available datasets are still limited, as well as it requires several processing steps and data augmentation to become usable. That's why we propose a private database in collaboration with the hospital Fattouma Bourguiba Monastir, Tunis. The subjects studied were 30% female and 70% male and ranged in age from 5 to 8 years.

Currently, the labeled data are ready. For the evaluation of our model, we randomly divide the data set into 80% for training, 10% for validation, and 10% for testing. This proposal provides 5176 images for the train, 647 slices for the test and validation sets.

To validate our proposed methods, we used another database "Multi-Disease, Multi-View & Multi-Center Right Ventricular Segmentation in Cardiac MRI (M&Ms-2)" provided by "MICCAI2021" challenge. The public database used consists of 160 patients with 3554 slices. The annotation of the slices integrates RV, LV, and LV myocardium. In addition, we randomly split our data into 80% for training, 10% for validation and 10% for testing. 355 slices are selected for each test and validation set. 2844 images are left for the training set.

3.2   Preprocessing

Due to the large variety of data, some preprocessing techniques are applied. Firstly, for private data sets, all the images are cropped to obtain a square image. Then, a resizing step to 384*384 is performed. Moreover, we apply a normalization technique to solve the problem of large pixel intensity plagiarism. Before the learning process, a Contrast Limited Adaptive Histogram Equalization (CLAHE) is applied to ensure a better contrast of the images.

For the M&M dataset, we start the preprocessing task by applying a binarization algorithm to remove the ground truth of LV and myocardium. Subsequently, we cropped all slices and also we resized them to 256*256. Lastly, we have realized the CLAHE method.

3.3 Data Augmentation

The private dataset is considerably large, as it contains healthy patients and patients with various cardiovascular diseases. For this reason, the data augmentation technique is not employed. However, the number of annotated slices for the public dataset is limited. To avoid overfitting during learning process of the Convolutional Neural Network, we implement translations, random rotations, zooms, and horizontal and vertical Random Flip. After data augmentation process, 5688 slices are used to train our model.

3.4 Inter-Expert Similarity

The assessment of the RV is a difficult task because of its complex and variable shape. Even the segmentation of the same patient by two different experts may be inconsistent. Therefore, we propose an inter-expert comparative study for a pathological patient and a healthy volunteer from our private dataset. This task is guided by three different experts from our original university hospital. Two metrics are used for the inter-expert similarity evaluation. The first metric provides an overlap measure named "Dice coefficient" which quantifies the similarity between two binary regions. The results are between 0 and 1. Values near 1 are the best [10], presented by formula 1. In addition, the second expression, the MSE (mean squared error), is used to measure the variability. This evaluation metric depends on the predicted variable. The evaluation results vary between 0 and 1. The value around 0 is the most favorable, illustrated by Eq. 2.

$$DC = \frac{2|A \cap B|}{|A| + |B|} \tag{1}$$

$$MSE(U, V) = \frac{1}{n} * \sum_{i=1}^{n} (U_i - V_i)^2 \tag{2}$$

The table below includes a comparison of the manual segmentation results between our experts. The significant variation between the results is noticeable. The assessment metrics show that the variance is higher for the healthy patient than for the pathological patient. For example, the average MSE for a healthy patient is equal to 0.002 while for a pathological patient is equal to 0.012. Also, the dice value varies between 0.82 and 0.86 for the pathological patient. However, between 0.87 and 0.90 for the healthy patient (Table 1).

Table 1. DC and MSE metrics for inter-expert similarity assessment.

Metrics	Pathological patient		Healthy patient	
Expert	DC	MSE	DC	MSE
Exp1/ Exp2	0.86	0.003	0.89	0.002
Exp1/ Exp3	0.85	0.013	0.87	0.003
Exp2/ Exp3	0.82	0.021	0.90	0.002
Average	0.84	0.012	0.89	0.002

3.5 Algorithm

In this section, we suggested an extended U-Net model in order to reduce the number of parameters while guaranteeing better accuracy. We illustrate the adopted U-Net model in Fig. 1.

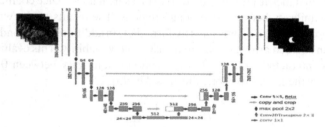

Fig. 1. Architecture of our modified U-Net model

As presented in Fig. 1, our modified U-Net architecture consists of 4 encoder blocks, one base block, and 4 decoder blocks [6]. Each encoder block consists of a convolution with a 5 × 5 kernel, a BatchNormalization layer, and the ReLu activation function. This block is repeated two times. The number of filters is reduced from 64 to 32 for the first encoder block. For each encoder block, the number of filters is duplicated by reducing the image size to half using maxPooling convolution. Then the base block consists of only two conv2D blocks, a BatchNormalization and the ReLu function. For the decoder blocks, we applied a Conv2DTranspose layer with a stride of 2, weights of 1, and kernel size equal to 2. This convolution is performed for oversampling. Also for multiplying the kernel with the pixel values of the image based on the stride in order to double the number of features. The size of the output image depends to the stride size. A very important concatenation step specific only to the U-Net model to make the semantic segmentation applicable. The encoder output convolution block is the one that will be concatenated with the output of the decoder block in order to obtain the context of the different levels. Finally, the block consisting of conv2D, BatchNormalization, and the ReLu function is repeated twice. After several iterations, the best hyper-parameters for learning our model are set to an Adam optimizer with a Learning Rate of 0.001 using an automatic reduction for the Learning Rate of a constant factor of 0.5 to 1e-7 for all epochs.

4 Result

To evaluate applied architectures, we adopted the Keras library and the Tensorflow back-end which are commonly used for Deep Learning. Nvidia GeForce RTX 3090 Graphics Processing Unit (GPU) with 24GB memory is used for powerful data computation acceleration. Python environment is used on Windows 11th generation with 32Gb of RAM with the Intel® core i9 processor. As evaluation metrics, we applied the same techniques used for manual segmentation. As well as the accuracy and precision metrics. Equations 3 and 4 were employed for the measurement of these metrics. Table 2 shows test results obtained for the 3 models using private and public datasets.

$$Accuracy = \frac{TN + TP}{FN + TN + FP + TP} \tag{3}$$

$$Precision = \frac{TP}{FP + TP} \tag{4}$$

Table 2. Various metrics to evaluate models

Models	Private dataset			Public dataset		
	DM	MSE	Acc	DM	MSE	Acc
U-Net 2015	0.892	0.0021	0.995	0.886	0.0022	0.994
DenseNet	0.896	0.0018	0.996	0.891	0.0020	0.995
Our model	0.903	0.0017	0.996	0.894	0.0019	0.995

The same preprocessing, batchSize, number of epochs, as well as the same hyper-parameters, loss function, and Learning Rate, were used to train all models. According to the table above, all the evaluation metrics used show that the best results are given by our model.

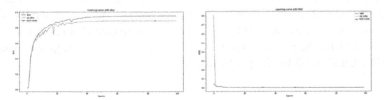

Fig. 2. The history graph of our proposed model based on DC and MSE metrics to the train ing and validation sets using the private dataset

Using our modified U-Net model, the values of DM, and MSE metrics are respectively 0.903, 0.0017 for the private dataset, and 0.894, 0.0019 for the public dataset. Figures 2 and 3 displays the DC and MSE graphs of our model for the evaluation and

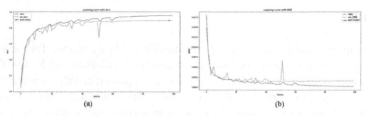

(a)   (b)

Fig. 3. The history graph of our proposed model based on DC and MSE metrics to the training and validation sets using the public dataset

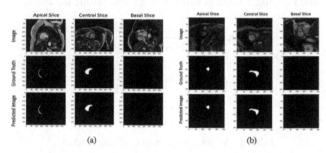

(a)   (b)

Fig. 4. Example of various cuts segmentation using our modified U-NET model using (a) private dataset (b) public dataset

validation sets using private and public datasets. We notice a remarkable stability during learning and validation phases of the private dataset compared to the training history of the public dataset. Figure 4 integrates 3 randomly selected slices of the test set with the ground truth and the image predicted by our model using both datasets.

5 Conclusion

In this paper, we propose a simple and efficient adapted U-Net approach for the segmentation of short-axis MRIs of the RV while ensuring the minimization of model complexity. We evaluate our proposed method on a private and public datasets. Experimental results show the efficiency of our model compared to other models. As a result, the RV segmentation assessment metrics DC, MSE, and Accuracy were provided respectively 0.903, 0.0017, and 0996 for the private dataset, as well as, these metrics were given respectively 0.894, 0.0019, and 0.995 for the public dataset.

References

1. Murphy, E., Shelley, B.: The right ventricle—structural and functional importance for anaesthesia and intensive care. BJA education **18**(8), 239 (2018)
2. Adegun, A., Viriri, S.: Fully Convolutional Encoder-Decoder Architecture (FCEDA) for Skin Lesions Segmentation. In: International Conference on Computational Collective Intelligence. Springer, Cham (2019)

3. Boukhris, K., et al.: U-Shaped Densely Connected Convolutions for Left Ventricle Segmentation from CMR Images. In: International Conference on Computer Analysis of Images and Patterns. Springer, Cham (2021)
4. Cabitza, F., Locoro, A., Banfi, G.: Machine learning in orthopedics: a literature review. Frontiers in bioengineering and biotechnology **6**, 75 (2018)
5. Luo, G., et al.: A deep learning network for right ventricle segmentation in short-axis MRI. In: 2016 Computing in Cardiology Conference (CinC). IEEE (2016)
6. Ronneberger, O., Fischer, P., Brox, T.: U-net: Convolutional networks for biomedical image segmentation. In: International Conference on Medical image computing and computer-assisted intervention. Springer, Cham (2015)
7. Campello, V.M., et al.: Multi-centre, multi-vendor and multi-disease cardiac segmentation: the M&Ms challenge. IEEE Transactions on Medical Imaging **40**(12) (2021)
8. Huang, G., et al.: Densely connected convolutional networks. In: Proceedings of the IEEE conference on computer vision and pattern recognition (2017)
9. Xingrong, Z., et al.: Segmentation of right ventricular MR image based on deep neural network: Dilated DenseNet of two level losses. In: 2018 14th IEEE International Conference on Signal Processing (ICSP). IEEE (2018)
10. Shamir, R.R., et al.: Continuous dice coefficient: a method for evaluating probabilistic segmentations. arXiv preprint arXiv:1906.11031 (2019)

Fast Unsupervised Residual Attention GAN for COVID-19 Detection

Najeh Nafti[1,2]([✉]) [ID], Olfa Besbes[3] [ID], Asma Ben Abdallah[2,4] [ID],
and Mohamed Hedi Bedoui[2] [ID]

[1] Sfax University, National Engineering School of Sfax, Sfax, Tunisia
naftinajeh9@gmail.com
[2] Monastir University, Research Laboratory of Technology and Medical Imaging,
Faculty of Medicine of Monastir, Monastir, Tunisia
[3] Sousse University ISITCOM and Research Laboratory COSIM,
SUPCOM Carthage University, Sousse, Tunisia
[4] Monastir University, Higher Institute of Computer Science and Mathematics
of Monastir, Monastir, Tunisia

Abstract. Recently, deep unsupervised learning methods based on Generative Adversarial Networks (GANs) have shown great potential for detecting anomalies. These last can appear both in global and local areas of an image. Consequently, ignoring these local information may lead to unreliable detection of anomalies. In this paper, we propose a residual GAN-based unsupervised learning approach capable of detecting anomalies at both image and pixel levels. Our method is applied for COVID-19 detection, it is based on the BigGAN model to ensure high-quality generated images, also it adds attention modules to capture spatial and channel-wise features to enhance salient regions and extract more detailed features. The proposed model is composed of three components: a generator, a discriminator, and an encoder. The encoder enables a fast mapping from images to the latent space, which facilitates the evaluation of unseen images. We evaluate the proposed method with by real-world benchmarking datasets and a public COVID-19 dataset and we illustrate the performance improvement at image and pixel levels.

Keywords: Unsupervised learning · Anomaly detection · Residual generative adversarial network · High quality images · Attention mechanism

1 Introduction

Detecting anomalies play a critical role in radiological assessment; it is often the first step in the diagnosis pipeline. It aims at discovering unexpected regions or occurrences in data sets that differ from the normal variation. Anomaly detection has many real-life applications such as credit card fraud detection in finance, radio-frequency anomaly detection in wireless networks, and lesion detection in medical imaging [1].

C. Bădică et al. (Eds.): ICCCI 2022, CCIS 1653, pp. 360–372, 2022.
https://doi.org/10.1007/978-3-031-16210-7_30

The application of deep learning techniques for the detection of anomalies requires large amounts of annotated data to provide better results. However, one of the core challenges in applying these techniques is the limited availability of annotated data, especially in the medical field. The difficulties are related to the fact that annotated databases of unhealthy patients are very hard to find, and data annotation is a hard, long, and expensive process that requires considerable time and effort from experts to correctly annotate a set of data with the right information of lesions. To overcome the necessity of expensive medical labeled data, unsupervised approaches are often used to learn the distribution of normal data, where only normal data is used for training.

Generative Adversarial Networks (GANs) [2] based on unsupervised learning methods have gained a great attraction for anomaly detection. GAN is composed of two sub-models, namely, a generator and a discriminator. The generator is trained to generate new data as realistically as possible to fool the discriminator, while the discriminator is trained to distinguish real data from ones created by the generator. Deep Convolutional Generative Adversarial Network (DCGAN) [3] is an extension of GAN and represents the first deep convolutional GAN model. It is composed of convolution layers without max pooling or fully connected layers. DCGAN uses convolutional stride and transpose convolution for the downsampling and the upsampling. In order to ensure a more stable training, a new type of GAN models is defined called Wasserstein GAN (WGAN) [4] based on the minimization of an approximation of the Earth-Mover's distance (EM).

AnoGAN [5] represents the first GAN-based algorithm for anomaly detection, which is trained only on normal samples and aims to learn a mapping from the latent space representation to the generated images. However, AnoGAN is computationally expensive. In [6] authors introduced a GAN-based anomaly detection method based on the BIGAN [7] architecture that aims to learn a direct mapping from input samples to the latent space during adversarial training. To ensure a fast mapping from the latent space to the image space, the authors of [8] proposed f-AnoGAN, a new fast anomaly detection approach that replaces the iterative algorithm in [5] with an encoder. In [9] authors proposed a new unsupervised anomaly detection method based on the auto-encoding generative adversarial network (α-GAN) framework. Authors of [10] proposed an image level GAN-based anomaly detection network. These GAN-based methods demonstrated the effectiveness of adding an encoder network to the architecture. Authors of [6] showed the importance of the encoder of the ALI [11] and the BiGAN [7] frameworks to ensure a visual representation learning for downstream tasks. In [8], authors illustrated the capacity of the encoder of the f-AnoGAN framework to speed up the anomaly scoring during the test time.

All these approaches are focused on the global information presented by the input image. However, anomaly segmentation requires the network to learn more information from the training data to achieve a better pixel-wise anomaly location [12]. Indeed, these approaches used DCGAN [3] and WGAN [4] style generators that are incapable of producing high-quality images. Recently, some works [9,10,13,14] have used and demonstrated the effectiveness of the attention mechanism in the extraction of relevant information and the suppress of redundancy in the image. The Convolutional Block Attention Module (CBAM) [15] is one of the recent attention mechanisms that shows great potential in extracting the important details of the input image.

In this paper, we introduce a new method for fast anomaly detection at both image and pixel levels. Our architecture is motivated by the state-of-the-art GAN, BigGAN [16] to generate high-quality images, by f-AnoGAN [8] to speed-up the anomaly detection. Indeed, our architecture is based on the attention blocks to focusing on local information. It is composed of three sub-models: a generator, a discriminator, and an encoder. Our contributions are as follows:

- We show that generating high-quality images as well as discriminating powerfully them can significantly improve unsupervised anomaly detection and localization.
- We propose a new unsupervised anomaly detection model based on residual blocks of BigGAN model.
- We show that adding the CBAM attention block improves the anomaly detection.

2   Proposed Method

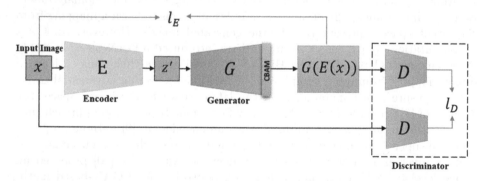

Fig. 1. An overview of the proposed framework.

2.1   Model Overview

Our model is inspired by the f-AnoGAN [8] framework, that is shown in Figure 1. Different from the f-AnoGAN, we built our model based on the BigGAN model instead of WGAN [4] for producing high-quality images. Besides, we change the activation function of the discriminator and the encoder from ReLU to LeakyReLU to handle the sparse gradients problem faced in training generative adversarial networks. Furthermore, we add Instance Normalization (also known as contrast normalization) at the discriminator and the encoder. This normalization process prevents instance-specific mean and covariance shift simplifying the learning process. Finally, we incorporate the CBAM [15] at the generator blocks to capture local information and improve the anomaly detection process.

2.2 Attention Mechanism

The attention mechanism is being one of the main mechanisms used in deep learning models to capture global dependencies and improve the representation capability of the neural network. The Convolutional Block Attention Module (CBAM) [15] is a multi-layer attention that combines two sequential sub-modules called the channel attention module and the spatial attention module, which are applied in a specific order. The channel attention module concentrates on what is meaningful in an input image by providing a weight for each channel and thus enhances or suppresses different channels for different images. As for the spatial attention module, it focuses to locate the region of interest in the image and obtain the weight distribution map for the image.

In our model, we use CBAM because of its capacity to extract main features in both channel and spatial-wise dimensions and to enhance the representation of specific regions without increasing the parameters and computational complexity [13]. Indeed, we add CBAM into the last layers of the generator.

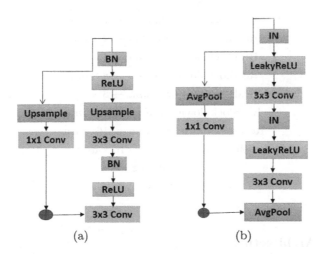

(a)   (b)

Fig. 2. An overview of the model architecture residual blocks. (a) shows the generator's residual block.(b) shows the residual block for the discriminator and the encoder.

Table 1. Generator, Discriminator and Encoder Architectures.

(a) Generator

$z \in R^{128} \sim N(0, I)$
Linear $128 \rightarrow 4 \times 4 \times 16 \times dim$
ResBlock up $16 \times dim \rightarrow 16 \times dim$
ResBlock up $16 \times dim \rightarrow 8 \times dim$
ResBlock up $8 \times dim \rightarrow 8 \times dim$
ResBlock up $8 \times dim \rightarrow 4 \times dim$
ResBlock up $4 \times dim \rightarrow 2 \times dim$
CBAM Attention block $(2 \times dim)$
ResBlock up $2 \times dim \rightarrow 1 \times dim$
CBAM Attention block $(1 \times dim)$
BN, ReLU, 3×3 Conv $dim \rightarrow 1$
Tanh

(b) Discriminator

Image $x \in R^{256 \times 256 \times 1}$
ResBlock down channel $\rightarrow 1 \times dim$
ResBlock down $1 \times dim \rightarrow 2 \times dim$
ResBlock down $2 \times dim \rightarrow 4 \times dim$
ResBlock down $4 \times dim \rightarrow 8 \times dim$
ResBlock down $8 \times dim \rightarrow 8 \times dim$
ResBlock down $8 \times dim \rightarrow 16 \times dim$
ResBlock down $16 \times dim \rightarrow 16 \times dim$
ResBlock $16 \times dim \rightarrow 16 \times dim$
LeakyReLU, Global sum pooling
Linear $\rightarrow 1$

(c) Encoder

Image $x \in R^{256 \times 256 \times 1}$
ResBlock down channel $\rightarrow 1 \times dim$
ResBlock down $1 \times dim \rightarrow 2 \times dim$
ResBlock down $2 \times dim \rightarrow 4 \times dim$
ResBlock down $4 \times dim \rightarrow 8 \times dim$
ResBlock down $8 \times dim \rightarrow 8 \times dim$
ResBlock down $8 \times dim \rightarrow 16 \times dim$
ResBlock down $16 \times dim \rightarrow 16 \times dim$
ResBlock $16 \times dim \rightarrow 16 \times dim$
Linear $\rightarrow z$
Tanh

2.3 Model Architecture

Our model architecture is built upon the state-of-the-art model BigGAN [16], where their residual blocks are defined as presented in Fig. 2. A ResBlock (without up or down) in the architecture does not include the Upsample or Average Pooling layers, and has identity skip connections. The model architecture as presented in Table 1 is defined for the COVID-19 dataset with an image size of 256×256.

Generator: The generator G as presented in Table 1(a) comprises six residual blocks with 3×3 filter kernels of size respectively $1024 - 512 - 512 - 256 - 128 - 64$. Each residual block is composed of two Batch Normalization layers (BN), two ReLU activation functions, two Upsample layers, two 3×3 convolutional layers and one 1×1 convolutional layer. G is based on Upsampling layers and takes as input a random noise vector z of size 128 with a base filter *dim* equals to 64. And at the end of last two layers of the generator (see Table 1), we added CBAM attention blocks.

Discriminator and Encoder: The discriminator D and the encoder E have the same residual blocks as shown in Fig. 2 (b). They used filter kernels of size $64 - 128 - 256 - 512 - 512 - 1024$. Each residual block of D and E is composed of two Instance Normalization layers (IN), two Leaky ReLU activation functions, two Average Pooling (AvgPool) layers, two 3×3 convolutional layers and one 1×1 convolutional layer. At the end of the discriminator architecture, we added the global sum pooling as used in Spectral Normalization for Generative Adversarial Networks (SN-GAN) [17] to ensure our model stability. D outputs a scalar score that should be high score for real images and low for fake images.

2.4   Model Training

We train our model based only on normal data for the detection of anomalies at both image and pixel levels. The training of the model networks involves two learning steps [6], the training of the generator/discriminator and the training of the encoder.

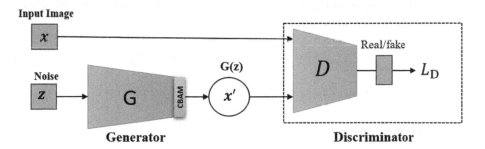

Fig. 3. The structure of the GAN framework.

Generator/Discriminator (GAN) Training: The GAN (Fig. 3) training is based on two networks: the generator network G and the discriminator network D. During training, G learns to generate images that follow the normal distribution and try to minimize the loss function to reduce the difference between the real and the generated images. However, D tries to maximize the loss function to maximize the difference between the real and the generated images. In our GAN model, we use the Wasserstein Gradient Penalty (WGAN-GP) [18] loss function in order to increase training stability. The loss of the discriminator is computed from the scalar output that determines whether the input comes from the real or generated image. The objective function of the discriminator is defined as:

$$L_D = E_{x' \sim P_g} \left[D\left(x'\right) \right] - E_{x \sim P_r} \left[D\left(x\right) \right] + \lambda E_{\hat{x} \sim P_{\hat{x}}} \left[\left(\left\| \nabla_{\hat{x}} D\left(\hat{x}\right) \right\|_2 - 1 \right)^2 \right], \quad (1)$$

where $D\left(x'\right)$ and $D\left(x\right)$ refer to the discriminator decision at image level for respectively the fake and the original images. The generator loss is defined as follows:

$$L_G = -E_{x' \sim P_g} \left[D\left(x'\right) \right]. \quad (2)$$

Encoder Training: After the GAN training is completed, G will be able to map from a latent vector z to a generated image x', $G\left(z\right) = x'$. While the encoder E makes the mapping from the image x to the latent vector z, $E\left(x\right) = z$. The trained generator and discriminator are used with fixed weights for subsequent encoder training. The encoder network is implemented with an architecture similar to the generator and based on the discriminator residual blocks. During the training of E, we minimize the mean squared error (MSE) between the input image x and its associated reconstructed image $G\left(E\left(x\right)\right)$. The loss of the encoder L_E is computed from the sum of the image space loss L_{img} and the discriminator features loss L_{feat}:

$$L_E\left(x\right) = L_{img}\left(x\right) + k\, L_{feat}\left(x\right), \quad (3)$$

where k is a weighting parameter. The image space loss L_{img} is computed as follows:

$$L_{img}\left(x\right) = \frac{1}{n} \left\| x - G\left(E\left(x\right)\right) \right\|^2, \quad (4)$$

where n is the number of pixels in the image, and x is the input image. Similarly, the discriminator features loss L_{feat} is determined as:

$$L_{feat}\left(x\right) = \frac{1}{m} \left\| f\left(x\right) - f\left(G\left(E\left(x\right)\right)\right) \right\|^2, \quad (5)$$

where m is the dimensionality of the discriminator features representation.

2.5 Anomaly Scores

An anomaly score is used to detect the anomalies in each test image. To obtain the anomaly score for the test images at image level, we are based on the weighted sum of reconstruction error and the discrimination error.

$$A_{image}\left(x\right) = \frac{1}{n} \left\| x - x' \right\|^2 + \frac{1}{m} \left\| D\left(x\right) - D\left(G\left(E\left(x\right)\right)\right) \right\|^2. \quad (6)$$

For pixel-level anomaly detection, we measured the reconstruction error between the test image x and the reconstructed image x' as their absolute difference:

$$A_{pixel}\left(x\right) = \left| x - x' \right|. \quad (7)$$

3   Datasets and Experimental Setup

In order to thoroughly illustrate the effectiveness of our model, we evaluated its performance on three different datasets.

3.1   Datasets

CIFAR-10. [19] This is a dataset for image recognition that consists of 60000, 32×32 color images, including 50000 training images and 10000 test images. This dataset is divided into 10 classes, namely airplane, automobile, bird, cat, deer, dog, frog horse, ship, and truck. In the experiments, one of the classes was randomly chosen as the anomalous class and the rest of them as normal.

MNIST. [20] This is a real-world dataset that consists of 70000, 28×28 gray images, including 60000 training samples and 10000 test samples. It is divided into 10 classes of handwritten digits from 0 to 9. In the experiment, one of the classes was treated as abnormal, while others as normal.

COVID-19 Dataset. For our specific task of COVID-19 anomaly detection, we consider two benchmarking datasets [21,22]. [21] includes 20 CT scans of patients with healthy and COVID-19 images with expert segmentation of lungs and infections. [22] is a large publicly available database of CT scans that includes COVID-19 and non-COVID-19 images with different pathology types. Both image datasets were stored in PNG format and resized to 256×256. Concerning the data augmentation, for the training set we first tailored the images according to the annotated cropping frame, followed by random horizontal flips and normalization. Indeed, all images were shuffled to avoid considering two subsequent images in a batch and avoid biasing the training. For the test set, we simply adjusted the images that were cropped according to the annotation.

3.2   Experimental Setup

We have performed experiments on a Ubuntu16.04 server with $24Gb$ memory and a single NVIDIA GeForce RTX 3090Ti GPU. We build our model upon the state-of-the-art model BigGAN. We trained our model based on the gradient penalty (WGAN-GP) [18] loss function. As in [8], we didn't use any batch normalization in the discriminator and the encoder, but we add an instance normalization.

The ReLU [23] activation function takes only the maximum between the input and zero. This will lead the network to produce sometimes nothing but zeros for all the outputs and this is known as the "dying ReLU" problem. However, the Leaky ReLU [24] activation function permits some negative values to pass through. So, in our architecture, we replace each ReLU in the discriminator and the encoder with a Leaky ReLU with $\alpha = 0.2$.

The model was implemented using Python and the deep learning framework, PyTorch. We trained and evaluated our model on the datasets described in subsection2.6 Regarding the choice of hyperparameters, we used the Adam optimizer for all models with 0.9 beta1 and 0.999 beta2. We set up the learning rate for all models at 0.0001, and the batch size at 24 for the COVID-19 dataset and 256 for MNIST and CIFAR-10 datasets.

4   Experimental Results

We evaluate our model performance at the image and pixels levels with the Precision, Recall, F-measure, and area under the receiver operating characteristic curve (AUC) [25]. Precision measures the number of actual anomalies detected relative to the total number of anomalies detected. Recall measures the number of detected anomalies against all actual anomalies. The F1-score is based on Precision and Recall and measures the amount of any type of false detection in the detection mechanism. The AUC indicates how much the model can distinguish between classes, and a high AUC implies a good result.

Table 2. The AUC of f-AnoGAN, f-AnoGAN with attention and our model on the MNIST and the CIFAR-10 datasets.

Models	MNIST	CIFAR-10
f-AnoGAN	0.921	0.530
f-AnoGAN with Attention	0.945	0.661
Our Model	0.991	0.761

Table 3. The performance of f-AnoGAN, f-AnoGAN with attention and our model on the COVID-19 dataset [10].

Models	Image Level				Pixel Level			
	Precision	Recall	F1	AUC	Precision	Recall	F1	AUC
f-AnoGAN	0.7654	0.7901	0.7775	0.9286	0.6711	0.6771	0.6740	0.7856
f-AnoGAN + Attention	0.7865	0.8484	0.8162	0.9498	0.6725	0.6814	0.6769	0.7923
Our Model	0.8396	0.9482	0.8906	0.9635	0.7254	0.7664	0.7453	0.8009

Table 2 illustrates the obtained AUC of the f-AnoGAN, f-AnoGAN with CBAM attention and our model on real-world datasets MNIST and CIFAR-10. And Table 3 presents an in-depth comparison on image and pixel levels of our model, f-AnoGAN and f-AnoGAN with CBAM modules.

Figure 4 illustrates the capacity of our model to produce high-quality realistic images that cannot be distinguished from real images. The obtained results prove our choice of using the BigGAN generator for the generation of images. They demonstrate besides the importance of adding attention blocks to the model that helps in capturing the information details in the images and then improves the anomaly detection process.

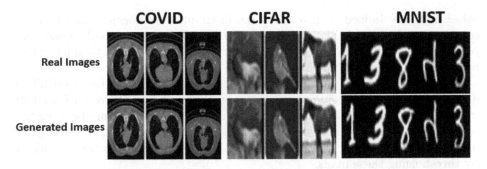

Fig. 4. Samples of our model image generation on COVID-19, CIFAR-10, and MNIST datasets.

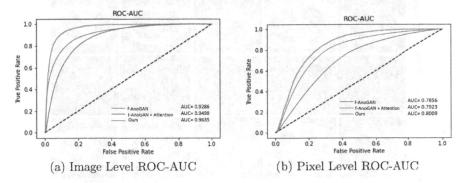

      (a) Image Level ROC-AUC   (b) Pixel Level ROC-AUC

Fig. 5. ROC-AUC on the COVID-19 dataset. (a) shows image-level ROC curve.(b) shows pixel-level ROC curve.

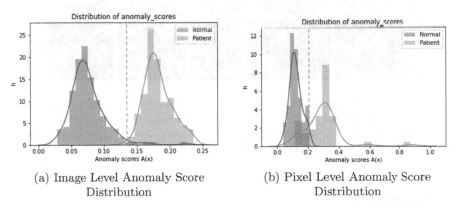

    (a) Image Level Anomaly Score   (b) Pixel Level Anomaly Score
            Distribution   Distribution

Fig. 6. Distribution of normal and abnormal scores on the COVID-19 dataset. (a) shows image-level anomaly score distribution.(b) shows pixel-level anomaly score distribution.

In Fig. 5, it is obvious from the ROC-AUC values on the COVID-19 dataset at both image and pixel levels that our proposed method clearly outperforms the other methods. Indeed, Fig. 6 shows the distribution of normal and abnormal scores with the threshold lines on the COVID-19 dataset at both image and pixel levels. It highlights the discriminative capacity of our model to differentiate between normal and anomalous images.

Figure 7, depicted the pixel-level anomaly detection on the COVID-19 dataset. The first two columns present normal images and the rest COVID-19 images. As demonstrated by anomaly score maps, i.e., the difference between the real image and its generated one, anomalous region, if they exist, present higher intensities than normal regions. Therefore, the predicted masks were obtained by thresholding these maps.

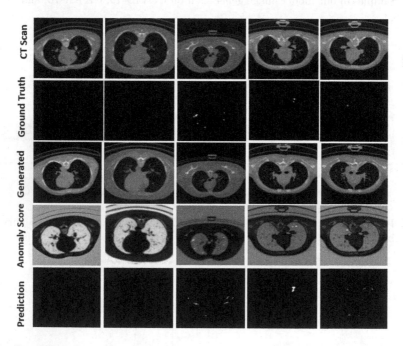

Fig. 7. Pixel level localization of anomalous image regions. The first row shows real input images. The second row shows the images ground-truth. The third row shows the generated images. The fourth row presents the obtained anomaly score. The last row shows the detected anomalous regions.

5   Conclusion

In this paper, we have presented a fast unsupervised anomaly detection method on the basis of the f-AnoGAN framework, by using the BigGAN residual blocks and incorporating an attention module on the generator blocks. Our experimental results for different datasets (MNIST, CIFAR-10, COVID-19) demonstrate the effectiveness of our method. We found that using BigGAN helps in producing high-quality images, adding CBAM blocks to the generator allows a better image generation that emphasizes salient regions, and the encoder ensures a faster anomaly detection.

Acknowledgements. We gratefully acknowledge the support of all members of the Research Laboratory of Technology and Medical Imaging, Faculty of Medicine of Monastir in Tunisia.

References

1. Pang, G., Shen, C., Cao, L., Hengel, A.V.D.: Deep learning for anomaly detection: a review. ACM Comput. Surv. (CSUR) **54**, 1–38 (2021)
2. Goodfellow, I., et al.: Generative adversarial nets. In: Advances in Neural Information Processing Systems 27, Curran Associates (2014)
3. Radford, A., Metz, L., Chintala, S.: Unsupervised representation learning with deep convolutional generative adversarial networks. arXiv preprint arXiv:1511.06434 (2015)
4. Arjovsky, M., Chintala, S., Bottou, L.: Wasserstein generative adversarial networks. In: International Conference on Machine Learning, pp. 214–223 (2017)
5. Schlegl, T., Seeböck, P., Waldstein, S.M., Schmidt-Erfurth, U., Langs, G.: Unsupervised anomaly detection with generative adversarial networks to guide marker discovery. In: Niethammer, M., et al. (eds.) IPMI 2017. LNCS, vol. 10265, pp. 146–157. Springer, Cham (2017). https://doi.org/10.1007/978-3-319-59050-9_12
6. Zenati, H., Foo, C.S., Lecouat, B., Manek, G., Chandrasekhar, V.R.: Efficient GAN-based anomaly detection. arXiv preprint arXiv:1802.06222 (2018)
7. Donahue, J., Krähenbühl, P., Darrell, T.: Adversarial feature learning. arXiv preprint arXiv:1605.09782 (2016)
8. Schlegl, T., Seeböck, P., Waldstein, S.M., Langs, G., Schmidt-Erfurth, U.: f-AnoGAN: fast unsupervised anomaly detection with generative adversarial networks. Med. Image Anal. **54**, 30–44 (2019)
9. Nakao, T., et al.: Unsupervised deep anomaly detection in chest radiographs. J. Digit. Imaging **34**, 418–427 (2021)
10. Liu, G., Lan, S., Zhang, T., Huang, W., Wang, W.: SAGAN: skip-attention GAN for anomaly detection. In: 2021 IEEE International Conference on Image Processing (ICIP), pp. 2468–2472 (2021)
11. Dumoulin, V., et al.: Adversarially learned inference. arXiv preprint arXiv:1606.00704 (2016)
12. Xia, X., et al.: GAN-based anomaly detection: a review. Neurocomputing **493**, 497–535 (2022)
13. Ma, B., Wang, X., Zhang, H., Li, F., Dan, J.: CBAM-GAN: generative adversarial networks based on convolutional block attention module. In: International Conference on Artificial Intelligence and Security, pp. 227–236 (2019)
14. Hu, J., Shen, L., Sun, G.: Squeeze-and-excitation networks. In: Proceedings of the IEEE Conference on Computer Vision and Pattern Recognition, pp. 7132–7141 (2018)
15. Woo, S., Park, J., Lee, J.-Y., Kweon, I.S.: CBAM: convolutional block attention module. In: Proceedings of the European Conference on Computer Vision (ECCV), pp. 3–19 (2018)

16. Brock, A., Donahue, J., Simonyan, K.: Large scale GAN training for high fidelity natural image synthesis. arXiv preprint arXiv:1809.11096 (2018)
17. Miyato, T., Kataoka, T., Koyama, M., Yoshida, Y.: Spectral normalization for generative adversarial networks. arXiv preprint arXiv:1802.05957 (2018)
18. Gulrajani, I., Ahmed, F., Arjovsky, M., Dumoulin, V., Courville, A.C.: Improved training of Wasserstein GANs. In: Advances in Neural Information Processing Systems 30 (2017)
19. Krizhevsky, A., Hinton, G., et al.: Learning Multiple Layers of Features from Tiny Images (2009)
20. LeCun, Y., Bottou, L., Bengio, Y., Haffner, P.: Gradient-based learning applied to document recognition. Proc. IEEE **86**, 2278–2324 (1998)
21. Ma, J., et al.: COVID-19 CT Lung and Infection Segmentation Dataset (2020)
22. Soares, E., Angelov, P., Biaso, S., Froes, M.H., Abe, D.K.: SARS-CoV-2 CT-scan dataset: a large dataset of real patients CT scans for SARS-CoV-2 identification. MedRxiv (2020)
23. Lu, L., Shin, Y., Su, Y., Karniadakis, G.E.: Dying ReLU and initialization: theory and numerical examples. arXiv preprint arXiv:1903.06733 (2019)
24. Maas, A.L., et al.: Rectifier nonlinearities improve neural network acoustic models. In: Proceedings ICML 30, p. 3 (2013)
25. Ling, C.X., et al.: AUC: a statistically consistent and more discriminating measure than accuracy. In: IJCAI 3, pp. 519–524 (2003)

Detection of Breast Masses in Mammograms by Incremental Discriminant Based Support Vector Machine Classifier and Active User Involvement

Marwa Salhi[1]([✉]), Riadh Ksantini[2], and Belhassen Zouari[1]

[1] Mediatron Lab, Higher School of Communications of Tunis, University of Carthage, Tunis, Tunisia
maroua.salhi@supcom.tn
[2] Department of Computer Science, College of IT. University of Bahrain, Sakhir, Bahrain

Abstract. Breast masses are among the most studied mammary pathologies on mammographic images. The complexity and diversity of mass forms require the use of appropriate descriptors and techniques. In this work, we propose a mass detection process based on our novel incremental Discriminant Based Support Vector Machine classifier coupled with the active involvement of domain experts. It is a three steps process. In the first step, mammographic images are pre-processed by eliminating noise and enhancing contrast. The second step is a feature engineering one. Multiple descriptors are extracted from the mammographic images and feature space transformation and reduction are performed by PCA (Principal Component Analysis). In the third step, the mass detection is performed based on the incremental classification guided by user involvement. The user is first provided with a simple user interface. Hence, this interface allows him to interact with the mammographic image and select some parts. Based on the selection, the pixels are incrementally classified using the IDSVM, which combines both local and near-global variational information of the training data into the input space. Experiments on mammograms from the INbreast database, by reference to the ground truth results, demonstrate the validity of our method.

Keywords: Breast cancer · Incremental classification · IDSVM · Mammographic images

1 Introduction

Medical imaging is certainly one of the areas of medicine that has made the most progress in the last 20 years. These recent developments not only allow a better diagnosis but also offer new hopes of treatment for many diseases. Breast

C. Bădică et al. (Eds.): ICCCI 2022, CCIS 1653, pp. 373–384, 2022.
https://doi.org/10.1007/978-3-031-16210-7_31

cancer, which represents one of the leading causes of early mortality in women, was the first to benefit from this progression. Mammography has been shown to be an essential tool in the screening and diagnosis of breast cancer. The use of mammography increases the rate of detection of cancerous tumors. In addition, the risk of death among women monitored by the screening program over a 10-year period decreased by 30% as mentioned in [1].

Radiologists use a visual examination of mammograms in order to search for abnormalities. The large volume of films to be analyzed makes the task so difficult for radiologists, tumors can be missed by them and screening errors become hard to avoid. Most of the research studies aim to develop automatic systems [2]. Computer-aided detection systems (CAD) serve as a second interpretation of different types of breast lesions. The combination of this second opinion with radiologists' reading improves performance for the detection and classification of breast cancer.

The mammographic image is the result of the X-ray attenuation of breast tissue. Tumors become visible in those X-ray images. Mass detection is more complicated compared to microcalcifications because of the variety of sizes and shapes [13]. The reading and detection of anomalies of mammogram images mainly rely on radiologists. This method largely depends on the subjective judgment of radiologists, which greatly increases the possibility of misdiagnosis in screening, especially with the increasing number of images. Many research works introduced several techniques for mass detection. The main challenge is the complexity of breasts in texture and density which make the tumors hidden by the different mass structures. Existing methods for mass detection generally fall into three categories: Supervised, Unsupervised, and Semi-supervised mass detection. The most common procedure of mass detection in literature is using the unsupervised approach. However, the unsupervised-based methods have many problems. First, the machine-learning model used in these previous studies learns from raw data without any prior knowledge. Also, the unsupervised method is a time-consuming process. The learning phase of the algorithm might take a lot of time, as it analyses and calculates all possibilities. In addition, unlike our proposed method, previous unsupervised-based approaches don't take into consideration the radiologist's experience, who is the one that has better knowledge about mammographic images and breast cancer.

In this paper, to overcome these problems, we propose a classification-based method to detect masses in mammograms. After pre-processing, feature enrichment, and selection, the detection phase is based on the incremental discriminant-based support vector machine classifier (IDSVM). In this step, a set of pixels selected by a radiologist are used to train the model. The experimental evaluation of mammographic images which are manually segmented shows high precision for mass detection with different shapes, sizes, and tissue densities. The rest of this paper is organized as follows. Section 2 overviews some related works. Then, Sect. 3 presents the mass lesion detection process based on IDSVM. Followed by Sect. 4 which is dedicated to the results and the evaluation. Finally, we conclude the paper.

2   Related Work

Several valuable attempts have been conducted to develop novel CAD systems for mammogram analysis and suspicious masses detection. Nanayakkara et al. [7] proposed an automatic technique for mass localization. This technique uses a modified region-growing algorithm known as fast marching to detect tumors. Mustra et al. [6] developed a robust and automatic segmentation method based on k-means clusters to obtain threshold values. Afterward, morphological operations were used to extract the breast region. Sreedevi et al. [14] reported on the use of gray-level thresholding in conjunction with the Canny edge detection technique for the detection and elimination of the pectoral muscle. Quyyoum [9] applied a median filter to suppress noise in a mammogram. Then, the Otsu technique is used to generate a binary mask. The binary mask generated contains the breast regions with labels and other artifacts. Afterward, labels and artifacts are eliminated using the labeling of connected components such that the resulting binary mask was used to extract the breast region from the original mammogram. Heath and Bowyer [4] proposed a new mass detection approach based on the filter of the average fraction under minimum (AFUM). This filter makes it possible to check the degree of decrease in intensity of a region surrounding a point. They used thresholding as the final step to identify the masses. Kom et al. [5] proposed a method of mass detection. A linear transformation filter algorithm is applied first to improve the image. The resulting image is subtracted from the image. A local adaptive thresholding technique is applied to the image to detect the mass. Several other methods have used texture features in the segmentation step or the classification step of a CAD. Djaroudib [3] used these matrices in an edge detection approach. The proposed approach is to use textural gray level information extracted from the GLCM (Gray Level Co-occurrence Matrix) in a segmentation approach by detecting the edge of the mass. Nithya et al. [8] presented a performance comparison of three extraction techniques with different characteristics for breast cancer detection. A supervised neural network classifier was used to evaluate the performance of the GLCM features, intensity histogram features, and intensity-based features for the detection of breast cancer in mammograms.

Recently, many methods have been proposed for the automatic detection of breast lesions. Zhang et al. used an improved Faster R-CNN to localize and detect breast masses in images from the DDSM dataset [16]. After improving the contrast of the breast image, they modified the size of the Anchor in the process of candidate box extraction and optimized the pooling method in the network to increase the tumor detection rate. Zeiser et al. [15] proposed an approach based on U-Net to diagnose breast cancer. The developed model contains four phases: image preprocessing, data augmentation, training, and testing. The first phase of the model is a preprocessing one to enhance the contrast of the acquired images and obtain the region of interest. Then, a phase of data augmentation was used for horizontal mirroring, resizing, and zooming of mammogram images. Lastly, the U-Net strategy was used to classify the images into malignant and benign. Sathiyabhama et al. [11] used a Grey Wolf Optimizer (GWO) to design a feature selection framework for analyzing the mammographic images. Therefore, they used the GWO-rough set theory to introduce a dimensionality reduction method. Then, the proposed algorithm was used to derive the appropriate features from the feature set. Shankar and Duraisamy [12] introduced a Versatile Duck Traveler Optimization (VDTO) algorithm based on the triple segmentation approaches. They used the VDTO to optimize threshold values for cancer segmentation. Then, they determine the desired region from the image using VDTO-ROI. However, the proposed method requires extending the VDTO version for disease diagnosing using medical image processing. Despite the efficiency of the above-mentioned methods, these approaches possess their limitations, making them less than ideal for mass detection. Firstly, they need a long run time because of using batch methods. Also, the absence of experts' knowledge in creating the final result discourages their use. Hence, in this paper, we present a new method for mass detection based on incremental classification coupled with expert involvement to provide real-time and efficient results.

3   Mass Detection by IDSVM

We propose a three-step process to detect masses with irregular shapes and sizes in mammograms. Figure 1 shows the high level system diagram for the proposed method. The first step is the preparation of images before analysis. The second step is a feature engineering one to obtain a better description of images through significant features. The third step is a classification method based on the incremental classifier IDSVM trained on some user-selected pixels. These steps are explained in more detail in the following section.

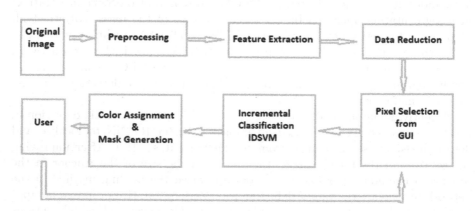

Fig. 1. Block diagram of proposed methodology.

3.1 Mammographic Images Preprocessing

Image preparation is essential to obtain unbiased and better quality analysis results. We have treated the noise and the contrast problem by using median filtering and contrast enhancement.

Median Filtering: Most mammograms usually contain low-intensity noise and sometimes artifacts. Therefore, we perform median filtering to remove the noise effect on the data classification without affecting the details of the image. It consists in making a modification to the value of the pixels of the image based on the neighborhood of each pixel in order to improve it. A new image is obtained using the pixel values of the original image. We have used a non-linear median filter of window size 3 * 3.

Enhancement of Mammogram: During the acquisition of mammograms, the radiation dose applied degrades the contrast between different regions in the image. This makes the detection of edges between the mass regions and their surrounding textural backgrounds becomes one of the most difficult tasks. This difficulty returns to be worse with small and subtle masses and also when mammographic masses overlap with dense breast tissues. Therefore, it is necessary to reduce the effect of the low contrast between the different regions in the image while preserving the features and patterns related to the masses. For this purpose, we have used the CLAHE method (Contrast Limited Adaptive Histogram Equalization) to improve the quality of the image. Indeed, CLAHE allows the reduction of the invisibility of the edges between the regions. CLAHE method is applied to the filtered images. The combination of the filtering method with the contrast enhancement method allows precise detection of the different regions of the image.

3.2 Feature Engineering

Once the step of image correction is finished, we generate new features that may be relevant for our analysis task. Better classification can be obtained from a better description. A feature enrichment is performed. Features are extracted from normal and abnormal breast tissues.

Feature Extraction: In our proposed methodology, this process consists of extracting for each pixel a set of relevant information from the pixel and its neighborhood to describe it. These features were extracted from normal as well as cancerous tissues.

1. The pixel intensity value x_i.
2. The rank of the pixel according to its gray level compared to these eight surrounding neighbors $|\{p_j \in V p_i / x_j < x_i\}|$.
3. The number of neighbors having values greater than p_i $|\{p_j \in V p_i / x_j > x_i\}|$.

4. The number of neighbors similar to p_i $|\{p_j \in Vp_i/x_j = x_i\}|$.
5. The dependence between p_i(with value equal to x_i) and its neighbors, each of which has its value x_v. This dependence function is given by:

$$r_{iv} = min\left\{\frac{x_i}{x_v}, \frac{x_v}{x_i}\right\}. \tag{1}$$

Here the dependence function returns value between 0 and 1. The dependence is optimal if its value is 1. Where x_i is the intensity value of pi and x_v is the intensity value of its neighbor.

6. The degree of homogeneity between p_i and its region is defined as,

$$h = \frac{1}{nv}\sum_{n=1}^{nv}(r_{in}). \tag{2}$$

Where n_v represents the number of neighbors of p_i and r_{iv} is equal to the dependence between p_i and its neighbor v_n.

7. The gradient magnitude at each pixel.
8. The average intensity value of the neighboring pixels.

Data Reduction: Features obtained in previous steps sum to a total of 15 attributes. In this section, a principal component analysis method is used to reduce the number of attributes extracted without loss of information. It's about extracting the most relevant and independent components that describe the image. The Principal Component Analysis (PCA) method allows, from a data table in which individuals are described by p variables, to extract important information from the table so as to remove the truly characteristic relationships (proximities between variables and individuals). It represents then the table as a set of new orthogonal variables called principal components. Several interpretations can be made from the new clouds. We can cite the interpretation of the principal axes, the study of the proximities between the points, and the choice of the number of axes to retain. Our goal of using PCA is to reduce the size of the data table in terms of the number of features while summarizing the information contained in the original table and attempting to give them meaning. Each component represents a new variable that carries some information. The choice of a new variable is based on the degree of inertia given by this component. All the first components that give sufficient cumulative inertia will be considered as the new descriptors of our image. We applied the PCA on images containing masses of the INbreast database after obtaining 15 new attributes for each pixel in the previous step. According to Fig. 2, the first four dimensions of PCA express 80% of the total inertia. As a consequence, the description will stand to these axes, since, according to studies, the dimensions carrying 80% of the information are sufficient to describe individuals. The principal component analysis also shows that all features extracted from the image contribute to the pixel description.

3.3   IDSVM Based Classification

IDSVM Classifier: The IDSVM [10] is an incremental classifier, that learns incrementally, as new data is available over time. It is inspired by combining the merits of both discriminant-based classifiers and the classical SVM. The IDSVM calculates the scatter matrices of the discriminant-based algorithm in the input space, by considering the k nearest neighbors for each training data point, to find the near-global characteristics of the data. Then, it incorporates these merits into the SVM optimization problem. The SVM is based only on the support vectors (local properties) to build the separating hyperplane. Since both of these sources of information are important, combining their characteristics results in accurate classification. Besides, calculating the matrices in the input space, rather than feature space can improve performance and response time. The IDSVM uses the singular value decomposition as a change of variable technique to transform the initial data and map the data to a higher dimensional feature space. This transformation enables the classifier to deal with large datasets. Furthermore, formulating the solution recursively, while preserving the benefit from the proposed classifier accuracy, will result in a high capability in manipulating complex datasets, which is the case with mammographic images. The computational complexity of IDSVM is $O(N_s^2)$, where N_s is the number of support vectors, $N_s \leq N$, and N is the number of training data points.

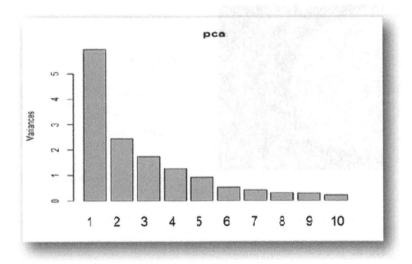

Fig. 2. Decomposition of the total inertia on the components of the PCA

Mass Detection: In this work, our purpose is to build a framework that can be used easily and gives efficient results in real-time. Since the radiologist is the only one who knows what to look for and has the domain knowledge about the breast masses and mammograms, our approach is based on involving him in the classification process. First, we present a simple GUI (Fig. 3) that contains the mammographic image with simple tools. The expert makes a selection on the proposed GUI to express his intention of how to classify the image. Then, the user assigns the selected pixels to groups. These pixels are used as training data to train the IDSVM. The most important utility of incremental learning derives from the gain in the computational complexity, both in terms of required memory and time. This is because the incremental classifier stores the estimated parameters related to the past training data and doesn't need retraining each time new examples become available. Hence, the key advantage of our method is that it uses incrementality for classification. Thus, the IDSVM separates the given set of user-labeled training data with a hyperplane controlled placed in an optimum way. Consequently, the whole image is classified using the separating hyperplane efficiently. After classifying the image, we assign color values for each detected class to differentiate among various structures and perform aesthetic attraction. The colored image is shown to the user in real-time. Then, the user can choose a label and ask the system to generate a mask. If the label corresponds to the masse class, then the user is presented with the mask containing the detected masse. Since the problem can be multiclass, we have used the one-versus-one classification with our IDSVM classifier.

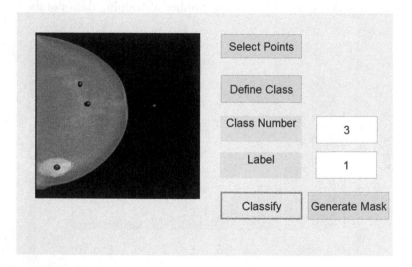

Fig. 3. The GUI with mammographic image and selected pixels.

4   Results and Discussion

This section quantitatively describes the usefulness of the proposed method in detecting masses in digitized mammograms. In this work, we test our algorithm by using mammograms from the INbreast database. The database was acquired at the Breast Center in CHSJ, Porto, under the permission of both the Hospital's

Ethics Committee and the National Committee of Data Protection. It includes examples of normal mammograms, mammograms with masses, mammograms with microcalcifications, architectural distortions, asymmetries, and images with multiple findings. The database consists of craniocaudal and mediolateral images which contained sometimes one or several tumors marked by experienced radiologists. We apply our method to these images to detect masses. The generated masks are used to evaluate our approach. An example of the obtained results is shown in Fig. 4. The algorithm is evaluated in terms of Recall, Precision, and accuracy metrics. We compare the detected masses found by our algorithm with those marked by the radiologists. We carry out this comparison study in the case of different shapes, sizes, and densities to study the robustness of our approach.

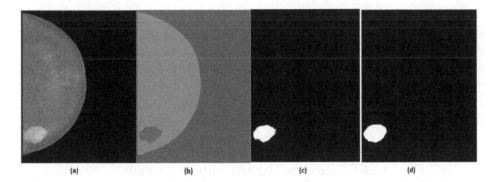

Fig. 4. (a) Original image. (b) Regions detected in the image. (c) Mass detected by algorithm. (d) Ground truth

4.1   Masses Shape Influence

We apply the algorithm to two sets of instances. In the first one, the masses have circular shapes and in the second they are irregular-shaped. Table 1 recapitulates results concerning the precision, recall, and accuracy. These results indicate that masses are well detected by our algorithm in both cases. According to the accuracy, the detection of irregular shapes is slightly better than circular ones. The cooperation of the incremental DSVM and the expert knowledge used in this approach allows for detecting the spicules of a lesion. Indeed, they allow bringing the pixels of the mass region even if they are arbitrary shaped.

4.2   Masses Size Influence

In order to appreciate the similarity between masses marked by radiologists and those detected by our algorithm, we used mammograms containing masses of different sizes. Results indicate that the algorithm yielded small, medium, and large masses with good detection. The influence of the size of the lesion on the accuracy of the algorithm is summarized in Table 2. The resemblance between

Table 1. Results comparison of mass detection with different shapes.

Shape	File Name	Precision	Recall	Accuracy
Circular	22614379	0.73993	0.98305	0.99618
	22678787	0.61936	1	0.88657
	22613650	0.80118	0.88371	0.99186
	22579730	0.96662	0.86218	0.98151
Irregular	20587612	0.52033	1	0.9984
	22613702	0.50307	0.79109	0.99
	24055274	0.71216	0.97783	0.98199
	24065530	0.7937	0.90576	0.98255

the precision results of the algorithm for the different shapes of the images is due to the fact that as the size of the masses increases, the variation in their shape also increases. And we have already visualized the independence of the algorithm of the shape of the lesion.

Table 2. Results comparison of mass detection with different sizes.

Shape	File Name	Precision	Recall	Accuracy
Large	22614379	0.73993	0.98305	0.99618
	22613650	0.80118	0.88371	0.99186
	20588562	0.54112	1	0.9643
	22678787	0.61936	1	0.88657
Average	50996352	0.50769	1	0.89117
	22613702	0.50307	0.79109	0.99
	22670094	0.19374	1	0.99508
	24055274	0.71216	0.97783	0.98199
Small	20587612	0.52033	1	0.9984
	20587664	0.744193	1	0.98191
	22614522	0.4107	0.83797	0.91585
	22427705	0.833019	0.89716	0.98501

4.3 Breast Tissue Density Influence

In order to test the influence of breast tissue density on the performance of our approach, the area of masses marked by radiologists was compared to those found by our algorithm throughout Table 3. Observing those results shows that, fat and glandular tissues are well detected by our method. We also note that, in dense breasts, even though marked masses are still detected, the accuracy value is reduced. We found that for dense tissue, IDSVM only detects one level of density. This model makes it possible to separate the breast region within the background of the image. The extension of the IDSVM to the mass detection problem in mammographic images realizes good results for masses with different shapes, sizes, and tissue densities. High recall and accuracy are obtained when comparing the generated masses with the expert result. But, the values of precision are lower. This is because of the breast tissue density. Also, the presence of the pectoral muscle in many images may mislead the detection due to its high-level similarity to the masse. In addition, imbalanced data distribution and imbalanced quality of the majority and minority classes lead to misclassification. In future work, the performance of the proposed method can be improved with the integration of another preprocessing step to eliminate the pectoral muscle before classification. Also, balancers can be used to optimize the performance of the classifier. Moreover, a post-processing step can be performed to delimitate the region of the lesion.

Table 3. Results comparison of mass detection with different tissue densities.

Shape	File Name	Precision	Recall	Accuracy
Fat	20587612	0.52033	1	0.9984
	22670094	0.19374	1	0.99508
	22614379	0.73993	0.98305	0.99618
	24055274	0.71216	0.97783	0.98199
Glandular	20587664	0.744193	1	0.98191
	22613650	0.80118	0.88371	0.99186
	22613702	0.50307	0.79109	0.99
	20588680	0.62307	0.93466	0.9584
Dense	20588562	0.54112	1	0.9643
	22678694	0.27374	1	0.90108
	22614522	0.4107	0.83797	0.91585
	24065584	0.5718	1	0.98895

5 Conclusion

In this work, we have proposed a novel algorithm for the user-guided detection of masses in mammography images. The method consists of three main steps which are image preprocessing, feature engineering, and image classification. A series of treatments are performed before classification: median filter, CLAHE method, feature enrichment, and principal component analysis. We apply next an incremental classifier, based on user selection, to detect masses. The algorithm overcomes the drawback of the clustering-based approach. Testing of the proposed algorithm is carried out and shows its effectiveness. The classification of detected masses in malignant lesions and benign lesions should be a complementary task to this one. Further improvement can be made to delimit the border of the masses.

References

1. Al-Hajj, M., Wicha, M.S., Benito-Hernandez, A., Morrison, S.J., Clarke, M.F.: Prospective identification of tumorigenic breast cancer cells. Proc. Natl. Acad. Sci. **100**(7), 3983–3988 (2003)
2. Chattaraj, A., Das, A., Bhattacharya, M.: Mammographic image segmentation by marker controlled watershed algorithm. In: Bioinformatics and Biomedicine (BIBM), 2017 IEEE International Conference on, pp. 1000–1003. IEEE (2017)
3. DJAROUDIB, K.: Détection Multicritères des Anomalies sur des Mammographies, Ph.D. thesis, Université de Batna 2 (2016)
4. Heath, M.D., Bowyer, K.W.: Mass detection by relative image intensity. In: 5th International Workshop on Digital Mammography, pp. 219–225 (2000)
5. Kom, G., Tiedeu, A., Kom, M.: Automated detection of masses in mammograms by local adaptive thresholding. Comput. Biol. Med. **37**(1), 37–48 (2007)
6. Mustra, M., Grgic, M.: Robust automatic breast and pectoral muscle segmentation from scanned mammograms. Sig. Process. **93**(10), 2817–2827 (2013)
7. Nanayakkara, R., Yapa, Y., Hevawithana, P., Wijekoon, P.: Automatic breast boundary segmentation of mammograms. Int. J. Soft. Comput. Eng. (IJSCE) **5**(1), 97–101 (2015)
8. Nithya, R., Santhi, B.: Comparative study on feature extraction method for breast cancer classification. J. Theo. Appl. Inf. Technol. **33**(2), 220–226 (2011)
9. Qayyum, A., Basit, A.: Automatic breast segmentation and cancer detection via svm in mammograms. In: Emerging Technologies (ICET), 2016 International Conference on, pp. 1–6. IEEE (2016)
10. Salhi, M., Ksantini, R., Zouari, B.: A real-time image-centric transfer function design based on incremental classification. J. Real-Time Image Process. **19**(1), 185–203 (2022)
11. Sathiyabhama, B., et al.: A novel feature selection framework based on grey wolf optimizer for mammogram image analysis. Neural Comput. Appl. **33**(21), 14583–14602 (2021). https://doi.org/10.1007/s00521-021-06099-z
12. Shankar, R., Duraisamy, S., et al.: Versatile duck traveler optimization (Vdto) algorithm using triple segmentation methods for mammogram image segmentation to improving accuracy (2021)
13. Sharma, M., Singh, R., Bhattacharya, M.: Classification of breast tumors as benign and malignant using textural feature descriptor. In: Bioinformatics and Biomedicine (BIBM), 2017 IEEE International Conference on, pp. 1110–1113. IEEE (2017)
14. Sreedevi, S., Sherly, E.: A novel approach for removal of pectoral muscles in digital mammogram. Procedia Comput. Sci. **46**, 1724–1731 (2015)
15. Zeiser, F.A., et al.: Segmentation of masses on mammograms using data augmentation and deep learning. J. Digit. Imaging **33**(4), 858–868 (2020)
16. Zhang, Z., et al.: Ultrasonic diagnosis of breast nodules using modified faster R-CNN. Ultrason. Imaging **41**(6), 353–367 (2019)

Analysis of Right Ventricle Segmentation in the End Diastolic and End Systolic Cardiac Phases Using UNet-Based Models

Rania Mabrouk[1,2(✉)] [iD], Ramzi Mahmoudi[1,3] [iD], Asma Ammari[4] [iD],
Rachida Saouli[4] [iD], and Mohamed Hedi Bedoui[1] [iD]

[1] Faculty of Medicine of Monastir, Medical Imaging Technology Lab – LTIM-LR12ES06,
University of Monastir, Monastir, Tunisia
ranyamab96@gmail.com
[2] National Engineering School of Sfax, University of Sfax, Sfax, Tunisia
[3] Gaspard-Monge Computer-Science Laboratory, Paris-Est University, Mixed Unit
CNRS-UMLV-ESIEE UMR8049, BP99, ESIEE Paris Cité Descartes,
93162 Noisy Le Grand, France
ramzi.mahmoudi@esiee.fr
[4] Department of Computer Science, Laboratory LINFI, University of Biskra, BP 145 RP 07000,
Biskra, Algeria
rachida.saouli@esiee.fr

Abstract. Segmentation is an important task held to assess and analyze the heart's Right Ventricular (RV) function using CMR images. It has a major role in extracting important information which helps radiologists and doctors with the proper diagnosis. Several approaches have been proposed for RV segmentation showing great results in the End Diastolic (ED) phase but lower results in the End Systolic (ES) phase explained by the great variability of the complex shape of this chamber and its thin borders especially in the last phase. In this work, we aim to analyze the effect of short-axis slices from ED to ES phases on the segmentation task using a U-Net based architecture and two different datasets. Thus, a total of six models were trained to monitor the segmentation behavior.

Keywords: CMRI segmentation · Right ventricle · End diastolic phase · End systolic phase · U-Net

1 Introduction

The clinical importance of the Right Ventricle in cardiovascular diseases [1] has been encouraging to assess its function for a better and a more accurate diagnosis [2, 3]. Various imaging modalities are used for the RV evaluation where Cardiovascular Magnetic Resonance Imaging (CMRI) is the gold standard reference [4, 5]. To analyze the RV function, radiologists have to delineate its boundaries over the entire slices which is a time-consuming task. For this reason, automatic segmentation of this cardiac cavity has been studied using multiple approaches [6]. Despite the inspiring results obtained in the

© The Author(s), under exclusive license to Springer Nature Switzerland AG 2022
C. Bădică et al. (Eds.): ICCCI 2022, CCIS 1653, pp. 385–395, 2022.
https://doi.org/10.1007/978-3-031-16210-7_32

End Diastolic (ED) phase, lower results were detected in the End Systolic (ES) phase for many proposed approaches [7]. Those results are explained by the great variability of the complex shape of this cavity and its thin borders especially in the ES phase where the chambers are found considerably narrowed.

This paper aims to analyze the impact of short-axis slices from ED to ES phases on the segmentation task. For this reason, we proposed a U-Net based architecture and used two different datasets (a private one and a public one). A total of six models were trained to observe the segmentation performance.

The remainder of this paper is organized as follows: In Sect. 2, a brief literature overview is presented. The used datasets and the proposed architecture are detailed in Sect. 3. The experimental results including a comparison with similar works are discussed in Sect. 4. Finally, Sect. 5 concludes the paper and proposes possible improvements.

2 Related Works

To tackle the challenges of Right Ventricle segmentation, various works were proposed employing different segmentation techniques [8]. As reviewed in [6] and [9], the most recently proposed methods are more oriented to use deep learning techniques. In fact, Good progress in the medical imaging field has been reached thanks to the introduction of Artificial Intelligence technologies that became a popular approach for detection and segmentation problems due to their powerful feature representation [10]. A Multi-Centre, Multi-Vendor and Multi-Disease Cardiac Segmentation Challenge was organized as part of the MICCAI 2020 Conference [7] where a total of fourteen teams submitted different techniques for CMR images segmentation, including Left Ventricle segmentation, myocardium segmentation and Right Ventricle segmentation, using the same proposed dataset. As we are only interested in the RV segmentation, we note that the best dice coefficient reached in the challenge for this task was 0.91 at the End Diastolic phase and 0.86 at the End Systolic phase.

3 Proposed Method

3.1 Datasets Description

We adopted two different datasets to monitor the behavior of U-Net-based models in accordance with data.

The first one is "LabTIM-RV" private dataset proposed within our laboratory collected from the University Hospital of Fattouma Bourguiba (Monastir, Tunisia) in collaboration with its radiology service. It constitutes a total of 160 patients with a total number of 3528 labeled RV CMR images at both ED and ES phases. We subdivided this dataset into two other subsets each containing a total of 1659 RV labeled images at ED and ES phases separately.

The second one is the publicly available dataset used in the Multi-Centre, Multi-Vendor and Multi-Disease Cardiac Segmentation M&Ms Challenge which was organized as part of the MICCAI 2020 Conference [7]. It contains a total of 160 patients with a total number of 3554 short-axis CMR images along with their corresponding ground truth images of Left Ventricle LV, LV myocardium, and Right Ventricle RV. As we are interested in segmenting the Right Ventricle, we only extracted its labels by applying a simple threshold on the original ground truth images. We subdivided this dataset as well into two other subsets each containing a total of 1777 RV labeled images at ED and ES phases separately.

Both datasets were resized to 256 × 256 as they had a wide variety of dimensions ranging from 174 × 208 to 512 × 512.

3.2 Architecture

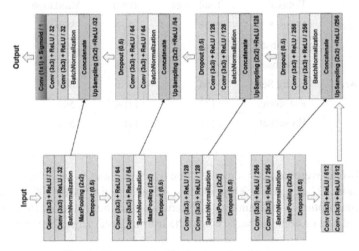

Fig. 1. The proposed U-Net-based architecture.

The U-Net-based architecture implemented for the analysis in this work consists of five blocks encoding path and a symmetric five blocks decoding path as detailed in Fig. 1. At each level of the encoder, a convolution operation and a ReLU activation function were applied two times consecutively followed by a batch normalization operation, a max-pooling operation then a dropout layer before moving to the next level. The decoder, then, recovers the original input size by applying the same sequence of operations with replacing the max-pooling operation with the transposed convolution as an upsampling operation at every level. The corresponding feature from the encoder is concatenated to the decoder's block input as well. A 1 × 1 convolution, with a sigmoid activation function, was then added at last for the generation of the final binary prediction map. The convolutions were applied with a kernel size of 3 × 3 and the transposed convolutions were applied with a kernel size of 2 × 2 in a stride of 2 × 2.

A total of six models were trained using this architecture with different datasets.

The first model (model1) was trained using the entire private dataset described above. The second model (model2) was trained using a subset that contains only the End Diastolic slices of the private dataset whereas the third model (model3) was trained using another subset that contains only the End Systolic slices of the private dataset. The forth model (model4) was trained using the entire public dataset described above as well. The fifth model (model5) was trained using a subset that contains only the End Diastolic slices of the public dataset whereas the sixth model (model6) was trained using another subset that contains only the End Systolic slices of the public dataset.

Each used dataset was subdivided into 10 patients for the testing process and 150 patients for the training process that itself was partitioned into 70% for the training set and 30% for the validation set as detailed in Table 1.

Table 1. Details of the different used datasets in the learning and test processes.

	Dataset	Total imgs	Train	Validation	Test
Private dataset	Entire Set	3528	2322	996	210
	ED subset	1764	1161	498	105
	ES subset	1764	1161	498	105
Public dataset	Entire Set	3554	2336	1002	216
	ED subset	1777	1168	501	108
	ES subset	1777	1168	501	108

All networks were trained using the same hyper parameters including Dice Loss as a loss function, 32 batch size, 100 epochs and Adam optimizer with 0.0005 as a learning rate. To further optimize the training procedure, we used the cosine annealing scheduler, implemented as a custom callback, where the learning rate ranges between 0.0005 and 0.0001.

4   Experimental Results and Discussion

In this section, we provide a detailed experimental analysis of the proposed models that demonstrates quantitative and qualitative results held with each of the datasets used in the training phase. We compare at last our results with state-of-the-art methods.

4.1   Evaluation Metrics

Various metrics are being used by the research community for medical image analysis to quantify the performance of segmentation models among which we can cite Dice Coefficient, Intersection over Union, Precision and Recall as the most popular choice.

Four measures are required to calculate these metrics:

True Positive (TP): is the number of RV pixels being correctly identified as RV pixels.
True Negative (TN): is the number of non-RV pixels being correctly identified as non-RV pixels.
False Positive (FP): is the number of non-RV pixels being wrongly identified as RV pixels.

False Negative (FN): is the number of RV pixels being wrongly identified as non-RV pixels.

Dice Coefficient: is the overlap ratio between the prediction and the ground truth with giving more weight to the intersection between them two and defined in (1). It ranges between 0 and 1 and the higher the value is, the better the segmentation result.

$$Dice\ Coefficient\ =\ 2TP/(2TP + FP + FN) \tag{1}$$

Intersection over Union (IoU): it measures the overlap between the prediction and the ground truth and is defined in (2).

$$Dice\ Coefficient = TP/(TP + FP + FN) \tag{2}$$

Precision: is a measure of exactness calculated as the ratio of true positive predictions divided by the number of predicted positives and defined in (3).

$$Precision = TP/(TP + FP) \tag{3}$$

Recall: is a measure of completeness calculated as the ratio of true positive predictions divided by the number of actual positives and defined in (4).

$$Recall = TP/(TP + FN) \tag{4}$$

4.2 Quantitative Evaluation

In this section a comparative experiment is presented to address RV segmentation challenging issues caused by the shape variation from End Diastolic and End Systolic slices. Consequently, we decided to study the impact of learning each slice level separately. For that, a total of six models were trained using the different datasets and the same U-Net based architecture as detailed above.

To evaluate and study the behavior of the RV segmentation among the different datasets, the dice coefficient and dice loss are computed.

Private Dataset
Figure 2 demonstrates the dice and loss curves of training and validation of the RV segmentation models, where the whole private dataset was used for training first (a) then the ED (b) and ES (c) private subsets were considered next separately.

The third model presented by Fig. 2(c) seems to be confused more than the other models. Whereas the first model presented by Fig. 2(a) demonstrates a better behavior along the training process where the Dice Coefficient curves/Dice Loss curves continued to increase/ decrease to a point of stability.

Public Dataset
Figure 3 demonstrates the dice and loss curves of training and validation of the RV segmentation models, where the whole public dataset was used for training first (a) then the ED (b) and ES (c) public subsets were considered next separately.

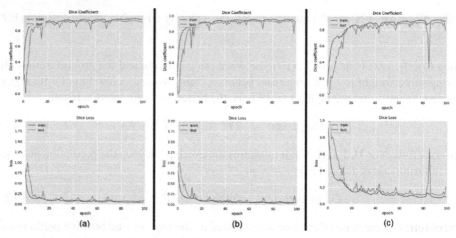

Fig. 2. Dice Coefficient and Dice Loss Training curves of the RV segmentation models of the private dataset. (a) model1: using the entire dataset. (b) model2: using the ED subset. (c) model3: using the ES subset.

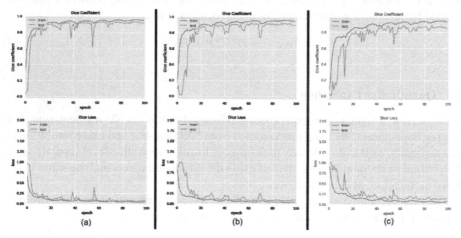

Fig. 3. Dice Coefficient and Dice Loss Training curves of the RV segmentation models of the public dataset: (a) using the entire dataset, (b) using the ED phase dataset, (c) using the ES phase dataset.

Same to the previous experiments, the third model presented by Fig. 3(c) seems to be confused more than the other models. Whereas the first model presented by Fig. 3(a) demonstrates a better behavior along the training process where the Dice Coefficient curves/Dice Loss curves continued to increase/decrease to a point of stability. Therefore, it is safe to assume that the challenging issues related to the End systolic phase may influence the segmentation results and even affect the segmentation of other slices.

Table 2/Table 3 reports a comparison of RV segmentation performance in the validation/test phase, in terms of Dice Coefficient, IoU, Precision and Recall when training

Table 2. Comparison of RV segmentation performance of the different models in the validation phase, in terms of Dice Coefficient, IoU, Precision and Recall.

	Metric	Dice	IoU	Precision	Recall
Private dataset	Model1	0.9272	0.8653	0.9378	0.9204
	Model2	0.9437	0.8940	0.9472	0.9445
	Model3	0.8931	0.8079	0.8944	0.8968
Public dataset	Model4	0.9322	0.8745	0.9362	0.9326
	Model5	0.9221	0.8569	0.9374	0.9116
	Model6	0.8514	0.7447	0.9463	0.7803

Table 3. Comparison of RV segmentation performance of the different models in the test phase, in terms of Dice Coefficient, IoU, Precision and Recall.

	Metric	Dice	IoU	Precision	Recall
Private test set	Model1	0.9058	0.8325	0.9603	0.8661
	Model2	0.9241	0.8609	0.9872	0.8727
	Model3	0.8243	0.7061	0.8987	0.7683
Public test set	Model4	0.8890	0.8125	0.9603	0.8661
	Model5	0.8704	0.8124	0.8855	0.8597
	Model6	0.7394	0.6103	0.9216	0.6346

with the whole private dataset (model1), with the private ED subset (model2), with the private ES subset (model4), with the entire public dataset (model4), with the public ED subset (model5) and with the public ES subset (model6).

Training with the private ED subset (model2) shows the best performance as it reached a validation Dice Coefficient of 0.9437 and test Dice Coefficient of 0.9241 which are the highest values in comparison with model1 and model3. Whereas training with the public whole dataset (model4) shows the best performance as it reached a validation Dice Coefficient of 0.9322 and test Dice Coefficient of 0.8890 which are the highest values in comparison with model5 and model6.

Training with the private ES subset (model3) and the public one (model6) both show the worst performance as model3 and model6 reached a validation Dice Coefficient of 0.8931 and 0.8514 respectively and test Dice Coefficient of 0.8243 and 0.7394 respectively which are the lowest values in comparison with the other models.

Table 4/Table 5 reports a comparison of RV segmentation performance in the validation/test phase, in terms of Dice Coefficient, IoU, Precision and Recall at the end-systolic (ED) and the end-diastolic (ES) phases, when training with the whole private dataset (model1) and the entire public dataset (model4). Both tables demonstrate that the segmentation performance in the End Systolic phase is lower than the End Diastolic phase for all computed metrics.

Table 4. Comparison of RV segmentation performance in the validation phase, in terms of Dice Coefficient, IoU, Precision and Recall at the end-systolic (ED) and the end-diastolic (ES) phases, when training with the whole private dataset (model1) and the entire public dataset (model4).

	Dice		IoU		Precision		Recall	
	ED	ES	ED	ES	ED	ES	ED	ES
Model1	0.9586	0.9148	0.9208	0.8442	0.9731	0.9181	0.9469	0.9159
Model4	0.9587	0.9352	0.9224	0.8821	0.9709	0.9338	0.9504	0.9424

Table 5. Comparison of RV segmentation performance in the test phase, in terms of Dice Coefficient, IoU, Precision and Recall at the end-systolic (ED) and the end-diastolic (ES) phases, when training with the whole private dataset (model1) and the entire public dataset (model4).

	Dice		IoU		Precision		Recall	
	ED	ES	ED	ES	ED	ES	ED	ES
Model1	0.9292	0.8783	0.8694	0.7867	0.9959	0.9179	0.8737	0.8470
Model4	0.8893	0.8416	0.8081	0.7453	0.9362	0.8904	0.9326	0.8098

Table 6. Comparison of End Systolic slices segmentation performance in the validation phase using the different models, in terms of Dice Coefficient, IoU, Precision and Recall.

	Metric	Dice	IoU	Precision	Recall
Private dataset	**Model1**	**0.9148**	**0.8442**	**0.9181**	**0.9159**
	Model2	0.8317	0.7200	0.7949	0.8875
	Model3	0.8931	0.8079	0.8944	0.8968
Public dataset	**Model4**	**0.9352**	**0.8821**	**0.9338**	**0.9424**
	Model5	0.8591	0.7601	0.8374	0.8948
	Model6	0.8514	0.7447	0.9463	0.7803

Table 7. Comparison of End Systolic slices segmentation performance in the test phase using the different models, in terms of Dice Coefficient, IoU, Precision and Recall.

	Metric	Dice	IoU	Precision	Recall
Private test set	**Model1**	**0.8783**	**0.7867**	**0.9179**	**0.8470**
	Model2	0.8517	0.7490	0.8555	0.8536
	Model3	0.8243	0.7061	0.8987	0.7683
Public test set	**Model4**	**0.8416**	**0.7453**	**0.8904**	**0.8098**
	Model5	0.8012	0.6739	0.8382	0.7768
	Model6	0.7394	0.6103	0.9216	0.6346

Table 6/Table 7 reports a comparison of End Systolic slices segmentation performance in the validation/test phase, in terms of Dice Coefficient, IoU, Precision and Recall when training with the whole private dataset (model1), with the private ED subset (model2), with the private ES subset (model4), with the entire public dataset (model4), with the public ED subset (model5) and with the public ES subset (model6).

Training with the private whole dataset (model1) and the public one (model4) both show the best performance as model1 and model4 reached a validation Dice Coefficient of 0.9148 and 0.9352 respectively and test Dice Coefficient of 0.8783 and 0.8416 respectively which are the highest values in comparison with the other models.

These results don't show a better impact of excluding End Systolic slices on the segmentation performance.

4.3 Qualitative Evaluation

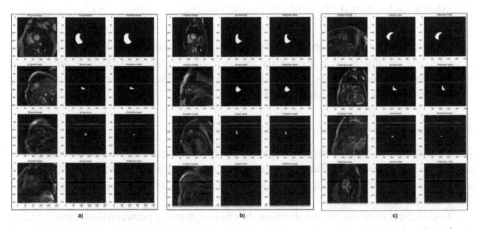

Fig. 4. Visual qualitative comparison of the right ventricle segmentation results using the private dataset. First column: original slice. Second column: ground truth. Third column: predicted masks. a) model1's results. b) model2's results. c) model3's results.

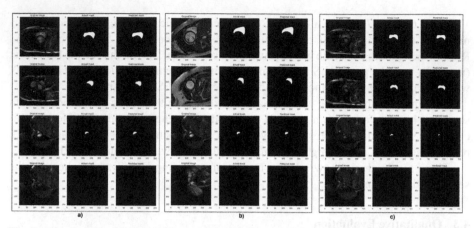

Fig. 5. Visual qualitative comparison of the right ventricle segmentation results using the public dataset. First column: original slice. Second column: ground truth. Third column: predicted masks. a) model4's results. b) model5's results. c) model6's results.

The Qualitative evaluation proved that the predicted masks of the different six models give a good agreement with the reality as the results are notably close to the original ones as demonstrated in Figs. 4 and 5 above displaying each four sample images from the test set and test subsets respectively.

4.4 Comparison with State of the Art Methods

In this section, we quantitatively compare the performance of our proposed RV segmentation model, trained using the whole public dataset (model4), with fourteen state of the art methods submitted within the M&Ms Challenge organized as part of the MICCAI 2020 Conference [7].

The dice coefficients obtained within the challenge range between 0.910 and 0.552 in the End Diastolic phase which are lower than the dice coefficient we obtained using our model (0.9587). The dice coefficients obtained in the End Systolic phase range between 0.860 and 0.517 which are also lower than the dice coefficient we obtained using our model (0.9352).

5 Conclusion

Inspite of the promising results reached with our proposed U-Net architecture that surpassed state of the art methods, we conclude that U-Net alone is still insufficient to tackle the RV segmentation challenging issues in the ES phase. Hence, further improvements and other approaches are needed. It may be wiser to propose a particular approach for each phase separately.

In addition, choosing a specific segmentation method is not the only concern but it would be interesting, as well, to study how to efficiently exploit the CMRI available slices to achieve higher results for the entire cardiac short-axis sequence. In fact, data augmentation, preprocessing and picking the most relevant clinical cases can have a great positive influence in the segmentation process.

References

1. Sheehan, F., Redington, A.: The right ventricle: anatomy, physiology and clinical imaging. Heart **94**, 1510–1515 (2008). https://doi.org/10.1136/hrt.2007.132779
2. Goetschalckx, K., Rademakers, F., Bogaert, J.: Right ventricular function by MRI. Curr. Opin. Cardiol. **25**, 451–455 (2010). https://doi.org/10.1097/HCO.0b013e32833b78e6
3. Tavano, A., et al.: MR imaging of arrhythmogenic right ventricular dysplasia: what the radiologist needs to know. Diagn. Interv. Imaging **96**, 449–460 (2015). https://doi.org/10.1016/j.diii.2014.07.009
4. Steen, H., et al.: Is magnetic resonance imaging the 'reference standard' for cardiac functional assessment? Factors influencing measurement of left ventricular mass and volumes. Clin. Res. Cardiol. **96**(10), 743–751 (2007). https://doi.org/10.1007/s00392-007-0556-2
5. Caudron, J., Fares, J., Lefebvre, V., Vivier, P.-H., Petitjean, C., Dacher, J.-N.: Cardiac MRI assessment of right ventricular function in acquired heart disease: factors of variability. Acad. Radiol. **19**, 991–1002 (2012). https://doi.org/10.1016/j.acra.2012.03.022
6. Ammari, A., Mahmoudi, R., Hmida, B., Saouli, R., Bedoui, M.H.: A review of approaches investigated for right ventricular segmentation using short-axis cardiac MRI. IET Image Process. (2021)https://doi.org/10.1049/ipr2.12165
7. Campello, V.M., et al.: Multi-centre, multi-vendor and multi-disease cardiac segmentation: the M&Ms challenge. IEEE Trans. Med. Imaging **40**, 3543–3554 (2021). https://doi.org/10.1109/TMI.2021.3090082
8. Petitjean, C., et al.: Right ventricle segmentation from cardiac MRI: a collation study. Med. Image Anal. **19**, 187–202 (2015). https://doi.org/10.1016/j.media.2014.10.004
9. Chen, C., et al.: Deep learning for cardiac image segmentation: a review. Front. Cardiovasc. Med. **7** (2020)
10. Voulodimos, A., Doulamis, N., Doulamis, A., Protopapadakis, E.: Deep learning for computer vision: a brief review. Comput. Intell. Neurosci. **2018**, c7068349 (2018). https://doi.org/10.1155/2018/7068349

An Original Continuous-to-Continuous Forward Model as a Universal Method for the Formulation of Reconstruction Methods for Medical Imaging Techniques

Robert Cierniak[(✉)] and Piotr Pluta

Department of Intelligent Computer Systems, Czestochowa University of Technology, Armii Krajowej 36, 42-200 Czestochowa, Poland
robert.cierniak@pcz.pl
http://www.iisi.pcz.pl/

Abstract. This original approach to the formulation of a continuous-to-continuous (C-C) forward model can be used as a universal way to design reconstruction algorithms. In this work, we show how to adapt this forward model to different medical imaging techniques, particularly computed tomography (CT) and positron emission tomography (PET). In the case of CT, we will discuss strategies for the formulation of a practical statistical iterative reconstruction algorithm for scanners with parallel-beam, fan beam, and spiral cone-beam geometries. Some possible practical implementation methods for the PET technique are also considered, however. Our method is compared with a statistical approach based on a forward model belonging to the discrete-to-discrete (D-D) category; our approach has some significant advantages when compared with this methodology. Firstly, in our method, we establish certain coefficients (the convolution kernel) but this is performed much more easily than in D-D methods. Secondly, we only need to carry out the reconstruction procedure for one plane in 2D space, greatly simplifying the reconstruction problem. Additionally, our approach outperforms the D-D methodology in regard to its much better conditioning of the reconstruction problem. This makes our reconstruction method more competitive in terms of its resistance to the influence of noise and errors in the forward model. But above all, thanks to the fact that our proposed model is derived as a shift- invariant system, it is possible to use an FFT algorithm to accelerate the most demanding calculations in the formulated reconstruction algorithms.

Keywords: Reconstruction methods · Iterative reconstruction · Data model

The project financed under the program of the Polish Minister of Science and Higher Education under the name "Regional Initiative of Excellence" in the years 2019 - 2022 project number 020/RID/2018/19 the amount of financing 12,000,000 PLN.

1 Introduction

Recent research in the area of tomography techniques for medicine is mostly focused on the challenge to reduce the dose of x-ray radiation absorbed by patients during examinations (computed tomography) and radiopharmaceutical dose absorption (positron emission tomography). This challenge is relevant because of the harmful effect that CT (and partly also PET) examinations have on human health [2]. The most interesting research directions in the area of CT [1] and PET [3,4] are statistical reconstruction methods, especially those belonging to the model-based iterative reconstruction (MBIR) class of methods [1]. Some commercial solutions have been developed, which perform the reconstruction process in an iterative way, which aims to suppress noise in the obtained images. These methods are consistent with a discrete-to-discrete (D-D) data model, where the reconstructed image only in discrete form is considered, and measurements are exclusively discrete. The D-D forward model used in those approaches is as follows [5]:

$$p = AF, \tag{1}$$

where p is a matrix representing measurements; A is a system matrix; F is a reconstructed image.

The MBIR methods used commercially (e.g. the iterative coordinate descent (ICD) algorithm described comprehensively in [6]) have some serious drawbacks, above all the calculation complexity of the problem is approximately proportional to I^4, where I is the image resolution. Moreover, the size of the forward model matrix A is extremely large and it has to be calculated online. All those drawbacks can be reduced by using an approach that is formulated based on a continuous-to-continuous (C-C) data model. In previous papers, we have shown how to formulate the analytical reconstruction problem consistent with the ML strategy for CT scanners with parallel geometry [7], [8], for fan-beam geometry [9], and we have proposed reconstruction methods for the spiral cone-beam scanners [10–13].

First of all, in our approach, the forward model is formulated as a shift invariant system, which allows for the use of FFT algorithms in the most computationally demanding elements of the reconstruction algorithm (realization of the 2D convolutions in the frequency domain). Furthermore, we can pre-calculate the model matrix (coefficients), i.e. we establish it before the algorithm is started. Additionally, the reconstruction process can be carried out in only one plane in 2D space, which greatly simplifies the reconstruction problem, and it is possible to obtain every slice of the body separately. In this paper, we present this forward model as a universal tool for the formulation of statistical iterative reconstruction methods for different medical imaging techniques.

2 Continuous-to-Continuous Data Model Formulation

The statistical reconstruction approach presented below is fundamentally formulated to parallel beam tomography. However, it can be adopted for the most existing geometries of the produced scanners.

Thus, let us start from the presentation of the basic definitions, i.e. the continuous function $f(x, y)$ that denotes the unknown image representing a cross-section of an examined object. Image $f(x, y)$ will be calculated using projections obtained by using the Radon transform. The function $p(s, \alpha)$ is the result of a measurement carried out at a distance s from the origin when a projection is made at a specific angle α, and that is written mathematically as

$$p(s, \alpha) = \int\limits_{-\infty}^{+\infty} \int\limits_{-\infty}^{+\infty} f(x, y) \cdot \delta(x \cos \alpha + y \sin \alpha - s)\, dx dy. \qquad (2)$$

It is worth noting that there is the following relation between the fixed coordinate system (x, y) and the rotated coordinate system (s, u): $s = x \cos \alpha + y \sin \alpha$. It should be also underlined that projection functions $p(s, \alpha)$ are considered as continuous.

If we consider the scheme of the reconstruction algorithm, we perform the first step of the reconstruction procedure: the back-projection operation. This operation is described by the following equation:

$$\tilde{f}(x, y) = \int\limits_{-\pi}^{\pi} p(s, \alpha)\, d\alpha, \qquad (3)$$

for a full revolution of the scanner.

Because in the real projection geometry it is highly likely that for any given projection angle no ray will pass through the point (x, y) of the reconstructed image, it will be necessary to apply interpolation to obtain the appropriate projection during the back-projection operation described by (3). Mathematically, in a continuous space, the interpolation can be expressed as follows:

$$\bar{p}(s, \alpha) = \int\limits_{-\infty}^{+\infty} \bar{p}(\bar{s}, \alpha) \cdot int(s - \bar{s})\, d\bar{s}, \qquad (4)$$

where $int(\Delta s)$ is an interpolation function.

Thus, we will introduce the interpolated projections $\bar{p}(s, \alpha)$ from equation (4) instead of $p(s, \alpha)$ into relation (3). In this way we obtain a blurred filtered image after the back-projection operation, which can be expressed by

$$\tilde{f}(x, y) = \int\limits_{-\pi}^{\pi} \int\limits_{-\infty}^{+\infty} p(\bar{s}, \alpha)\, int(s - \bar{s})\, d\bar{s} d\alpha. \qquad (5)$$

According to Eq. (2), we can transform relation (5) into the following form:

$$\tilde{f}(x, y) = \int\limits_{-\pi}^{\pi} \int\limits_{-\infty}^{+\infty} \int\limits_{-\infty}^{+\infty} \int\limits_{-\infty}^{+\infty} f(\bar{x}, \bar{y}) \cdot \delta(\bar{x} \cos \alpha + \bar{y} \sin \alpha - \bar{s})\, d\bar{x} d\bar{y} \cdot int(s - \bar{s})\, d\bar{s} d\alpha,$$
$$\qquad (6)$$

and further:

$$\tilde{f}(x,y) = \int\limits_{-\infty}^{+\infty} \int\limits_{-\infty}^{+\infty} f(\bar{x},\bar{y}) \int\limits_{-\pi}^{\pi} \left(\int\limits_{-\infty}^{+\infty} \delta\left(\bar{x}\cos\alpha + \bar{y}\sin\alpha - \bar{s}\right) int\left(s - \bar{s}\right) d\bar{s} \right) d\alpha d\bar{x} d\bar{y}. \quad (7)$$

Finally, we can present a compact form of the above model, as a shift-invariant system, as follows:

$$\tilde{f}(x,y) = \int\limits_{-\infty}^{+\infty} \int\limits_{-\infty}^{+\infty} f(\bar{x},\bar{y}) h\left(\varDelta x, \varDelta y\right) \bar{x} d\bar{y}. \quad (8)$$

where the kernel $h\left(\varDelta x, \varDelta y\right)$ is determined according to the following expression:

$$h\left(\varDelta x, \varDelta y\right) = \int\limits_{0}^{2\pi} int\left(\varDelta x\cos\alpha + \varDelta y\sin\alpha\right) d\alpha, \quad (9)$$

and $int\left(\varDelta s\right)$ is an interpolation function used during the back-projection operation.

Obviously, regarding our possibilities to perform calculation, it is necessary to discretize some above formulas, i.e.:

$$\tilde{f}(x_i,y_j) = \varDelta_\alpha\varDelta_s \sum_{\psi=0}^{\Psi-1}\sum_{l} p\left(l\varDelta_s, \alpha_\psi\right) int\left(s_{ij} - l\varDelta_s\right). \quad (10)$$

where: $s_{ij} = i\varDelta_s\cos\alpha_\psi + j\varDelta_s\sin\alpha_\psi$ is the coordinate defining the position of point (i,j) on the screen, during a projection carried out at angle α_ψ; (x_i, y_j) are coordinates of pixels; I is a dimension of the reconstructed image; l is an index of the parallel beams, $\varDelta_s$ is a distance between these beams, ψ is an index of the performed views, and the kernel $h_{\varDelta i,\varDelta j}$ is precalculated, as follows:

$$h_{\varDelta i,\varDelta j} = \varDelta_\alpha \sum_{\psi=0}^{\Psi-1} int\left(\varDelta i\cos\psi\varDelta_\alpha + \varDelta j\sin\psi\varDelta_\alpha\right). \quad (11)$$

3   Model-based Iterative Reconstruction Method

The presented formulas (8) and (9) are fundamentals for the proposed here D-D data model. It is the so-called forward model which can be used to design the statistical reconstruction methods for different imaging modalities. We propose two methods: the dedicated to transmission tomography (x-ray Computed Tomography) and the designed especially for emission tomography (Positron Emission Tomography). In both cases, methods are based on the popular Maximum Likelihood (ML) estimation. A form of the objective in the ML method depends on the statistical conditions in a given imaging modality. Generally, in the PET scanners, there is preferred to take into account the Poisson distribution of measurement noise. It means that the Kullback-Leibler (KL) divergence will be utilized at the method formulation. In turn, in the CT scanners, it is preferred the least squares method (W-LS). In further considerations, we will only present the results of the performed statistical analyses because it would exceed the size of this short report.

3.1   Model-based Iterative Reconstruction Method for PET

The method here relates strictly to the positron emission tomography (PET) belonging to a class of emission tomography techniques. The standard reconstruction method used in this is the maximum likelihood-expectation maximization (ML-EM) algorithm [14].

The goal of the PET technique is to reconstruct the distribution of the radioactive tracer in the investigated tissues based on a set of projections acquired by a PET scanner. We propose a new approach to reconstruction problem which is based on the C-C data model presented in the previous section. Our reconstruction algorithm is performed in iterative way, according to the following formula:

$$f^{t+1}(x,y) = f^t(x,y) \frac{1}{g(x,y)} \int_{\bar{x}} \int_{\bar{y}} \frac{\tilde{f}(\bar{x},\bar{y})}{\int_{\bar{\bar{x}}} \int_{\bar{\bar{y}}} f^t(\bar{\bar{x}},\bar{\bar{y}}) h_{\Delta x,\Delta y} d\bar{\bar{x}} d\bar{\bar{y}}} h_{\Delta x,\Delta y} d\bar{x} d\bar{y} \quad (12)$$

where $\tilde{f}(x,y)$ is an image obtained by way of a back-projection operation, theoretically determined according to the relation (8), wherein $p(s,\alpha)$ are measurements carried out using a hypothetical parallel beam PET scanner, coefficients $h_{\Delta x,\Delta y}$ can be precalculated according to the formula (9), and $g(x,y)$ is a sum of all coefficients $h_{\Delta x,\Delta y}$ taken into account at the calculation of a given expression $\frac{\tilde{f}(\bar{x},\bar{y})}{\int_{\bar{\bar{x}}} \int_{\bar{\bar{y}}} f^t(\bar{\bar{x}},\bar{\bar{y}}) h_{\Delta x,\Delta y} d\bar{\bar{x}} d\bar{\bar{y}}} h_{\Delta x,\Delta y}$.

The image processing in this algorithm is entirely consistent with the continuous-to-continuous data model. Now, to perform calculation, it is possible to discretize above formula, as follows:

$$f^{t+1}(x_i,y_j) = f^t(x_i,y_j) \frac{1}{g_{ij}} \sum_{\bar{i}}^{I} \sum_{j=1}^{I} \frac{\tilde{f}(x_{\bar{i}},y_{\bar{j}})}{\sum_{\bar{\bar{i}}} \sum_{\bar{\bar{j}}} f^t(x_{\bar{\bar{i}}},y_{\bar{\bar{y}}}) h_{\Delta i,\Delta j}} h_{\Delta i,\Delta j} \quad (13)$$

wherein g_{ij} is a sum of all coefficients $h_{\Delta i,\Delta j}$ taken into account at the calculation of a given expression $\frac{\tilde{f}(x_{\bar{i}},y_{\bar{j}})}{\sum_{\bar{\bar{i}}} \sum_{\bar{\bar{j}}} f^t(x_{\bar{\bar{i}}},y_{\bar{\bar{y}}}) h_{\Delta i,\Delta j}} h_{\Delta i,\Delta j}$, and $h_{\Delta i,\Delta j}$ are determined according to the formula (11).

3.2   Model-based Iterative Reconstruction Method for CT

In turn, this method relates strictly to the computed tomography (CT) belonging to a class of transmission tomography techniques. The goal of the CT technique is to reconstruct the distribution of the x-ray attenuation coefficient in the investigated tissues based on a set of projections acquired by a CT scanner. Although the standard reconstruction algorithms used in this are Filtration/Back-Projections (FBP) methods, methods based on the maximum likelihood (ML) estimation are gaining more and more popularity.

We present an approach to the reconstruction problem dedicated to the CT technique. This approach is based on the C-C data model presented in the previous section. Our reconstruction algorithm is performed in iterative way, according to the following formula:

$$
\mathbf{f}_{\min} = \arg\min_{\mathbf{f}} \left(\int\limits_x \int\limits_y \left(\int\limits_{\bar{x}} \int\limits_{\bar{y}} f\left(\bar{x}, \bar{y}\right) \cdot h_{\Delta x, \Delta y} d\bar{x} d\bar{y} - \tilde{f}\left(x, y\right) \right)^2 dx dy \right), \quad (14)
$$

where $\tilde{f}\left(x, y\right)$ is an image obtained by way of a back-projection operation, theoretically determined according to the relation (8), wherein $p\left(s, \alpha\right)$ are measurements carried out using a hypothetical parallel beam CT scanner, coefficients $h_{\Delta x, \Delta y}$ can be precalculated according to the formula (9).

Again, the image processing in this algorithm is entirely consistent with the continuous-to-continuous data model, and, for performing calculations, it is possible to discretize the above optimization problem, as follows:

$$
\mathbf{f}_{\min} = \arg\min_{\mathbf{f}} \left(\sum_i \sum_j \left(\sum_{\bar{i}} \sum_{\bar{j}} f\left(x_{\bar{i}}, y_{\bar{j}}\right) \cdot h_{\Delta i, \Delta j} - \tilde{f}\left(x_i, y_j\right) \right)^2 \right), \quad (15)
$$

Although, there are several methods of searching for the optimal solution for the optimization problem (15), we propose the gradient descent method, because of its simplicity. In this case, the pixels in the reconstructed image will take the following values:

$$
\mathbf{f}^{(t+1)}\left(x_i, y_j\right) = \mathbf{f}^{(t)}\left(x_i, y_j\right) - c \cdot \sum_{\bar{i}=1}^{I} \sum_{\bar{j}=1}^{I} e^{(t)}\left(x_{\bar{i}}, y_{\bar{j}}\right) h_{\Delta i, \Delta j}, \quad (16)
$$

, where c is a constant coefficient, and

$$
e^{(t)}\left(x_{\bar{i}}, y_{\bar{j}}\right) = \sum_i \sum_j f^{(t)}\left(x_i, y_j\right) \cdot h_{\Delta i, \Delta j} - \tilde{f}\left(x_{\bar{i}}, y_{\bar{j}}\right), \quad (17)
$$

wherein $h_{\Delta i, \Delta j}$ are determined according to the formula (11).

4   Experimental Results

We divided our computer simulations into two phases: first, we will try to show that the C-C data model gives better quality of the reconstructed images for the PET application, and then, we will perform experiments dedicated to the CT application.

It was convenient to establish coefficients $h_{\Delta i, \Delta j}$ using relation (11) before the reconstruction process was started. In both cases, the quality of the reconstructed image has been evaluated by a well-known MSE measure.

In the first phase, we have adapted the well-known Shepp-Logan mathematical phantom (all values divided by 10^{-3}). During the simulations, for parallel projections, we fixed L = 512 virtual detectors on the virtual screen. The number of views was chosen as $\Psi = 1456$ per full-rotation and the size of the processed image was fixed at I × I = 512 × 512 pixels.

It is possible to conduct the virtual measurements and complete all the required parallel projections which relate to the measurements. Then, through suitable rebinning operations, the back-projection operation was carried out to obtain an image $\tilde{f}(x_i, y_j)$. Next, the iterative reconstruction procedure was realized. There is depicted the reconstructed image after 25000 iterations in the Fig. 1.a. For comparison, a view of the reconstructed image using a reconstruction algorithm based on the D-D data model is also shown in Fig. 1.b.

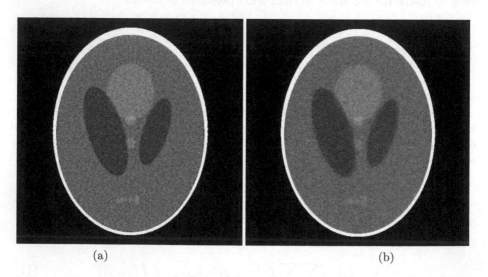

(a)   (b)

Fig. 1. Views of the images ($C = 1.05 \cdot 10^{-3}$, $W = 0.1 \cdot 10^{-3}$): reconstructed image using the C-C statistical approach proposed in this paper obtained after 25 000 iterations ($MSE = 2,84 \cdot 10^{-9}$) (a), reconstructed image using the D-D statistical approach obtained after 60 iterations ($MSE = 3,22 \cdot 10^{-9}$).

In the next phase of our experiments, we have adapted the FORBILD phantom [15] (all the values of the attenuation coefficients placed in the original model were divided by a factor 10^{-3}). During our experiments, we fixed L = 1024 measurement detectors on the screen, the number of projections was chosen as $\Psi = 3220$ rotation angles per full-rotation, and the size of the processed image was fixed at I × I = 1024 × 1024 pixels.

At this time, we have taken into account one form of regularization for the algorithm based on the D-D data model: the total variation (TV) prior [16]. The result obtained are shown in Fig. 2.a. For comparison, the referential ICD algorithm (D-D data model) in Fig. 2.b is also presented.

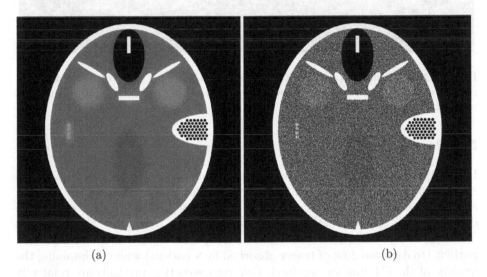

(a) (b)

Fig. 2. Views of the images ($C = 1.05 \cdot 10^{-3}$, $W = 0.1 \cdot 10^{-3}$): (a) reconstructed image using the C-C statistical approach proposed in this paper obtained after 20 000 iterations ($MSE = 3.17 \cdot 10^{-9}$) (b) reconstructed image using the D-D statistical approach obtained after 15 iterations ($MSE = 3.37 \cdot 10^{-9}$).

Finally, we would show an application of our conception in an practical implementation. Experiments in the this phase were carried out using projections obtained from a Somatom Definition AS+ commercial CT scanner. Figure 3 depicts results obtained using measurements at the full-dose (recently used in clinical practice), and an image reconstructed using a quarter-dose.

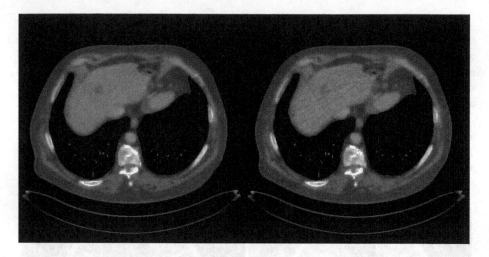

Fig. 3. Obtained image (a case with pathological change in the liver) using full-dose projections (left) quarter-dose projections (right) with application of the statistical method presented in this paper.

5   Conclusions

It has been shown that the forward model formulated by us can be used to solve reconstruction problems in different medical applications, e.g. in positron emission tomography and in computed tomography. In this way, it is possible to design iterative reconstruction algorithms that allow to improve the resolution of reconstructed images and/or decrease x-ray dose absorbed by an examined patient (to decrease dose of tracer absorbed by a patient) while maintaining the quality of the CT images obtained. Our reconstruction methods are relatively fast (thanks to the use of the FFT algorithms) and give satisfactory results with suppressed noise regarding results obtained using the referential D-D algorithms. For both techniques, in total, the computational complexity is approximately $O\left(8log_2 4I^2\right)$ operations per one iteration of the iterative reconstruction procedure (totally it takes less than 10s). This is rewarding result regarding possibilities of the commercial Veo system (referential MBIR approach), where reconstruction times range between 10 to 90 min depending on the number of reconstructed slices [17]. It means an unacceptable delay between data acquisition and availability for interpretation, especially for emergent indications.

References

1. Zhou, Y., Thibault, J.-B., Bouman, C.A., Hsieh, J., Sauer, K.D.: Fast model-based X-ray CT reconstruction using spatially non-homogeneous ICD optimization. IEEE Tran. Image Proc. **20**, 161–175 (2011)
2. Mathews, J. D., et al.: Cancer risk in 680 people expose to computed tomography scans in childhood or adolescent: data linkage study of 11 million Australians. British Medical Journal, f2360, 346–360 (2013)

3. Sauer, K., Bouman, C.: A local update strategy for iterative reconstruction from projections. IEEE Tran. Signal Proc. **41**, 534–548 (1993)
4. Bouman, C.A., Sauer, K.: A unified approach to statistical tomography using coordinate descent optimization. IEEE Tran. Image Proc. **5**, 480–492 (1996)
5. Censor, Y.: Finite series-expansion reconstruction methods. Proc. IEEE **71**, 409–419 (1983)
6. Thibault, J.-B., Sauer, K.D., Bouman, C.A., Hsieh, J.: A three-dimensional statistical approach to improved image quality for multislice helical CT. Med. Phys. **34**, 4526–4544 (2007)
7. Cierniak, R.: A new approach to tomographic image reconstruction using a Hopfield-type neural network. Int. J. Artif. Intell. Med. **43**, 113–125 (2008)
8. Cierniak, R.: A new approach to image reconstruction from projections problem using a recurrent neural network. Int. J. Appl. Math. Comput. Sci. **183**, 147–157 (2008)
9. Cierniak, R.: New neural network algorithm for image reconstruction from fan-beam projections. Neurocomputing **72**, 3238–3244 (2009)
10. Cierniak, R.: A three-dimensional neural network based approach to the image reconstruction from projections problem. Lect. Notes Artif. Intell. **6113**, 505–514 (2010)
11. Cierniak, R.: Analytical statistical reconstruction algorithm with the direct use of projections performed in spiral cone-beam scanners. In: Proceedings of the 5th International Meeting on Image Formation in X-Ray Computed Tomography, Salt Lake City, pp. 293–296 (2018)
12. Cierniak, R., Pluta, P., Kaźmierczak, A.: A practical statistical approach to the reconstruction problem using a single slice rebinning method. J. Artif. Intell. Soft Comput. Res. **10**, 137–149 (2020)
13. Cierniak, R., et al.: A new statistical reconstruction method for the computed tomography using an X-ray tube with flying focal spot. J. Artif. Intell. Soft Comput. Res. **11**, 271–286 (2021)
14. Shepp, L.A., Vardi, Y.: Maximum likelihood reconstruction for emission tomography. IEEE Tran. Med. Imag. **1**(2), 113–122 (1982)
15. FORBILD project. http://www.imp.uni-erlangen.de/forbild/deutsch/results/head/head.html Accessed 12 Dec 2020
16. Rudin, L.I., Osher, S., Fatemi, E.: Nonlinear total variation based noise removal algorithms. Phys. D Nonlin. Phenom. **60**, 259–268 (1992)
17. Geyer, L.L., et al.: State of the art: iterative CT reconstruction techniques. Radiology **276**, 339–357 (2017)

Applications for Industry 4.0

Towards a Dynamic Vehicular Clustering Improving VoD Services on Vehicular Ad Hoc Networks

Bechir Alaya[1,2(✉)], Lamaa Sellami[1,3], and Mutiq Al Mutiq[1]

[1] Department of Management Information Systems and Production Management, College of Business and Economics, Qassim University, 6633, Buraidah 51452, Saudi Arabia
{b.alaya,l.sellami,m.almutiq}@qu.edu.sa
[2] Hatem Bettaher Laboratory (IResCoMath), FSG, Gabes University, Gabes, Tunisia
[3] Commande Numérique des Procédés Industriels Laboratory (CONPRI), ENIG, Gabes University, Gabes, Tunisia

Abstract. Nowadays, video-on-demand (VoD) applications are becoming one of the tendencies driving vehicular network users. In this paper, considering the unpredictable vehicle density, the unexpected acceleration or deceleration of the different cars included in the vehicular traffic load, and the limited radio range of the employed communication scheme, we introduce the "Dynamic Vehicular Clustering" (DVC) algorithm as a new scheme for video streaming systems over VANET. The proposed algorithm takes advantage of the concept of small cells and the introduction of wireless backhauls, inspired by the different features and the performance of the Long Term Evolution (LTE)- Advanced network. The proposed clustering algorithm considers multiple characteristics such as the vehicle's position and acceleration to reduce latency and packet loss. Therefore, each cluster is counted as a small cell containing vehicular nodes and an access point that is elected regarding some particular specifications.

Keywords: Video-on-demand · Vehicular ad-hoc network · Mobility · Vehicular traffic load · Small cell · Wireless backhaul · LTE-Advanced · Latency · Packet loss

1 Introduction

Vehicular Ad-Hoc Networks (VANET) are highly mobile wireless ad-hoc networks that were implemented to support passenger safety, driving assistance and emergency warning services. VANET is designed to grant vehicular self-organized formation [1, 2]. Generally, smart car designers have shown increasing attention to the employment of Dedicated Short Range Communication (DSRC) based on IEEE 802.11p [3–5]. However, DSRC is not a suitable solution for vehicle to infrastructure communication because of its limited radio range [6]. Therefore, there have been various studies in the literature [7, 8] suggesting the deployment of the fourth-generation Long Term Evolution

C. Bădică et al. (Eds.): ICCCI 2022, CCIS 1653, pp. 409–422, 2022.
https://doi.org/10.1007/978-3-031-16210-7_34

(LTE) systems, as well as the next-generation LTE, advanced to deal with vehicular communications [9, 10].

Video streaming applications' requirements in terms of network resource management and QoS specifications have been the main issue for numerous studies during the last decade [11–13]. Vehicular networks are more concerned with video streaming issues due to their high mobility, dynamic topology, and unpredictable user density. Therefore, video streaming among vehicular networks raises more QoS requirements challenges. The wireless network supporting vehicular communication must deal carefully with interference, frequent handover issues, and video storage locations to enhance the streaming quality in terms of content availability, low latency, and minimum frame loss.

We have more communication challenges to report considering video streaming over vehicular networks [14, 15]. High mobility and unpredictable users' density make the process of delivering video content with the desired QoS, challenging in terms of resource allocation, content distribution, and interference reduction. Therefore, the use of heterogeneous schemes to separate signaling traffic links and content flows seems to be a promising paradigm to reduce interference among vehicular networks [16]. However, mobile nodes among a VANET system are not restricted to a predefined traffic network since its multiple degrees of freedom (i.e. high mobile node) [17].

In this paper, we propose a dynamic algorithm called Dynamic Vehicular Clustering (DVC) to enhance both vehicle-to-vehicle and vehicle-to-Base station connectivity among high mobility networks. The proposed algorithm exhibits the impact of small cell deployment on connectivity and mobility performance in Long Term Evolution (LTE)-Advanced-based vehicular network. Furthermore, the introduction of 5G features into vehicular ad-hoc networks [18, 19] such as the concept and communication of the small cell over wireless backhaul networks will enhance video content transmission due to its low latency and the utilized schemes to deal effectively with congestion and interference issues.

The remainder of the paper is organized as follows: Sect. 2 introduces an overview of the related issues to video streaming and vehicular networks; Sect. 3 illustrates the proposed algorithm and highlights the different features of the clustering scheme; Sect. 4 evaluates the solution based on simulations results analysis and compares its performance to existing studies; Finally, Sect. 5 concludes the paper.

2   Related Work

In the literature, there are numerous schemes to boost V2V and V2I communications regarding their features [20–23]. The common strategy promotes the use of a separate solution for each type of link. V2V communication links two or more vehicles directly (i.e. without infrastructure's relaying) to minimize control traffic and cope with range limitation among the mobile network [24]. Moreover, smart vehicles are nowadays equipped with high-performance processors and large caches. Hence, short-range networks can perfectly support this type of vehicular link since data management and storage are available using the car's smart-board without the infrastructure's involvement. DSRC has been a highly recommended scheme to serve V2V communication with effective support, high throughput, low latency, and low cost. V2I communication needs a robust wireless network to deal properly with interference between different vehicles communicating with the infrastructure. The devoted scheme must support long-range communications to manage the vehicle's high mobility. Therefore, LTE and LTE Advanced are becoming very popular as the most promising techniques for V2I communications. The next generation will be more attractive to be deployed in vehicular networks, especially with its tendency to establish communication with almost no latency, no more concerns about bandwidth capacity, very high throughput, etc. [25, 26]. However, the case of dense cells remains a critical concern for vehicular networks that need effective employment of the existing schemes.

It is considered a promising paradigm to have cooperative communication established directly between two or more wireless nearby devices (i.e. without having the base station involved). Device-to-Device communication shows major benefits in terms of reliability, spectral efficiency, storage capacity, and transmission range issues. A D2D communication involves source, destination, and device relays which are the intermediate devices utilized as relaying nodes to transmit content over a massive ad-hoc mesh network. In the context of vehicular networks, video content relaying requires device dynamic location discovery to ensure durable communication within its neighbors to enhance content availability and minimize packet loss rate [27, 28].

The BS will normally continue supervising and serving the devices through the macro cell regardless of the established D2D link. However, in the case of congested cells, the devices will create an ad-hoc mesh network and the BS services will be abolished. This type of D2D link is established and supervised by the BS which continues its communication with the devices (Fig. 1).

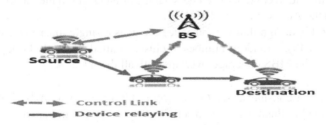

Fig. 1. D2D communication with BS controlled link.

Another possible scenario for D2D communication is when the BS control is replaced by device-controlled links (Fig. 2). Hence, a direct link is established between devices from the source to destination to carry content over device relays without the BS control. Each device should be self-assisted to use effectively system resources. On the other hand, devices should exchange content using smart interference management schemes to reduce packet loss rate and performance degradation. Compared to the schemes surveyed above, our work introduces a dynamic clustering process to deal with road load frequent updates and high mobility environments problems. Moreover, the scheme does not rely on broadcasting but it is more target-oriented communication. For each cluster, a head node is elected not as a "forwarding node" but as an access point to handle all exchanges between the cluster and the roadside units. In the following section a detailed description of our proposed algorithm.

Fig. 2. D2D communication with self-controlled links.

3   The Proposed Solution

The small cells concept is considered an unavoidable solution for the next-generation 5G network's architecture. Regardless of its drawbacks, we are developing in this paper an adaptive system model inspired by the features of small cells and a 5G wireless backhaul network's management in ultra-dense small cells.

3.1   System Model and Problem Formulation

We introduce the concept of Dynamic Vehicle Clustering (DVC) for video content delivery over next-generation macrocells (MC). A cluster contains the Client Vehicle (i.e. the car requiring the video content), the Peers having already stored the video, the Relaying Vehicles, and the Access Point (AP).

The network's design that we introduce includes a single macro-cell with a Macro Base Station (MBS), a random number of clusters called 'Friendly Groups' (FG), and car users (CU), the MBS coverage overlaps with all the other FG.

Architecture. We consider a set $FG \triangleq \{fg(1, AP_1), \ldots, fg(K, AP_K)\}$ of K Friendly Groups contained in the macro cell, a set $CU \triangleq \bigcup_{n=1}^{K}(FG_n)$ of car users, a set.

$AP \triangleq \{(AP_1), \ldots, (AP_K)\}$ of K selected access points and a set $V = \sum_{i=0}^{n} V_i$ of videos pre-stored in the Cloud data centers [29, 30].

We take into account the use of disjoint sub-channel allocation among different APs while we are defining the friendly groups' formation referring to the concept of small cells [31]. Furthermore, to improve system performances we recommend the use of enhanced Inter-Cell. Interference Coordination Techniques (eICIC) are proposed in LTE Rel. 10 to deal with interference between neighboring APs. It offers resource partitioning between the macro cell and small cell to improve the offload of traffic to the small cell layer [32, 33]. Hence, the technique optimizes the scheduling process by offering the possibility to coordinate the resource usage between the MBS and each AP.

Video requests. In this paper, user requests are modeled by RQ_m. We consider as well a set of users friendly lists $FL \triangleq \bigcup_{k=1}^{S}[fl(V_K, Z_1), \ldots, fl(V_k, Z_N)]$ where:

- Z_i (I = 1...N) refers to a sub-region consisting of the subset of users in the same location as the user CU_j.
- fl (V_K,Z_i) is the friendly list containing users nearby the user CU_j (at a sub-region of 60 GHz) having already downloaded the requested video V_K and having accepted to share it?
- S refers to the total number of videos having been delivered in the macro cell.

The main use of Dynamic Vehicles Clustering (Fig. 3) is to reduce signalization messages exchanged among the macro cell. Therefore, this scheme can help reduce interference, which will normally decrease the frame loss rate. On the other hand, it defines a heterogeneous scheme for vehicular communications, which deals separately with V2V and V2I links. Direct V2V communication can be ideally supported by the DSRC scheme described in the Sect. 2, while the next-generation 5G network's features will be used for AP to MBS backhaul link. Hence, combining these communication schemes can provide a streaming service with low latency and better performances.

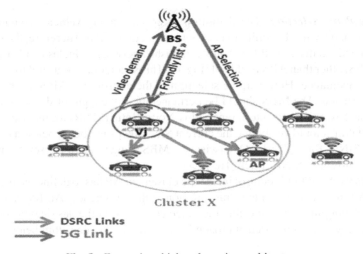

Fig. 3. Dynamic vehicles clustering architecture.

3.2 Dynamic Vehicles Clustering Features

Friendly List. The MBS creates dynamic lists of vehicles storing each video to facilitate content location. The macrocell is subdivided into N sub-region Z(i = 1..N) based on users' density (i.e. a sub-region is a geographical zone where the number of users is upper than a predefined Density-Threshold DT). Among each sub-region where users have already downloaded the video V_K, all considered users are invited to join the friendly list of video V_K corresponding to the sub-region Z_i. Hence, users who have sent back an acknowledgment to the MBS are automatically added to the concerned friendly list.

Moreover, the idea of the deployment of friendly lists is used for security measurements besides its role in content location. It makes sure that the MBS in charge is permanently aware of the identity of the members ensuring the content delivery among the macro cell.

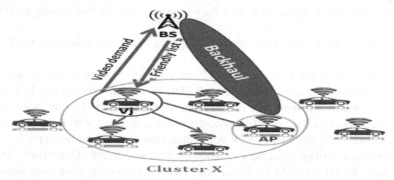

Fig. 4. Dynamic vehicles clustering architecture with backhaul establishment.

Access Point Selection. The definition of an AP among vehicles contained in a cluster aims mainly for the limitation of backhauls' congestion. Therefore, the proposed strategy intends to discard all backhauls established between vehicles inside the cluster and the MBS, other than AP's backhaul (Fig. 4). This scheme can be useful for backhauls congestion avoidance. However, the selection of the appropriate AP in each cluster is a critical decision. The MBS should be permanently at the sight of the selected AP to maintain the best Signal-to-Interference-plus-Noise-Ratio (SINR) for the backhaul link. The base station should verify that the current SINR keeps not being below a predefined threshold (SINR_Back_Tresh). Otherwise, the MBS triggers a new AP selection process (i.e. When current < SINR_Back_Tresh >).

Besides the V2V link's control inside the cluster, an AP has to define the best Relays Vector (RV) that ensures content transmission with low latency. An RV refers to the different relaying nodes transporting the video content from the destination source.

A summary of the proposed approach is presented in the algorithm below:

Algorithm: *Dynamic Vehicles Clustering*

1- *Initialize a video V_k request RQ_m from CU_j to MBS*

2- *MBS defines the location Z_i of the CU_j*

3- *MBS checks the availability of $\mathrm{fl}(V_K, Z_i)$ in*
$$FL \triangleq U_{k=1}^S[fl(V_K, Z_1), \dots, fl(V_k, Z_N)]$$
if ($\mathrm{fl}(V_K, Z_i)$: available) {

4- *MBS sends $\mathrm{fl}(V_K, Z_i)$ to CU_j*

5- *CU_j establishes the clustering process*

6- *AP_i selection*

7- *V_K segments' transmission is trigged }*
else {MBS initializes V_K to V_K}

4 Simulation Results and Analysis

In the proposed study, the major intention is to develop a suitable technique based on the exceptional features of the LTE-Advanced network (small cells and wireless backhauls) for the controlling of video streaming services over VANET systems and to providing trust-based communication. DVC algorithm is implemented using MATLAB in the windows platform on the PC with Intel Core i7 and 8 GB RAM. The proposed system is analyzed based on the performances such as packet failure, bandwidth utilization, response time, and network scalability. The simulation parameters of VANET using the DVC algorithm are given in Table 1.

Table 1. Simulation parameters

Parameters	Setting
Number of nodes/Vehicle	100
Simulation area	100 m × 100 m
Paquet size	512 bytes
Transmission range	50 m – 150 m
Traffic type	Two Ray Ground
Vehicle speed	0–50 km/h
Number of clusters	4
PHY/MAC layer	IEEE 802.11p

The vehicle nodes (VN) act as 802.11p wireless access points (APs) to communicate between them in the coverage range in 100 m x 100 m and we set the bandwidth as 20 Mbps. In created network given in Fig. 5, we have included 100 vehicles moving on the paths in random directions and uniformly distributed and with a speed between 0–50 km/h.

Fig. 5. Initial topology for the experiments.

The virtual topology of the VANET network is created with four clusters as given in Fig. 5 and each cluster has a node to analyze the trustability. The nodes are represented as "●" and the four clusters are differentiated by spotting different colors.

The packets failure report without application of a management algorithm is given in Fig. 6. This report (packet loss) shows the measurement of the number of lost packets compared to the total number of transmitted packets. We can discover that packet loss randomly increases with the number of vehicle nodes.

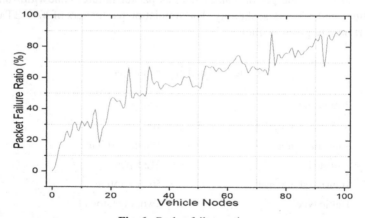

Fig. 6. Packet failure ratio.

Figure 7 illustrates the average probability of packet loss on the arrival rate of vehicle nodes with the application of our DVC algorithm and by comparing it with other algorithms such as VTD [34], NDN (Named Data Networking) [35], and SASMF [36]. The arrival rate of packets varies between 50 and 100 packets/s. It is clear that more than 80% of packets are delivered so that the loss is reduced by less than 20% with DVC in the interval from 0 to 50 vehicle nodes, also more than 50% of packets are delivered, so that the loss is reduced by less than 50% in the case of higher loads, in particular between 50 and 100 vehicle nodes. In cases where the arrival rate (n) of vehicle nodes is low (n < 20), the packet loss rates between DVC and VTD are almost similar. Indeed, with this low number of vehicle nodes, the collisions are limited. When n becomes big (n > 50), our algorithm gives better results to avoid excessive packets collisions and reduce the packet error rate. Take n = 100, the probability of packet loss decreases by more than 20% with our proposed algorithm compared to the VTD algorithm, more than 25% compared to the NDN algorithm, and more than 40% compared to the SASMF algorithm. Figure 7 clearly shows that the proposed DVC algorithm has reduced the average packet failure rate of normal VANET communication. Consequently, the proposed technique then improves the packet delivery rate. The use of bandwidth is shown in Fig. 10.

Figure 10 clearly shows that the bandwidth with the DVC algorithm is efficiently used in our VANET network. Our VANET network uses around 98% of the bandwidth, while the DVC algorithm reduces it and uses up to 92%. Therefore, integrating the DVC algorithm into VANET has effectively managed bandwidth usage.

We can see that our new algorithm gives better results of simulation in all the spectrum of n, notably, an average and equitable use of the bandwidth in all load situations.

On the other hand, the other algorithms give either a maximum or minimum use of the bandwidth which is not preferable for VANET networks.

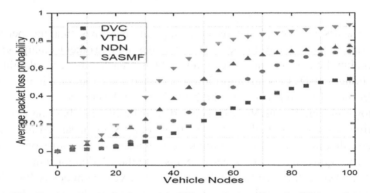

Fig. 7. Average packet loss probability vs the number of vehicle nodes.

As n increases, the use of bandwidth increases and decreases with DVC but in an interval of 89% to 92% which is still bearable by the VANET network. The figures also show that bandwidth usage increases and decreases randomly, rather than growing completely with n.

In Fig. 9 we compare the scalability of our VANET network. We evaluate the scalability of the network according to the response time. As the rate of arrival of vehicle nodes increases, the average response time is calculated and illustrated in Fig. 9.

Figure 9 shows the comparison results of response time for DVC, VTD, NDN, and SASMF algorithms under different numbers of vehicle nodes. Figure 8 shows the network scalability by varying the number of vehicle nodes. We can observe that the DVC algorithm has reached between 0.2 and 4 ms response time in terms of 50 at 250 vehicle nodes. On the other hand, compared to the other algorithms, one can also observe that DVC reached between 10% and 25% of the value of response time less than VTD, NDN, and SASMF algorithms with the same density of traffic. However, in the scenario of 100 car knots or less, DVC produces better response time values with less than 1 ms.

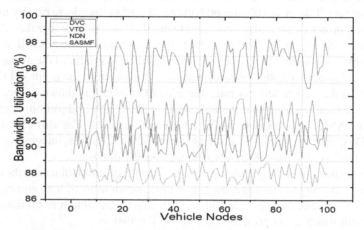

Fig. 8. Bandwidth utilization with and without DVC algorithm.

The comparison between the different algorithms shows that the performance degrades while increasing the number of vehicle nodes, among other techniques using the DVC algorithm the performances are better and have reached better scalability. These results indicate that DVC is an algorithm well suited for an application that requires reliable delivery of video packets in a high traffic VANET network.

As shown in Fig. 10 our VANET network will be busier when the rate of video requests from each vehicle node increases. From our results presented in Fig. 10, We can conceive that the guarantee of optimal performances of transmission of real-time video packets requires a delay of at least 1.8 ms with the DVC algorithm.

Likewise, even in the case where the number n of vehicle nodes is 100, the transmission delay is also acceptable (no more than 3 ms) mainly due to our algorithm and the high bandwidth of the VANET network.

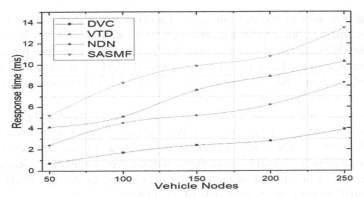

Fig. 9. Response time with and without DVC algorithm.

Increasing traffic generally leads to frequent changes in the network topology. Thus, the results show that the transmission delay increases in high-speed scenarios. The proposed algorithm allows a significant reduction in the transmission delay compared to other schemes. DVC creates stable clusters that can guarantee sufficient connectivity and a reliable link.

As a result, the retransmission times and the transmission delay are reduced, which results in a reduction of the transmission delay. Another reason is that using stable connected clusters, packets can be delivered to the next hop with reduced conflict, which leads to short network latency.

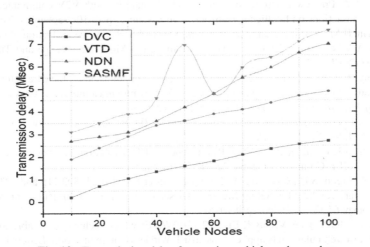

Fig. 10. Transmission delay for varying vehicle node number.

5   Conclusion

In this paper, we have proposed a dynamic algorithm "Dynamic Vehicle Clustering" (DVC) as a new scheme for video streaming systems on VANET taking into account the unpredictable density of vehicles, unexpected acceleration or deceleration of different cars included in the vehicle traffic load and the limited radio range of the communication scheme used. We have introduced a wireless link inspired by the different functionalities and performance of the Long Term Evolved Network (LTE)-Advanced. Our algorithm is proposed to enhance both vehicle-to-vehicle and vehicle-to-Base station connectivity among high mobility networks.

Our policy has allowed us to dynamically divide traffic into several clusters. Another objective of this article is to guarantee a certain balance of load and resources available between the various VANET network vehicle nodes. We also noted that the cooperation and the distribution of the load between the various clusters simplify the calculations and accelerate the task of diffusion of the packets and also reduce the time of convergence of the VANET network towards the state of equilibrium.

The results of theoretical analysis and experiences illustrate the effectiveness of our application of "Dynamic Vehicle Clustering" (DVC) due to the reduction of delays for the VANET network and the convergence towards a steady-state is greatly improved.

References

1. Wassim, D., Kyoung, H., Hesham, R., Fethi, F.: Development and Testing of a 3G/LTE Adaptive Data Collection System in Vehicular Networks. IEEE Transactions on Intelligent Transportation Systems 17 (2016)
2. Araniti, G., Campolo, C., Condoluci, M., Molinaro, A.: LTE for vehicular networking: a survey. IEEE Commun. Mag. 51(5), 148–157 (2013)
3. Seong, J.Y.: Preview controller design for vehicle stability with V2V communication. In: IEEE Transactions on Intelligent Transportation Systems, pp. 1–10 (September 2016)
4. Zeeshan, H.M., Fethi, F.: Large-scale simulations and performance evaluation of connected cars - A V2V communication perspective. Simulation Modeling Practice and Theory 72, 88–103 (2017)
5. Ruifeng, Z., Libo, C., Shan, B., Jianjie, T.: A method for connected vehicle trajectory prediction and collision warning algorithm based on V2V communication. Int. J. Crashworthiness (2016). https://doi.org/10.1080/13588265.2016.1215584
6. Kenney, J.: Dedicated short-range communications (DSRC) standards in the United States. Proc. IEEE 99(7), 1162–1182 (2011)
7. Hanbyul, S.K.L., Shinpei, Y., Ying, P., Philippe, S.: LTE evolution for vehicle-to-everything services. IEEE Commun. Mag. 54, 22–28 (2016). June
8. Ucar, S., Ergen, S.C., Ozkasap, O.: Multihop-cluster-based IEEE 802.11p and LTE Hybrid Architecture for VANET Safety Message Dissemination. IEEE Transactions on Vehicular Technology 65, 2621–2636 (April 2015)
9. Vinel, A.: 3GPP LTE Versus IEEE 802.11p/WAVE: which technology is able to support cooperative vehicular safety applications? IEEE Wireless Communications Letters 1, 125–128 (2012)
10. Alaya, B., Sellami, L.: Clustering method and symmetric/asymmetric cryptography scheme adapted to securing urban VANET networks. Journal of Information Security and Applications 58 (2021). https://doi.org/10.1016/j.jisa.2021.102779
11. Mendiboure, L., Chalouf, M.-A., Krief, F.: Edge computing based applications in vehicular environments: comparative study and main issues. J. Comput. Sci. Technol. 34(4), 869–886 (2019). https://doi.org/10.1007/s11390-019-1947-3

12. Sajid Mushtaq, M., Fowler, S., Augustin, B., Mellouk, A.: QoE in 5G Cloud Networks using MultimediaServices. In: IEEE Wireless Communications and Networking Conference (WCNC) (April 2016)
13. Zribi, N., Alaya, B., Moulahi, T.: Video streaming in vehicular Ad Hoc networks: applications, challenges and techniques. In: 2019 15th International Wireless Communications & Mobile Computing Conference (IWCMC), pp. 1221–1226 (2019). https://doi.org/10.1109/IWCMC. 2019.8766443
14. Neelakantan Pattathil Chandrasekharamenonand Babu AnchareV: Connectivity analysis of one-dimensionalvehicular ad hoc networks in fading channels. EURASIP Journal on Wireless Communications and Networking (December 2012)
15. Jeon, S., Kim, G., Kim, B.: Study on V2V-based AEB system performance analysis in various RoadConditions at an intersection. Int. J. Softw. Eng. Its Applic. 9(7), 1–10 (2015)
16. Ge, X., Cheng, H., Guizani, M., Han, T.: 5G wireless backhaul networks: challenges and research advances. IEEE Network 28(6), 6–11 (December 2014)
17. Abbas, M.T., Muhammad, A., Song, W.-C.: Road-aware estimation model for path duration in internet of vehicles (IoV). Wireless Pers. Commun. 109(2), 715–738 (2019). https://doi. org/10.1007/s11277-019-06587-5
18. Afaq, M., Iqbal, J., Ahmed, T., Ul Islam, I., Khan, M., Khan, M.S.: Towards 5G network slicing for vehicular ad-hoc networks: An end-to-end approach. Computer Communications 149, 252-258 (2020)
19. Iqbal, J., Iqbal, M.A., Ahmad, A., Khan, M., Qamar, A., Han, K.: Comparison of spectral efficiency techniques in device-to-device communication for 5G. IEEE Access 7, 57440–57449 (2019)
20. Storck, C.R., Duarte-Figueiredo, F.: A 5G V2X ecosystem providing internet of vehicles. Sensors 19(550), 1–20 (2019)
21. Takai, I., et al.. Optical VEHICLE-TO-VEHICLE communication system using LED transmitterand camera receiver. IEEE Photonics Journal 6(5) (October 2014)
22. Siddiqi, K., Raza, A.D., Sheikh Muhammad, S.: Visible light communication for V2V intelligent transport system. In: Broadband Communications for Next Generation Networks and Multimedia Applications (CoBCom), International Conference on (October 2016)
23. Lin, D., Kang, J., Squicciarini, A., Wu, Y., Gurung, S., Tonguz, O.: MoZo: a moving zone based routing protocol using pure V2V communication in VANETs. IEEE Transactions on Mobile Computing, pp. 1 (July 2016)
24. Alaya, B.: Payoff-based dynamic segment replication and graph classification method with attribute vectors adapted to urban VANET. ACM Trans. Multimedia Comput. Commun. Appl. 17(3), 22 (August 2021). Article 85 https://doi.org/10.1145/3440018
25. Montero, R., Agraz, F., Pagès, A., Spadaro, S.: Enabling multi-segment 5G service provisioning and maintenance through network slicing. J. Netw. Syst. Manage. 28(2), 340–366 (2020). https://doi.org/10.1007/s10922-019-09509-9
26. Zhang, X., Cheng, W., Zhang, H.: Heterogeneous statistical QoS provisioning over 5G mobile. In: Computer Communications (INFOCOM) IEEE Conference on (August 2015)
27. Jabbar, R., et al.: Blockchain technology for intelligent transportation systems: a systematic literature review. IEEE Access 10, 20995–21031 (2022). https://doi.org/10.1109/ACCESS. 2022.3149958
28. Khairnar, V.D., Pradhan, S.N.: V2V Communication survey - (wireless technology). Int. J. Computer Technology & Applications 3(1), 370–373 (February 2012)
29. Martín, J.R., Pérez-Leal, R., Navío-Marco, J.: Towards 5G: techno-economic analysis of suitable use cases. NETNOMICS: Economic Research and Electronic Networking 20(2–3), 153–175 (2019). https://doi.org/10.1007/s11066-019-09134-3
30. Afaq, M., Song, W.C.: A novel framework for resource orchestration in OpenStack cloud platform. KSII Trans. Internet Inf. Syst. 12, 5404–5424 (2018)

31. Kishiyama, Y., Benjebbour, A., Ishii, H., Nakamura, T.: Evolution concept and candidate technologies for future steps of LTE-A. In: Proc. of IEEE ICCS (2012)
32. Noorani, N., Seno, S.A.H.: SDN-and fog computing-based switchable routing using path stability estimation for vehicular ad hoc networks. Peer-to-Peer Netw. (Appl. 2020)
33. Astely, D., et al.: LTE: the evolution of mobile broadband. IEEE Communications Magazine **47**(4) (2009)
34. Charles, R., Balasubramanian, P., Protocol, V.T.D.: A cluster based trust model for secure communication in VANET. Int. J. Intelli. Eng. Sys. **13**, 35–45 (2020)
35. Jain, V., Kushwah, R.S., Tomar, R.S.: Named data network using trust function for securing vehicular Ad Hoc network. In: Proc. Soft Computing: Theories and Applications, pp. 463–471 (2019)
36. Xia, H., Zhang, S.S., Li, B.X., Li, L., Cheng, X.G.: Towards a novel trust-based multicast routing for VANET. Security and Communication Networks **2018**(1), 1–12 (2018)

RVT-Transformer: Residual Attention in Answerability Prediction on Visual Question Answering for Blind People

Duy-Minh Nguyen-Tran[1,2], Tung Le[1,2], Khoa Pho[3], Minh Le Nguyen[3], and Huy Tien Nguyen[1,2(✉)]

[1] Faculty of Information Technology, University of Science, Ho Chi Minh, Vietnam
20C11041@student.hcmus.edu.vn, {lttung,ntienhuy}@fit.hcmus.edu.vn
[2] Vietnam National University, Ho Chi Minh city, Vietnam
[3] Japan Advanced Institute of Science and Technology, Nomi, Ishikawa, Japan
{khoapho,nguyenml}@jaist.ac.jp

Abstract. Answerability Prediction on Visual Question Answering is an attractive and novel multi-modal task that can be regarded as a fundamental filter to eliminate the low-qualified samples in practical systems. Instead of focusing on the similarity between images and texts, the critical concern in this task is to accentuate the conflict in visual and textual information. However, the fusion function of the multi-modal system unwittingly decreases the original features of image and text that are essential in answerability prediction. Therefore, inspired by the VT-Transformer, we propose a Residual VT-Transformer model utilizing a residual attention module to combine the single and multiple modality features of images and texts in an aggregated representation. Our architecture allows us not only to maintain the residual signals but also to emphasize the attentive features of vision and text. Through detailed experiments and ablation studies, our model achieves promising results against the competitive baselines in VizWiz-VQA 2020 dataset for blind people.

Keywords: Answerability prediction · Visual Question Answering · VizWiz · Multi-head attention · Residual attention · Blind people

1 Introduction

In the recent explosion of multimedia information, multi-modal problems get more and more attention, especially in the combination of Vision and Language. Some typical challenges need to be addressed in this branch such as Visual Question Answering [10,13], Visual Question Classification [12], Visual Commonsense Reasoning [16,17], Image Captioning [8] and so on. The critical question of these problems is how to digest and represent visual-textual information together and their mutual relationship. It requires huge efforts in both single-modal and multi-modal areas. Despite its great challenges, vision-language problems are innovative and attractive to researchers.

C. Bădică et al. (Eds.): ICCCI 2022, CCIS 1653, pp. 423–435, 2022.
https://doi.org/10.1007/978-3-031-16210-7_35

Among many interesting vision-language tasks, Visual Question Answering receives encouragement in both research and industry. There are much more efforts in collecting and employing fundamental materials for VQA such as datasets, visual and textual tools, etc. Unfortunately, most of them tend to concentrate on answerable samples. This consideration is highly ideal in practice. Towards the specific domains, especially to blind people, we focus on the Predicting Answerability on Visual Question Answering (VQA) task firstly introduced in 2018 in the contest of VQA for blind people [4,5]. In particular, the goal of this task is to determine the answerability score between image and question. It is considered a stepping stone towards practical VQA systems. With a shallow elimination against unanswerable samples, we can take advantage of available VQA approaches. Besides, Answerabity Prediction also points out another aspect in understanding visual and textual information. Instead of emphasizing the relationship between image and question to answer the questions, this task gives a central viewpoint on textual and visual conflicts.

In practice, detecting the unanswerable VQA samples is critical for research and applicability. However, there are only a few approaches to this challenge. This paucity comes from the lack of practical datasets for this task. Fortunately, in the effort to support blind people, the Answerability Prediction is regarded as one of the fundamental tasks at the beginning of the VizWiz competition. Besides the answerable samples, VizWiz-VQA for blind people contains a lot of unanswerable ones. The reason for unanswerability comes from the low quality of images and the challenge of natural questions. In particular, all images are taken by blind people in their real life, which leads to no assurance in vision quality. Besides, ambiguous questions recorded by blind people and the inconsistency of annotators also cause difficulties for automatic systems.

Traditionally, prediction answerability of a Visual Question is not considered as a stand-alone task. The answerability of a question is extended from a VQA system as a classification task. However, Le et al. [11] introduced the VT-Transformer model and firstly considered this task as a regression approach. VT-Transformer has been shown to be effective with Answerability Prediction on Visual Question Answering problems against classification approaches. Nevertheless, this model utilizes simple operations including either multiplication or concatenation to combine visual and textual features. Despite its simplicity, the performance of the VT-Transformer is unstable when we try to reproduce it. It may come from the impact of mutual vision and text interactions.

Through many previous works, the combination between image and text plays an important role in the success of vision-language tasks. In another way, in many recent approaches based on the stack of Deep Learning layers, these mutual signals are gradually transformed during the learning process. This procedure is effective to emphasize the important factors in the vision-text relationship. However, as we mentioned above, Answerability Prediction addresses the conflict between image and text instead of their relationship. Therefore, visual and text combinations may degrade the original signals in later layers. To enhance the visual and textual features in multi-modal architecture, we propose a Residual Vision Text Transformer (RVT-Transformer) model utilizing our proposed residual attention module in vision-language tasks. In previous image processing works, residual learning proves its strength to intensify the identical features through the stacked layers in Deep Learning architecture. It inspires us to take advantage of residual learning into vision-language tasks, especially in Deep Learning-based approaches. Besides, we also make use of vanilla Transformer architecture to enhance both multi-modal and residual signals. Through the detailed experiments and ablation studies in the VizWiz dataset, our proposed architecture obtains promising results against the competitive baselines. Our main contributions are as follows: (i) We propose a residual attention architecture for a delicate combination of both multi-modal and residual signals to address Answerability Prediction; (ii) Through the details of ablation studies and discussion, we also highlight the importance of residual learning vision-language tasks. (ii) Our proposed model achieves a promising performance against the existing approaches in a practical dataset for blind people.

2 Related Works

In the early stages of Visual Question Answering tasks, researchers often utilize Convolution Neural Networks (CNNs) and Recurrent Neural Networks (RNNs) to learn the visual and textual features [3]. Recently, the strength of transfer learning in Deep Learning approaches motivates many researchers to integrate the pre-trained components in their systems. The typical works should be mentioned as FT-VQA [9], VT-Transformer [11], BERT-RG [10,13] and so on. Particularly, these approaches utilize pre-trained vision models such as ResNet [6], VGG [14], and Vision Transformer [2] for image embedding and language models such as BERT for question embedding. The most related model to this task, VT-Transformer [11], integrates pre-trained models including BERT and Vision Transformer for extracting features of both question and image. Through the experiments on the VizWiz dataset for blind people, this model achieved the best performance in the answerability prediction task.

In general, feature extraction gradually evolves through the development of transfer learning. The critical factor in current systems is about multi-modal fusion function. Traditionally, researchers often use the fundamental fusion operations such as point-wise multiplication, concatenation, and so on. These functions are simple and easy to set up in practice. In recent years, with the significant performance of Attention and Transformer architectures, this information aggregation has shown many remarkable results in many different tasks. The typical example is LXMERT [15] which proposes a cross-modality function combining modalities through a bi-directional cross-attention layer. In vision-language models, a few works point out the importance of residual signals. In SelRes+SelMask model [7], Hong et al. integrate the visual features into the self-attention layer via residual operations, which is similar to ResNet [6]. Nevertheless, it is an effort to intensify vision signals into a multi-modal fusion process instead of maintaining the characteristics of original inputs.

In the Answerability Prediction task, the most recent model, VT-Transformer [11], obtains significant results in the VizWiz dataset. As we mentioned above, the feature extraction of this model also takes advantage of transfer learning via BERT and Vision Transformer. In the multi-modal fusion function, this approach only employs the fundamental operations including concatenation and multiplication between visual and textual features. Inherited by the simplicity of VT-Transformer and inspired by the strength of residual process, our Residual Attention VT-Transformer proposes a delicate combination and transmission between visual and textual features to emphasize their relationship and difference through deep neural layers.

3   Our Model

3.1   Feature Extraction

Inspired by VT- Transformer [11], our model takes advantage of pre-trained models for extracting features. Details of the question and image embedding are shown in Fig. 1.

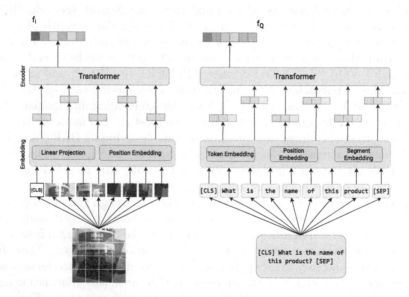

Fig. 1. Feature Extraction: extracts textual features of words in question by BERT and extracts visual features of image by Vision Transformer model

In particular, questions are embedded by the most popular language model, BERT [1]. This model can create contextual representations of tokens based on surrounding words. In our architecture, we add two special characters $[CLS]$ and $[SEP]$ in the first and last positions respectively. After processing through BERT, question features f_T are extracted from the $[CLS]$ representation vector.

For image embedding, we use a pre-trained Vision Transformer [2] model. This model is inspired by the Transformer model with the fewest modifications. The Vision Transformer model splits the image into a sequence of regions called patches and treats them as tokens in a sentence. Similar to BERT, a special patch $[CLS]$ is added to the first position of the patch sequence. Then, the outputs of $[CLS]$ vector are utilized as image features f_I. Different from VT-Transformer [11], our model considers both BERT and Vision Transformer as the internal components which are fine-tuned during the training process.

3.2 Residual Attention

The necessity of original signals via residual learning is proved in many previous works of image processing. However, in vision-language systems, the highlighted factor is on multi-modal fusion function that combines the visual and textual features. In general, this aggregation is effective to emphasize the relationship between image and text in multi-modal systems. However, the insights of Answerability Prediction come from the conflicts between vision and text information. In another way, these features are also considered to take part in predicting process instead of only contributing from multi-modal features.

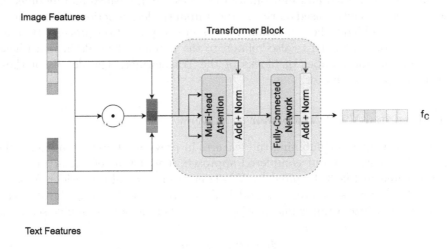

Fig. 2. Architecture of residual attention

To preserve the original textual and visual features, we propose a Residual Attention architecture for combining the single and multiple modalities' features. Our proposed component is visualized in Fig. 2. Our attention consists of two sub-modules. In the first part, we combine three kinds of signals that include visual, textual, and multi-modal ones via concatenation in Eq. 1. In our model, three elements have equal contributions in predicting answerability. Besides the multi-modal features f_M in VT-Transformer, we provide two extra signals of vision and text. Although this change seems quite negligible, its effect is highly valuable in performance. Our proposed component provides the original features for later full-connected layers.

$$f_R = CAT(f_I, f_M, f_T) \tag{1}$$

where the multi-modal signals are calculated by multiplication function like VT-Transformer [11]. Based on the results of VT-Transformer, the visual and textual features are combined by multiplication operations in Eq. 2.

$$f_M = MUL(f_I, f_T) \tag{2}$$

Secondly, these signals are intensified by a Transformer block. In particular, with each head h in multi-head block, it is similar to self-attention calculated by Eq. 3 and Eq. 4.

$$f_R^h = Self - Attention(f_R, f_R, f_R) \tag{3}$$

$$Self - Attention(q, K, V) = softmax(\frac{qW^Q(KW^K)^T}{\sqrt{d}})VW^v \tag{4}$$

With the effort of multi-head attention, the input signals containing the information of original and multi-modal features are intensified and modified in many different heads. Based on the gradient from the loss function, this attention is useful to highlight the important factors in the prediction process. Besides, the success of our model is also related to the number of heads in multi-head attention and the number of blocks of the Transformer. The details of these factors are presented later.

3.3   Residual VT-Transformer

After extracting and combining the features in previous steps, we integrate the Residual Attention in our completed approach. The details of our architecture are presented in Fig. 3. Inspired by VT-Transformer, we also consider Answerability Prediction as a regression model. Therefore, after obtaining the attentive features, we utilize a full-connected layer to predict the answerability score via Eq. 5.

$$f_a = W_R^T f_R' + b_R \tag{5}$$

where f_R' is the outputs of Transformer block in Residual Attention.

Finally, the Answerablity score is normalized by the sigmoid function in Eq. 6.

$$score = \sigma(W_a^T f_a + b_a) \tag{6}$$

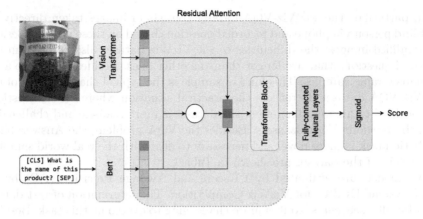

Fig. 3. VT-Transformer: combines Vision and Text features by residual attention to predict answerable score

For the loss function, we also use Mean Squared Error in Eq. 7.

$$Loss = \frac{1}{N} \sum_{i=1}^{n} (s_i - \hat{s}_i)^2 \tag{7}$$

where $s_i = 0$; 1 corresponds to unanswerable and answerable sample.

4 Experiments

4.1 Dataset and Evaluation Metrics

All experiments are conducted on the VizWiz-2020 dataset which is a typical one for blind people. The details of the dataset are shown in Table 1.

Table 1. Detail of VizWiz-2020 dataset on answerability prediction

	Type	Train	Val	Test
No. Samples	Answerable	14991	2934	8000
	Unanswerable	5532	1385	
	All	20523	4319	
Question Length (token)	Answerable	6.33±4.91	6.72±5.30	6.64±5.25
	Unanswerable	7.89±6.47	8.39± 6.91	
	All	6.76±5.42	7.26±5.91	

In particular, the VizWiz-VQA dataset consists of images taken directly by the blind person via phone and recorded questions based on these images. Besides low-qualified images, the difficulties of the VizWiz dataset also come from the recorded questions that are longer than the other ones. Besides, there are a lot of unanswerable samples. This kind of sample is the typical characteristic of the VizWiz-VQA dataset. It reflects the practical situation where visual questions are too hard to answer. Therefore, the dataset is more realistic and challenging than the previous VQA datasets. Besides the VQA problem, the Answerability Prediction task is more novel and necessary to deal with the real-world samples. The details of the dataset are shown in Table 1.

All models are evaluated by F1-score and Average Precision (AP) by an online system, EvalAI, for VizWiz Competition. The information of test data is blind for all researchers, so it is more challenging to overcome this task. Besides, the online system has two modes that include test-standard and test-dev. The difference between them is the number of submissions per day. Therefore, we only use the test-standard mode in the comparison against the previous works. In the discussion and ablation studies part, all results are extracted by the test-dev mode.

For the evaluation metric, mathematically, Average Precision calculated by Eq. 8 reflects the system's performance in many pre-defined thresholds. In the competition, AP is also regarded as the main metric for ranking the participants.

$$AP = \sum_n (R_n - R_{n-1})P_n \qquad (8)$$

where P_n and R_n are the precision and recall at the nth threshold.

4.2 Experimental Settings

In our model, we take advantage of pre-trained models for extracting features from images and questions. The name of initial version in our feature extraction modules are presented in Table 2. Besides, we also provide more details to make the reproducing process easier. For Multi-head Attention and Transformer components, we also show the range of our tuning process. These choices come from the results and the infrastructures in the experimental environment.

Table 2. Detail of Component Setting

Component	Value
Vision Transformer	google/vit-base-patch16-224-in21k
BERT	bert-base-uncased
No. Transformer Block	$I \in \{1, 2, 3, ..., 8\}$
No. Multihead	$i \in \{4, 8, 12, 16, 20, 24\}$
Fully-connected layers	768 - 512 - 1
Optimizer	AdamW(lr = 3e-5, eps = 1e-8)

4.3   Results

Due to the practical challenges of the VizWiz-VQA dataset, a few approaches are proposed on this topic since 2018. Therefore, we compare our model against two kinds of competitive baselines. The first one includes HawkTeam and rf-model in the leader-board[1] of VizWiz-2021 Competition. Secondly, we also compare our model against BERT-RG [13] Regression and VT-Transformer. For BERT-RG [13] model, the result is extracted from the publication of the VT-Transformer model. Besides, we also reproduce the VT-Transformer model to provide more details for comparison. All experiments of our model and VT-Transformer are conducted in 10 running times. Then, the best and average results are also presented in Table 3 as **Previous Works** and **10 Times Evaluation** mode. The results of our model come from the best configuration settings discussed later. The details of the comparison are shown in Table 3.

Table 3. The comparison of our model and competitive baselines (test-standard)

Mode	Model	Average Precision	F1- score
Leader-board VizWiz-2021	HawkTeam	75.99	69.94
	rf-model	55.27	52.49
Previous works	BERT-RG	52.22	41.85
	VT-Transformer (Reproduced)	72.28	65.71
Our model	RVT-Transformer	**76.47**	**69.61**
10 Times Evaluation	VT-Transformer	71.71 ± 0.56	62.88± 1.71
	RVT-Transformer	**75.19 ± 0.79**	**69.24 ± 0.39**

Firstly, our model obtains promising results among the previous works in both research and competition. Despite the significant results of VT-Transformer in the competition's leaderboard, its performance is not stable. Besides the best results of VT-Transformer and our model, we also show detailed observation in evaluation. In particular, VT-Transformer and our model are evaluated by 10 times in the experiment. Their results are presented in the range of mean and standard deviation to highlight the dispersion of VT-Transformer and our model. With the detailed comparison by **10 Times Evaluation** model, our model proves its strength and robustness in the practical dataset for blind people. In both two metrics, the performance of our model is better than the competitive baselines. Especially, our model also achieves the significant improvement of F1-score, even in the competition's leaderboard against VT-Transformer.

---

[1] https://eval.ai/web/challenges/challenge-page/743/leaderboard/2023.

4.4   Ablation Studies

In this section, we conduct some ablation experiments to demonstrate the effectiveness of our proposed components. Due to the lack of submissions on the EvalAI system, we only consider the results of test-dev mode. Firstly, VT-Transformer is considered as the baseline architecture to deploy our system. Then, we integrate residual attention to intensify the original signal into multimodal representation. In a general viewpoint, residual attention is an aggregation of residual transmission and multi-head attention. Therefore, it is valuable to highlight the contribution of each component in the architecture.

Table 4. The effect of residual attention in our architecture (test-dev)

	Average Precision	F1- score
VT-Transformer (MUL) (SOTA in VizWiz-2021)	74.18	65.22
+ Residual Transmission (Eq. 1)	77.14	68.48
+ Multi-head Attention	76.24	69.82
ResComb + MH Attention (Our model)	**78.70**	**70.85**

The details of the ablation studies are presented in Table 4. Accentuating the effect of residual attention, we utilize the same feature extraction module in all experiments. Specifically, the dimension of visual and textual representation is 768 instead of 512 in the original version of VT-Transformer. Firstly, the results of ablation studies prove the strength of our proposed components in both two measurements. In particular, the enhancement of residual transmission is higher than multi-head attention. It reflects the importance of original signals in this task. Even that, the performance has been considerably improved by a simple integration of residual information in our architecture. Besides, the efficiency of multi-head attention is also clarified in many previous works and our system.

5   Discussion

In our architecture, residual attention is based on multi-head attention via Transformer Block. In this module, the number of heads and blocks plays a critical role in the system. However, these hyper-parameters are based on the quantity and quality of samples. Therefore, the effect of these factors is worthy of detailed consideration. Firstly, for highlighting the tendency of our model via the number of Transformer blocks, we consider the same 12 heads in Multi-head Attention. The effect of the Transformer block is visualized in Fig. 4.

The change of both Average Precision and F1-score reflects the dependency of our system on the Transformer Block. In this experiment, the best performance is in the block of 1. It is less effective to optimize the stacked structure of attention blocks with only a tiny number of samples. It is also similar to BERT-RG [10] with stacked attention where the best one is on the layer of 10 over 100.

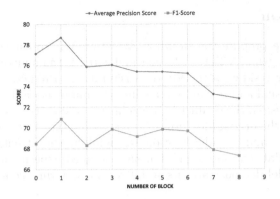

Fig. 4. The effect of transformer block in RVT-Transformer model (test-dev)

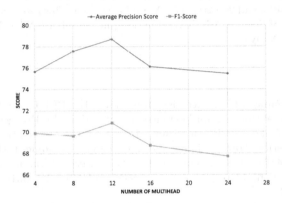

Fig. 5. The effect of the number of heads in multihead-attention module (test-dev)

Secondly, in the block of 1 in Transformer Block, it is valuable to highlight the effect of the number of heads in the Multi-head Attention module. With the dependency of head and feature dimension, we conduct the comparison in the range of head between 4 and 24 with a step of 4. The visualization of our experiment in the head of Multi-head Attention is presented in Fig. 5. Each head reflects the different considerations of features via the different learnable matrices. Therefore, the performance of our system is also improved gradually through the growth of multi-heads. On the other hand, the size of our model also increases quickly because of the stack mechanism in multi-head attention. Based on our observation and experiment, the tipping point of the head is 12. This number of the head is also popular in many famous systems. With the suitable head and block in our attention, our model obtains promising results against the competitive baselines.

6 Conclusion

In this paper, we propose the Residual Attention VT-Transformer model that inherits the strength of VT-Transformer and extends the multi-modal representation. With our residual attention to Answerability Prediction, our approach integrates the visual and textual signals into the multi-modal features. Through residual transmission, the conflict between images and texts has remained in the architecture via the original features of single modalities. Besides, our approach also incorporates multi-head attention to highlight the attentive relationship in the multi-modal representation. Through detailed experiments and ablation studies, our model demonstrates its stability and performance against the competitive baselines.

Acknowledgment. This work was supported by JSPS Kakenhi Grant Number 20H04295, 20K20406, and 20K20625 for Minh Le Nguyen. This research was also funded by the University of Science, VNU-HCM under grant number CNTT 2022–05 for Tung Le and Huy Tien Nguyen.

References

1. Devlin, J., Chang, M.W., Lee, K., Toutanova, K.: BERT: pre-training of deep bidirectional transformers for language understanding. In: Proceedings of the 2019 Conference of the North American Chapter of the Association for Computational Linguistics: Human Language Technologies, Volume 1 (Long and Short Papers), pp. 4171–4186. Association for Computational Linguistics, Minneapolis, Minnesota (2019). https://doi.org/10.18653/v1/N19-1423, https://aclanthology.org/N19-1423
2. Dosovitskiy, A., et al.: An image is worth 16x16 words: transformers for image recognition at scale. In: International Conference on Learning Representations (2021)
3. Goyal, Y., Khot, T., Agrawal, A., Summers-Stay, D., Batra, D., Parikh, D.: Making the V in VQA matter: elevating the role of image understanding in visual question answering. Int. J. Comput. Vis. **127**(4), 398–414 (2019)
4. Gurari, D., et al.: Vizwiz-priv: a dataset for recognizing the presence and purpose of private visual information in images taken by blind people. In: 2019 IEEE/CVF Conference on Computer Vision and Pattern Recognition (CVPR), pp. 939–948 (2019). https://doi.org/10.1109/CVPR.2019.00103
5. Gurari, D., et al.: Vizwiz grand challenge: answering visual questions from blind people. In: Proceedings of the IEEE Conference on Computer Vision and Pattern Recognition (CVPR) (2018)
6. He, K., Zhang, X., Ren, S., Sun, J.: Deep residual learning for image recognition. In: Proceedings of the IEEE Conference on Computer Vision and Pattern Recognition (CVPR) (2016)
7. Hong, J., Park, S., Byun, H.: Selective residual learning for visual question answering. Neurocomputing **402**, 366–374 (2020). https://doi.org/10.1016/j.neucom.2020.03.098. www.sciencedirect.com/science/article/pii/S0925231220304859
8. Jiang, W., Wang, W., Hu, H.: Bi-directional co-attention network for image captioning. ACM Trans. Multimedia Comput. Commun. Appl. **17**(4), 1–20 (2021). https://doi.org/10.1145/3460474

9. Kazemi, V., Elqursh, A.: Show, ask, attend, and answer: a strong baseline for visual question answering. arXiv preprint arXiv:1704.03162 (2017)
10. Le, T., Nguyen, H.T., Nguyen, M.L.: Multi visual and textual embedding on visual question answering for blind people. Neurocomputing **465**, 451–464 (2021). https://doi.org/10.1016/j.neucom.2021.08.117
11. Le, T., Nguyen, H.T., Nguyen, M.L.: Vision and text transformer for predicting answerability on visual question answering. In: 2021 IEEE International Conference on Image Processing (ICIP), pp. 934–938 (2021). https://doi.org/10.1109/ICIP42928.2021.9506796
12. Le., T., Pho., K., Bui., T., Nguyen., H.T., Nguyen., M.L.: Object-less vision-language model on visual question classification for blind people. In: Proceedings of the 14th International Conference on Agents and Artificial Intelligence - Volume 3: ICAART, pp. 180–187. INSTICC, SciTePress (2022). https://doi.org/10.5220/0010797400003116
13. Le, T., Tien Huy, N., Le Minh, N.: Integrating transformer into global and residual image feature extractor in visual question answering for blind people. In: 2020 12th International Conference on Knowledge and Systems Engineering (KSE), pp. 31–36 (2020). https://doi.org/10.1109/KSE50997.2020.9287539
14. Simonyan, K., Zisserman, A.: Very deep convolutional networks for large-scale image recognition. In: International Conference on Learning Representations (2015)
15. Tan, H., Bansal, M.: Lxmert: learning cross-modality encoder representations from transformers (2019)
16. Wang, T., Huang, J., Zhang, H., Sun, Q.: Visual commonsense R-CNN. In: Proceedings of the IEEE/CVF Conference on Computer Vision and Pattern Recognition (CVPR) (2020)
17. Zhang, X., Zhang, F., Xu, C.: Explicit cross-modal representation learning for visual commonsense reasoning. IEEE Trans. Multimedia **24**, 2986–2997 (2021). https://doi.org/10.1109/TMM.2021.3091882

Automatic Processing of Planning Problems: Application on Representative Case Studies

Sabrine Ammar[1], Taoufik Sakka Rouis[2](✉), Mohamed Tahar Bhiri[1], and Walid Gaaloul[3]

[1] MIRACL Laboratory, ISIMS, University of Sfax, Sakiet Ezzit, Tunisia
[2] LIPAH Laboratory, FST, University of Tunis El Manar, Tunis, Tunisia
srtaoufik@yahoo.fr
[3] SAMOVAR Laboratory, Telecom SudParis, Evry, France

Abstract. Automatic planning is a full-fledged discipline in artificial intelligence. It allows describing and solving planning problems in many fields such as robotics, project management, internet navigation, crisis management, logistics and games. The PDDL language, planners and validators associated with this language allow the description, resolution and validation of planning problems. In this paper, we recommend a formal process based on the PDDL language that favors the obtaining of reliable PDDL descriptions. Our process is successfully experimented on a set of representative case studies like the Hanoï Towers and the Sliding puzzle game.

Keywords: PDDL · Automatic planning · Planning domain · Sliding puzzle game · Hanoï Towers

1 Introduction

Automatic planning is a full-fledged discipline in artificial intelligence. It allows describing and solving planning problems in many fields such as robotics, project management, internet navigation, crisis management, logistics and games. The planning problems are expressed in a concise language of state change operators. A state models a stable situation of the addressed planning problem. It can be an initial, final (also called goal) or intermediate state. Moving from one state to another is governed by labeled transitions. A labeled transition has an origin state, a destination state and a well-defined action. The automatic planning community has developed a de facto standard PDDL (Planning Domain Definition Language) (McDermott et al. 1998) to formally describe planning problems. In addition, this community has been interested in the generation of plans. Moreover, it has developed validation tools (Howey et al. 2004) to check whether a given solution plan can be derived from a PDDL description. The formal PDDL[1] language is used to describe the two components of a planning problem: state and state change operators. The state is described by types-containing unstructured objects-and logical predicates. State change operators are described in PDDL by actions with Pre/Post

---

[1] In this work we limit ourselves to the initial PDDL language known as PDDL1.2.

C. Bădică et al. (Eds.): ICCCI 2022, CCIS 1653, pp. 436–445, 2022.
https://doi.org/10.1007/978-3-031-16210-7_36

semantics. The precondition describes the applicability condition and the post condition describes the effect of the action. PDDL descriptions are difficult to write, read and develop. Complex PDDL descriptions are subject to errors that are difficult to identify a priori, i.e. when writing PDDL specifications. This is because the planners and validators associated with the PDDL language make it possible, at most, to detect errors a posteriori. Locating errors in a PDDL description is not easy. This is also true for error correction.

In this work, we advocate the correct by construction paradigm for the formal modeling of planning problems. To achieve this, we propose a formal process based on the PDDL language. The formal PDDL description is considered to be correct by construction. Our process is illustrated on a set of representative case studies like the Hanoï Towers and the Sliding puzzle game.

Section 2 presents the related planning problem's works. Our automatic processing of planning problems solution is presented in Sect. 3. A first application of our planning process is validate on the Hanoi Hanoï Towers in Sect. 4. A second application of our planning process is validate on the Sliding puzzle game in Sect. 5. Finally, Sect. 6 provides the conclusion and a set of future perspectives.

2 Related Works

In artificial intelligence, planning designates a field of research aiming at automatically generate, via a formalized procedure, a hinged result called plan. This is intended to orientate the action of one or more executors (robots or humans). Such executors are called upon to act in a particular world to achieve a predefined goal. Automatic planning concerns various fields such as: robotics, crisis management, logistics, web services composition, resource management, games, assembly of complex objects, storage management, transportation, elevator management, etc.

In (Haslum et al. 2019), a more or less exhaustive list of planning domains is established. Automatic planning makes a clear distinction between two activities: modeling and resolution. The modeling activity aims to describe a planning problem using an appropriate formalism in PDDL, in this case. As for the resolution activity, it concerns the automatic generation of solution plans using planning algorithms (Ghallab et al. 2004) from a PDDL description, knowing that a plan is a sequence of elementary actions leading from an initial state to a goal state. The software tools used to automatically generate solution plans are called planners (Roberts and Howe 2009). They are based on a planning algorithm. In this work, we will use these planners as black boxes. In order to correct the generated PDDL plan-solutions, the authors of (Abdulaziz and Lammich 2018) recommend the use of the proof assistant Isabelle/HOL to formally develop a certified validator. To achieve this, they formalize the PDDL language in HOL.

In more or less completed jobs, automatic scheduling is seen as a model checking problem. For example, the work described in (Hörne and van der Poll 2008) explores the use of two model-checkers ProB and NuSMV for modeling and solving planning problems. It empirically compares these two model-checkers on five planning problems described by B (for ProB) and BDD (Binary Decision Diagrams) for NuSMV. Similarly, the work described in (Li et al. 2012) proposes an approach for translating PDDL to CSP# in order to use the PAT model-checker in the planning domain.

3   Automatic Processing of Planning Problems

The automatic planning community has developed a defacto standard planning language called PDDL (Planning Domain Definition Language) (McDermott et al. 1998) is a language for formal modeling of planning problems. Given that a planning problem is defined by states and state change operators. PDDL is based on the first-order predicate language to model the states and on a precondition/post-condition specification to model the state change operators. In this section, we will describe the main components of the PDDL formal language. First of all, we will introduce the discipline of automatic planning as an integral part of Artificial Intelligence (AI). Then, we will present the two macroscopic components of the PDDL, namely: **Domain** and **Problem**. In addition, we will illustrate our point by addressing the Hanoï Towers problem as a planning problem. Finally, we will describe the functionalities of the software tools associated with the PDDL language, namely planners and validators.

3.1   Domain and Problem Constructs

A PDDL description has two parts: **domain** and **problem**. The **domain** part encompasses the static and dynamic aspects of a planning domain, while the **problem** part includes the definition of an initial state and the logical condition of the goal states of a given planning problem bearing in mind that a planning domain contains several planning problems. PDDL is a **declarative** language and has a prefixed syntax: operator followed by operands. The **domain** construct offered by the PDDL language essentially allows to define the state and state change operators of a planning domain. A state has several properties and each property is defined by a PDDL predicate. The state change operators are formalized in PDDL by elementary actions. Technically speaking, the Domain construct has several clauses. The construction **problem** depends on the **domain** construct. It reuses the modeling elements coming out from the **domain** construct in order to define its constituents.

3.2   Planner and Validator

A planner (Roberts and Howe 2009) is a rather complex software tool. It is based on heuristic planning algorithms. A planner accepts as input a PDDL description (both **domain** and **problem** parts) and produces, as output, plan-solutions. In addition to the generation of plan-solutions, a planner provides more or less elaborate lexico-syntactic checks. A validator (Howey et al. 2004) is used to check whether a given solution plan can be generated from a PDDL description.

4   Formal Planning of Hanoï Towers

In this section, we will illustrate the possibilities offered by PDDL on the famous Hanoï Towers algorithmic problem. This area is a representation of the famous game of Hanoï Towers. In this very constrained domain, a problem is constituted by p pegs and n discs of decreasing size stacked in a pyramid on one of the rods. The pyramid must be moved on another rod. The disks can only be transferred to another rod by respecting the constraint that no larger disk may be placed on top of a smaller disk.

4.1 Planning Domain Hanoï

We have studied, retrieved and adapted a PDDL model of the Hanoï Towers. Indeed, we have attributed a type of the said modeling by bringing two types for efficiency and readability reasons (Listing 1). The state of this domain has three predicates: *on, clear* and *smaller.* The predicate *on* admits two parameters: *?x* and *?y.* The first one is of type *disc* and the other one is of type **object**. Thus, *?y* is polymorphic: it can be either *disc* type or *peg* type. This facilitates inter-pegs displacements. Indeed, we can move either a disc on another disc, or a disc on an empty peg. In conclusion, the predicate **codifies** in PDDL the stacks (or pyramids) of discs including the pegs. The predicate "clear "admits a polymorphic parameter (*?x*) of **object** type and allows to know the availability of a disk or a peg. In other words, the *clear* predicate **codifies** in PDDL the vertices of the stacks. Finally, the predicate *smaller* admits two parameters (*?x* and *?y*): one of disc type and the other polymorphic of **object** type. Such a predicate is supposed to answer the following query: is *?x* smaller than *?y* ?. Naturally, the predicate *smaller* is static and it remains unchanged during the evolution of the state of the planning domain by the *move* action. The other two predicates *on* and *clear* are dynamic subject to modification by the *move* action. The *move* action moves a disk from an origin to a destination and admits three parameters (*?disc, ?from* and *?to*). The first parameter is of type *disc* and the two others are polymorphic of type **object**. The precondition of the *move* action stipulates its applicability. It is a non-atomic predicate obtained by composing the atomic predicates (*on, clear* and *smaller*) using the two logical connectors "**and**" and "**not**". The post-condition (clause **effect**) updates the state of the planning domain by adding and removing (**not**) from atoms or facts.

```
(define (domain hanoi)
(:requirements :strips :equality :typing )
(:types disc - object peg - object)
(:predicates (clear ?x - object) (on ?x - disc  ?y - object) (smaller ?x  - disc  ?y - object) )
(:action move
  :parameters (?disc - disc  ?from - object ?to - object)
  :precondition (and (smaller ?disc ?to) (smaller ?disc ?from) (on ?disc ?from)
          (clear ?disc) (clear ?to) (not (= ?from ?to)) )
  :effect (and (clear ?from) (on ?disc ?to) (not (on ?disc ?from)) (not (clear ?to)))))
```

Listing 1: Hanoï planning domain

4.2 The Three-Disk Hanoï Problem

Listing 2 describes in PDDL the three-disk Hanoï problem using the planning domain described in Sect. 4.1. The **objects** clause introduces the three pegs (*peg1, peg2* and *peg3*) and disks (*d1, d2* and *d3*). The **init** clause initializes the static predicate *smaller* and the two dynamic predicates *clear* and *on* stipulating the initial state of the planning problem handled: all the disks are on the peg peg1 and the available vertices are the two pegs peg2 and peg3 and the disk d1. The goal clause expresses the condition on the goal states: the pyramid on peg peg1 is moved to peg peg3.

```
(define (problem pb3)
    (:domain hanoi)
    (:objects peg1 peg2 peg3 - peg d1 d2 d3 - disc)
    (:init (clear peg2) (clear peg3) (clear d1) (on d3 peg1) (on d2 d3) (on d1 d2)
        (smaller d1 peg1) (smaller d1 peg2) (smaller d1 peg3) (smaller d2 peg1)
        (smaller d2 peg2) (smaller d2 peg3) (smaller d3 peg1) (smaller d3 peg2)
        (smaller d3 peg3) (smaller d1 d2) (smaller d1 d3) (smaller d2 d3) )
    (:goal (and (on d3 peg3) (on d2 d3) (on d1 d2))))
```
Listing 2: Three-disk Hanoï problem

4.3 Plan-Solution

Listing 3 gives the solution plan corresponding to the three-disk Hanoï problem described in PDDL in 2.3.3. Such a plan is generated by the planner supported by the Web Planner (Magnaguagno et al. 2017) platform. It includes seven instantiated *move* actions, i.e. the parameters are replaced by suitable objects declared in the **objects** clause of the **problem** part. The optimality of the generated plan is $2^3 - 1$.

```
(move d1 d2 peg3)
(move d2 d3 peg2)
(move d1 peg3 d2)
(move d3 peg1 peg3)
(move d1 d2 peg1)
(move d2 peg2 d3)
(move d1 peg1 d2)
```
Listing 3: Obtained plan-solution

Using the validator (Howey et al. 2004) on the obtained plan-solution we can easily checked the solution plan associated to the three-disk Hanoï problem.

5   Formal Planning of Sliding Puzzle Game

Sliding puzzle game is a solitaire game in the form of a checkerboard created around 1870 in the United States by Sam Loyd. This problem consists of moving numbered tokens on an n × n grid to achieve a given configuration. The constraints imposed on displacements are as follows:

– A movement can be carried out horizontally or vertically (diagonal movements are prohibited).
– To move a token numbered t_i, the destination location on the grid must be empty.

In this section, we will present two PDDL models of the Sliding puzzle game case study. The first one comes from (Bibai 2010). The second one is established by ourselves. Then, we will compare these two models and question the means offered by PDDL to describe **a rigorous relationship** between both models.

5.1 First Modeling

The modeling proposed here is derived from (Bibai 2010). It has a state described by three predicates: two dynamic and one static. Also, it has a single state change operator that allows browsing the state space associated with the Sliding puzzle game.

5.1.1 Domain Construct

Listing 4 provides the **Domain** part of the Sliding puzzle game. The predicates *at* and *empty* are the dynamic predicates. They are modified by the state change operator *move*. While the predicate *neighbor* is static. It remains unchanged by the *move* action. The types construction introduces the types of objects used: *position* and *tile*. The predicate *at* allows to see if the object *?tile* of type *tile* is in the position (*?position*) of type *position*. The predicate *empty* models the notion of empty position. It allows to see if the object *?position* of type *position* is indeed the empty position. The predicate *neighbor* models the notion of neighbor with respect to two directions: horizontal and vertical. It allows to see if two objects *?p1* and *?p2* of type *position* are two neighbors.

```
(define (domain n-sliding-puzzle)
    (:types position tile)
    (:predicates (at ?position - position ?tile - tile)
                 (neighbor ?p1 - position ?p2 - position)
                 (empty ?position - position))
    (:action move
        :parameters (?from ?to - position ?tile - tile)
        :precondition (and (neighbor ?from ?to) (at ?from ?tile) (empty ?to))
        :effect (and (at ?to ?tile) (empty ?from) (not (at ?from ?tile)) (not (empty ?to)))))
```

Listing 4: Domain construct of the first modeling

The move action allows three parameters: *?from*, *?to* of type position and *?tile* of type *tile*. Intuitively, move allows to move the *?tile* object from the *?from* position to the *?to* position. The formal before/after semantics of move are in two parts:

- a precondition (**precondition** clause) described by the connector **and** three elementary predicates, namely *neighbor*, *at* and *empty*. It states that the two objects *?from* and *?to* are neighbors via the predicate *neighbor*, the object *?to* is empty via the predicate *empty* and the object *?tile* is in position *?from* via the predicate *at*.
- a post-condition (clause **effect**) described by the connector **and**. It updates the current state: addition of atoms (*(at ?to ?tile)* and *(empty ?from)*) and deletion of atoms indicated by **not**.

5.1.2 Problem Construct

Listing 5 provides an instance of the Sliding puzzle game. The **objects** clause introduces all the objects of type *position* and *tile* introduced in the domain part (Listing 4). The **init** clause initializes the three predicates *at*, *empty* and *neighbor* describing the initial configuration. The **goal** clause describes in PDDL the final configuration.

```
(define (problem p-sliding-puzzle)
    (:domain n-sliding-puzzle)
    (:objects p_1_1 p_1_2 p_1_3 p_2_1 p_2_2 p_2_3  p_3_1 p_3_2 p_3_3 - position
              t_1 t_2 t_3 t_4 t_5 t_6 t_7 t_8 - tile)
    (:init   (at p_1_1 t_4) (empty p_1_2) (at p_1_3 t_8) (at p_2_1 t_6) (at p_2_2 t_3)
        (at p_2_3 t_2) (at p_3_1 t_1) (at p_3_2 t_5) (at p_3_3 t_7)
        (neighbor p_1_1 p_1_2) (neighbor p_1_2 p_1_1) (neighbor p_1_2 p_1_3)
        (neighbor p_1_3 p_1_2) (neighbor p_2_1 p_2_2) (neighbor p_2_2 p_2_1)
        (neighbor p_2_2 p_2_3) (neighbor p_2_3 p_2_2) (neighbor p_3_1 p_3_2)
        (neighbor p_3_2 p_3_1) (neighbor p_3_2 p_3_3) (neighbor p_3_3 p_3_2)
        (neighbor p_1_1 p_2_1) (neighbor p_2_1 p_1_1) (neighbor p_1_2 p_2_2)
        (neighbor p_2_2 p_1_2) (neighbor p_1_3 p_2_3) (neighbor p_2_3 p_1_3)
        (neighbor p_2_1 p_3_1) (neighbor p_3_1 p_2_1) (neighbor p_2_2 p_3_2)
        (neighbor p_3_2 p_2_2) (neighbor p_2_3 p_3_3) (neighbor p_3_3 p_2_3))
    (:goal (and  (at p_1_1 t_1) (at p_1_2 t_2) (at p_1_3 t_3) (at p_2_1 t_4)
                (at p_2_2 t_5) (at p_2_3 t_6) (at p_3_1 t_7) (at p_3_2t_8))))
```

Listing 5: Problem construct of the first modeling

5.1.3 Plan-Solution

We submitted the PDDL description of the Sliding puzzle game (Listing 4 and Listing 5) to the WEB PLANNER (Magnaguagno et al. 2017). This planner established a solution plan including a sequence, of length 25, of execution of the action move.

5.2 Second Modeling

The *move* action from the previous modeling of the Sliding puzzle game (Listing 4) is a non-deterministic action. It expresses a movement in a generic sense: left, right, up and down.

5.2.1 Domain Construct

Here we propose a less abstract modeling (Listing 6) than the one provided in Sect. 5.1. To achieve this, we decompose the *move* action of the first modeling into four elementary actions: *move_right*, *move_left*, *move_up* and *move_down*. In the same way, the predicate *neighbor* of the first modeling is broken down into four predicates: *neighbor_right*, *neighbor_left*, *neighbor_up* and *neighbor_down*. Moreover, we keep the introduced types (*position* and *tile*) and the two predicates *at* and *empty* introduced in the first modeling. Finally, the four actions *move_right*, *move_left*, *move_up* and *move_down* are strongly inspired by the *move* action of the first modeling.

```
(define (domain n-sliding-puzzle)
  (:types position tile)
  (:predicates (at ?position - position ?tile - tile) (empty ?position - position)
               (neighbor_left ?p1 - position ?p2 - position)
               (neighbor_right ?p1 - position ?p2 - position)
               (neighbor_up ?p1 - position ?p2 - position)
               (neighbor_down ?p1 - position ?p2 - position))
  (:action move_left
    :parameters (?from ?to - position ?tile - tile)
    :precondition (and (neighbor_left ?from ?to) (at ?from ?tile) (empty ?to))
    :effect (and (at ?to ?tile) (empty ?from) (not (at ?from ?tile)) (not (empty ?to))))
  (:action move_right
    :parameters (?from ?to - position ?tile - tile)
    :precondition (and (neighbor_right ?from ?to) (at ?from ?tile) (empty ?to))
    :effect (and (at ?to ?tile) (empty ?from) (not (at ?from ?tile)) (not (empty ?to))))
  (:action move_up
    :parameters (?from ?to - position ?tile - tile)
    :precondition (and (neighbor_up ?from ?to) (at ?from ?tile) (empty ?to))
    :effect (and (at ?to ?tile) (empty ?from) (not (at ?from ?tile)) (not (empty ?to))))
  (:action move_down
    :parameters (?from ?to - position ?tile - tile)
    :precondition (and (neighbor_down ?from ?to) (at ?from ?tile) (empty ?to))
    :effect (and (at ?to ?tile) (empty ?from) (not (at ?from ?tile)) (not (empty ?to)))))
```

Listing 6: Domain construct of the second modeling

5.2.2 Problem Construct

Listing 7 provides the same instance of the Sliding puzzle game dealt in the first modeling. It is almost identical to the one provided by the Listing 5 except the *neighbor* initialization replaced by *neighbor_left*, *neighbor_right*, *neighbor_up* and *neighbor_down*.

```
(define (problem p-sliding-puzzle)
   (:domain n-sliding-puzzle)
   (:objects p_1_1 p_1_2 p_1_3 p_2_1 p_2_2 p_2_3 p_3_1 p_3_2 p_3_3 – position
             t_1 t_2 t_3 t_4 t_5 t_6 t_7 t_8 – tile)
   (:init (empty p_1_2) (at p_1_1 t_4) (at p_1_3 t_8) (at p_2_1 t_6) (at p_2_2 t_3)
          (at p_2_3 t_2) (at p_3_1 t_1) (at p_3_2 t_5) (at p_3_3 t_7)
          (neighbor_left p_1_1 p_1_2) (neighbor_right p_1_2 p_1_1)
          (neighbor_left p_1_2 p_1_3) (neighbor_right p_1_3 p_1_2)
          (neighbor_left p_2_1 p_2_2) (neighbor_right p_2_2 p_2_1)
          (neighbor_left p_2_2 p_2_3) (neighbor_right p_2_3 p_2_2)
          (neighbor_left p_3_1 p_3_2) (neighbor_right p_3_2 p_3_1)
          (neighbor_left p_3_2 p_3_3) (neighbor_right p_3_3 p_3_2)
          (neighbor_up p_1_1 p_2_1) (neighbor_down p_2_1 p_1_1)
          (neighbor_up p_1_2 p_2_2) (neighbor_down p_2_2 p_1_2)
          (neighbor_up p_1_3 p_2_3) (neighbor_down p_2_3 p_1_3)
          (neighbor_up p_2_1 p_3_1) (neighbor_down p_3_1 p_2_1)
          (neighbor_up p_2_2 p_3_2) (neighbor_down p_3_2 p_2_2)
          (neighbor_up p_2_3 p_3_3) (neighbor_down p_3_3 p_2_3))
   (:goal (and (at p_1_1 t_1) (at p_1_2 t_2) (at p_1_3 t_3) (at p_2_1 t_4)
               (at p_2_2 t_5) (at p_2_3 t_6) (at p_3_1 t_7) (at p_3_2 t_8))))
```

Listing 7: Problem construct of the second modeling

5.2.3 Plan-Solution

We submitted the PDDL description associated to second modeling of the Sliding puzzle game (Listing 6 and Listing 7) to the same planner used for the first modeling: WEB PLANNER. We notice that the generated solution plan includes the same number of trips (here 25) as the one provided in Sect. 5.1.3. Such a plan-solution **explains** the direction of the legal movements of the tiles via the names of the operators executed, i.e. *move_right*, *move_left*, *move_up* and *move_down*.

5.3 Comparison

Intuitively, the second model (Listing 6) **refines** the first model (Listing 4). **The states** of two models are equivalent. The union of four predicates *neighbor_left*, *neighbor_right*, *neighbor_up* and *neighbor_down* is equal to *neighbor*. And the other two predicates *at* and *empty* remain the same. The four state change **operators** *move_left*, *move_right*, *move_up* and *move_down* of the second model are derived from the generic operator *move* of the first model. But the PDDL language cannot **formally verify** the refinement relationship between the two models.

6 Conclusion

In this paper, the PDDL language is used to describe the states and actions of a planning problem. However, not all the semantic aspects related to the formalization of a state of a planning problem are easy to describe in PDDL. This concerns the intra-atomic and inter-atomic semantic properties. For example, in the planning problem of the Sliding puzzle game treated previously, we want to attach the following property to the predicate *empty*: at any state, one and only one position is empty. Thus, the actions are specified in a totally separate way. Moreover, the basic properties (mainly typing) related to the entities of a planning problem are insufficient to judge the coherence of a PDDL description. More or less elaborated properties should be attached to static and dynamic predicates in particular. This makes it possible to check the consistency of the initial state, the goal state and the actions.

Finally, we can conclude that the PDDL language, planners and validators associated with this language allow the description, resolution and validation of planning problems. However, they only allow the reliability of PDDL descriptions to be examined in **a posteriori**. As a perspective, we recommend a formal process based on the coupling of Event-B method and the PDDL language. This favors the obtaining of reliable PDDL descriptions from an **ultimate** Event-B model that is **correct by construction**.

References

Abdulaziz, M., Lammich, P.: A formally verified validator for classical planning problems and solutions. In: IEEE 30th International Conference on Tools with Artificial Intelligence (2018). https://doi.org/10.1017/CBO9781139195881

Bibai, J.: Segmentation et Evolution pour la Planification : Le Système DivideAndEvolve. Paris Sud University, THALES Research and Technology France (2010)

Ghallab, M., Nau, D., Traverso, P.: Automated planning: theory & practice (2004)

Howey, R., Long, D., Fox, M.: VAL: automatic plan validation, continuous effects and mixed initiative planning using PDDL. In: Tools with Artificial Intelligence. ICTAI (2004). https://doi.org/10.1109/ICTAI.2004.120

Haslum, P., Lipovetzky, N., Magazzeni, D., Muise, C.: An introduction to the planning domain definition language. In: Synthesis Lectures on Artificial Intelligence and Machine Learning (2019). https://doi.org/10.2200/S00900ED2V01Y201902AIM042

Magnaguagno, M.C., Pereira, R.F., More, M.D., Meneguzzi, F.: WEB PLANNER: A tool to develop classical planning domains and visualize heuristic state-Space search. ICAPS, User Interfaces for Scheduling & Planning (UISP) Workshop (2017)

Roberts, M., Howe, A.: Learning from planner performance. Elsevier, Artificial Intelligence 173(5–6), 536–561 (2009)

Hörne, T., van der Poll, J.A.: Planning as model checking: the performance of ProB vs NuSMV. In: Proceedings of the 2008 annual research conference of the South African Institute of Computer Scientists and Information Technologists on IT research in developing countries: riding the wave of technology (2008)

Li, Y., Sun, J., Song Dong, J., Liu, Y., Sun, J.: Translating PDDL into CSP# - the PAT Approach, In: Proceedings of the 17th IEEE International Conference on Engineering of Complex Computer Systems (2012)

Application of Software Defined Networks for Collection of Process Data in Industrial Real-Time Systems

Ireneusz Smołka[1] , Jacek Stój[1]([✉]) , and Marcin Fojcik[2]

[1] Silesian University of Technology, Gliwice, Poland
{ireneusz.smolka,jacek.stoj}@polsl.pl
[2] Western Norway University of Applied Sciences, Førde, Norway
marcin.fojcik@hvl.no

Abstract. Modern computer systems are expected to be more and more advanced and therefore their complexity is ever increasing. Some solutions make control systems more open and flexible. Whereas the main goal of others is to improve reliability. Such services may adding failure detection and even failure prediction features. Knowing the possibility of failures with a high level of accuracy may bring excellent management and economic benefits and refers to predictive maintenance. However, it is based on process, and diagnostic data gathered from the monitored system, which sometimes is not straightforward. In this paper, we present a way of obtaining knowledge about the system state without introducing significant modifications to the system itself. It is based on Software Defined Networks SDN, which allows for controlling of communication network traffic on the software level as well as obtaining information about the state of the network or even about the user data that are sent in it. Data gathered in such a way may be forwarded to machine learning services, e.g., to perform predictive maintenance. The conceptual solution presented in this paper was verified during some experimental research performed in a system based on Beckhoff industrial controllers and EtherCAT communication network. In the role of SDN switch and SDN controller Raspberry Pi development boards were used.

Keywords: Software Defined Network · SDN · Networked control system · Real-time systems · Industrial Ethernet · Industry 4.0 · EtherCAT

1 Introduction

Originally, industrial systems were developed for supervision and control tasks. Consequently, the communication systems were tailored to this purpose. However, as complexity of systems increased, more and more information about the process was needed. It increased requirements on available resources like computational power or communication networks throughput. There were also new demands considering planning, efficiency, management, etc. Moreover, failure detection, and failure prediction was expected. As a result, common trend called Industry 4.0 emerged. It refers to the current shift towards the complete integration of physical objects, people, and production systems into a single communication system. This change increased productivity through cost reduction, improved quality, and allowed for better planning [22].

Industry 4.0 is based on the logical connection of data from elements present in industrial system [12]. Such integration requires flexible and efficient networking with suitable network protocols [13]. Unfortunately, these systems often consist of many different subnetworks, with different protocols providing real-time behavior. Therefore, it is often almost impossible to prepare new communication structures in existing systems. An interesting solution seems to be the usage of Software Defined Network technology (SDN) [15], which separates control and data planes of the network. However, SDN was designed for general-purpose LANs and thus may be incompatible with specific industrial systems that require real-time and fault tolerance.

On the other hand, many industrial networking systems require timeliness and in particular low latency and low jitter. Traditionally, such guarantees were provided by dedicated fieldbus networks. However, with the proliferation, ever-increasing performance, and decreasing cost of Ethernet that technology is nowadays more often used in areas where real-time operation is required. The paper shows some practical solutions of SDN for a specific industrial case and results of experiments conducted to measure the delay (jitter) when using industrial networks connected via SDN.

Generally speaking, SDN technology is used to programmatically define the way datagrams should be forwarded by switching devices from one point in the network to another. In comparison to typical Ethernet networks (with switches operating on L2 or L3 ISO/OSI layer), application of SDN makes it possible to transfer datagrams not in typical way, i.e. basing only on MAC or IP addressing. Among other things, in SDN datagrams may be duplicated to make similar functionality the port mirroring does. That option could be implemented for data extraction from Ethernet based networks. However, regular port mirroring has got its limitations and the presented solution based on SDN gives much more than mere port mirroring as described latter in the paper.

The main contribution of the research work presented in this paper is:

– a solution that allows for obtaining of user data from any Ethernet based communication system. Concerning industrial systems to which the paper mainly refers to, the user data should be understood by process data (the state of inputs and outputs of the system), i.e. any data that is transferred between system nodes using Ethernet Protocol (like EtherCAT, Profinet, Ethernet Powerlink are any other),
– the solution is based on port mirroring but is far more than that; among other things it may be transparent to topology detection protocols,
– the solution allows for selective user data extraction and therefore may be implemented very efficiently considering computational power of the device to which the duplicated datagrams are forwarded to.

The paper is structured as follows. Section 2 outlines a background of the research work Sect. 3 presents the SDN concepts. The presentation of data extraction concept follows in Sect. 4. Section 5 shows the experimental testbed architecture. Section 6 describes the experimental results concerning the SDN switch latency and jitter introduced in the communication network in the presented solution. Finally, Sect. 7 contains some discussion and concludes the paper mentioning also planned future works.

2 Background

Modern, reliable industrial systems contain real-time communication for the control of the process together with many other services. Real-time communication is necessary for proper operation and the safety of the process and staff. But, in addition, it is also needed to have other elements such as quality of operation, effectivity, maintenance, flexibility, failure detection or even fault prediction. Sometimes new features must be introduced after the systems is developed and started up. Therefore, a question arises: is it possible to obtain data from a distributed computer system without any significant modification to its configuration and hardware? Here, the *data* is to be understood as both user data and diagnostic data including monitoring communication quality.

In newly created systems, it is possible to add some functionality on the planning step. The situation is much worse for already working systems with the real-time paradigm. Often all process data is available on the logical level, but there may be no devices capable of processing the data. For example, a control device (often Programmable Logic Controller PLC) receives data from a temperature sensor for processing and detecting warnings levels. When it is needed to add the new functionality – to see the quality of communication with the temperature sensor (or device with the sensor) or analyze how the temperature changes in time, it can be done in various ways: directly in the new code on this device, in the PLC or by introducing a new device on the network performing the required new functionality. Unfortunately, adding new code to computing devices typically increases program execution time and increases delays in data processing. On the other hand, adding a new network device requires changing network communication – making additional data exchanges also leads to increasing delays. Yet another solution can be implementation of a transparent "sniffer" or at least a managed switch with port mirroring for capturing of network traffic together with the process data (see: Fig. 1). This requires knowledge about protocols that are used in the system and the structure of the system. This solution can be based on Software Defined Network technology (SDN). As shown in the paper, this idea allows for creation of a flexible tool for monitoring and control of traffic without modifying the existing system as well as extraction of user data from the communication system.

To see significance of the presented solution it should be noted, that apart from improving the reliability of computer systems [23], there is also a need for failure prediction. Such solutions are implemented in various scenarios: in Smart Grids [3], intelligent workshops [10], oil fields [27], and others. In all cases, the basis of fault prediction is vast amounts of data.

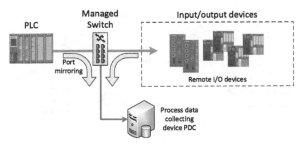

Fig. 1. An example of a Network Control System with a managed Ethernet switch used to obtain datagrams (by the means of port mirroring) from the process network to forward them to the data collecting device.

The paper concerns Network Control System (NCS), i.e. distributed systems performing control services over industrial objects – plants, machines, etc. [14, 25]. For many years, the NCSs have been based on industrial Ethernet Protocols like Profinet [28], EtherCAT [18], EthernetIP [9], etc. Nowadays, the TSN networks and OPC UA are also introduced to industrial systems [6]. The Ethernet standard is going to be present in the industry for many years. Therefore, mechanisms of diagnostics and obtaining process data from Ethernet-based systems are worth considering.

There are more and more fault prediction systems and early warning platforms, like [8] in Smart Grids. Such systems allow for fault prediction with over 90% accuracy, which brings great benefits from the point of view of the economy and system management. Among other things, it may reduce the equipment failure rates significantly. For any kind of system, when operation analysis or faults prediction is to be performed, it is crucial to have data that describes how the state of the system changes in time. Solution presented in this paper shows how to obtain data from Ethernet based systems without introducing significant modifications to the system itself.

3 Software Defined Networks

Software Defined Network SDN is a networking paradigm that transforms classical network infrastructures. Firstly, it breaks vertical integration by separating the network control logic (control plane) from the underlying routers and switches that transmit traffic (data plane). Secondly, the control logic is implemented in a logically centralized controller, which simplifies policy egress and network (re)configuration and evolution. Thirdly, network switches are transformed into simple forwarding devices without logic implemented in them [15].

A necessary consequence of software-defined networking principles is the separation between the definition of network policies, their implementation in the switching hardware, and traffic forwarding rules.

The basic idea of SDN is to control network datagrams flows through a centralized intelligent controller with "common" routing devices in the network data plane [16]. By monitoring the state of the entire network, the controller obtains an up-to-date picture of the network and can dynamically adjust flows according to current needs. The SDN concept allows for a wide range of traffic engineering, security, and other applications.

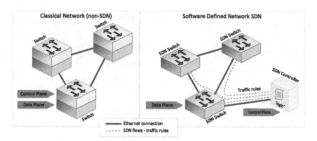

Fig. 2. The idea of decoupling the control and the data plane in SDN.

SDNs are being applied in many areas: industrial systems [11] real-time systems [31], Internet of Things and Wireless Sensor Networks [20, 29], on the factory floor [1], and in Industry 4.0 systems [5, 19]. It is used to improve management and maintenance of the networks and increase security, e.g. against eavesdropping attacks [17] or cybersecurity, in general, using Intrusion Detection Systems [26]. There are also papers concerned with communication determinism [21]. The OpenFlow protocol is the de facto standard for communication between SDN switches and controllers [4]. Regular switches may also be implemented in SDN networks, and hybrid solutions may be built [2]. In this paper it is shown, that SDN may be implemented yet for another purpose – for data collection of user data from industrial control systems. It may be done by duplicating chosen Ethernet datagrams and sent them to a data collecting device for further processing.

4 Process Data Extraction Using SDN

Application of Ethernet-based communication networks enables the use of cost-effective, pervasive, and high-throughput Ethernet technology in industrial environments such as automation, process control, and transportation, where one of the critical challenges is real-time communication, i.e., communication with guaranteed upper limits on latency and latency variation (jitter). In such systems there is usually a kind of controller and one or more remote input/output devices, here called RIO (see: Fig. 1). The controller may be a Programmable Logic Controller (PLC) that communicates with other devices using real-time communication network. The role of the controller is to read input data from RIOs to get information about the industrial process. The data are then analyzed in the PLC program. The result of the analysis is the required state of the system outputs according to the industrial process to be controlled. The state of the inputs and outputs signals is the process data.

The PLC has got all the process data. If the process data should be obtained from the system, in principle it may be read from the PLC. Configuration and possibly program implemented in the PLC should be altered for that purpose. However, it may not be allowed or even possible. Among other things, the PLC may be protected from modification for the reason of "know-how" protection, or the owner may have no engineering tools or source files to alter the PLC user program or configuration.

Additionally, NCSs are real-time systems, which means that they must operate in a timely manner. Modification in the PLC software will change the time needed for the execution of the user program, extending the PLC operation cycle time. This extension could lead to violation of the time constraints that are defined for the real-time system. Besides, the transfer of the process data also will increase netload in the network and possibly lengthen the network communication cycle. Here again, the communication network is used for real-time data exchange. Therefore, sending additional data from the PLC to some outside systems could delay the communication process. In that case, additional device could be installed in order to obtain the date without altering the existing PLC. That device would be called to the Process Data Collecting (PDC). The problem is how to supply the PDC with process data without making significant modifications in the system.

One solution for obtaining the process data from Ethernet base NCS could be port mirroring (see: Fig. 1). In NCS, all process data are sent through the communication link between the PLC and I/O devices. To collect all the process data, one point of monitoring is sufficient. A managed switch with port mirroring could send all the PLC datagrams on that link to the PDC device. The problem is that the managed switch is another network device installed in the communication network. In some industrial protocols, like Profinet, the network topology is often defined to simplify management or provide some additional diagnostics information. Definition of topology may even be required when using some of the network's features, like operation in the ring with Media Redundancy Protocol or fast device replacement in Profinet networks. Therefore, another switch between the PLC and the remote I/O devices would yet again require modifications in the PLC. Moreover, when using Profinet IRT communication protocol, applying a switch with port mirroring is not possible as there are no IRT switches with the mirroring feature.

In some networks, regular Ethernet devices cannot be applied at all. In EtherCAT networks, when another than line topology is needed, EtherCAT junction modules must be installed [7]. Typical L2 switches cannot be used because EtherCAT datagrams are sent as broadcasts and are routed from one EtherCAT device to another, forming a logical ring [30]. However, is it possible to use Open vSwitch OVS (an SDN switch) by implementing the solution shown in this paper.

The main goal of the presented research is to provide means of obtaining process data from an NCS without introducing changes into the system. This can be done by application of Software Defined Networks SDN [32]. It may be used for protocols such as Profinet RT (with some restrictions), EtherCAT, and others.

In classical Ethernet networks, decisions about datagrams routing are made by switching devices. In contrast, in an SDN, an additional autonomous device controls the data traffic – called the SDN controller. In SDN, the control plane is separated from the data plane. The central SDN controller controls the data flow in the network, while SDN switches are only for forwarding datagrams according to SDN controller instructions.

The idea of SDNs is to make the control of the network traffic centralized. SDN switches do not decide on the network datagrams routing on their own, as is done in regular networks, but from that SDN controller with a broader view of the network. Therefore, traffic control may be performed in a more comprehensive way.

Decoupling the control and the data plane together with centralized network control brings great advantages. Above all, decisions made by the SDN controller are based on the global view of the network, which makes them more relevant to the current condition of the network. In SDN networks, it is also possible to easily duplicate datagrams. Datagrams may be defined such that datagrams received on one port of an SDN switch may be transferred to more than one destination port. In other words, datagrams transferring the process data may be routed to their destination, which is the I/O device and the PDC device. This is the basis of the presented solution.

Using the SDN concept, Ethernet port mirroring can be easily defined. For that purpose, a rule has to be defined to send datagrams received on one port (the mirrored port) to two other ports: one port where the destination host is and another serving as the mirroring port (see: Fig. 2).

Port mirroring based on SDN may be performed in a more flexible way with possible online adjustment (comparing to regular port mirroring performed in managed L2 switches), e.g.:

- it is possible to mirror not all of the datagrams, but only datagrams with specific source or destination addresses (MAC, IP or other) or according to the EtherType field of the Ethernet datagrams or any other filtering rule based on the datagram contents,
- the mirroring may be done from more than one mirrored port (in contrast to most managed switches) and from any number of SDN switches in the network,
- datagrams that are mirrored from the source port may be may be sent directly to a device that collects them (see PDC device in Fig. 1), but also to some remote device available in LAN (by definition of appropriate SDN flows that direct the datagrams to the recipient).

The above idea of duplication of frames is the basis of the presented research. It is purposefully not called here 'port mirroring' being more than that. It is shown that it may be used for user data extraction from the network datagrams. The duplicated datagrams are sent to the Process Data Collecting (PDC) device. The process data are obtained from the datagrams to be sent to some cloud services for further processing, e.g., to perform predictive maintenance using deep learning tools.

5 Testbed

The presented solution realizing process data extraction from Ethernet-based communication networks is shown in Fig. 3. It consists of an SDN controller, an SDN switch, and a PDC device as presented in Fig. 3.

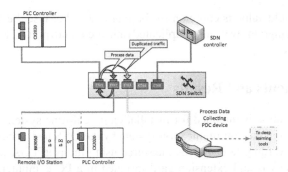

Fig. 3. The experimental testbed.

Both the SDN controller and the SDN switch are based on Raspberry Pi. The SDN controller was serviced by RYU software. The controller user program was implemented in Python. The SDN switch was equipped with 5 Ethernet interfaces (using USB Ethernet cards). One of the Ethernet ports was connected to the SDN controller, which provided rules for traffic forwarding (SDN flows). The OpenFlow 1.4 protocol was used to communicate with the controller.

The PDC device was implemented on BeagleBone Black platform. It was connected to the SDN switch to receive datagrams captured from the monitored network. It was assumed that it may be needed to do some filtering of the datagrams in the PDC (in addition to the selective datagrams mirroring performed in the SDN switch), so the processing of the datagram was implemented in C++, and the LIBPCAP library was included for application of filtering rules as they are defined in the Wireshark software tool.

Moreover, the PDC was extended by one Ethernet port connected through the USB interface to allow communication with an external service – Microsoft Azure, to which the process data obtained from the Ethernet datagrams were sent for further processing using deep learning tools. However, description of that part of the system is beyond the scope of this paper. The additional Ethernet port does not influence the PDC operation regarding the data collection.

The PLC controller for this study was a Beckhoff CX2020 embedded device. For the realization of remote I/O stations, RIO and a BK9050 Real-Time Ethernet bus coupler was used. In the final system developed in this paper, there were two RIO stations connected to two models of a conveyor belt with a pressing machine. In this way, the process data corresponded to a model control process.

During the experimental research, the system presented in Fig. 3 was implemented. The data exchange between the Beckhoff devices was done using the EtherCAT industrial Ethernet protocol. The SDN controller was applied to control network traffic using an SDN switch, called an Open vSwitch (OVS). Then, the process data was being sent between the PLC controller and remote I/O stations or another PLC (here, Real-Time Ethernet RTE was used). The SDN controller programmed the OVS to forward the datagrams with the process data going through Ethernet ports ETH1 and ETH2 (see: Fig. 3). The EtherCAT and RTE datagrams used for communication were distinguished by the EtherType field of the Ethernet datagram. In both cases, it was set to 0x88A4.

This EtherType field value is common for both protocols because the RTE is based on EtherCAT. The datagrams were also duplicated (mirrored) onto port ETH3 and forwarded to the PDC device.

6   Measurements and Results

The presented solution is intended for installation in real-time systems. Therefore, the latency introduced in the communication system by the OVS had to be measured.

The OVS forwarding latency was measured using the NetFPGA tool described in [24]. The NetFPGA is and extension card installed in a PC computer. It has got four Ethernet interfaces, referred here as PHY1-PHY4 (see: Fig. 4).

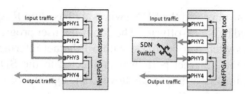

Fig. 4. Measurement of SDN switch latency.

The input traffic from the PLC received on the PHY1 interface was forwarded by the NetFPGA onto the PHY2 interface using an internal bridge implemented in the NetFPGA (the same was done for PHY3 and PHY4). Then, datagrams sent on PHY2 were directed back to the PHY3 in two ways (in two research scenarios): by a patchcord or through an SDN switch.

Datagrams received on every interface were captured and timestamped with a high precision of 4 ns, then sent to a PC application using a PCIe interface and stored in a *pcap* file. By comparing the timestamps of the registered frames, it was possible to calculate the latency of the SDN switch.

The OVS latency was measured for network traffic in two scenarios:

- datagrams exchanged between the PLC controller and the RIO stations; the Real-Time Ethernet protocol, based on EtherCAT, was used, and 8 bytes of data were transmitted,
- datagrams sent from one PLC controller to another (used in place of the RIO station); The EtherCAT Automation Protocol EAP and variable producer-subscriber mechanisms were used with one variable of two lengths: 1 byte and 1k byte.

In both case described above, over 200,000 datagrams were captured and analyzed. The results are presented in Fig. 5 for PLC-RIO communication and in Fig. 6 for PLC-PLC communication. Parts a) of the figures present latency measured with a patchcord connection (for the needs of comparison, i.e. without OVS switch), and parts b) of the figures show the OVS latency. Therefore, the latency introduced by the OVS switch was measured. The x-axis is the latency in microseconds, and the y-axis is the number of samples (one sample is a delay between reception of a datagram on the PHY1 port of the NetFPGA and the same datagram on the PHY3). The y-axis is scaled logarithmically.

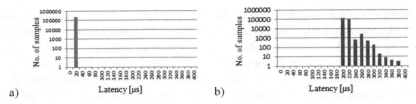

a)   Latency [µs]   b)   Latency [µs]

Fig. 5. OVS latency measurement results during PLC-RIO communication using EtherCAT protocol and 100 Mb/s; a) latency with patch cable connection, b) latency with OVS connection.

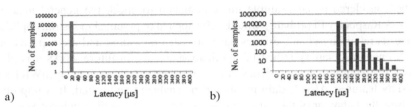

a)   Latency [µs]   b)   Latency [µs]

Fig. 6. OVS latency results during PLC-PLC communication using EtherCAT protocol while sending 128 bytes of user data with 1 Gb/s link speed; a) latency with patchcord connection, b) latency with OVS connection.

According to the experimental research results, the OVS introduces additional latency of values between 200 µs to 380 µs, no matter the speed of the communication link (EtherCAT with 1 Gb/s and Real Time Ethernet with 100 Mb/s). In both cases, about 98% from over 200,000 of taken measurements, most of the measurements had the value of 200 µs and 220 µs.

In the presented figures it is clearly visible that the additional delays introduces by the OVS switch is not constant. The switch increases the jitter of data exchange significantly. However still, the jitter is less than 200 µs. But even when referring it to very low communication cycle like 1 ms, the jitter would be below 20% of the cycle which in most cases is most acceptable.

7   Conclusions

This paper presents an SDN-based solution dedicated to obtaining data from NCSs. A programmable definition of datagram routing rules allows selective and flexible duplication of datagrams in OVSs (SDN switches). The presented solution is far more flexible than typical port mirroring as described in the paper. It is applicable in an Ethernet-based communication system. It may be implemented even in systems with defined network topologies. It is so due to the OVS being transparent to the topology detection datagrams, like Link Layer Discovery Protocol and the Simple Network Management Protocol.

It is worth mentioning, that data that may be obtained from an NCSs may be the process data of an industrial system (e.g. the state of inputs and outputs of a networked control system) as well as data about traffic in the monitored network, state of communication channels (e.g. information whether a set of devices communicate with each other), etc.

During the experimental research, the latency of the OVS was measured using a NetFPGA analyzing tool. Summarizing the results, the OVS introduces some delays into the system and increases the jitter of real-tiem data exchange. However, from the point of view of a typical NCS, these delays are so small that in many cases they may be neglected. Importantly, the considered switch was based on a Raspberry Pi with additional Ethernet interfaces. A dedicated OVS would provide much better results, and most probably would be applicable in even more demanding systems with cycle times of about 1 ms.

In this paper, in the role of an OVS switch, a Raspberry Pi device was used. It should only be considered as an example implementation to check the general idea of the system. A Raspberry Pi probably wouldn't be applied in practical industrial applications because its reliability characteristics have not been measured and are expected not to be high enough to satisfy industrial applications needs. In future works it is planned to check the temporal characteristics of the presented solution on an OpenWRT switch with SDN features. Also scalability should be analyzed and tested. It is important to know how the behavior of the solution changes when volume of data increases.

As already mentioned in the introduction, extraction of process data from NCS is done for the latter application of failure prediction mechanisms. What is worth noting, the implementation of SDN makes the data exported cyber-secure because the process data flow is only in one direction – from the NCS outside. A potential intruder trying to access the monitored system would first have to break into the PDC device. After that, a change in the Ethernet communication interface of the OVS configuration would be required to let datagrams flow in the other direction – from the outside system to the attacked NCS.

Acknowledgement. The research leading to these results received funding from the Norway Grants 2014–2021, which the National Centre operates for Research and Development under the project "Automated Guided Vehicles integrated with Collaborative Robots for Smart Industry Perspective" (Project Contract no.: NOR/POLNOR/CoBotAGV/0027/2019-00) and partially by the Polish Ministry of Science and Higher Education Funds for Statutory Research.

References

1. Ahmed, K., et al.: Software defined networking for communication and control of cyber-physical systems. In: 2015 IEEE 21st International Conference on Parallel and Distributed Systems (ICPADS), pp. 803–808 (2015)
2. Amin, R., et al.: Hybrid SDN networks: a survey of existing approaches. IEEE Commun. Surv. Tutor. **20**(4), 3259–3306 (2018)
3. Andresen, C.A., et al.: Fault detection and prediction in smart grids. In: 2018 IEEE 9th International Workshop on Applied Measurements for Power Systems (AMPS), pp. 1–6 (2018). https://doi.org/10.1109/AMPS.2018.8494849
4. Benzekki, K., et al.: Software-defined networking (SDN): a survey. Secur. Commun. Netw. **9**(18), 5803–5833 (2016). https://doi.org/10.1002/sec.1737
5. Bolanowski, M., et al.: Analysis of possible SDN use in the rapid prototyping process as part of the Industry 4.0. Bull. Pol. Acad. Sci. Tech. Sci. **67**(1), 21–30 (2019)

6. Bruckner, D., et al.: An introduction to OPC UA TSN for industrial communication systems. Proc. IEEE **107**(6), 1121–1131 (2019)
7. ETG.1600G (R)V1.0.2: EtherCAT Installation Guideline: Guideline for Planning, Assembling and Commissioning of EtherCAT Networks (2017)
8. Fan, L., et al.: Research and application of smart grid early warning decision platform based on big data analysis. In: 2019 4th International Conference on Intelligent Green Building and Smart Grid (IGBSG), Hubei, Yi-chang, China, pp. 645–648. IEEE (2019). https://doi.org/10.1109/IGBSG.2019.8886291
9. Fischer, S., Doran, H.D.: Embedding Real Time Ethernet: EtherNet/IP on resource constricted platforms. In: ETFA 2011, pp. 1–4 (2011)
10. Han, Q., et al.: On fault prediction based on industrial big data. In: 2017 36th Chinese Control Conference (CCC), pp. 10127–10131 (2017). https://doi.org/10.23919/ChiCC.2017.8028970
11. Henneke, D., et al.: Analysis of realizing a future industrial network by means of Software-Defined Networking (SDN). In: 2016 IEEE World Conference on Factory Communication Systems (WFCS), pp. 1–4 (2016)
12. Kampen, A.-L., Fojcik, M., Cupek, R., Stoj, J.: Low-level wireless and sensor networks for Industry 4.0 communication – presentation. In: Wojtkiewicz, K., Treur, J., Pimenidis, E., Maleszka, M. (eds.) ICCCI 2021. CCIS, vol. 1463, pp. 474–484. Springer, Cham (2021). https://doi.org/10.1007/978-3-030-88113-9_38
13. Kampen, A.-L., et al.: The requirements for using wireless networks with AGV communication in an industry environment. In: 2021 17th International Conference on Wireless and Mobile Computing, Networking and Communications (WiMob), pp. 212–218 (2021). https://doi.org/10.1109/WiMob52687.2021.9606399
14. Kottenstette, N., et al.: Design of networked control systems using passivity. IEEE Trans. Control Syst. Technol. **21**(3), 649–665 (2013). https://doi.org/10.1109/TCST.2012.2189211
15. Kreutz, D., et al.: Software-defined networking: a comprehensive survey. Proc. IEEE **103**(1), 14–76 (2015). https://doi.org/10.1109/JPROC.2014.2371999
16. McKeown, N., et al.: OpenFlow: enabling innovation in campus networks. SIGCOMM Comput. Commun. Rev. **38**(2), 69–74 (2008). https://doi.org/10.1145/1355734.1355746
17. Ndonda, G.K., Sadre, R.: A low-delay SDN-based countermeasure to eavesdropping attacks in industrial control systems. In: 2017 IEEE Conference on Network Function Virtualization and Software Defined Networks (NFV-SDN), pp. 1–7 (2017)
18. Nguyen, V.Q., Jeon, J.W.: EtherCAT network latency analysis. In: 2016 International Conference on Computing, Communication and Automation (ICCCA), pp. 432–436 (2016). https://doi.org/10.1109/CCAA.2016.7813815
19. Okwuibe, J., et al.: SDN enhanced resource orchestration of containerized edge applications for industrial IoT. IEEE Access. **8**, 229117–229131 (2020). https://doi.org/10.1109/ACCESS.2020.3045563
20. Romero-Gázquez, J.L., Bueno-Delgado, M.V.: Software architecture solution based on SDN for an industrial IoT scenario. Wirel. Commun. Mob. Comput. **2018**, e2946575 (2018). https://doi.org/10.1155/2018/2946575
21. Schneider, B., et al.: Evaluating software-defined networking for deterministic communication in distributed industrial automation systems. In: 2017 22nd IEEE International Conference on Emerging Technologies and Factory Automation (ETFA), pp. 1–8 (2017)
22. Schrauf, S., Berttram, P.: Industry 4.0: opportunities and challenges of the industrial internet. PwC (2014)
23. Stój, J.: Cost-effective hot-standby redundancy with synchronization using EtherCAT and real-time Ethernet protocols. IEEE Trans. Autom. Sci. Eng. **18**, 2035–2047 (2020)
24. Stój, J., et al.: FPGA based industrial Ethernet network analyser for real-time systems providing openness for Industry 4.0. Enterp. Inf. Syst. **0**(0), 1–21 (2021). https://doi.org/10.1080/17517575.2021.1948613

25. Stój, J.: State machine of a redundant computing unit operating as a cyber-physical system control node with hot-standby redundancy. In: Świątek, J., Borzemski, L., Wilimowska, Z. (eds.) ISAT 2019. AISC, vol. 1051, pp. 74–85. Springer, Cham (2020). https://doi.org/10.1007/978-3-030-30604-5_7

26. Wang, F., et al.: A dynamic cybersecurity protection method based on software-defined networking for industrial control systems. In: 2019 Chinese Automation Congress (CAC), pp. 1831–1834 (2019)

27. Xu, B., et al.: Internet of things and big data analytics for smart oil field malfunction diagnosis. In: 2017 IEEE 2nd International Conference on Big Data Analysis (ICBDA), pp. 178–181 (2017). https://doi.org/10.1109/ICBDA.2017.8078802

28. Yang, M., Li, G.: Analysis of PROFINET IO communication protocol. In: 2014 Fourth International Conference on Instrumentation and Measurement, Computer, Communication and Control, pp. 945–949 (2014). https://doi.org/10.1109/IMCCC.2014.199

29. Yoon, H., et al.: Dynamic flow steering for IoT monitoring data in SDN-coordinated IoT-Cloud services. In: 2017 International Conference on Information Networking (ICOIN), pp. 625–627 (2017)

30. EtherCAT Automation Protocol. EtherCAT for Plant Automation (2012)

31. Real-Time Wireless Data Plane for Real-Time-Enabled SDN. https://www.it.pt/Publications/PaperConference/34712. Accessed 09 June 2022

32. SDN (software-defined networking). In: Software Networks, pp. 13–32. Wiley (2020). https://doi.org/10.1002/9781119694748.ch2

ITS Traffic Violation Regulation Based on Blockchain Smart Contracts

Nihed Yousfi[1]([envelope])[iD], Mourad Kmimech[1][iD], Imed Abbassi[1][iD], Hedi Hamdi[2,3][iD], and Mohamed Graiet[1][iD]

[1] UR-OASIS Laboratory, University of Tunis El-Manar, Tunis, Tunisia
nihed.youssfi@gmail.com
[2] College of Computer Science, Jour University, Sakakah, Kingdom of Saudi Arabia
[3] University of Manouba, Manouba, Tunisia

Abstract. In the intelligent transportation system, many challenges have been identified to achieve a fully functional, practical and integrable ITS network. Some of these challenges include the regulation of traffic violations. Therefore, a proposed blockchain smart contract-based method has been formulated to address this challenge. This method includes vehicle speed detection, vehicle information collection through vehicle re-identification technique and a blockchain part containing smart contracts. The smart contract is a conditioned filter that follows regulatory rules from reporting violation points and fines for each violation to penalties. We have implemented the proposed algorithm and presented an evaluation of the proposed method, which gives satisfactory results and finally compare it with other known methods.

Keywords: ITS · Blockchain · Smart contract · Traffic violation · Vehicle re-identification

1 Introduction

Intelligent Transportation Systems (ITS) represent a combination of emerging technologies for improved safety and mobility to monitor, evaluate, and manage transportation systems. It is revolutionizing the way cities handle traffic and emergency response, while reducing congestion on city streets through sensors, advanced communications technology, automation and high-speed technology to move around a convenient city [1]. Their development is based on functions related to intelligence, such as sensory abilities, memory, communication, information processing and adoption processing (Fig. 1). ITS can be found in several areas of activity, including optimizing the use of transportation infrastructure as well as improving road safety and security. These possibilities can only be realized if road authorities have a clear and well-thought-out strategy to integrate the different systems and services along with the operational approaches that exist over time. One of the attributes that make up smart transportation is safety, which reduces the human element through a combination of machine learning,

C. Bădică et al. (Eds.): ICCCI 2022, CCIS 1653, pp. 459–471, 2022.
https://doi.org/10.1007/978-3-031-16210-7_38

IoT and 5G. Furthermore, since data collection is a key to a responsible public management of infrastructure, it enables a better management of intelligent transportation, by providing detailed data points for all aspects of the transportation system and enabling managers to better monitor operations. Smart transportation is more efficient by a good management and is cost-effective by making a good use of the available resources [2]. There are several integrated components of an ITS. These components include:

- Smart vehicles: As the transportation industry continues to evolve, the evolution of smart cars will have the greatest impact on how we travel and on our transportation infrastructure.
- Public transportation: Public transportation systems in many cities are the primary means of getting around metropolitan areas.
- Internet of things devices: IoT devices are increasingly being used in every aspect of ITS, from public transportation systems to stop signs that relay vacancy information to travelers looking for a parking space.
- Controllers: administer, control, or change the dynamics of the transportation system.

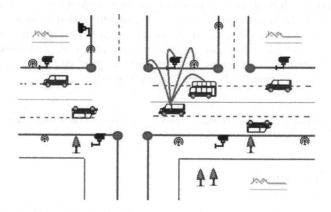

Fig. 1. Intelligent transportation system in smart city.

The intelligent traffic controller executes the decision-making actions generated by the intelligent components of the ITS. Routing algorithms and traffic schemes, which are adapted based on the observations made by smart vehicles, public transportation, and IoT devices, are sent to the smart traffic controllers for implementation [3]. Smart traffic controllers are not only responders to the observed data but are also a part of the data generation process. By connecting multiple smart traffic controllers together over a communication network, the data observed by one controller can be propagated to the rest of the system to further enhance the systems' ability to efficiently respond to traffic dynamics including emergency events. At the center of smart traffic control system are the TMCs that combine and synthesize data from the rest of the system into a useable form that can be utilized by traffic algorithms and Artificial Intelligence (AI) components of ITS [4]. In the fields of information technology, security and data exchange, one answer is blockchain. In fact, using blockchain provides high-level transparency and security standards because it does not require a central control. Allows connected users to exchange data without intervention. In the field of vehicles, blockchain can take care of this aspect, but also other aspects, such as vehicle traffic control to manage the license or the payment of fines committed by vehicle drivers. If blockchain technology is a solution, it is carried by communication technologies, such as IoT. In fact, blockchain requires data exchange to send tasks, share tasks and get results. Control-ling the vehicle network of an intelligent transportation system in a way that is not tight enough will increase the time needed to solve the problem (note that delay is an important parameter in a vehicle network).

We propose a solution to manage vehicle network control via blockchain and smart contracts. Consider a blockchain smart contracts-based approach, the TMC receives all relevant traffic information from the infrastructure, creates a complete picture of the traffic topology and derives events. Our research focuses on the use of smart contracts to manage violations. In fact, this is an important factor in controlling driver behavior. However, this approach can be extended to other parameters and there is no restriction on the type of actor. This paper proposes a method to automatically regulate traffic violations for a vehicle without stopping the vehicle and without the intervention of human resources. An algorithm has been developed and incorporated into smart contracts to verify vehicle data and automatically regulate traffic violations. The implementation and experimental results of the proposed algorithm are presented in a concise manner.

2   Related Work

Many industries, such as finance, medicine, manufacturing, and education, are using blockchain applications to take advantage of the technology's unique set of features. Blockchain Technology (BT) promises benefits in collaboration, organization, identification, trustworthiness, and transparency [5]. With immutability, additional functionality, and a visible record of all transactions, BT can provide transparency to all users at every stage of the system. Research revealed that this technology had significant, under-researched potential to support and improve the efficiencies of the revolution and identified areas for future research [6]. One of these research areas is intelligent traffic management systems. [7] focused on the real-time management of all available parking spaces in the city. By keeping track of the occupancy status of all the parking spaces available within a city, it is possible to aid not only the driver to locate his/her preferable parking spot quickly but also the city authorities in generating revenues by proper utilization of the parking spaces. [8] offered the opportunity for toll facility operators to supply a substantially greater amount of traffic capacity than any other currently available form of toll collection. The current interest in the Electronic

Toll Collection (ETC) derives from the proposals in a number of countries to introduce urban toll ways, using the net toll receipts to recover the cost of the capital investment plus an acceptable profit margin for those taking the financial risk.

[9] aimed not only to reduce fatal accidents related to speeding, but also to change the drivers' speeding behavior. The speed control strategy of the fixed Automated Speed Enforcement (ASE) system is to reduce the proportion of speeding vehicles in dangerous sections, and to increase the distance affected by the camera. [10] automatically identified trucks, simplified registration and co-operation with the management information system of railways, the visibility of shipments in real time, and ensured data integrity, lower error rates in the process of record of the consignments, and eliminated time-consuming documentation.

Although blockchain application is starting to be implemented in various fields [11], it has not yet reached the field of ITS as a real traffic violation system.

3   Smart Contract-Based Regulation of Traffic Violations in ITS

In ITS, the increase in vehicular traffic in urban areas is creating a mess for the authorities to manage urban traffic. Faced with a lack of human resources, authorities are turning to the use of intelligent and automatic traffic control systems to manage the increasing volume of traffic [12]. In most cases, these systems monitor traffic using street cameras and identify illegal behavior, such as traffic light violations [13], as described at Table 1. Furthermore, automatic license plate recognition [14] is complicated by the fact that it must operate in real time. It must be able to detect the license plate of every passing vehicle. Intelligent transport systems need the road user's data to function, and the optimal use of roads, traffic and travel data is a priority area for ITS development. Therefore, it seems necessary to designate additional safeguards for the personal data collected and processed by ITS services in order to make road traffic flow more smooth, while ensuring and improving user safety. However, in a normal system, a record in the database can be easily modified to reduce penalty points, fines, or even a driver's license status. This can be done as long as someone has access to the data-base. In a blockchain, though, even if a person has access to the server, he or she cannot do anything with the record for several reasons, the least of which is that every block stored in a blockchain is secured by a unique hash. TMCs help manage traffic to meet policy goals and positively impact throughput, pollution, and safety. Their main function is to collect and disseminate real-time traffic information for efficient traffic management as well as co-ordinate assistance for highway users who need it. A TMC uses loop detectors and cameras on the road as a part of its safety monitoring duties, aiming to achieve traffic efficiency by minimizing traffic problems. It provides users with prior information about traffic, local convenience, real-time operational information, seat availability, and more. This reduces travel time for

Table 1. Example of dataset reflects the daily volume of violations that occurred in Children's Safety Zones for road surveillance cameras in Chicago 2014.

Address	Camera ID	Date	...	Violation	Location
10318S INDIANAPOLIS	CHI120	05/22/2022	...	91	(41.7°, −87.5...°)
1111 N N HUMBOLDT	CHI010	05/22/2022	...	104	****
115 N OGDEN	CHI077	05/22/2022	...	109	(41.8...°, −87.6...°)
140 N ASHLAND	CHI076	05/22/2022	...	31	(41.8°, −87.6...°)
...	...	...	...	...	...

commuters and improves their safety and comfort. Even with a high volume of data, emergency scenarios still require "eyes on the road" technology to monitor and control traffic conditions as much as possible, allowing them to make quick traffic management and safety decisions.

ITS works through partners that exchange information with each other using a standardized set of messages. Technically, there are three data transmitters: the vehicles and the infrastructure leading to communication paths between vehicles (vehicle-to-vehicle), between vehicle and infrastructure (vehicle-to-infrastructure), and between infrastructure elements (infrastructure-to-infrastructure) [15]. Vehicles and infrastructure systems are wirelessly connected. The receiving TMC analyzes the data and makes use of the information depending on the service and application. In this article, we will explore the interaction between the TMC and the vehicle, as shown in Fig. 2 below. Figure 3 shows the overall architecture, which is composed of vehicles that can collect traffic-related data and send such data to nearby vehicles or they can send such data to a TMC through an access network. Like vehicles, a TMC can collect traffic-related data and send them to be analyzed. Additionally, the core network connects the access network to the cloud, providing many important functions, such as aggregation, authentication, switching, and routing. Moreover, many different sources can provide their data to the cloud through the core network,

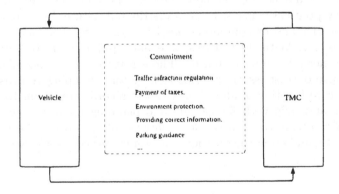

Fig. 2. Interaction between the TMC and the vehicle.

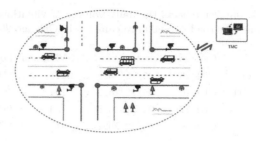

Fig. 3. Communication between the TMC and vehicles.

improving the services delivered by the TMC. All data is collected and analyzed here for further operation and control management of traffic in real time or to provide information about local transport vehicles. Well-organized and proficient operations of TMC depend more on automated data collection with precise information location than the analysis of that data to generate accurate information and then transmitting it back to travelers.

Intelligent Transportation systems introduce new privacy concerns [3] through the data they collect about passengers and their vehicles. The increasing integration of loosely secured devices and applications with the transportation system presents opportunities for attackers to exploit these systems. In a traffic violation system, TMC, police, and vehicle drivers may not have complete trust in each other. This could even reduce a decision affected by political reasons. Therefore, it is important to have a blockchain. The decentralized structure combined with the use of cryptographic procedures ensures that a user cannot secretly manipulate any information in the database. However, once the data is added to the ledger it cannot be removed or edited as with a database. In this case, blockchain also requires smart contracts between different companies to collect data in any uncertain situation. Information can be more easily interpreted to define the situation and help create a safe environment. In a TMC equipped with a traffic violation system, the trust between the police and the vehicle operator may not be complete. This could even reduce decisions that are influenced by political reasons. From a distributed nature, blockchain provides a wide range of nodes or computers participating in the network to distribute computing power. With its features, it enables public users to verify records without the need for intermediaries. These features serve the main purpose of an automated trustless traffic violation system. Keeping records of transactions is a core function of all systems. These records are meant to track past performance and help with forecasting and planning for future actions. Most processes of resolving cases of traffic violations' records take a lot of time and effort to create, and often the creation and storage processes are prone to errors.

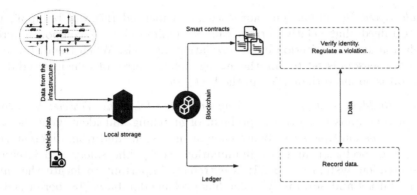

Fig. 4. Overview of the intelligent transportation system platform.

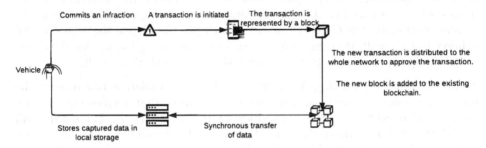

Fig. 5. Blockchain-based structure to regulate traffic violations.

Currently, transactions can be executed immediately, but settlement can take from several hours to several days. In addition, the regulation rules often take days and may involve lawyers and government employees. Each party maintains its own ledger, and cannot access the ledgers of the other parties. However, when a transaction is recorded in the blockchain, details of the transaction such as price, asset, and ownership, are recorded, verified and settled within seconds across all nodes. A verified change registered on any one ledger is also simultaneously registered on all other copies of the ledger. Since each transaction is transparently and permanently recorded across all ledgers, there is no need for third-party verification as shown in Fig. 4. The method introduced [16] by has the advantage that Toll-Tax (TA) from the highway driver is automatically collected using the smart contract. The results of the proposal appear to be consistent with this simple procedure, but not with more complex traffic rules such as violation management. To address the above objective, we propose an approach based on a blockchain smart contracts that automatically regulate traffic violations (Fig. 5). This approach can be divided into the following three parts:

Vehicle Speed Detection: The autocorrelation method [17] will be applied. It is determined that relative errors can be minimized by Z-component cross-correlation and K_z criterion cross-correlation methods. When the distance between the sensors is set to 2m, the average relative error of vehicle speed determination is no more than 1.5% in the best case.

Vehicle Re-Identification for Tracking and Identifying the Vehicle: Vehicle re-identification aims to solve the problem of matching and identifying the same vehicle across multiple surveillance cameras in a scene and from different viewpoints with occlusion and low illumination. For public safety and intelligent transportation systems (ITS), it is extremely important to locate the target vehicle quickly and accurately in the huge vehicle database. [18] performed the vehicle re-identification based on approximate string matching. The experimental results show that the proposed method can improve the matching performance when compared to the existing approximate string matching techniques. In our experiment, the GED [19] achieved high precision while the 2-Grams [20] achieved high recall. By combining the two methods using the proposed weighting technique, precision is further improved without reducing recall.

Smart Contract for Identity Verification and Traffic Violation Regulation: The idea is to design a smart contract model on request that verifies the identity of the vehicle, as well as the regulations for traffic violations. The details will be processed in a smart contract module to see if any conditions are met, then hashed and stored in the blockchain. If the process is successful, the transaction will appear in the interface. The block transaction patterns are designed to match the regulatory rules [21], which are then used as inputs to the smart contracts. The details of the block include: license plate number (which serves as an identifier to which penalty points and other contracts can refer), date of violation, type of violation, penalty points, fines, penalty, and driver's license status. Since all the regular security mechanisms protecting blockchain transactions are involved, the smart contract has access to the user's identity (address) and users cannot fake a transaction by using another user's address because he/she does not have other people's private keys. Hence, violations will be billed to the vehicle owner's bank account.

Execute Algorithm 1 below for all violations reported by TMC. For each violation reported, make sure the ID V_{id} is true and the offender's $D_{account-balance}$ is not empty. If it is empty, the offender will be notified. If there is such a violation category vlt_Type (Band_A, Band_B, or Band_C), the smart contract will automatically extract the amount of the violation penalty from the Daccount-balance and add points to the penalty plty_Pts according to the vlt_Type. As soon as the total number of penalty points reaches a certain number (here 100) or more the Boolean variable License-Disqualification is displayed as True and the value of Num_Susps is incremented so that the driver's license will be suspended for a period of time if the penalty point limit is exceeded. If there are too many suspensions in the driver's traffic history, the license will be revoked.

Algorithm 1: Algorithm IVIRTV

Data: V_{id} , vlt_Type, $D_{account}$
Result: fines, plty, license_status, T_Plty_Pts
if $V_{id} = true$ && $D_{account\_balance}$ ¿0 then
    if $vlt\_Type = Band\_A$ then
        $plty\_pts \leftarrow 4$;
        $fines \leftarrow 150$;
    end
    if $vlt\_Type = Band\_B$ then
        $plty\_pts \leftarrow 6$;
        $fines \leftarrow 200$;
    end
    if $vlt\_Type = Band\_C$ then
        $plty\_pts \leftarrow 8$;
        $fines \leftarrow 300$;
    end
    $D_{Account\_balance} \leftarrow D_{Account\_balance} -$ fines;
    $T\_Plty\_Pts \leftarrow T\_Plty\_Pts + plty\_Pts$;
else
    Warn the owner
end
if $T\_Plty\_Pts \geq 100$ then
    License_Disq=true ;
    $Num\_Susps \leftarrow Num\_Susps + 1$;
end
if $Num\_Susps = 1$ then
    $plty \leftarrow Suspended - for - 3 - months$;
end
if $Num\_Susps = 2$ then
    $plty \leftarrow Suspended - for - 6 - months$;
end
if $Num\_Susps \geq 3$ then
    $plty \leftarrow License\_revoked$;
    $License\_status \leftarrow Revoked$;
end

---

4 Experiment and Discussion

Using the proposed method, the automated traffic violation system will optimize trips, eliminate unnecessary trip miles, and reduce traffic jam times. First, the individual vehicle data is collected and stored in a local storage at the TMC. A record is completed at the time of registration. For each vehicle, the speed is calculated and recorded automatically in the local storage. If the TMC records an alleged speeding, a traffic violation will be issued to the vehicle's registrar. The record will contain: the vehicle details, date, and the speed rating categories.

Three rating categories are described at Table 2, highlighting the extent to which the speed limit is exceeded.

Table 2. Speed limits categories, fines, and penalty.

Speed limit	Band$_A$	Band$_B$	Band$_C$
20 mph	21–30 mph	31–40 mph	41+ mph
30 mph	31–40 mph	41–50 mph	51+ mph
40 mph	41–55 mph	56–65 mph	66+ mph
50 mph	51–65 mph	66–75 mph	76– mph
60 mph	61–80 mph	81–90 mph	91+ mph
70 mph	71–90 mph	91–100 mph	101+ mph
Fine	150	200	300
Penalty points	3 points	4 points	6 points

As shown in the example below (Fig. 6), the vehicle starts its journey and has to pass through different zones that have different speed limits. In the first and third zones, the vehicle is traveling at the speed limit. However, in the fourth zone, the speed limit is 40 mph and the vehicle does not meet it. Immediately, a traffic violation is recorded with the vehicle data. The smart contracts will then verify the identity and work by following simple statements that are written into the code on a blockchain "if speed > speed limit then regulation". When the predetermined conditions are met and verified, the transaction is executed. The blockchain is then updated when the transaction is completed. According to the proposed method and the example, a contract is applied: each traffic violation has its referential penalty points and will be fined according to the penalty points, as described at Table 2 above. Based on the accumulated penalty points, if a driver has exceeded 100 points, the driver license will be suspended and follows the penalty of the third contract. Once a driver's penalty points racked up to 100 points or above, the first driving license suspension will be given. The first suspension does not exceed 6 months. If, after being revoked, the driver violates the law again despite the demerit points, he will be subject to the penalty of

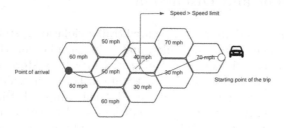

Fig. 6. Example of a vehicle's journey.

having his driver's license revoked for a period of not more than 12 months. If the offense is repeated within 5 years of the second suspension, the driver's license will be revoked.

To test the functionality of the system we evaluated the proposed method using the example in Fig. 6. Blocks are received during the testing and recorded correctly on the blockchain system. The purpose of this test is to verify the rigidity of the smart contract in terms of filtering various conditions in the transaction, and to check that blocks are created, then hashed and stored in the blockchain. In conclusion, the decentralized model has been successful (Fig. 7). This means it is implemented correctly and works as expected.

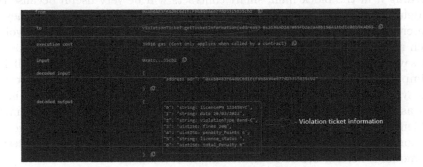

Fig. 7. Output of the block.

Penalty and penalties received from the input match the actual regulations, as described at Table 2. Data will be updated based on the total penalties and the number of sus-pensions. In conclusion, the smart contract is properly executed. Thus, in a practical situation, a smart contract can filter out any input, reducing human error in deciding how many penalty points to assign in a particular violation. The above Table 3 provides a comparison between our proposed method and well-known traffic violation detection methods. Most of these methods are at best able to detect traffic violations without providing a truly automated settlement, which means it will require human intervention. In addition, the processing of the violation ticket through to settlement is time and resource intensive. Our proposed method, on the other hand, is based on smart contracts that run automatically as soon as a violation is detected, thus automatically handling traffic

Table 3. Comparison table of existing methods and the proposed method.

Method	Settlement of infraction/toll-tax				Resources			
	Real time	Toll-Tax	Infraction	Automatic regulation	Policeman	Camera	Sensor	Toll reader
ASE	✗	✗	✓	✗	✓	✓	✗	✗
ETC	✓	✓	✗	✓	✓	✓	✗	✓
Proposed method	✓	✓	✓	✓	✗	✓	✓	✗

violations that saves time and resources without human intervention. It also classifies violations and determines the status of the driver's license based on this classification (revoked, suspended, etc.).

5   Conclusion and Perspective

The main goal of ITS, is to help people and vehicles move more safely and efficiently by providing information links between travelers, vehicles and infrastructure. Thus, in a real-life traffic violation situation and after detecting the vehicle's speed, capturing its information using the vehicle's Re-Id technique and recording it in the blockchain, smart contracts will be very useful because they are defined only once and can filter all entries since then. In addition, they are tamper-proof and guarantee greater security since no intermediaries are involved, which reduces human errors. They offer faster resolution than manual processes and save time for both parties while reducing vehicle travel, which will have an impact on carbon consumption and therefore on environmental protection. This system shows that it is possible to implement and apply blockchain in ITS such as for traffic violation regulation, but since it is a blockchain system, the problem of forking still exists. In addition, many different technologies have been mentioned to implement the model. Therefore, a real-world performance test for this model is needed before implementing it in a real ITS.

References

1. Ang, K.L.-M., Seng, J.K.P., Ngharamike, E., Ijemaru, G.K.: Emerging technologies for smart cities' transportation: geo-information, data analytics and machine learning approaches. ISPRS Int. J. Geo-Inf. **11**(2), 85 (2022)
2. Ma, S., Wolfson, O.: A survey on trust management for intelligent transportation system. In: Proceedings of the 4th ACM SIGSPATIAL International Workshop on Computational Transportation Science, pp. 18–23 (2011)
3. Hahn, D., Munir, A., Behzadan, V.: Security and privacy issues in intelligent transportation systems: classification and challenges. EEE Intell. Transp. Syst. Mag. **13**(1), 181–196 (2019)
4. Hilmani, A., Maizate, A.: Automated real-time intelligent traffic control system for smart cities using wireless sensor networks. Wirel. Commun. Mobile Comput., 1–28 (2020)
5. Leible, S., Schlager, S.: A review on blockchain technology and blockchain projects fostering open science. Front Blockchain **2**(16), 28 (2019)
6. Sikorski, J.J., Haughton, J.: Blockchain technology in the chemical industry: machine-to-machine electricity market. Appl. Energy **195**(2), 234–246 (2017)
7. Sadhukhan, P., Talukdar, A.: Automated real-time parking management for smart cities. In: Kundu, S., Acharya, U.S., De, C.K., Mukherjee, S. (eds.) Proceedings of the 2nd International Conference on Communication, Devices and Computing. LNEE, vol. 602, pp. 655–667. Springer, Singapore (2020). https://doi.org/10.1007/978-981-15-0829-5_61
8. Groves, T.: Emergency vehicle notification. International Application No. PCT/CA2010/OOO962 (2015)

9. Kang, J.-G.: Changes of speed and safety by automated speed enforcement systems. IATSS Res. **26**(2), 38–44 (2002)
10. Andrea Rosová, M.B.: The use of the RFID in rail freight transport in the world as one of the new technologies of identification and communication. Acta Montanistica Slovaca **18**(1), 26–32 (2013)
11. Hawlitschek, F., Notheisen, B.: The limits of trust-free systems: a literature review on blockchain technology and trust in the sharing economy. Electron. Commer. Res. Appl. **29**(1), 50–63 (2018)
12. Hiroshi Makinoa, K.T.: Solutions for urban traffic issues by ITS technologies. IATSS Res. **42**(2), 49–60 (2021)
13. Rathore, M.M.: Smart traffic control: identifying driving-violations using fog devices with vehicular cameras in smart cities. Sustain. Cities Soc. **71**(1), 102986 (2021)
14. Gonçalves, G.R., Diniz, M.A.: Real-time automatic license plate recognition through deep multi-task networks, pp. 110–117. IEEE (2018)
15. Hasan, M., Mohan, S., Shimizu, T., Hongsheng, L.: Securing vehicle-to-everything (V2X) communication platforms. IEEE Trans. Intell. Veh. **5**(4), 693–713 (2020)
16. Das, D., Banerjee, S.: Design and development of an intelligent transportation management. Cluster Comput. **25**(3), 1899–1913 (2022)
17. Markevicius, V., Navikas, D.: Dynamic vehicle detection via the use of magnetic field sensors. Sensors **16**(1), 78–78 (2016)
18. Watcharapinchai, N., Rujikietgumjorn, S.: Approximate license plate string matching for vehicle re-identification, pp. 1–6. IEEE (2017)
19. Oliveira-Neto, F.M., Han, L.D.: Online licenseplate matching procedures using license-plate recognition machines and new weighted edit distance. Transp. Res. Part C Emerg. Technol. **21**, 1–6 (2017)
20. Karen, K.: Technique for automatically correcting words in text. Transp. Res. Part C Emerg. Technol. **24**(1), 377–439 (1992)
21. Aditya Pradana, G.O.: Blockchain traffic offence demerit points smart contracts: proof of work. (IJACSA) Int. J. Adv. Comput. Sci. Appl. **9**(11), 375–382 (2018)

Distributed Architecture of an Intrusion Detection System in Industrial Control Systems

Ahlem Abid(✉)[ID], Farah Jemili[ID], and Ouajdi Korbaa[ID]

MARS Research Lab LR17ES05, ISITCom, University of Sousse, 4011 H. Sousse, Tunisia
ahlemabid95@gmail.com, ouajdi.korbaa@centraliens-lille.org

Abstract. Industry 4.0 refers to a new generation of connected and intelligent factories that is driven by the emergence of new technologies such as artificial intelligence, Cloud computing, Big Data and industrial control systems (ICS) in order to automate all phases of industrial operations. The presence of connected systems in industrial environments poses a considerable security challenge, moreover with the huge amount of data generated daily, there are complex attacks that occur in seconds and target production lines and their integrity. But, until now, factories do not have all the necessary tools to protect themselves, they mainly use traditional protection. To improve industrial control systems in terms of efficiency and response time, the present paper propose a new distributed intrusion detection approach using artificial intelligence methods including machine learning, Big Data techniques and deployed in a cloud environment. We use the industrial dataset SWat for the experiment. Our system achieved good results in terms of Accuracy (99%) and response time by using Gradient-Boosted Trees (GBTs) classifier due to the performance of Databricks and Apache Spark.

Keywords: Intrusion detection · Industry 4.0 · Industrial control systems · Artificial intelligence · Machine learning · Cloud computing

1 Introduction

Artificial intelligence in cyber security increases efficiency and precision of the system to detect any potential threat in Manufacturing Systems. Manufactories expanding their horizon to different geographies are generating voluminous data to gain insights and are also using analysis techniques to enhance their product offerings. Global AI in cyber security market [7] is predicted to grow at 35.0% during the forecast period with the market size reaching USD 31.2 billion by 2024. The market is driven by the factors such as increasing stringent data privacy regulations, increasing number of cyber-attacks, increasing adoption of digital solutions, and increasing inclination towards cloud-based solutions from onpremise. The continuous research and development for technologically advanced systems for anomaly detection, web filtering, intrusion detection, and data loss prevention among others. The market for AI in cyber security devices is primarily driven by increasing data frauds and cyber-attacks worldwide. The increasing use of connected technologies makes the smart manufacturing system vulnerable to cyber risks. This creates utmost need of certain systems and programs

C. Bădică et al. (Eds.): ICCCI 2022, CCIS 1653, pp. 472–484, 2022.
https://doi.org/10.1007/978-3-031-16210-7_39

which can detect predict process and analyze such threats and keep manufactories safe from cyber-attacks. AI offers the solution to the threat to a great extent and therefore different industry players are focusing on utilizing AI for cyber security, thereby fueling the growth of the global market. Security is a broad term, and in industry there are a myriad of "security" contexts on a variety of levels wide.

Artificial intelligence and machine learning technologies are being applied and developed across this spectrum. Artificial intelligence and security were - in many ways - made for each other, and the modern approaches of machine learning seem to be arriving just in time to fill in the gaps of previous rule-based data security systems. The recent White House report on Artificial Intelligence (AI) [4] highlights the significance of AI and the necessity of a clear roadmap and strategic investment in this area. As AI emerges from science-fiction to become the frontier of world-changing technologies, there is an urgent need for systematic development and implementation of AI to see its real impact in the next generation of industrial systems, namely Industry 4.0. This fourth revolution [1] refers to a new generation of connected, robotic, and intelligent factories that is driven by the emergence of new technologies such as industrial artificial intelligence, the Cloud, Big Data and industrial control systems (ICS) intelligent and interconnected in order to automate all phases of industrial operations from design to maintenance, which could allow production to operate efficiently, flexibly and economically, with a consistent high quality and low cost. The presence of connected systems in industrial environments poses a considerable security challenge as only 16% of companies are well prepared to meet the challenges of cyber security [13] which plays a leading role in preventing the loss of competitiveness of companies, this is mainly due to the lack of accurate standards that companies can refer to as well as the lack of management skills and the techniques needed to implement them; this increases the surface of vulnerability and the risk of intrusions into industrial IT systems. This creates the greatest need for certain systems and programs that can detect and predict the process and analyze such threats and keep factories safe from cyber attacks. In addition, with the huge amount of data generated on a daily basis, there are also more complex attacks that occur in seconds that target production lines and their integrity or are related to the lack of data control at the Cloud. In fact, in the last few years, modern ICS have been victims of cyber attacks, these attacks can cause ICS malfunction and result in financial losses and have the ability to damage physical equipment and cause human casualties. However, until now, factories do not have all the necessary tools to protect themselves, they mainly use traditional protection tools such as firewalls and antivirus which are not effective enough to protect against complex attacks because their protection capabilities are very limited and only allow access control.

Considering the importance of an intrusion detection system, some factories deploy IDS to obtain information about potentially vulnerable activities occurring in their technological environment to allow maintaining system security and transferring information between departments and organizations with an increasingly secure and reliable way. But currently, factories mainly use traditional IDS such as Snort and Bro as intrusion detection mechanisms that are limited due to their inability to detect attacks that do not belong to their databases. In order to improve industrial control systems in terms of efficiency and response time, the present paper aims to propose a new distributed intrusion detection approach using artificial intelligence methods including machine learning based on Big Data techniques and deployed in a cloud environment.

Based on the motivations described above, the authors have chosen to organize the paper as follows. In Sect. 2, a brief overview of related works in the area of Intrusion detection based on ICS is presented. Section 3 presents our proposed approach, Sect. 4 evaluates the experimental results. Finally, some conclusions and the future works are presented in Sect. 5.

2 Related Work

The purpose of this section is to present related work and methods currently used to detect intrusions in an industrial context Table 1.

Table 1. Related Work.

Work	Dataset	Data Preprocessing	Deployment Architecture	Intrusion Detection Technique
[11]	Gas pipeline	❑ Remove missing values, Feature extraction	No	❑ Machine Learning (Naive Bayes, PART, Random Forest)
[15]	SWaT	❑ One-hot encoding, Correlation filter, Kolmogorov-Smirnov filter, variance filter, Feature extraction	No	❑ Deep Learning (LSTM)
[6]	KDDCup'99	❑ No	No	❑ Machine Learning (J48, Naive Bayes, Random Forest)
[12]	SWaT	❑ Converting continuous and categorical values to scale (0,1), Feature extraction	No	❑ Deep Learning (CNN and LSTM)
[10]	SWaT	❑ No	No	❑ Deep Learning (DNN), Machine Learning (OCSVM)

In conclusion, all these related works have proposed solutions to detect cyber attacks in ICS and based on different Machine Learning and Deep Learning models, but their main limitation is the use of a local environment so the distributed environment is absent. Based on the methods of existing work, we will present a new distributed approach to detect intrusions in industrial control systems using a Cloud deployment architecture, Databricks Community, and the Apache Spark tool to manipulate and analyze our industrial data, SWaT dataset, in a short time and to give best results.

3 A New Distributed Approach of Intrusion Detection System in Industrial Control Systems

Our approach aims to provide an efficient and distributed intrusion detection system by adding additional processing power. Our approach is divided into four steps:

- The collection of industrial data for water treatment via the ITrust[1].

---
[1] https://itrust.sutd.edu.sg/testbeds/secure-water-treatment-swat/.

- Data storage using a deployment architecture: the Databricks Cloud Platform which allows us to have a distributed and scalable system and which solves several problems, mainly the problem of storing alert databases.
- Data structuring through data preprocessing techniques to obtain clean and usable data through data transformation by converting data from the original format to another format, the study of correlation between data and data cleaning by eliminating irrelevant features and redundant rows.
- Data analysis by using AI learning mechanisms such as machine learning to properly detect and classify intrusions.

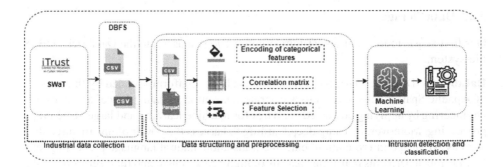

Fig. 1. Overview of the proposed approach.

To realize our approach, we choose Databricks as our data analysis, processing and storage platform, which is based on AWS and already has Spark installed and configured.

3.1   Industrial Data Collection

In the literature [8], there are several datasets for ICS intrusion detection such as: the datasets of Morris et al. [14] who published five different power generation, gas and water treatment datasets for their intrusion detection research, the dataset of Lemay et al. who provided the network traffic dataset related to command and control of secret channels in the Supervisory Control and Data Acquisition (SCADA) field, and the datasets published by SWaT that represent a scaled-down version of an industrial water treatment plant and collected sensors, actuators, input/output signals, and network traffic for seven days of normal operation and four days of attack scenario. However, these datasets contain unintended patterns that can be used to easily identify attacks and non-attacks using machine learning algorithms. Although the gas dataset was updated in 2015 to provide more randomness, it was obtained from a small-scale testbed that may not reflect the true complexity of ICS. Therefore, there is no realistic dataset of sufficient complexity from a modern ICS that contains both network traffic and physical properties of the ICS except the SWaT dataset which is a large-scale labeled dataset collected from a realistic testbed of sufficient complexity [9].

Secure Water Treatment Dataset (SWaT). SWaT [9] represents a scaled-down version of an actual industrial water treatment plant producing 5 gallons per minute of filtered water through ultrafiltration and reverse osmosis membrane units. The SWaT data set was collected over 11 d of continuous operation. The first 7 d of data were collected under normal operation (no attacks) while the remaining 4 d were collected with 36 attack scenarios. All network traffic and physical data (sensors and actuators) were collected. The dataset contains a total of 53 features: 1 for the timestamp, 1 for the label ("Attack" and "Normal"), and the remaining 51 are numerical values indicating the data recorded by 51 sensors and actuators. The sensors and actuators were sampled every second.

3.2   Data Storage

Our first step is to load our SWaT intrusion detection dataset into the Databricks DBFS file system.

Databricks. Databricks(AWS) [3] is a data analytics platform founded by the creators of Apache Spark whose goal is to accelerate innovation in data science, analytics and engineering by applying advanced analytics for machine learning and large-scale graph processing. Moreover, by using deep learning to harness the power of unstructured data such as AI, image interpretation, machine translation, natural language processing, etc. In addition, it performs real-time analysis of high-speed sensor and time-series IoT data. A free version is provided by AWS called Databricks Community Edition. This platform is a cloud-based Big Data solution designed for developers and data engineers. It provides users with access to a micro-cluster and cluster manager as well as a notebook environment. It's a higher level platform that allows users to become proficient with Apache Spark. This platform offers a variety of features, It allows cluster sharing where multiple users can connect to the same cluster. In addition, it offers a security feature and provides a data management.

DBFS. DBFS is a distributed file system available on Spark Cluster in Databricks. It allows mounting storage objects to access data without the need for credentials. In addition, it allows you to interact with the storage objects using directory and file semantics. In addition, this system keeps files in the object storage so that data is not lost after closing clusters.

Apache Spark. Apache Spark is a powerful, flexible and distributed data processing framework. It uses in-memory computation to run jobs thus making it much faster than Apache Hadoop. It is the most active open source project in the big data field. Spark provides support for a range of libraries, including the scalable machine learning library MLlib which contains many machine learning algorithms, such as classification, clustering and regression algorithms.

3.3   Data Structuring and Preprocessing

Data Transformation. Since Apache Spark offers the ability to convert data from the original format to another format, we first read the CSV files from DBFS and convert them to Apache Parquet format for compressing and partitioning it and therefore we can minimize storage costs and get better performance [5].

Deal with Categorical Label and Features. This step consists in carrying out the encoding of categorical features, so that we can form our model, with the help of the StringIndexer() method in which the indices are attributed according to the frequency of the attribute, thus the most frequent attribute obtains the index 0.0. In our dataset, mainly categorical features from motorized valves and pumps. The list of categorical features encoded using the StringIndexer() method are : MV101, P101, P102, MV201, P201, P202, P203, P204, P205, P206, MV301, MV302, MV303, MV304, P301, P302, P401, P402, P403, P404, UV401, P501, P502, P601, P602, P603.

Correlation Matrix. A correlation matrix is used to evaluate the dependency between several variables at the same time. The result is a table containing the correlation coefficients between each variable and the others. The correlation matrix for our features is shown below in Fig. 2:

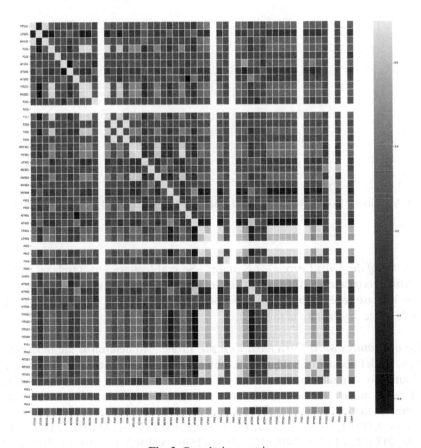

Fig. 2. Correlation matrix.

Feature Selection. It is the automatic selection of attributes in our data (such as columns in tabular data) that are most relevant to the classification problem we are working on. Feature Selection is the process of selecting a subset of relevant features to use in model building. Feature selection is different from dimension reduction. Both methods seek to reduce the number of attributes in the dataset, but a dimension reduction method does so by creating new combinations of features, whereas feature selection methods include and exclude attributes present in the data without changing them.

Elimination of Features That Do Not Vary Over Time. After studying the variation of the features, we found that the features P202, P401, P404, P502, P601 and P603 which correspond to those of the pumps have a null variation. Figure 3 shows a visualization of the variation of these features.

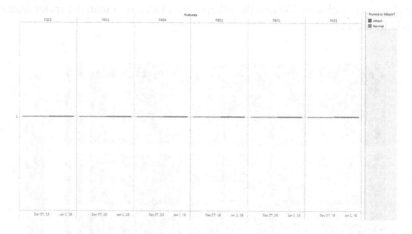

Fig. 3. Visualization of the variation of the features P202, P401, P404, P502, P601 and P603.

Elimination of the Most Correlated Features. Several features are correlated with each other with a correlation of 100%. This kind of correlation is habitual in industrial control systems because several sensors (or actuators) depend and based on each other [15]. So, we can't delete any feature in this step.

Choice of Features Most Correlated with the Target. To determine the most relevant features, we defined a threshold of 0.25, which corresponds to the average of the thresholds found, for a judicious choice that allows us to develop a powerful and efficient classification model. The selected features are those which have a correlation with our target higher than 0.25. At the end, we can define a dataset composed of 24 features as follows: LIT101, P101, AIT201, P203, DPIT301, FIT301, MV302, MV304, P302, AIT402, FIT401, LIT401, P402, UV401, AIT501, AIT502, FIT501, FIT502, FIT503, FIT504, P501, PIT501, PIT502, PIT503.

3.4   Intrusion Detection and Classification

After applying the necessary preprocessing and once our database is ready, we arrive at the last step of this approach which is classification. A judicious choice of Machine Learning algorithms represents a fundamental step for the development of a classification system capable of efficiently distinguishing the different classes with a high accuracy rate and a low error rate. In our work, We tested the performance of our intrusion detection system against several ML classification algorithms Multi-layer Perceptron (MLP), Decision Tree, Random Forest, Logistic Regression, Gradient-Boosted Trees (GBTs) and Naïve Bayes, by using Apache Spark and its MLlib library.

Model Optimization. Most machine learning models need to be adjusted to provide the best results. For example, for a random forest, each time you divide a node, you have to choose the number of trees to create and the number of variables to use. If you set the parameters manually, it quickly becomes very time consuming. This is where the ParamGridBuilder and the CrossValidator come in. This is an optimization method (hyperparameter optimization) that allows you to test a series of parameters and compare the performances to deduce the best parameterization. There are several ways to test model parameters, and the ParamGridBuilder and CrossValidator is one of the simplest methods. For each parameter, we determine a set of values to test.

4   Evaluation and Validation of Results

This last section summarizes the classification results obtained across several models. We will present the results of each model to evaluate the effectiveness and efficiency of the proposed method. Then we will discuss and validate these results.

4.1   Evaluation Metrics

Model evaluation is an integral part of the model development process. It is useful to find the best model that represents our data and how well the chosen model will perform in the future. For classification algorithms, two evaluation measures are commonly used [2]:

Confusion Matrix. A confusion matrix is used to have a complete picture of the performance of a model. It is defined as follows:

Main Indicators. The following indicators are commonly used to evaluate the performance of classification models Table 2:

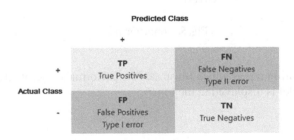

Fig. 4. Confusion matrix

Table 2. IDS Performance Metrics

Metric	Description
Accuracy	The fraction of correctly classified objects and the total number of objects
Precision	The ratio of data instances predicted as positive that are actually positive
Recall	The proportion of positive examples that were classified correctly
F-Measure	The harmonic mean of precision and recall

4.2   Results

After having parameterized the models used, we can confirm that the ParamGridBuilder and the CrossValidator have allowed the optimization of the results of different models for a better performance. In the rest of this section, we illustrate the results found for each classifier. The confusion matrix of each classifier is displayed in the Fig. 5:

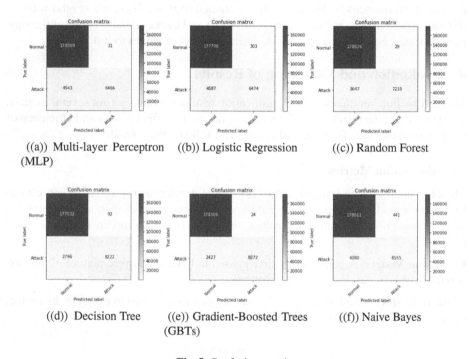

((a)) Multi-layer Perceptron (MLP)   ((b)) Logistic Regression   ((c)) Random Forest

((d)) Decision Tree   ((e)) Gradient-Boosted Trees (GBTs)   ((f)) Naive Bayes

Fig. 5. Confusion matrix

The classification report which illustrates the performance across the different metrics for each model is displayed in the Fig. 6:

```
         precision recall f1-score support
Normal   0.98      1.00   0.99     178110
Attack   1.00      0.59   0.74     11009

accuracy                0.98     189119
macro avg 0.99     0.79  0.86     189119
weighted avg 0.98  0.98  0.97     189119
```

```
         precision recall f1-score support
Normal   0.97      1.00   0.99     178099
Attack   0.96      0.59   0.73     11061

accuracy                0.97     189160
macro avg 0.97     0.79  0.86     189160
weighted avg 0.97  0.97  0.97     189160
```

```
         precision recall f1-score support
Normal   0.98      1.00   0.99     178665
Attack   1.00      0.86   0.80     10857

accuracy                0.98     189522
macro avg 0.99     0.83  0.89     189522
weighted avg 0.98  0.98  0.98     189522
```

((a)) Multi-layer Perceptron (MLP)   ((b)) Logistic Regression   ((c)) Random Forest

```
         precision recall f1-score support
Normal   0.98      1.00   0.99     177624
Attack   0.99      0.75   0.85     11018

accuracy                0.98     188642
macro avg 0.99     0.87  0.92     188642
weighted avg 0.98  0.98  0.98     188642
```

```
         precision recall f1-score support
Normal   0.99      1.00   0.99     178330
Attack   1.00      0.77   0.87     10699

accuracy                0.99     189029
macro avg 0.99     0.89  0.93     189029
weighted avg 0.99  0.99  0.99     189029
```

```
         precision recall f1-score support
Normal   0.98      1.00   0.99     178452
Attack   0.94      0.60   0.73     10935

accuracy                0.97     189387
macro avg 0.96     0.80  0.86     189387
weighted avg 0.97  0.97  0.97     189387
```

((d)) Decision Tree   ((e)) Gradient-Boosted Trees (GBTs)   ((f)) Naive Bayes

Fig. 6. Classification report

4.3 Comparison and Discussion of Results

The table below compares the different models used for the detection and classification of intrusions in our dataset Table 3:

Table 3. Models comparison

Model	Accuracy	Precision	Recall	F1-score
Multi-layer Perceptron (MLP)	0.98	0.98	0.98	0.97
Logistic Regression	0.97	0.97	0.97	0.97
Random Forest	0.98	0.98	0.98	0.98
Decision Tree	0.98	0.98	0.98	0.98
Gradient-Boosted Trees (GBTs)	**0.99**	**0.99**	**0.99**	**0.99**
Naive Bayes	0.97	0.97	0.97	0.97

The results showed that the Gradient-Boosted Trees (GBTs) classifier gave the best performance in terms of Accuracy (0.99), Precision (0.99), Recall (0.99) and F1-score (0.99) with a low number of FNs(24) and FPs(2427). This was followed by the Random Forest classifier then the Decision Tree classifier, while the Naïve Bayes and Logistic regression classifiers gave the lowest detection accuracy (0.97).

In terms of speed, as well as implementation and data processing, thanks to Apache Spark, we received a response from the system within seconds. The table shows the time spent by each model in the learning and prediction phases Table 4.

Table 4. Response time

Model	Training (s)	Prediction (s)
Multi-layer Perceptron (MLP)	5.97	0.57
Logistic Regression	6	1.56
Random Forest	4.11	0.54
Decision Tree	5.22	0.71
Gradient-Boosted Trees (GBTs)	**3.1**	**0.53**
Naive Bayes	3.54	0.94

In our investigation we have demonstrated in the following Table 5 that our approach has given a better performance in terms of precision, recall and F1-score compared to other intrusion detection works that used the SWaT dataset.

Table 5. Comparison of our approach with other works

Work	Precision	Recall	F1-score
[15]:LSTM	0.99	0.75	0.85
[12]:1D CNN	0.97	0.79	0.87
[10]:DNN	0.98	0.68	0.80
[10]:OCSVM	0.92	0.70	0.80
Our approach: Gradient-Boosted Trees (GBTs)	**0.99**	**0.99**	**0.99**

By comparing our work with other intrusion detection works that used the SWaT dataset, we notice that by using the Gradient-Boosted Trees (GBTs) classifier, our distributed system achieved the best results in terms of performance and response time and this is thanks to the advantages of Databricks and Apache Spark.

5   Conclusion and Future Work

In this paper, we aimed to propose a new distributed intrusion detection system in industrial control systems based on Cloud computing and Apache Spark big data tool. We used SWaT, the industrial dataset to evaluate our proposed system. Our system achieved good results in terms of Accuracy and response time, thanks to the performance of Databricks Community which solved several problems, including dataset storage and high availability of our cluster, despite its limited version. The proposed research presents several perspectives: a first axis aims to merge two or more datasets in streaming in order to produce more consistent information, increase the reliability of intrusion detection and improve the evaluation schemes. A second axis is to improve the data processing speed by opting for continuous streaming (data processing in milliseconds and not only in seconds). A third axis focuses on automating the decision making process to deal with intrusions through the development of an expert system to provide appropriate recommendations for each intrusion to stop the attack.

References

1. Industry 4.0 challenges and solutions for the digital transformation and use of exponential technologies. Finance, Audit Tax Consulting Corporate, Zurich, Swiss (2015)
2. Apache spark: Evaluation metrics. https://spark.apache.org/docs/latest/mllib-evaluation-metrics.html Accessed 25 Oct 2021
3. Databricks architecture overview. https://docs.databricks.com/getting-started/overview.html Accessed 25 Oct 2021
4. Executive office of the president of the united states: office of science and technology policy. Summary of the 2018 White House Summit on Artificial Intelligence for American Industry Product of the White House Office of Science And Technology Policy (2018)
5. Abid, A., Jemili, F.: Intrusion detection based on graph oriented big data analytics. Procedia Comput. Sci. **176**, 572–581 (2020). Proceedings of the 24th International Conference on Knowledge-Based and Intelligent Information Engineering Systems, KES 2020
6. Alhaidari, F.A., AL-Dahasi, E.M.: New approach to determine DDoS attack patterns on SCADA system using machine learning. In: 2019 International Conference on Computer and Information Sciences (ICCIS), pp. 1–6 (2019). https://doi.org/10.1109/ICCISci.2019.8716432
7. Channe, C.: Artificial intelligence in cyber security market - global trends, market share, industry size, growth, opportunities, and market in us forecast, 2019–2025. Industry Daily Observer (2019)
8. Choi, Seungoh, Yun, Jeong-Han., Kim, Sin-Kyu.: A comparison of ICS datasets for security research based on attack paths. In: Luiijf, Eric, Žutautaitė, Inga, Hämmerli, Bernhard M.. (eds.) CRITIS 2018. LNCS, vol. 11260, pp. 154–166. Springer, Cham (2019). https://doi.org/10.1007/978-3-030-05849-4_12
9. Goh, Jonathan, Adepu, Sridhar, Junejo, Khurum Nazir, Mathur, Aditya: A dataset to support research in the design of secure water treatment systems. In: Havarneanu, Grigore, Setola, Roberto, Nassopoulos, Hypatia, Wolthusen, Stephen (eds.) CRITIS 2016. LNCS, vol. 10242, pp. 88–99. Springer, Cham (2017). https://doi.org/10.1007/978-3-319-71368-7_8
10. Inoue, J., Yamagata, Y., Chen, Y., Poskitt, C., Sun, J.: Anomaly detection for a water treatment system using unsupervised machine learning. In: 17th IEEE International Conference on Data Mining Workshops ICDMW, 18–21 Nov 2017, New Orleans, pp. 1058–1065 (2017). https://doi.org/10.1109/ICDMW.2017.149
11. Khan, A.A.Z., Serpen, G.: Misuse intrusion detection using machine learning for gas pipeline SCADA networks. In: International Conference on Security and Management (SAM), Las Vegas, NV, USA (2019)
12. Kravchik, M., Shabtai, A.: Detecting cyber attacks in industrial control systems using convolutional neural networks. In: Proceedings of the 2018 Workshop on Cyber-Physical Systems Security and Privacy, CPS-SPC 2018, pp. 72–83. Association for Computing Machinery, New York, USA (2018). https://doi.org/10.1145/3264888.3264896, https://doi.org/10.1145/3264888.3264896
13. Lezzi, M., Lazoi, M., Corallo, A.: Cybersecurity for industry 4.0 in the current literature: a reference framework. Comput. Ind. **103**, 97–110 (2018). https://doi.org/10.1016/j.compind.2018.09.004. www.sciencedirect.com/science/article/pii/S0166361518303658

14. Morris, Thomas, Gao, Wei: Industrial control system traffic data sets for intrusion detection research. In: Butts, Jonathan, Shenoi, Sujeet (eds.) ICCIP 2014. IAICT, vol. 441, pp. 65–78. Springer, Heidelberg (2014). https://doi.org/10.1007/978-3-662-45355-1_5
15. Perales Gomez, L., Fernandez Maimo, L., Huertas Celdran, A., Garcia Clemente, F.J.: MADICS: a methodology for anomaly detection in industrial control systems. Symmetry **12**(10), 1583 (2020). https://doi.org/10.3390/sym12101583. https://www.mdpi.com/2073-8994/12/10/1583

MAFC: Multimedia Application Flow Controller for Big Data Systems

Takoua Abdellatif[1,2](✉), Houcem Eddine Testouri[2](✉),
and Aymen Yahyaoui[1,3](✉)

[1] SERCOM Lab, University of Carthage, 2078 La Marsa, Tunisia
{Takoua.Abdellatif,Aymen.Yahyaoui}@ept.rnu.tn
[2] ENISO/ University of Sousse, 4000 Sousse, Tunisia
houcem.testouri@ept.u-carthage.tn
[3] Military Academy of Fondouk Jedid, 8012 Nabeul, Tunisia

Abstract. A lot of research has been conducted on different areas of Big Data technology in the multimedia domain, such as multimedia Big Data capture, storage, indexing and retrieval. Nevertheless, ensuring real-time processing for multimedia Big Data is still a big challenge. Indeed, when the streaming speed is higher than the processing time, data can be lost or the processing no longer respects real-time constraints even though efficient streaming technology is used. In this context, we propose MAFC, a Multimedia Application Flow Controller that filters incoming multimedia data so that only significant data is sent for processing. Data extraction is executed following application-based policies. MAFC is a building block that can be embedded in the management layer of Big Data systems. The main contribution of our work is a Big Data architecture that couples multimedia data filtering with the Big Data streaming technology in order to reduce the stress on the processing layer. As a use-case, the integration of MAFC in a Big Data-based surveillance system for video frame extraction shows a significant performance improvement compared to the initial system.

Keywords: Real-time analysis · Massive multimedia streams · Control policy · Information flow control · Big Data systems

1 Introduction

Big Data and the Internet of Things (IoT) are evolving rapidly, affecting many aspects of technology and business and increasing the benefits to companies and individuals. The explosion of data generated by the IoT has a significant impact on the Big Data landscape [12]. Multimedia data, such as text, audio, images and videos are rapidly increasing and becoming the main channels for controlling, processing, exchanging and storing information in the modern era [14]. The fact that 2.5 quintillion bytes (2.5 e+9 GB) of data is generated every day is a huge challenge for this undertaking. Approximately 90% of the world's data has

© The Author(s), under exclusive license to Springer Nature Switzerland AG 2022
C. Bădică et al. (Eds.): ICCCI 2022, CCIS 1653, pp. 485–497, 2022.
https://doi.org/10.1007/978-3-031-16210-7_40

been created in the last two years [2]. Video streaming and downloading are expected to account for 82% of global Internet traffic by 2022 [3], according to estimates. To put this in perspective, in 2018, 56 exabytes (equivalent to one billion gigabytes) of Internet video were used each month [3].

We can therefore predict the amount of data that will be generated in the coming years. The enormous development of multimedia data accessible to users poses a whole new set of problems in terms of data control and processing.

Many crucial data is transferred in the IoT context. For example, due to the growing relevance of public security in many locations, the demand for intelligent visual surveillance has increased. It is necessary to build computer vision-based controlling and processing tools for real-time detection of intrusions, suspicious movements and criminal suspect vehicles among other things. The detection and subsequent tracking of moving objects is an important task for computer vision based surveillance systems. The identification of an object in a video that varies its position according to the field of view of a scene is defined as the process of recognizing moving objects. The detection process can be characterised as the detection of the trajectory of an object in a video. These tasks have to be performed in real-time. For this reason, recent Big Data technologies are currently deployed in modern surveillance systems.

Figure 1 presents a typical Big Data system where big volumes of data can be derived from different sources and are treated either in real-time (at the streaming layer) or in batch mode. The service layer creates added values like visualization or emergency notifications in the case of surveillance use-case. The security and governance layer is a cross-layer used for data security and management throughout the process, from data sources to services. While the underlying technologies provide real-time multimedia processing, scalability remains a nightmare due to the increasing volume and velocity of this data. Indeed, in many cases, these current Big Data systems cannot keep pace with the addition of multimedia sources such as cameras with exponentially higher bandwidth and processing rates deployed in large geographical areas like smart cities. More memory, computing power and energy consumption are required with higher bandwidth [15]. Indeed, data bandwidth can exceed the processing time, which can lead to data loss or delay in real-time processing. In addition, intensive data processing can impact on power consumption and even damage the system hardware. For mission-critical applications like surveillance systems, information loss or long notification delays after a security breach are not acceptable.

A valuable solution to this issue is data filtering which consists in controlling and verifying the data flow based on specifications and rules depending on the application and its related well-defined policies. The main idea is to reduce data complexity and volume by removing redundant and irrelevant information. For video streaming data, filtering is classically done by a key feature selection which consists in an extraction of a keys set of frames from data flow with a minimum loss of information [9]. In our work, the key frame selection is application-based and depends on defined policies.

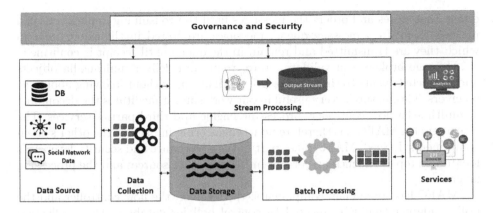

Fig. 1. Traditional Big Data system

More precisely, we approach the scalability issue by a real-time control of massive multimedia data to avoid stressing the processing engines in Big Data systems. The idea is to intercept data coming from data sources and pre-process it to filter interesting events making the stream processing engine keep pace with the multimedia throughput which prevents latency and data loss. We propose MAFC, a Multimedia Application Flow Controller for Big Data systems. MAFC filters the incoming multimedia stream with intelligent dropping system based on application-based policies. The main contribution of our work is a Big Data architecture that couples multimedia data filtering with the Big Data streaming technology in order to reduce the stress on the processing layer. As a use-case, the integration of MAFC in a Big Data-based surveillance system for video frame extraction shows the significant performance improvement compared to the initial system. Furthermore, MAFC can be plugged at the governance layer without interfering with existent Big Data applications. Consequently, the re-engineering effort is minimal to use MAFC in current Big Data applications.

The remainder of this paper is structured as follows. Section 2 describes the system architecture of the proposed solution. Section 3 presents the application to surveillance systems. Section 4 presents the experimental evaluation. Section 5 is devoted for related works, and Sect. 6 concludes the paper.

2   System Architecture and Operations

In the remaining part of the paper, we focus on video data from cameras, which represents the most challenging case when considering real-time processing performance. Figure 2 depicts the integration of MAFC in a classical Big Data architecture. The message broker serves as a distributed communication layer that allows application spanning multiple platforms to communicate internally. In order to provide reliable multimedia data storage and guaranteed delivery, message brokers often rely on a substructure or component called a message queue that stores and orders the messages until the consuming applications can process them. In a message queue, messages are stored in the exact order in which they are transmitted and remain in the queue until receipt is confirmed.

Message brokers can validate, store, route and deliver multimedia objects and extracted events to the appropriate destinations without knowing about the receivers. This feature is very useful in our work since it facilitates the decoupling of multimedia flow controller, processing engine and third parties services. The integration of MAFC has therefore no re-engineering impact on the other system components. Indeed, MAFC takes part of the governance and security layer. It is located on top of the message broker in-between data sources and the processing layers.

MAFC has three main components: the receiver, the flow controller and the policy adapter that is connected to control policies database. Data collection is in charge of ingesting video data from either unbounded video streaming data or from stored multimedia sequences. Once the multimedia data has been acquired, MAFC receiver component intercepts data and decomposes it into a sequence of individual multimedia objects that will be fed one by one to the flow controller. The flow controller respects a set of policies defined by the system administrator through the policy adapter that notifies the flow controller each time the policy changes. The flow controller selects the frames to be published through the message broker on a general topic of the message broker, called "Frame Processing". Then, the extracted events are published to the concerned topics to be consumed by third-party services. We describe, hereafter, the main MAFC components.

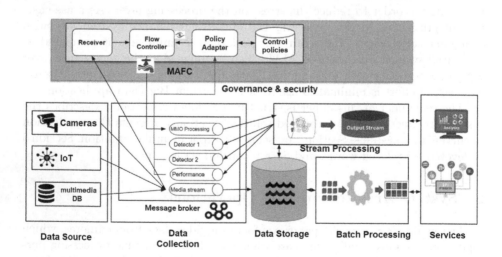

Fig. 2. System architecture

2.1   Receiver

The main role of the receiver is to break down an incoming multimedia stream into discrete elements called multimedia objects that can be examined one by one. The type of "individual multimedia object" depends on the application concerned. In a surveillance system, the object is a single image extracted from a camera video sequence. In this case, the receiver acts as a video-to-frame converter.

2.2   Flow Controller

The flow controller is the process of managing the rate of incoming multimedia objects from the receiver before sending them to the processing engine through the message broker. It provides a mechanism for the receiver to control the transmission rate based on the information from the policy adapter to ensure system scalability and real-time processing with low latency, so that the processing engine is not overwhelmed by the incoming multimedia data. It is notified about any change in control policies by the policy adapter. Then, it applies the new policy adapter's incoming policies on the multimedia objects.

2.3   Policy Adapter

The policy adapter acts as an intermediary between the control policies database and the flow controller. It provides a user-interface for the administrator to prioritize policies based on needs and application context, also it provides a full access to the source code to add or update a specific policy. In addition, it calculates and updates automatically policies based on extracted events from the processing engine and previous policies. Then, it notifies the flow controller for this update and saves it in the control policies database.

2.4   Control Policies Database

The control policy database contains all the control policy data that models the multimedia flow controller, and that will be modified or accessed by the policy adapter. This provides a significant persistence advantage. Initially, it contains preconfigured control policies based on the application context.

In MAFC, there are four kinds of possible control policies:

1. **Time-based flow control:** the incoming stream is adapted following the hour range in the day. For example, in a surveillance system, we may increase the multimedia stream in the daytime when there is a large movement of people and decrease it at night to make it possible to add cameras inside to provide security in prohibited areas.
2. **Priority-based flow control:** in this context, the administrator chooses which cameras have priority over others. According to this policy, the controller increases the throughput of the prioritized cameras over the others.

3. **Event-based flow control:** in this case, the controller changes the through-put according to a specific event triggered by the processing engine, such as the detection of an intrusion to increase the throughput of cameras in the intruder's area, or by the system administrator, such as the reception of a VIP in a surveyed region.
4. **Performance-based flow control:** in order to keep the system running smoothly and remain scalable with low checkpoint, MAFC controls the incoming data flow according to the system performance. Thus, when a new media source is added, the system automatically decreases the data flow to allow the new stream to be processed without data loss.

In addition to these principle policies, the user can add other custom policies according to his needs and prioritize those policies to choose which order to follow to control the multimedia stream.

In MAFC control policies are either statically configured in flow policies database or can be dynamically updated following incoming events. For example, in the performance-based flow control, when the frame bandwidth exceeds a threshold, the system may automatically enable the processing of only the most important cameras following a priority classification. To communicate the information between the receiver, the policy adapter and the flow controller, we use the message broker for event notification about the bandwidth rate and about the policy update.

3   Application to Surveillance Systems

MAFC is implemented to enhance the performance of a surveillance system deployed for a smart city. The considered system supervises a protected area and aims at detecting intruders in real-time. To cover the whole area, 20 cameras are deployed and are sending continuously the videos. The deployed server-side system is a classical Big Data system using the streaming technologies for real-time image processing as presented in Fig. 2. Deep learning is used for image processing to detect the intruders. Despite the large adopted resources, the server cannot keep pace with the processing throughput. This induces data loss and a high latency to detect the intruders. Indeed, the system can handle only 20 fps (frames per second) whereas the required processing is 30 fps at minimum. The first solution was to adopt the horizontal scalability by deploying further machines to parallelize the processing. The one we adopted in our work is to deploy MAFC on the existent system while keeping the already adopted infrastructure and reducing, consequently, the scalability cost.

In the following, we present the adopted flow control policies and the implementation details.

3.1   MAFC Operations and Flow Control Policies in a Surveillance System

We have noticed that, for some cameras, it is not necessary to send the whole camera frames for an intruder detection. Only 1 frame over 10 is sufficient. Consequently, we configured MAFC to adopt the "performance-based control policy" that allows a reduction of the frame rate. The second policy to be adopted consists in classifying the cameras per priority. The cameras deployed on the critical parts of the supervised areas have their frames reduced only of 50% in order to accelerate the detection of a potential intruder. When a specific camera detects an intruder, the system automatically increases the processing throughput of this camera and its neighbors by 10 to increase the intruder detection accuracy and to reduce the latency time. This throughput adaptation follows the "event-based flow control policy". Therefore, we combined three kinds of policies to reduce the system frame throughput at processing layer. The flow controller ensures that overall throughput does not exceed the threshold of 20 fps supported by the system. MAFC is efficient to ensure the intrusion detection in real-time for large IoT systems like smart cities while avoiding extra-expenses for the infrastructure expansion to support the system scalability.

3.2 Implementation

Regarding the Big Data system, recent technologies are deployed. For the message broker, Apache Kafka [1] is used. It is a platform for real-time environment using distributed messaging system and it can handle a large volume of data. Furthermore, Kafka is partitioned, replicated, distributed and fault tolerant. In order to process all the real-time data coming through Kafka, we use Apache Flink which is an open-source, distributed stream processing framework with a high-throughput, low-latency engine widely adopted in the industry. We adopted Apache Flink for a number of reasons. First, it is robust enough to continuously support a large number of frames with the built-in state management and check-pointing features for failure recovery. Second, it is easy to scale and can handle back-pressure efficiently when faced with a massive input Kafka flow. Third, it has a large and active open source community as well as a rich ecosystem of components and toolings. We associate Kafka with Flink for its persistent channel that prevents immediate back pressure processing and avoids data loss. On top of Flink, we use tensorflow with SSD-mobilnet as an object detection model for its high accuracy with low latency.

The MAFC module was implemented using Python for its compatibility with major platforms and systems [4]. Also, it provides a large and robust set of libraries compared to other programming languages. MAFC is integrated to the system as a consumer and a publisher of Kafka broker. It intercepts all the video frames arriving at Kafka and after filtering and pre-processing, these frames are injected again to Kafka for the "MMO processing". All MAFC components communicate through Kafka, namely the receiver, the flow controller and the policy adapter.

4   Experimental Evaluation

In this section, we evaluate MAFC performance considering the surveillance system we introduced in the previous section. Therefore, we performed a series of

Table 1. Experimental environment.

		CPU	RAM (GB)
Local environment	VM1	2	8
	VM2	4	8
Cloud environment	VM3	4	16
	VM4	4	32

experiments on different machines by changing the CPU and RAM performance. These tests were performed on 4 Virtual Machines (VM1, VM2, VM3 and VM4) in two different environments (local and cloud) as described in Table 1. For tests on the local environment, we run two VMs (VM1 and VM2) on a PC with an i5-8300h CPU @2.3 GHz, equipped with 16 GB of RAM. For tests on the cloud environment, we used two VMs (VM3 and VM4) on the Microsoft Azure cloud. The first set of experiments aims at evaluating the time spent for each processing step in the data life-cycle, starting from acquiring the video to sending the extracted objects to third parties. The goal is to evaluate the flow control time compared to the overall data processing. We demonstrate clearly that this time is negligible. The second evaluation aims at assessing the impact of the adopted infrastructure and resources on MAFC processing time. Clearly, the more we have resources in terms of CPU and memory, the more the processing time is improved. The third test shows MAFC scalability with an increasing number of cameras. We detail hereafter each experiment set-up and result.

4.1   Processing Time Evaluation

Figure 3 plots the four evaluation measures for the different VM. For the first one, it took half a second to process an image, almost 0.45 s on detection and classification. The second VM was faster, taking quarter of a second to process a frame. This demonstrates that the processing time was halved if we doubled the RAM or processor performance.

On the other hand, according to Fig. 4, the bottleneck of the system is the image processing part that comprises the object detection and classification phases. Indeed, about 90% of the latency time is spent on object detection processing, while the image splitting and image sending tasks are relatively fast. In particular, the flow control processing part takes a relatively negligible time compared to the other processing tasks. This result does not depend on the available resources (CPU and RAM) of the used infrastructure.

4.2   Infrastructure Resources' Impact

In this experience, we consider an end-to-end latency which refers to the time taken from the capture of the video stream by the camera to the reception of the extracted event on the notification web page. Figure 5 illustrates that

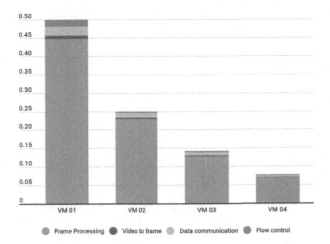

Fig. 3. Processing time per frame

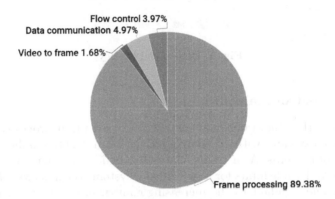

Fig. 4. Percentage of processing time

on VM1, the system can process 2 fps in real-time without latency, but the latency increases exponentially by increasing the video rate. For the second virtual machine, the system can process 4 fps in real-time without latency and then, the latency increases as the video rate increases. The same evolution time is noticed for the other virtual machines.

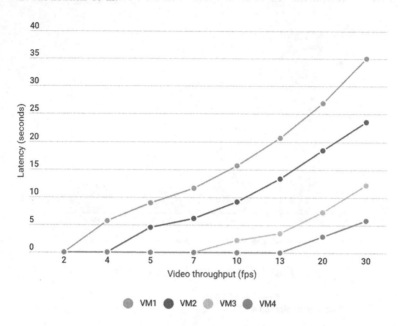

Fig. 5. End-to-end latency

4.3   Flow Control Scalability

Figure 6 shows that the traditional surveillance system that processes all incoming multimedia streams without control has not been able to handle the increasing number of cameras. As a result, the end-to-end latency has increased exponentially to intolerable limits for a surveillance system. Whereas with MAFC, the system was able to adapt to the increasing number of cameras and to preserve acceptable performance.

5   Related Works

Many research works have studied multimedia Big Data systems using several methods such as incoming stream control and pre-processing method optimization. In this section, recent works in this field are presented.

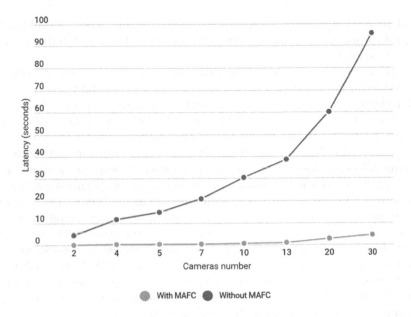

Fig. 6. Flow controller impact

In literature, there are several techniques to extract key frames. Authors in [10,13] presents the key frame selection techniques: sequential comparison of frames, global comparison of frames, minimum correlation between frames, minimum reconstruction error in frames, temporal variance between frames, maximum coverage of video frames, reference key frame, curve simplification, key frame extraction using clustering, object and event-based key frame extraction and paper panoramic key frames. In [9] authors compare and analyses those techniques in terms of characteristics, advantages, and shortcomings. MAFC can embed any of these techniques even though we have chosen a static key frame selection in our implemented surveillance system. The novelty in our work is that we couple these techniques with the powerful streaming features of Big Data technology to provide more scalability than previous systems.

In a previous work, a tool called AMSEP [6] is proposed for scalable multimedia processing. Cameras are not activated all the time in order to avoid unnecessary broadcasting of video data. Indeed, scalar sensors activate the cameras only when a motion is detected. This optimization can be used in combination with MAFC for further reduction of frame throughput.

In RAM^{3}S [7], authors describe a software framework for the real-time analysis of massive multimedia streams. Like in MAFC receiver, the framework embeds a Receiver component that breaks down a single incoming media stream into discrete elements that can be examined one by one. Another component called Analyzer is used for analyzing the individual multimedia elements. Each media object is compared to the underlying event classes to determine whether or not an alarm should be triggered. Like in Big Data systems, the usage of several processing engines allows for scalability. In our work, we additionally take profit from backpressure features avoiding data loss and filtering to reduce frames' throughput.

In [11], authors present an adaptation strategy for SDN-based networks. The proposed technique estimates the appropriate level of scalability based on information about the user's device and network capabilities. The identified scalability level is then used to transmit data. Rate adaptation with the SDN controller improves video quality and facilitates decision making. Scalable video levels are determined by the dynamic condition of the network. Therefore, multirate video streaming offers an alternative approach to improve resource utilization in multicast communication using available routers and switches. At this stage, the video is encoded at multiple bitrates and stored on the media server. The video data is broadcast by the media server, and users join a session based on their ability to process it. Compared to unicast transmission, the bandwidth consumption in multi-bitrate multicast transmission is lower. This research work provides a frame rate adapting mechanism at network level while MAFC is an adaptation at application level. Their proposed solution requires special devices and impacts communication protocols whereas, MAFC can be plugged to any existing Big Data applications with minimal engineering effort.

In addition to research works, a set of industrial solutions like Netflix [8] has also integrated Kafka with Flink with backpressure feature to handle the huge Netflix text-based content during production. Similarly, Uber [5] combines Apache Flink and Kafka to power streaming applications to calculate updated pricing, improve driver dispatch and combat fraud on its platform.

In comparison to Netflix and Uber, to our knowledge, we apply the backpressure feature to multimedia data processing rather than text. Additionally, we propose application-based policy integration for data streaming flow control.

6   Conclusion

This paper presents MAFC, a solution to the overcome the challenging multimedia streaming in Big Data systems. The idea consists in filtering and controlling the incoming video flow following application-based policies. The implementation and evaluation of MAFC in a surveillance system use case shows its efficiency compared to a system processing all data flow while keeping the same infrastructure resources. Although, the number of used machines and simulated cameras is relatively small due to limited resources, the conducted experiments provides a proof of concept for the proposed approach, and MAFC may be used to handle a larger number of machines and cameras for a high scalable system. Besides the integration of MAFC can be performed smoothly without re-engineering overhead. Indeed, the filtering module is added at the message broker level in the Big Data ingestion layer and intercepts incoming video frames before sending them to their destinations.

As a future work, for further optimization in IoT systems, we plan to deploy and test MAFC from the server side to the edge in order to optimize the network bandwidth and to reduce the delay due to data communication. Indeed, with edge-based systems, the data is processed locally or in nearby edge data centers and only filtered data flows through the network to reach servers. Furthermore, edge computing spreads processing, storage and applications across a variety of devices and data centers, which provides fault tolerance and makes it impossible for a single outage to bring the entire network down.

Furthermore, we are interested in extending MAFC with security and data protection policies. Indeed, with the same architecture, we can filter information following privacy policies avoiding the disclosure of personal data to non authorized parties.

References

1. Apache Kafka. https://kafka.apache.org/. Accessed 21 June 2021
2. Big Data, for better or worse: 90% of world's data generated over last two years
3. Cisco Annual Internet Report - Cisco Annual Internet Report (2018–2023) White Paper. https://www.cisco.com/c/en/us/solutions/collateral/executive-perspectives/annual-internet-report/white-paper-c11-741490.html
4. Python.org. https://www.python.org/doc/. Accessed 21 June 2021
5. Keystone real-time stream processing platform, 10 September 2018
6. Abdallah, H.B., Abdellatif, T., Chekir, F.: AMSEP: automated multi-level security management for multimedia event processing. Procedia Comput. Sci. **134**, 452–457 (2018). The 15th International Conference on Mobile Systems and Pervasive Computing (MobiSPC 2018)/The 13th International Conference on Future Networks and Communications (FNC-2018)/Affiliated Workshops
7. Bartolini, I., Patella, M.: A general framework for real-time analysis of massive multimedia streams. Multimedia Syst. **24**(4), 391–406 (2017). https://doi.org/10.1007/s00530-017-0566-5
8. Fu, Y., Soman, C.: Real-time data infrastructure at Uber (2021)
9. Gawande, U., Hajari, K., Golhar, Y.: Deep learning approach to key frame detection in human action videos. Recent Trends Comput. Intell. **1**, 1–17 (2020)
10. Hannane, R., Elboushaki, A., Afdel, K., Naghabhushan, P., Javed, M.: An efficient method for video shot boundary detection and keyframe extraction using sift-point distribution histogram. Int. J. Multimedia Inf. Retriev. **5**(2), 89–104 (2016)
11. Ramakrishna, M., Karunakar, A.K.: Rate adaptive multicast video streaming over software defined network. J. Theor. Appl. Inf. Technol. **96**, 6163–6171 (2018)
12. Sestino, A., Prete, M.I., Piper, L., Guido, G.: Internet of things and big data as enablers for business digitalization strategies. Technovation **98**, 102173 (2020)
13. Sujatha, C., Mudenagudi, U.: A study on keyframe extraction methods for video summary. In: 2011 International Conference on Computational Intelligence and Communication Networks, pp. 73–77. IEEE (2011)
14. Wang, Z., Mao, S., Yang, L., Tang, P.: A survey of multimedia big data. China Commun. **15**(1), 155–176 (2018)
15. Zikria, Y., Afzal, M., Kim, S.W.: Internet of multimedia things (IOMT): opportunities, challenges and solutions. Sensors **20**, 1–8 (2020)

Experience Enhanced Intelligence to IoT and Sensors

On-wrist Based Datasets Exploration for an IoT Wearable Fall Detection

Farah Othmen[1,2](✉)(iD), Mouna Baklouti[2](iD), and André Eugenio Lazzaretti[3](iD)

[1] Tunisia Polytechnic School, University of Carthage, Marsa, Tunisia
farah.othmen@ept.rnu.tn
[2] CES Lab, National School of Engineers of Sfax, University of Sfax, Sfax, Tunisia
[3] Federal University of Technology – Paraná (UTFPR), Curitiba, Brazil

Abstract. Fall presents a vulnerable health burden, especially in the elderly, due to its after-affecting longnsequences. Wrist-based fall detection presents an accessory-like comfortable solution yet very unsteady as to IMU sensors. Hence, this paper focuses on inspecting the impact of the use of IMU sensors and their sampling rates in the efficacy of a wrist worn fall detector, a subject still underexplored in the recent literature. We assessed benchmark datasets using supervised dictionary learning. We also introduced an IoT-based framework for monitoring using a mobile application. Various exploration experiments showed that an optimal accuracy of 99.5% is attained when using only an accelerometer with 20 Hz sampling rate using SRC algorithm. Tests in real situations of the prototype were also carried out, demonstrating adequate performance in facing several ADL and fall-alike activities, with an autonomy of 14 running hours.

Keywords: Fall detection · Dataset · Wrist worn · SDL algorithm · IoT · Sampling rate · IMU sensors

1 Introduction

According to a study by the UN Department of Economic and Social Affairs [1], the number of elderly people aged 60 years or more is expected to reach 21% of the world's population by 2050. With an average growth of 2.4% per year, their number should exceed that of the young generations. One of the most serious problems facing older people is the risk of falling. In fact, about 30% of people aged 65 and over fall each year. Most of this elderly population are likely to be susceptible to accidental falls caused mostly by illness dependency and environmental factors [2]. Thus, remote monitoring of this age range is vital nowadays, especially since the long period after a fall can sometimes lead to disastrous consequences. These are essentially traumatic, with a significant

This research and innovation work was supported in a part by MOBIDOC grants from the EU and National Agency for the Promotion of Scientific Research under the AMORI project and in collaboration with Telnet Innovation Labs.

mortality rate. The leading cause is the delay in intervention. According to the WHO [2], every year, 646,000 people die from falls. In fact, after a fall, an older person is, in most cases, unable to report an alert. Generally, it is because the latter does not have the reflex to reach his manual alert device or is unconscious in most cases. Therefore, it is absolutely necessary that a fall is reported immediately and autonomously to receive emergency assistance.

The detection of falls can be achieved through several approaches and technologies [3]. Some approaches are context-based, either using external cameras or ambient sensors. In contrast, other approaches consist of mobile sensor analysis through body worn Inertial Measurement Unit (IMU) sensors, e.g., accelerometers, gyroscopes, and magnetometers [4]. Due to its leading advantages, wearable-based sensors devices are considered one of the main types to present a promising direction for fall detection and prediction. Indeed, the latter presents an optimal cost-effective system assuring mobility, wearability, availability, and guaranteeing privacy. Moreover, it increasingly becomes more comfortable with the emergence of technological devices and the familiarity of their use given by their ubiquity, such as smart bands and smartphones.

Wrist-based offers an optimal solution considering user/patient comfort and easy use. Still, it is very challenging to meet the steadiness and robustness requirements of the system. Two main wearable fall classification and prediction methods have been proposed in the related literature [3,4], namely, threshold-based or knowledge-based and machine learning-based. Knowledge-based methods are considered the easiest. A fall is detected through the analysis of the fall phases by calculating orientation and thresholds through sensor readings of specific features. On the other hand, machine learning-based methods are more likely to distinguish falls from ADL (Activities of Daily Living) in an autonomous way based on observation or training.

We assume that designing an optimal feature extraction and classifier chemistry is the most strenuous procedure in determining an accurate fall detection system. In addition, dataset configuration may display an additive ambiguity. In this context, sensors' sampling rate does heavily influence wearable system reliability depending on the implemented classification model in one side, and the device energy consumption and computational complexity in other side. Several previous works have discussed this aspect using machine learning [19] and deep learning [20] algorithms to extract system behaviours when facing re-sampling techniques.

We have proved in previous works [5,6] the efficiency and robustness of our proposed novel Supervised Dictionary Learning (SDL) on a wrist-based fall detection system. Subsequently, we propose in this paper a new automatic BLE-based fall detection system using only an accelerometer sensor embedded in a wristband prototype. An Android smartphone collects kinematic information about the monitored person, detects falls, and real-time GPS location. This study aims to:

– Explore wrist-based datasets in regards of data configuration, mainly the impact of the used sensors and the sampling rate;

– Build a totally autonomous and robust IoT system based on wrist fall detection using Supervised Dictionary Learning.

The remainder of this paper is organized as follows. Section 2 describes the IoT-based framework for the on-wrist fall detection system and details the different processing steps. This Section also presents datasets exploration results to choose the most appropriate one. Section 3 highlights the experimental test and evaluation considering various sensors and datasets. Finally, Sect. 4 concludes this paper with a brief outlook on future works.

2 Methodology: IoT-Based Framework for Wrist-Based Fall Detection System Using SDL

In this section, we will introduce our proposed IoT framework for on-wrist fall detection system. A comprehensive description of the main components of the system will be also given.

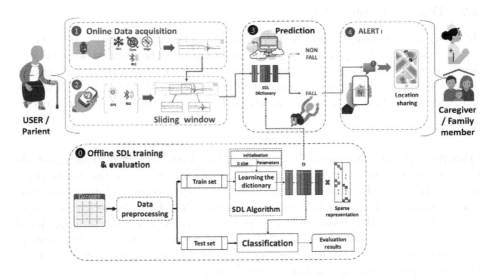

Fig. 1. Proposed IoT-based fall detection.

2.1 Overview of the Proposed Framework

Figure 1 illustrates an overview of the proposed IoT-based pipeline for an on-wrist fall detection system. Subsequently, the system presents two main phases: (i) offline phase and (ii) online phase.

The offline phase, denoted in the Fig. 1 by the number zero, presents a fundamental phase in building and defining an efficient fall detector. Thus, three datasets will be evaluated: UMAfall [7], UPFALL [8], and Quadros et al.'s dataset [9]. Considering the impact of adding sensors and the variety of their sampling rates, a preprocessing component will be consequently introduced for the filtering, down/upsampling, and representing raw data. The obtained preprocessed data will be subdivided into training and testing sets. The train set is to be dressed into the learning process of the SDL algorithm. The learned Dictionary D will then be used for the test set's offline evaluation.

As for the online phase, it is composed of four partitions denoted in the Fig. 1 from number 1 to number 4. First, a device attached to the wrist will be used to acquire online raw data through embedded sensors (accelerometer, gyroscope, and magnetometer). Later on, the collected data will be then sent via Bluetooth protocol to an android-based mobile application. The GPS must be activated in the latter for the location's sake. Therefore, a sliding window technique is implemented to set up the real-time windowing complexity facing lost information and misdetection issues. An online detection process is indeed triggered to differentiate falls from ADLs. If a fall is detected, an alert notification will be sent to the concerned family member or caregiver with a sharing of the user/patient location.

2.2 Dataset Exploration

To select an adequate dataset, we have considered two main criteria: (i) A Wrist-based dataset and (ii) A dataset that must include the studied sensors, i.e., accelerometer, gyroscope, and magnetometer. We have chosen three dataset categories following this selection, namely Quadros et al., UMAfall, and UPfall. A detailed description of the three mentioned datasets will be conducted in this section.

Quadros et al. Dataset. The dataset has been collected throughout de Quadros et al. study [9]. The signal acquisition was made by the use of three primary triaxial IMU sensors, i.e., accelerometer, gyroscope, and magnetometer, which are embedded in the GY-80 IMU model device. An Arduino Uno was integrated with the IMU device into a wrist-worn band at the non-dominant hand to acquire and register data signals from the latter sensors. The raw sensors data were obtained at 100 Hz sampling rate and 4 g, 500°/s, and 0.88 Gs for the accelerometer, gyroscope, and magnetometer.

In order to make the dataset more generalized and accurate, twenty-two volunteers of different ages, heights, and weights were engaged in this experimental protocol. Each one performs two main event categories: fall incidents and Activities of Daily Living (ADL). The recorded fall incident covers forward to fall, backward fall, right-side fall, left-side fall, fall after rotating the waist clockwise, and fall after rotating the waist counterclockwise. The ADLs performed activities enclosing walking, clapping hands, moving an object, tying shoes, and sitting on a chair. The average duration of the recorded activities is 9.2 s, assuming that each one starts with a resting arm (resting state) followed by a few steps before the activity's performance.

UMAFall. UMAFall [7] is a wearable multi-position fall detection dataset in which several predefined ADLs and falls have been systematically emulated. They were acquired through the traces of tree wearable sensing points located on five different body spots (chest, ankle, right trouser pocket, waist, and wrist). The traces include the acceleration, gyroscope, and magnetometer data captured simultaneously. All the experiments were simulated by 17 subjects of different sex and features. Each participant performed eight different ADLs: body bending, climbing stairs up, climbing stairs down, hopping, lying down on a bed, sitting on a chair, and walking at a normal pace. Also, three typologies of fall were considered: backward, forwards, and lateral fall. The overall data include 322 ADLs and 209 falls obtained from the SensorTag nodes at 20 Hz sampling rate.

UPFALL. UP-Fall Detection Dataset [8] is an open-source dataset available on google covering raw and extracted feature sets collected from 17 healthy young volunteers who performed five fall examples: forward using hands, forward using knees, backward, sideward, and falling sitting in a chair; and six ADLs simulations: walking, standing, sitting, picking up an object, jumping, and laying. The dataset comprises more than 850 GB of information from different wearable sensors placed in multiple body points, ambient infrared sensors, and vision devices. Taking into account only wearables, the experiment was based on five body spots: neck, wrist, waist, pocket, and ankle, using IMU sensors (Accelerometer and gyroscope) at 20 Hz data rate and luminosity sensor.

2.3   Data Preprocessing

In general, data preprocessing presents a key element in impacting the performance of machine learning classifiers. Considering wearable fall detection systems, various techniques for data preprocessing, including feature extraction, feature selection, and data mapping, have been introduced in the existing literature to minimize the system's error rate [4]. Subsequently, finding significant attributes that better illustrate the raw data has always been challenging depending on numerous factors, i.e., the device's on-body position, the used sensors and their corresponding configuration, and signal preparation. In this sense, wrist-attached IMU sensors are most vulnerable to a more challenging preprocessing task regarding their unsteady and moving placement. The aim here is to shortlist the right features that better categorize the raw dataset and discriminate ADL events from a fall event, especially facing similar overlapped data events.

This work presents extended experimentation on our former works [5, 6]. Here we will focus on the impact of the sampling rate and the use of sensors in defining an accurate wrist fall detection system using the SDL techniques. Using SDL capacity to generate higher discriminative features mapped by a sparse representation, we consider processing a time window of raw acquired data from sensors. The accelerometer data were preprocessed with a low pass filter with a window size of 40 to clear any external influence that may affect it. Additionally, subtraction of a fixed value equal to 1g to eliminate the gravity-related information is performed.

Resampling Technique. The previously presented datasets illustrate different sampling rate configurations. Appropriately, we have implemented the down and upsampling techniques to examine the SDL robustness regarding the usage of low and high sampling rates. The resampling technique is the sampling rate converting process in which the sampling of digital signal changes from one rate to another. It can be sub-categorized into downsampling and upsampling. In fact, for a desired N number of samples, the downsampler selects every N^{th} sample and discards the rest. In comparison, the upsampling is described by a stretching operation [10] aiming to fill the gap in-between the existing ones using a symmetric FIR filter. The resampling techniques are implemented using the *interp()* and *downsample()* Matlab functions for upsampling and downsampling, respectively.

Window Segmentation. In the offline mode, each studied dataset presents a different time window for event simulation. Nevertheless, the classification process of the SDL algorithm claims a specific fixed window size of raw data as input. Thus, we assume that a fall is defined by a sudden burst of acceleration amplitude denoted by impact [4], likewise similar to ADL events as clapping. In order to extract the most relevant window segment in each of the dataset samples, we acknowledge the vertical component (VA) of the total acceleration (TA) described by the following Eq. (1):

$$TA = \sqrt{x(t)^2 + y(t)^2 + z(t)^2}, \tag{1}$$

where $x(t)$, $y(t)$, and $z(t)$ represents respectively the registered x, y and z axis of the accelerometer, respectively.

We implemented a threshold algorithm that extracts a fixed window of the period where VA has attained the highest amplitude. Thus, we maintain the same period of time in extracting the fixed segment of the gyroscope and magnetometer data samples.

Sliding Window. When working in an online mode, the sliding window technique plays an elementary process in achieving an accurate event detection when dealing with time complexity. Accordingly, two windowing categories are presented: (i) The fixed-length non-overlapping sliding window (FNSW) and (ii) The fixed-length overlapping sliding window (FOSW). Based on [11], the FOSW model gives the most suitable real-time solution to cover precise segments following time constraints. Thus, the collected data is windowed into equal frames in a predefined time overlap rate.

2.4 Dictionary Learning-Based Classification for Wristband Fall Detection

The Dictionary Learning technique is commonly illustrated as a sub-branch of the machine learning paradigm by highlighting the learning and testing phases.

It has proven its efficiency in several literature fields as a representation-based method, mainly in computer vision such as information retrieval, image restoration and denoising, and classification [12].

More specifically, given a learning set $\mathbf{X} = [\mathbf{x}_1,\dots,\mathbf{x}_m]$ of m samples, the objective is to generate a dictionary $\mathbf{D}$ which depicts a sparse representation denoted $\mathbf{A} = [\mathbf{a}_1,\dots,\mathbf{a}_m]$ in a higher dimensional map for each input sample. This problem is solved via an optimization Eq. 2:

$$\min_{\mathbf{D},\mathbf{A}} \sum_{i=1}^{m} (\frac{1}{2}||\mathbf{x}_i - \mathbf{D}\mathbf{a}_i||_2^2 + \lambda_1||\mathbf{a}_i||_1), \tag{2}$$

where, λ_1 defines the regularization parameter that affects the number of nonzero coefficients.

To be adapted to the supervised task, several SDL categorizations have been recently presented in the literature [12,13]. They include shared, class-specific, commonality and particularity, auxiliary, and domain adaptive dictionary learning. The labeled information is jointly learned either in the dictionary atoms, the coefficients of the sparse representation, or both. Thus, the objective is to optimise $\mathbf{D}$ through a sparse representation $\mathbf{X}$ while respecting extra constraints $f_A(.)$ and $f_D(.)$ through an optimization problem generally defined by the following Eq. 3:

$$\min_{\mathbf{D},\mathbf{A}} \{ \sum_{i=1}^{N} (\frac{1}{2}||\mathbf{x}_i - \mathbf{D}\mathbf{a}_i||_2^2 + \lambda_1||\mathbf{a}_i||_q) + \lambda_2 f_A(\mathbf{A}) + \lambda_3 f_D(\mathbf{D})\}, \tag{3}$$

where, $f_A(.)$ could be a logistic function, a linear classifier, a label consistency term, a low-rank constraint, or the Fisher discrimination criterion. $f_D(.)$ allows forcing the incoherence of the dictionary for different classes. Hence, it is possible to jointly learn the dictionary and classification model, which attempt to optimize the learned dictionary for classification tasks [14]. λ_2 and λ_3 are two scalar parameters corresponding to the associated function [12].

The label of each test sample is assigned while maintaining the class with the minimum reconstruction error rate according to Eq. 4:

$$Label(\mathbf{x}_{test}) = \min_{i} r_i(\mathbf{x}_{test}), \tag{4}$$

where, $r_i = ||\mathbf{x}_{test} - \mathbf{D}\sigma_i(\mathbf{a}_{test})||_2^2$ designs the error rate equation, σ_i is the selective function of the coefficient vector associated to the class i, and used as a feature descriptor of the data. Thus, the test samples are represented as a linear combination of just the training samples corresponding to the same class.

Assuming that supervised dictionary learning methods and sparse representation differ in how they exploit class labels, we focused on the most popular and utilized ones in the experimentation. For this purpose, five different SDL algorithms for classification were evaluated and compared in terms of performance: sparse representation-based classifier (SRC) [15], Dictionary Learning with Structured Incoherence (DLSI) [16], Fisher Discrimination Dictionary Learning (FDDL) [17], and Low-Rank Shared Dictionary (D2L2R2) [18].

3   Experimental Test and Evaluation

3.1   Evaluation Metrics

Three metrics were considered throughout this experiment evaluation, including the system Accuracy (AC), Sensitivity (SE), and Specificity (SP). Accordingly, AC is the simplest form to evaluate a fall classifier; it is used to determine how often the classifier is overly correct. SE, also known as recall, is depicted by the rate of how correctly the system detects a fall over the set of fall instances. SP is described by how adequately a fall detection system detects ADL over the whole set of ADL instances.

3.2   Experimental Setup

Offline Evaluation Setup. Throughout the conducted offline evaluation, we assume that 75% of each investigated dataset for the training set and 25% will be used as an offline testing set. We assume considering the same settings used in configuring each used SDL hyper-parameters in our previous study [5, 6].

Online Evaluation Setup. To proceed with the online evaluation, we considered a hardware prototype composed of an Arduino Nano microcontroller platform to process the data acquired from an MPU6050 module embedding a triaxial accelerometer, gyroscope, and magnetometer. The data is transmitted via the HC-05 Bluetooth module to a mobile application. We assume using an overlapping rate of 50% for the sliding window.

3.3   Offline Experiment

In the offline experiment evaluation, we consider varying the sampling rate in [20, 50, 100] in Hz. Moreover, we study the influence of the addition of each of the previously mentioned sensors through three scenarios: (i) Accelerometer, (ii) Accelerometer + Gyroscope, and (iii) Accelerometer + Gyroscope + Magnetometer. Throughout this experiment, UMAfall [7], UPfall [8], and Quadros et al. [9] fall will be studied and compared regarding the SE, SP and AC metrics.

(i) Accelerometer only {Acc}. Tables 1, 2 and 3 represent the best results achieved by the assessed datasets when using 20, 50, 100 Hz respectively for sampling rate. Overall, the Quadros et al. dataset has overpassed UMAfall and UPfall in all three resampling values. Thus, it has reached an accuracy of 99.5%, 99%, and 99.8% 20 Hz, 50 Hz, 100 Hz, respectively. UMAfall attained its best performance of 99.5% via the SRC algorithm when upsampled to 100 samples per second versus 97.2% using the DLSI algorithm. A considerable performance was attained by the Quadros et al. dataset when resampled 20 Hz, reaching 99.5%, 100%, and 99% of accuracy, sensitivity, and specificity accordingly.

Table 1. Evaluation using {Acc} scenario 20 Hz

SDL	SRC			DLSI			FDDL			D2L2R2		
	AC	SE	SP	AC	SE	SP	AC	SE	SP	AC	SE	SP
UMAfall	96.6	97.6	97.6	**97.2**	97.6	97.1	92.41	97.6	90.4	92.4	100	90.4
UPfall	90.5	85.4	94.7	94.3	89.6	98.3	**95.2**	91.7	98.3	93.3	85.4	98.3
Quadros	**99.5**	100	99.0	**99.5**	100	99.0	97.4	99.0	95.8	96.9	96.88	96.88

Table 2. Evaluation Using {Acc} scenario 50 Hz

SDL	SRC			DLSI			FDDL			D2L2R2		
	AC	SE	SP	AC	SE	SP	AC	SE	SP	AC	SE	SP
UMAfall	97.4	94.8	100	**98.4**	97.9	99.0	95.9	97.9	93.8	92.7	90.6	94.8
UPfall	90.1	96.9	83.3	**97.4**	95.8	99.0	96.9	96.9	96.9	95.8	92.7	99.0
Quadros	97.9	96.9	99.0	**99.0**	97.9	100	97.9	95.8	100	97.4	95.8	99.0

(ii) Accelerometer + Gyroscope { Acc + Gyro}. We have added the triaxial gyroscope data information to the previously tested dataset, and a resampling process of 20, 50, 100 Hz is applied accordingly. The obtained results are shown in Tables 4, 5 and 6. The observed performance shows a noticeable decrease in SDL performances compared with those obtained using only an accelerometer. Subsequently, the performance when using various datasets has considerably decreased while increasing the sampling rate. The best performance was fulfilled using the Quadros et al. dataset set to 50 Hz sampling rate, obtaining an accuracy of 98.4%, a sensitivity of 99%, and a specificity of 97.9%. The worst performance was attained by the UPfall dataset upsampled 100 Hz.

(iii) Accelerometer + Gyroscope + Magnetometer {Acc + Gyro + Mag}. We only consider UMAfall and Quadros et al. datasets in this evaluation process since UPfall considers only the Accelerometer and Gyroscope as IMU sensors. Tables 7, 8, and 9 illustrate the resampling impact of 20, 50 100 Hz respectively on the SDL performance. As the sampling rate increases, the SDL performance decreases, especially for the UMAfall that has reached a

Table 3. Evaluation Using {Acc} scenario 100 Hz

SDL	SRC			DLSI			FDDL			D2L2R2		
	AC	SE	SP	AC	SE	SP	AC	SE	SP	AC	SE	SP
UMAfall	**99.5**	100	99.0	98.4	100	96.9	96.4	99.0	93.8	96.9	99.0	94.8
UPfall	91.2	100	82.3	**97.9**	95.8	100	**97.9**	100	95.8	**97.9**	100	95.8
Quadros	**99.8**	100	99.6	99	100	97.9	98.0	98.0	98.0	97.4	97.9	96.9

Table 4. Evaluation Using {Acc + Gyro} scenario 20 Hz

SDL	SRC			DLSI			FDDL			D2L2R2		
	AC	SE	SP	AC	SE	SP	AC	SE	SP	AC	SE	SP
UMAfall	93.1	78.1	99.0	94.5	78.8	95.2	95.9	87.8	99.0	**97.2**	90.5	98.1
UPfall	78.1	72.9	82.5	**84.8**	87.5	82.5	79.1	85.4	73.7	82.9	70.8	91.2
Quadros	97.4	96.9	97.9	97.4	96.9	97.9	**97.9**	99.0	96.9	**97.9**	99.0	96.9

Table 5. Evaluation Using {Acc + Gyro} scenario 50 Hz

SDL	SRC			DLSI			FDDL			D2L2R2		
	AC	SE	SP	AC	SE	SP	AC	SE	SP	AC	SE	SP
UMAfall	93.1	78.1	99.0	**97.4**	99.0	95.8	96.4	95.8	96.9	96.9	100	93.6
UPfall	89.1	99.0	79.2	**94.7**	97.9	91.7	88.5	89.6	87.5	91.2	99.0	83.3
Quadros	97.9	99.0	96.9	97.9	99.0	96.9	97.9	99.0	96.9	**98.4**	99.0	97.9

Table 6. Evaluation Using {Acc + Gyro} scenario with 100 Hz

SDL	SRC			DLSI			FDDL			D2L2R2		
	AC	SE	SP	AC	SE	SP	AC	SE	SP	AC	SE	SP
UMAfall	84.4	88.5	80.2	83.3	84.4	82.3	**88.0**	89.6	86.5	89.6	90.6	88.5
UPfall	71.9	88.5	55.2	**84.9**	84.3	85.4	77.1	84.3	69.8	84.4	88.5	80.2
Quadros	**90.6**	90.6	90.6	88.5	91.7	854	**90.6**	93.8	87.5	90.1	93.8	86.5

Table 7. Evaluation using {Acc + Gyro + Mag} scenario 20 Hz

SDL	SRC			DLSI			FDDL			D2L2R2		
	AC	SE	SP	AC	SE	SP	AC	SE	SP	AC	SE	SP
UMAfall	95.8	100	91.7	**97.4**	94.8	100	95.8	99.0	92.7	94.3	97.9	90.6
Quadros	**99.0**	99.0	99.0	99.0	100	97.9	97.9	97.9	97.9	98.4	99.0	97.9

Table 8. Evaluation using {Acc + Gyro + Mag} scenario 50 Hz

SDL	SRC			DLSI			FDDL			D2L2R2		
	AC	SE	SP	AC	SE	SP	AC	SE	SP	AC	SE	SP
UMAfall	**93.2**	97.9	88.5	91.7	96.9	86.46	91.1	96.9	85.42	92.7	100	85.4
Quadros	**98.4**	100	96.9	97.9	99.0	96.9	97.4	97.9	96.9	96.4	97.9	94.8

Table 9. Evaluation using {Acc + Gyro + Mag} scenario 100 Hz

SDL	SRC			DLSI			FDDL			D2L2R2		
	AC	SE	SP	AC	SE	SP	AC	SE	SP	AC	SE	SP
UMAfall	62.3	62.3	62.3	52.7	26.2	63.5	61.4	64.3	60.6	56.2	14.3	67.3
Quadros	**97.4**	96.9	97.9	96.4	100	92.7	96.4	96.9	95.8	**97.4**	96.9	97.9

deteriorated performance of 52.7% when using the DLSI algorithm. Even though Quadros et al. has decreased in terms of performance, it has maintained a fair accuracy of 99.0% and 97.4%, making this latter dataset more reliable than UPfall and UMAfall datasets.

3.4 Prototype

We assume 20 Hz presents an optimal sampling rate when respecting the energy consumption condition and a satisfactory SDL model accuracy. Based on the achieved results in the offline experiment, we chose to implement the learned SRC model using an accelerometer with a sampling rate 20 Hz. Indeed, the latter reached 99.5%, 100%, and 99% of accuracy, sensitivity, and specificity, respectively.

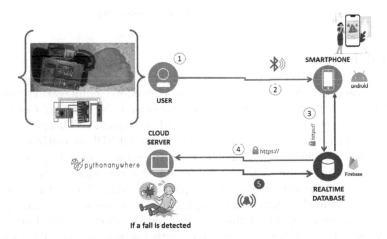

Fig. 2. On-wrist device prototype.

Figure 2 presents the on wrist prototype, in which we attached a 9 V alkaline battery with a 550 mAh capacity. The user will then open an android application illustrated in Fig. 3 and log in either as a patient or as a supervisor. As a supervisor, a request must be sent to the concerned patient to enable the latter's supervision notification. As for the patient, the supervisor will receive a request for either acceptance or decline. The smartphone GPS and Bluetooth must be enabled to maintain data acquisition and patient localization when a fall is detected. The data is received via a real-time database and processed via a cloud-based SDL model.

A volunteer wore the device band on his non-dominant left hand and carried out his daily living activities using his smartphone. The system showed good autonomy in facing several ADL activities like walking, raising hands, and sitting. Nevertheless, it has exhibited some ambiguity for fall-alike activities like jumping and realizing hands, leading to false alerts. The system device has shown an autonomy of 14 running hours.

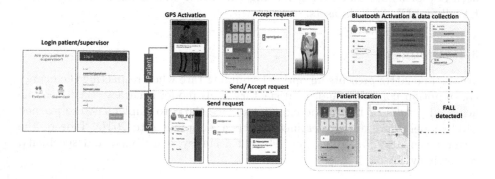

Fig. 3. Mobile application processing.

4   Conclusion

Wearable-based systems present an optimal cost-effective, increasingly comfortable with the emergence of technological devices and the familiarity of their use given their ubiquity, such as smartwatches and smartphones. This paper presents a datasets exploration using the previously proposed SDL algorithms regarding two main benchmarks. Firstly, when varying the sensors' sampling rate and secondly, when adding some IMU sensors, including accelerometer, magnetometer, and gyroscope. A Smartphone-based application using Bluetooth communication with the wearable device was implemented to assess and locate patients when a fall is detected. The Offline evaluation has shown optimal system efficiency when using only an accelerometer with low energy and 20 Hz sampling rate.

As future work, we intend to focus more on the efficiency of the IoT-based system in order to optimize the energy consumption of the wearable device and to enhance system reliability in SDL algorithm facing false alerts.

References

1. U.N: Living arrangements of older persons. in World Population Ageing 2020 Highlights, 2020 ed. New York, USA: United Nations Department of Economic and Social Affairs, Population Division, 2020 (2021). https://www.un.org/development/desa/pd/. Accessed 21 Feb 2021
2. W.H.O; WHO Global Report on Falls Prevention in Older Age. In: Ageing and Life Course Family and Community Health, 2008 ed.: World Health Organisation, pp. 23 (2021)
3. Wang, X., Ellul, J., Azzopardi, G.: Elderly fall detection systems: a literature survey. Front. Robot. AI. **7** (2020). https://doi.org/10.3389/frobt.2020.00071
4. Ramachandran, A., Karuppiah, A.: A survey on recent advances in wearable fall detection systems. BioMed Res. Int. **2020**, Article ID 2167160, 17 pages (2020). https://doi.org/10.1155/2020/2167160
5. Othmen, F., Baklouti, M., Lazzaretti, A.E., Jmal, M.., Abid, M.: A novel on-wrist fall detection system using Supervised Dictionary Learning technique. In: 18th International Conference On Smart Living and Public Health (2020)
6. Othmen, F., Lazzaretti, A., Baklouti, M. , Jmal, M., Abid, M.: A sparse representation classification for noise robust wrist-based fall detection. In: Proceedings of the 14th International Joint Conference on Biomedical Engineering Systems and Technologies - HEALTHINF, pp. 409–416 (2020). https://doi.org/10.5220/0010238804090416
7. Casilari, E., Santoyo-Ramón, J.A., Cano-García, J.M.: UMAFall: a multisensor dataset for the research on automatic fall detection. Procedia Comput. Sci. **110**, 32–39 (2017). ISSN 1877–0509. https://doi.org/10.1016/j.procs.2017.06.110
8. Martínez-Villaseñor, L., Ponce, H., Brieva, J., Moya-Albor, E., Núñez-Martínez, J., Peñafort-Asturiano, C.: UP-Fall Detection Dataset: A Multimodal Approach. Sensors (Basel) **19**(9), 1988 (2019). https://doi.org/10.3390/s19091988
9. de Quadros, T., Lazzaretti, A.E., Schneider, F.K.: A movement decomposition and machine learning-based fall detection system using wrist wearable device. IEEE Sens. J. **18**(12), 5082–5089 (2018)
10. Smith, J.O.: Upsampling and Downsampling. In: Spectral Audio Signal Processing. https://www.dsprelated.com/freebooks/sasp/UpsamplingDownsampling.html 2011 edition. Accessed 23 Oct 2021
11. Putra, I.P.E.S., Vesilo, R.: Window-size impact on detection rate of wearable-sensor-based fall detection using supervised machine learning. In: IEEE Life Sciences Conference (LSC) 2017, pp. 21–26 (2017). https://doi.org/10.1109/LSC.2017.8268134
12. Gangeh, M.J., Farahat, A.K., Ghodsi, A., Kamel, M.S.: Supervised Dictionary Learning and Sparse Representation-A Review, arXiv (2015)
13. Xu, Y., Li, Z., Yang, J., Zhang, D.: A survey of dictionary learning algorithms for face recognition. IEEE Access **5**, 8502–8514 (2017)
14. Jiang, Z., Lin, Z., Davis, L.S.: Learning a discriminative dictionary for sparse coding via label consistent K-SVD. In: CVPR 2011, Providence, RI, 2011, pp. 1697–1704
15. Wright, J., Yang, A.Y., Ganesh, A., Sastry, S.S., Ma, Y.: Robust face recognition via sparse representation. IEEE Trans. Pattern Anal. Mach. Intell. **31**(2), 210–227 (2009)

16. Ramirez, I., Sprechmann, P., Sapiro, G.: Classification and clustering via dictionary learning with structured incoherence and shared features. In: 2010 IEEE Computer Society Conference on Computer Vision and Pattern Recognition, San Francisco, CA, 2010, pp. 3501–3508 (2010)
17. Yang, M., Zhang, L., Feng, X., Zhang, D.: Fisher discrimination dictionary learning for sparse representation. In: 2011 International Conference on Computer Vision, Barcelona, pp. 543–550 (2011)
18. Vu, T.H., Monga, V.: Fast low-rank shared dictionary learning for image classification. IEEE Trans. Image Process. **26**(11), 5160–5175 (2017)
19. Liu, K., Hsieh, C., Hsu, S.J., Chan, C.: Impact of sampling rate on wearable-based fall detection systems based on machine learning models. IEEE Sens. J. **18**(23), 9882–9890 (2018). https://doi.org/10.1109/JSEN.2018.2872835
20. Santoyo-Ramón, J.A., Casilari, E., Cano-García, J.M.: A study of the influence of the sensor sampling frequency on the performance of wearable fall detectors. Measurement **193**, 110945 (2022). ISSN 0263-2241

UML Profile for IoT-Based Applications

Malek Ltaief[1]([✉])[iD], Sarah Hussein Toman[2,3][iD], and Lazhar Hamel[1][iD]

[1] Computer Science Department ISIMM, University of Monastir, Monastir, Tunisia
ltaief.maleek@gmail.com, lazhar.hamel@isimm.rnu.tn
[2] Computer Science Department FSM, University of Monastir, Monastir, Tunisia
[3] University of Al-Qadisiyah, Al Diwaniyah, Iraq
sarah.toman@qu.edu.iq

Abstract. In the last few years, the Internet of Things (IoT) has emerged as a new paradigm aimed at providing technological solutions for the monitoring and control of physical entities (so-called objects - cars, furniture, buildings). These new solutions encompass heterogeneous devices capable of: capturing information about the physical entities to which they are attached and/or the environment in which they are inserted, performing sensing tasks; acting on the physical domain, performing actuation tasks; and communicating with each other and/or with other systems via the Internet to achieve common goals. However, Designing systems of this kind is a real challenge and modeling with UML is consolidating itself as a resource to surmount this challenge. To deal with this situation, we contribute by proposing an adaptation of UML2.5 to IoT systems. It is in this context that we have defined a UML2.5 profile for the IoT system. This profile includes a set of stereotypes applied to meta-classes from the UML2.5 meta-model. These stereotypes are complemented by formal constraints in OCL. These extensions allow to improve the consistency checking of reusable system architectures.

Keywords: Internet of Things · UML · Software architecture · Model · Profile · Object Constraint Language (OCL)

1 Introduction

Software engineering enables us to comprehend the system and to think about its characteristics by offering a high-level model of its architecture. Software and digitalization have taken over everything. The Internet of Things (IoT) paradigm comes with very distinctive properties like the heterogeneity of its physical and virtual components that have to be integrated. Designing systems of this kind is a big challenge and the modelisation using UML is emerging as a resource to overcome this challenge.

To handle the complexity of software engineering, the notion of software architecture was proposed in the beginning of the 1990s. It facilitates the decomposition of big and complex software applications in terms of manageable elements and connectors and their high level logic [15], [9] and [4]. The use of

C. Bădică et al. (Eds.): ICCCI 2022, CCIS 1653, pp. 515–527, 2022.
https://doi.org/10.1007/978-3-031-16210-7_42

software engineering concepts to support the development of IoT systems is currently still in the process of being adapted.

Despite the necessity of a formal foundation and a well-structured project, modeling IoT systems remains a challenge. The objectives of software design include the best understanding of the problem, by using resources such as UML diagrams for designing complex systems. Based on [20], software engineering, as a domain, has to identify the resources and broader issues that characterize IoT systems, to describe the inclusion of its components in a model.

The UML uses diagrams that provide a graphical view of system components and their integration, although it requires an extension and customization for a representation of IoT systems. According to [18], [17] [16] suggest the use of UML for IoT systems, implying extensions. One of the advantages of using UML for IoT is the extensive number of available tools. The challenge of designing an IoT system is the adequate level of detail for developers to design it and at the same time abstracting the complexities for a high-level comprehension for the system implementation. In this paper we have proposed a UML profile to model an IoT system. This profile includes a set of stereotypes applied to metaclasses from the UML metamodel. The proposed stereotypes have usage constraints formally expressed in OCL [19].

The remainder of this paper is structured as follows. In Sect. 2, we discuss the related work. In Sect. 3, we give an overview of UML dedicated to model UML profile and IoT. The Sect. 4 introduces the IoT system modeling. In Sect. 5 we details the proposed IoT system based on UML profile. In Sect. 6, we will present an IoT application to a case study of our proposed approach. Finally, Sect. 6 concludes the paper.

2 Related Work

The rise of the Internet of Things has created numerous new challenges for architects and developers of complex systems. In order to assist and orient designers, various modeling and design approaches have been proposed such as tools, UML profiles and Design Patterns.

Despite the fact that there is no standard and adequately representative language for IoT systems, UML is one of the available visual modeling support resources that allows extensions to be employed to describe these systems. In this context, there are several works that have realized IoT-specific UML extensions [8,18]. Some of these profiles are those that design the security functions [17], the other one enables to design the IoT applications [5]. In a further work [13], the authors established a framework that provides the opportunity to design the architecture of an IoT system using patterns as well as to check these models using a logic programming language.

On the other side, The authors of [14] suggested an embedded approach to support the development of IoT systems through applying a development methodology that splits the process into various concerns and gives a conceptual framework for this purpose. [7] provides a definition of a design and analysis process and a supporting framework called SysML4IoT; a SysML profile based on the IoT-A reference model [2], to assist application designers in precisely specifying the IoT application system models and checking their QoS characteristics. An extension of this paper is presented in [6] to offer a modeling language for the specification of SOA-based IoT applications, named SoaML4IoT. Furthermore, [12] propose a model-driven approach to enhance the reusability and flexibility of sensor based software systems called FRASAD (FRAmework for Sensor Application Development). [10] concentrated on adaptive IoT systems and introduced a model-driven approach to facilitate the modeling and realization of such systems by adopting SysML4IoT. SysML is further adopted and extended by [11], though in this case with the aim of implementing a model-based design approach in IoT eHealth systems. The contributors of this paper concentrate on the Remote Elderly Monitoring System (REMS) use case by identifying its criticalities and modeling them as SysML requirements, whereas SysML constraints and parametric diagrams are employed to specify and verify the quantitative criticality requirements.

Despite the large number of works focused on IoT systems, to the best of our knowledge, there is no work focused on designing 'IoT systems while taking into consideration behavioral and structural requirements. In this paper, we seek to fill this gap by defining a UML2.5 profile includes a set of stereotypes applied to the metaclasses of the UML2.5 metamodel. The proposed stereotypes have usage constraints formally expressed in OCL.

3   Background

In this section, we provide a broad overview of the main concepts of UML modeling language. Then, we introduce the basic concepts of the IoT system which are necessary for the comprehension of the present paper.

3.1   UML Profile

UML is a "general-purpose" modeling language for software system specification, visualization, construction and artifacts documentation [3].

One of its goals is the standardization of the several existing methods to describe object-oriented systems. Its current version (2.5) has 14 diagrams that show the static and behavioral aspects of a of a system (OMG, 2017). With the growing complexity of today's systems, the UML has an aggregation extension to further specify several features of systems, which incorporates pervasive processing, distributed computing, cross-platform systems, etc.

It can be adapted to each domain thanks to the extensibility mechanisms offered by this language such as stereotypes, tagged values and constraints.

- Stereotypes are employed to identify a new type of model as an extension or a classification of an already existing base feature (for example, « IoTSystem » as a class classification). The concept of a stereotype permits the element to "behave as if it were instantiated from the meta-model construction".

- Tagged values indicate keyword-value pairs of model components to denote a new feature for an already existing UML model element or they can be applied to stereotypes.
- Constraints are a collection of conformance rules. To do so, three methods are authorized:
  - Predefined constraints: ordered, subset, xor, addOnly, frozen, ...
  - Constraints expressed in natural language (comments)
  - Constraints expressed in Object Constraint Language (OCL)

The UML extensions targeting a particular domain form UML profiles.

The profile is the light extension mechanism given by UML to permit the extension and specialization of the UML meta-model with constructs that are specific to a particular domain without modifying the UML metamodel.

3.2 IoT

The Internet of Things (IoT) is a novel paradigm that is made up of heterogeneous objects that communicate with each other by both sending and receiving information in heterogeneous formats (e.g., JSON, XML) through heterogeneous protocols (e.g., Long Range Wide-area network (LoRaWAN), Zigbee, Message Queuing Telemetry Transport (MQTT) and more) to accomplish common goals. In the context of IoT, architecture is an environment that defines the physical components, the functional organization and configuration of the network, the operational methods and the types of data to be used. The IoT architecture can be very different depending on the execution; it must be flexible enough for open protocols to handle many network applications. A standard IoT architecture that could capture all aspects of IoT scenarios is far from a reality, mainly due to the complex nature of the IoT. This means that there is no simple blueprint that can be followed for all possible implementations. However, a number of IoT architectures are commonly used in the literature, such as three-layer architecture, four-layer architecture, five-layer architecture, middleware-based architecture, SOA-based architecture. While there is no single, universally accepted IoT architecture, the most basic and widely accepted format is the three-layer architecture. It was first introduced in the early research on the Internet of Things. For this reason we have decided to adopt it as our reference model. This architecture proposes three layers: *Perception, Network* and *Application*.

Thanks to the adoption of the component-based conception method, we have identified three main types of classification for the devices and services that interact within the proposed architecture

- End devices that collect data from the surroundings and receive commands from the IoT platform to interact.
- The IoT gateway is the middleware between the other components.
- The IoT platform in witch we perform the necessary device processing, analysis, storage and management to deliver applications to users.

4 Proposed IoT System Profile

IoT system implementations using UML based resources are discussed in this section. While there is no standard and properly representative language for IoT systems, the UML is one of the modeling tools that provides the ability to use extensions to represent such systems.

A meta-model describes the various components required to define a specific domain and specifies the semantic dependencies between them. It provides a domain-specific vocabulary to allow designers to establish a commonly shared view of the domain and to enable them to collaborate more easily. The main contribution of this paper consists, first, in a generic profile for IoT systems. We propose a profile to describe the architecture of such systems from different perspectives while taking into account their structural and behavioral constraints. Our UML2.5 profile for the IoT system includes a set of stereotypes applied to metaclasses from the UML2.5 meta-model. Actually, it is composed of nine stereotypes (see Fig. 1):

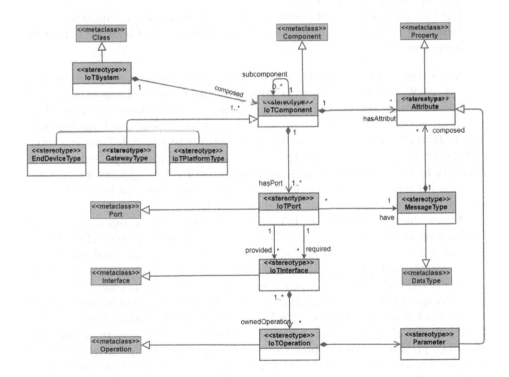

Fig. 1. IoTSystem profile

- *IoTSystem* this simply represents a generic IoTSystem, which is essentially a set of *IoTComponent*.

- *IoTComponent* These are generic components that represent the architecture components of the IoT, which can be primitive or composite components. An IoTComponent is abstracted and specialized by the three substereotypes end device, gateway and IoT platform
- *IoTPort* Each IoT component has a port that represents the point of inter-action with the other components.
- *IoTInterface* communications with the environment are made through both types of interface. The Provided interface and the Required interface.
- *IoTPort* Each IoT component has a port that represents the point of inter-action with the other components.
- *IoTOperation* describes the operations provided by an interface. This stereo-type extends the UML Operation meta-class.
- *MessageType* In every system, there are a lot of messages that are circulating. For that, we need to define the type of each message in such a way that we can differentiate the messages exchanged by the different elements of the system. These messages can be either of XML or JSON type. This stereotype extends the UML DataType meta-class.
- *Attribute* represents a data definition for an instance of a component.
- *Parameter* is a specific argument that passes information between behavioral characteristics

Then we refined this profile by specifying the communication technology (we chose LoRaWAN) used. In fact, to implement the behavioral concepts we need to choose a communication protocol. In our work we have chosen the LoRaWAN standard which is one of the most common protocols used in IoT applications. The LoRaWAN architecture considers a star-of-star topology, IoT devices trans-mit data for neighbor gateways that send the message to the application server (IoT platform). Depended to such architecture, LoRaWAN produces connectiv-ity to a big number of IoT devices deployed over a large area by employing a control access mechanism with less complexity [1].

As previously mentioned an IoT system has three basic components: an IoT component which can be either IoT platform or connected object(End Device ED) or gateway, an IoT port which can have four subtypes and component interfaces. An IoT platform is composed by a device management component, a connectivity and normalization component, a data analysis component and a data storage component. According to the LoRaWAN communication protocol a connected object can be extended by three types of class: class A object, class B object and class C object. Figure 2 illustrates the IoT system architecture described previously. The proposed stereotypes have usage requirements formally expressed in OCL. The elaborated IoT system profile representing most of the concepts of such a system. This profile allows, in our context, to express in a semi-formal way the concepts of an IoT system to be modeled in UML2.5.

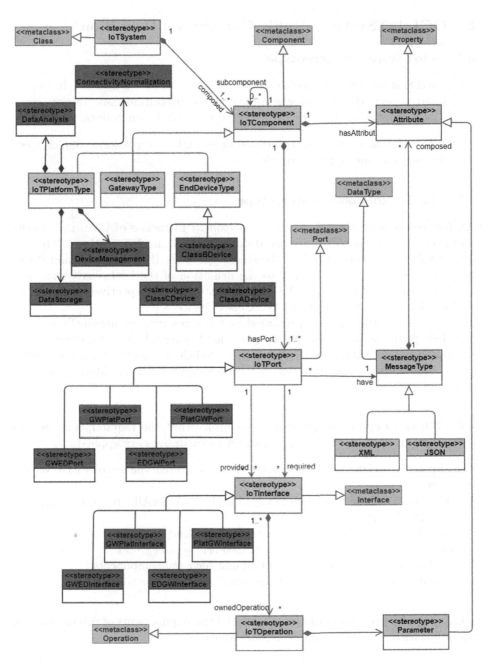

Fig. 2. Refined IoTSystem meta-model

5   OCL IoTSystem Profile Constraints Definition

5.1   « IoTSystem » stereotype

The « IoTSystem » stereotype extends the UML *Class* meta-class. It can be composed of several IoT components but this composition must respect some conditions. For this we have defined the following OCL constraints.

– An IoT system have to be composed of a single IoT platform, one or more gateways and one or more end devices.

5.2   « IoTComponent » stereotype

An IoT component is applied to the *Component* metaclass of UML metamodel and it can have three sub-types end device, gateway and IoT platform. The end device subtype is represented by the stereotype « EndDeviceType » and it can have three class types, according to the definition of the LoRaWAN standard, class A class B and class C . These three subtypes are respectively stereotyped « ClassADevice » « ClassBDevice » « ClassCDevice »
The gateway component is represented by the stereotype « GatewayType »
The IoT platform is represented by the « IoTPlatformType » stereotype. It is composed of four sub-components of type «IoTComponent» which are respectively stereotyped «DataStorage » « DataAnalysis» « DeviceManagement» « ConnectivityNormalisation »

« EndDeviceType » stereotype. To ensure that the requirements for this stereotype are met, the following set of OCL constraints are applied :

– All ports associated with the EndDeviceType stereotype are of « EDGWPort » stereotype
   ➡ self.oclAsType(EndDeviceType).hasPort → forAll (p |p.stereotype = EDGWPort)
– One or more ports can be associated to each End Device
   ➡ self.oclAsType(EndDeviceType).hasPort → size() =>1
– A « EndDeviceType » component cannot have subcomponents :
   ➡ self.oclAsType(EndDeviceType).subComponent → >isEmpty()

« GatewayType » stereotype. To control the requirements of this stereotype, the following set of OCL constraints are applied:

– All ports associated with the GatewayType stereotype are of « GWEDPort » stereotype or « GWPlatPort » stereotype
   ➡ self.oclAsType(GatewayType).hasPort → forAll (p |(p.stereotype = GWEDPort) OR (p.stereotype = GWPlatPort))
– One or more ports of « GWEDPort » stereotype and only one port of « GWPlatPort » stereotype can be associated to each GatewayType:

➥ self.oclAsType(GatewayType).hasPort → exists (p |(p.stereotype = GWEDPort)) and self.oclAsType(GatewayType).hasPort → select (p |(p.stereotype = GWPlatPort))→ size() = 1
- A « GatewayType » component cannot have subcomponents :
  ➥ self.oclAsType(GatewayType).subComponent → isEmpty()

« IoTPlatformType » stereotype. The following set of OCL constraints are applied in order to verify the requirements of this stereotype:

- All ports associated with the IoTPlatformType stereotype are of « PlatGWPort » stereotype :
  ➥ self.oclAsType(IoTPlatformType).hasPort → forAll (p |p.stereotype = PlatGWPort)
- One or more ports can be associated to each IoT Platform
  ➥self.oclAsType(IoTPlatformType).hasPort → size() =>1
- An iot platform component is composed of four subcomponents a component for the Data Storage services, one for the Data Analysis services, one for the Device Management services and one for the Connectivity and Normalisation services
  ➥ self.oclAsType(IoTPlatformType).subComponent → size() = 4
  ➥ self.oclAsType(IoTPlatformType).subComponent → select (p |(p.stereotype = DataStorage))→ size() = 1
  ➥ self.oclAsType(IoTPlatformType).subComponent → select (p |(p.stereotype = DataAnalysis))→ size() = 1
  ➥ self.oclAsType(IoTPlatformType).subComponent → select (p |(p.stereotype = DeviceManagement))→ size() = 1
  ➥ self.oclAsType(IoTPlatformType).subComponent → select (p |(p.stereotype = ConnectivityNormalisation))→ size() = 1

5.3 « IoTPort » stereotype

An IoT port is described by the *Port* meta-class of UML stereotyped by « IoTPort » . It is divided into four subtypes which are respectively stereotyped « PlatGWPort » « GWPlatPort » « GWEDPort » « DGWPort »

- Each port admits only one message type :
  ➥ self.have → size() = 1

« PlatGWPort » stereotype. In order to check the stereotype requirements, the following set of OCL constraints are applied:

- All required interfaces associated with the PlatGWPort type are of the « GWPlatInterface » stereotype:
  ➥ self.oclAsType(PlatGWPort).required → forAll (i |i.stereotype = GWPlatInterface)
- All provided interfaces associated with the PlatGWPort type are of the « PlatGWInterface » stereotype
  ➥ self.oclAsType(PlatGWPort).provided → forAll (i |i.stereotype = PlatG-WInterface)

« GWPlatPort » **stereotype.** In order to ascertain the requirements related to this stereotype, the following set of OCL constraints are applied:

– the GWPlatPort has only one interface offered and only one interface required:
  ➥ self.oclAsType(GWPlatPort).provided -> size() = 1
  and self.oclAsType(GWPlatPort).required -> size() = 1
– the required interface associated with the GWPlatPort type is of « PlatGWInterface » stereotype
  ➥ self.oclAsType(GWPlatPort).required → forAll (i |i.stereotype = PlatG-WInterface)
– the provided interface associated with the GWPlatPort type is of « GWPlatInterface » stereotype
  ➥ self.oclAsType(GWPlatPort).provided → forAll (i |i.stereotype = GWPlatInterface)

« GWEDPort » **stereotype.** In view of checking the requirements related to this stereotype, the following set of OCL constraints are applied:

– All required interfaces associated with the GWEDPort type are of the « GWEDInterface » stereotype
  ➥ self.oclAsType(GWEDPort).required → forAll (i |i.stereotype = EDG-WInterface)
– All provided interfaces associated with the GWEDPort type are of the « GWEDInterface » stereotype
  ➥ self.oclAsType(GWEDPort).provided → forAll (i |i.stereotype = GWED-Interface)

« EDGWPort » **stereotype** in order to check the requirements related to this stereotype a set of OCL constraints are applied:

– All required interfaces associated with the EDGWPort type are of the « GWEDInterface » stereotype
  ➥ self.oclAsType(EDGWPort).required → forAll (i |i.stereotype = GWED-Interface)
– All provided interfaces associated with the EDGWPort type are of the « EDGWInterface » stereotype
  ➥ self.oclAsType(EDGWPort).provided → forAll (i |i.stereotype = EDG-WInterface)

5.4   « IoTInterface » stereotype

An IoT interface is described by the UML *Interface* meta-class and stereotyped by « IoTInterface ». It is divided into four subtypes which are respectively stereotyped « PlatGWInterface » « GWPlatInterface » « GWEDInterface » « EDGWInterface »

– Each IoTInterface can have one or more operations. These operations are of stereotype IoTOpertion
  ➥ self.ownedOperation → size()= >1 and self.ownedOperation → forAll (o |o.stereotype =IoTOpertion)

6   Use Case: A Smart Home System

The IoT has rendered the world completely digitized by interconnecting the physical world with the numerical world. The smart home is a representation of this technology, and these homes are equipped with a large number of connected objects (e.g., air conditioner, smoke sensor, smart window, gas leakage sensor, noise sensor, light control sensor, body sensor, infrared camera, etc.) to control everything in the home. The cooperation of these components enables services to be offered. In our case, we chose to take a part of the smart home system which is smart room to do some experiments to validate our approach. The system is composed of three layers that are coherent with the general IoT architecture in order to have a scalable intelligent environment that supports a diversity of services. The software and hardware components used:

- Perception layer: is composed by an air conditioner, it used to cool the temperature by removing the existing heat and humidity in the room, and a light sensor which is used to control the lighting.
- Network layer: is a gateway that it is an intermediary between the Perception layer and the application layer. We opt for LoRaWAN as communication technology because it is supported by a lot of devices.
- application layer: contain the IoT platform, it permits to do the necessary processing, storage and management.

Now we will instantiate the model from the proposed meta-model to model our scenario. As shown in Fig. 3, we have specified the type of each component while respecting the constraints defined previously. Indeed, we have defined two

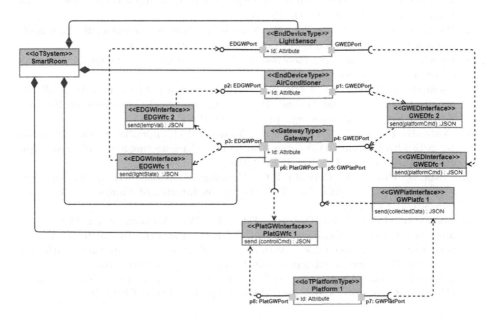

Fig. 3. Smart room system model

IoTComponent of type *EndDeviceType* one *IoTComponent* of type *GatewayType* and only one *IoTComponent* of type *IoTPlatformType*. Then we defined the port of each component of the system as well as the operations offered by each interface while keeping the constraints related to these stereotypes.

7 Conclusion

This work, has presented an approach to model the architecture of the Internet of Things. Our IoT System has been designed as a UML profile so to leverage standard languages and practices. Our approach consists in offering an IoT system meta-model that represent a high level of abstraction. Also, We have taken particular care in developing the formal OCL requirements associated with stereotypes. This allows us to better define the environment in which these stereotypes are used. Such a meta-model allows UML users to use IoT system's architectural concepts to design and build applications according to a UML-induced approach.

Much work can be built around the IoTSystem-profiled UML model. Some of the research avenues we think should be explored are automatic code generation from profiled UML models through automatic skeleton generation. Furthermore, an inclusion of the Event-B method to specify structural and behavioral properties, to have valid and correct models, is possible

References

1. Ballerini, M., Polonelli, T., Brunelli, D., Magno, M., Benini, L.: NB-IoT versus lorawan: an experimental evaluation for industrial applications. IEEE Trans. Industr. Inf. **16**(12), 7802–7811 (2020)
2. Bassi, A., Bauer, M., Fiedler, M., Kramp, T., Van Kranenburg, R., Lange, S., Meissner, S.: Enabling things to talk. Springer Nature (2013)
3. Booch, G., Rumbaugh, J., Jacobson, I.: The unified modeling language user guide addison-wesley. Reading (1999)
4. Clements, P., Garlan, D., Little, R., Nord, R., Stafford, J.: Documenting software architectures: views and beyond. In: 25th International Conference on Software Engineering, 2003. Proceedings, pp. 740–741. IEEE (2003)
5. Costa, B., Pires, P.F., Delicato, F.C.: Modeling IoT applications with sysml4iot. In: 2016 42th Euromicro Conference on Software Engineering and Advanced Applications (SEAA), pp. 157–164. IEEE (2016)
6. Costa, B., Pires, P.F., Delicato, F.: Modeling SOA-based IoT applications with soaml4iot. In: 2019 IEEE 5th World Forum on Internet of Things (WF-IoT), pp. 496–501. IEEE (2019)
7. Costa, B., Pires, P.F., Delicato, F.C., Li, W., Zomaya, A.Y.: Design and analysis of IoT applications: a model-driven approach. In: 2016 IEEE 14th Intl Conf on Dependable, Autonomic and Secure Computing, 14th Intl Conf on Pervasive Intelligence and Computing, 2nd Intl Conf on Big Data Intelligence and Computing and Cyber Science and Technology Congress (DASC/PiCom/DataCom/CyberSciTech), pp. 392–399. IEEE (2016)

8. Fleurey, F., Morin, B.: Thingml: a generative approach to engineer heterogeneous and distributed systems. In: 2017 IEEE International Conference on Software Architecture Workshops (ICSAW), pp. 185–188. IEEE (2017)

9. Garlan, D.: Software architecture (2008)

10. Hussein, M., Li, S., Radermacher, A.: Model-driven development of adaptive IoT systems. In: MODELS (Satellite Events), pp. 17–23 (2017)

11. Kotronis, C., Nikolaidou, M., Dimitrakopoulos, G., Anagnostopoulos, D., Amira, A., Bensaali, F.: A model-based approach for managing criticality requirements in e-health iot systems. In: 2018 13th Annual Conference on System of Systems Engineering (SoSE), pp. 60–67. IEEE (2018)

12. Nguyen, X.T., Tran, H.T., Baraki, H., Geihs, K.: Frasad: a framework for model-driven IoT application development. In: 2015 IEEE 2nd World Forum on Internet of Things (WF-IoT), pp. 387–392. IEEE (2015)

13. Ogata, S., Nakagawa, H., Aoki, Y., Kobayashi, K., Fukushima, Y.: A tool to edit and verify IoT system architecture model. In: MODELS (Satellite Events), pp. 571–575 (2017)

14. Patel, P., Cassou, D.: Enabling high-level application development for the internet of things. J. Syst. Softw. **103**, 62–84 (2015)

15. Perry, D.E., Wolf, A.L.: Foundations for the study of software architecture. ACM SIGSOFT Softw. Eng. Notes **17**(4), 40–52 (1992)

16. Reggio, G.: A UML-based proposal for IoT system requirements specification. In: Proceedings of the 10th International Workshop on Modelling in Software Engineering, pp. 9–16 (2018)

17. Robles-Ramirez, D.A., Escamilla-Ambrosio, P.J., Tryfonas, T.: IoTsec: UML extension for internet of things systems security modelling. In: 2017 International Conference on Mechatronics, Electronics and Automotive Engineering (ICMEAE), pp. 151–156. IEEE (2017)

18. Thramboulidis, K., Christoulakis, F.: UML4IoT-a UML-based approach to exploit IoT in cyber-physical manufacturing systems. Comput. Ind. **82**, 259–272 (2016)

19. Warmer, J.B., Kleppe, A.G.: The object constraint language: getting your models ready for MDA. Addison-Wesley Professional (2003)

20. Zambonelli, F.: Towards a general software engineering methodology for the internet of things. arXiv preprint arXiv:1601.05569 (2016)

A Formal Verification Model for IoT Based Applications Using Event-B

Rihab Omri[1][(✉)] , Zinah Hussein Toman[2,3] , and Lazhar Hamel[1][(✉)]

[1] Computer Science Department ISIMM, University of Monastir, Monastir, Tunisia
`riihab.77@gmail.com`, `lazhar.hamel@isimm.rnu.tn`
[2] Computer Science Department FSM, University of Monastir, Monastir, Tunisia
`Zinah.hussein@qu.edu.iq`
[3] University of Al-Qadisiyah, Al Diwaniyah, Iraq

Abstract. The Internet of Things (IoT) defines the collection of devices and systems that connect real-world sensors and actuators to the Internet. This interconnection is accomplished by the use of various protocols and appropriate communication technologies for heterogeneous objects and services. However, the modeling of these different IoT protocols for various purposes and domains becomes complicated. In this context, a study of the requirements becomes necessary to overcome these problems of heterogeneity and interconnectivity related to IoT applications. Indeed, the challenge here is to formalize an IoT system model to verify its requirements. In this paper, we propose a formal model to verify IoT components, as well as their requirements based on LoRaWAN technology. To achieve so, we used Event-B to fomalize an IoT system and its desired requirements. Event-B method allows decomposing these problems thanks to its refinement capabilities. On the other hand, it allows the verification of the model, following its structure, using proof obligations.

Keywords: IoT · Event-B · LoRaWAN · Formal verification · Proofs

1 Introduction

Over the past few years, there has been increasing interest in the verification of IoT systems. Particularly with the growth of connected devices, IoT systems use a variety of heterogeneous IoT network and connection technologies, with different devices processing data everywhere [18].

As a consequence, the specification of the requirements of these systems and their combination can increases the complexity of the development and evaluation of the IoT applications. Thus, meeting these requirements becomes a fundamental step for the success of IoT software. However, to ensure that the system meets these requirements, it is necessary to discover how the evaluation of these IoT applications is done. However, despite their similarities, such as interoperability, mobility, addressing, and routing; IoT applications have also some

C. Bădică et al. (Eds.): ICCCI 2022, CCIS 1653, pp. 528–541, 2022.
https://doi.org/10.1007/978-3-031-16210-7_43

singularities, such as interconnectivity, dynamicity, security and heterogeneity related to devices; which can be defined as a properties that a system must respect [18]. In this context, the first challenge we face when we talk about IoT applications is the sheer variety of heterogeneous devices and the different ways in which these devices share data and connect to each other. For this aim, there are several IoT communication protocols that can allow the network manager to meet some problems caused by this diversity [8].

Nowadays, the right choice of communication network between different objects defined a crucial necessity [8,17]. The communication protocols used in IoT environments are numerous, for example Bluetooth, LoWPAN, LoRaWAN, MQTT, ZigBee, etc. In recent years, the LoRaWAN protocol is the one who attract the attention of many enterprises because of its ability to deploy LoRa devices on its own LoRaWAN network. This, motivated us to choose it as a communication protocol to define our formal model based on IoT communications. However, we focus on a Formal Verification to requirements and communication protocols in the IoT domain, based on the Event-B formal method that facilitates the modeling of complex systems through its refinement capabilities. To this end, our work based on the proof and refinement of IoT components, as well as their requirements based on LoRa technology and event-B formal method.

The remainder of this article is organized as follows: In Sect. 2, we present some studies presented in the literature related to the IoT field. Hence, we give an overview of the Event-B method in Sect. 3. In Sect. 4, we present our model in an informal way. Next, in Sect. 5, we present our formal model using Event-B. Finally, in Sect. 6 we conclude by opening the perspectives of our future work.

2   Related Work

Several works have been carried out in the field of the IoT in recent years. Where several approaches have been proposed. For this, let us quote some examples: Authors in [13] proposes an approach based on The Tree Query Logic (TQL) in order to formally express and verify some structural and behavioral properties related to different IoT devices. In [5], the authors propose a runtime model-driven that centers on describing device models in IoT application development. On the other hand, [6] propose an MDE4IoT approach based on model-driven engineering (MDE) to model IoT objects by supporting their intelligence as self-adaptation for emerging configurations in IoT environments.

Reaching out a bit to the IoT domain, some work has been done on several IoT protocols such as MQTT [3], ZigBee [11], Bluetooth [16], as well as the LoRaWAN protocol that we are interested in. Most of the work, such as [14,19] and [7], focuses on improving solutions related to the security and properties of LoRaWAN. Concerning the works based on formal model, [9] propose a formal verification model to verify the security mechanisms of the IoT architecture layers using the Event-B method. Also, [12] present an abstract model of IoT application.

Despite the efforts to support the description, formalization and modeling of IoT applications and their communication protocols, these researches do not consider the structural and behavioral verification of IoT applications using Event-B method based on the LoRaWAN protocol and its interconnection properties between different entities.

3   Event-B Method

According to [4], Event-B defines an evolution of the B method where it reuses the same theoretical and logical notations of sets by providing new notations to express abstract systems based on the notion of events. This method allows the development of the software step by step, starting from the abstract level to the more detailed one. This is done by using the concept of refinement. The latter allows to know the level of complexity of such a system where it introduces step by step the different parts of the system starting from the abstract model to the most concrete one.

Event-B can be connected to several other tools in order to validate a formal development such as the provers with the help of the RODIN platform that supports it.

In general, Event-B is composed by two main concepts: CONTEXT and MACHINE. First, the CONTEXT which describes the static part of an Event-B specification where it includes the SETS clause which describes the set of abstract and enumerated types, the CONSTANTS clause which represents the constants of the model and the AXIOMS clause which indicates the properties and types of the constants clause. The EXTENDS clause allows to extend the context by calling it by its name, while the SEES clause allows to reference it by a machine. Secondly, the MACHINE which describes the dynamic part of an Event-B specification where it has three main clauses: VARIABLES, INVARIANTS and EVENTS. The VARIABLES clause represents the state variables of the model. The INVARIANTS clause defines the properties of the system and the typing of the variables. An event is constituted by GUARD and ACTION. Where GUARD presents the conditions that an event must satisfy and ACTION presents the action that an event must establish.

4   Informal Description

An IoT system contains an infinite number of objects. We cannot verify a model on this basis. Therefore, we work on a finite number of objects as a demonstrative example. Our example is represented by Fig. 1. Where we have three devices. Each device has data to send to another device. This figure represents the general IoT communication between different devices.

Reaching out a bit at the communication and interconnection between IoT objects according to LoRaWAN protocol, we need to extract the main requirements in order to build our model correctly. These requirements are based on two main types of requirements: structural and behavioral requirements.

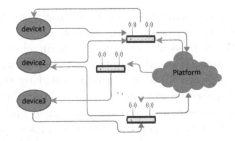

Fig. 1. Case study.

4.1 Structural Requirements

In this subsection, we focus on analyzing the structure of IoT application based on the literature to provide an overview of the basic relationships and mapping constraints.

According to [1], [10] and [15], the 3-layer architecture model defines the most well-known model for IoT applications. It consists of: **Perception Layer:** (the devices collect data and then transmit it to the network layer through the gateways), **Network Layer:** (enables reliable and secure data routing by connecting different devices and gateways) and **Application layer:** (the application/End Device allowing to analyze the messages received by another one). The same architecture is used for LoRa communications, where devices communicate with the gateways via LoRa, and the gateways communicate with the server via the IP network.

According to this architecture and based on Fig. 1, Table 1 present the structural rules that must be defined in our model.

Table 1. Structural requirements.

Struct1	The model must contain three main components which are the devices, the gateways and the IoT platform
Struct2	Within a communication infrastructure, the different objects of an IoT application can be connected and share information
Struct3	The state of the objects and their context change dynamically to facilitate data transfer without external intervention
Struct4	Two connected objects cannot communicate directly. Communication is done only through the gateways

4.2 Behavioral Requirements

In this section, we explain how an IoT object can send its data to another object, and how the latter can receive it. According to [2], LoRa devices are classified into 3 classes: 'class A' which defines the basic class for all IoT devices, and 'class

B and 'class C' which are defined as intermediate classes. Each class based on its Downlink accessibility and power consumption.

Since the LoRaWAN class A presents the main class of all IoT objects, we present the interconnection and data transmission between different objects according to it. Class B and C devices are extended by the Class A. Class B devices open scheduled receive windows to receive Downlink messages from the network server. They use synchronized beacons timed and transmitted by the gateway. While Class C devices keep the receive windows open until they transmit data. We present our behavioral requirement in Table 2.

Table 2. Behavioral requirements.

Beh1: An object can only join the LoRaWAN Network if it admits three types of necessary information: Device Address, Network Session Key and Application Session Key. These three pieces of information, as well as the data to be transferred, are sent in a same frame to the network server via gateways
Beh2: Each object joins the LoRa Network as a class A
Beh3: Each Device can transmit (Uplink) to the Gateway without checking the availability of the receiver
Beh4: An object is initially in standby. If it has data to transmit, it must goes to the active state
Beh5: The object must choose the Uplink channel and then send the data
Beh6: After transmission, the object returns to the standby state during a delay RxDelay1
Beh7: If there is RX1 Downlink transmission, the object listens one more time after RxDelay1 by opening a first window RX1
Beh7': After the Downlink RX1 transmission, the device goes to the standby state until the next Uplink transmission without waiting for an additional RX2 delay
Beh8: If there is RX2 Downlink transmission, after an additional RxDelay2 the object listens by opening a second window RX2
Beh9: The object returns to the standby state until the next Uplink transmission
Beh10: The Network can use a single gateway during the Downlink

5   Event-B Formal Model

In this section, we apply the Event-B formalism to develop our IoT model and prove the LoRaWAN protocol requirements.

5.1 Formal Development

In general, for any formal system development, an informal description of the system specifications and requirements must be established. Therefore, a formal development process must capture all of these informal specifications and requirements. In this context, our model includes five levels of abstraction to model the set of requirements according to the different LoRaWAN classes.

5.1.0.1 Abstract level: abstractMachine sees abstractContext. defines the abstract machine where we define the structural property model. Figure 2 presents the abstractContext sets: DEVICES, GATEWAYS, PLATFORM and finally DATA (data to be shared). Also, it represents the abstract invariants where the four sets described previously are denote by **@inv1** (as a finite set), **@inv2**, **@inv3** and **@inv4**. The Uplink transmission denotes by **@inv5**, **@inv6** and **@inv7**, and the Downlink transmission denotes by **@inv8**, and **@inv9**. Figure 3 represents the abstractMachine events where *dataFromGtwToPlt*, *dataFrom PltToGtw* and *dataFromGtwToDev* have the same concept as the *dataFromDevToGtw* event.

```
CONTEXT  abstractContext
SETS
    DEVICES
    GATEWAYS
    PLATFORM
    DATA
CONSTANTS

AXIOMS
    axm1:  partition(DEVICES,
           {dev1}, {dev2}, {dev3})
    axm2:  partition(GATEWAYS,
           {gtw1}, {gtw2}, {gtw3})
    axm3:  partition(PLATFORM,
           {plt1})
    axm4:  partition(DATA,
           {data1}, {data2}, {data3}, {id1},
           {id2}, {id3}, {net1})
END
```

```
MACHINE  abstractMachine
SEES  abstractContext
VARIABLES

INVARIANTS
    inv1:  device ⊆ DEVICES
    inv2:  gateway ⊆ GATEWAYS
    inv3:  platform ⊆ PLATFORM
    inv4:  data ⊆ DATA
    inv5:  dataDev ∈ data ↣ device
    inv6:  dataGtw ∈ data ↔ gateway
    inv7:  dataPlt ∈ data ↔ platform
    inv8:  feedbackGtw ∈ data ↠ gateway
    inv9:  feedbackDev ∈ data ↠ device
END
```

Fig. 2. Abstract Context and Machine.

```
dataFromDataToDevice (ordinary)  ≙

any
    dev
    dat
where
    grd1:  dev ∈ device
    grd2:  dat ∈ data
    grd3:  dat ∉ dom(dataDev) ∧ dev ∉
           ran(dataDev)
then
    act1: dataDev(dat) := dev
end
```

```
datafromDevToGtw (ordinary)  ≙

any
    dev
    gtw
    dat
where
    grd1:  dev ∈ device
    grd2:  gtw ∈ gateway
    grd3:  dat ∈ dom(dataDev) ∧
           dataDev(dat) = dev
    grd4:  dat ∉ dom(dataGtw)
    grd5:  dom(dataDev) ≠ dom(dataGtw)
then
    act1: dataGtw(dat) := gtw
end
```

Fig. 3. abstractMachine events.

5.1.0.2 First Refinement: joiningMachine Refines abstractMachine. In this level of refinement, we model **Beh1** requirement by adding three events.

Those events ares: addIdToDevice(**inv0**), addAppKeyToDevice(**inv1**) and add-NetKeyToDevice(**inv2**). These information must be sent in the same data frame. This is presented by (**inv4**) as shown in Fig. 4. Concerning *addIdToDevice* event: @grd3 requires that initially, the device has no identifier and we need to add it by the action @act1. The same concept made for *addAppKeyToDevice* and *addNetKeyToDevice*. Eq. 1 present the added to *dataFromDataToDevice* event which refers to the sent data frame where the information must belong to the same device.

$$\boxed{sender \in ran(idDev) \wedge sender \in ran(appKey) \wedge sender \in ran(netKey)} \quad (1)$$

5.1.0.3 Second Refinement: machineClassA Refines joiningMachine.

defines the second refinement where we add, respectively, to this machine ten other events so that we can detail the Uplink and Downlink transmission of this class. As shown in Fig. 5, we add to contextClassA three sets CONNEC-TIVITY, CLASSES and CHANNELS that define respectively the state of the object (connected or disconnected), the class to which it belongs and the channel used for transmission. Figure 4 presents the additional variables described by the clause of the invariants: **@inv1/2:** to describe the state of each device; **@inv3/4:** which class belongs the device; **@inv5..8:** channel used whether uplink or down-link transmission; **@inv9..11:** Boolean invariants to know which transmission is launches; **@inv12/13:** Boolean invariants to know which reception window is open; **@inv14:** an object cannot have two types of transmission at the same time; **@inv15/17..19:** used for the incrementing time; **@inv16:** The device cannot have two Downlinks RX1 and RX2 at the same time; **@inv20:** boolean variable refers to the start of sending data from the gateway to the platform.

```
inv0:   deviceIdentifier ⊆ data
inv1:   NetworkKey ⊆ data
inv2:   applicationKey ⊆ data
inv3:   dataDevice ⊆ data
inv4:     data  =  dataDevice ∪ deviceIdentifier ∪
          NetworkKey ∪ applicationKey
inv5:   idDev ∈ deviceIdentifier ↣ device
inv6:   appKey ∈ applicationKey ↣ device
inv7:   netKey ∈ NetworkKey ↔ device
inv8:   idDevToGtw ∈ deviceIdentifier ↠ gateway
inv9:   netKeyToGtw ∈ NetworkKey ↔ gateway
inv10:  appKeyToGtw ∈ applicationKey ↠ gateway
inv11:  idDevToPlt ∈ deviceIdentifier ↠ platform
inv12:  appKeyToPlt ∈ applicationKey ↠ platform
inv13:  netKeyToPlt ∈ NetworkKey ↔ platform
inv14:  weight ∈ device → N
inv15:  pltKey ∈ NetworkKey ↣ platform
inv16:  idReceiver ∈ deviceIdentifier ↠ gateway
```

```
addIdToDevice (ordinary) ≙

any
      sender
      uiSender
where
      grd1:   sender ∈ device ∧ sender ∉
              ran(idDev)
      grd2:   uiSender ∈ deviceIdentifier ∧
              uiSender ∉ dom(idDev)
then
      act1: idDev(uiSender) := sender
end
```

Fig. 4. joiningMachine.

```
CONTEXT  contextClassA
EXTENDS  joiningContext
SETS
     CONNECTIVITY
     CLASSES
     CHANNELS
CONSTANTS
     delayRX1
     delayRX2
     CLASS_A
     CLASS_B
     CLASS_C
     connectedDevice
     disconnectedDevice
     RX2Channel
     RX1Channel
     RX3Channel
AXIOMS
     axm1:  partition(CLASSES, {CLASS_A}, {CLASS_B}, {CLASS_C})
     axm2:  partition(CONNECTIVITY, {disconnectedDevice}, {connectedDevice})
     axm3:  partition(CHANNELS, {RX1Channel}, {RX2Channel}, {RX3Channel})
     axm4:  delayRX1 ∈ N
     axm5:  delayRX2 ∈ N
END
```

Fig. 5. contextClassA

Figure 6 presents the refined event *dataFromDevToGtwA* where we add some conditions: Initially, a device must be in standby state (**@grd10**). It must wake up to transfer its data (**@act5**) in case of Uplink transmission (**@grd11**). After that, it must choose a channel to complete the transmission (**@act6**). After that, the device must go into sleep mode which is presented by *sleepDevice* event. While sending and receiving data between the gateway and the platform, the device remains in sleep mode until a specific delayRX1 if there is a Downlink in the first RX1 window, or adding another delayRX2 if there is a Downlink in the second RX2 window. This is represented by the adding of the time incrementation in both of the event *dataFromGtwToPltA* and the event *dataFromPltToGtwA* (Fig. 7). Figure 8, 9 presents the RX1 downlink transmission. The same concept done for the RX2 downlink transmission case.

```
datafromDevToGtwA (ordinary) ≙
datafromDevToGtw

any
     .....
     chnl
where
     ...:
     grd10:    deviceConnectivity(sender)     =
          disconnectedDevice
     grd11:  thereIsAnUplinkToSend(sender) =
          TRUE
     grd12:  chnl ∈ channel
     grd13:  deviceClass(sender) = CLASS_A
then
     ...:
     act5:    deviceConnectivity(sender)     :=
          connectedDevice
     act6: UplinkChannel(sender) := chnl
end
```

```
sleepDevice (ordinary) ≙

any
     sender
where
     grd1:  sender ∈ device
     grd2:  thereIsAnUplinkToSend(sender) =
          TRUE
     grd3:    deviceConnectivity(sender)     =
          connectedDevice
     grd4:  deviceClass(sender) = CLASS_A
     grd5:  startGtwToPlt(sender) = FALSE
then
     act1:  thereIsAnUplinkToSend(sender) :=
          FALSE
     act2:    deviceConnectivity(sender)     :=
          disconnectedDevice
     act3: startGtwToPlt(sender) := TRUE
end
```

Fig. 6. machineClassA part1 of events.

```
datafromGtwToPltA (ordinary) ≙
datafromGtwToPlt

any
      .....
      sender
where
      ...:
      grd13:  sender ∈ device
      grd14:  thereIsAnUplinkToSend(sender) =
              FALSE
      grd15:    deviceConnectivity(sender)    =
              disconnectedDevice
      grd16:  time ≤ delayRX1_1 + 1
      grd17:  deviceClass(sender) = CLASS_A
      grd18:  startGtwToPlt(sender) = TRUE
then  grd19:  gtw ∈ ran(dataGtw)
      ...:
      act5:  startGtwToPlt(sender) := FALSE
      act6:  time := time + 1
end
```

```
datafromPltToGtwA (ordinary) ≙
datafromPltToGtw

any
      ......
      receiver
where
      ...:
      grd8:  receiver ∈ device
      grd9:    deviceConnectivity(receiver)    =
             disconnectedDevice
      grd10: thereIsAnUplinkToSend(receiver) =
             FALSE
      grd11: time ≤ delayRX1
      grd12:        deviceClass(receiver)      =
             CLASS_A
then
      ...:
      act3: time := time + 1
end
```

Fig. 7. machineClassA part2 of events.

5.1.0.4 Third Refinement: machineClassB Refines machineClassA. In this refinement, we keep the same Uplink Transmission as class A. But we add six other events to present the periodic Downlink transmission from the gateway to the end devices according to B class. In this machine, we extend the same Uplink events but we add new Downlink transmission events. We add to the context *contextClassB* five constants as shown in 'Fig. 10': beaconPeriod, beaconGuard, beaconReserved, beaconWindow and pingSlot. The purpose of these constants is represented in the AXIOMS clause as follows: all constants are of type integer (**@axm1,4..7**). Such that beaconPeriod defines the sum of beaconGuard, beaconReserved and beaconWindow(**@axm3**). However, we add six events to *machineClassB* machine: First event *moveToClassB* (Fig. 10), refers to the moving from class A to class B. Figure 11, Fig. 12 and Fig. 13 describe

```
datafromGtwToDevA (ordinary) ≙
datafromGtwToDev

any
      .....
where
      ...:
      grd14:  time ≤ delayRX1
      grd15:  thereIsAnUplinkToSend(receiver) = FALSE
      grd16:  thereIsAnRX1Downlink(receiver) = TRUE
      grd17:        deviceConnectivity(receiver)        =
              disconnectedDevice
      grd18:  deviceClass(receiver) = CLASS_A
then
      ...:
      act3: deviceConnectivity(receiver) := connectedDevice
end
```

Fig. 8. datafromGtwToDevA event.

```
rx1DownlinkA (ordinary) ≘

any
        receiver
        chnl
        ui
        rcvDevId
        gtw
where
        grd1:  receiver ∈ device
        grd2:  time ≤ delayRX1
        grd3:     thereIsAnUplinkToSend(receiver)    =
               FALSE
        grd4:     thereIsAnRX1Downlink(receiver)    =
               TRUE
        grd5:        deviceConnectivity(receiver)    =
               connectedDevice
        grd6:     rcvDevId   ∈   deviceIdentifier  ∧
               rcvDevId ∈ dom(idReceiver)
        grd7:  ui ⊂ dom(idDev)
        grd8:  ui = rcvDevId
        grd9:  idDev(rcvDevId) = receiver
        grd10: gtw ∈ ran(idReceiver)
        grd11:  receiver ∈ ran(idDev) ∧ receiver ∉
               ran(feedbackDev)
        grd12: chnl ∈ channel
        grd13: deviceClass(receiver) = CLASS_A
then
        act1: rx1_channel(receiver) := chnl
        act2: openRX1_window(receiver) := TRUE
end
```

```
endRX1DownlinkTransmissionA (ordinary) ≘

any
        receiver
where
        grd1:  receiver ∈ device
        grd2: thereIsAnUplinkToSend(receiver) =
               FALSE
        grd3: thereIsAnRX1Downlink(receiver) =
               TRUE
        grd4:     deviceConnectivity(receiver)    =
               connectedDevice
        grd5:        openRX1_window(receiver)    =
               TRUE
        grd6:          deviceClass(receiver)    =
               CLASS_A
then
        act1: thereIsAnRX1Downlink(receiver) :=
               FALSE
        act2:  openRX1_window(receiver)    :=
               FALSE
        act3:  deviceConnectivity(receiver)    :=
               disconnectedDevice
end
```

Fig. 9. machineClassA part3 of events.

the beacon period, which is divided into four periods: the beacon guard time (constant period where the total beacon period is protected by it), the beacon reserved time (where the gateway broadcasts the beacon), the ping slot period (differs from one device to another) and the ping reception slots (the downlink reception is performed periodically until the end of the time).

```
inv1:  time2 ∈ N
inv2:  time3 ∈ N
inv3:  beacon ∈ gateway ⤖ device
inv4:  pngOff ∈ device → N
inv5:  pingReception ∈ device → N
inv6:  deviceConnectivity2 ∈ device → connectivity
inv7:  deviceClassB ∈ device ⤗ class
inv8:  openWindow ∈ device → BOOL
inv9:  time4 ∈ N
inv10: guardEnd ∈ device → BOOL
inv11: startBeaconB ∈ gateway → BOOL
inv12: offsetEnd ∈ device → BOOL
inv13: receptionEnd ∈ device → BOOL
inv14: reservedEnd ∈ device → BOOL
inv15: extraDownlink ∈ device → BOOL
inv16: time22 ∈ N
```

```
moveToClassB (ordinary) ≘
datafromPltToGtw

any
        .....
        receiver
where
        ...:
        grd8:  receiver ∈ device ∧ receiver ∈
               dom(deviceClassB)
        grd9:     deviceClassB(receiver)    =
               CLASS_B
        grd10:       startBeaconB(gtw)    =
               FALSE
        grd11:
               deviceConnectivity2(receiver) =
               disconnectedDevice
then
        ...:
        act3: startBeaconB(gtw) := TRUE
end
```

Fig. 10. machineClassB part 1.

```
beaconGuardPeriodB (ordinary) ≙

any
        gtw
        receiver
        rcvDevId
where
        grd1:  gtw ∈ gateway
        grd2:  gtw ∈ ran(idReceiver)
        grd3:  receiver ∈ device ∧ receiver ∈
               dom(deviceClassB)
        grd4:  receiver ∉ ran(feedbackDev)
        grd5:  deviceConnectivity2(receiver) =
               disconnectedDevice
        grd6:  deviceClassB(receiver)       =
               CLASS_B
        grd7:  time2 ≤ beaconGuard
        grd8:  guardEnd(receiver) = FALSE
        grd9:  startBeaconB(gtw) = TRUE
        grd10: rcvDevId ∈ deviceIdentifier ∧
               rcvDevId ∈ dom(idReceiver)
        grd11: idDev(rcvDevId) = receiver
then
        act1: time2 := time2 + 1
        act2: deviceConnectivity2(receiver) :=
              connectedDevice
        act3: startBeaconB(gtw) := FALSE
        act4: guardEnd(receiver) := TRUE
end
```

```
beaconReservedPeriodB (ordinary) ≙

any
        gtw
        receiver
        rcvDevId
where
        grd1:  gtw ∈ gateway
        grd2:  receiver ∈ device ∧ receiver ∈
               dom(deviceClassB)
        grd3:  deviceConnectivity2(receiver)  =
               connectedDevice
        grd4:  deviceClassB(receiver) = CLASS_B
        grd5:  time22 ≤ beaconReserved
        grd6:  reservedEnd(receiver) = FALSE
        grd7:  guardEnd(receiver) = TRUE
        grd8:  startBeaconB(gtw) = FALSE
        grd10: rcvDevId ∈ deviceIdentifier ∧
               rcvDevId ∈ dom(idReceiver)
        grd11: idDev(rcvDevId) = receiver
then
        act1: time22 := time22 + 1
        act2: deviceConnectivity2(receiver)  :=
              disconnectedDevice
        act3: beacon(gtw) := receiver
        act4: startBeaconB(gtw) := FALSE
        act5: reservedEnd(receiver) := TRUE
end
```

Fig. 11. machineClassB part2 of events.

5.1.0.5 **Fourth Refinement:** The machineClassC refines the machineClassB. In this refinement, we add some modifications to the uplink and downlink transmissions. However, due to space limitation, we do not explain the whole code, we only introduce the specificity of class C compared to other classes. Class C continuously listens for a downlink transmission on the RX2 window after each uplink transmission. This is presented by the notion of each device connectivity must be *connectedDevice*.

```
pingOffsetPeriodB (ordinary) ≙

any
        receiver
        rcvDevId
        gtw
        ui
where
        grd1:  receiver ∈ device ∧ receiver ∈
               dom(deviceClassB)
        grd2:  deviceConnectivity2(receiver)  =
               disconnectedDevice
        grd3:  time3 ≤ pngOff(receiver)
        grd4:  deviceClassB(receiver)       =
               CLASS_B
        grd5:  thereIsAnUplinkToSend(receiver) =
               FALSE
        grd6:  reservedEnd(receiver) = TRUE
        grd7:  offsetEnd(receiver) = FALSE
        grd8:  guardEnd(receiver) = TRUE
        grd9:  receiver ∈ ran(idDev) ∧ receiver ∉
               ran(feedbackDev)
        grd10: rcvDevId ∈ deviceIdentifier ∧
               rcvDevId ∈ dom(idReceiver)
        grd11: ui ∈ dom(idDev)
        grd12: ui = rcvDevId
        grd13: idDev(rcvDevId) = receiver
        grd14: gtw ∈ ran(idReceiver)
then
        act1: time3 := time3 + pingSlot
        act2: offsetEnd(receiver) := TRUE
end
```

```
pingReceptionSlotsB (ordinary) ≙
datafromGtwToDev

any
        .....
where   ...:
        grd14: receiver ∈ dom(deviceClassB)
        grd15: deviceConnectivity2(receiver)  =
               disconnectedDevice
        grd16: thereIsAnUplinkToSend(receiver) =
               FALSE
        grd17: extraDownlink(receiver) = TRUE
        grd18: deviceClassB(receiver)       =
               CLASS_B
        grd19: time4 ≤ pingReception(receiver)
        grd20: openWindow(receiver) = FALSE
        grd21: guardEnd(receiver) = TRUE
        grd22: reservedEnd(receiver) = TRUE
        grd23: offsetEnd(receiver) = TRUE
        grd24: receptionEnd(receiver) = FALSE
then
        ...:
        act3: time4 := time4 + pingSlot
        act4: deviceConnectivity2(receiver)  :=
              connectedDevice
        act5: openWindow(receiver) := TRUE
        act6: receptionEnd(receiver) := TRUE
end
```

Fig. 12. machineClassB part3 of events.

---

endBeaconPeriod (ordinary) $\hat{=}$

any
    receiver
where
    grd1: $receiver \in device \wedge receiver \in dom(deviceClassB)$
    grd2: $deviceConnectivity2(receiver) = connectedDevice$
    grd3: $thereIsAnUplinkToSend(receiver) = FALSE$
    grd4: $extraDownlink(receiver) = TRUE$
    grd5: $deviceClassB(receiver) = CLASS\_B$
    grd6: $openWindow(receiver) = TRUE$
    grd7: $guardEnd(receiver) = TRUE$
    grd8: $reservedEnd(receiver) = TRUE$
    grd9: $offsetEnd(receiver) = TRUE$
    grd10: $receptionEnd(receiver) = TRUE$
then
    act1: $deviceConnectivity2(receiver) := disconnectedDevice$
    act2: $openWindow(receiver) := FALSE$
    act3: $extraDownlink(receiver) := FALSE$
end

Fig. 13. endBeaconPeriod event.

5.2 Verification

The model obtained by the development process presents the different contexts and machines. Typically, contexts contain sets to express the structure or behavior of an IoT application. While machines contain invariants that must be proved. This means that each initial state (i.e., initialization) must satisfies the invariant. This is the case as shown in Fig. 14 where all invariants have been proven in all machines level.

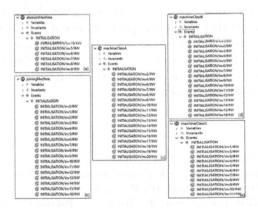

Fig. 14. Initialisation proof.

In the initialization event, we associate all events with the empty set, except those corresponding to the system state.

Our refinement model generate 259 proof obligations. As described in the Fig. 15. Some of these are discharged automatically (175 OPs) using the provers associated to Rodin platform. The others are discharged manually (39 OPs). While the rest still undischarged (45 OPs). The obligations of the undischarged proofs cannot be discharged because of the change of state that can occur during the transmission of the data (Fig. 16).

Element Name	Total	Auto	Man.	Rev.	Und.
IoTModelingApp	259	175	39	0	45
abstractContext	0	0	0	0	0
contextClassA	0	0	0	0	0
contextClassB	0	0	0	0	0
joiningContext	0	0	0	0	0
abstractMachine	11	10	1	0	0
joiningMachine	26	23	3	0	0
machineClassA	90	61	15	0	14
machineClassB	76	42	17	0	17
machineClassC	56	39	3	0	14

Fig. 15. Review of proof obligations.

Fig. 16. inv2 proof obligations.

6   Conclusion and Future Work

In this paper, we focus on modeling and verification of an IoT model application based on LoRaWAN protocol, using Event-B method. The refinement strategy partitions all requirements into 5 levels of refinement. The model presented in this paper has been proven by construction using the Rodin Prover. In the case of the number of pages that we cannot pass, we do not put the total code that we have made but we present in this paper as much as possible of the code with its description. This model can be a starting point for modeling an IoT application based on LoRaWAN communication. Furthermore, it can be improved by adding more details and more requirements.

References

1. Al-Qaseemi, S.A., Almulhim, H.A., Almulhim, M.F., Chaudhry, S.R.: IoT architecture challenges and issues: lack of standardization. In: 2016 Future Technologies Conference (FTC), pp. 731–738. IEEE (2016)
2. Ayoub, W., Samhat, A.E., Nouvel, F., Mroue, M., Prévotet, J.C.: Internet of mobile things: LoRaWAN, DASH7, and NB-IoT in LPWANs standards and supported mobility. IEEE Commun. Surv. Tutorials **21**(2), 1561–1581 (2018)
3. Aziz, B.: A formal model and analysis of an IoT protocol. Ad Hoc Netw. **36**, 49–57 (2016)
4. Cansell, D., Méry, D.: The event-B modelling method: concepts and case studies. In: Bjørner, D., Henson, M.C. (eds.) Logics of Specification Languages. MTC-SAES, pp. 47–152. Springer, Heidelberg (2008). https://doi.org/10.1007/978-3-540-74107-7_3

5. Chen, X., Li, A., Zeng, X., Guo, W., Huang, G.: Runtime model based approach to IoT application development. Front. Comp. Sci. **9**(4), 540–553 (2015)
6. Ciccozzi, F., Spalazzese, R.: MDE4IoT: supporting the internet of things with model-driven engineering. In: IDC 2016. SCI, vol. 678, pp. 67–76. Springer, Cham (2017). https://doi.org/10.1007/978-3-319-48829-5_7
7. Eldefrawy, M., Butun, I., Pereira, N., Gidlund, M.: Formal security analysis of lorawan. Comput. Netw. **148**, 328–339 (2019)
8. Elhadi, S., Marzak, A., Sael, N.: Operating models of network protocols IoT: short-range protocols. In: 2020 International Symposium on Advanced Electrical and Communication Technologies (ISAECT), pp. 1–6. IEEE (2020)
9. Elsayed, E.K., Diab, L., Ibrahim, A.A.: Formal verification of an efficient architecture to enhance the security in IoT
10. Ertürk, M.A., Aydın, M.A., Büyükakkaşlar, M.T., Evirgen, H.: A survey on lorawan architecture, protocol and technologies. Future Internet **11**(10), 216 (2019)
11. Gawanmeh, A.: Embedding and verification of zigbee protocol stack in event-b. Procedia Comput. Sci. **5**, 736–741 (2011)
12. Jarrar, A., Gadi, T., Balouki, Y.: Modeling the internet of things system using complex adaptive system concepts. In: Proceedings of the 2nd International Conference on Computing and Wireless Communication Systems, pp. 1–6 (2017)
13. Marir, S., Belala, F., Hameurlain, N.: A formal model for interaction specification and analysis in IoT applications. In: Abdelwahed, E.H., Bellatreche, L., Golfarelli, M., Méry, D., Ordonez, C. (eds.) MEDI 2018. LNCS, vol. 11163, pp. 371–384. Springer, Cham (2018). https://doi.org/10.1007/978-3-030-00856-7_25
14. Naoui, S., Elhdhili, M.E., Azouz Saidane, L.: Novel enhanced lorawan framework for smart home remote control security. Wireless Pers. Commun. **110**(4), 2109–2130 (2020)
15. Navani, D., Jain, S., Nehra, M.S.: The internet of things (IoT): a study of architectural elements. In: 2017 13th International Conference on Signal-Image Technology & Internet-Based Systems (SITIS), pp. 473–478. IEEE (2017)
16. Pek, E., Bogunovic, N.: Formal verification of logical link control and adaptation protocol. In: Proceedings of the 12th IEEE Mediterranean Electrotechnical Conference (IEEE Cat. No. 04CH37521), vol. 2, pp. 583–586. IEEE (2004)
17. Sharma, C., Gondhi, N.K.: Communication protocol stack for constrained IoT systems. In: 2018 3rd International Conference on Internet of Things: Smart Innovation and Usages (IoT-SIU), pp. 1–6. IEEE (2018)
18. Vermesan, O., Friess, P.: Internet of things: converging technologies for smart environments and integrated ecosystems. River publishers (2013)
19. You, I., Kwon, S., Choudhary, G., Sharma, V., Seo, J.T.: An enhanced lorawan security protocol for privacy preservation in IoT with a case study on a smart factory-enabled parking system. Sensors **18**(6), 1888 (2018)

Machine Learning and IoT for Stress Detection and Monitoring

Sami Hadhri[1](✉) (iD), Mondher Hadiji[1](✉) (iD), and Walid Labidi[2](✉)

[1] Higher Institute of Technological Studies Sfax, Sfax, Tunisia
hadhri.sami@gmail.com, mondherhadiji@gmail.com
[2] Faculty of Sciences Sfax, Sfax, Tunisia
walid.labidi001@gmail.com

Abstract. In this paper, we propose a Machine Learning and IoT based system for the detection and monitoring of patient stress. This system consists of a medical kit that uses sensors placed on top of the patient's hand to measure oxygen saturation, heart rate, and galvanic skin response before sending the data to the Firebase server. Five Machine Learning algorithms (Logistic Regression, K-Nearest Neighbors, Support Vector Machine, Decision Tree, and Random Forest) were implemented using holdout and K-fold cross-validation on a Raspberry board installed in the doctor's office. Our system can make predictions with the Random Forest classifier with a value that reaches 87%.

Keywords: IoT · Stress monitoring · Pulse oximetry · Heart rate · Machine Learning

1 Introduction

Stress is typically defined as a disturbance in one's normal psychological equilibrium. It is a physical or mental pressure that might occur when a person is unable to balance the demands placed on him with his ability to cope. This puts a strain on mental health and leads to stress [1].

In addition, the whole world is experiencing an unprecedented health crisis because of COVID-19. This can affect people physically, but also psychologically. Governments across the world have taken serious measures to contain this pandemic, including confinement, movement restrictions, and the closing of retail and leisure areas. In result, many people experience many psychological disorders like anxiety, depression and stress.

During this epidemic, the world saw a surge in e-health when the healthcare system was utterly disrupted. Indeed, for the recent years, health has been the ideal playground for new technologies: teleconsultations, connected objects, and robots infiltrating hospitals. As evidence, more than 14 million connected watches were sold around the world in the first quarter of 2020, a 12% increase over the same period in 2019. Furthermore, connected healthcare devices represent a third of the IoT (Internet of Things) market, and mobile health apps have doubled in popularity [2].

C. Bădică et al. (Eds.): ICCCI 2022, CCIS 1653, pp. 542–553, 2022.
https://doi.org/10.1007/978-3-031-16210-7_44

IoT designates all the infrastructures and technologies put in place to operate various objects via an Internet connection. People can access or control these objects remotely using a computer, smartphone, or tablet to simplify their daily lives, ensure their safety, or conserve energy.

IoT is used in various fields, including modern health care (or IoMT - The Internet of Medical Things), to provide a solution to meet the evolving needs of users, which have been amplified by the health crisis: heart attack prevention and alert, support for patients with chronic diseases, detection of stress, …

In fact, the IoT can help identify the stress level of patients in advance. This could be achievable by collecting data and exploit it with Machine Learning (ML) classification algorithms, allowing patients' stress states to be detected and communicated to doctors in real-time.

This article is organized as follows: Sect. 2 deals with related work carried out in the literature to detect the stress state by presenting the employed technological solutions. Section 3 presents the materials and methods used to develop our solution. Section 4 explores the proposed system by splitting it into interconnected sub-layers. Results and Discussion are presented in Sect. 5. Finally, Sect. 6 concludes this article.

2 Related Work

A variety of methods can be used to classify and recognize the stress state. The first approach is traditional statistical and based on surveys. Harville et al. analyzed data from 1,587 pregnant women and used questionnaires and interviews to measure perceived stress and pregnancy-specific anxiety. They used multiple correlations and regressions to describe the relationship between stress measures [3].

In [4], authors examined the characteristics and correlates of posttraumatic stress symptoms in a group of young adult cancer survivors. Data on socio-demographic and illness information, as well as posttraumatic information, was collected using self-reported questionnaires.

Another approach is based on the biological signals' measurements retrieved from the sensors on which ML algorithms are applied. Smets et al. [5] proposed a study to examine different ML algorithms for measuring stress in a controlled environment based on physiological responses. During a laboratory stress test, the electrocardiogram (ECG), galvanic skin response (GSR), temperature, and respiration were all recorded. A generic and personal approach were used to investigate 6 ML algorithms. The results demonstrate that personalized Dynamic Bayesian Networks and generalized Support Vector Machine produce the best classification results with respectively 84% and 82%.

Garg et al. proposed different ML models for individuals stress detection using the WESAD Dataset [6]. Sensor data including ECG, body temperature (TEMP), respiration (RESP), electromyogram (EMG), and electrodermal activity (EDA) are collected. They used ML algorithms such as K-Nearest Neighbors, Linear Discriminant Analysis, Random Forest, AdaBoost and Support Vector Machine to generate and compare F1-score and accuracy for the 3 classes (Neutral, Stress and Fun) and the binary classes (Stress vs Without Stress). The Random Forest model beat the other models in binary and 3 classes classification, with F1-scores of 83% and 65%, respectively.

The last approach focuses on body users' features and interactions. In many studies, video sequences of conversations are used to automatically detect blinks' eyes [7]. It consists of extracting an ocular region of interest from the face followed by the supervised descent method [8]. Using it as an input to a classifier, the different parts of the eye are also segmented. Finally, the system measures the variation in the opening of the eyelid to detect blinking.

In [9], the author proposed a user-tailored, game-based emotion detection process. It is based on a trained Neural Network capable of detecting the emotional states of boredom and stress of a given subject. The automated process relies on computer vision and remote photoplethysmography (rPPG) to capture user data using an ordinary camera.

Pepa et al. conducted a study under laboratory conditions to identify stress in 62 computer users [10]. The data was obtained using a specifically created online program to deduce stress state by asking each subject to complete eight computer tasks under various stress situations. The designed system was able to successfully detect three classes of stress level using keyboard data (76% accuracy) and mouse data using Multiple Instance Learning (MIL) and Random Forest classification (63% accuracy).

In another study [11], the scientists presented StayActive, a system that analyzes user activity via their smartphone to detect the risk of stress. This service recommends and shows a variety of "just in time" relaxation activities, allowing users to complete and solve daily tasks and problems at work. Data on users' phone usage, such as sleep patterns, social interactions, and physical activity was collected. Then, StayActive assign a weighting factor to each of these 3 dimensions of well-being based on the user's personal perception to build a stress detection system. Finally, the system was evaluated based on a personalized score to calculate stress level.

Aigrain et al. extracted physical features reflecting the state of stress in a population of 44 people from videos, and then assigned annotations to them [12]. They derived behavioral variables like self-touch, hand, and head movements from the video data. A similar procedure was used in [13], where people were asked to watch their recorded videos. The aspects of body language (body movement and facial features) were then extracted using a software that gave a mental arithmetic test with 6 stages of increasing difficulty.

3 Materials and Methods

3.1 Data Collection

It was collected by a doctor from 25 volunteered of his patients, 11 men and 14 women (mean age $= 45 \pm 10$ years). The patients' measurements were divided into 2 categories: Stressed and No Stressed. Experiments were conducted in the doctor's office using the realized kit. Two sensors were used to measure oxygen saturation, heart rate, and electrodermal activity. We used our own Dataset since the other existing Datasets in the stress field do not use the 3 biological measurements recommended by the doctor.

Table 1. Part of the dataset

spo2	bpm	sweat	status
78	121	269	0
95	77	207	1
87	94	382	0
84	76	235	1
99	68	141	1

Table 1 shows a sample of our Dataset. It has a well-defined structure with 1072 rows and 4 columns along with the column headers, each one representing an attribute or feature (spo2, bpm & sweat) except the last one which represents stress state (status): 1 if stressed, 0 if not. Based on his knowledge, the doctor determined the stress condition from the measurements taken on his patients (588 Stressed instances and 484 No Stressed instances).

3.2 Features Extraction

The complete list of features is reported in this table:

Table 2. Features descriptive list

N°	Feature	Abb.	Sensor	Ref.
1	The amount of oxygen-carrying hemoglobin in the blood compared to non-oxygen carrying	spo2	MAX30100	[14]
2	The number of heart beats per minute	bpm	MAX30100	
3	The property of the human body that causes continuous variation in the skin's electrical characteristics	sweat	GSR	[15]

Before modelling, the Dataset was analyzed to detect outliers and missing values. After check, a total of 19 instances were removed. Therefore, our study was conducted using the remaining Dataset of 1053 instances with 3 different extracted features and 1 binary target (576 Stressed and 477 No Stressed). Finally, to prevent algorithms from getting biased, we normalized and scaled data features.

3.3 Analysis Methods

ML is a subdomain of Artificial Intelligence (AI) that allows a system to learn from data not through explicit programming. Nevertheless, ML is not a simple process. As algorithms ingest training data, it becomes possible to create more accurate models based on that data. However, when providing input data to a model, it would be able to predict the output result. ML techniques are needed to improve the predictive model accuracy. Depending on the nature of the problem being solved, there are different approaches that vary depending on the data type and volume namely supervised, unsupervised and reinforcement.

In this work, we selected the supervised learning approach which typically begins with a well-defined Dataset and some understanding of how that data is classified. This data includes features associated with labels that define their meaning. The supervised ML can be subdivided into 2 types:

- **Classification:** the output variable is a category.
- **Regression:** the output variable is a specific value.

Classification is a type of supervised learning allowing to classify new data in one of the existing classes so that it is closer in the sense of a similarity criterion to one class than to others. Generally, we go through a first so-called learning stage where it is a question of learning a classification rule from annotated data to predict the classes of new unknown data.

In fact, detecting the stress from clinical signals is a typical classification task of discriminating data, in a supervised way. Two classes are available for classification purposes. Class '0' represents No Stressed state and class '1' represents Stressed state.

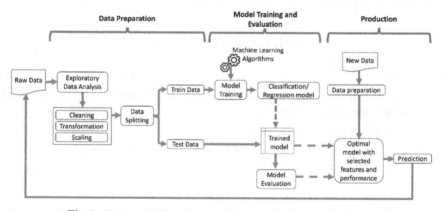

Fig. 1. Schematic flow diagram of stress detection methodology

In this paper, we used ML classification to identify patients' stress states and anticipate it in advance, allowing to prevent substantial damage to their lives before it occurs. Figure 1 shows the schematic flow diagram of stress detection methodology: this includes a full Dataset, preprocessing, features extraction and applying 5 ML algorithms (Logistic Regression, K-Nearest Neighbors, Support Vector Machine, Decision Tree, and Random Forest) and comparing their performance parameters. The extracted features, detailed above, are preprocessed according to suitability to the 5 classification algorithms:

Logistic Regression (LR). It is a method of statistical analysis to predict a dependent binary outcome by analyzing the relationship between one or more existing independent variables. It is a generalized linear model using a logistic function as a link function. It also makes it possible to predict the probability that an event will happen (value of 1) or not (value of 0) from the optimization of the regression coefficients.

This result always varies between 0 and 1. When the predicted value is above a threshold, the event is likely to occur, while when this value is below the same threshold, it is not. [16].

K-Nearest Neighbors (K-NN). It is a nonparametric method in which the model stores observations from the training set for test set classification. Qualified as lazy learning (it learns nothing during the learning phase), it makes it possible to predict the class of a new input data by searching for its K nearest neighbors (using the Euclidean distance, or others) and will choose the neighboring majority class. [17].

Support Vector Machine (SVM). It is a linear classifier algorithm allowing to find the border between different data categories each occupying a different region of the plan. The objective is to properly classify a new point in the appropriate category. To find this border, it is necessary to provide training data from which SVM will estimate his most plausible position. [18].

Decision Tree (DT). This is a decision support or data mining classifier tool that allows to represent a set of choices in the graphical form of a tree. It is one of the most popular supervised learning methods for data classification problems. Concretely, a decision tree models a hierarchy of tests to predict an outcome. [19].

Random Forest (RF). This classifier generates numerous unique decision trees, thus forming a forest. Considered among the most accurate learning algorithms, RF reduces the variance observed in DT. This algorithm attempts to find out best feature from all the features at random. [20].

3.4 Models Evaluation and Performance Measures

After the data preprocessing and before modeling, it is important to have a strategy for evaluating our models that doesn't involve training data. In our study, for every ML algorithm, multiple models were trained depending on the used method of dividing the Dataset:

- The first one using a "holdout" Dataset with the scikit-learn Python library's train_test_split() method to split the Dataset into training (80%) and test (20%) sets for the experiments.
- The second one performs K-fold cross-validation. K refers to the number of groups that a given data sample is to be split into. One of the groups is used as the test set and the rest are used as the training set. Then the process is repeated until each unique group has been used as the test set. We used 3-fold, 5-fold, 7-fold and 10-fold cross-validation by applying GridSearchCV() method.

As evaluation measures, we can choose between the precision and the F1-score. Precision represents the number of correctly classified instances among all samples while F1-score is defined as the harmonic mean of precision, which indicates the reliability of results in each class, and recall, which is a measure of completeness. Precision and recall were calculated independently for each class and then averaged to obtain the final F1-score.

Since our Dataset is balanced (576 Stressed and 477 No Stressed), the F1-score is not the best evaluation metric but rather the accuracy which will be used as the main evaluation metric.

4   Design and Implementation

The block diagram of the proposed solution is described in this section. The system is made up of two blocks, as shown in Fig. 2. The first block is the Service Layer which is represented by a mobile application interacting with the cloud. While the second, named Processing Layer, is made up of two sub-layers, one for data collecting and the other for the AI system.

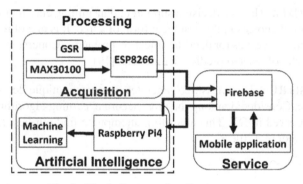

Fig. 2. Block diagram of realized prototype

4.1   Acquisition Layer

This layer consists of an ESP8266 board (NodeMCU) connected to a GSR sensor to measure the galvanic skin response through an analog communication and to a MAX30100 sensor to detect pulse oximetry and heart rate signals. A strong emotion such as stress can generate a nervous stimulus which will cause sweat secreted by the sudoriferous glands and makes the heart beats faster [21]. Every second, the sensors' measurements are transmitted to the cloud.

4.2   Service Layer

The Service Layer is composed of a mobile application interacting with the Firebase cloud:

- The user of the mobile application (doctor or patient) can consult in real time the heart rate, the oxygen saturation and the galvanic skin response once authenticated. The mobile application also includes a comprehensive dashboard that displays the history of these physiological measurements in the form of curves. The doctor can also consult the patient's stress status.
- Firebase offers a NoSQL (Not Only SQL) database called Realtime Database, used in our solution to store the values measured by the MAX30100 and GSR sensors and sent by the ESP8266 board.

Every second, the mobile app retrieves data from Firebase service allowing users to view the physiological measurements in real-time. Similarly, the Raspberry Pi board (RPi) retrieves the values saved in the cloud in real-time with each update.

4.3 AI Layer

This layer is made up of a RPi 4 board with embedded ML algorithms (Fig. 3). The RPi 4 model was chosen because of its AI capabilities and processing capacity (1.5GHz CPU, 8GB RAM) in combination with a tiny form factor and low energy requirements, making it a perfect choice for this project.

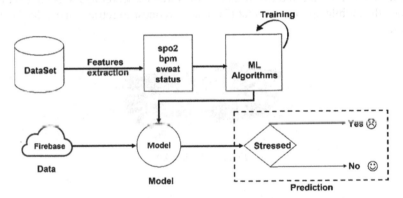

Fig. 3. Stress detection system based on ML techniques

The ML process starts with features extraction from Dataset (spo2, bpm, sweat, status) and then applying five ML algorithms. Models are generated after the training phase. Thenceforth, there are supplied with input data from the Firebase server representing the patient's physiological measurements to predict his stress state.

5   Results and Discussion

Figure 4 illustrates the scenario adopted by the proposed solution:

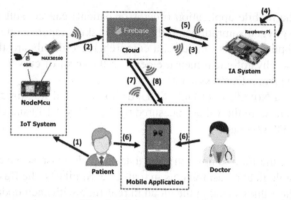

Fig. 4. Illustrative scenario

First, (1) the patient wears the medical kit (Fig. 5) composed of NodeMCU and sensors in the upper part of his hand (weight ≈ 250 g, cost ≈ 180 $ and powered by a small size power bank with a power of 20000 MAh). Then, (2) this kit measures and sends the values retrieved from the sensors to the Firebase server.

After that (3) RPi retrieves the values from Firebase, (4) performs ML algorithms to deduce the stress state and (5) saves it in the Firebase server again. Next, (6) the user launches the mobile application that (7) sends a request to retrieve the values (8) from Firebase.

Fig. 5. Medical kit

The proposed work used the classification to predict patients' stress state based on their clinical data. In this study, 5 classifiers were implemented for the purpose of stress detection. For each one, multiple models were trained: holdout and cross-validation with 3-fold, 5-fold, 7-fold, and 10-fold respectively.

Hyperparameters are hugely important in getting good performance with models. They were tuned for the different algorithms to provide the best results. For LR threshold was set to 0.7 while in the K-NN algorithm, the optimum number of neighbors which has the best score is 5 (default value) or 7 (Fig. 6).

Concerning the SVM algorithm, the radial basis function kernel was used. DT best hyperparameters were gini method to measure the quality of a split and 9 as a max depth. Finally, for the RF classifier, minimum number of samples for splitting a node was set to 5 and the number of estimators was set to 50.

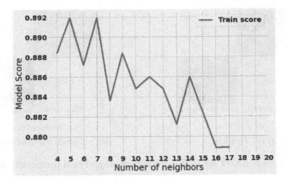

Fig. 6. K-NN score in function of neighbors' number

The performance of models (Table 3) was calculated with precision metric as evaluation measure as previously explained since the Dataset is balanced.

Table 3. Accuracies result on the 5-classification task

Classifier	Holdout	Cross-Validation			
		3-folds	5-folds	7-folds	10-folds
Logistic Regression	84.83	83.89	84.36	84.36	84.36
K-Nearest Neighbors	85.78	–	–	–	–
Support Vector Machine	86.83	85.31	85.31	85.31	84.83
Decision Tree	83.41	84.36	86.23	84.83	84.83
Random Forest	84.62	86.73	87.26	86.73	86.26

This table shows the performance of given classifiers. When all the classifiers mentioned above are employed and their performance is compared, it becomes apparent that the RF classifier reached the highest classification accuracy with 3-folds, 5-folds, 7-folds & 10-folds cross-validation with respectively 86.73%, 87.26%, 86.73% and 86.26% of accuracy. 87.26% is the best accuracy for all classifiers and all methods of dividing the Dataset (holdout or cross-validation).

Concluding from Table 2, with holdout method, the DT classifier had the overall worst performance, whereas SVM outperformed other ML models with 86.83% accuracy. We deduct that cross-validation has increased accuracy for only DT and RF classifiers and for other classifiers, holdout is more appropriate.

Confusion matrix for holdout using DT and 3-fold cross-validation using RF were plotted. From Fig. 7 (a), we observed that the DT classifier did not perform well. We noticed that the percentage of correctly predicted Stressed and No Stressed classes is only 35% and 47% respectively. However, it is evident from Fig. 7 (b), RF classifier yield better results with respectively 37% and 49% stressed and no stressed classes.

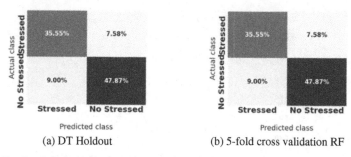

Fig. 7. Confusion matrix for worst prediction (a) and best prediction (b) scenarios

6   Conclusion and Future Work

In this paper, we have proposed a ML and IoT based system for the detection and monitoring of patient stress made up of 3 layers: acquisition, service and artificial intelligence. This low-cost system consists of 2 sensors (MAX30100, GSR) that measure the patient's physiological data and are connected to a NodeMCU board on the patient's arm. A RPi 4 installed in the doctor's office, retrieves the data that has already been saved in the cloud.

Five ML algorithms (LR, K-NN, SVM, DT, RF) were investigated using holdout and cross-validation with 3-fold, 5-fold, 7-fold, and 10-fold. Our system can make a reasonable prediction with RF classifier which reached the highest classification accuracy with a value of 87.26%.

The results are displayed on a dashboard with real-time and historical data, as well as the patient's stress level, through a developed mobile application.

This prototype is poised for more autonomy and scalability by using other components and technologies. Thus, many aspects of this solution still need to be improved, such as the detection of multiple stress categories (No Stressed, Low Stress, Medium Stress, High Stress, Acute Stress) rather than just 2 (Stressed, No Stressed) and the use of Deep Learning models such as Convolution Neural Networks (CNN) and Recurrent Neural Network (RNN) for stress detection.

References

1. Rizwan, M.F., Farhad, R., Mashuk, F., Islam, F., Imam, M.H.: Design of a biosignal based stress detection system using machine learning techniques. In: Proceedings of the International Conference on Robotics, Electrical and Signal Processing Techniques (ICREST) (2019)
2. www.pandasecurity.com/fr/mediacenter/mobile-news/technologie-sante
3. Harville, E.W., Savitz, D.A., Dole, N., Herring, A.H., Thorp, J.M.: Stress questionnaires and stress biomarkers during pregnancy. J. Women's Health **18**, 1425–1433 (2009)
4. Lee, Y.L., Santacroce, S.J.: Posttraumatic stress in long-term young adult survivors of childhood cancer: a questionnaire survey. Int. J. Nurs. Stud. **44**(8), 1406–1417 (2007)
5. Smets, E., et al.: Comparison of machine learning techniques for psychophysiological stress detection. In: Serino, S., Matic, A., Giakoumis, D., Lopez, G., Cipresso, P. (eds.) MindCare 2015. CCIS, vol. 604, pp. 13–22. Springer, Cham (2016). https://doi.org/10.1007/978-3-319-32270-4_2

6. Garg, P., Santhosh, J., Dengel, A., Ishimaru, S.: Stress detection by machine learning and wearable sensors. In: 26th International Conference on Intelligent User Interfaces, pp. 43–45 (2021)

7. Marcos-Ramiro, A., Pizarro-Perez, D., Marron-Romera, M., Pizarro-Perez, D., Gatica-Perez, D.: Automatic blinking detection towards stress discovery. In: Proceedings of the 16th International Conference on Multimodal Interaction (ICMI 2014), pp. 307–310 (2014)

8. Xiong, X., De la Torre, F.: Supervised descent method and its applications to face alignment. In: Proceedings of the IEEE Conference on Computer Vision and Pattern Recognition (CVPR), pp. 532–539 (2013)

9. Bevilacqua, F.: Game-calibrated and user-tailored remote detection of emotions. Doctoral dissertation in Informatics, University of Skövde, Sweden. Dissertation Series No. 27 (2018)

10. Pepa, L., Sabatelli, A., Ciabattoni, L., Monteriù, A., Lamberti, F., Morra, L.: Stress detection in computer users from keyboard and mouse dynamics. IEEE Trans. Consum. Electron. **67**(1), 12–19 (2021)

11. Kostopoulos, P., Kyritsis, A.I., Deriaz, M., Konstantas, D.: Stress detection using smart phone data. In: Giokas, K., Bokor, L., Hopfgartner, F. (eds.) eHealth 360°. LNICSSITE, vol. 181, pp. 340–351. Springer, Cham (2017). https://doi.org/10.1007/978-3-319-49655-9_41

12. Aigrain, J., Dapogny, A., Bailly, K., Dubuisson, S., Detyniecki, M., Chetouani, M.: On leveraging crowdsourced data for automatic perceived stress detection. In: Proceedings of the 18th ACM International Conference on Multimodal Interaction (ICMI 2016), pp. 113–120 (2016)

13. Aigrain, J., Dubuisson, S., Detyniecki, M., Chetouani, M.: Person-specific behavioural features for automatic stress detection. In: 11th IEEE International Conference and Workshops on Automatic Face and Gesture Recognition (FG), pp. 1–6 (2015)

14. Annapurna, B., Manda, A.P., Raj, A.C., Indira, R., Srivastava, P.K., Nagalakshmi, V.: Max 30100/30102 sensor implementation to viral infection detection based on Spo2 and heartbeat pattern. Ann. R.S.C.B. **25**(2), 2053–2061 (2021). ISSN: 1583–6258

15. Nagai, Y., Jones, C.I., Sen, A.: Galvanic skin response (GSR)/electrodermal/skin conductance biofeedback on epilepsy: a systematic review and meta-analysis, in systematic review article, Front. Neurol. **10** (2019). https://doi.org/10.3389/fneur.2019.00377. Article 377

16. LaValley, M.P.: Logistic regression. Circulation **117**(18), 2395–2399 (2008)

17. Kramer, O.: K-nearest neighbors. In: Kramer, O. (ed.) Dimensionality Reduction with Unsupervised Nearest Neighbors. Intelligent Systems Reference Library, vol. 51, pp. 13–23. Springer, Heidelberg (2013). https://doi.org/10.1007/978-3-642-38652-7_2

18. Mammone, A., Turchi, M., Cristianini, N.: Support vector machines. Nat. Biotechnol. **24**(12), 1565–1567 (2009)

19. Myles, A.J., Feudale, R.N., Liu, Y., Woody, N.A., Brown, S.D.: An introduction to decision tree modeling. J. Chemom. J. Chemom. Soc. **18**(6), 275–285 (2004)

20. Biau, G., Scornet, E.: A random forest guided tour. TEST **25**(2), 197–227 (2016)

21. Darrow, C.W.: The rationale for treating the change in galvanic skin response as a change in conductance. Psychophysiology **1**, 31–38 (1964)

Long Short-Term Memory Based Photoplethysmography Biometric Authentication

Khawla Ben Salah[1,2](✉) , Mohamed Othmani[3,4] , and Monji Kherallah[5]

[1] National Engineering School of Sfax, University of Sfax, Sfax 1173, Tunisia
[2] Research Lab: Technology, Energy, and Innovative Materials (TEMI), University of Gafsa, Gafsa, Tunisia
khawla.bensalah@fsgf.u-gafsa.tn
[3] Faculty of Sciences of Gafsa, University of Gafsa, 2100 Gafsa, Tunisia
[4] Department of Applied Natural Sciences, Applied College, Qassim University, Buraydah, Saudi Arabia
[5] Faculty of Sciences of Sfax, University of Sfax, 1173 Sfax, Tunisia
monji.kherallah@fss.usf.tn

Abstract. Spoofing attacks remain one of the most inherent problems with traditional biometrics. Therefore, the investigation into other solutions for subject recognition is warranted. Physiological signals are recently employed as new biometrics traits that are not readily visible, like Electroencephalography (EEG), Electrocardiography (ECG), and Photoplethysmography (PPG). In particular, we are interested in PPG since its simple acquisition and its liveness clue. In this study, we have proposed an effective ppg-based biometric model compromising between minimizing the complexity of the model as regards trainable parameters while keeping high performance by using a long short-term memory (LSTM) network for the classification of ppg waveforms by modeling time series sequences. The proposed model relies on three sequential - LSTM layers to capture the sequential feature of ppg recordings. Our proposed model outperforms previous state-of-the-art studies.

Keywords: PPG · Biometric authentication · LSTM · Spoofing attacks · Vivacity

1 Introduction

Biometrics as a terminology refers to the mixture of the (Bio) and (Metrics) Greece words which signify "life measurements". It recommends the use of human physiological and behavioral characteristics for various security pursuits such as identification/verification of one's self-identity, user's grant, data safety, and access control. Secure authentication techniques have become an indispensable critical means to protect sensitive data with the grown dominance and wide

The original version of this chapter was revised: Author's name has been changed to "Ben Salah" and the affiliation has been revised as "Technology, Energy, and Innovative Materials (TEMI), Gafsa, Tunisia". The correction to this chapter is available at https://doi.org/10.1007/978-3-031-16210-7_59

vogue of IT applications. Currently, there is a global transformation in lifestyle that is driving more toward the usage of e-services and smart devices which require the confirmation of user identity. Different institutions have placed a spectrum of technologies to establish user's authentication using various biometric traits such as fingerprints, iris recognition, and so forth. Nevertheless, cost, reliability, and viability are significant impediments to the use of such technologies. Passwords, login, and Pin have delivered access control, but have revealed their inherent vulnerabilities. To overcome the boundaries of the conventional biometric methods, photoplethysmography (PPG) has received a considerable amount of attention from the biometrics community due to the liveness nature of the PPG signals and the fact that they are omnipresent and hard to counterfeit. PPG is a biomedical signal that can be employed to evaluate the cardiovascular response by measuring the blood flow changes and they are generally measured by cost-effective PPG signal sensors integrated into wearable gadgets or even estimated from facial video [1]. As the heart pumps blood through the body, fluid dynamics drive subtle expansions and contractions of the vasculature, which in turn delivers rise to a pulsating PPG signal. PPG signals fulfill the primary properties: Universality, Permanence, Distinctiveness, and Collectability [2] of the biometric traits. This paper proposes a photoplethysmography Biometric Authentication approach using a long short-term memory network. In opposite to many previous deep-learning based approaches that are computationally intensive, the proposed approach boosts the classification accuracy without particularly rising the computational costs. We select deep learning as the core base of our approach due to its varied capabilities including Feature extraction. Deep learning has become broadly applied in many fields [3–6] and reporting great success. In order to make the main problem of this study tractable, we formulate it as a classification problem. We demonstrate the effectiveness of our proposed model on Mendeley benchmark databases. As a result, the proposed approach was found to be capable of recognizing 35 subjects with an accuracy of 98.79 % by extracting feature values derived from PPG sequences.

2 Literature Review

Biometric authentication using PPG signals has been extensively investigated in the literature. The PPG-based approach for human authentication was firstly presented by Gu et al. [7] They chose four feature parameters which are the number of peaks on each single PPG signal, and determining the slope between the bottom to the first peak, then the Downward slope, and finally the time interval between the bottom point and the first peak point in order to complete feature vector. The study reached 94% accuracy. Authors in [8] performed 1st and 2nd derivatives of PPG signal to form a 40 dimensional time-domain feature vector to fed to the k-NN classifier. They accomplished 94.44% of accuracy. Sarkar et al. decomposed ppg signals as a sum of Gaussians and then the parameters will be used in a discriminant analysis framework to differentiate subjects [9]. Authors in [10] introduce a two-stage technique based on biometric identification using Deep Belief Networks and Restricted Boltzmann Machines and they achieved an accuracy of 96.1%. The study in [11] proposed a nonfiducial authentication approach relying on convolutional neural networks they achieved an accuracy of 78.2%. W. Karlen et al. [12] proposed a four-layer deep neural network for subject identification and they achieved an average accuracy of 96%. Recently [13] presented a nonfiducial PPG-based subject authentication method that relies on statistical features and support vector machine as a classifier and they achieved an average authentication accuracy of 99.3%.

3   Methodology

This section highlights and details the proposed research methodology for PPG signal classification. The proposed method is mainly represented in three steps. First, we conducted signal preprocessing. Secondly, we performed data preparation before we fed data to the proposed model. Then, we thoroughly elaborated on the proposed LSTM-based approach and its architecture to detect and classify PPG rows into different subject ID.

3.1   Signal Preprocessing

PPG signals are often adjoined with measurement artifacts and sensor noise. Low-frequency noise may be put in place at the moment of acquisition of data by movements of the measuring zone (e.g., head, a finger), by simple actions such as coughing, smiling, or even breathing. In some cases, the noise may have a huge effect on the shape of the PPG signal. In order to filter the different signal rows from the power line interference, baseline wanders, and motion artifacts, Butterworth Bandpass filter of cutoff frequencies 0.5–4.5 Hz and order 10 has been used. then we proceeded to normalization of amplitude to have a dynamic range of one.

3.2   PPG Data Preparation

The data used in this study are publicly available from the Mendeley data [14]. The PPG dataset englobes PPG signals from 35 healthy subjects. It consists of 300 samples per signal and each subject have 50 to 60 signals. Before we can fed a dataset to the model, We segmented signal into frames. Each frame consists of 50 points rather than 300 points. Features then will be extracted from the frames of each signal band to assemble the feature vectors. The original dataset contains two folders devised to about 66% for training, and 34% for testing. Thus we proceed to combine the two parts. The new generated dataset contain 80% for training and 20% for testing of PPG signals. Figure 1 shows the description of the new generated dataset.

3.3 Proposed Deep Learning Solution for Feature Extraction and Classification:

In order to perform a good classification, we are invited to detect every subtle spatio-temporal change in the PPG rows. Thus, we needed a solution capable of recognizing and eventually aggregating these changes across all signals of the dataset. Addressing all these requirements developed the idea behind our proposed model of using an LSTM network. The chosen network model has been illustrated in Fig. 2. LSTM is suitable for exploring PPG data due to its ability to investigate the temporal correlation between PPG signals. The first model used with sequences data was RNN, However, RNN has a vanishing gradient problem in which a given input affects the hidden layer and, thereafter, network output. The present research deploys LSTM network. It is composed of related subnetworks, jointly named a memory block, which remembers inputs for a long time. Each one of them hold at least one self-connected accumulator cell and various multiplicative units, such as the three main operations: The input gate,

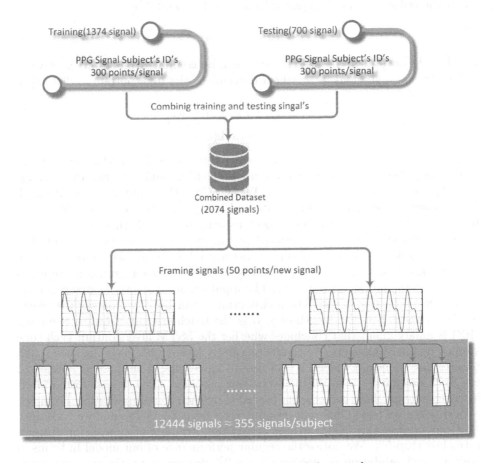

Fig. 1. The new generated structure of the ppg dataset

forget gate and output gate, detailed from eq 1 to eq 6. Information is stowed and reached through the gates. Figure 3 illustrates the basic structure of LSTM cell used in this research. The main key of LSTM is the cell state (Ct). LSTM controls which information to remove or to add to (Ct) by using three gates. The first one is named forget gate which decide what information to abandon from the cell state, this decision is performed with a sigmoid layer.

$$f_t = \sigma(W_f \cdot [h_{t-1}, x_t] + b_f) \tag{1}$$

The second gate called input gate which relies on sigmoid layer to determine which values will be adjusted, and tanh layer which constructs a vector of new revised values as described in (2) and (3).

$$i_t = \sigma(W_i \cdot [h_{t-1}, x_t] + b_i) \tag{2}$$

$$\tilde{C}_t = \tanh(W_c \cdot [h_{t-1}, x_t] + b_c) \tag{3}$$

Then the cell state will be changed from Eqs. 1, 2, and 3 by

$$C_t = f_t * C_{t-1} + i_t * \tilde{C}_t \tag{4}$$

Finally, the output of the present state will be computed based on the revised cell state and a sigmoid layer which determines the final output as defined in Eqs. 5 and 6.

$$o_t = \sigma(W_o \cdot [h_{t-1}, x_t] + b_o) \tag{5}$$

$$h_t = o_t * \tanh(C_t) \tag{6}$$

where σ is sigmoid activation function which returns results into the range (0, 1), tanh is hyperbolic tangent activation function which yields results into the range (−1, 1) the weight matrices are: Wf, Wi, Wc, Wo, the input vector is xt and h (t−1) mark the precident hidden state and finally the biasvectors are: bf, bi, bc, bo. In our LSTM -based PPG subject recognition model, time-series features of every subject's signal are extracted by our custom LSTM-based model. The proposed model is composed of three consecutive LSTM layers composed of each one of 1024 units. As detailed previously LSTM network regroups an input, a memory block, and an output layer. The inputs in our case are the ppg segments or frames y= f1, f2, f3..., fn. The architecture of our proposed network is shown in Fig. 2 where L is the length of y, b is the batch size, and Return Sequence (RS) is an argument that concludes whether the LSTM layers output each time step or its final time step. We conducted firstly layers with low units such as 32, 64 etc. but it doesn't indeed reveal promising results. A dropout is applied to the first three layers to avoid the overfitting problem. Time series information is learned through these three layers preceded by each 2% dropout rate. From our experiments, we tested different dropout rates from 1% to 7%, and we encounter that our proposed model showcases more raised training accuracies for dropout rates less than 5%. We notice the regular performance of our model in terms of training and validation accuracies with a 2% dropout rate. Features extracted from the LSTM Layers are then passed into the last dense layer to generate a 1 ×35 vectors. This vector is finally then given into the Softmax activation function to classify ppg segments into their corresponding class. The last layer which is the output layer involves the softmax activation function which normalizes the dense layer output exponentially and delivers a distribution of probabilities across the 35 different subject'IDS which will be compared with the target probability distribution. The softmax function in our model depends upon the following formula:

$$\sigma(V')_i = \frac{eV'_i}{\sum_{j=1}^{35} e^{V'_j}} \text{ for i=1,2,...,35 and } V' = (V'_1, ..., V'_{35}) \in \mathbb{R}^{35} \quad (7)$$

where V' is one-dimensional vector of size 35. We pass the training PPG signals with 50 epochs as there is no further progress in training and validation accuracies noticed. We test the model and the related parameters through the set of testing rows. We opt for "Categorical Cross-Entropy" as the loss function for our model and Adam Optimizer is used to optimizing the loss function. The categorical cross-entropy loss function computes the loss of an example by calculating the following sum:

$$Loss = - \sum_{i=1}^{\text{output size}} y_i \cdot \log \hat{y}_i \quad (8)$$

y_i is the i-th scalar value corresponding to the model output. $\hat{y}_i$ is the related target value, and the output size consists of the number of scalar values in the model output. During 51st to 52nd epochs, the validation accuracy is at its peak but validation loss and training loss are very close in addition the training accuracy is still expanding. From these observations, we fixed the 50th epoch for stopping the training of our model. Batch size has a decisive impact on the learning of each model. We employ dominant used batch sizes such as 32 and 64 in our proposed model, we notice that our model achieves the best when the batch size is set to 64.

4   Experimental Results

Our proposed approach was evaluated on a PC workstation with 2.6 GHz CPU, 32 GB of memory, and NVIDIA GeForce GTX1650 GPU card. The comparison of the obtained results of the proposed approach with the methods in the literature is illustrated in Table 1. The table incorporates the authors with their specific feature extraction methods, the number of subjects evaluated in their approach, and the average authentication accuracy. It is important to mention that authors in [12] who conceived the augmented features extracted from the four filtered signals approach accomplished the highest achieved accuracy of 99.3% using a 15 s, the same authors proposed in the same study an augmented features method that achieved the best average accuracy of 97.89% using a 3 s frame length. The first method that is illustrated in the first row which is based on fiducial features of 1st and 2nd derivative of PPG signal, The authors have used upward downward slopes, and peak time as features. Accordingly, they have achieved 94% accuracy, nevertheless the method was tested with only 17 subjects and one out of the 17 subjects could not be verified correctly as reported. In the same regard, Kavsaoğlu et al. opt for fiducial features but with 30 subjects, the k-nearest neighbor classifier algorithm was employed and leave-one-out transposition for k 1, 3, 5, 7, and 10 values but the best classification success was achieved as 94.44% for the k = 1 value of the classification algorithm with the first 20 features from 40 features. Sarkar et al. proposed to transform the signal from time domain to angular domain, and performed a decomposition into a sum-of-Gaussians representation: 2 Gaussians to model two fiducial points at the systolic and diastolic peaks, 5 Gaussians, and receipts three additional fiducial points: the starting foot, the dicrotic notch, and the negative slope in the catacrotic phase, their experimental results that indicate 90% and 95% with 2 s and 8 s of PPG test signal data respectively. V. Jindal et al. involved clustering of individual PPG sources into different groups and employ Deep Belief Networks and Boltzmann machines as classification models reaching an average accuracy of 96.1%. Jordi Luque et al. reported an average accuracy of 78.2% 83.2% with 43 and 20 subjects respectively. D. Biswas et al. proposed a four-layer network was evaluated on the 22 PPG records and achieved an average accuracy of 96% on 20 subjects. We reported evaluation results on Table 2. The proposed authentication approach achieved an average authentication accuracy of 98.79% using frames with 50 to 60 points length. As well We achieved f1 measure, recall, and precision of 98.16%, 98.14% and 98.19% respectively over 35 subjects. The proposed network ensures automatic feature extraction, where LSTM layers capture complex temporal properties. Figure 4 and Fig. 5 shows the results of the accuracy and loss of our proposed model on Mendeley dataset during training phase. The blue graph illustrates the training set and the red graph illustrates the validation set. We trained our network in 50 epochs with

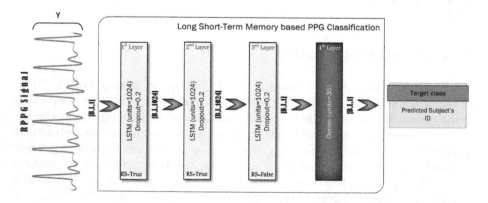

Fig. 2. Proposed LSTM network. RS = Return sequences, T = True, F = False.

64 batch size. The results could be classified as favorable since to the best of knowledge, it achieved one of the best accuracies in comparison to state-of-the art methods of biometric authentication based photoplethysmography.

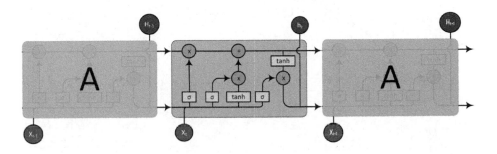

Fig. 3. LSTM cell architecture

Table 1. Comparison of photoplethysmography PPG signal methods.

Authors	Feature extraction methods	Subjects	Classification models	Maximum accuracy obtained (%)
Y. Y. Gu et al. 2003	Fiducial features	17	None	94
A. R. Kavsaoğlu et al. 2014	Fiducial features of 1st & 2nd derivatives	30	k-Nearest neighbors	94.44
A. Sarkar et al. 2016	Dynamical system model	23	linear discriminant analysis (LDA) and quadratic discriminant analysis (QDA)	95
V. Jindal et al. 2016	Clustering	12	Deep Belief Networks and Boltzmann machines	96.1
Jordi Luque et al. 2018	Automatic feature extraction	43/20	Convolutional neural network	78.2/83.2
Dwaipayan Biswas et al. 2019	Automatic feature extraction	22	Four-layer-deep neural network	96
Turky N. Alotaiby et al. 2020	extracting statistical features from each preprocessed frame	42	support vector machine (SVM)	97.89 /99.3
Proposed Approach 2022	Automatic feature extraction from each preprocessed frame	35	Long short-term memory (LSTM)	98.79

Table 2. Parameters and results of our proposed method.

Authors	Feature extraction methods (%)
Epoch	50
Batch size	64
Accuracy	98.79
Precision	98.19
Recall	98.14
F1-measure	98.16

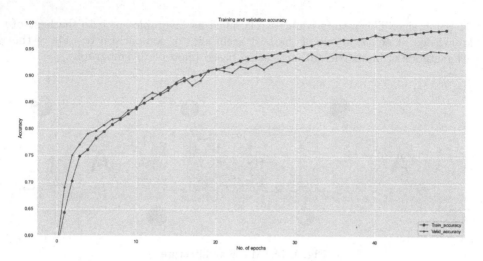

Fig. 4. The accuracy curve of the proposed method.

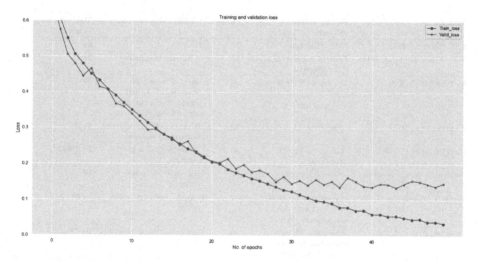

Fig. 5. The loss curve of the proposed method.

5 Conclusion

This paper discussed another biometric modality of cardiac sensing known as photoplethysmography (PPG). We have introduced a robust biometric subject recognition approach using long short-term memory. The premise of our work is that it should be possible to characterize different subjects based on practical PPG physiological variations in the cardiovascular system. In addition to personalizing training procedures for the classification of the subject's PPG signal.

Future work contains extracting more discriminating features for PPG signals using hybrid models with larger datasets.

References

1. Ben Salah, K., Othmani, M., Kherallah, M.: Contactless heart rate estimation from facial video using skin detection and multi-resolution analysis. In: WSCG (2021). http://dx.doi.org/10.24132/CSRN.2021.3002.31
2. Jain, A.K., Ross, A., Prabhakar, S.: An introduction to biometric recognition. IEEE Trans. Circuits Syst. Video Technol. **14**(1), 4–20 (2004)
3. Othmani, M.: A vehicle detection and tracking method for traffic video based on faster R-CNN. Multimed. Tools Appl., March 2022. https://doi.org/10.1007/s11042-022-12715-4
4. Fourati, J., Othmani, M., Ltifi, H.: A Hybrid Model based on Convolutional Neural Networks and Long Short-term Memory for Rest Tremor Classification, pp. 75–82, January 2022. https://doi.org/10.5220/0010773600003116
5. Salah, K.B., Othmani, M., Kherallah, M.: A novel approach for human skin detection using convolutional neural network. Vis. Comput. **38**(5), 1833–1843 (2021). https://doi.org/10.1007/s00371-021-02108-3
6. Fourati, J., Othmani, M., Ltifi, H.: A hybrid model based on bidirectional long-short term memory and support vector machine for rest tremor classification. Signal, Image and Video Processing, pp. 1–8 (2022)
7. Y. Y. Gu, Y. Zhang, and Y. T. Zhang: A novel biometric approach in human verification by photoplethysmographic signals. In: 4th International IEEE EMBS Special Topic Conference on Information Technology Applications in Biomedicine, 2003, pp. 13–14, Birmingham, UK, April (04 2022)
8. Kavsaoğlu, A.R., Polat, K., Bozkurt, M.R.: A novel feature ranking algorithm for biometric recognition with PPG signals. Comput. Biol. Med. **49**, 1–14 (2014)
9. Sarkar, A., Lynn Abbott, A., Doerzaph, Z.: Biometric authentication using photoplethysmography signals. In: IEEE 8th International Conference on Biometrics Theory, Applications and Systems (BTAS), Niagara Falls, NY, USA, September 2016
10. Jindal, V., Birjandtalab, J., Baran Pouyan, M., Nourani, M.: An adaptive deep learning approach for PPG-based identification. In: 38th Annual International Conference of the IEEE Engineering in Medicine and Biology Society (EMBC), Orlando, FL, USA, August 2016
11. Luque, J., Cortès, G., Segura, C., Maravilla, A., Esteban, J., Fabregat, J.: End-to-end photoplethysmography (PPG) based biometric authentication by using convolutional neural networks. In: 26th European Signal Processing Conference. (EUSIPCO), Rome, Italy, September 2018
12. Karlen, W., Raman, S., Ansermino, J.M., Dumont, G.A.: Multiparameter respiratory rate estimation from the photoplethysmogram. IEEE Trans. Biomed. Eng. **60**(7), 1946–1953 (2013)
13. Alotaiby, T. N., Aljabarti, F., Alotibi, G., Alshebeili, S.A.: A Nonfiducial PPG-based subject authentication approach using the statistical features of DWT-based filtered signals. J. Sensors (2020)
14. Siam, A., El-Samie, A., Fathi, A.E., Atef, E.-B., Nirmeen, E.: Ghada: real-World PPG dataset, Mendeley Data, V1. https://doi.org/10.17632/yynb8t9x3d

Extended U-net for Retinal Vessel Segmentation

Henda Boudegga[1,3](✉) 🅓, Yaroub Elloumi[1,3](✉) 🅓, Rostom Kachouri[2] 🅓,
Asma Ben Abdallah[1] 🅓, and Mohamed Hédi Bedoui[1] 🅓

[1] Medical Technology and Image Processing Laboratory, Faculty of Medicine, University of
Monastir, Monastir, Tunisia
{henda.boudegga,yaroub.elloumi}@esiee.fr
[2] LIGM, Univ Gustave Eiffel, CNRS, ESIEE Paris, 77454 Marne-la-Vallée, France
[3] ISITCom Hammam-Sousse, University of Sousse, Sousse, Tunisia

Abstract. The retinal vascular tree is an important biomarker for the diagnosis
of ocular disease, where an efficient segmentation is highly required. Recently,
various standard Convolutional Neural Networks CNN dedicated for segmentation are applied for retinal vessel segmentation. In fact, retinal blood vessels are
presented in different retinal image resolutions with a complicated morphology.
Thus, it is difficult for the standard configuration of CNN to guarantee an optimal
feature extraction and efficient segmentation whatever the image resolution is. In
this paper, new retinal vessel segmentation approach based on deep learning architecture is propounded. The idea consists of enlarging the kernel size of convolution
layer in order to cover the vessel pixels as well as more neighbors for extracting
features. Within this objective, our main contribution consists of identifying the
kernel size in correlation with retinal image resolution through an experimental
approach. Then, a novel U-net extension is proposed by using convolution layer
with the identified kernel size. The suggested method is evaluated on two public
databases DRIVE and HRF having different resolutions, where higher segmentation performances are achieved respectively with 5 * 5 and 7 * 7 convolution
kernel sizes. The average accuracy and sensitivity values for DRIVE and HRF
databases are respectively in the order of to 0.9785, 0.8474 and 0.964 and 0.803
which outperform the segmentation performance for the standard U-net.

Keywords: Retinal vessel · Segmentation · Convolution kernel size

1 Introduction

The main anatomical components of the retina are the optic disc (OD), the macula and
the blood vessels. Retinal blood vessels are represented in the retinal texture with various
anatomical criteria, distinguished by the elongated structure, the variety of thicknesses
and the curvilinear or the tortuous form.

Several ocular pathologies are associated with abnormal variation of vessel
anatomies. As in the proliferative stage of diabetic retinopathy [1], new tortuous vessels appear with lower thickness with respect to the predecessor ones. Further, in the
non-proliferative diabetic retinopathy stages, numerous lesions such as microaneurysms

© The Author(s), under exclusive license to Springer Nature Switzerland AG 2022
C. Bădică et al. (Eds.): ICCCI 2022, CCIS 1653, pp. 564–576, 2022.
https://doi.org/10.1007/978-3-031-16210-7_46

and exudates appear close to the vessel tree [2, 3]. Therefore, the analysis of vascular anatomy is the primary mission to diagnose and detect the ocular pathology severity. Hence, it is indispensable to segment the entire retinal vascular tree.

However, due to the complicated vascular morphologies, their manual segmentation is a tedious task and considered as a challenging step. Therefore, an automatic and an accurate vessel segmentation is required. With the development of deep learning and especially Convolutional Neural Networks (CNNs), various architecture are proposed and have been applied in various medical domains [1, 4, 5]. Certain of these architectures have been propounded for the segmentation tasks such as [6]. However, due to the complicated vessel structures, the standard CNN architectures still insufficient to extract complexes features and guarantee an efficient segmentation whatever the image resolution is and to tolerate the segmentation challenge.

In this work, we propound to put forward a deep learning based method for the segmentation of blood vessels. The idea consists of enlarging kernel size of convolution layer in order to cover the vessel pixels as well as more neighbors for extracting features. Within this objective, the main contribution consists of identifying the kernel size in correlation with retinal image resolution through an experimental approach. Within this context, a novel U-net extension is propounded throw applying convolution layers parameterized by the identified kernel size. The proposed architecture is trained and tested into retinal sub-image datasets, where the produced segmented patches will be merged to generate the final vessel segmentation map. The remainder of this paper is organized into five sections. In Sect. 2, we review some related works based Deep learning architecture. Thereafter, the patch extraction processing is described in Sect. 3. Section 4, the proposed network is detailed. The experimentation results are presented in Sect. 5, where segmentation performances are evaluated and compared to extended networks based methods. The conclusion is given in the last section.

2 Related Works

Blood vessel segmentation in fundus imaging was subject of various reviews such as [7], where different categories of approaches have been studied. In this paper, we suggest briefly reviewing Deep learning based approaches.

Several well-known networks have been applied such as Alexnet [8], VGG [9], U-net [6]. However, these networks still insufficient to achieve the segmentation challenge. Within this context, various well-known networks have been extended in order to enhance the segmentation results, as the case of U-net architecture. Certain extension consists of applying advanced convolution layers, as the case of [10–12], where standard ones have been replaced respectively by dilated convolution layers and deformable convolution layer. Their aim is respectively to enlarge the convolution receptive field for learning more distributed information and to adapting the convolution receptive field form to the vessel structure. However, their proposed convolution processing still insufficient to properly extract features, where the same dilation rate is applied for all vessel resolutions. In addition, vessels information are dropped caused by the spaced convolution kernel samples of the dilated convolution kernel.

In addition, other extension consists of varying the size of kernel convolution layers, such as [13], where the convolution kernel size is hierarchically decreased over the network. The aim is to extract hierarchical vessel information and address vessel scale variation. However, the features extracted from the earlier layers will be used for all the remainder of the network, causing a leakage of vessels information.

In other hand, some works suggest improving the performances by further going in depth of the applied architecture as [14]. In this work, the networks AlexNet, LeNet, VGG and ZF-net are modified by further adding convolution layers at the beginning of the network. Nevertheless, the performances of those methods based extended networks have achieved reduced sensitivity rates in the order of 69% and 79%, which are insufficient to gain the segmentation challenge.

3   Patch Extraction

As the retina is characterized by a large number of vessels, then a rejected segmentation of the entire image may be achieved. Therefore, a patch extraction process is suggested in this paper, where the fundus images are sliced into sub-images containing a portion of vessels to be segmented separately. The cropping principle allows modeling blood vessels without burdening the patch content. Thus, an experimental study is propounded to determine the appropriate crop size. The experiment consists in iteratively performing several training processes while increasing the cropping size and keeping the training parameters. As a result, experience shows that the 128 * 128 and 192 * 192 sizes of patches are the most suitable respectively for DRIVE and HRF images, allowing an appropriate presentation of blood vessels without overloading the crop by several information. This patch extraction process is applied for the process of training and testing. The training patches were extracted from the training images by overlapping with its neighbors to take benefit in increasing the size of the training dataset. In contrast, the testing patches were extracted from testing images without the overlapping strategy. Thereafter, the predicted result was reconstructed with respect to the image size to produce a segmented retinal blood vessel map.

4   Proposed Architecture for Retinal Blood Vessel Segmentation

The U-net is a CNN architecture characterized by a U-form to segment biomedical images [6]. It is designed with the U-form having the downsampling and upsamling paths, structured on blocks. Containing essentially convolution layers allowing the model to automatically and adaptively detect features.

4.1   Convolution Processing

The convolution layers of U-net blocks are parameterized by a convolution kernel having the size of "n × n = 3 × 3", applied to extract vessel features to generate a segmentation vessels tree map. The convolution processing is a linear operation, consists of an element-wise multiplication between the weight values "W" of the convolution kernel "K" and the kernel-sized patch of the input feature map "I". Then, the results are summed to obtain an output value in the corresponding position (i, j) of the output feature map "O".

This processing is computed as (1), where (Kpx, Kpy) denotes the coordinates of the kernel points.

$$O(i, j) = \sum_{p=0}^{n \times n} W\left(Kp_x, Kp_y\right) * I\left(i + Kp_x, j + Kp_y\right) \qquad (1)$$

Upon the extraction of the vessel features, the convolution operation with "n × n = 3 × 3" receptive field is applied to the centered element boxed in red as well as to its local neighbors highlighted in blue in the upper part of Fig. 1, iteratively by moving the convolution kernel on the input feature map "I", respecting the same stride on the width and on the length. Nevertheless, as the blood vessels are presented in the retina with a straight structure, characterized by thickness variation and curvilinear or tortuous form, the convolution kernel with tight neighbors as highlighted with blue box in the upper part of Fig. 1 cannot cover pixels of the same segment of the image sharing common vessel features. Accordingly, the application of small convolution kernels leads to low feature quality. Consequently, this results in a weak segmentation quality, where the continuity of vessels and their neighbors may not be modeled and detected. In addition, it may be difficult for the small kernels receptive field to distinguish pathological regions, leading to an incorrect segmentation of blood vessels.

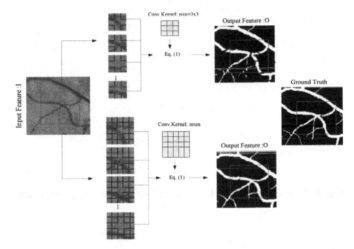

Fig. 1. Segmentation of blood vessels: (Upper part) convolution processing with small convolution kernel size = 3 × 3, (Lower part) Convolution processing with a larger convolution kernel receptive field "m × m". (Color figure online)

Within the context of improving the quality of vessels features extraction, the main purpose is to identify the ideal convolution kernel size, which allows extracting optimal vessel features from the earlier layers to be used in the innermost layers.

Thus, the idea is to make the kernel look at more surrounding neighbors while computing the convolution processing as boxed in Fig. 1 with blue, in order to compute relevant neighbors and to share more vessel features. Thereupon, the suggestion consists of enlarging the convolution kernel receptive field to "m × m", where "m > 3" as shown in the lower part of Fig. 1.

Therefore, to consolidate the choice of the enlarged convolution kernel size "m ×
m", an identification approach of the convolution kernel size is proposed and the outline
processing is illustrated in Fig. 2. The approach consists of continually updating the
size of convolution kernel until achieving the suitable convolution kernel size. Hence,
the convolution kernel size "m × m is firstly initialized" to "1 × 1" and the maximal
result "Seg_Acc_max" is set to zero. Thereafter, the size of the convolution kernel "m ×
m" is increased with step equal to two, and the U-net architecture is configured by the
increased convolution kernel size. Subsequently, the configured U-net architecture is
evaluated, where the increased convolution kernel size is saved, if their segmentation
results "Seg_Acc" is higher than the maximal result "Seg_Acc_max". These treatments
are repeated iteratively until obtaining the appropriate kernel size. This identification
approach is experimentally described in detail in Sect. 5.2, where two different dataset
described in Sect. 5.1 is applied.

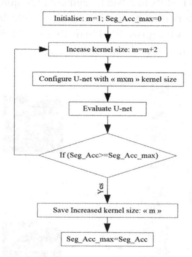

Fig. 2. Flowchart of convolution kernel size identification approach.

4.2 Proposed Network

The main contribution of this work consists in extending the well-known architecture
U-net through configuring their convolution layers by a larger convolution kernel having
the size of "m × m". The objective is to guarantee accurate performance by adopting the
U-form and making the model able to cover the vessel structure by applying the "m × m"
convolution kernel size. As U-net is structured in blocks containing convolution layers
having with the same kernel sizes, hence the convolution kernel substitution is applied
over the downsample and upsample blocks.

The downsampling path of the extended U-net network is composed by five blocks.
Each block is composed of two convolution layers as shown with pink boxes in Fig. 3,
parameterized by "m × m" convolution kernel illustrated with blue points framed with

red as shown in Fig. 3. Those convolution layers are configured by a stride "s = 1" and activated with the RELU function, in order to avoid the non-linearity of convolution operation. This ReLu is defined as (2), allows setting to zero the negative value "z" of the neuron "x":

$$Relu(x) = Max(0, z) \qquad (2)$$

Each block of the downsampling path excepting the last is composed of two convolution layers followed by a max pooling layer as illustrated with red arrows in Fig. 3. This layer is parameterized by a pooling window having the size "pxp = 2 × 2" and a stride "s = 2", allows taking the maximum value of the pooling window of the input feature map "I". Hence, the size of the output feature map is defined in (3). For the first downsampling block, 64 feature maps are convolved. Thereafter, the number of output feature maps is doubled as shown in Fig. 3.

$$Out\_Maxpool = Floor(I - p/s) + 1 \qquad (3)$$

Similarly to the original U-net architecture, the upsampling path is mirrored to dowsampling path, where four blocks are deployed. Each of which is composed by upsampling layer as illustrated with green arrows in Fig. 3, followed by two convolution layers having the same configuration as downsampling convolution layers. The applied upsampling layers are parameterized by a kernel size "n × n = 2 × 2" and a stride "s = 2", allows reproducing the spatial size and information of the image. Thus, the output feature map size can be calculated as (4), where "M" corresponds to the input image size and the padding is set to zero.

$$Out\_Up = (M - 1) * 2 + n - 2 * padding \qquad (4)$$

Contrary to the downsampling path, the number of the output feature map is reduced by half for each block, as shown in Fig. 3. The network is achieved by a 1 × 1 convolution layer activated with the softmax function as shown with a purple box in Fig. 3, allows the mapping of 64 feature maps to produce the prediction of vessels and background. Furthermore, a skip connection between the downsampling blocks and their corresponding of the upsampling blocks illustrated with grey arrows is performed, promoting the fusion of the lower details information with the global information.

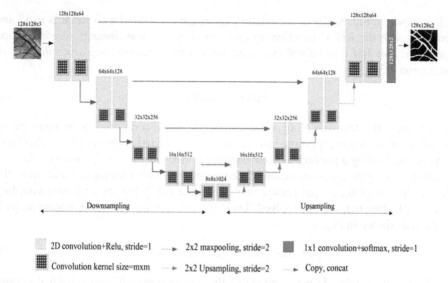

Fig. 3. Proposed network for retinal blood vessel segmentation method (Color figure online)

4.3   Training Parameter Setting

The suggested network is conducted for a training process, to modify the node weights until having an accurate model. This processing is performed using a set of training parameters, where several ones are chosen experimentally, while others are used by referring to recent studies. As for the optimizer and the learning rate value, some training experiences are conducted while modifying for each experience the value of one parameter. Thereafter, we select the one performing the higher result rates. Hence, the ADAM optimizer parameterized with learning equal to 0.001 is chosen for training the proposed network. Furthermore, the Xavier initialization technique is applied. Added to that, to minimize the gap between the predicted output and the ground truth, the cross entropy "CE" loss function defined in (5) is applied, where "P_out" and "d_out" respectively correspond to the predicted output and the desired one.

$$CE = -\sum(d_{out}.\log(P_{out}) + (1 - d_{out}).\log(1 - P_{out})) \tag{5}$$

In the same vein, the dropout regularization technique is applied for regularizing the training, which consists in temporarily switching a subset of nodes. The applied technique is defined in (6), where "L_Out" corresponds to the layer output, "F" is the activation function of the weight matrix "W" of layer "x", and "1 − d_p" is the dropout mask where the "d_p" value is chosen experimentally and is set to 0.5.

$$L\_Out = F(W_x)(1 - d_p) \tag{6}$$

5   Experiments

The method is evaluated with respect to its background through using well-known retinal image database and computing the evaluation metrics described in Subsect. 5.1.

The experiment is carried out by distinctly identifying the convolution kernel size and evaluating the segmentation performance respectively in Subsect. 5.2 and 5.3. Further a comparative assessment with respect to the state-of-the-art methods detailed in Subsect. 5.4.

5.1 Dataset, Evaluation Metrics and Experiment Setup

Dataset: The validation of the proposed method is ensured by the deployment of the public retinal database DRIVE [7] and HRF [7]. Both databases are composed respectively by 40 and 45 retinal images with different resolution respectively in the order of 565×584 and 3504×2336. Those retinal images are joined with its manual blood vessel segmentation and its masks. For the DRIVE database, seven retinal images are characterized by the signs of diabetic retinopathy [7]. In Addition, 30 HRF retinal images have the signs of proliferative diabetic retinopathy and glaucoma [7].

Evaluation Metric: Four classes of pixel classification results, namely True Positive (TP), True Negative (TN), False Positive (FP) and False Negative (FN), can be generated depending on the correct or incorrect segmentation of pixels, with respect to the manual annotation of blood vessel segmentation. Various evaluation metrics can be conducted from these pixel classification results, including Accuracy (Acc), sensibility (Sens), specificity (Spec) and DICE, where Sensitivity is the indicator that reflects the proportion of positives correctly identified. All those evaluation metrics are computed respectively as in (7–10).

$$\text{Accuracy(Acc)} = TN + TP/(TP + FP + FN + TN) \tag{7}$$

$$\text{Sensitivity(Sens)} = TP/(TP + FN) \tag{8}$$

$$\text{Specificity(Spec)} = TN/(TN + FP) \tag{9}$$

$$\text{DICE} = 2 * TP/((2 * TP) + FN + FP) \tag{10}$$

Experiments Setup: All the experiments are done on Intel core i7 configured with a 3.67 GHZ frequency processor, 8Go RAM and a NVIDIA GTX 980 GPU. This method is implemented with the Python 3.5.2, the OpenCV library 3.4 and Tensorflow GPU framework 1.12, using CUDA 9.0 with CUDNN 7.6.3.

5.2 Identification of Convolution Kernel Size

We suggest in this section, implementing the identification approach of the convolution kernel size proposed in Sect. 4.2. Within this context, we suggest iterating three times throw configuring the architecture U-Net respectively with three different kernel sizes in the order of 3×3, 5×5 and 7×7. The aim is to identify the suitable convolution kernel sizes correlated with vessel representation into DRIVE and HRF images patches.

For this experiment, both DRIVE and HRF are processed where three segmentation measurements are depicted in Table 1 for the different U-Net configuration.

Form Table 1, the three different convolution kernel size have depicted Acc and Spec rates respectively greater than 95% and 97% of the two databases. Nevertheless, the miss segmentation of the thin-vessel pixels hardly affects the Acc and Spec rates. On other hand, the Sens rate increases with the correct extraction of fine vessels and maintain of connectivity, where the numbers of false positives pixels are reduced and the true positives pixels are increased. Thus, the higher Sens rates in the order of 86% and 80% generated respectively by the 5×5 U-net kernel size configuration of DRIVE and 7×7 U-net kernel size configuration of HRF. Those Sens rates indicate the ability of models to generate accurate segmentation of retinal vessels. Accordingly, we can confirm that using of these larger kernel sizes for both databases can reduce the number of false positives and increased the true positives. Further, for the case of DRIVE images shown in Fig. 4, the largest U-net configuration with 7×7 kernel samples disperses and drops vessel information. In contrast, it is revealed that the U-net configuration with the enlarged convolution kernel size in the order of 5×5 can more accurately detect the retinal vessels, with respect to the other U-net configuration. Moreover, the propounded network preserves more the connectivity of vessel tree with respect to the other configuration.

Table 1. Average performance for the 3 different Convolution kernel sizes of U-net on DRIVE and HRF databases.

Convolution kernel size	DRIVE			HRF		
	Acc	Sens	Spec	Acc	Sens	Spec
3×3 (original U_net)	0.9594	0.7698	0.9798	0.9577	0.6577	0.9701
5×5	0.9759	0.86	0.9853	0.958	0.78	0.975
7×7	0.975	0.5916	0.9982	0.964	0.803	0.963

5.3 Segmentation Performance

We suggest evaluating the suggested U-net extension for both DRIVE and HRF basing on the Acc, Sens, Spec and DICE metrics. Figure 5 shows examples of segmentation results. Further, within the aim of evaluating the robustness of the suggested method across the testing images, we suggest applying the four-fold cross validation approach on DRIVE database as proposed in [15]. Hence, the retinal fundus images are splitted into four subsets, three are conducted for the training process and one subset is used for testing. Therefore, four experiments are performed, where the average performance measurements of the four experiments are indicated in Table 2. Consequently, the U-net extension have confirming a higher segmentation performance of the proposed network whatever the image used for the training or testing procedure.

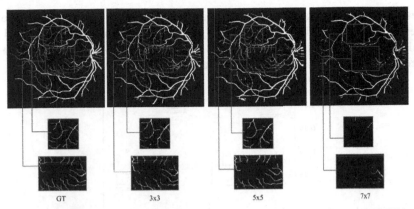

GT   3x3   5x5   7x7

Fig. 4. Comparison of segmentation results of different U-net configuration on DRIVE images; (Row 1) segmentation vessel maps, (Row 2) local thin vessel region of fundus images, (column 1) ground truth, (column 2–4) segmentation result generated respectively by $3 \times 3, 5 \times 5$ and 7×7 U-net configuration

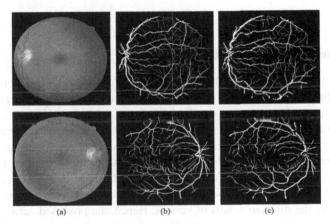

(a)   (b)   (c)

Fig. 5. Segmentation results for DRIVE database; (a) Retinal images, (b) Ground truth, (c) Segmented results.

Table 2. Average performance of DRIVE and HRF database.

Database	Acc	Sens	Spec	DICE
DRIVE	0.9785	0.8474	0.9892	0.8461
HRF	0.964	0.803	0.9637	0.778

To evaluate the robustness of the U-net extension for DRIVE database and confirm a higher correlation with respect to the used images, the box plots in Fig. 6 illustrate the four performances Acc, Sens, Spec and DICE measures of the four experiments. The representation demonstrates a high correlation between 4-fold datasets, where the Acc values are very close to their average with a variation in the order of 0.01. Reduced gaps are also deduced between values for Sens, Spec and DICE with variation values, are respectively in the order of 0.0462, 0.0047 and 0.028 for the DRIVE database.

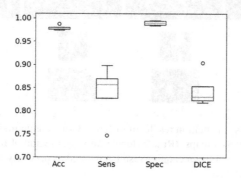

Fig. 6. Boxplot of four-fold cross validation results.

5.4   Comparison with State of the Art

To evaluate the propounded method, we compare our segmentation performance on DRIVE database with the state-of-the-art methods. Thus, we propose to evaluate our segmentation results with respect to standard-DL-based methods and extended-DL-based methods, where the Acc, Sens and Spec values on the DRIVE database are presented in Table 3. From these results, we deduce that the proposed average Sens rate is better than the extended-DL-based methods [10–14] and the standard DL based methods [8] and [6], where a significant difference in the range of 0.12 is distinguished. Sensitivity is a particular indicator in the context of segmentation. It shows the capability of the model to detect the discrete details of vessels. Hence, the proposed network presents a powerful ability to detect vessel pixels. This relevant performance is explained by the growth of the receptive field vision of the convolution kernel, where a single pixel in a 5 × 5 activation map is able to look at every 5 × 5 region of the input feature map. As a consequence, such increase in the receptive field vision allows modeling vessel neighborhood and learning deeper vessel details similar to ground truth segmentation. In the same vein, the contribution put forward in [10] consists in enlarging the receptive field convolution kernel by applying dilated convolution layers. However, a reduced Sens rate compared to ours is generated in the order of 0.79. Thus, the reduction is explained by the applied dilation rate, which introduces striding between the kernel samples that result in the drop of information and vessel features.

Table 3. Comparison of segmentation performances on DRIVE database

	Works	DRIVE		
		Acc	Sens	Spec
Standard DL architecturebased methods	[8]: Alexnet	0.9624	0.754	0.9825
	[6]: U-net	0.9594	0.7698	0.9798
Extended DL architectures based methods	[10]: EEA-U-net	0.9577	0.7918	0.9708
	[11]: D-U-net	0.9641	0.7595	0.98
	[13]: Joint loss U-net	0.9542	0.7653	0.9818
	[12]: MA-U-net	0.9557	0.789	0.9799
	[14]: M-Alexnet	0.9628	0.7995	0.9804
	[14]: M-VGG	0.9585	0.8404	0.9802
Proposed method(average)		0.9785	0.8474	0.9892

6 Conclusion

The segmentation of the retinal vessel tree is an indispensable element for the detection and diagnosis of ocular and cardiovascular diseases. Thus, the clinical contexts expect precise and sensitive segmentation of blood vessels. Within this objective, an identification of convolution kernel size in correlation with vessel representation on different retinal image resolution is propounded. Thus, the convolution kernel size is enlarged in order to cover the vessel pixels as well as more neighbors for extracting features.

On other hand, several automatic ophthalmological diagnostic systems such as [16–18] expect sensitive segmentation of retinal vascular tree. In this context, our automated method can be directly employed to take benefit from its segmentation performance. As future work, the method proposed in [18] can be extended in function to this approach in order to take benefit to the accurate segmentation performance while keeping computation time.

References

1. Akil, M., Elloumi, Y., Kachouri, R.: Detection of retinal abnormalities in fundus image using CNN deep learning networks. In: State of the Art in Neural Networks, vol. 1. Elsevier (2020)
2. Kaur, J., Mittal, D.: A generalized method for the segmentation of exudates from pathological retinal fundus images. Biocybern. Biomed. Eng **38**(1), 27–53 (2018)
3. Elloumi, Y., Abroug, N., Bedoui, M.H.: End-to-end mobile system for diabetic retinopathy screening based on lightweight deep neural network. In: Bouadi, T., Fromont, E., Hüllermeier, E. (eds.) IDA 2022. LNCS, vol. 13205, pp. 66–77. Springer, Cham (2022). https://doi.org/10.1007/978-3-031-01333-1_6
4. Elloumi, Y.: Cataract grading method based on deep convolutional neural networks and stacking ensemble learning. Int. J. Imaging Syst. Technol. **32**, 798–814 (2022)
5. Elloumi, Y., Akil, M., Boudegga, H.: Ocular diseases diagnosis in fundus images using a deep learning: approaches, tools and performance evaluation. In: Real-Time Image Processing and Deep Learning, vol. 10996, pp. 221-228. SPIE (2019)

6. Ronneberger, O., Fischer, P., Brox, T.: U-Net: convolutional networks for biomedical image segmentation. In: Navab, N., Hornegger, J., Wells, W.M., Frangi, A.F. (eds.) MICCAI 2015. LNCS, vol. 9351, pp. 234–241. Springer, Cham (2015). https://doi.org/10.1007/978-3-319-24574-4_28

7. Fraz, M.M., et al.: Blood vessel segmentation methodologies in retinal images – a survey. Comput. Methods Programs Biomed **108**(1), 407–433 (2012)

8. Krizhevsky, A., Sutskever, I., Hinton, G.E.: ImageNet classification with deep convolutional neural networks. Commun. ACM **60**(6), 84–90 (2017)

9. Badrinarayanan, V., Kendall, A., Cipolla, R.: SegNet: a deep convolutional encoder-decoder architecture for image segmentation. arXiv:1511.00561 (2016)

10. Sathananthavathi, V., Indumathi, G.: Encoder Enhanced Atrous (EEA) Unet architecture for retinal blood vessel segmentation. Cogn. Syst. Res. **67**, 84–95 (2021)

11. Jin, Q., Meng, Z., Pham, T.D., Chen, Q., Wei, L., Su, R.: DUNet: a deformable network for retinal vessel segmentation. Knowl. Based Syst. **178**, 149–162 (2019)

12. Li, H., et al.: MAU-Net: a retinal vessels segmentation method. In: 2020 42nd Annual International Conference of the IEEE Engineering in Medicine and Biology Society (EMBC), pp. 1958–1961 (2020)

13. Yan, Z., Yang, X., Cheng, K.-T.: Joint segment-level and pixel-wise losses for deep learning based retinal vessel segmentation. IEEE Trans. Biomed. Eng. **65**(9), 1912–1923 (2018)

14. Jin, Q., Chen, Q., Meng, Z., Wang, B., Su, R.: Construction of retinal vessel segmentation models based on convolutional neural network. Neural Process. Lett. **52**(2), 1005–1022 (2020)

15. Boudegga, H., Elloumi, Y., Akil, M., Hedi Bedoui, M., Kachouri, R., Abdallah, A.B.: Fast and efficient retinal blood vessel segmentation method based on deep learning network. Comput. Med. Imaging Graph. **90**, 101902 (2021)

16. Boukadida, R., Elloumi, Y., Akil, M., Hedi Bedoui, M.: Mobile-aided screening system for proliferative diabetic retinopathy. Int. J. Imaging Syst. Technol. **31**, 1638-1654 (2021)

17. Mrad, Y., Elloumi, Y., Akil, M., Hedi Bedoui, M.: A fast and accurate method for glaucoma screening from smartphone-captured fundus images. IRBM **43**, 279-289 (2021)

18. Sayadia, S.B., Elloumi, Y., Akil, M., Hedi Bedoui, M., Kachouri, R., Abdallah, A.B.: Automated method for real-time AMD screening of fundus images dedicated for mobile devices. Med. Biol. Eng. Comput. **60**, 1449–1479 (2022)

Cooperative Strategies for Decision Making and Optimization

Spatial Clustering by Schelling's Ants

László Gulyás[(✉)] [iD]

Faculty of Informatics, Institute for Industry-Academy Innovation Department
of Artificial Intelligence, ELTE Eötvös Loránd University, Budapest, Hungary
lgulyas@inf.elte.hu

Abstract. This paper revisits a distributed, collective spatial clustering
algorithm motivated by ants and points out its fundamental similarity
to one of the most cited and earliest agent-based models. Based on this
observation, a novel variant of the algorithm is proposed and its behavior
and performance is studied.

1 Introduction

Distributed collective intelligence is concerned with the joint problem solving
behavior of large groups of autonomous agents, typically with relatively simple capabilities. The last decade of the previous millennium has seen a surge of
interest in the observation of the surprisingly rich and efficient problem solving
behavior of various species of social insects and in the application of bio-inspired
algorithms resulting from these observations to computational problems. These
early studies were the precursor of the research domain now known as *Swarm
Intelligence (SI)*, [1,2]. The majority of these algorithms originated in the foraging behavior of ant colonies (cf. *Ant Colony Optimization*) [3,4]. However,
several other bio-inspired methods were discussed in the 1990s, including ones
applicable to problem domains different from those of SI today. This paper revisits an early 'ant algorithm' and proposes a novel variant, inspired by Schelling's
Segregation model, one of the most cited agent-based models of computational
social science [5,6]. The potential applications and generalisations of the new
variant are discussed in the last Section.

2 Spatial Clustering by Ants

The Task. Let's consider a 2D regular lattice (grid). Each cell of the lattice
may contain a single object. Objects can be of different types (or color). The

The author acknowledges the support of the "Application Domain Specific Highly
Reliable IT Solutions" project, which has been implemented with the support provided
from the National Research, Development and Innovation Fund of Hungary, financed
under the Thematic Excellence Programme TKP2020-NKA-06 (National Challenges
Subprogramme) funding scheme. This research was also supported by the European
Union within the framework of the Artificial Intelligence National Laboratory Program
(grant id: RRF-2.3.1-21-2022-00004).

task is to reorganize (move) the objects in such a way that objects of the same type are placed next to each other (i.e., they are grouped or spatially clustered). In the simplest version of this problem, all objects are of the same type, but there are empty locations on the grid. The task is to collect the objects together in a single, contiguous patch.

The Problem. We have a group of simple, identical agents (ants) that are capable of moving around on the grid and picking up, carrying and putting down objects as they go. Ants are always located at one of the cells. They can also step on cells holding objects. Ants can pick up the object at their current location, provided they are not carrying. Similarly, they can put down the object that they have with them at their current location, if the cell is empty. Ants are assumed to be simple, having limited processing power and no ability to communicate with one another. Their vision is constrained to their immediate neighborhood. Given these serious limitations of capabilities, the agents are assumed to be cheap and thus available in larger quantities.

Classic Ant Clustering. Ants wander around randomly on the grid, always moving to one of the neighboring cells, observing the object at their current location [9]. They have a limited short term memory and remember the objects at the last couple of cells. If a non-carrying ant encounters an object, it will decide stochastically, whether to pick it up. The probability of picking up will decrease proportionally to the number of objects of the same type recently observed. Similarly, if an object-carrying ant visits an empty cell, it will put it down with a probability proportional to the number of similar objects recently encountered. This simple algorithm, inspired by the brood sorting or cemetery organisation behavior of ants, places minimal processing burden on the agents, yet it is capable of improving the spatial clustering of objects with surprising efficiency [7,8].

Proposed New Variant: Clustering by Schelling's Ants. This variant[1] does not require ants to have memory. They wander around randomly on the lattice as above, but their pick-up/put-down decisions are based only on the local neighborhood: on the ratio of neighboring cells with same color objects. A non-carrying ant will pick up an object if the local ratio is below a predefined threshold (a parameter). Similarly, a carrying ant will put down its object at an empty cell if the ratio is above the threshold.

---

[1] The algorithm is inspired by *Thomas C. Schelling*'s residential segregation model that studies residential segregation on an abstract 2D grid [5]. The model shows that moving decisions by residents, based on the similarity of nearest neighbors, will lead to highly segregated (i.e., spatially clustered) residential configurations, even when decision makers are highly tolerant.

3   Methods

We implemented the above distributed spatial sorting algorithm as an agent-based computational simulation. We used NetLogo [10], a popular platform for multi-agent simulations. This implementation (available from GitHub[2]) allows for the extensive computational testing and analysis of the algorithm, but it is not suitable for any particular application domain.[3]

The simulation takes the size of the world ($s > 0$), the number of ants ($n > 0$), as well as the number of object types (or colors, $c > 1$) as parameters. The world is initialized with a certain percentage of the locations ($d \in [0, 1]$, for *density*) holding objects – the object holding locations are determined randomly. The types (color) of the objects are also uniform random – each type having equal probability. Initially, ants are randomly located and their 'hands' are empty. Finally, the ants' threshold for picking up or dropping an object ($t \in [0, 1]$), that is the same for all ants, is a tuneable parameter of the implementation.

Our implementation works with periodic boundary conditions, i.e., the world is 'wrapped around' so that cells at the edges are neighbors with the cells at the opposite end of the world. This torus topology ensures that all locations in the world are structurally similar, having the same number of neighbors and same average distances to other locations, etc. In our implementation, 8 neighbors are considered for each cell (*north, south, west* and *east*, as well as *northwest, northeast, southwest* and *southeast*). This implies that the possible values for ratio of same-color neighbors are 0, 0.125, 0.25, 0.375, 0.5, 0.625, 0.75, 0.875 and 1. Correspondingly, these are the meaningful choices for parameter t as well.

4   Results

Our computer simulations confirm that the Schelling-inspired collective ant algorithm results in efficient spatial clustering of objects. The left half of Fig. 1 illustrates the workings of the algorithm in the case of a single object type (top row) and in the case of 3 colors (bottom row). The left panels show the initial, random distribution of objects, while the right ones display the world after 1000 time steps. White cells are empty, while cells of color contain objects. The improvement of spatial clustering is clearly visible. Following the 719th time step, the state of the world does not change anymore. However, by the nature of the algorithm, the ants (not shown) keep wandering around randomly. This can be useful in a dynamic environment where objects may disappear, or new ones may appear, or external forces may disturb the spatial allocation of objects. In such cases, the algorithm is capable of dynamically reacting to the changes.

To measure the performance of the algorithm, we need a measure of spatial order, or of randomness in a spatial configuration. A natural idea would be a

---

[2] https://github.com/lgulyas1972/Schelling-s-Ants.

[3] For reference, the typical time-to-convergence on a 15 × 15 grid with 10 agents was 1s on a Dell Latitude 5300 laptop with Intel(R) Core(TM) i7-8665U CPU @1.90GHz and 16GB RAM running 64 bit Windows.

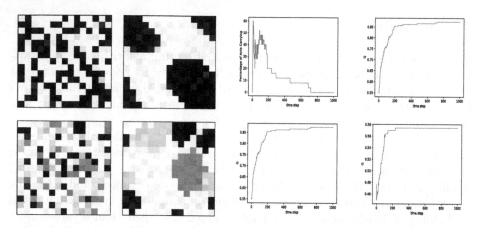

Fig. 1. Workings of the algorithm (left half) and its measurements (right half). The initial configuration (col 1) and the state after 1000 steps (col 2) for a case of $s = 15, n = 25, d = 0.45$ and $c = 1, t = 0.4$ (top row), $c = 3, t = 0.3$ (bottom row). White cells are empty, darker ones contain objects. In-run time series of the % of agents carrying objects (col 3, top) and that of q (col 4, top) during the run with $c = 1$. The Q of the same run (col 3, bottom) and that of a non-converging run (col 4, bottom).

spatial version of *entropy*. However, the interpretation of *spatial entropy* is not straightforward as it involves the partitioning of space with varying resolutions [11,12]. Instead, we calculate the ratio of neighboring cells containing same color objects for each location, handling empty cells as if containing objects of a special color. The average of this ratio across all cells will be denoted by q. This measure, in effect, approximates the total length of boundaries between cells containing objects of different types. The higher the average ratio of same color neighbors, the fewer the number of 'edges' between cells that are part of the boundary. The shorter the length of the boundary is, the larger the patches containing same color object and thus the higher the quality of spatial clustering. The top of column 4 of Fig. 1 shows the evolution of q during the course of the simulation with a single color.

Depending on t, in relation to c and d, ants may never find the final location of all objects, but may keep carrying them. In these cases the spatial order 'on the ground' may increase without solving the original problem, as ants, in effect, remove a significant number of objects from the grid. Thus we introduce a new measure, denoted by Q, that penalizes objects in carry. The ρ_i ratio of same color neighbors of ant i will be 1 if the ant is not carrying, as this is the best possible ratio, and it will be 0 for carrying ants.

$$q = \frac{\sum_{i=1}^{s}\sum_{j=1}^{s}\rho_{ij}}{s^2} \qquad Q = \frac{\sum_{i=1}^{s}\sum_{j=1}^{s}\rho_{ij}+\sum_{i=1}^{n}\rho_i}{s^2+n} \qquad (1)$$

where ρ_{ij} is the ratio of same color neighbors of the cell at location (i, j).

The bottom row of the right half of Fig. 1 shows the in-run evolution of Q for the single color case (left panel) and for a non-converging case (right panel)

In the following, we will use the difference of Q between the emerging final state and that of the initial configuration as a concise way to discuss the improvement of quality achieved by the algorithm. We will denote this value by Δ_Q.

We also consider the time it takes for the collective of ants to achieve the above measured improvement on spatial clustering. This is the number of time steps from the start until the last time step in which there are ants carrying objects. We denote this by t_{conv}, or time to converge. To decouple from the number of ants working, we also count the number of moves ants make carrying an object. That is, the number of elementary moves objects need to go through in order to reach the spatial configuration with improved order. This measure will be called the 'number of carrying hops' and will be denoted by H_c.

For the runs of Fig. 1 the values of these measures are $t_{conv} = 719$, $\Delta_Q = 0.321999$ and $H_c = 3306$ (top row) and $t_{conv} = 483$, $\Delta_Q = 0.33$ (reaching a top of $Q = 0.754$) and $H_c = 5192$ (bottom row). Consequently, the effectiveness of these runs was $\varepsilon = \Delta_Q/H_c = 0.000097$ and 0.000064, respectively. The value of ε gives the average increment of quality per carrying move. Notice that as H_c goes to infinity for non-converging runs, this measure of effectiveness (ε) goes to 0 in such cases.

4.1 Dependence on Parameters

We studied the performance of the algorithm by extensive computational experiments exploring the parameter space (for explored parameter combinations, see Table 1). For each combination 10 sample runs were made (13500 runs in total) that were stopped after 2000 time steps.

Table 1. The parameter configurations of the computational experiments

Name	Meaning	Value(s)
s	Size of grid (world)	15
n	Number of ants	10, 30, 50
d	Density of objects	0.1, 0.2, 0.3, 0.4, 0.5, 0.6, 0.7, 0.8, 0.9 1
c	Number of object types	1, 2, 3, 4, 5
t	Threshold (pick-up/put-down)	0, 0.125, 0.25, 0.375, 0.5 0.625, 0.75, 0.875, 1.0

Figure 2 summarizes our results for selected parameter combinations. The top panel shows the convergence properties: a converging and a non-converging regime, a phase transition between them as a function of t with large variance around the critical value. This critical t value depends on c and d. In the converging region, t_{conv} grows with t. Note, however, that quick convergence may not mean optimal results. It may also signal the algorithm's inability to perform its task. The quality increase (Δ_Q) achieved during the runs is shown on the middle panel. Again, two regimes with a high-variance critical threshold separating them. In the convergence region Δ_Q increases with t (except for regions

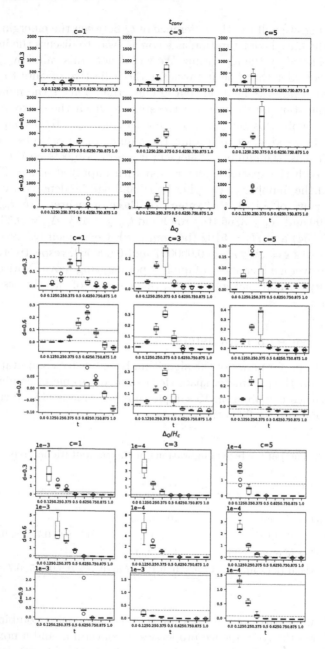

Fig. 2. Boxplots summarizing the results of 10 runs for $n = 10$ as a function of d, c and t. Top: t_{conv}, middle: Δ_Q, bottom: ε, i.e., Δ_Q/H_c. The boxes extend from the Q1 to Q3 quartile values of the data, with a line at the median (Q2). The whiskers extend from the edges of the boxes to show the range of the data. Outliers are plotted as separate dots. Non-converging runs have no data points. Note the varying range of the vertical axis on the individual plots. For comparison, the red lines show the best (solid) and mean (dashed) performance of the Classic Algorithm for the given problem across that algorithm's parameter combinations. Notice the lack of convergence in many cases.

of likely premature convergence, e.g. at high densities and few colors). In the non-convergence region Δ_Q decreases as t grows, due to the correction factor of Q, i.e., the penalty for ants still carrying. The negative values are also due to this (no ant is carrying at the beginning). The effectiveness is plotted on the bottom panel. Due to the construction of ε (non-convergence means ever increasing H_c and thus ε going to 0), the two regimes have disappeared. Also notice the missing values for high densities and few colors, when the agents could not even start – yielding $H_c=0$. On the other hand, in the convergence region we see a monotonic decrease with increasing t. This suggests that with lower t the ants are able to find the highest-gain moves, but fine-tuning the spatial configuration requires a threshold closer to the critical value. Overall, Fig. 2 shows that there is a sweet spot of $t \in [0.25, 0.675]$ for all combinations of c and d, yielding best results. For comparison, the red lines show the best (solid) and mean (dashed) performance of the Classic Algorithm for the given problem across a pool of that algorithm's parameter combinations. Notice the lack of convergence in many cases.

5   Conclusion and Future Works

This paper revisited the task of spatial clustering and one of the early SI algorithms and introduced a novel variant inspired by the problem's qualitative similarity to Schelling's Segregation model. We studied the new variant both by discussing individual runs and by analysing the algorithm's performance as a function of task and algorithm parameters. Such a method for the collective clustering of objects in 2D space may find applications in *swarm robotics*, but it may also be generalised to distributed *edge computing* environments of 5G communication networks populated by *mobile software agents* [13,14]. For this, generalisations of both the task and algorithm will be necessary (e.g., allowing several objects on a cell and working with network-based spatial topologies, etc.). These will be reported in subsequent papers.

References

1. Chakraborty, A., Kar, A.: Swarm Intelligence: A Review of Algorithms (2017). https://doi.org/10.1007/978-3-319-50920-4_19
2. Lones, M.A.: Mitigating Metaphors: A Comprehensible Guide to Recent Nature-Inspired Algorithms. SN COMPUT. SCI. **1**, 49 (2020). https://doi.org/10.1007/s42979-019-0050-8
3. Beckers, Ralph, Goss, S., Deneubourg, J.-L., Pasteels, J.: Colony size, communication and ant foraging strategy. Psyche **96** (1989). https://doi.org/10.1155/1989/94279.
4. Dorigo, M., Birattari, M., Stutzle, T.: Ant colony optimization. IEEE Comput. Intell. Mag. **1**(4), 28–39 (2006)
5. Schelling, T.C.: Micromotives and macrobehavior. Norton, New York (1978)
6. The powers and perils of using digital data to understand human behaviour (Editorial). Nature **595**, 149–150 (2021). https://doi.org/10.1038/d41586-021-01736-y

7. Sendova-Franks, A.B., Scholes, S.R., Franks, N.R., Melhuish, C.: Brood sorting by ants: two phases and differential diffusion. Anim. Behav. **68**(5), 1095–1106 (2004)
8. Bonabeau, E., Theraulaz, G., Fourcassié, V., Deneubourg, J.-L.: The Phase-Ordering Kinetics of Cemetery Organization in Ants. Santa Fe Institute, Working Papers. 57 (1998). https://doi.org/10.1103/PhysRevE.57.4568
9. Parunak, H.V.: "Go to the ant": engineering principles from natural multi-agent systems. Ann. Oper. Res. **75**, 69–101 (1997)
10. Wilensky, U.: NetLogo (1999). https://ccl.northwestern.edu/netlogo/ Center for Connected Learning and Computer-Based Modeling, Northwestern University, Evanston, IL
11. Batty, M.: Spatial Entropy. Geograph. Anal. **6**, 1–31 (1974). https://doi.org/10.1111/j.1538-4632.1974.tb01014.x
12. Wang, C., Zhao, H.: Spatial heterogeneity analysis: introducing a new form of spatial entropy. Entropy **20**(6), 398 (2018). https://doi.org/10.3390/e20060398
13. Guo, Y., Jiang, C., Wu, T.-Y., Wang, A.: Mobile agent-based service migration in mobile edge computing. Int. J. Commun Syst. **34**, e4699 (2021)
14. Sittón-Candanedo, I., Alonso, R.S., Corchado, J.M., Rodríguez-González, S., Casado-Vara, R.; A review of edge computing reference architectures and a new global edge proposal, Future Generation Computer Systems, vol. 99, 2019, pp. 278–294. https://doi.org/10.1016/j.future.2019.04.016

A New Variant of the Distributed Permutation Flow Shop Scheduling Problem with Worker Flexibility

Tasnim Mraihi[1,4]([✉]) [iD], Olfa Belkahla Driss[2,4] [iD], and Hind Bril EL-Haouzi[3] [iD]

[1] Ecole Nationale des Sciences de l'Informatique,
Université de la Manouba, Manouba, Tunisia
tasnimmraihi@gmail.com
[2] Ecole Supérieure de Commerce de Tunis,
Université de la Manouba, Manouba, Tunisia
olfa.belkahla@esct.uma.tn
[3] Université de Lorraine, CRAN, UMR 7039, Campus Sciences,
BP 70239, 54506 Vandœuvre-lès-Nancy cedex, France
hind.el-haouzi@univ-lorraine.fr
[4] LARIA La Recherche en Intelligence Artificielle, ENSI,
Université de la Manouba, Manouba, Tunisia

Abstract. This paper studies for the first time a new variant of the Distributed Flow Shop named Distributed Permutation Flow Shop Scheduling Problem with worker flexibility (DPFSPw). The DPFSPw is a type of distributed production systems in which the production tasks are first assigned to different factories, then, the sequencing of the workers and jobs on machines will be executed. The optimization criterion is the minimization of the maximum completion time or makespan among the factories regarding the availability of the workers on machines. Motivated by the good performances of some heuristics in the literature, we present a constructive heuristic to deal with the DPFSPw. This paper highlights the need to study human factors introduced into the DPFSP that will lead to more realistic insights to enhance the precision and usefulness of operations scheduling models.

Keywords: Scheduling problems · Distributed flow shop · Worker flexibility · Heuristic

1 Introduction

Scheduling problems are ubiquitous in various areas of manufacturing industry engineering and science. They play a significant role in enhancing the productivity, improving the utilization of resources, reducing cost and raising customer satisfaction. It can be applied in different domains including production planning, manufacturing system, logistics and computer design. One of the most competing combinatorial optimization problems in scheduling area is the Flow Shop [1].

C. Bădică et al. (Eds.): ICCCI 2022, CCIS 1653, pp. 587–597, 2022.
https://doi.org/10.1007/978-3-031-16210-7_48

The idea of Flow Shop sequencing was given by the well-known Johnson in 1954 [2]. It can be described as follows: there are m machines that should process n jobs. Job Jj consists of a number of operations. All operations are having strict order to be performed without preemption. The jobs cannot be processed in parallel, and the machines can execute only one operation at any given instant.

The Permutation Flowshop Scheduling Problem (PFSP) is one of the most investigated scheduling problems in the fields of Operational Research and management science [3]. The PFSP can be described as follows: each job from the set $J = 1, 2, \ldots, n$ has to be processed on m machines $1, 2, \ldots, m$ in the same order and meanwhile all the machines should process the jobs in the same sequence [4]. The target of the PFSP is to seek a job sequence on machines so as to optimize the given performance metric.

Nevertheless, in today's highly competitive marketplace, the multi-factory production pattern has become increasingly popular because distributed manufacturing reduces risks, cuts costs and improves product quality [5–8]. Therefore, enterprises start to shift from traditional centralized environment to multi-site production shops in order to increase the efficiency of resource utilization and the satisfaction of customers, improve the capacity of resisting risk, reduce economic cost, and meet environmental policy.

Among this type of decision problems, Naderi and Ruiz extended the regular PFSP to the Distributed Permutation Flowshop Scheduling Problem (DPFSP) where more than one factory is available to process jobs [5]. More specifically, a set of n jobs has to be processed in one of F identical factories, each one consisting of m machines that all jobs must visit in the same order. The decisions involved in this problem are to simultaneously decide in which factory the jobs have to be processed and which is the sequence of the jobs for each factory. The execution times of all the tasks of a given job do not change from one factory to another. All factories are capable of handling all jobs. Once a job is assigned to a factory, it cannot be transferred to another factory and it must be completed once it has started before the resource runs another job. This problem is known to be NP-hard in the strong sense (when $n > F$) [5]. An optimization criterion for a scheduling problem corresponds to the objective function to be optimized. The most commonly studied criterion is the minimization of the maximum completion time, commonly referred to as makespan or Cmax.

Nowadays manufacturing systems have reached a high automation level in all phases of production. The human role evolved towards the control of the operation rather than the manual executions of the activity. Workers are able to perform setup, to deal with machine operations or software, or to handle raw materials and components at a greater pace. The effects of human characteristics such as learning and forgetting, aging, fatigue, etc. can affect the manufacturing processes and their processing times. So, it should be considered when seeking to develop systems-wide scheduling methods to increase productivity of a system [9]. In this context, motivated by the profound impact human resources undoubtedly exert on the performance of manufacturing systems, taking into account human resources in production systems is a field that is worth studying.

However, to our knowledge, there is no study in the literature that addresses this problem of introducing worker flexibility into distributed workshop scheduling issues. It is therefore interesting to study a new variant of the DPFSP with worker flexibility. The aim of this paper is to present for the first time a new variant of Flow Shop scheduling problem named Distributed Permutation Flow Shop Scheduling Problem with worker flexibility, denoted as DPFSPw, which can be defined as a combination of two problems, Distributed Permutation Flow Shop Scheduling Problem (DPFSP) and Flow Shop with worker Flexibility (FSPw).

The paper is arranged as follows: Sect. 2 presents a brief literature review on previous and related research. The DPFSPw is described in Sect. 3. Section 4 describes an heuristic method for the jobs and workers assignment. Finally, Sect. 5 concludes the paper and points several future research directions.

2 Related Literature Review

To the best of our knowledge, the DPFSPw has not been previously studied in the literature. In this section, we first survey the literature on the Distributed Permutation Flow Shop Scheduling Problem and then we continue with the literature on the Flow Shop Scheduling Problem with Worker flexibility.

2.1 Distributed Permutation Flow Shop Scheduling Problem

The Distributed Permutation Flow Shop Scheduling Problem DPFSP was proposed by Naderi and Ruiz. To minimize the makespan, Naderi and Ruiz [5] first proposed two factory-assignment rules (denoted as NEH1 and NEH2) together with 14 heuristic methods and two variable neighborhood descent methods. Lin and Ying [10] formulated a mixed integer Linear programming (MILP) model and developed an iterated cocktail greedy (ICG) algorithm for solving distributed no-wait Flow shop problem. Bargaoui et al. [11,12] proposed an artificial chemical reaction optimization (CRO) algorithm to solve the DPFSP with makespan criterion. Shao et al. [13] designed a constructive heuristics version of variable neighborhood descent to solve the distributed no-wait flexible Flow Shop scheduling problem. Ochi et al. [14] presented a bounded search iterated greedy algorithm BSIG to solve the distributed assembly permutation Flow Shop scheduling problem with the makespan minimization as objective. Naderi and Ruiz in 2014 [15] presented a scatter search (SS) method for the DPFSP problem to optimize makespan. Meng et al. [16] developed three meta-heuristics, a variable neighborhood descent (ORVND), an artificial bee colony (ORABC) and an iterated greedy (ORIG) to solve the distributed permutation Flow Shop scheduling problem with the customer order constraint with the objective of minimizing the makespan among factories. In another way, Xiong et al. [17] focused on the distributed concrete precast Flow Shop scheduling problem to minimize total weighted earliness and tardiness with 3 hybrid metaheuristics, a hybrid iterated greedy algorithm (HIG), a hybrid tabu search and iterated greedy (HTS-IG) and a hybrid genetic algorithm and variable neighborhood search (HGA-VNS). Also, Fernandez-Viagas et al. [18] designed eighteen constructive heuristics to obtain high-quality solutions in reasonable CPU times for DPFSP to minimize the total flowtime.

Through the discussion in the previous paragraph, it can be seen that the DPFSP is a current research hotspot. A large number of heuristic algorithms and meta-heuristic algorithms have been proposed to solve the DPFSP and its variants due to the NP-hardness of the problem.

2.2 Flow Shop Scheduling Problem with Worker Flexibility

The impact of the workforce on the performance of manufacturing planning and scheduling has been widely addressed by the literature in the last decades. Costa et al. [19] presented a backtracking search algorithm powered by a tabu search BSATS to study new hybrid Flow Shop scheduling problem wherein a limited workforce is employed to perform sequence independent setup operations. Gong et al. [20] proposed a hybrid evolutionary algorithm (HEA) to present a new model of energy-efficient flexible Flow Shop scheduling with worker flexibility considering 3 related indicators: green production, time and worker cost simultaneously. Pargar et al. [21] presented non-dominated sorting and ranking water flow-like algorithms (NSWFA and NRWFA) to solve the hybrid Flow Shop scheduling problem with learning effect while minimizing both total tardiness and makespan simultaneously. Bai et al. [22] proposed an effective branch and bound algorithm and a discrete artificial bee colony algorithm to study the Flow Shop Scheduling problem to optimize maximum lateness, where learning effects are introduced for each task. Also, Marichelvam et al. [23] proposed a particle swarm optimization (PSO) algorithm to solve hybrid Flow Shop scheduling problems with the effect of human factors to minimize both makespan and total flow time. Kerdsiri et al. [24] proposed a FEAL, Fatigue Concerned Employee Assignment Technique with Flow Shop Scheduling Optimization using Genetic Algorithm to minimize makespan.

To sum up, we can see that existing research on the DPFSP has assumed that there are no constraints among workers. Besides, there is sufficient work considering human factors in Flow Shop scheduling problems, which can be regarded as the basis and inspiration to study the DPFSP with human factors. Thus, there is a need to aggregate studies including human factors into the DPFSP to improve the production process.

The new Distributed Permutation Flow Shop Scheduling Problem with Worker flexibility is presented in the next section.

3 Description of the Distributed Permutation Flow Shop Scheduling Problem with Worker Flexibility

The proposed Distributed Permutation Flow Shop Scheduling Problem with Worker flexibility (DPFSPw) can be defined as follows: a set of n jobs that must be executed in a set of f identical factories, each of the factories contains the same set of m machines, each job requires the presence of one of the w workers for the duration of its treatment. In addition, a machine is idle until there is a worker available to run it. The change of assignment of employees on the different machines is operated according to the end-of-operation mode, that is, an employee cannot interrupt the processing of an operation before its completion. The worker can then either start processing another operation on the same machine or start processing a job on another machine or simply remain idle. The processing time of each operation, which is operated by a worker on a machine, is fixed. Notably, workers must not be transferred from one factory to another. Figure 1 shows a realistic example for the considered problem.

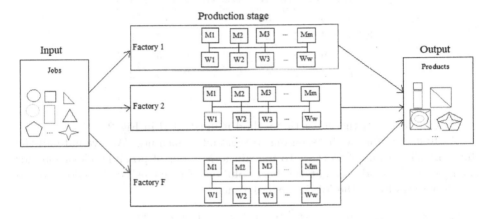

Fig. 1. Illustration of the DPFSPw

Therefore, the DPFSP is more difficult than the classical FSP due to the consideration of both factory selection and job scheduling. The FSP is strongly NP-hard [25] while the DPFSP is much more complicated [5]. Hence, it can be concluded that DPFSPw is also NP-hard. In this work, we had the interest to study the DPFSPw with the objective of minimizing the makespan. In distributed scheduling, makespan minimisation becomes the minimisation of maximum makespan among all factories.

4   Heuristic Method for the DPFSPw

Recall that the DPFSPw requires dealing with two interdependent decisions:

1. Determination of the production sequence in each factory.
2. Distribution of jobs in factories

In order to determine how the worker assignment and job distribution are generated, a re-implemented heuristic based on 2 very known existing heuristics in the literature [5, 26] is presented. Recall that for the regular PFSP, studies show that NEH proposed by Nawaz, Enscore and Ham in 1983 [26] is the best heuristic algorithm to solve this problem [27, 28].

Table 1 shows a situation where we have 2 factories, 4 jobs and 3 workers which we want to assign to 3 machines (let us remind that factories are identical which means that both factories have 3 identical machines with 3 workers to handle it).

Table 1. Processing times for the DPFSPw

	Machine 1			Machine 2			Machine 3		
	W1	W2	W3	W1	W2	W3	W1	W2	W3
J1	4	3	9	3	4	5	7	4	2
J2	9	4	7	6	10	4	8	7	1
J3	7	9	8	8	3	7	9	6	4
J4	7	4	6	6	5	7	9	5	2

The flowchart of the heuristic method is illustrated in Fig. 2.

At first, we start with assigning workers into machines. We evaluate all the different allocations of workers to machines. Number of possible allocations for each job is $A = m!$. We get the best solution after choosing the allocation in which workers finish the job in earliest time:

- For *J1*, we assign *W1* to *M2*, *W2* to *M1* and *W3* to *M3*.
- For *J2*, we assign *W1* to *M2*, *W2* to *M1* and *W3* to *M3*.
- For *J3*, we assign *W1* to *M1*, *W2* to *M2* and *W3* to *M3*
- For *J4*, we assign *W1* to *M2*, *W2* to *M1* and *W3* to *M3*.

To find the best job sequencing, let us first recall the NEH algorithm:

First, we order the n jobs by decreasing sums of processing times on the machines.

Second, we take the first two jobs and schedule them in order to minimize the partial makespan as if there were only these two jobs.

Third, for k = 3 to n do: we insert the kth job at the place, among the k possible ones, which minimizes the partial makespan.

When applying these steps we get the best job sequencing S:

$$S = (J3\text{-}J4\text{-}J2\text{-}J1)$$

We complete by assigning jobs into factories. We have $f = 2$, $n = 4$, $m = 3$ and $w = 3$. Regarding the availability of the workers (a worker is unable to have 2 jobs at the same time and also unable to work in 2 machines at the same time), by applying the first assignment rule of Naderi and Ruiz [5] with S, each job is inserted in all possible positions of all existing factories. The job is finally

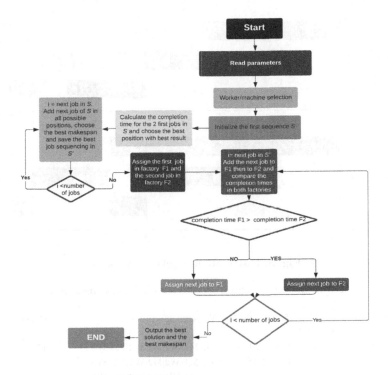

Fig. 2. Flowchart of the proposed heuristic

placed in the position of the factory resulting the lowest makespan value. When processing *J3*, the first in the sequence, there is no difference in allocating it to factories 1 or 2. Therefore, factory 1 is arbitrarily selected. Worker1, worker2, worker3 are fixed in machine1, machine2, machine3, respectively. After scheduling *J3*, the next job to process is *J4*. Since no job has been so far allocated to factory 2, it has the completion time of 0. Therefore, *J4* is allocated to factory 2. Worker1, worker2, worker3 are fixed in machine2, machine1, machine3, respectively. The next job in the sequence is *J2*. The completion times of factories 1 and 2, prior to scheduling *J2*, are 14 and 12 time units, respectively. So, *J2* is assigned to factory 2 because it has the lowest partial makespan all respecting workers/ machines allocation. The procedure repeats similarly for all unscheduled jobs.

The best job sequence is *S* where Jobs *J3* and *J1* are assigned to factory 1 with a lowest makespan value = 17 and jobs *J4* and *J2* are assigned to factory 2 with a lowest makespan value = 17.

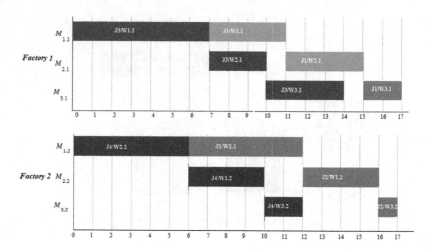

Fig. 3. Distribution of jobs in factories

Table 2. Experimental results for small-sized instances

Instance	Size (f × n × m × w)	Job scheduling	Workers affectation	Cmax
1	2 × 4 × 3 × 3	F1: J3-J1 F2: J4-J2	J1: M1-W1|M2-W2|M3-W3 J2: M1-W2|M2-W1|M3-W3 J3: M1-W1|M2-W2|M3-W3 J4: M1-W2|M2-W1|M3-W3	17
2	2 × 4 × 2 × 2	F1: J1-J4 F2: J2-J3	J1: M1-W1|M2-W2 J2: M1-W2|M2-W1 J3: M1-W2|M2-W1 J4: M1-W1|M2-W2	18
3	2 × 5 × 4 × 4	F1: J4-J5 F2: J2-J3-J1	J1: M1-W3|M2-W4|M3-W1|M4-W2 J2: M1-W3|M2-W4|M3-W1|M4-W2 J3: M1-W3|M2-W4|M3-W1|M4-W2 J4: M1-W4|M2-W3|M3-W2|M4-W1 J5: M1-W4|M2-W3|M3-W2|M4-W1	21
4	2 × 6 × 4 × 4	F1: J3-J4-J5 F2: J2-J6-J1	J1: M1-W3|M2-W1|M3-W4|M4-W2 J2: M1-W3|M2-W1|M3-W4|M4-W2 J3: M1-W4|M2-W1|M3-W2|M4-W3 J4: M1-W4|M2-W1|M3-W2|M4-W3 J5: M1-W4|M2-W1|M3-W2|M4-W3 J6: M1-W3|M2-W1|M3-W4|M4-W2	17

Figure 3 shows the resulting Gantt chart for the best solution obtained in factory 1 starting with *J3* on machine *M1.1* (Machine 1; Factory1) by worker *W1.1* (Worker1; Factory1) and factory 2 starting with *J4* on machine *M1.2* (Machine1; Factory2) by worker *W2.2* (Worker2; Factory2) respectively with a makespan value equals to 17.

Lastly, it is easy to see that each job is assigned to one of the factories and no factory should be left empty to have the best results, taking into consideration the availability of the workers on machines.

To test the efficiency of this heuristic method, and since we are the first to study this new variant of the Distributed Permutation Flow Shop Scheduling problem with Worker flexibility, we generated 4 different scales of instances. In this paper, only small-scale instances are concerned, whereas the number of jobs is up to 6 and the number of machines is between 3 and 4 generated by the same number of workers. Table 2 indicates the results.

5   Conclusion and Future Directions

In this paper, we have studied a new variant of the Distributed Flow Shop Scheduling Problem. This problem comes after considering that human factors should be taken into account in real-world production systems to improve production performance for the reason that worker's production efficiency often greatly affects other workers and even the entire operation process (i.e. constraints among workers exist and should be considered). We named this setting Distributed Permutation Flow Shop Scheduling Problem with Worker flexibility, denoted as DPFSPw. We have characterized this problem by analyzing a feasible solution. We have also demonstrated that for maximum makespan minimization, no factory should be left empty. Notably, workers must not be transferred from one factory to another. Also, a worker cannot interrupt the processing of a job before its completion. The worker can then either start processing another operation on the same machine or start processing a job on another machine or simply remain idle.

Last but not least, based on this study, it is interesting to work on the DPFSPw considering other assumptions such as learning and forgetting effects, fatigue consideration, aging effects and so on with mono or multi-objective functions such as total flow time, maximum lateness, maximum completion times, etc. This research is also applicable to the distributed extensions of other scheduling problems.

References

1. Reza Hejazi, S., Saghafian, S.: Flowshop-scheduling problems with makespan criterion: a review. Int. J. Prod. Res. **43**(14), 2895–2929 (2005)
2. Johnson, S.M.: Optimal two- and three-stage production schedules with setup times included. Naval Res. Logist. Quart. **1**(1), 61–68 (1954)
3. Bargaoui, H., Driss, O.B.: Multi-agent model based on Tabu search for the permutation flow shop scheduling problem. In: Omatu, S., Bersini, H., Corchado, J.M., Rodríguez, S., Pawlewski, P., Bucciarelli, E. (eds.) Distributed Computing and Artificial Intelligence, 11th International Conference. AISC, vol. 290, pp. 519–527. Springer, Cham (2014). https://doi.org/10.1007/978-3-319-07593-8_60

4. Grabowski, J., Wodecki, M.: A very fast tabu search algorithm for the permutation flow shop problem with makespan criterion. Comput. Oper. Res. **31**(11), 1891–1909 (2004)

5. Naderi, B., Ruiz, R.: The distributed permutation flowshop scheduling problem. Comput. Oper. Res. **37**(4), 754–768 (2010)

6. Fernandez-Viagas, V., Framinan, J.M.: A bounded-search iterated greedy algorithm for the distributed permutation flowshop scheduling problem. Int. J. Prod. Res. **53**(4), 1111–1123 (2015)

7. Bargaoui, H., Belkahla Driss, O., Ghedira, K.: Minimizing makespan in multi-factory flow shop problem using a chemical reaction metaheuristic. In: 2016 IEEE Congress on Evolutionary Computation (CEC) (2016)

8. Chaouch, I., Driss, O.B., Ghedira, K.: A survey of optimization techniques for distributed job shop scheduling problems in multi-factories. In: Silhavy, R., Senkerik, R., Kominkova Oplatkova, Z., Prokopova, Z., Silhavy, P. (eds.) CSOC 2017. AISC, vol. 574, pp. 369–378. Springer, Cham (2017). https://doi.org/10.1007/978-3-319-57264-2_38

9. Lodree, E.J., Geiger, C.D., Jiang, X.: . Taxonomy for integrating scheduling theory and human factors: Review and research opportunities. Int. J. Ind. Ergon. **39**(1), 39–51 (2009)

10. Lin, S.-W., Ying, K.-C.: Minimizing makespan for solving the distributed no-wait flowshop scheduling problem. Comput. Ind. Eng. **99**, 202–209 (2016)

11. Bargaoui, H., Belkahla Driss, O., Ghédira, K.: A novel chemical reaction optimization for the distributed permutation flowshop scheduling problem with makespan criterion. Comput. Ind. Eng. **111**, 239–250 (2017)

12. Bargaoui, H., Belkahla Driss, O., Ghédira, K.: Towards a distributed implementation of chemical reaction optimization for the multi-factory permutation flowshop scheduling problem. Procedia Comput. Sci. **112**, 1531–1541 (2017)

13. Shao, W., Shao, Z., Pi, D.: Effective constructive heuristics for distributed no-wait flexible flow shop scheduling problem. Comput. Oper. Res. **136**, 105482 (2021)

14. Ochi, H., Belkahla Driss, O.: Scheduling the distributed assembly flowshop problem to minimize the makespan. Procedia Comput. Sci. **164**, 471–477 (2019)

15. Naderi, B., Ruiz, R.: A scatter search algorithm for the distributed permutation flowshop scheduling problem. Eur. J. Oper. Res. **239**(2), 323–334 (2014)

16. Meng, T., Pan, Q.-K., Wang, L.; A distributed permutation flowshop scheduling problem with the customer order constraint. Knowledge-Based Systems, 104894 (2019)

17. Xiong, F., Chu, M., Li, Z., Du, Y., Wang, L.: Just-in-time scheduling for a distributed concrete precast flow shop system. Comput. Oper. Res. **129**, 105204 (2021)

18. Fernandez-Viagas, V., Perez-Gonzalez, P., Framinan, J.M.: The distributed permutation flow shop to minimize the total flowtime. Comput. Ind. Eng. **118**, 464–477 (2018)

19. Costa, A., Fernandez Viagas, V., Framinam, J.M.: Solving the hybrid flow shop scheduling problem with limited human resource constraint. Comput. Ind. Eng. **146**, 106545 (2020)

20. Gong, G., Chiong, R., Deng, Q., Han, W., Zhang, L., Lin, W., Li, K.; Energy-efficient flexible flow shop scheduling with worker flexibility. Expert Syst. Appl. **141**, 112902 (2019)

21. Pargar, F., Zandieh, M., Kauppila, O., Kujala, J. (2018). The Effect of Worker Learning on Scheduling Jobs in a Hybrid Flow Shop: A Bi-Objective Approach. J. Syst. Sci. Syst. Eng. 27, 265–291

22. Bai, D., Bai, X., Yang, J., Zhang, X., Ren, T., Xie, C., Liu, B.: Minimization of maximum lateness in a flowshop learning effect scheduling with release dates. Comput. Ind. Eng. **158**, 107309 (2021)
23. Marichelvam, M.K., Geetha, M., Tosun, Ö.; An improved particle swarm optimization algorithm to solve hybrid flowshop scheduling problems with the effect of human factors - a case study. Comput. Oper. Res. **114**, 104812 (2019)
24. Kerdsiri, S., Aramkul, S., Champrasert, P.: Fatigue consideration optimization model for employee allocation in flow shop scheduling problems. In: 2019 IEEE 6th International Conference on Industrial Engineering and Applications (ICIEA) (2019)
25. Garey, M.R., Johnson, D.S., Sethi, R.: The Complexity of Flowshop and Jobshop Scheduling. Math. Oper. Res. **1**(2), 117–129 (1976)
26. Nawaz, M., Enscore, E.E., Jr., Ham, I.: A heuristic algorithm for the m-machine, n-job flow shop sequencing problem. OMEGA Int. J. Manage. Sci. **11**(1), 91–95 (1983)
27. Kalczynski, P.J., Kamburowski, J.: An improved NEH heuristic to minimize makespan in permutation Flow shops. Comput. Oper. Res. **35**, 3001–3008 (2008)
28. Framinan, J.M., Leisten, R., Rajendran, C.: Different initial sequences for the heuristic of Nawaz, Enscore and Ham to minimize makespan, idletime or flowtime in the static permutation flowshop sequencing problem. Int. J. Prod. Res. **41**, 121–148 (2003)

Resource Allocation Strategy on Yarn Using Modified AHP Multi-criteria Method for Various Jobs Performed on a Heterogeneous Hadoop Cluster

Emna Hosni[1]([✉])(iD), Nader Kolsi[2], Wided Chaari[3], and Khaled Ghedira[4]

[1] National School of Computer Sciences, LARIA, Manouba, Tunisia
emna.hosni@ensi-uma.tn
[2] School of Business, LARIA, Tunis, Tunisia
nader.kolsi@esct.uma.tn
[3] National School of Computer Science, LARIA, Tunis, Tunisia
wided.chaari@ensi-uma.tn
[4] Ibn Khaldoun University, UIK, Tunis, Tunisia
khaled.ghedira@esprit.tn

Abstract. Recently, Hadoop has been used extensively to process a large amount of data. However, it still faces resource allocation and load imbalance issues in a heterogeneous environment. The objective of this work is to present an efficient resource allocation approach based on multi-criteria decision making to assign resources required by the given job in a heterogeneous Yarn cluster. The proposed model considers node and job heterogeneity as constraints to achieve the best resource allocation while maintaining multiple performance criteria (CPU, Disk, Network and Memory) in real time. It is applied to Yarn architecture using a modified analytical hierarchy process (AHP). This work aims at mitigating load imbalance and improve the resource use when jobs and machines have heterogeneous characteristics. The implemented model provided better cluster resource utilization and reduced the job completion time over comparable Hadoop schedulers FIFO, Fair and TMSA, by 38.3%, 19.4% and 15%, respectively.

Keywords: Resource utilization · Yarn heterogeneous cluster · Job allocation · Multi-criteria decision · Load balancing

1 Introduction

Hadoop Apache[1] is the most popular framework that manages data processing and storage for Big Data applications in scalable clusters. Yarn (Yet another Resource Negotiator) is responsible to schedule jobs to be executed on different clusters and manage resources for various applications [7]. In the last decades,

---

[1] https://hadoop.apache.org/.

C. Bădică et al. (Eds.): ICCCI 2022, CCIS 1653, pp. 598–611, 2022.
https://doi.org/10.1007/978-3-031-16210-7_49

Hadoop system has been studied in several research works [1,2,6,8,11] in order to enhance job allocation and resource utilization, especially in a heterogeneous Hadoop cluster. In fact, when managing jobs in heterogeneous nodes in real time, it is more difficult to ensure cluster balance, which reduces the overall performance of Yarn. Therefore, efficient resource allocation becomes a crucial challenge in a heterogeneous cluster for Hadoop [13,14]. In this context, different types of heterogeneity should be considered when managing resources. However, the existing resource management [1] approaches designed for homogeneous Hadoop environments are not efficiently used in a heterogeneous cluster. They may also cause load imbalance. To overcome this problem, researchers focused on the heterogeneity issues in order to achieve the best trade-off between the required resources and the current capacities of a given node. In fact, heterogeneity factors are mainly due to the various resources requested by each type of submitted job (e.g., CPU-Bound, Memory-Bound, etc.) and the different CPUs, RAMs, disks and network bandwidths of nodes. In fact, dealing with node heterogeneity and task characteristics plays a critical role in improving Hadoop performance. In this paper, the use of a multi-criteria decision-making approach improves the load balancing and the resources utilization in the overall Hadoop system, which represents the main motivation of this work. In this article, the status of the Node Managers (NM) and the types of jobs submitted by the user are taken into account and formulated as multi-criteria decision problems using a modified AHP. The proposed work is a dynamic multi-criteria model for resources allocation in a heterogeneous Yarn cluster called DMRAH. Three main phases describe the introduced model: first, the required resources by each submitted job are identified based on historical job information, then the jobs with similar resource utilization are classified by job type in order to dynamically assign a score to the jobs according to their needs. Secondly, the dynamic scores is obtained in an iterative process, which is based on each job type and the current state of the Node Managers capacities. Finally, DMRAH is performed to allocate the appropriate resources to the different jobs. Experimental results show that DMRAH achieved a better load balancing considering a heterogeneous environment. The rest of the paper is organized as follows. Section 2 presents related work. Section 3 describes the proposed model. Section 4 formulates the problem statement. Section 5 defines the applied algorithm and Sect. 6 illustrates the experimental results. Finally, Sect. 6 provides some concluding remarks and presents a brief conclusion and future works.

2 Related Work

Over the past few years, resources optimization and performance improvements of heterogeneous Hadoop cluster have become important research hotspots. In fact, several studies have been conducted to address the heterogeneity issues in Hadoop system, mainly load imbalance and resource wastage. The heterogeneous environment may cause an imbalance in resource utilization between over-loaded and under-loaded hosts, which degrades resource utilization. For this reason, many authors [1,2,12] have developed new dynamic resource allocation approaches to deal with the heterogeneity challenges, essentially in terms of resource use. We may cite, for instance, the mechanism of the default Hadoop schedulers. The First-in First-out method [3] uses a FIFO queue where the jobs submitted earlier get priority over those submitted later. The second job has to wait till the first job is accomplished or resources are made available. In fact, nodes that do not have resources to perform an assigned task, cannot continue to execute tasks, which deteriorates the system performance, results in imbalance between nodes and decreases the system performance. On the other hand, Fair Scheduler [4] use multiple queues for resource allocation based on each queue assignment for different resources. Nevertheless, they were designed initially to be employed in homogeneous Hadoop clusters. However, these policies cause load imbalance while distributing data over a heterogeneous cluster. In [8] suggested performance-based clustering of Hadoop nodes to load data among the cluster nodes. However, the author did not take into account the heterogeneity of nodes when loading data, which leads to load imbalance and inefficient resource allocation. A scheduler, named H-fair, was proposed [2] and applied in heterogeneous Yarn system. Obviously, it showed good performance in balancing Google workload trace and resource utilization. This scheduler demonstrated higher cluster resource utilization, compared to the Fair Scheduler. Besides, TMSA algorithm [6] improved the resource allocation in Yarn. It considered the node heterogeneity using a prediction model integrated on each Node Manager to estimate the end time of a task. However, this algorithm was developed at a small-scale and only with 10 jobs, which does not clearly reflect the scalability of the approach. In [9] the authors designed an approach to allocate the workload based on the processing capacity of the node. However, in this work, it uses the static resource to determinate the processing capabilities of the node, which may result in inaccurate node computing capacities. It can also cause load imbalance in a heterogeneous environment, which degrades the overall performance of Hadoop system. In the heterogeneous Hadoop environment, nodes have different performance capabilities, especially when executing different types of tasks. This leads to variation in the system loads. Most strategies do not ensure load balancing and efficient resource allocation while maintaining node and jobs heterogeneity in real time. Thus, an optimal selection of nodes must be made to achieve a good degree of matching between the required resource and the capacities of the nodes having different characteristics. This matching constitutes our main motivation when considering the heterogeneity issues in Yarn. Therefore, in this paper, a multi-criteria decision-making approach strategy is proposed for Yarn resources allocation in a heterogeneous environment. We modify the AHP method [5] to create a dynamic scores according to the demanded resources and node capability to efficiently allocate resources to jobs.

3 Dynamic Multi-criteria Decision-Making for Resource Allocation in a Heterogeneous Yarn Cluster

In this section, we design a mapping between Yarn resource management mechanism and our DMRAH approach applied in heterogeneous environment. This approach is proposed mainly to assign efficiently various jobs to the available current nodes in order to achieve the best load balancing in Hadoop cluster. Figure 1 presents an overview of the proposed model in Yarn architecture. Six dynamic interaction phases which are adapted in Yarn are described as follows: First, when a client submits a job to the Resource Manager (RM), the latter communicates with a Node Manager (NM) to launch an Application Master (AM) to execute the job. In fact, the AM is responsible for submitting resource requests to the RM and negotiating with a set of NMs to launch containers in order to process the tasks of the job. The NM depends on RM to maintain the global view of the cluster resource availability.

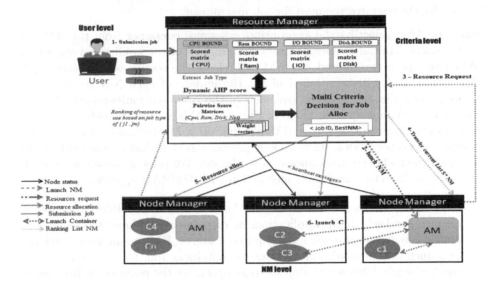

Fig. 1. Proposed model based on multi-criteria method for resource allocation in yarn

Step 1. The client submits a job to the Resource Manager (RM). Then, the NM sends the heartbeat messages, containing the resources availability to RM.

Step 2. DMRAH identifies continuously the requested resource of each job.

Step 3. A dynamic AHP scoring driven by Job information is performed. The scoring step is developed using an iterative process: this step is carried out by improving the accuracy of the AHP method. This improvement consists by collecting the historical log file form the nodes using the APIs provided by Hadoop by creating four score matrices based on the type of job considered in our work. Then, we classified the new jobs by job type using the information of the jobs already executed. At each iteration a submitted job will be scored exactly based on its requested resources. When submitting a job, the relative importance of the resources is dynamically rated based on the client's request. This process is applied dynamically depending on the current state.

Step 4. AM demands resources required by RM to negotiate and launch the appropriate resources containers.

Step 5. After obtaining the dynamic scores of the previous step, the weights of jobs are calculated using the AHP method. Based on this weights, the corresponding computing resources are allocated. The proposed strategy in RM manages the resources of a particular job. It is detailed in the following substeps: 1) after obtaining the appropriate score matrices, the scheduler calculates the global score of all NMs in the cluster. 2) The RM provides AM with a list of high performance NMs to run the submitted jobs. This approach provide the best trade-off between the relative importance of NMs in terms of each criterion driven by the resource required for job assignment.

Step 6. After selecting the appropriate resources container from the RM, the AM launches container and monitors the progress of the application execution. When the job is terminated, the AM will release the resources for the next job. After that, RM will be notified about the update of each NM status. These steps present the architectural overview of the proposed multi-criteria decision for resource management in Yarn. In the rest of this section, we detail each used component. Yarn consists of a RM residing on a Master node, while the NM resides on worker nodes. Yarn runs a job on a NM within a container, which specifies the node resources allocated to the job. We present the components of the Yarn architecture and their interaction with DMRAH approach.

- **Resource Manager RM**: is the Master Node responsible for managing resources and scheduling applications in Yarn. In the developed model, we integrated a dynamic adjustment of required resource. RM communicate with NM to launch the most adequate resources containers and, thus, to perform this particular job. This scheduling strategy optimizes the resources utilization on the overall system and the load balancing in a heterogeneous Hadoop cluster.
- **Node Manager NM**: it runs on each slave of the Yarn cluster. The Node Manager NM first sends periodic heartbeat messages to the Resource Manager [12]. Then, the heartbeats messages describe the node status and the containers running on it. Each NM takes instructions from RM. It also reports and launch containers.
- **Application Master AM**: one AM runs by application and negotiates resources for it. Indeed, each AM requests resources from RM before contacting the corresponding NMs. After that, it launches the containers provided by NM.
- **Container**: the container is represented by the performance resources allocated by RM in which the application tasks are executed.

4   Problem Statement

The Hadoop cluster considered in the present work is described below. A set of m jobs $J = \{j_1, \ldots, j_m\}$ submitted to a heterogeneous Hadoop cluster H. The latter contains a set of nodes having different performance capacities. We define the different AHP criteria in our model based on the types of heterogeneous hardware resources (*CPU, Disk, etc.*) provided by each node. The Hadoop cluster H is a group of related nodes including a Master Node, represented by RM, and worker nodes which are the Node managers. DMRAH compares several criteria of each node N_i when assigning a different jobs on the cluster. The network traffic between the nodes in the cluster is also considered as a decision criterion in our multi-criteria approach. The network traffic is reduced by increasing a data-local on the machines. The suggested solution guarantees the best trade-off between required job and the resource available in the cluster.

We define a cluster $H = \{N_1, \ldots, N_n\}$ which is composed of a set of heterogeneous nodes. Each node N_i is assumed to have different capacities denoted criterion according to AHP model [5]. In this paper, We also use the network traffic between two nodes as a criterion for the job allocation decision. A set of jobs J run in cluster H where each job j_i has a different resource demand resources. We can define a job as follows: $j_i = \{id_i, Dcpu_i, Dr_i, Dd_i, Dnet_i\}$ $i = 1, \ldots, m$, where id_i is a unique number that identifies a job j_i, and $Dcpu_i, Dr_i, Dd_i$ and $Dnet_i$ represent the different resources requested by each job according to the criteria of N_k, $k = 1, \ldots, n$, which are based on the usage of CPU, RAM, Disk and Network. In this system, we consider disk utilization, CPU utilization, network utilization and Memory utilization during processing job. We can calculate the disk utilization as follow [10]:

$$U(D_i) = \frac{Use(D_i)}{T(D_i)} \quad i = 1, \ldots, n \tag{1}$$

where, $U(D_i)$ is the disk utilization of the ith node, $Use(D_i)$ is the used disk capacity of the Node N_i and, $T(D_i)$ is the total disk capacity of the Node N_i. Then, we can carry out the CPU utilization as [10]:

$$U(cpu_i) = (1 - Dcpu) \times 100 \tag{2}$$

where, $U(cpu_i)$ is the CPU utilization of the Node, $Dcpu$ is the time spent to job execution. We carry out the Memory Utilization as:

$$U(M_i) = \sum_{i=1}^{k} \frac{Dr_i}{T(M)} \tag{3}$$

Here $U(M_i)$ is the memory utilization of the ith node, Dr_i is the size of the requested memory by the job, and T(M) is a total memory in the node. We also consider the network traffic between NM nodes during job assignment $U(Net)$.

$$U(net) = L_{ij} + (D_{size} \times TT_{Dsize}) \tag{4}$$

where L_{ij} corresponds to the transmission latency between two nodes, d_{size} is the size of data to transfer and TT_{Dsize} designates the transfer time of a data size on network. We also take into account different job types belonging

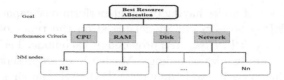

Fig. 2. The AHP hierarchy of the proposed multi-criteria approach

to (CPU-Bound, I/O-Bound, memory-Bound, disk-Bound). These job types are denoted by $Type_J = \{CPU_j^B, I/O_j^B, M_j^B, Disk_j^B\}$. In this paper, the decision of resource allocation is driven by the resources required for jobs running on cluster H by taking into account the available performance criteria of each NM in a real-time. Note that in the Yarn system, only two resources are included $< RAM, CPU >$. Therefore, DMRAH is based on multiple resources evaluation in a heterogeneous environment. The goal of this paper is to achieve the optimal nodes with the highest score or degree of job satisfaction while respecting the current resource constraints in H. This approach connects all levels of the hierarchy from the highest to the lowest level as shown in Fig. 2. This structure helps to define the best representation of heterogeneous nodes performance and to satisfy the different resource requirements. The Yarn resource allocation model is structured on three main levels: goal, set of criteria and alternatives. The hierarchical structure of DMRAH is shown in Fig. 2. The goal is placed at the top of the hierarchy while the evaluation criteria are at the lower level, and the n alternatives are at the bottom of the model which defines the set of NM. AHP determines the relative score of the decision criteria level. Based on the used criteria, a global score of nodes was build at the lower level. In fact, the best nodes of job execution were selected by modifying the AHP score integrated into the resource manager RM. The optimisation problem of job allocation in Yarn was mathematically formulated as follows: Let consider a matrix M with $M = (m_{ij})_{1 \leq i,j \leq n}$. The elements of matrix M demonstrate how much the alternative n_i is preferred to alternative n_j represented by heterogeneous nodes in the cluster H. The assumed reciprocity axiom defines the score ratio (or weight) of node n_i to node n_j depending on their resources use. The pairwise comparison matrix M is given in (5):

$$M = (m_{ij})_{1 \leq i,j \leq n} \quad with \quad m_{ij} = \begin{cases} \frac{w_i}{w_j} & i \neq j \\ 1 & i = j \end{cases} \tag{5}$$

The elements of m_{ij} are represented by the weighing of the different performance criteria of the nodes defined by $\frac{w_i}{w_j}$. The degree of heterogeneity taken into account in this paper concerns the $Type_j$ and the performance of the nodes. It ensures load balancing and cluster resources utilization and maintains the parallel processing of jobs. We modified the criteria score of AHP method to make it more efficient in assigning various jobs in a heterogeneous Hadoop cluster. After receiving the current resource information by the NMs, we gave scores and measured weights for all nodes at the lower level depending on the score and weight already assigned to the resource at the criterion level of AHP structure. The aim of this work is to dynamically select the best current available nodes in the cluster to allocate the resources required by different types of jobs $Type_j$. We first present the pairwise comparison matrix M for criteria level as follows:

$$\textbf{Criteria} \begin{array}{c} Memory \\ Cpu \\ Disk \\ Network \end{array} \begin{array}{cccc} Memory & CPU & disk & Network \\ \left(\begin{array}{cccc} 1 & m_{12} & m_{13} & m_{14} \\ 1/m_{12} & 1 & m_{23} & m_{24} \\ 1/m_{13} & 1/m_{23} & 1 & m_{34} \\ 1/m_{14} & 1/m_{24} & 1/m_{34} & 1 \end{array} \right) \end{array}$$

The next step is to get a normalized matrix. The elements of the matrix $M^{'}$ were calculated as:

$$M^{'} = (m^{'}_{ij})_{1 \leq i,j \leq n} \quad with \quad m^{'}_{ij} = \frac{m_{ij}}{\sum\limits_{i=1}^{n} m_{ij}} \tag{6}$$

The calculation of the weights, i.e. eigenvector (priority vector) $W = [W_i]$ form the normalized matrix $M^{'}$ was achieved by computing the arithmetic mean for each row of the matrix shown by the formula written below.

$$W = [W_i] \quad with \quad W_i = \frac{\sum\limits_{j=1}^{n} m^{'}_{ij}}{n} \quad i = 1 \ldots n \tag{7}$$

The consistency of the comparison Matrix M should be checked. This step results in coherent scoring regarding the pairwise comparisons. According to [5], a matrix is considered consistent if the transitivity rule is valid for all pairwise comparisons. Mathematically, M is consistent iff [5]: $m_{ij}m_{jk} = m_{ik} \quad \forall i,j,k = 1,2,\ldots n$. In order to compare consistency ratio at lower level of hierarchy, the column vectors of the scoring matrix must be first multiplied by their respective weights. The values of rows are summed. The mean of the obtained vector divided by the weight vector constitutes the maximal eigenvalue of $M^{'} = (m^{'}_{ij})$ denoted by λmax. The latter is calculated from the sum of products between each element of Eigenvector and the sum of columns of the matrix. After that, the consistency index CI was calculated by using the formula below [5]:

$$CI = \frac{\lambda_{\max} - n}{n - 1} \tag{8}$$

where n is the number of criteria considered in the Scoring matrix representing the number of the compared elements. In addition, M is consistent iff $\lambda_{max} \geq n$. Subsequently, the consistency ratio CR was obtained by dividing CI value by using the Random Consistency Index RI[2]. In AHP, the consistency ratio CR was obtained using the formula below [5]:

$$CR = \frac{CI}{RI} \tag{9}$$

Saaty [5] showed that $CR \leq 0.1$ is acceptable to continue the AHP analysis. Otherwise, $CR > 0.1$ is a inconsistency matrix and the comparison should be recalculated. Consequently, the consistency validation of all the matrices guarantees the consistency of the ranking established by AHP method. Finally, a synthesis of local weights on all the criteria was performed in order to determine the global weights. AHP approach adopts an additive aggregation by normalizing the sum of the local weights to unity. We consider S^*_{Yarn} as the best score of AHP Yarn approach used to determine the best node manager for job allocation. The global score is given bellow:

$$S^*_{Yarn} = \max_{i=1...n} \sum_{j=1}^{n} W_i \times a_{ij} \tag{10}$$

where a_{ij} is the position of the weight of node N_i with the weight of node N_j is represented in a $(m \times n)$ matrix noted A where m is the number of nodes and n is the number of criteria. This matrix was created at the lower level of the AHP hierarchy using the relative importance of the cluster nodes in terms of each criterion C. W_i designates the weight vector relative to the normalized criteria matrix M' calculated to the next higher level after the top level representing the goal. At the lower level, the algorithm applied the same previous steps to calculate the normalized matrix of NMs (alternatives) in order to obtain a matrix A. The NMs level depends on the elements of the criteria level. After that, the weight vector of the NMs level was multiplied using the weight coefficient of the criteria level elements. The steps were repeated at each level until reaching the top of the hierarchy. The global scores of each decision alternative is then obtained. The results of pairwise comparisons relative to the NM at the lower level of the AHP hierarchy is illustrated by the following matrix $A = (a_{ij})_{\substack{1 \leq j \leq n \\ 1 \leq i \leq m}}$.

In this paper, we consider 3 elements (goal, criteria and alternatives). The proposed approach makes an efficient Yarn job allocation decision to dynamically accommodate the required resources. Therefore, the RM identifies the types of jobs submitted by the user to allow the scheduler to schedule the job efficiently using dynamic score based on each request in order to optimize the resources containers in NM. Finally, based on the heartbeat messages, RM establishes a global scores and sends the list of the best NMs satisfying the resource required to NM. The Node Manager with the highest score value S^*_{Yarn} represents the best trade-off between the node performance and the resource requirements of the given job.

---

[2] RI is the average CI of 500 randomly-filled matrices defined by Saaty.

5   Proposed Algorithm

The algorithm starts by determining the resources required by the jobs and then dynamically groups them to optimize the next process in order to better satisfy the demands of the new jobs. Then the information about the requested resources is saved in RM per job type. For each type of job the Algorithm computes the comparison matrices by AHP but in an iteratively and more efficient. These scores measuring NM's ability to perform a given type of job (Sect. 4). The matrices dynamically calculated uses the AHP scale [5]. DMRAH assigns preference scores to the requested resources in order to achieve a better job allocation to the resources available in Yarn heterogeneous cluster. The scores associated to the types of jobs are based on the node resources used to execute these jobs. DMRAH modifies the attribution of Saaty's preferences [5], because we have different requests in a heterogeneous cluster, which explains the real time change in the scores of the nodes and the importance of calculating new rankings according to a new user's request. DMRAH applied to assign job achieved the best resource allocation driven by the user's demand in heterogeneous Yarn cluster. The global score is defined by S^*. The decisions obtained in certain cases can also be taken as the best alternative. After that, the best node allocates the most

---

Algorithm 1. Dynamic Yarn Multi-criteria Resource Allocation DMRAH

Input: $J = (id_i, Dcpu_i, Dnet_i, Dri, Ddi)$, historical job inf, Resource Criteria C
Output: Best NMs to run a given job j
    for all $j_k \in J$ **do**
        Determine the resource demand per job j_i
        Jobs with similar demand are grouped by $Type_j$
    end for
    for each $Type_j$ **do**
        Create pairwise comparison matrices M_c for a given j
        Calculate AHP weight W_c
    end for {*The matrices of criteria are stored dynamically in RM* }
    Receive status from NMs through a heartbeat messages
    if $NM \neq \emptyset$
    for all C **do** { $C = \{CPU, Disk, Network, RAM\}\}$
    Create pairwise comparison matrices for all nodes M_n
    Calculate AHP weight W_n
    end for
    Calculate the Global Weight (See Eq.10)
    for i **in** list of ranked NMs **do**
        for all j **in** C **do**
        $S^*[i][j] = S^*[i][j] + W_c[j] \times W_n[i]$
    end for { *Obtain the best S^* which equal to S^*_{Yarn} in Eq.10*}
    Update of the nodes ranking in RM
    else
    The system wait for the node to release the resource and return to step 2.
    end if

---

appropriate resource containers to perform a given job while respecting multiple constrains during job assignment in Yarn architecture. Finally, the system waits until the container will be released and will return to step 2. The system run the job and collect the results, which will be used as historical information for the next process allocation.

6   Experimental Results

In this section, we evaluate the performance of DMRAH by conducting experiments in a Hadoop Yarn heterogeneous cluster. Our cluster consists of 10 virtual machines (VM), among these VM nodes: one is configured as Resource Manager node and 9 are configured as worker nodes with heterogeneous performances capacities. All nodes were deployed using VMware and ran the Ubuntu 16.04 operating system. Our experimental environment was deployed in a physical node (CPU Intel Core i9-7960X, 2.8 GHz, 16 Cores) and 64G of RAM. We used Hadoop Yarn 2.7.6 to run the experiments. We implemented our algorithm in all VMs. The HDFS block size and the replication level were set to 128 MB and 3, respectively. We used a historical information in order to identify the job resource type of each submitted job. DMRAH algorithm was applied to deal with how to set appropriate resources requirements for each job type under heterogeneous nodes. The submitted jobs might be bounded by the resources of memory intensive, CPU intensive, network I/O-intensive, etc. We used various types of jobs: a CPU-Bound job depending highly on CPU resource; a IO-Bound job specified by the I/O operation and maintaining a low CPU utilization rate; and jobs having memory access intensity classified as memory-Bound. The obtained results were evaluated using various job types available in Hadoop such as TeraSort (CPU-Bound and I/O-Bound Job), WordCount (CPU-Bound) and Sort (IO-Bound). However, compared with FIFO, Fair and TMSA [6], DMRAH reduced noticeably the completion time of jobs. When the number of jobs was equal to 10, DMRAH registered an improvement of 11%, 34.0% and 21% compared respectively to TMSA and FIFO and Fair. When executing 20 jobs our approach achieve the minimum completion time compared to FIFO, Fair and TMSA by 38,1 %, 17% and 21.4%, respectively. We notice that DMRAH algorithm enhanced the job completion time when the number of jobs increased, which ameliorated the performance of the overall Yarn cluster. Figure 3(e) presents the resource utilization of the FIFO, Fair schedulers, TMSA and DMRAH. The proposed approach provided the best resource utilization results. It gave a resource utilization rate of 82% when executing CPU-Bound job. This rate is higher than those provided by TMSA [6], Fair and FIFO by 28.04%, 32.9% and 39% respectively. The results reveal that Fair and FIFO schedulers have a low rate of resource utilization when running IO-Bound and Memory-Bound compared to TMSA [6] and DMRAH due to the fact that our work has a more accurate allocation based on a multi-criteria model which allocates resources with high utility while satisfying the required resources of various job and, subsequently, optimizing the resource consumption on heterogeneous Yarn cluster. DMRAH provided dynamically the best node to execute a given job considering the heterogeneity of its capacities. A graphic representation exposes the ranks of the NMs based on CPU Bound job Fig. 3(a), on memory-Bound Fig. 3(b), and I/O-bound Fig. 3(c). For example, the NM rankings obtained in Fig. 3(a) show that N9 is the most efficient node able to execute a CPU-Bound job in the real time on a heterogeneous environment.

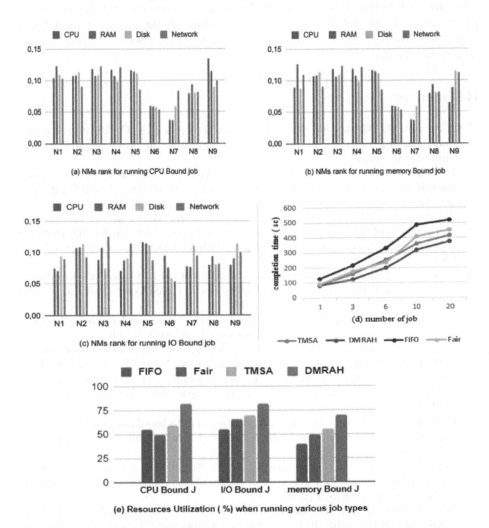

Fig. 3. (a). NMs rank for CPU Bound job, (b). NMs rank for memory Bound job, (c) NMs rank for running IO Bound job, (d). The completion time (sec), (e). Resource Utilization (%) of Fair, TMSA, FIFO and DMRAH.

7 Conclusion and Future Works

In this paper, we proposed a dynamic multi-criteria model for resource allocation in a heterogeneous Yarn cluster called DMRAH. This model efficiently allocates resources that have a high score based on the different resources requested allowing for a better match between the available resources and the job needs. In future work, we will evaluate the performance of our approach on a larger scale with different job sizes to achieve more accurate resource allocation in a real environment.

References

1. Awaysheh, F., Alazab, M., Garg, S., Niyato, D., Verikoukis, C.: Big data resource management & networks: taxonomy, survey, and future directions. IEEE Commun. Surv. Tutor. (2021)
2. Postoaca, A., Pop, F., Prodan, R.: h-Fair: asymptotic scheduling of heavy workloads in heterogeneous data centers. In: 18th IEEE/ACM International Symposium on Cluster, Cloud and Grid Computing (CCGRID), pp. 366–369 (2018)
3. Shu-Jun, P., Xi-Min, Z., Da-Ming, H., Shu-Hui, L., Yuan-Xu, Z.: Optimization and research of Hadoop platform based on FIFO scheduler. In: 7th International Conference on Measuring Technology and Mechatronics Automation, pp. 727–730 (2015)
4. Sharma, G., Ganpati, A.: Performance evaluation of fair and capacity scheduling in Hadoop Yarn. In: 2015 International Conference on Green Computing and Internet of Things (ICGCIoT), pp. 904–906 (2015)
5. Saaty, T.: Decision Making for Leaders: The Analytic Hierarchy Process for Decisions in a Complex World. RWS Publications, Pittsburgh (1990)
6. Wang, M., Wu, C., Cao, H., Liu, Y., Wang, Y., Hou, A.: On mapReduce scheduling in Hadoop yarn on heterogeneous clusters. In: 2018 17th IEEE International Conference on Trust, Security and Privacy in Computing and Communications/12th IEEE International Conference On Big Data Science And Engineering, pp. 1747–1754 (2018)
7. Bawankule, K., Dewang, R., Singh, A.: Historical data based approach for straggler avoidance in a heterogeneous Hadoop cluster. J. Amb. Intell. Hum. Comput. **12**, 9573–9589 (2021)
8. Paik, S., Goswami, R., Roy, D., Reddy, K.: Intelligent data placement in heterogeneous Hadoop cluster. In: International Conference on Next Generation Computing Technologies, pp. 568–579 (2017)
9. Naik, N., Negi, A., Br, T., Anitha, R.: A data locality based scheduler to enhance MapReduce performance in heterogeneous environments. Futur. Gener. Comput. Syst. **90**, 423–434 (2019)
10. Thu, M., Nwe, K., Aye, K.: Replication based on data locality for Hadoop distributed file system. In: 9th International Workshop on Computer Science (2019)
11. Delgado, P., Didona, D., Dinu, F., Zwaenepoel, W.: Kairos: preemptive data center scheduling without runtime estimates. In: Proceedings of the ACM Symposium on Cloud Computing, pp. 135–148 (2018)
12. Pandey, V., Saini, P.: How heterogeneity affects the design of Hadoop MapReduce schedulers: a state-of-the-art survey challenges. Big Data, 72–95 (2018)

13. Javanmardi, A., Yaghoubyan, S., BagheriFard, K., Parvin, H.: An architecture for scheduling with the capability of minimum share to heterogeneous Hadoop systems. J. Supercomput. **77**(6), 5289–5318 (2021)
14. Xu, H., Lau, W.: Optimal job scheduling with resource packing for heterogeneous servers. IEEE/ACM Trans. Netw. **29**, 1553–1566 (2021)

A Memetic Approach for Routing Problem with Capacity and Time Constraints

Imen Boudali[1,2]([⊠]) [iD] and Marwa Ragmoun[3]

[1] SERCOM Laboratory, University of Carthage, 1054 Carthage, Tunisia
imen.boudali@enit.utm.tn
[2] National Engineering School of Tunis, University of Tunis El Manar, Tunis, Tunisia
[3] High Institute of Computer Sciences, University of Tunis El Mnar, Tunis, Tunisia

Abstract. In this paper, we propose a memetic approach to deal with routing problem with capacity and time constraints. Our approach aims to determine least-cost trips for a homogenous fleet of vehicles that serve a set of geographically dispersed customers with deterministic demands. Customers time constraints and vehicle capacity have to be rigorously respected during the solving process. Our approach is based on a bio-inspired stochastic algorithm that mimics the reaction process of chemical molecules, which interact until attaining a stable state with minimum free energy. Through the sequence of elementary reactions, molecules explore different regions of the solution space toward the lowest energy state. Since the effectiveness of the optimization process mainly depends on the quality of initial population, we integrated a two-step procedure involving greedy randomized construction with local search. In order to assess our approach, we present a wide variety of computational experiments. The obtained results are compared to those of the best metaheuristics. These results confirm the effectiveness and good performances of our approach.

Keywords: Optimization · Planning · Capacity and time constraints · Memetic algorithm · Population-based method · Local search

1 Introduction

Logistics and transport planning are crucial concern in the economic development of any country since they ensure individual mobility, supplying industries, distribution management, etc. The vehicle routing problem with time windows is one of the most common issue in this context. It consists in finding least-cost vehicle routes that deliver a set of geographically scattered points with known demands while satisfying vehicle capacity and hard time windows for customers. All the routes have to start from one depot, which also corresponds to the endpoint. Each point must be visited only once by exactly one vehicle within a given time interval known as time window. When time windows have to be rigorously respected, the problem is known as the VRP with Hard Time Windows (VRPHTW). However, if these windows may be violated by adding penalties in the objective function, the problem is called VRP with Soft Time Windows (VRPSTW). In

© The Author(s), under exclusive license to Springer Nature Switzerland AG 2022
C. Bădică et al. (Eds.): ICCCI 2022, CCIS 1653, pp. 612–626, 2022.
https://doi.org/10.1007/978-3-031-16210-7_50

literature, the VRPTW and its variants have received a lot of attention from both communities of Operation Research and Artificial Intelligence given their complexity NP-Hard and their importance in many real-world applications [6, 7]. Several exact algorithms have been presented such as exact branch and price algorithm [10], column generation [3, 24], subset-row inequalities [12] and set portioning based model [4]. A literature review of exact methods for VRPTW is provided in [17]. A Hybrid exact method for a variant of VRPTW was proposed in [2] by embedding the column generation method into branch and bound algorithm leading to branch and price algorithm. Let us notice that most exact methods have shown their limitations in solving large instances of VRPTW and its variants. Thus, many heuristic approaches have been proposed in literature. We mainly find Construction methods, two phase methods and improvement methods [7]. We also notice the wide application of many metaheuristics and their hybridization for solving the VRPTW and its variants [7, 9]. We find Genetic algorithms [1, 21], Tabu search [8], Harmony Search algorithm [5, 23], Ant Colony optimization [20], Particle Swarm Optimization [11]. Surveys on metaheuristics and their hybridization for VRPTW are provided in [7, 9]. Experimental results of these metaheuristic based approaches have shown their effectiveness and efficiency for solving the VRPTW.

In this paper, we propose to deal with the VRP with Hard Time Windows by using a memetic approach based on Chemical Reaction inspired metaheuristic. This method is a population-based metaheuristic that was firstly proposed in [13] where its applicability to solve some NP-hard problems in operation research is demonstrated. In fact, it has been applied to tackle diverse real-world problems in both discrete and continuous domains [14, 22]. These applications have shown the splendid performance of Chemical Reaction Optimization method. In order to enhance the intensification and diversification throughout the solving process, we embedded in our approach Greedy Randomized Adaptive Search Procedure. This local search based method has been successfully applied to a big number of classical and real-world combinatorial optimization problems in different fields of science, business and technology [18]. The remainder of this paper is organized as follows. Section 2 formally describes the Vehicle Routing Problem with Hard Time Windows. In Sect. 3 and 4, we present the basic methods of our proposed approach and which are the greedy randomized adaptive procedure and the chemical reaction optimization. In Sect. 5, we focus on our memetic approach GRASP-CRO. In Sect. 6, we discuss the performances of our algorithm through simulations based on benchmark problems. We conclude this paper and give some potential future work in Sect. 7.

2 Problem Description

In order to provide a mathematical description of our problem [7], we assume $G(N, A)$ a non oriented graph where N represents the set of nodes $\{0, .., n\}$ including n customers (C) and the depot 0; and A is the set of arc (i, j) between two customers i and j with a cost c_{ij}. We also consider V a homogenous fleet of m vehicles with identical capacity Q. Each customer i is defined by a fixed demand q_i; a time interval $[e_i, l_i]$ indicating the earlier and latest date of its service; and s_i the service time of customer i. We also denote by a_i^v the arriving date of vehicle v at customer i. The decision variable x_{ij}^v indicates whether arc (i, j) is travelled by vehicle v. The objective function corresponds to the minimization of total distances that are travelled by vehicles. Formally, it is defined by Eq. (1), subject to capacity constraint in Eq. (2) and time constraints in Eq. (3).

$$Minimize \sum_v \sum_i \sum_j c_{ij}x_{ij}^v \quad \forall v \in V, \forall i, j \in N \tag{1}$$

$$\sum_i q_i \sum_j x_{ij}^v \leq Q \tag{2}$$

$$e_i \leq a_i^v \leq l_i \tag{3}$$

Let us notice that a vehicle must wait when he arrived at customer i before e_i, but it is not accepted when it arrived after l_i. Others constraints are also considered in this problem: each customer is visited by exactly one vehicle and each vehicle route must start and finish at the depot.

3   Greedy Randomized Adaptive Search Procedure

GRASP is an iterative metaheuristic, in which each iteration is defined by two steps: construction and local search. The first step generates a greedy randomized solution by progressively inserting elements to the solution set and preserving feasibility. The inserted elements are randomly selected from a list of candidates that are ranked according to the quality of the solution they will achieve. Well-ranked candidate elements are memorized in a Restricted Candidate List (RCL). Once a feasible solution is generated, local search is performed in its neighborhood until a local minimum is found. The best overall solution is retained as the result. In Algorithm 1, we illustrate the main instructions of the greedy randomized construction phase [18]. The generated solutions from the first step are not necessarily optimal. Therefore, a local search step is applied to these solutions for improvements. Local search technique consists in successively replacing the current solution by a better one in its neighborhood N. The end of the search is detected when no better solution is found (see Algorithm 2) [18].

Algorithm 1. Greedy Randomized Construction
Input: Objectif function f, Constraints, the set of elements E
Output: S
1. $S \leftarrow \emptyset$
2. $C \leftarrow E$; /* initialization of the candidate set C*/
3.   For $\forall e \in C$
4.   Evaluate the incremental cost $f(e)$
5.   While $C \neq \emptyset$ Do
6.   Build RCL $\leftarrow \{e \mid f(e)$ are the smallest costs$\}$
7.   Select randomly $s \in$ RCL
8. $S \leftarrow S \cup \{s\}$
9.   Update the candidate set C;
10.   For $\forall e \in C$
11.   Revaluate the incremental cost $f(e)$
12. return S;

> **Algorithm 2. Local Search**
> **Input**: Objectif function f, Constraints, Solution S
> **Output**: S
>
> 1. while S is not locally optimal do
> 2.   Find $S' \in N(S)$ with $f(S') < f(S)$;
> 3. $S \leftarrow S'$;
> 4. return S:

4 Chemical Reaction Optimization

4.1 Basic Concepts

CRO has been designed on the base of interactions between molecules in chemical reactions [13, 15, 16]. In fact, molecules continuously change in order to attain a stable state with the lowest free energy. Each molecule maintains a certain number of attributes: molecular structure, potential energy (PE), kinetic energy (KE), the number of hits, the minimum hit number, and the minimum value. These attributes are further explained as follows [15, 16]:

- Molecular structure: corresponds to feasible solution of the optimization problem;
- **PE**: represents the cost function value for a molecular structure;
- **KE**: indicates the solution's ability of escaping local optima. When the value of KE is large, the molecular structure could have a rigorous change.
- **NumHit**: represents the number of hits undergone by the molecule.
- **MinHit**: corresponds to the number of hit when the molecule has the best solution. The value of (NumHits – MinHit) is the number of hits the molecule has faced without improving the solution cost.
- **MinVal**: is the least **PE** encountered by the molecules.

In order to explain the chemical reaction process, we assume a closed container with a certain number of molecules. These molecules undergo a sequence of elementary reactions that may change their molecular structures and the related energies. Thus, elementary reactions act as operators under the following four forms: on-wall ineffective collision, decomposition, inter-molecular ineffective collision and synthesis. In the two ineffective collisions, molecules are modified to new molecular structures close to the original ones. Thus, the two operators enable the molecules to search their immediate surroundings on the solution space known as the potential energy surface (PES). However, decomposition and synthesis produce new molecular structures, which may be very dissimilar from the original ones. So, the later operators provide the molecules with the ability to jump to other regions on the PES for better solutions. Consequently, the degrees of diversification and intensification are subject to the actual mechanisms used in the elementary reactions. Through the sequence of elementary reactions, molecules explore different regions of the PES toward the lowest energy state. In this way, the system tries to redistribute the energies (PE and KE) among the different molecules and central energy buffer with respect to the law of conservation of energy. With the evolving process, molecules are getting more stable with lower PE in each subsequent change. This is the key feature of CRO to guarantee convergence to lower energy state.

Algorithm 3. CRO
Input: Objectif function f, Constraints, Dimension of the problem N
Output: M_{Best} and $f(M_{Best})$

1. Initialize *PopSize, KELossRate, MoleColl and InitialKE*
2. *Pop: set of Molecules M* with $|Pop|=PopSize$
3. For each $M \in Pop$ Do
4.   Assign a random molecular structure x
5. $PE = f(x)$
6. $KE = InitialKE$
7. *Buffer = 0*
8. While Not(Stopping_Criterion) Do
9.   Generate $t \in [0, 1]$
10.   if ($t \geq MoleColl)$ then
11.   Select randomly a molecule M from *Pop*
12.   if *(decomposition criterion)* then
13. $(M_1', M_2', Success) = Decomposition(M, Buffer)$
14.   if *Success* then
15. $Pop = Pop\backslash \{M\}$
16. $Pop \cup \{M_1', M_2'\}$
17.   else
18.   ineffective Collision On wall (M, Buffer)
19.   else
20.   Select randomly molecules M_1, M_2 from *Pop*
21.   if (Synthesis Criterion) then
22.   (M', Sucess) = Synthesis (M1, M2)
23.   if (Success) then
24.   Pop = Pop\ {M1, M2}
25.   Pop $\cup$ { M'}
26.   else
27.   inter-ineffective Collision (M_1, M_2)
28. Check for any new minimum solution

4.2   CRO Algorithm

As shown in Algorithm 3, three stages are defined: Initialization, iteration and the final stage [13]. In initialization, some control parameters have to be defined (line 1). Then, initial population of solutions has to be assigned to the set Pop (line 2–7). Let us notice that the size of Pop is variable during the iteration stage according to the effects of decomposition and synthesis. In the iteration stage (line 8–28), a number of iterations are performed until a stopping criterion is matched. This criterion may be defined based on the maximum amount of CPU time, the maximum number of iterations performed without improvements, etc.

At each iteration, a random number t in $[0, 1]$ is generated to decide whether a unimolecular or an inter-molecular collision will be applied (line 9). If t is larger than MoleColl (line 10), a unimolecular collision (decomposition, on-wall ineffective collision) will be performed. Otherwise, an inter-molecular collision (Synthesis, inter-molecular collision) will occur. We notice that we will always perform a unimolecular collision when there is only one molecule in Pop. Afterwards, we check the criteria of decomposition (line 12) or synthesis (line 21) to decide which type of collision (Decomposition or On wall ineffective collision; Synthesis or inter-molecular collision). Then, we verify any new minimum point found and record it. Let us notice that the decomposition criterion (line 12) is specified in the original CRO with a parameter α, which represents the maximum time that a selected molecule is allowed to stay in a stable state. So, the decomposition criterion is defined as: (NumHit − MinHit > α). When this condition is met, decomposition will happen to drive the molecule to search other regions of the Potential Energy Surface (PES). Similarly, the synthesis criterion is specified with parameter β, which describes the least amount of KE a molecule should possess. When the two selected molecules M1, M2 have both KE lower than β, synthesis will occur. So, the synthesis criterion is defined as: ($KE_{M1} \leq \beta$) and ($KE_{M2} \leq \alpha$). Otherwise, an inter-molecular ineffective collision will occur (line 27). This iteration stage is performed repeatedly until a stopping criterion. In the final stage, the solution with the minimum value of f is determined.

5 Memetic Approach

In this section, we present our memtic approach for solving the VRPHTW. This approach is based on a stochastic algorithm that mimics the reaction process of chemical molecules until reaching a stable state. Since the effectiveness of the optimization process highly depends on the quality of starting solutions, we embedded random procedure with the greedy randomized adaptive search procedure for generating the initial population. This feature will provide more diversification for the search process. The percentage of solutions that were generated from the two procedures is the same. Afterwards, the optimization process is performed according to the CRO scheme by considering its different operators. In the following subsections, we detail our solution representation as well as the initialization phase and the optimization process of our approach.

5.1 Solution Representation

A problem solution is a set of feasible routes that begin and end at the depot. Therefore, the molecular structure w of a solution M is defined by a succession of customer identifiers as the example illustrated in Fig. 1. In this solution structure, two routes are defined. We notice that the ending of a route is detected in this sequence when capacity and/or time windows constraints are no longer satisfied.

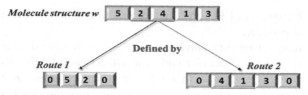

Fig. 1. Example of molecular structure w for a solution M.

5.2 Initialization Stage

During this stage, the solution population is initialized by integrating greedy randomized adaptive search procedure and random procedure. The initial population Pop_{init} is filled with feasible good quality solutions and random solutions, which offer more diversification of the search space. Therefore, an initialization of the GRASP parameters is required (RCL_size and candidate element set E). The generated population is a 2-D matrix where each row carries a molecular structure of one molecule (see Fig. 2). For each solution M, different attributes are computed:

- PE_M: the objective function value;
- KE_M: is initialized with InitialKE;
- $NumHit_M$: is initialized with 0, since no hits were performed for initial solutions;
- $MinHit_M$: is initialized with 0;
- $MinVal_M$: is initialized with PE_M.

Once Pop_{init} is initialized, it is sorted according to PE (see Fig. 2).

Molecule Mi	Molecular Structures Xi					PE (x)
M1	1	5	3	2	4	161.3
M2	5	2	1	4	3	180.8
M3	2	1	5	4	3	199.4

Fig. 2. Structure of Pop and the PE vector.

Afterwards, CRO parameters are configured before launching the optimization process:

- PopSize: initial number of solutions in Pop, i.e. number of rows in Pop.
- KELossRate: upper limit of KE reduction in on-wall ineffective collisions.
- MoleColl: faction of all elementary reactions corresponding to intermolecular reactions.
- InitialKE: initial value of KE for each solution in Pop_{init}.
- Buffer: the central energy buffer which is initially empty (Buffer $= 0$);
- α: maximum time that a selected molecule is allowed to stay in a stable state. We recall that α specifies the decomposition criterion.
- β: least amount of KE a molecule should possess to undergo a synthesis.

5.3 Optimization Process

After the initialization stage, the optimization process is started. In each iteration, we first decide whether the collision is uni-molecular or inter-molecular according to a randomly generated variable t in [0, 1]. When t exceeds the system parameter MoleColl. If t > MoleColl, the collision is considered to be uni-molecular. Otherwise, the collision is inter-molecular. In the first case, one molecule M is randomly selected from Pop and the decomposition criterion is checked. As mentioned above, the decomposition criterion is defined by the following condition: $NumHit_M - MinHit_M > \alpha$. If this criterion is satisfied, the molecule will undergo a decomposition. Otherwise, an on-wall ineffective collision will be performed. For an inter-molecular collision, two molecules M1 and M2 are randomly selected from Pop and the synthesis criterion is checked. As explained above, the synthesis criterion is described with parameter β, which defines the least amount of KE the both molecules should possess. Formally, it is defined by the condition: $(KE_{M1} \leq \beta)$ and $(KE_{M2} \leq \alpha)$. When this criterion is satisfied, the molecules will undergo a synthesis. Otherwise, the collision is an inter-molecular ineffective collision. At the end of every iteration, the population is updated. This iteration stage is repeated until a stopping criterion. Here, we considered a maximum number of iterations. In the final stage, the best solution, i.e. the molecule with the lowest PE value is outputted.

5.4 Collision Operators

Here we detail the different collisions operator as adapted to our routing problem.

On-Wall Ineffective Collision. To illustrate this collision, we assume the molecular structure x of the selected solution M. When M hits a wall and bounces back, its molecular structure does not change rigorously and turns into a new neighboring molecule M'. So, we perform a neighborhood search operator such as pair-exchange or 2-opt (Fig. 3). For instance, we randomly pick two distinct elements from the structure x. Then, we form a new one x' by exchanging their positions. The corresponding $PE_{M'}$ is computed and energy conservation law is checked: $PE_M + KE_M \geq PE_{M'}$. After, $KE_{M'}$ is computed and Buffer is updated. Then, the solution M is updated with the new molecular structure x' and the corresponding energies: $PE_{M'}$ and $KE_{M'}$.

Molecular structure x of M   *Molecular structure x' of M'*

Fig. 3. Example of neighboring Molecule M'

Decomposition. In this collision the randomly selected molecule M hits a wall and decomposes into two molecules M_1 and M_2. The two new molecular structure x_1 and x_2 are obtained from the original structure x by firstly generating two random indexes ind_1, ind_2 within the interval $[- n, +n]$, where n is the size of a solution. The generated values indicate the direction and the number of cyclic swaps to be performed on molecular structure x to obtain x_1 and x_2. As shown in Fig. 4, we assume $ind_1 = 2$, $ind_2 = -1$. So,

x_1 is obtained from x by performing 4 cyclic permutations in the left-right direction; x_2 is obtained by 3 cyclic permutations in the reverse direction. The performance of each molecular structure is computed and the conservation energy law is checked. When the decomposition succeeds, the population Pop is updated with the new solutions M_1, M_2 instead of M.

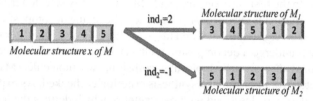

Fig. 4. Example of molecule decomposition

Inter-molecular Ineffective Collision. This collision happens when two molecules M_1 and M_2 collide with each other and then bounce away. Similarly, to on-wall ineffective collision, the molecularity is unchanged before and after the process. The energy management is the same but without involving buffer. We may apply the same operator for on-wall ineffective collision to produce the new molecules from the selected ones (see Fig. 5). For each new molecular structure, PE is computed and the law of energy conservation is checked. If the condition is satisfied, KE of the transformed molecules share the remaining energy in the sub-system. Then, the population is updated with the new molecules.

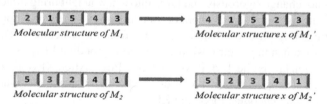

Fig. 5. Example of Inter-molecular ineffective collision

Synthesis. This collision does the opposite of decomposition. A synthesis happens when two molecules hit against each other and fuse together. In order to illustrate this operator, we assume two molecules M_1 and M_2 that have been randomly selected from Pop. First we randomly pick two distinct elements from the structure x_1; $x_1(i)$ and $x_1(j)$. Then, we put them at the same position i and j in the new molecular structure x'. The rest cases are filled with the remainder values according to their appearance in x_2. Each customer identifier appears once in the resulting solution (Fig. 6).

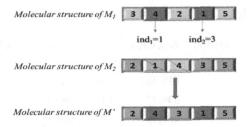

Fig. 6. Example of molecule synthesis.

6 Experimental Study

In order to study the performance of our memetic approach for our routing problem, we first implemented it with JAVA language, on a laptop Intel® Core(TM) i3-3217U CPU @ 1.80 GHZ with 4Go of RAM. Then, we performed an experimental study on the base of Solomon's benchmark problems [19], which are organized in three different classes: C-Clustered, R-Random and RC-Random & Clustered). In our study, we considered 18 instances of these problems. In each instance, we performed different tests by varying the customer number: 25, 50 and 100 customers. Before, presenting the obtained results, we first introduce our algorithm configuration. In fact, we performed preliminary tests to define the parameters values: maximum number of iteration NI, the rate KELoss, MoleColl, InitialKE, α and β. According to our study, we found that the solution performance is getting better when the maximum number of iteration NI increases, the values of KELoss and α raise with a decreasing quantity of MoleColl and β. After our empirical study, we retained the following parameter configuration: InitialKE = 10; KELoss = 0.9; MoleColl = 0.1; α = 100; β = 0.1.

In Table 1, 2 and 3, we provide the obtained results with this configuration by considering instances with 25, 50 and 100 customers, respectively. In each table, we illustrate the best found solution by the metaheuristic CRO, the best solution found by the proposed approach Memetic GRASP-CRO, the best known solution from literature, as well as the percentage of deviation (PD) of our solution from the best known one. As we can see in Table 1, the percentage of deviation does not exceed 6% for instances with 25 customers. Moreover, this percentage is very close to 0% for most instances here (for 14 instances among 18) especially in the case of instances of class C and RC. We notice that the percentage of deviation very close to the results obtained by the metaheuristic CRO only.

Table 1. Comparative study for the case of 25 customers.

Instances	Best-Known solution	Best CRO	PD CRO	Best GRASP- CRO	PD GRASP-CRO
R101	617.1	618.32	0.19	618.32	0.19
R102	547.1	549.35	0.41	548.95	0.34
R103	454.6	461.55	1.51	461.55	1.51
R201	463.3	465.18	0.40	464.37	0.23
R202	410.5	429.35	4.39	425.32	3.48
R203	391.4	425.51	8.02	419.78	6.76
C101	191.3	191.81	0.26	191.81	0.26
C102	190.3	191.81	0.26	190.74	0.23
C103	190.3	192.53	1.16	190.74	0.23
C201	214.7	215.54	0.39	215.54	0.39
C202	214.7	215.54	0.39	215.54	0.39
C203	214.7	219.21	2.01	219.1	2.01
RC101	461.1	463.0	0.41	463.0	0.41
RC102	351.8	352.78	0.27	352.78	0.27
RC103	332.8	334.37	0.47	334.11	0.39
RC201	360.2	361.24	0.28	361.24	0.28
RC202	338.0	339.61	0.47	338.87	0.26
RC203	326.9	330.23	1.01	328.44	0.47

Table 2. Comparative study for the case of 50 customers

Instance	Best-known solutions	Best CRO	PD CRO	Best GRASP-CRO	PD GRASP-CRO
R101	1044.0	1068.42	2.29	1068.42	2.29
R102	822.5	925.75	11.15	944.64	12.93
R103	710.9	791.90	10.23	791.90	10.23
R201	684.4	829.59	17.50	824.61	17
R202	613.6	751.47	18.35	746.25	17
R203	605.3	662.14	8.58	662.14	8.58
C101	362.4	438.69	17.39	438.69	17.39
C102	361.4	434.30	16.79	418.82	13.71

(continued)

Table 2. (*continued*)

Instance	Best-known solutions	Best CRO	PD CRO	Best GRASP-CRO	PD GRASP-CRO
C103	361.4	392.31	7.88	385.15	6.16
C201	360.2	457.53	21.27	395.21	8.86
C202	360.2	431.59	16.54	388.51	7.28
C203	359.8	387.33	7.11	377.37	4.65
RC101	944.0	984.65	4.3	984.65	4.3
RC102	822.5	880.66	6.60	848.58	3.07
RC103	710.9	**735.56**	**3.35**	**679.2**	**−4.66**
RC201	684.8	778.35	12.02	687.65	0.41
RC202	613.6	708.11	13.35	624.61	1.76
RC203	555.3	643.88	13.76	572.85	3.06

In Table 2, we notice that the percentage of deviation from the best known results is less than 21% for the case of problems with 50 customers. This percentage is relatively inferior for instances of class R since it does not exceed 12%. The obtained results for class RC are also promising and even competitive to the best known from literature since the deviation percentage does not exceed 4%. Moreover, for instance RC103 we found a better solution than the best known one with a deviation of −4.66%. Thus, we notice that the percentage of discrepancy is improved compared to the obtained results with CRO metaheuristic.

Table 3. Comparative study for the case of 100 customers.

Instance	Best-known solutions	Best CRO	PD CRO	Best GRASP-CRO	PD GRASP-CRO
R101	1645.79	1721.11	4.38	1715.17	4.05
R102	1486.12	1545.36	3.83	1537.81	3.36
R103	1292.68	**1268.39**	**−1.92**	**1263.92**	−2.28
R201	1252.37	1296.00	3.37	1274.25	1.72
R202	1191.70	**1191.39**	**−0.03**	**1137.49**	−4.77
R203	939.34	1027.29	8.56	993.54	5.45
C101	828.94	1197.03	30.75	1136.31	27.05
C102	828.94	1112.34	25.48	1032.60	19.72
C103	828.06	1029.15	19.54	1032.60	19.81
C201	591.56	988.50	40.16	693.24	14.67

(*continued*)

Table 3. (*continued*)

Instance	Best-known solutions	Best CRO	PD CRO	Best GRASP-CRO	PD GRASP-CRO
C202	591.56	910.23	35.01	695.85	14.99
C203	591.17	816.52	27.60	702.46	15.84
RC101	1696.94	1827.18	7.13	1763.32	3.76
RC102	1554.75	1618.16	3.92	1565.16	0.66
RC103	1261.67	1423.28	11.35	1330.27	5.16
RC201	1406.91	1516.65	7.24	1433.03	1.82
RC202	1367.09	**1335.08**	**−2.40**	**1277.40**	**−7.02**
RC203	1049.62	1105.34	5.04	1074.0369	2.91

In Table 3, we show the obtained results for problems with 100 customers. As we can see, the deviation of our solutions from the best known ones is negligible for instances of class R and RC since it does not surpass 5%. In these two classes, we have even found competitive solutions with lower cost than the best known solutions for the following problems: R103, R202 and RC202. Nevertheless, this percentage is relatively higher for problems of class C since it varies between 14% and 27%. Thus, we notice that the percentage of deviation is improved compared to the results obtained by the metaheuristic CRO in all the classes.

7 Conclusions

In this paper, we proposed to deal with the Vehicle Routing Problem with Hard Time Windows by using a memetic approach based on two metaheuristics that have been successfully applied to many optimization problems: Greedy Randomized Adaptive Search Procedure and Chemical Reaction Optimization. After detailing our solution representation, the preliminary stage and the optimization process of our approach GRASP-CRO, we carried out an experimental study in order to assess its performance.

Therefore, we considered Solomon's benchmark problems by varying the customer number and involving different classes R, RC and C. Preliminary tests have been performed to define the best configuration of our algorithm. Experimental results have shown the competitive performance of the proposed approach GRASP-CRO since competitive solutions to the best known ones, have been found and the overall percentage deviation is low. Given the good performance of our algorithm, we intend to apply it to other theoretical and real-world combinatorial optimization problems.

References

1. Alvarenga, G., Mateus, G., De Tomi, G.: A genetic and set partitioning two-phase approach for the vehicle routing problem with time windows. Comput. Oper. Res. **34**(6), 1561–1584 (2007)

2. Alvarez, A., Munari, P.A.: An exact hybrid method for the vehicle routing problem with time windows and multiple deliverymen. Comput. Oper. Res. **83**, 1–12 (2017)

3. Azi, N., Gendreau, M., Potvin, J.-Y.: An exact algorithm for a vehicle routing problem with time windows and multiple use of vehicles. Euro. J. Oper. Res. **202**(3), 756–763 (2010)

4. Baldacci, R., Mingozzi, A., Roberti, R.: Recent exact algorithms for solving the vehicle routing problem under capacity and time window constraints. Euro. J. Oper. Res. **218**(1), 1–6 (2012)

5. Boudali, I., Mlayah, I.: A hybrid stochastic HS-GRASP algorithm for the VRP with time windows. In: Proceedings of the Mediterranean Conference on Pattern Recognition and Artificial Intelligence - MedPRAI, pp. 64–70 (2016)

6. Boujlil, M., Lissane Elhaq, S.: The vehicle routing problem with time window and stochastic demands: review. In: Proceedings of IEEE 13th International Colloquium of Logistics and Supply Chain Management (LOGISTIQUA), pp. 1–6 (2020)

7. Desaulniers, G., Madsen, O.-B.G., Ropke, S.: The vehicle routing problems with time windows. In: Toth, P., Vigo, D. (eds.) Vehicle Routing: Problems, Methods, and Applications, 2nd edn., Chapter 5, pp. 119–159. MOS-SIAM Series on Optimization, Philadelphia (2014)

8. Desaulniers, G., Lessard, F., Hadjar, A.: Tabu search, generalized k-path inequalities, and partial elementarity for the vehicle routing problem with time windows. Transp. Sci. **42**, 387–404 (2008)

9. Elshaer, R., Awad, H.: A taxonomic review of metaheuristic algorithms for solving the vehicle routing problem and its variants. Comput. Ind. Eng. **140**, 106242 (2020)

10. Gutiérrez-Jarpa, G., Desaulniers, G., Laporte, G., Marianov, V.: A branch-and-price algorithm for the vehicle routing problem with deliveries, selective pickups and time windows. Eur. J. Oper. Res. **206**(2), 341–349 (2010)

11. Gong, Y.-J., Zhang, J., Liu, O., Huang, R., Shu-Hung Chung, H., Shi, Y.: Optimizing the vehicle routing problem with time windows: a discrete particle swarm optimization approach. IEEE Trans. Syst. Man Cybern. Part C **42**(2), 254–267 (2012)

12. Jepsen, M., Petersen, B., Spoorendonk, S., Pisinger, D.: Subset-row inequalities applied to the vehicle routing problem with time windows. J. Oper. Res. **56**, 497–511 (2008)

13. Lam, A.Y.S., Li, V.O.K.: Chemical-reaction-inspired metaheuristic for optimization. IEEE Trans. Evol. Comput. **14**(3), 381–399 (2010)

14. Lam, A.Y.S., Li, V.O.K, Yu, J.J.Q.: Real-coded chemical reaction optimization. IEEE Trans. Evolut. Comput. **16**(3), 339–353 (2012)

15. Lam, A.Y.S., Li, V.O.K., Xu, J.: On the convergence of chemical-reaction optimization for combinatorial optimization. IEEE Trans. Evolut. Comput. **17**(5), 605–620 (2013)

16. Lam, A.Y.S., Li, V.O.K.: Chemical reaction optimization: a tutorial. Memetic Comput. **4**, 3–17 (2012). https://doi.org/10.1007/s12293-012-0075-1

17. Michelini, S., Arda, Y., Crama, Y., Küçükaydin, H.: Exact and heuristic solution methods for a VRP with time windows and variable service start time. QuantOM – HEC- Université de Liège. In: ORBEL 29th Meeting of the Belgium Operational Research Society (2015)

18. Resende, M.G.C., Ribeiro, C.C.: Greedy randomized adaptive search procedures. In: Glover, F., Kochenberger, G. (eds.) Handbook of Metaheuristics, pp. 219–249. Kluwer Academic Publishers (2003)

19. Solomon, M.M.: Algorithms for the vehicle routing and scheduling problems with time windows constraints. J. Oper. Res. **35**(2), 254–265 (1987)

20. Tan, X., Zhuo, X., Zhang, J.: Ant colony system for optimizing vehicle routing problem with time windows (VRPTW). In: Huang, DS., Li, K., Irwin, G.W. (eds.) ICIC 2006. LNCS, vol. 4115, pp. 33–38. Springer, Heidelberg (2006). https://doi.org/10.1007/11816102_4

21. Thangiah, S.: Vehicle routing with time windows using genetic algorithms. In: Chambers, L. (eds.) Application Handbook of Genetic Algorithms: New Frontiers, vol. 2, pp. 253–277. CRC Press, Boca Raton (1995). https://doi.org/10.1201/9781420050073.ch11

22. Xu, J., Lam, A.Y.S., Li, V.O.K.: Chemical reaction optimization for task scheduling in grid computing. IEEE Trans. Parallel Distrib. Syst. **22**(10), 1624–1631 (2011)
23. Yassen, E-T., Masri, A. et al.: Harmony search algorithm for vehicle routing problem with time windows. J. Appl. Sci. **13**, 633–638 (2013)
24. Yuan, Y., Cattaruzza, D., Ogier, M., Semet, F., Vigo, D.: A column generation based heuristic for the generalized vehicle routing problem with time windows. Transp. Res. Part E Logist. Transp. Rev. **152**, 102391 (2021)

A Novel Unfeasible Space Exploring Matheuristic Proposal to Solve the Sum Coloring Problem

Olfa Harrabi[1]([⊠])([iD]) and Jouhaina Chaouachi Siala[2]([iD])

[1] Higher Institute of Management of Tunis, Tunis University,
41, Liberty Street, Bouchoucha 2000, Bardo, Tunisia
olfaharrabikhlif@gmail.com
[2] Institute of Advanced Business Studies of Carthage, Carthage University,
IHEC Carthage Presidency-2017 Tunis, Carthage, Tunisia

Abstract. This research paper deals with a novel matheuristic approach to solve the Sum Coloring Problem. This problem is an extension of the classic graph coloring problem that simply focuses on coloring a given graph with the minimum number of colors. Indeed, the sum coloring problem is a hard-to-solve combinatorial optimization problem that imposes a minimal sum of colors where colors are integers. The work deals with a two-phase infeasible space matheuristic approach for solving the examined problem. The first phase relies on a relaxation of the sum coloring problem using a weight-based formulation to enable the exploration of non feasible solutions and diversify the conducted search. In the second phase, we refer to a hybrid evolutionary approach that efficiently explores the search space and oscillates between the feasible and unfeasible solutions. The computational performance of our approach, based on a set of benchmark instances, turned out to be effective and demonstrate that operating with non feasible solutions leads to promising results on both computation time and solution quality.

Keywords: Sum coloring problem · Chromatic sum · Weight-based formulation · Matheuristic · Evolutionary algorithm · Simulated annealing

1 Introduction

1.1 Review and State-of-the-art

In this paper, we tackle the sum coloring problem (SCP) which is known to be NP-hard [23]. Due to its theoretical and practical importance, the problem has recently begun to attract attention. From a theoretical point of view, SCP is related to other variants of problems like sum multi-coloring [2], sum list coloring [5] and bandwidth coloring [20]. The sum coloring problem can also model many applications in VLSI design [30], scheduling [12] and resource allocation

© The Author(s), under exclusive license to Springer Nature Switzerland AG 2022
C. Bădică et al. (Eds.): ICCCI 2022, CCIS 1653, pp. 627–639, 2022.
https://doi.org/10.1007/978-3-031-16210-7_51

[1]. Given the computational complexity of the problem, polynomial-time algorithms exist on specific graphs: trees, interval graphs and bipartite graphs for instance [22] [3]. Therefore, much effort has been devoted to propose various approximation algorithms.

In 2007, an early Parallel Genetic Algorithm was proposed by Kokosiński and Kwarciany [21]. The algorithm reports upper bounds on 16 small DIMACS graphs. Li et al. [24], in 2009, elaborated two greedy algorithms (MDSAT & MRLF). Experimental results showed that [MDSAT & MRLF] are more performant than the recent DSATUR & RLF [9]. Later in 2010, Bouziri et al. [8] adapted a tabu search technique to tackle SCP. The approach was tested only on seven DIMACS instances. In 2011, Helmar et al. [16] proposed a local search heuristic (MDS(5)+LS) for the sum coloring problem. The approach relies on the use of a variable neighborhood search and iterated local search. MDS(5)+LS outperforms all recent methods. In 2012, a Breakout Local Search algorithm (BLS) was developed by Benlic et al. [4]. BLS improved upper bounds for 4 instances out of 27 tested graphs. In 2012, Wu et al. [32] elaborated a heuristic based on independent set extraction: EXSCOL. The proposed algorithm performs well on large graphs. In 2014, an evolutionary algorithm introduced by Moukrim et al. [27], improved upper and lower bounds on tested instances. In the same year, another evolutionary algorithm (MASC) was elaborated by Jin et al. [19]. MASC reported 15 new upper bounds for the sum coloring problem. Later, Yan et al., in [18], propose a hybrid evolutionary search. Computational results show that the latter algorithm obtained the best-known result for most of tested instances. Moreover, it improved upper and lower bounds for 51 instances out of 94. In 2017, in the research work of Harrabi et al. [14], it was proved that it's possible to solve the SCP by referring to a bi-objective evolutionary approach combined with a tabu search method for diversification interests. Therefore, later in 2019, the same authors proposed in [15] to effectively tune the parameters of the developed evolutionary approach. Indeed, when detecting the promising set of parameters, the evolutionary method provided a practical performance in term of experimental results. In addition, Harrabi et al. integrated in [13] a generally applicable modeling methodology Hyper-Heuristic. The approach incorporates the most performing low-level heuristics to improve the obtained solutions and maintain the balance between exploration and exploitation. Experimental results show that the hyper-heuristic yields to better or equal bounds for 25 tested instances out of 42. Recently, new lower bounds were proposed in [28] using a column generation algorithm that is enhanced by several procedures and avoids the exact solution relative to the pricing problems. Experimental study shows the efficiency of the approach in term of the gap comparing to the best known bounds. For an overview of the sum coloring problem, interested the reader can refer to [17].

1.2   Contributions

The concept of operating with infeasible solutions turned out to be advantageous when referring to the original graph coloring problem [11]. Such research papers enabled the search procedure to use intermediate infeasible solutions in terms of color violations within several metaheuristic approaches. In the same context, some advanced works focused on elaborating approximate methods that exploit infeasible solutions to produce promising results in the SCP literature [15], [8], [14] and [13].

In this paper, we propose a novel matheuristic approach to solve the sum coloring problem. Indeed, the conception of matheuristic approaches refers the inter-operation aspect between mathematical programming models and meta-heuristics techniques [6]. According to Talbi [31], the matheuristics could be classified into three categories:

1. Decomposition class: it handles the complexity of the principle problem by decomposing it into different subproblems to be effectively solved.
2. Improvement metaheuristics/heuristics class: the mathematical formulations are used to ameliorate the quality of the metaheuristic/heuristic solutions.
3. A class that employs the mathematical models to deliver approximate solutions by performing some relaxation of the principle problem.

Our proposed method performed in the context of the second matheuristic class. This paper attracts more attention from researchers to benefit from the effectiveness of operating with infeasible space search. In specific, we present a new matheuristic approach that oscillates between infeasible and feasible space of the sum coloring problem model.

Specifically, we adopt for the resolution a novel algorithm that combines the use of a Weight-Based Formulation (WBF) proposed in [13] with a hybrid evolutionary algorithm. The main contributions of the proposed algorithm can be summarized as follows:

- The new proposed hybrid evolutionary approach is based on a bi-objective algorithm Vector Evaluated Genetic Algorithm (VEGA) [29]. The VEGA approach optimizes independently each treated objective functions by decomposing the initial population and performing the genetic operators on each sub-populations. This fact will help us in enhancing quality of the obtained solutions by giving more freedom to discover other promising regions in the search space.
- The evolutionary algorithm employs a novel Iterated Simulated Annealing (ISA) during the mutation step. The latter combines two neighborhood operators: destroy/repair method and a new one-move operator. Such combination is designed to handle both feasible and unfeasible solutions.

The remainder of this paper is organized as follows. Section 2 describes the sum coloring problem considered in this work. Section 3 presents in details the weight-based formulation. Section 4 explains the proposed matheuristic approach. Section 5 presents the obtained simulation results.

2   Problem Statement: Preliminary Definitions and Properties

Formally, the sum coloring problem could be defined using an simple undirected graph $G = (V; E)$ where V is the set of $|V| = n$ vertices and E the set of $|E| = m$ edges. Let us consider a set of k colors $\{1, \ldots, k\}$. A **proper k-coloring** of the graph is an application $C : V \to \{1, \ldots, k\}$ such as $C(x) \neq C(y)$, $\forall (x, y) \in E$. If $(x, y) \in E$ and $C(x) = C(y)$, then the vertices x and y are termed **conflicting** vertices and the obtained coloring is **non proper**. Equivalently, a k-coloring could also be considered as a partition of V into k **colors classes** $\{V_1, \ldots, V_k\}$. Color classes V_i are composed of vertices having the same color. V_i could be defined using its cardinality $|V_i|$ which corresponds to its containing vertices. The smallest integer k for which we can color the graph properly is called the **chromatic number**. It is usually denoted by $\chi(G)$. Note also that, the k-coloring problem is about coloring a graph using k colors. However, **graph coloring problem** consists on looking for a proper coloring using χ colors. The sum coloring problem studied in this paper asks to find a proper k-coloring of G using natural numbers such that the following sum of colors is minimized:

$$f(c) = \sum_{j=1}^{k} (j * |V_j|) \tag{1}$$

where $|V_j|$ is cardinality of the color class $|V_j|$ and $k > c(G)$. This minimal sum is called **chromatic sum** and usually denoted by $\sum(G)$. The number of colors used to obtain the chromatic sum $\sum(G)$ is called **the strength s(G)** of the graph. Although the SCP is a variant of the classic graph coloring problem, the problems have different objective functions. To better illustrate the difference between the two considered problems, we provide an illustrative example in Figure 1.

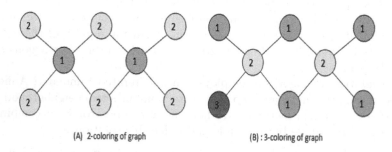

(A) 2-coloring of graph   (B) : 3-coloring of graph

Fig. 1. Relation between graph coloring problem and sum coloring problem.

The graph has a chromatic number $\chi(G) = 2$ (left figure). With the given 2-coloring, we achieve a sub-optimal sum of 14. However, this graph requires 3 colors to achieve its chromatic sum which is equal to 12 (right figure). Clearly, we can note that $\chi(G)$ is a lower bound of $s(G)$, i.e. $\chi(G) \leq s(G)$.

3   A Novel Weight-Based Formulation WBF

A relaxation of sum coloring problem could be performed using the WBF [13]. The incentive behind using such model is offering the opportunity to explore the search space solutions and driving the population toward the optimum using the appropriate weights. We carefully point out in what follows the decision variables and definitions.

- V: is a set of vertices.
- E: is a set of edges.
- K: is a set of colors.
- c_k: is the value of color k.
- w_1: is a scalar weight assigned to the objective 1.
- w_2: is a scalar weight assigned to the objective 2.
- β_{ij}: is the coefficient of term j in response function i, for each $j \in J$ and $i \in I$.

- $x_{ik} = \begin{cases} 1 \text{ if vertice i is colored with color } k, \\ \forall k \in K, \forall i \in V \\ 0 \text{ otherwise} \end{cases}$

- $y_{ij} = \begin{cases} 1 \text{ if edge } (i,j) \text{ violated the proper coloring,} \\ \forall (i,j) \in E \\ 0 \text{ otherwise} \end{cases}$

Hence, the proposed weight-based formulation is as follows:

$$Minimize \quad \left[\frac{w_1}{\sqrt{\sum_{j \in J} \beta_{1j}^2}} \right] \sum_{i \in V} \sum_{k \in K} c_k x_{ik} + \left[\frac{w_2}{\sqrt{\sum_{j \in J} \beta_{2j}^2}} \right] \sum_{(i,j) \in E} y_{ij} \quad (2)$$

$$subject\ to: \quad \sum_{k \in K} x_{ik} = 1 \quad \forall i \in V \quad (3)$$

$$y_{ij} \geq x_{ik} + x_{jk} - 1 \quad \forall k \in K, \forall (i,j) \in E \quad (4)$$

$$x_{ik} \in \{0,1\} \quad \forall k \in K, \forall i \in V \quad (5)$$

$$y_{ij} \in \{0,1\} \quad \forall (i,j) \in E \quad (6)$$

The objective (2) is an aggregate objective function. Constraints (3) ensure that each vertice is colored only once. Constraints (4) indicate if the solution is proper or not. Finally, constraints (5) and (6) state that the decision variables x_{ik} and y_{ij} are binary-valued.

4   Methodology

This section details the proposed matheuristic approach for the resolution of the SCP. It starts with the outline of the algorithmic scheme. Next, the core of an iterated simulated annealing integrated with an evolutionary algorithm is described.

4.1   The Proposed Matheuristic Approach

Hybrid evolutionary approaches have emerged as successful alternatives to tackle the tightly related graph coloring problem [11]. Indeed, within reasonable running time, these approaches find sub-optimal solutions while providing a guarantee on its quality. In light of the progress achieved by these techniques, we investigate a matheuristic approach based on a hybrid algorithm to solve the SCP. Our resolution method combines the use of a VEGA schema [29] with a new Iterated Simulated Annealing algorithm ISA. The general flow chart of the proposed matheuristic is illustrated in Fig. 2. Moreover, all the elements of the Hybrid Evolutionary approach based on an Iterated Simulated Annealing HE-ISA are separately explained in the following subsections.

The proposed matheuristic starts by randomly generate the initial population[1]. Afterword, our algorithm performs different generations[2] to generate the best solution until a timeout limit is reached[3]. Then, the matheuristic divides at each generation the obtained population into two sub-populations. Interestingly, in order to guide the search through and ameliorate quality of the initial population, we apply the WBF model on one selected sub-population and generate optimal solutions. From each sub-population, we select randomly two parent solutions. Motivated by the performance of the SPX operator[4] proved in [7], we adopt it to result an offspring solution. Next, an Iterated Simulated Annealing ISA is used to improve the quality of the obtained coloring solution. In the next, we detail the ISA basic components.

4.2   An Iterated Simulated Annealing for the Sum Coloring Problem: ISA

Simulated annealing approaches have emerged as successful alternatives for delivering tight bounds of the chromatic number in the context of graph coloring problem [10].

Interestingly, this local search method performs well as it could escape from getting trapped into local minima [25]. Indeed, simulated annealing accepts both of better and worse solutions with a probability $exp(\Delta/T)$ stipulated by the criterion of Metropolis criterion [26]. Thus, this strategy has the potential ability of intensifying the current solution. The outline of the overall simulated annealing framework is presented in Fig. 3.

---

[1] The population size was experimentally set to be 20.
[2] The maximum number of generations was experimentally set to be 100.
[3] The timeout limit was experimentally set to be 2 h except for large instances.
[4] The SPX rate was experimentally set to be 0.9.

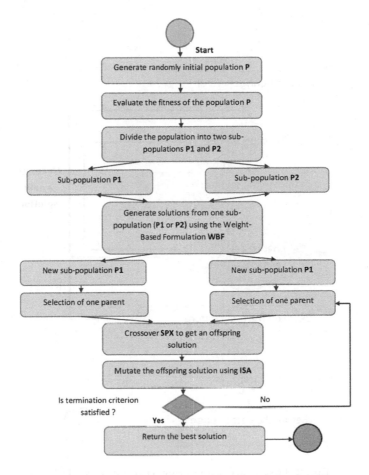

Fig. 2. Flow chart of the proposed matheuristic algorithm.

The proposed iterated simulated annealing procedure performs different generations of neighboring solutions. ISA performs with an initial temperature related to an initial solution[5]. Then, it intensifies the search and selects different neighbor solutions[6]. ISA relies on two neighborhood structures during the search: a *destruction/construction* and a *one move operator*.

The destroy/repair operator guarantees the feasibility of the obtained coloring solution as follows. It selects all the conflicting vertices and assigns it to a possible color class having a maximum cardinality. Such move is performed without creating color conflicts. A new color class could be created to respect the coloring hard rules and not violate the sum coloring constraints. Concerning the one move operator, it randomly chooses one vertice in conflict and assigns it to a different color class with a maximum cardinality without resulting a non proper solution.

---

[5] The initial temperature of was experimentally set to $\sqrt{n}$ as suggested by [10].

[6] The cooling ratio was experimentally chosen from $[0.8, \ldots, 0.99]$.

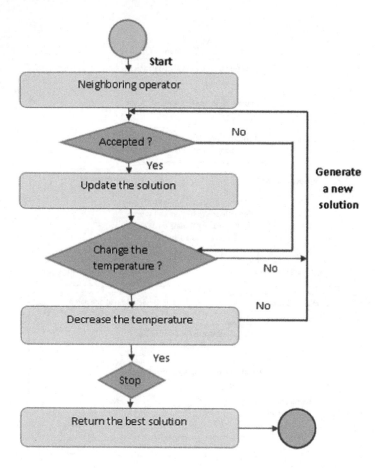

Fig. 3. Flow chart of the proposed local search ISA.

5   Computational Study

This section summarizes computational results obtained by the matheuristic approach when dealing with the NP-hard sum coloring problem. Initially, the benchmark instances are introduced. To motivate the design of the proposed algorithm, we conduct analytic comparisons with state-of-the-art SCP methodologies.

5.1   Experimental Setup and Tested Instances

The proposed matheuristic approach was coded using C++. Moreover, we used cplex 12.6 to solve the WBF mathematical formulations. Experiments were conducted on a i5 processor with 2.53 Ghz and 8 Gb of available memory. The running times are expressed in minutes.

The used test-bed consists of a set of graphs used to report computational results for the SCP: DIMACS challenge[7] and the COLOR 2002-2004 competitions[8].

5.2   Used Metrics

We have evaluated the performance of the matheuristic approach according to its improvements on the obtained Lower bounds. Accordingly, we have measured the gaps of the obtained upper bounds as follows:

- $Gap=[\frac{(Sol-f_{LB}^b)}{f_{LB}^b}]*100$

  where f_{LB}^b value is the current best known lower bound for the sum coloring problem [17].

5.3   Evaluation of the Proposed Matheuristic and Comparisons

This section has two major goals. It is noteworthy to exhibit the impact of the matheuristic main components. Afterword, it is significantly relevant to carry out a comparisons with some recent performing algorithms in order to assess the performance of our proposed solution approach.

In a first step of experimental analysis, we exhibit the influence of the matheuristic features: the evolutionary algorithm (EA) and the Iterated simulated annealing approach (ISA). To this end, we compare the results of the matheuristic approach against each of the two separately used algorithms: EA and ISA. Tests were conducted using these resolution approaches for 10 times in order to deliver upper bounds for the chromatic sum. In Table 1, we display for each approach the obtained upper bounds f_{UB}^*, the average of $Gap(\%)$ value and the CPU computational running time t. f_{UB}^b is the best reported upper bounds from the literature [17]. From Table 1, we note that the matheuristic approach is extremely the best coloring algorithm since it outperforms the tested approaches (the results are indicated in bold). Moreover, it is noteworthy that for 4 cases out of 16, the proposed approach matches the best upper bounds (underlined entries). Indeed, the matheuristic achieves the best results with an average Gap of only 1.473% compared to 1.535% for EA and 1.567% for ISA. Surprisingly, our resolution approach was also the fastest since it requires only 41.1 min. In summary, the use of EA, ISA and WBF has allowed the matheuristic method to performs clever movements during the search process.

Pushing our analysis a step further, in Table 2, we compare the obtained results with bounds reported by the most recent hybrid algorithms from the literature, namely HESA [18] and the hype-heuristic HHA-SCP [13].

---

[7] http://dimacs.rutgers.edu/Challenges/.
[8] http://mat.gsia.cmu.edu/COLOR02.

Table 1. Comparative results of Matheuristic, EA and ISA algorithms.

Instances	f^b_{UB}	Matheuristic			EA			ISA		
		f^*_{UB}	Gap(%)	t	f^*_{UB}	Gap(%)	t	f^*_{UB}	Gap(%)	t
DSJC125.5	1012	**1013**	0.845	6	1017	0.852	7	1018	0.854	5
DSJC125.9	2503	**2505**	0.481	7	2520	0.490	15	2520	0.490	9
DSJC250.5	3210	**3212**	1.495	27	3240	1.517	25	3249	1.524	18
DSJC250.9	8277	8277	0.919	8	8280	0.920	15	8290	0.922	8
DSJC500.1	2836	**2841**	1.272	36	2860	1.288	28	2890	1.312	12
DSJC500.5	10886	**10891**	2.725	54	10905	2.730	30	11100	2.797	38
DSJC500.9	29862	**29900**	1.705	45	29937	1.708	40	29946	1.709	30
DSJC1000.1	8991	**9000**	2.258	98	9100	2.294	110	9160	2.316	50
DSJC1000.5	37575	**37595**	4.604	25	37687	4.618	35	38551	4.747	29
DSJC1000.9	103445	**103464**	2.895	62	103480	2.896	65	104290	2.927	61
flat300.20-0	3150	3150	1.057	50	3257	1.127	25	3241	1.127	25
flat300.26-0	3966	3966	1.562	2	4015	1.593	7	4012	1.593	1
flat300.28-0	4238	**4279**	1.765	133	5495	2.552	125	5270	2.406	102
flat1000.50-0	25500	**25512**	2.864	9	26780	3.056	18	26870	3.070	7
flat1000.60-0	30100	30100	3.533	11	32160	3.843	16	32200	3.849	10
flat1000.76-0	37164	**37168**	4.604	21.5	35235	4.614	40	38420	4.793	20
Average	-	-	1.473	41.1	-	1.535	41.86	-	1.567	30.16

Table 2. Comparative results of Matheuristic, EA and ISA algorithms.

Instances	f^b_{UB}	Matheuristic			HHA-SCP			HESA		
		f^*_{UB}	Gap(%)	t	f^*_{UB}	Gap(%)	t	f^*_{UB}	Gap(%)	t
DSJC125.5	1012	1013	0.845	6	1012	0.843	5	1012	0.843	10.1
DSJC125.9	2503	2505	0.481	7	2503	0.480	7	2 503	0.480	0.3
DSJC250.5	3210	3212	1.495	27	3211	1.494	27	3 210	1.494	47.1
DSJC250.9	8277	8277	0.919	8	8277	0.919	8	8 277	0.919	24.6
DSJC500.1	2836	2841	1.272	36	2841	1.272	37	2 836	1.268	82.6
DSJC500.5	10886	10891	2.725	54	10890	2.725	55	10 886	2.724	97
DSJC500.9	29862	29900	1.705	45	29910	1.706	45	29 862	1.701	95.4
DSJC1000.1	8991	9000	2.258	98	9000	2.258	99	8 991	2.255	101.6
DSJC1000.5	37575	37595	4.604	25	37596	4.604	25	37 575	4.601	33.5
DSJC1000.9	103445	103464	2.895	62	103464	2.895	63	103 445	2.895	103.1
flat300.20-0	3150	3150	1.057	50	3150	1.057	50	3 150	1.057	0
flat300.26-0	3966	3966	1.562	2	3966	1.562	2	3 966	1.562	0.4
flat300.28-0	4238	4279	1.765	133	4289	1.772	133	4 260	1.753	49.7
flat1000.50-0	25500	25512	2.864	9	25513	2.865	10	25 500	2.863	0.3
flat1000.60-0	30100	30100	3.533	11	30100	3.533	12	30 100	3.533	2.7
flat1000.76-0	37164	37168	4.604	21.5	37168	4.604	22.5	37 164	4.603	36.8
Average	-	-	1.4733	41.1	-	1.4735	41.34	-	1.469	56.84

Looking at Table 2, one can note that the shown methods exhibit very similar performance. Precisely, the average Gap are 1.4733% for the matheuristic, 1.4735% for the hyper heuristic HHA-SCP and 1.469% for the HESA algorithm. Moreover, a striking observation can be drawn since the matheuristic approach outperforms the hyper heuristic in term of GAP and computation time speed (41.1 min against 41.34 min). Compared to the recent hybrid HESA algorithm, our matheuristic approach behaves favorably well in term of Gap. But, surprisingly, our approach was faster than HESA algorithm. Success of the matheuristic method could be explained by operating with both feasible and non feasible solutions that has offered the opportunity to effectively control the search process.

6 Conclusion

This research paper proposes a new matheuristic approach for the challenging sum coloring problem. The construction of a coloring solution relies of two phases, a coloring relaxation using the weight-based formulation and a hybrid evolutionary algorithm that enables feasible and unfeasible space exploring.

Operating with unfeasible solutions diversifies the search towards new promising regions of the solution space. In addition, the employed hybrid evolutionary algorithm results in significant modifications of the solution structure. These diversification effects are controlled by the proposed iterated simulated annealing method which can quickly intensify local optimal solutions. Experimentation show the performance of our proposed matheuristic approach when comparing the results with the two most recent state-of-the-art methods in term of solution quality and computation CPU efforts.

Future research directions focus on proposing novel neighborhood structures that aim at maximizing the benefits of tunneling through unfeasible space search.

References

1. Bar-Noy, A., Bellare, M., Halldórsson, M.M., Shachnai, H., Tamir, T.: On chromatic sums and distributed resource allocation. Inf. Comput. **140**(2), 183–202 (1998)
2. Bar-Noy, A., Halldórsson, M., Kortsarz, G., Salman, R., Shanhnai, H.: Sum multicoloring of graphs. In: Algorithms-ESA'99, pp. 693–693 (1999)
3. Bar-Noy, A., Kortsarz, G.: Minimum color sum of bipartite graphs. J. Algorithms **28**(2), 339–365 (1998)
4. Benlic, U., Hao, J.-K.: A study of breakout local search for the minimum sum coloring problem. In: Bui, L.T., Ong, Y.S., Hoai, N.X., Ishibuchi, H., Suganthan, P.N. (eds.) SEAL 2012. LNCS, vol. 7673, pp. 128–137. Springer, Heidelberg (2012). https://doi.org/10.1007/978-3-642-34859-4_13
5. Berliner, A., Bostelmann, U., Brualdi, R.A., Deaett, L.: Sum list coloring graphs. Graphs Combinatorics **22**(2), 173–183 (2006)
6. Boschetti, M.A., Maniezzo, V., Roffilli, M., Bolufé Röhler, A.: Matheuristics: Optimization, Simulation and Control. In: Blesa, M.J., Blum, C., Di Gaspero, L., Roli, A., Sampels, M., Schaerf, A. (eds.) HM 2009. LNCS, vol. 5818, pp. 171–177. Springer, Heidelberg (2009). https://doi.org/10.1007/978-3-642-04918-7_13

7. Bouziri, H., Harrabi, O.: Behavior study of genetic operators for the minimum sum coloring problem. In: 2013 5th International Conference on Modeling, Simulation and Applied Optimization (ICMSAO), pp. 1–6. IEEE (2013)
8. Bouziri, H., Jouini, M.: A tabu search approach for the sum coloring problem. Electron. Notes Discrete Math. **36**, 915–922 (2010)
9. Brélaz, D.: New methods to color the vertices of a graph. Commun. ACM **22**(4), 251–256 (1979)
10. Chams, M., Hertz, A., De Werra, D.: Some experiments with simulated annealing for coloring graphs. Eur. J. Oper. Res. **32**(2), 260–266 (1987)
11. Galinier, P., Hao, J.K.: Hybrid evolutionary algorithms for graph coloring. J. Comb. Optim. **3**(4), 379–397 (1999)
12. Halldórsson, M.M., Kortsarz, G., Shachnai, H.: Sum coloring interval and k-claw free graphs with application to scheduling dependent jobs. Algorithmica **37**(3), 187–209 (2003)
13. Harrabi, O., Chaouachi, J.: Towards effective resolution approaches for solving the sum coloring problem. J. Exp. Theor. Artif. Intell. **32**(1), 31–57 (2020)
14. Harrabi, O., Fatnassi, E., Bouziri, H., Chaouachi, J.: A bi-objective memetic algorithm proposal for solving the minimum sum coloring problem. In: Proceedings of the Genetic and Evolutionary Computation Conference Companion, pp. 27–28 (2017)
15. Harrabi, O., Siala, J.C.: An effective parameter tuning for a bi-objective genetic algorithm to solve the sum coloring problem. In: Bansal, J.C., Das, K.N., Nagar, A., Deep, K., Ojha, A.K. (eds.) Soft Computing for Problem Solving. AISC, vol. 816, pp. 107–119. Springer, Singapore (2019). https://doi.org/10.1007/978-981-13-1592-3_8
16. Helmar, A., Chiarandini, M.: A local search heuristic for chromatic sum. In: Proceedings of the 9th Metaheuristics International Conference, vol. 1101, pp. 161–170 (2011)
17. Jin, Y., Hamiez, J.-P., Hao, J.-K.: Algorithms for the minimum sum coloring problem: a review. Artif. Intell. Rev. **47**(3), 367–394 (2016). https://doi.org/10.1007/s10462-016-9485-7
18. Jin, Y., Hao, J.K.: Hybrid evolutionary search for the minimum sum coloring problem of graphs. Inf. Sci. **352**, 15–34 (2016)
19. Jin, Y., Hao, J.K., Hamiez, J.P.: A memetic algorithm for the minimum sum coloring problem. Comput. Oper. Res. **43**, 318–327 (2014)
20. Johnson, D.S., Mehrotra, A., Trick, M.A.: Preface: special issue on computational methods for graph coloring and its generalizations. Discret. Appl. Math. **156**(2), 145–146 (2008)
21. Kokosiński, Z., Kwarciany, K.: On sum coloring of graphs with parallel genetic algorithms. In: Beliczynski, B., Dzielinski, A., Iwanowski, M., Ribeiro, B. (eds.) ICANNGA 2007. LNCS, vol. 4431, pp. 211–219. Springer, Heidelberg (2007). https://doi.org/10.1007/978-3-540-71618-1_24
22. Kroon, L.G., Sen, A., Deng, H., Roy, A.: The optimal cost chromatic partition problem for trees and interval graphs. In: d'Amore, F., Franciosa, P.G., Marchetti-Spaccamela, A. (eds.) WG 1996. LNCS, vol. 1197, pp. 279–292. Springer, Heidelberg (1997). https://doi.org/10.1007/3-540-62559-3_23
23. Kubicka, E., Schwenk, A.J.: An introduction to chromatic sums. In: Proceedings of the 17th Conference on ACM Annual Computer Science Conference, pp. 39–45. ACM (1989)
24. Li, Y., Lucet, C., Moukrim, A., Sghiouer, K.: Greedy algorithms for the minimum sum coloring problem. In: Logistique et transports, pp. LT-027 (2009)

25. Lin, S.W., Vincent, F.Y., Lu, C.C.: A simulated annealing heuristic for the truck and trailer routing problem with time windows. Expert Syst. Appl. **38**(12), 15244–15252 (2011)
26. Metropolis, N., Rosenbluth, A.W., Rosenbluth, M.N., Teller, A.H., Teller, E.: Equation of state calculations by fast computing machines. J. Chem. Phys. **21**(6), 1087–1092 (1953)
27. Moukrim, A., Sghiouer, K., Lucet, C., Li, Y.: Upper and lower bounds for the minimum sum coloring problem (2014)
28. Mrad, M., Harrabi, O., Siala, J.C., Gharbi, A.: A column generation-based lower bound for the minimum sum coloring problem. IEEE Access **8**, 57891–57904 (2020)
29. Schaffer, J.D.: Multiple objective optimization with vector evaluated genetic algorithms. In: Proceedings of the First International Conference on Genetic Algorithms and Their Applications, 1985. Lawrence Erlbaum Associates. Inc. (1985)
30. Sen, A., Deng, H., Guha, S.: On a graph partition problem with application to vlsi layout. Inf. Process. Lett. **43**(2), 87–94 (1992)
31. Talbi, E.G.: A unified taxonomy of hybrid metaheuristics with mathematical programming, constraint programming and machine learning. In: Talbi, EG. (eds) Hybrid Metaheuristics. Studies in Computational Intelligence, vol 434, pp. 3–76. Springer, Heidelberg (2013)
32. Wu, Q., Hao, J.K.: An effective heuristic algorithm for sum coloring of graphs. Comput. Oper. Res. **39**(7), 1593–1600 (2012)
33. Zadeh, L.: Optimality and non-scalar-valued performance criteria. IEEE Trans. Autom. Control **8**(1), 59–60 (1963)

Machine Learning Methods

Addressing the Complexity of MOBA Games Through Simple Geometric Clues

Alexis Mortelier[(✉)] and François Rioult[(✉)]

Normandie Univ, UNICAEN, ENSICAEN, CNRS, GREYC, 14000 Caen, France
{alexis.mortelier,francois.rioult}@unicaen.fr

Abstract. Recently, the analysis of e-sport data has particularly attracted the attention of machine learning researchers. We contribute here by proposing, on the MOBA (Multiplayer Online Battle Arena) game DotA2 (Defense of the Ancients 2), an analysis of the relevance of geometric clues relating to the behavior of the players. The geometric clues we have chosen concern the trajectories of the players and the characteristics of the polygon described by the players of a team. More precisely, for the polygon clues, we computed, for each second of the game: the convex area, the diameter, the grouping capacity (average of the distances to the barycenter), the inertia (second order moment of the distances to the barycenter) and finally the distance to the opponent's fortress. During a regression on the number of alive heroes, the learning performance of an RNN (precisely a LSTM) fed by our simple clues allowed us to evaluate their relevance in describing this complex game.

Keywords: Trajectory analysis · MOBA games · Important moments highlighting · RNN

1 Introduction

Context Electronic sport or e-sport consists of the competitive playing of video games. This activity provides numerous traces that data science researchers like to study. Indeed, these researchers are often gamer themselves so they are familiar with the subject of their study. Moreover, e-sport has emerged as a serious discipline, operating in a similar way to sport, with the arrival of classic clubs such as Paris SG, AS Monaco, AS Roma and FC Grenoble. This craze is reflected in the particularly attractive financial amounts (up to millions of dollars) offered to the teams participating in the tournaments. For example, in 2018, The International 2018 tournament allowed the first 18 teams to share more than 25 millions Dollars (40 millions this year).

E-sport is a boon for data science research because activity traces are easily and massively available. Unlike traditional sports where it is difficult to obtain accurate data, each e-sport game is archived on servers in a very precisely exploitable format. The interest of e-sport also lies in the expression of human and collective organizations, for example the tactics and strategy of a team of players, which are comparable to those implemented in real sport.

C. Bădică et al. (Eds.): ICCCI 2022, CCIS 1653, pp. 643–649, 2022.
https://doi.org/10.1007/978-3-031-16210-7_52

Motivations Our main motivation is to analyze MOBA games (Multiplayer Online Battle Arena games) in order to better understand the performance of the best teams. This understanding would allow us to explain the reasons for the failure or success of a team and would provide means of analysis for the games. These means could then be used to automatically produce game summaries by characterizing highlights.

However, MOBA games are particularly complex to analyze: each player can choose his avatar from among a hundred, each avatar can cast four exclusive spells and improve his skills (movement speed, attack frequency, armor, mana regeneration, etc.) thanks to six items of equipment to be chosen from among a hundred. It is therefore desirable to reduce this complexity.

We believe that the spatial organization of the players is crucial for analyzing performance in these games and that it is not necessary to examine all the minute details of a game to characterize its important moments. Moreover, MOBA games are team games and the study of spatial organization allows us to focus attention on the collective aspects rather than on individual details.

Position Compared to other works in the field, our proposal presents two originalities. Firstly, we focused our study on the *collective* character of the practice of a MOBA, because it is fundamentally a team game emphasizing group actions to the detriment of individual ones [3]. To do so, we compared the relevance of clues related to the individual position of the players on the field and the geometry of the collective organization. We are looking for simple clues to calculate and exploit and we do not wish to focus our attention on individual behaviors and characteristics (equipment, skill tree).

We therefore compared the contribution to a learning method of the individual trajectories of the heroes *versus* the geometric measurements on the polygon described by the players (area, diameter, distance to the objective, etc.). This approach is qualified as *wrapper* in [4]: the relevance of a descriptor is measured by its contribution to the classification or regression model, it is a method of feature selection.

Secondly, we have decided to work only on data from games played by e-sport professionals, grouped in renowned teams. We wanted to study games performed by players who are used to play together and producing a high level of performance. This position is original in the literature [3,5]. In order to privilege quality over quantity, we did not wish to study millions or even billions of games [2]. Indeed, the matchmaking of occasional players is based on their expectation of winning, which leads to the constitution of balanced teams.

2   Related Work

Due to the lack of space in this short version, this section is available on the extended version of this article at this address[1].

---

[1] https://hal.archives-ouvertes.fr/hal-03699200/file/Addressing_the_Complexity_of_MOBA_Games_through_Simple_Geometric_Clues.pdf.

3   Addressing the Complexity Through Geometric Clues

DotA2 is a team game where coordinated and synchronized movements are paramount, independently of individual behavior. We believe (as [2]) and show here that geometric clues from player trajectories are sufficient to reveal the complexity of this game. Considering these geometric clues alone rather than examining individual player behaviors in terms of inventory and skill tree allowed us to propose a generic approach for the MOBA genre and to work on the basis of simple hypotheses.

We therefore compared the relevance of three types of geometric or positional clues: (i) player trajectories, (ii) trajectories *enriched* by the coordinates of the hero's orientation vector (this data is simply provided by the game engine) and (iii) the characteristics of the polygon described by all the players of a team. We normalized the data provided by the game engine so as to obtain one measurement per second of game time.

We considered that a game is divided into three major phases of play : the early-game, the first 15 min during which the heroes are weak and seek to obtain gold and experience to gain power. It is during this phase that ambushes are attempted to gain an advantage and ruin the opponent's progress; the mid-game (from 16 to 35 mn), some heroes are powerful enough to make team fights possible; the late-game: (36 mn and beyond), the heroes have their maximum power and no longer seek to collect gold or experience: towers and the enemy fortress becomes the only objective.

DotA2 provides traces of game activities in the form of a *replay* file that can be retrieved after each game. The 258 games we analyzed were those of a major tournament of the game, The International 2018[2]. Our goal was to determine clues, characteristic of the spatial organization of the players. Highlights occur approximately every three minutes and correspond to the confrontations of the players giving rise to the disappearance of some (virtual *death* followed by a resurrection after a variable time). In order to obtain results that are sufficiently general and do not depend on the intrinsic complexity of the game, we focused our attention on geometric clues linked to the positions of the heroes.

3.1   *Wrapper* Approach with RNN

We used a *wrapper* approach [4] which assumes that the relevance of a feature is related to its capacity to improve the quality of learning. Unlike the *filter* approach, more common in statistics, which attempts to evaluate the credit of features from the data alone, the wrapper approach attempts to identify the best subset of features to use with a learning algorithm. We used this approach to compare the suitability of trajectories with that of polygon features by examining the performance obtained by models computed on these clues.

---

[2] see https://www.dota2.com/esports/ti10 for this year's edition.

The learning algorithm we used was a Long Short Term Memory (LSTM), a particular recurrent neural network (RNN) [6] architecture. RNNs are designed to handle temporally evolving data: if a cell computes an output signal from the inputs, it additionally transmits a hidden state to the next cell, that influences it. The cells of an LSTM additionally include a memory/forget mechanism that solves the problem of vanishing gradient.

The LSTM was here well adapted to our goal which was the study of a long game (35 to 50 mn x 60 measures/mn). The target was the number of players alive 5 s into the future (as recommended by [1]), because the position of a dead hero was conventionally frozen at the place of its death, and then it was reborn at the fortress position. If this time lag was not introduced, the LSTM could use this information and introduce a bias in the results.

The results we report in the next section were obtained on a single-layer LSTM with 128 cells, which allowed us to best assess the difference in relevance between our choices of clues. However, adding additional layers allowed the network to acquire a universal approximator behavior and thus, fed by the trajectories, to potentially capture the expressive power of the geometric clues of the polygon. The experiments we have carried out in this sense show that the more layers we added, the less noticeable the differences between the types of clues (see Fig. 3). Finally, we performed a Student's t test to check whether there was a significant difference in relevance between the use of trajectories, enriched trajectories or polygon clues. The Student test calculates a value between two distributions called p-value. If the score is less than 0.05, then the hypothesis that the means are equal can be rejected.

3.2 Experimental Conditions

In the experiments whose results are presented in the next section, we fed an LSTM with either player coordinates or polygon geometric clues and evaluated the relative relevance of these attributes by examining the MSE. The objective function was the number of living heroes in each team (from 0 to 5). We considered that the LSTM worked in *regression* because it had to predict two continuous quantities on the interval $[0, 5]$. Figure 1 shows a schematic of our training process.

During our experiments, we also considered two types of chronology for the LSTM inputs:

Learning since the beginning of the game phase: the LSTM was fed *continuously* by a single sequence, with data between instants 0 and t and predicted a value at $t + 5$;

Sliding window learning: the LSTM was fed with multiple sequences from $t - w$ to t and predicted at $t + 5$, for w a window width that we let vary between 5 and 120 s.

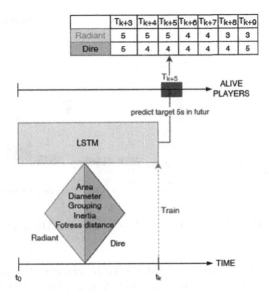

	Tk+3	Tk+4	Tk+5	Tk+6	Tk+7	Tk+8	Tk+9
Radiant	5	5	5	4	4	3	3
Dire	5	4	4	4	4	4	5

Fig. 1. LSTM training scheme on the continuity of the game.

4   Results

4.1   Learning Since the Beginning

Figure 2 represents the MSE boxplots, for each phase of the game. It can be observed that, independently of the phase, the polygon clues allowed a better prediction: the median of the MSE is the lowest and the dispersion is less important. Table 1 provides the values of the corresponding Student's tests: when the cell has a green background, the means are not equal.

Table 1. P-values of Student test for regression.

Phase	Poly vs traj	Poly vs enriched traj	Enriched traj vs traj
Early	$2.989.10^{-6}$	$1.104.10^{-10}$	0.113
Mid	$1.121.10^{-11}$	$4.633.10^{-13}$	0.782
Late	$4.366.10^{-9}$	$1.761.10^{-16}$	$4.043.10^{-5}$

During the early and middle of the game, the trajectories induced a slightly lower median error than the enriched trajectories, but the dispersion for the enriched trajectories is lower. For the end of the game, the results were more marked, the dispersion increased for the three types of clues and there were many more outliers. This could be explained by the fact that at the end of the game the virtual deaths are much more punitive (their duration depends linearly on the level of the player, maximum at this period). When a collective behavior led

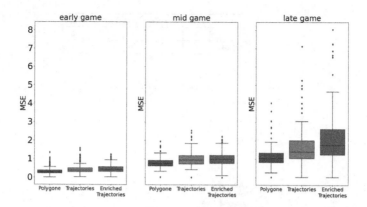

Fig. 2. Distribution of the MSE over the continuity of the game in regression.

to an important moment, the model detected it, however the players were more cautious because of the stake and canceled their action at the last moment.

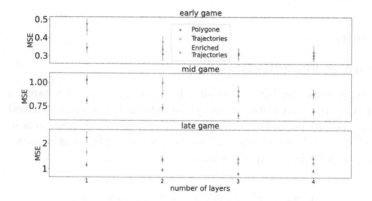

Fig. 3. Evolution of the MSE according to the number of layers for the regression.

Figure 3 shows the evolution of the relevance when increasing the number of layers of the LSTM (each one has 128 cells). Although the polygon clues were still the most relevant, there was a convergence of the three types of clues when the number of layers increased. However, the addition of layers had a significant algorithmic cost, particularly in terms of the number of epochs.

Finally, the polygons were the most relevant geometric clues for the regression problem, regardless of the game phase, both from an evaluation and computational time perspective. We also found that the LSTM converged faster when fed by the polygon clues rather than the trajectories.

4.2 Sliding Window Learning

When using sliding windows, the performance of the different types of clues, depending on the width of the window. Switching to sliding windows greatly improved the results obtained with the clues on the trajectories, equally for the trajectories and the enriched trajectories. The performance of the clues on the polygon was much poorer, and using sliding windows did not allow them to be sufficiently highlighted. These clues need to be taken into account for the entire period to reveal their potential relevance.

5 Conclusion

Using an LSTM that predicted the number of living heroes, we have shown that it was possible, by valuing geometric clues about the players' positions, to draw attention to important moments in a DotA2 game. Although DotA2 is a complex game, there is a strong relationship between simple positional clues and the occurrence of important moments.

Among the examined clues (geometry of the polygon described by the heroes, trajectories and trajectories enriched by orientations), those on the polygon proved to be more relevant for all phases, but it was necessary to learn on the continuity of the game. When using windows of variable size, the trajectories relatively gave better results but did not reach the performance of the polygon on the continuity of the game.

We have also found that increasing the number of layers in the LSTM allowed it to behave as a universal approximator: the more layers, the less sensitive the differences in performance between the feature types, although trajectories still required more learning epochs. The polygon clues, with the development of a small amount of preliminary computation, thus allowed for a reduction in the computation required for learning.

References

1. Chu, W.T., Chou, Y.C.: Event detection and highlight detection of broadcasted game videos. In: Computational Models of Social Interactions, pp. 1–8 (2015)
2. Deja, D., Myślak, M.: Topological clues for predicting outcomes of multiplayer online battle arena games. In: IADIS, July 2015
3. Katona, A., et al.: Time to die: death prediction in dota 2 using deep learning. In: 2019 IEEE Conference on Games (CoG), pp. 1–8. IEEE (2019)
4. Kohavi, R., John, G.H.: The wrapper approach. In: Feature extraction, construction and selection, pp. 33–50. Springer (1998)
5. Mora-Cantallops, M., Sicilia, M.Á.: MOBA games: a literature review. Entertainment Comput. **26**, 128–138 (2018)
6. Sherstinsky, A.: Fundamentals of recurrent neural network (RNN) and long short-term memory (LSTM) network. Physica D **404**, 132306 (2020)

Bots and Gender Detection on Twitter Using Stylistic Features

Sarra Ouni[1](✉) ⓘ, Fethi Fkih[1,2] ⓘ, and Mohamed Nazih Omri[1] ⓘ

[1] MARS Research Laboratory, LR 17ES05, University of Sousse, Sousse, Tunisia
sarraouni93@gmail.com, mohamednazih.omri@eniso.u-sousse.tn
[2] Department of Computer Science, College of Computer, Qassim University,
Buraydah, Saudi Arabia
f.fki@qu.edu.sa

Abstract. This paper describes our proposed method for the author profiling task at PAN 2019. The aim of this task is to identify the type of a Twitter user (i.e. bot or human). Then, in case of a human, determine its gender (i.e. male or female). Our approach uses a set of language-independent features and it applies machine learning algorithms. After an in-depth experimental study, conducted on English and Spanish datasets, we show that by using a simple set of stylistic information, we can surpass other existing methods that mainly depend on the content of the tweets. For the English dataset, accuracies of 93.06% and 90.04% are obtained for bot an gender classification tasks respectively. Using Spanish tweets, accuracies of 90.53% and 89.11% are achieved for bot and gender detection task respectively.

Keywords: Bot detection · Gender classification · Author profiling · Style-based features · Machine learning · Twitter

1 Introduction

Recently, with the rise of social media, online communication and social interaction have become an essential part of our daily life. These online platforms allow social media users, independently of their traits or behavior, to instantly and freely express their opinions by posting and sharing content related to any topic. Twitter is one of the main leading online social networking sites. It is a 'microblogging' system that is becoming a critical source of communication nowadays, because of its open access, quickness and reliability. With this increasing popularity, Twitter has drawn the attention of researchers and academics in recent years. Author profiling (AP) on Twitter is the main task that has been treated by many researchers in the field of natural language processing (NLP). The goal of AP is to identify some attributes of the authors by analyzing their written texts. These characteristics include gender [1], age [2], personality traits [3], etc. AP has proven to be useful in various fields such as politics, forensics, marketing, and security [4]. Twitter mostly deals with short and informal textual information [2]. These unstructured data make the task of AP tough, because extracting some features from such texts is a challenging process.

Recently, bots have become omnipresent on Twitter [5]. These profiles are being used to appear as humans in order to affect legitimate users. Twitter bots usually publish texts containing malicious information in order to spread rumours and fake news or to promote certain services. Consequently, there is a need to develop effective techniques which can distinguish between bot accounts and human ones on Twitter. The objective of the AP task at PAN 2019 [6] is to identify the type of the author of a given tweet (i.e. bot or human), and in case of a human, to determine its sex (i.e. male or female) in two different languages (English and Spanish). Bot detection (bot/human) and gender identification (male/female) are two binary classification problems. In this manuscript, we will present our language-independent method to address the task of bot and gender profiling [6]. Our approach is purely statistical and uses mainly a set of stylistic features. The great strength behind our approach is that is generic. It can be used for other languages and other Twitter profiles than those available in this task. The major contributions of this work are as follow:

- We propose a novel method based on style-based features to differentiate between bots and humans, and to determine the gender of human users on Twitter. The features we propose have a discriminative power for this challenging task;
- We assess the performance of the proposed system using supervised learning algorithms with cross-validation technique;
- We Compare our performance with that of some existing methods.

The remainder of this paper is organized as follows. Section 2 describes and discusses the main studies related to the identification of bots and gender on social networks. Section 3 introduces our proposed approach which aims to address the task of bot and gender profiling. Section 4 is reserved for the description of the experimental study that we have conducted on two different datasets. In addition, a comparative study is presented. In the final Sect. 5, we conclude the paper and we suggest certain futures direction.

2   Related Work

The AP task has been treated as a text classification issue. Researchers have been focused on extracting features from texts which are based on the author's writing style [7], as well as on the content of texts [8]. They also used machine learning and deep learning algorithms for the prediction step. Indeed, these techniques showed good performance results in different texts classification problems [9–15]. Recently in 2019, in the field of AP, many researchers have been focused on predicting the gender of Twitter users and also on identifying their types (i.e., bot or human). In this section, we describe previous important studies which deal with tasks of identifying the bot and gender of social media users.

2.1 Bots Detection

Many researchers have worked on developing automatic bots detection methods. They have considered the bots detection task as a texts classification issue. For example Hall et al. [16] developed a bot prediction system using machine learning classification. This model aims to remove bots from Wikidata. The authors used some behavioural features and applied random forest technique to train and test their model. Experimental findings showed that this method achieved a precision score of 88%. Botometer [17] is the most popular bot prediction system. It uses the random forest technique and a number of account-based features such as number of followers, number of followed, sentiment texts, mention users, retweets, among others. SentiBot [18] is another Twitter bot identification system. The authors focused on extracting sentiment-based features from a large Twitter dataset and applying Traditional machine learning algorithms in order to distinguish bots from humans. Using this system, the Area under the ROC Curve (AUROC) increased from 65% to 73%. In [19], the author proposed a machine learning model that aims to classify Twitter profiles into different classes: bot, cyborg, and human. Twitter features were employed as input to the random forest classifier. Using a collection of 500000 Twitter accounts, this method achieved 96% of accuracy for bots, 91% for cyborgs, and 98% for humans. In [8], a behavior enhanced deep model (BeDM) for bot detection was presented. This model used content and behavior information in order to capture the latent features. It also applied deep neural network with 10-fold cross-validation and achieved 88.41%, 86.26% and 87.32% of precision, recall and F1-measure, respectively.

2.2 Gender Identification

Gender detection is another challenge in the AP task. This challenge has been also approached as a binary texts classification problem. Stylometry-based and content-based approaches are the most widely used techniques in the literature. For example, in [2] the authors used a combination of stylometric features and content-based features for the prediction of gender and age on multilingual dataset. Stylometric features include word-based and character-based features, and vocabulary richness. The features based on the content include word and character n-grams. Experimental findings showed that the random forest and naive bayes classifiers are relevant for the gender identification task. In [1], Daneshvar et al. proposed a new method for Twitter users gender detection. This method used word and character n-grams as input to the Support Vector Machine algorithm, achieving an accuracy of 82% on the English dataset. In [20], the authors described their style-based model for predicting gender and age of Twitter users. They used 56 style-based features including syntactic features, lexical features, and vocabulary richness. Several machine learning algorithms were used to test the proposed method such as random forest, J48 and LADTree. This approach reached an accuracy or 57.6% for the gender prediction task. In [21], the authors proposed a new method based on deep learning architecture (Windowed Recurrent Convolutional Neural Network (WRCNN)) for identifying the gender of blog authors. WRCNN outperforms existing methods and it reached an accuracy of 86% on a large blog dataset. Safara et al. [22] proposed an author gender detection model based on deep learning techniques. They extracted some stylistic features from a public email dataset. Then, they trained an artificial neural network (ANN) to determine the sex of the email authors. The Whale Optimization Algorithm (WOA) was also employed to find optimal settings for the ANN algorithm. This hybrid model reached a good accuracy of 98%.

3 Proposed Approach

This section details our method for the AP task at PAN-19 [6]. The main focus of this study is on data pre-processing and features extraction. We assume that cleaning the data is as important as model building. We also suppose that using some carefully engineered style-based features can be an efficient method that overcomes the limits and the shortcomings of other existing methods. In the next subsections, we first explain the task of data preprocessing. Next, the set of features that we extract from the datasets are presented.

3.1 Pre-processing

The preprocessing is an essential step for any text classification task. Most of the profiles data collected from social networks contain many noisy and missing data, because of the unstructured and informal texts shared on these online platforms. Therefore, there is a need to clean the collected dataset so that the set of features that will be extracted for profiling the authors would produce a good performance result. In our work, various actions are performed on tweets:

- We combine each user tweets in a single document
- We lowercase all characters
- Tokenization of the tweets (with nltk TweetTokenizer)
- Lemmatization of all words
- We remove all stopwords from all tweets
- We cut repeated character sequences of length superior or equal to 3
- We remove all extra spaces

All operations in this stage are performed using the Natural Language Toolkit (NLTK).

3.2 Features Extraction

Based on some in-depth experiences, we choose to use stylistic features to address the task at hand. Indeed, the writing style of social media users can be effective in differentiating between texts shared by different groups of users (humans, bots, etc.) [23]. In addition, stylistic features have been successfully applied to various AP tasks such as gender and age classification [20]. This motivates us to use a set of style-based features to tackle the AP challenge at PAN-19 [6].

The proposed features used in this work are language independent, therefore our proposed method can be used for any language. In the following, we describe the different features that we extracted from the datasets and used in this work.

- Number of punctuation marks
- Number of hashtags (i.e. words starting with #)
- Number of retweets (start with "rt")
- Number of user mentions (start with @)
- Number of url links (start with http)
- Number of characters
- Number of special characters (such as %,&,*, +, - {, }, etc.)
- Number of characters between parentheses
- Number of words per sentence
- Number of words per document
- Number of Words between parentheses
- Number of short words (including 3 characters)
- Number of long words (including more than 5 characters)
- Number of sentences
- Number of Acronyms and Abbreviations (from a predefined list)
- Number of emoticons
- Number of determiners
- Number of verbs
- Number of pronouns
- Number of first person pronoun
- Number of second person pronoun
- Number of lines
- Number of digits
- Number of vocabulary richness

Many studies in AP use style-based features. The novelty in our work is the use of a combination of some of these features carefully chosen. In this work, the same set of features is used for both tasks (i.e. bot and gender classification).

It is worth noting that, initially, we have considered different combination of features to finally get the best results in the classification task. In fact, the main challenge of the task at hand is associated with the detection of writing style on Twitter. The simple set of features used in this study plays an important role in AP. For example, the punctuation marks are the most stylistically relevant features. In particular, the comma is a simple but very useful feature. Commas can be used to denote a simple pause when reading. They can be also removed to speed up the pace of a text. From the datasets, we have observed that tweets produced by humans have a high amount of commas compared to bots tweets. Thus, the usage of commas can be a very effective way to characterize the writing style of an author. Also bots tweets contain a high amount of hashtags, URLs, and mentions, compared to human tweets. In addition, tweets written by women contains more emoticons than men tweets. So, these features are valuable for the task of classifying gender. According to [24], humans make frequent use of verbs and pronouns. Therefore, these features can be helpful in distinguishing bot profiles from human ones.

The number of words per sentence is also a very powerful profiling feature. It is a way to characterize sentence complexity. Using too long sentences implies complex writing. This is certainly related to characteristics of the author (gender for example). Measuring the number of characters between parentheses is a very stylistic feature. Parentheses are often used to clarify some aspects of the text. This feature can be a very powerful profiling feature. Furthermore, measuring the usage of the first or second person pronoun is very useful when analyzing short texts such as Twitter content. It reveals the tendencies of a user to write about themselves as individual or as a group, and is thus useful in the context of gender detection.

4   Experimental Study and Result Analysis

This section describes the experimental protocol. We first provide a brief description of the datasets used. Then, we present the different classification algorithms used to evaluate the approach. Finally, we illustrate and discuss the obtained classification results.

Note that, for our experimentation, we use an Acer Aspire $E5 - 573$ laptop with 2.4 GHz Core i5 5th generation CPU and $16GB$ of RAM. Windows 10 (64 bit) and Python 3.6 are used for the software part.

4.1   Datasets

The PAN19-author-profiling-training dataset provided to address the task of bot and gender prediction at PAN-2019 [6] contains tweets in English and Spanish languages, and presented as XML files. Each XML file corresponds to an author and includes 100 tweets. Table 1 lists the number of Twitter users and the total number of tweets in each dataset (English and Spanish), and in each category (bots, male and female).

Table 1. Statistics of the datasets used

Language	Bots	Male	Female	All Authors	All tweets
English	2060	1030	1030	4120	412000
Spanish	1500	750	750	3000	300000

4.2   Classification Algorithms and Hyperparameters Tuning

In this work, the tasks of bot identification and gender detection are approached as supervised texts classification problems. For this end, various supervised machine learning algorithms are used to train and test the proposed approach including Random Forest (RF), Naive Bayes (NB), Logistic Regression (LR), Support Vector Machine (SVM) (with rbf and linear kernel), and Convolution Neural Network (CNN).

After performing an extensive research and after various experiments using the hyperopt library to set the best settings for each classifier, Table 2 illustrates the optimal parameters of each used algorithm.

Table 2. Parameters of all used classifiers obtained with the hyperopt library

Algorithms	Parameters
RF	number_estimators = 500
SVM with linear kernel	C = 1.0
SVM with rbf kernel	C = 1.0, gamma = 0.1
LR	C = 1e2, fit_intercept = False,
NB	alpha = 1.0
CNN	Convolutional filter size = 64, Convolutional kernel size = 4, MaxPooling: pooling size = 4, Dropout rate = 0.5, Dense layer units = 256 units, Layers Activation function = ReLu, Optimizer: Adam, Learning Rate: Adaptive (0.001 ⟶ 0.00001), Loss function: Binary crossentropy, Batch Size = 32, Dense (Output): SoftMax activation

4.3   Results Analysis

To validate the proposed approach, 10-cross-fold-validation technique is used for each algorithm. First of all, some experiments are performed to examine the usefulness of each type of features for both tasks (i.e., bot detection and gender classification). According to the results, we observed that for both tasks, the best performances are attained when using all the features. So, we present here findings with the combination of all the proposed features. Table 3 and Figs. 1, 2, 3 and 4 report the classification results obtained in terms of accuracy. Accuracy measure is defined using formula presented in [25].

Table 3. Accuracy results of our approach for the bot and gender prediction task

Algorithm	English (%)		Spanish (%)	
	Bot	Gender	Bot	Gender
LR	80.78	79.66	79.42	74.15
NB	81.31	79.63	80.27	74.24
SVM RBF	87.25	86.79	85.19	83.46
SVM Linear	89.47	87.61	88.57	86.67
CNN	91.14	89.15	88.21	88.01
RF	**93.06**	**90.04**	**90.53**	**89.11**

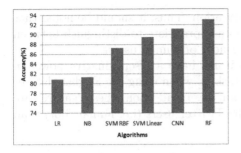

Fig. 1. Accuracy result of our approach for bot detection using the English dataset.

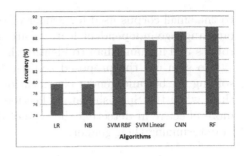

Fig. 2. Accuracy result of our approach for gender detection using the English dataset.

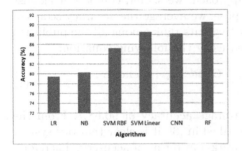

Fig. 3. Accuracy result of our approach for bot detection using the Spanish dataset.

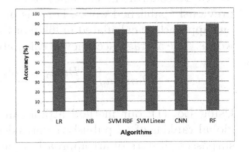

Fig. 4. Accuracy result of our approach for gender detection using the Spanish dataset.

From the findings illustrated in Table 3 and in Figs. 1, 2, 3 and 4 we can observe that the best performances are obtained when using the proposed stylometric features as input to the RF algorithm. First of all, for the bot detection task, an accuracy of 93.06% is achieved when using the English data collection and 90.53% is obtained for the Spanish dataset. SVM, LR, NB and CNN also reached acceptable performances scores (79.42%–91.14%). For the identification of gender, RF classifier achieved accuracies of 90.04% and 89.11% when using the English and Spanish tweets, respectively. With regard to the other classifiers, CNN reached encouraging results (88.01%–91.14%). SVM, LR, and NB also achieved promising accuracies.

An important remark to note is that all accuracy results are higher when using the English dataset than when the Spanish corpus is used, although we used the same features for both languages. An explanation for this may be that the Spanish tweets contain words or sentences with more than one language. This can affect the performance classification result. We also observed from Table 3 that all algorithms give significantly higher accuracy scores when tested for bot identification than when the same algorithms are used for sex classification. This can be due to the fact that we use a large dataset for bot detection compared to the small corpus used for gender classification. Thus, it should be noted that our language-independent features are more appropriate to distinguish between robots and humans than to identify the gender of human users.

To sum up, the proposed stylistic features have a discriminative power in solving the bot and gender classification task [6] when using the English dataset than when the Spanish data collection is used. In addition, these features are more effective in detecting the type of the Twitter users (i.e. human/bot) than in determining their gender.

4.4   Comparative Study

In this section, we consider the most efficient approach (that is, when RF is used). To confirm the efficiency of our approach, we should compare it against previously published works. For this purpose, we average the accuracy scores of our approach as calculated in [6] in order to get its rank among all the published works. The average accuracy is calculated using the following equation:

$$Ranking = \frac{Bot_{en} + Bot_{es} + Gender_{en} + Gender_{es}}{4} \tag{1}$$

Using Eq. (1), our method attains an average accuracy of 90.68%. From the global ranking of all published works described in [6], it is clear that our system surpasses all state of art approaches (56 works) in terms of accuracy. Therefore, it should be noted that combining the proposed features with the RF technique is the most relevant method for this challenge.

5   Conclusion

In this paper we have described a new approach for the bot and gender identification task at PAN 2019. Our approach consists of three majors parts: (i) the pre-processing of the data, (ii) the extraction of the features from the datasets, and (iii) the classification step. One of the most important challenges in this study is the features extraction step, because it was necessary to obtain a high classification result with a simple set of features. To achieve this purpose, we carefully extracted some style-based features from both datasets (English and Spanish). For the classification step, we tested various machine learning and deep learning algorithms. The final experimental outcomes showed that the proposed features were very useful in distinguishing bots from humans using the English tweets when they are used as input to the RF algorithm. However, Spanish corpus needs more cleaning operations to increase the performance results. Likewise, predicting humans gender requires further work.

As future work, we plan to expand our proposed set of features and to use a features selection technique in order to ameliorate the performance of our approach. In addition, we suggest to test the proposed method on other AP tasks such as detecting the age, native language, personality traits, occupation, among others.

References

1. Daneshvar, S., Inkpen, D.: Gender identification in twitter using n-grams and lsa. In: Proceedings of the Ninth International Conference of the CLEF Association (CLEF 2018) (2018)
2. Fatima, M., Hasan, K., Anwar, S., Nawab, R.M.A.: Multilingual author profiling on Facebook. Inf. Process. Manage. **53**(4), 886–904 (2017)
3. Rangel Pardo, F.M., Celli, F., Rosso, P., Potthast, M., Stein, B., Daelemans, W.: Overview of the 3rd Author Profiling Task at PAN 2015. In: CLEF 2015 Evaluation Labs and Workshop Working Notes Papers, pp. 1–8 (2015)
4. Juola, P.: Industrial uses for authorship analysis. Mathematics and Computers in Sciences and Industry, pp. 21–25 D(2015)
5. Subrahmanian, V., Azaria, A., Durst, S., Kagan, V., Galstyan, A., Lerman, K., et al.: The DARPA Twitter bot challenge. Computer **49**(6), 38–46 (2016)
6. Rangel, F., Rosso, P.: Overview of the 7th author profiling task at PAN 2019: bots and gender profiling in Twitter. In: Working Notes Papers of the CLEF 2019 Evaluation Labs. CEUR Workshop, vol. 2380 (2019)
7. Ouni, S., Fkih, F., Omri, M.N.: Toward a new approach to author profiling based on the extraction of statistical features. Soc. Netw. Anal. Min. **11**(1), 1–16 (2021). https://doi.org/10.1007/s13278-021-00768-6
8. Cai, C., Li, L., Zengi, D.: Behavior enhanced deep bot detection in social media. In: 2017 IEEE International Conference on Intelligence and Security Informatics (ISI), pp. 128–30. IEEE (2017)
9. Fkih, F., Omri, M.N.: Hidden data states-based complex terminology extraction from textual web data model. Appl. Intell. **50**(6), 1813–1831 (2020). https://doi.org/10.1007/s10489-019-01568-4
10. Mabrouk, O., Hlaoua, L., Omri, M.N.: Exploiting Ontology Information in Fuzzy SVM Social Media Profile Classification. Applied Intelligence, September 2020
11. Mahmoud, R., Belgacem, S., Omri, M.N.: Deep signature-based isolated and large scale continuous gesture recognition approach. J. King Saud Univ.-Comput. Inf. Sci. (2020)
12. Mahmoud, R., Belgacem, S., Omri, M.N.: Towards wide-scale continuous gesture recognition model for in-depth and grayscale input videos. Int. J. Mach. Learn. Cybern. **12**(4), 1173–1189 (2021). https://doi.org/10.1007/s13042-020-01227-y
13. Mabrouk, O., Hlaoua, L., Omri, M.N.: Exploiting ontology information in fuzzy SVM social media profile classification. Appl. Intell. **51**(6), 3757–3774 (2020). https://doi.org/10.1007/s10489-020-01939-2
14. Mabrouk, O., Hlaoua, L., Omri, M.N.: Profile categorization system based on features reduction. In: ISAIM (2018)
15. Mabrouk, O., Hlaoua, L., Omri, M.N.: Fuzzy twin SVM based-profile categorization approach. In: 2018 14th International Conference on Natural Computation, Fuzzy Systems and Knowledge Discovery (ICNC-FSKD), pp. 547–553. IEEE (2018)
16. Hall, A., Terveen, L., Halfaker, A.: Bot detection in Wikidata using behavioral and other informal cues. In: Proceedings of the ACM on Human-Computer Interaction, vol. 2(CSCW), pp. 1–18 (2018)
17. Yang, K.C., Varol, O., Davis, C.A., Ferrara, E., Flammini, A., Menczer, F.: Arming the public with artificial intelligence to counter social bots. Hum. Behav. Emerg. Technol. **1**(1), 48–61 (2019)

18. Dickerson, J.P., Kagan, V., Subrahmanian, V.S.: Using sentiment to detect bots on twitter: are humans more opinionated than bots? In: 2014 IEEE/ACM International Conference on Advances in Social Networks Analysis and Mining (ASONAM 2014), p. 620–7. IEEE (2014)
19. Chu, Z., Gianvecchio, S., Wang, H., Jajodia, S.: Detecting automation of twitter accounts: Are you a human, bot, or cyborg? IEEE Trans. Dependable Secure Comput. 9(6), 811–24 (2012)
20. Ashraf S, Iqbal HR, Nawab RMA. Cross-Genre Author Profile Prediction Using Stylometry-Based Approach. In: CLEF (Working Notes). Citeseer, pp. 992–9 (2016)
21. Bartle A, Zheng J. Gender classification with deep learning. Stanfordcs, 224d Course Project Report. 2015:1–7
22. Safara, F., Mohammed, A.S., Potrus, M.Y., Ali, S., Tho, Q.T., Souri, A., et al.: An Author Gender Detection Method Using Whale Optimization Algorithm and Artificial Neural Network. IEEE Access. 8, 48428–48437 (2020)
23. Flekova, L., Preoţiuc-Pietro, D., Ungar, L.: Exploring stylistic variation with age and income on Twitter. In: Proceedings of the 54th Annual Meeting of the Association for Computational Linguistics (Volume 2: Short Papers), pp. 313–319 (2016)
24. Kovács G, Balogh V, Mehta P, Shridhar K, Alonso P, Liwicki M. Author Profiling using Semantic and Syntactic Features. In: CLEF (Working Notes); 2019
25. Fkih, F., Omri, M.N.: Estimation of a priori decision threshold for collocations extraction: an empirical study. Int. J. Inf. Technol. Web Eng. (IJITWE) 8(3), 34–49 (2013)

How Differential Privacy Reinforces Privacy of Machine Learning Models?

Sana Ben Hamida[1,2](✉) , Hichem Mrabet[3] , and Abderrazak Jemai[4]

[1] Higher Institute of Technological Studies of Gabes, General Directorate of Technological Studies, 2098 Rades, Tunisia
Sana_benhamida@yahoo.fr
[2] Research Team on Intelligent Machines, National Engineering School of Gabes, Gabes University, 6072 Gabes, Tunisia
[3] ESST-HS, SERCOM-Laboratory, Tunisia Polytechnic School, Carthage University, 1054 Tunis, Tunisia
[4] INSAT, SERCOM-Laboratory, Tunisia Polytechnic School, Carthage University, 1080 Tunis, Tunisia

Abstract. Image classification, facial recognition, health care and graph data analysis are just a few of the areas where machine learning (ML) models were widely applied. Recent research has revealed that ML models are subject to membership inference attacks (MIAs), which attempt to determine whether or not a data record was used to train a target model. The success of MIAs is due to the data leakage during the training phase. Differential Privacy (DP) has been applied in ML to restrict inference of training samples. That's why in our experimentation, we try to mitigate the impact of MIAs using Differentially Private Stochastic Gradient Descent (DP-SGD) algorithm based on modifying the minibatch stochastic optimization process and adding noise in order to provide a way to get useful information about data without revealing much about any individual information. In this paper, we evaluate DP-SGD as a countermeasure against MIAs on Conventional Neural Networks (CNN) training over MNIST dataset. We consider different combinations of DP-SGD's noise multiplier and clipping norm parameters in our evaluation. Through experimental analysis, we show that this defense strategy can mitigate the impact of MIAs on the target model while guaranteeing the accuracy of the target model. Evaluation results reveal that our suggested solution for safeguarding privacy against MIA is successful.

Keywords: Machine learning · Security and privacy · Defense techniques · Membership inference attacks · Differential privacy

1 Introduction

Artificial intelligence and machine learning (ML) are making captions in scientific publications, and a high-level discussion over its advancements is being researched. ML uses algorithms to examine massive volumes of data and come up with a solution to a problem. However, while many people are working on inventing and upgrading algorithms today, just a few are looking into the security of those approaches. As a result, it's critical to be more cautious about security risks and the resulting ML defense approaches.

Any type of software development, including ML, carries security concerns [1]. To design a safe ML system, these risks must be considered at every stage of the ML life cycle. We have to investigate the risks of ML in order to improve its security. Indeed, based on the adversary's specific purpose and the phases of ML (training or testing), there are several types of attacks against ML models [2].

Liu et al. [3] divide ML security threats into two categories: training and test-ing/inferring. Moreover, the authors give a synopsis of several ML security threats. We mention the poisoning attack which is a sort of causal assault that disturbs the avail-ability and integrity of classify models by adding adversarial samples into the training data set, causing model predictions to be distorted. However, evasion attack consists of altered samples in order to avoid detection. Impersonate attack, prefers to imitate data samples from victims, especially in image recognition application settings. Inversion attack collects some basic information about target system models using the APIs pro-vided by ML systems. In our research, we are interested in one of the most popular attacks which affects data privacy, it is known as membership inference attacks (MIA).

MIA measures how much information a classify model leaks about its training data, which might include personal and sensitive data. The team's approach looks at the ML model's predictions to see whatever a certain data record was utilized in the training set [4].

The aim of this research is to study the vulnerability of ML models against MIAs and looking for the reasons of their success. Then, trying to mitigate privacy risks of such models.

As a principal contribution in this paper, we propose a strategy to safeguard the datasets used to train a ML model from MIA. The suggested technique seeks to train ML models while maintaining the privacy of data. Adversaries should be unable to discern between the model's prediction on its training dataset and other data samples not utilized on the training dataset if this countermeasure is applied. Our method seeks to provide membership privacy while maintaining a reasonable level of model accuracy. Overfitting has been recognized as the major source of a successful MIA in several studies [4–6].

Therefore, to mitigate the impact of our attack, we develop a method based on Differential privacy (DP) approach. In this study, we use a Conventional Neural Network (CNN) model to design and evaluate MIAs. After that, we examine our suggested defense approach to the test to see how effective it is at strengthening the model's security against MIA attacks. We have tested our solution using CNN model trained on MNIST dataset. It is shown from testing that our defense strategy may limit privacy leaks also reducing the effect of MIA, while guaranteeing a good accuracy of the model.

The following is a breakdown of the paper's structure. The background of MIA is briefly discussed in Sect. 2. In Sect. 3, we expose DP before going into our contribution in Sect. 4, when we reported experimental setup and results. Before ending in Sect. 6, similar works are analyzed in Sect. 5.

2   Membership Inference Attacks (MIA)

2.1   Overview on MIAs

In order to secure ML models against membership inference attacks, we began our studies by understanding how MIAs works and why it is successful. In practice, MIAs are one of the most common ways to assess privacy leaks.

Shokri et al. [5] were the first to describe MIAs in 2017. Since then, much research works have been done to improve the efficiency of these attacks, quantify the membership risk of a particular model, and reduce the dangers. The idea behind MIAs is that given a trained ML model, we try to discover which data points were used in the training set and which one were not used. As a result, MIAs are the most basic and extensively used attack for checking training data privacy [7].

Likewise, Nasr et al. [8] explain how MIAs runs: the attacker compares the released statistics from the dataset, and the same statistics computed on random samples from the population, to see which one is closer to the target data record. Alternatively, the adversary can compare the target data record and samples from the population, to see which one is closer to the released statistics. In either case, once the target is closer to the released statistics, then there is a high chance that it was a member of the dataset.

Figure 1 shows how MIAs seek to predict if a specific data record was used in the trained dataset of the target model or not.

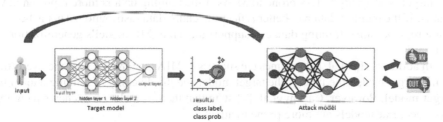

Fig. 1. How membership inference attacks perform: the attacker requests the target model with a data record (input) and gets the model's prediction on that input. The prediction is a vector of probabilities, one per class that the record belongs to a certain class. The attack model receives this prediction vector, together with the target record's label, and determines whether the record was in or out of the target model's training dataset.

Salem et al. [9] explain that MIA occurs when an adversary wants to know if one target data point was used to build a certain ML model. A MIAs may be characterized as the following function given a target data point x_{Target}, a trained ML model M, and external adversary information, represented by K:

$$A: x_{Target}, M, K \rightarrow \{0, 1\}$$

0 indicates that x_{Target} is not a part of M's training dataset D_{Train}, whereas 1 indicates that it is included in D_{Train}.

Most membership inference attacks operate in the same way as the original example described by Shokri et al. [5], namely by constructing a binary meta-classifier f_{attack} that determines whether or not a data point x_i was part of the model's training sample X given a model f and a data point x_i.

K shadow models f_{shadow} are created in order to train this meta-classifier f_{attack}. Those models are designed to behave similarly to the original ML model f.

2.2 Factors Influencing the Risk of Membership Inference Attacks

A lot of study has been done on the elements that facilitate MIAs. [3–6, 9, 10] and [11] are concerned with finding characteristics that increase MIAs in ML models.

Authors in [5, 6, 9] and [11] present overfitting as the major source of a successful membership inference attacks. When a model is over trained on the training component of a dataset, it produces less-than-expected results when it meets new data. Ying et al. [12] define overfitting as a key problem in supervised ML that stops researchers from completely generalizing models to fit observed data on training data as well as unknown data on testing data.

Song et al. [10] announce that robustness of the target model is an important factor for the success of MIAs.

The type of target model used in MIAs has a significant impact on their performance. In general, a target model with a decision boundary that is unlikely to be significantly influenced by a single data record will be more resistant to MIAs [13].

Diversity of training data is another factor that influences the risk of MIAs. In fact, the target model will be less prone to MIAs if the training data is more representative, that is, if the training data can better reflect the entire data distribution. This is because more representative training data can support the target ML model's generalization on test data.

In addition, Hu et al. [4] resumes the success of MIAs in three factors: the overfitting of the target model, the type of the target model and the diversity of training data of the target model. However, Carlini et al. [7] state that there is a clear tendency saying that more accurate models are more prone to attack.

3 Differential Privacy

3.1 Overview on DP

DP was introduced by Dwork [14] as a rigorous idea to quantify and assess privacy assurance based on a parameter called privacy budget to fight ML privacy threats. DP has been the most generally used method for determining how much personal information is divulged [15]. Indeed, DP allows a way to obtain useful information about sensitive data without disclosing too much about a single person.

Let the output space of a randomized mechanism M be S for two nearby datasets D1 and D2 that differ by only one data point. DP ensures that an observer (adversary) cannot tell whether the output of a randomized mechanism M is based on D1 or D2 (see Fig. 2). The following expression is how author in [14] formulate (ϵ, δ)-DP. (ϵ, δ)-DP is preserved by a mechanism M if:

$$Pr[M(D1) \in S] \le e^{\epsilon} \times Pr[M(D2)] \in S] + \delta$$

where ϵ is the privacy budget and δ is the failure probability. Differential privacy is a compromise between privacy and utility or model accuracy.

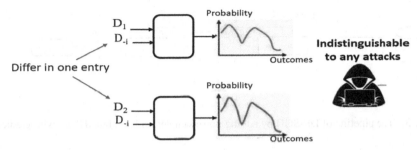

Fig. 2. How differential privacy guarantees that attacker cannot distinguish whether the output is based on D1 or D2.

DP has three qualities that make it particularly effective in similar situations: composability, group privacy, and auxiliary information resilience [16]. Composability allows for the modular construction of mechanisms: if all of a mechanism's components are differentially private, so is its composition. If datasets contain linked inputs, such as those given by the same individual, group privacy implies a gentle deterioration of privacy guarantees. Robustness against auxiliary information indicates that any side information available to the adversary has no effect on privacy promises.

As a result, regardless of how specific an individual's information is, or how specific the details of any other person in the database are, the guarantee of differential privacy holds true and provides a formal assurance that individual-level information about database participants will be preserved or will not be leaked.

DP protects an individual's privacy by introducing random noise into the dataset during data processing. Simply put, adding noise would make it impossible to detect individual data based on the results of an analysis.

However, once noise is introduced, the analysis' outcome becomes an estimate rather than the correct conclusion that would have been achieved if it had been run on the real dataset. Furthermore, because the unpredictability of the noises is included in the datasets, it is very likely that if a differential private analysis is run numerous times, it would provide different results each time.

Finally, ϵ (Epsilon) is defined as the privacy loss parameter, which controls the amount of noise injected. The epsilon may be calculated using the Laplace Distribution, which determines how much divergence there is in the computation when one of the data qualities is removed from the dataset.

3.2 Differentially Private SGD Algorithm

The Differentially Private Stochastic Gradient Descent (DP-SGD) algorithm modifies the famous deep learning minibatch stochastic optimization procedure to make it differentially private. The basic notion is that you may train a model by accessing its parameter gradients, or the gradients of the loss with respect to each of your model's parameters.

According to the post-processing feature of differential privacy, if this access preserves differential privacy of the training data, so does the generated model.

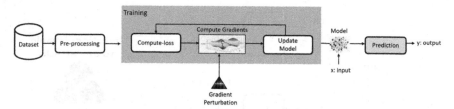

Fig. 3. The pipeline of DP-SGD by adding noise samples and combined them with gradient.

Abadi et al. [16] define DP-SGD as being similar to traditional stochastic gradient descent. The algorithm starts by randomly initializing the parameters, then picking a batch of data points at random, computing their gradients, and then updating the parameters using those gradients. However, in DP-SGD, we first clipped the gradient's sensitivity to make it more manageable. Second, we've taken random noise samples and combined them with the gradient as depicted in Fig. 3.

We can resume the DP-SGD algorithm into four steps: first we compute the per-sample gradients. Second, we clip them to a fixed maximum norm. Then we aggregate them back into a single parameter gradient. Finally, we add noise to it [17].

4 Related Works

Hu et al. [4] have classified the defense techniques against MIA on four classes. First class is **confidence masking**. In this context Shokri et al. [5] propose to provide only top-K confidence. Whereas Li et al. [21] proposed to deliver only prediction label, they offer a defense against MIA that purposely decreases training accuracy to reduce the gap between training accuracy and test accuracy which is, referenced to the authors the main cause of success of MIA. Choquette-Choo et al. [22], introduce a label-only attack that evaluates the robustness of the model's predicted labels under perturbations of the input, to infer membership. Jia et al. [23] revealed a new defense named MemGuard, it is based on adding noise to each confidence score vector predicted by the target classifier rather than interfering with the target classifier's training process. To protect models against MIA, Yang et al. [24] present a unified strategy called the purification framework. It reduces the dispersion of the confidence score vectors predicted by the target classifier. Hanzlik et al. [25] exposed MLCapsule method, it executes the machine learning model locally on the user's client and therefore the data never leaves the client.

The second class is based on **regularization,** Shokri et al. [5], Salem et al. [9], Choquette-Choo et al. [22], Nasr et al. [8] and Ben Hamida et al. [26] exposed L1 or L2 regularization as recent defenses that significantly decrease leakage of sensitive information. Some data augmentation strategies, according to studies, may lower the danger by combating overfitting, a significant component that increases leakage [27, 28]. Hayes et al. [29] presented weight normalization as a strategy to mitigate the inference attacks. Salem et al. [9], Hayes et al. [29] and Ben Hamida et al. [26] tested dropout as an effective defense to avoid overfitting which is the main cause of MIA's success. Nasr et al. [8] designed min-max privacy game an optimization problem to reduce the model's classification error and the inference accuracy of the attack. Another defense strategy presented by Salem et al. [9] is model stacking, which works regardless of the ML classifier utilized. This technique involves training the model with diverse subsets of data, which reduces the probability of overfitting.

The third category is **differential privacy**, we have identified different algorithms like DP-SGD [8, 13, 29, 30] and [21], PATE [31, 32] and LPD [3, 33]. These investigations showed that by perturbing model weights, differential privacy (DP) has been employed to protect against MIA with a strict privacy guarantee.

The fourth class is named **knowledge distillation**. V. Shejwalkar et A. Houmansadr [32] presented a new defense against MIAs termed distillation for membership privacy (DMP), which greatly improves the usefulness of the derived models over previous defenses. To limit membership inference attacks, authors presented a novel method for training privacy-preserving models that induces identical behavior on member and non-member inputs. SELENA, the framework, is made up of two fundamental components. Tang et al. [34] presented a defense technique defined in two components: new ensemble architecture for training is the primary and most important component of this strategy. This design divides the training data into random subgroups before training a model on each one. Self-Distillation, the second component of this architecture, is employed to defend against such harsher attacks. Zheng et al. [35] proposed two deep learning methods, complementary knowledge distillation (CKD) and pseudo complementary knowledge distillation (PCKD), to better address the trade-off between privacy and utility.

Firstly, Ben Hamida et al. [26] showed that in the context of ML, a practical challenge is establishing a suitable balance between the model's accuracy and the privacy of the data. In fact, authors revealed that using dropout and L2 regularization as defense technique against MIAs has mitigate the impact of the studied attack. However, model accuracy was affected. On the other hand, Zheng et al. [35] announced that defense systems that rely on DP mechanisms or adversarial training struggle to balance privacy with utility.

Liu et al. [3] declared that despite significant progress in DP [16, 33, 36], present privacy-preserving approaches have low cost efficiency owing to complicated cryptographic operations on a high number of parameters in ML algorithms. As a result, extremely efficient privacy-preserving technology in hostile environments is an important issue that should be investigated further.

5 Our Contribution

In this section, we describe our implementation of MIA, as well as our defense strategy against it, before analysing our results. Our approach focuses on protecting CNN models from MIAs. The goal of this study is to demonstrate the robustness of our privacy-preserving approach based on DP-SGD algorithm against MIA attacks empirically. Next, we describe in more detail each step of this experimentation and our expectations.

Steps of our experimentation
1- Load data
2- Pre-processing data
3- Define CNN model-1
4- Train model-1
5- Test MIA on model-1
6- Train model-2 with DP-SGD. Parameters: learning rate ηt, noise multiplier σ, Number micro-batches N
7- Test MIA on model-2
8- Compare impact of MIA on model-1 and model-2

5.1 Dataset

We test our experimentation using the standard MNIST dataset for handwritten digit recognition, which has 60,000 training and 10,000 testing instances [18]. Each sample is a gray-level picture with a size of 28 by 28 pixels. With cross-entropy loss and Adam as an optimizer function, we employ a basic feedforward neural network with ReLU units and SoftMax of 10 classes (corresponding to the 10 digits).

5.2 Implementation

First, we test our model's sensitivity to MIA on one trained model on the MNIST dataset, and then we evaluate the usefulness of DP-SGD algorithm as a defense strategy since the training phase. We apply the "membership inference attack" against these models to see if the attacker can "predict" if a particular sample belongs to the training set by training a simple image classification model on the MNIST dataset. Then, to prevent the model from leaking sensitive data, we train it with our defense technique. The MIA attack is then retested against the model to see if it has been mitigated.

To undertake MIA attacks on our trained models, we employ an open-source MIA library [19]. We create one shadow model to replicate the target model on the shadow dataset, and we develop the basis to train the attack model. The attack dataset is created by concatenating the shadow model's probability vector output with true labels. The concatenated input for the attack dataset is labeled 'in' if a sample is utilized to train the shadow model, and 'out' otherwise.

For evaluating our suggested solution, we have implemented the DP-SGD algorithms in TensorFlow as presented by Abadi et al. [16].

DP-SGD Optimizer, which minimizes a loss function using a differentially private SGD, and DP Train, which iteratively executes DP-SGD Optimizer using a privacy accountant to constrain the overall privacy loss, are shown in Fig. 3.

In our analysis, we look at several combinations of the noise multiplier and clipping norm parameters in DP-SGD. The evaluation of these combinations will be detailed in the next section.

5.3 Evaluation of Our Strategy Against MIAs and Discussion

In our experimentation, we begin by training the model and evaluate his accuracy. Then, we have tested the effectiveness of MIA on it. Figure 4 illustrates the accuracy of the target model trained on MNIST with epoch $= 10$ (training accuracy $= 0.9871$, testing accuracy $= 0.9839$).

After that, we run a MIA against the previously trained models on the MNIST training dataset. MIA, as described in Sect. 2.1, is the measurement of how much personal and sensitive information a ML model leaks about its training data. The fundamental idea behind MIA is to look at the model's predictions to see if a given data sample was utilized in the training dataset or not. We chose the Area Under the Curve (AUC) statistical metric to analyze our attack. The latter is a popular statistic for determining a classifier's ability to distinguish across classes. It is based on a summary of the ROC (Receiver operating characteristic) curve. The ROC curve [20] is a graph that shows the relationship between sensitivity and specificity (1-specificity). True Positive rate is also known as sensitivity, while false positive rate is also known as 1-specificity. The most significant benefit of adopting a ROC curve is that it is unaffected by changes in the proportion of responders.

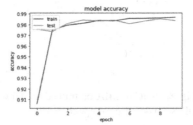
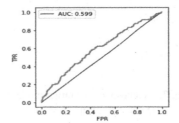

Fig. 4. The accuracy of the target model: epoch $= 10$

Fig. 5. AUC curve of MIA on the target model: epoch $= 10$

An AUC of less than 0.5 indicates that the attack was unable to identify training samples, implying that the model is free of privacy concerns. Higher levels, on the other hand, suggest significant privacy risks. Figure 5 shows how successful our membership inference attacks are in this scenario (AUC $= 0.599$). For more comprehension of how MIA works, we have testing it on some model with raising the number the epoch (i.e., AUC $= 0.599$ for epoch $= 10$, AUC $= 0.612$ for epoch $= 20$ and AUC $= 0.641$ for epoch $= 30$). As it is shown in Fig. 6, the performance of the attack was decreased by limiting the number of epochs when training the models on the same dataset. This can be explained by the fact that we reduced the model's overfitting when we stopped training it early.

In order to reduce privacy leakage, we investigate DP-SGD to mitigate the leakage about the sensitive data of the target model. The modified model is more resistant to the MIA attack, according to our tests. Indeed, our results demonstrate a slight improvement maintaining membership privacy for the MNIST with epoch $= 10$ (from AUC $= 0.595$ to AUC $= 0.589$). Yet, as it is shown in Fig. 7, after defining our defense method, the accuracy of the target model has been maintained (from 98% to 97% with epoch $= 10$).

Experimental results show that the attack performance using DP-SGD optimizer in the training phase, is lower than the same attack without using defense from AUC $= 0.599$ to AUC $= 0.589$ (according to Fig. 8). Figure 9 approves this result. According to Fig. 9. The performance of MIA was decreased from 0.612 to 0.555 with epoch $= 20$. As a consequence, an improvement of model privacy equal to 9.3% is observed.

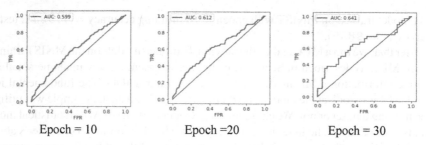

Epoch = 10   Epoch =20   Epoch = 30

Fig. 6. AUC curve of MIA on the target model with different values of epoch

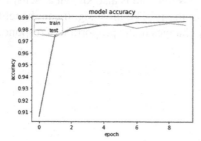

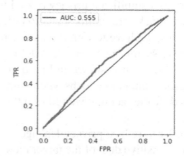

Fig. 7. Accuracy of the target model with DP-SGD defense for epoch = 10

Fig. 8. AUC of MIA on trained model with DP-SGD defense for epoch = 10

At the end, we have demonstrated empirically that our strategy presents a favourable impact on preserving the privacy of our model since the training phase with a slight degradation of the model's accuracy.

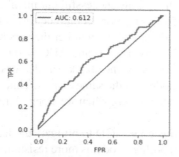

AUC of MIA before applying DP-SGD defense with = Epoch 20

AUC of MIA after applying DP-SGD defense with = Epoch 20

Fig. 9. AUC curve of MIA on the target model before and after applying our defense with epoch = 20

6 Conclusion

In this paper, we tested our MIA implementation over the CNN model trained on MNIST dataset. Then, we offered our defense approach based on DP-SGD algorithm to evaluate its usefulness in strengthening the model's privacy against these assaults. Experimentation was carried out to determine the efficiency of applying DP-SGD algorithm as a defense mechanism to mitigate the impact of MIAs as function of accuracy and AUC metrics. It is demonstrated in this work that the AUC of the attack was reduced from 0.612 to 0.555 (with epoch = 20 for MNIST dataset) thanks to the implemented DP-SGD. Also, it is shown from experimental results that our defense strategy may limit privacy leaks while reducing the effect of MIAs as well. Finally, we showed that the degradation of the accuracy of the target model was acceptable.

References

1. He, Y., Meng, G., Chen, K., Hu, X., He, J.: Towards security threats of deep learning systems: a survey. arXiv:1911.12562 [cs], October 2020
2. Papernot, N., Mcdaniel, P., Sinha, A., Wellman, M.: SoK: towards the Science of security and privacy in machine learning, p. 20 (2016)
3. Liu, Q., Li, P., Zhao, W., Cai, W., Yu, S., Leung, V.C.M.: A survey on security threats and defensive techniques of machine learning: a data driven view. IEEE Access **6**, 12103–12117 (2018). https://doi.org/10.1109/ACCESS.2018.2805680
4. Hu, H., Salcic, Z., Sun, L., Dobbie, G., Yu, P.S., Zhang, X.: Membership inference attacks on machine learning: a survey. arXiv:2103.07853 [cs], November 2021
5. Shokri, R., Stronati, M., Song, C., Shmatikov, V.: Membership inference attacks against machine learning models. arXiv:1610.05820 [cs, stat], March 2017
6. Yeom, S., Giacomelli, I., Menaged, A., Fredrikson, M., Jha, S.: Overfitting, robustness, and malicious algorithms: a study of potential causes of privacy risk in machine learning. JCS **28**(1), 35–70 (2020). https://doi.org/10.3233/JCS-191362
7. Carlini, N., Chien, S., Nasr, M., Song, S., Terzis, A., Tramer, F.: Membership inference attacks from first principles. arXiv:2112.03570 [cs], December 2021
8. Nasr, M., Shokri, R., Houmansadr, A.: Machine learning with membership privacy using adversarial regularization. In: Proceedings of the 2018 ACM SIGSAC Conference on Computer and Communications Security, New York, NY, USA, pp. 634–646, October 2018. https://doi.org/10.1145/3243734.3243855
9. Salem, A., Zhang, Y., Humbert, M., Berrang, P., Fritz, M., Backes, M.: ML-leaks: model and data independent membership inference attacks and defenses on machine learning models. arXiv:1806.01246 [cs], December 2018
10. Song, L., Shokri, R., Mittal, P.: Privacy risks of securing machine learning models against adversarial examples. In: Proceedings of the 2019 ACM SIGSAC Conference on Computer and Communications Security, pp. 241–257, November 2019. https://doi.org/10.1145/3319535.3354211
11. Yeom, S., Giacomelli, I., Fredrikson, M., Jha, S.: Privacy risk in machine learning: analyzing the connection to overfitting. arXiv:1709.01604 [cs, stat], May 2018
12. Ying, X.: An overview of overfitting and its solutions. J. Phys. Conf. Ser. **1168**, 022022, February 2019. https://doi.org/10.1088/1742-6596/1168/2/022022
13. Truex, S., Liu, L., Gursoy, M.E., Yu, L., Wei, W.: Towards demystifying membership inference attacks. arXiv:1807.09173 [cs], February 2019

14. Dwork, C.: Differential privacy. In: Bugliesi, M., Preneel, B., Sassone, V., Wegener, I. (eds.) ICALP 2006. LNCS, Part II, vol. 4052, pp. 1–12. Springer, Heidelberg (2006). https://doi.org/10.1007/11787006_1

15. Chen, J., Wang, W.H., Shi, X.: Differential privacy protection against membership inference attack on machine learning for genomic data. In: Proceedings of the Pacific Symposium Biocomputing, vol. 26, pp. 26–37 (2021)

16. Abadi, M., et al.: Deep learning with differential privacy. In: Proceedings of the 2016 ACM SIGSAC Conference on Computer and Communications Security, pp. 308–318, October 2016. https://doi.org/10.1145/2976749.2978318

17. Du, J., Li, S., Feng, M., Chen, S.: Dynamic differential-privacy preserving SGD (2021)

18. Yann, L., Corinna, C., Christopher, J.C.B.: MNIST handwritten digit database, Yann LeCun, Corinna Cortes and Chris Burges. http://yann.lecun.com/exdb/mnist/

19. TensorFlow Privacy. Tensorflow (2022). https://github.com/tensorflow/privacy. Accessed 8 Mar 2022

20. Fawcett, T.: ROC graphs: notes and practical considerations for researchers. Mach. Learn. **31**, 1–38 (2004)

21. Li, J., Li, N., Ribeiro, B.: Membership inference attacks and defenses in classification models. In: Proceedings of the Eleventh ACM Conference on Data and Application Security and Privacy, New York, NY, USA, pp. 5–16 (2021). https://doi.org/10.1145/3422337.3447836

22. Choquette-Choo, C.A., Tramer, F., Carlini, N., Papernot, N.: Label-only membership inference attacks. In: Proceedings of the 38th International Conference on Machine Learning, pp. 1964–1974, July 2021

23. Jia, J., Salem, A., Backes, M., Zhang, Y., Gong, N.Z.: MemGuard: defending against black-box membership inference attacks via adversarial examples. arXiv:1909.10594 [cs], December 2019

24. Yang, Z., Shao, B., Xuan, B., Chang, E.-C., Zhang, F.: Defending model inversion and membership inference attacks via prediction purification. arXiv:2005.03915 [cs], August 2020

25. Hanzlik, L., et al.: MLCapsule: guarded offline deployment of machine learning as a service, pp. 3300–3309 (2021)

26. Ben Hamida, S., Mrabet, H., Belguith, S., Alhomoud, A., Jemai, A.: Towards securing machine learning models against membership inference attacks. Comput. Mater. Continua (2021)

27. Kaya, Y., Dumitras, T.: When does data augmentation help with membership inference attacks?. In: Proceedings of the 38th International Conference on Machine Learning, pp. 5345–5355, July 2021

28. Yu, D., Zhang, H., Chen, W., Yin, J., Liu, T.-Y.: How does data augmentation affect privacy in machine learning? (2021)

29. Hayes, J., Melis, L., Danezis, G., De Cristofaro, E.: LOGAN: membership inference attacks against generative models. In: Proceedings on Privacy Enhancing Technologies, vol. 2019, no 1, pp. 133–152, January 2019. https://doi.org/10.2478/popets-2019-0008

30. Leino, K., Fredrikson, M.: Stolen memories: leveraging model memorization for calibrated {white-box} membership inference, pp. 1605–1622 (2020)

31. Saeidian, S., Cervia, G., Oechtering, T.J., Skoglund, M.: Quantifying membership privacy via information leakage. IEEE Trans. Inf. Forensics Secur. **16**, 3096–3108 (2021). https://doi.org/10.1109/TIFS.2021.3073804

32. Shejwalkar, V., Houmansadr, A.: Membership privacy for machine learning models through knowledge transfer | researchain. In: AAAI Conference on Artificial Intelligence, pp. 9549–9557 (2021)

33. Bernau, D., Robl, J., Grassal, P.W., Schneider, S., Kerschbaum, F.: Comparing local and central differential privacy using membership inference attacks. In: Barker, K., Ghazinour,

K. (eds.) DBSec 2021. LNCS, vol. 12840, pp. 22–42. Springer, Cham (2021). https://doi.org/10.1007/978-3-030-81242-3_2. https://www.springerprofessional.de/en/comparing-local-and-central-differential-privacy-using-membershi/19361800

34. Tang, X., et al.: Mitigating membership inference attacks by self-distillation through a novel ensemble architecture. arXiv:2110.08324 [cs], October 2021. http://arxiv.org/abs/2110.08324. Consulté le: 12 mars 2022. [En ligne]. Disponible sur

35. Zheng, J., Cao, Y., Wang, H.: Resisting membership inference attacks through knowledge distillation. Neurocomputing **452**, 114–126 (2021). https://doi.org/10.1016/j.neucom.2021.04.082

36. Jarin, I., Eshete, B.: DP-UTIL: comprehensive utility analysis of differential privacy in machine learning. arXiv:2112.12998 [cs], December 2021

Stochastic Expectation Propagation Learning for Unsupervised Feature Selection

Wentao Fan[1] , Manar Amayri[2] , and Nizar Bouguila[3(✉)]

[1] Computer Science and Technology, Huaqiao University, Xiamen, China
fwt@hqu.edu.cn
[2] Univ. Grenoble Alpes, CNRS, Grenoble INP (Institute of Engineering Univ.),
G-SCOP, 38000 Grenoble, France
manar.amayri@grenoble-inp.fr
[3] CIISE, Concordia University, Montreal, Canada
nizar.bouguila@concordia.ca

Abstract. We introduce a statistical procedure for the simultaneous clustering and feature selection of positive vectors. The proposed method is based on well-principled infinite generalized inverted Dirichlet (GID) mixture models. Unlike most currently existing learning algorithms, based on frequentist or Bayesian approaches, that have been proposed for GID mixtures, our framework is based on stochastic expectation propagation that offers a good compromise. The performance of the proposed algorithm is examined using both simulated and real world data sets.

Keywords: Clustering · Feature selection · Mixture models · Stochastic expectation propagation

1 Introduction

Clustering is a challenging task with applications in information processing, computer vision, pattern recognition, and data mining [9,10,20,22]. The main goal is discover hidden underlying structures of a given data set and classify objects into different groups, so that similarities are high among members of the same group and low among members from different groups. Existing clustering approaches can be roughly grouped into two families of approaches, partition algorithms and hierarchical algorithms. In this paper, we focus on partition approaches and in particular mixture models that have been shown to provide a formal approach to clustering [4,5]. Most of the available mixture-based approaches have been developed to deal with unbounded data, and very few have been specifically proposed to semi-bounded data. Semi-bounded data (e.g. positive vectors) are widely and naturally generated in practice. Three crucial problems when clustering this kind of data using mixture models are: 1) the choice of the per-components distribution, 2) the selection of the optimal number of components, and 3) the selection

© The Author(s), under exclusive license to Springer Nature Switzerland AG 2022
C. Bădică et al. (Eds.): ICCCI 2022, CCIS 1653, pp. 674–686, 2022.
https://doi.org/10.1007/978-3-031-16210-7_55

of the relevant features for the clustering task. These three problems have been tackled simultaneously in [2] via an infinite generalized inverted Dirichlet mixture model that has been learned by a variational inference approach.

Variational learning can be viewed as a deterministic approximation to purely Bayesian learning and has provided good learning results in the past few years. Another approximation has received some attention recently namely expectation propagation (EP) learning. Compared with variational inference, EP can offer analytic and computational advantages due to its nature of local approximations. During the last decade, expectation prorogation (EP) [17,18] has been adopted as an effective deterministic approximation algorithm for learning Bayesian mixture models [6,7]. It is built from the sequential approximation method namely assumed-density filtering (ADF) [16] and is a recursive approximation algorithm based on the minimization of a Kullback-Leibler (KL) divergence between the posterior distribution and its corresponding approximation. Compared to other Bayesian approximation methods, such as variational inference, or Markov chain Monte Carlo, EP has the advantages of learning large-scale data sets due to local computations. The interested reader is referred to [3, Chapter 10.7] for a complete and detailed introduction to EP. However, as indicated in [13], EP algorithm suffers from memory overhead that grows with the number of data points caused by the storage of local approximating factors for each data point. In order to address this issue, an extension to EP, namely stochastic expectation prorogation (SEP) has been proposed based on stochastic estimates on a subset of data points. Thus, the main goal of this paper is propose an SEP learning framework to learn infinite generalized inverted Dirichlet mixture models with feature selection.

The article is organized as follows. Section 2 presents our general statistical clustering with feature selection framework. The SEP learning approach is developed in Sect. 3. Section 4 illustrates the experimental results. Finally, Sect. 5 gives some concluding remarks.

2   The Infinite GID Mixture with Feature Selection

The GID distribution of a D-dimensional random vector $\boldsymbol{Y} = (Y_1, \ldots, Y_D)$ with parameters $\boldsymbol{\alpha}$ and $\boldsymbol{\beta}$ has the probability density function defined as [15]:

$$\text{GID}(\boldsymbol{Y}|\boldsymbol{\alpha}, \boldsymbol{\beta}) = \prod_{l=1}^{D} \frac{\Gamma(\alpha_l + \beta_l)}{\Gamma(\alpha_l)\Gamma(\beta_l)} \frac{Y_l^{\alpha_l - 1}}{(1 + \sum_{l=1}^{D} Y_l)^{\vartheta_l}} \tag{1}$$

where $\boldsymbol{\alpha} = (\alpha_1, \ldots, \alpha_D)$, $\boldsymbol{\beta} = (\beta_1, \ldots, \beta_D)$, $\vartheta_l = \alpha_l + \beta_l - \beta_{l+1}$ for $l = 1, \ldots, D$, and $\beta_{l+1} = 0$. $\Gamma(\cdot)$ is the gamma function: $\Gamma(x) = \int_0^{\infty} u^{x-1} e^{-u} du$. By considering GID as the basic distribution, we can construct the infinite GID mixture model with an infinite number of mixture components as

$$p(\boldsymbol{Y}|\boldsymbol{\alpha}, \boldsymbol{\beta}, \boldsymbol{\pi}) = \sum_{j=1}^{\infty} \pi_j \text{GID}(\boldsymbol{Y}|\boldsymbol{\alpha}_j, \boldsymbol{\beta}_j) \tag{2}$$

where $\boldsymbol{\pi}$ represents the mixing proportions, such that $\sum_{j=1}^{\infty} \pi_j = 1$.

2.1   Infinite GID Mixture Models with Feature Selection

As we may notice from (2), the infinite GID mixture model is built by considering all features (i.e., dimensions) of Y. However, in practice some features (e.g., irrelevant features, or noise) may not contribute to the learning process, or even degrade the performance, especially when dealing with high-dimensional data. Therefore, *feature selection*, the process of selecting a subset of relevant features may be integrated into the infinite GID mixture model to improve modeling capability. In our work, in order to perform feature selection, we first transform the data vector Y into another D-dimensional vector X with independent features, based on the geometric transformation as discussed in [15]: $X_1 = Y_1$ and $X_l = Y_l/(1 + \sum_{s=1}^{l-1} Y_s)$ for $l > 1$. Through this transformation, the GID distribution of D-dimensional vector Y can be represented by the product of D inverted Beta distributions, one for each feature X_l:

$$\text{GID}(Y|\alpha, \beta) = \prod_{l=1}^{D} \text{IB}(X_l|\alpha_l, \beta_l) \tag{3}$$

where $\text{IB}(X_l|\alpha_l, \beta_l)$ is an inverted Beta distribution with parameters α_l and β_l:

$$\text{IB}(X_l|\alpha_l, \beta_l) = \frac{\Gamma(\alpha_l + \beta_l)}{\Gamma(\alpha_l)\Gamma(\beta_l)} X_l^{\alpha_l - 1}(1 + X_l)^{-(\alpha_l + \beta_l)} \tag{4}$$

Recently, an unsupervised feature selection scheme has demonstrated prosimian performance when considered together with mixture models [2,7,12]. Its main idea is that, the lth feature of an observed data is considered as "irrelevant" if its distribution is independent of the class labels (i.e., it follows a common distribution). By exploiting this feature selection scheme and the geometric transformation of the GID distribution as described in (3), the infinite GID mixture model with feature selection is then given by

$$p(X) = \sum_{j=1}^{\infty} \pi_j \prod_{l=1}^{D} \left[\epsilon_l \text{IB}(X_l|\theta_{jl}) + (1 - \epsilon_l)\text{IB}(X_l|\theta_l') \right] \tag{5}$$

where $\theta_{jl} = (\alpha_{jl}, \beta_{jl})$ and $\theta_l' = (\alpha_l', \beta_l')$ are the parameters of inverted Beta distributions for the relevant and irrelevant features, respectively. The feature saliency parameter ϵ_l represents the probability that feature l is relevant.

2.2   Prior Distributions

Since the infinite GID mixture model is a nonparametric Bayesian model, each parameter should be assigned with a prior distribution. π follows a Dirichlet process prior [11,19] with a stick-breaking representation [21]:

$$\pi_j = \lambda_j \prod_{k=1}^{j-1} (1 - \lambda_k), \quad G = \sum_{j=1}^{\infty} \pi_j \delta_{\theta_j}, \quad d_j \sim \text{Beta}(1, d_j), \quad \theta_j \sim H, \tag{6}$$

where G is distributed according to the Dirichlet process $G \sim DP(d, H)$, δ_{θ_j} is a probability measure concentrated at θ_j, and d_j is a positive real number. For the parameter λ of the stick-breaking representation, its prior is a particular Beta distribution Beta$(1, d)$ as shown in (6):

$$p(\lambda) = \prod_{j=1}^{\infty} \text{Beta}(c_j, d_j) = \prod_{j=1}^{\infty} d_j (1 - \lambda_j)^{d_j - 1} \tag{7}$$

where $c_j = 1$. Here the hyperparameter c_j is introduced in order to facilitate the update of the Beta distribution later in the model learning process. For the feature saliency parameter ϵ, a Beta prior is adopted as

$$p(\epsilon) = \prod_{l=1}^{D} \text{Beta}(\epsilon_l | a, b) = \prod_{l=1}^{D} \left[\frac{\Gamma(a+b)}{\Gamma(a)\Gamma(b)} \epsilon_l^{a-1} (1 - \epsilon_l)^{b-1} \right] \tag{8}$$

Lastly, for the parameters θ_{jl} and θ_l' of the inverted Beta distributions, we consider Gaussian distributions as their priors. This choice is inspired from [6,7,14], in which Gaussian priors are used for several mixture models. In our case, adopting Gaussian prior can provide analytically tractable calculation and can model the correlation between the parameters of inverted Beta distributions (i.e., α_{jl} and β_{jl}, α_l' and β_l', respectively). Thus, two-dimensional Gaussians are adopted as the priors for θ_{jl} and θ_l' with parameters (μ_{jl}, A_{jl}) and (μ_l', A_l'), respectively.

3 Model Learning via SEP

Given a set of N i.i.d (independent and identically distributed) data vectors $\mathcal{X} = (X_1, \ldots, X_N)$ that is distributed according to the infinite GID mixture model with parameters $\Theta = \{\lambda, \epsilon, \theta, \theta'\}$. As discussed in [14,17], we can form the joint distribution of $\mathcal{X}$ and Θ as a product of factors in the form $p(\mathcal{X}, \Theta) = \prod_i f_i(\Theta)$, where each data point X_i is associated with one factor $f_i(\Theta) = p(X_i | \Theta)$, $i = 1, \ldots, N$, along with a prior factor $f_0(\Theta) = p(\Theta)$. Then, the posterior distribution of Θ is given by

$$p(\Theta | \mathcal{X}) = \frac{\prod_i f_i(\Theta)}{\int \prod_i f_i(\Theta) d\Theta} \tag{9}$$

In SEP learning algorithm, the posterior $p(\Theta | \mathcal{X})$ is approximated by the product of N copies of a single approximating factor $\widetilde{f}(\Theta)$ and the prior

$$q^*(\Theta) \approx \widetilde{f}(\Theta)^N f_0(\Theta) \tag{10}$$

where $\widetilde{f}(\Theta)$ is a global factor that captures the average contribution a likelihood function has on the posterior. The first step of SEP learning algorithm is to initialize the global approximating factor $\widetilde{f}(\Theta)$ by initializing all the involved hyperparameters $\{a, b, c_j, d_j, \mu_{jl}, A_{jl}, \mu_l', A_l'\}$. We also truncate the stick-breaking representation of the infinite GID mixture model at a value of M as

$$\lambda_M = 1, \qquad \pi_j = 0 \text{ when } j > M, \qquad \sum_{j=1}^{M} \pi_j = 1 \tag{11}$$

where M is the truncation level that can be freely initialized and will be inferred automatically during the learning process. Then, based on the idea of SEP, we initialize the posterior approximation by setting $q^*(\Theta) \propto \tilde{f}(\Theta)^N$ with hyperparameters calculated by

$$a^* = Na - N, \qquad b^* = Nb - N \tag{12}$$

$$c_j^* = Nc_j - N, \qquad d_j^* = Nc_j - N \tag{13}$$

$$\mu_{jl}^* = (NA_{jl}^{-1})(NA_{jl}\mu_{jl}), \qquad A_{jl}^* = NA_{jl} \tag{14}$$

$$\mu_l'^* = (NA_l'^{-1})(NA_l'\mu_l'), \qquad A_l'^* = NA_l' \tag{15}$$

To update $\tilde{f}(\Theta)$, we remove one of the copies from the posterior $q^*(\Theta)$ as

$$q^{\backslash 1}(\Theta) = \frac{q^*(\Theta)}{\tilde{f}(\Theta)} \tag{16}$$

where the corresponding hyperparameters of $q^{\backslash 1}(\Theta)$ can be calculated by

$$a^{\backslash 1} = a^* - a + 1, \qquad b^{\backslash 1} = b^* - b + 1 \tag{17}$$

$$c_j^{\backslash 1} = c_j^* - c_j + 1, \qquad d_j^{\backslash 1} = d_j^* - d_j + 1 \tag{18}$$

$$\mu_{jl}^{\backslash 1} = (A_{jl}^{\backslash 1})^{-1}(A_{jl}^*\mu_{jl}^* - A_{jl}\mu_{jl}), \tag{19}$$

$$A_{jl}^{\backslash 1} = A_{jl}^* - A_{jl} \tag{20}$$

$$\mu_l'^{\backslash 1} = (A_l'^{\backslash 1})^{-1}(A_l'^*\mu_l'^* - A_l'\mu_l'), \tag{21}$$

$$A_l'^{\backslash 1} = A_l'^* - A_l' \tag{22}$$

Next, we sample a data point $\boldsymbol{X}_i$ uniformly from the data set: $i \sim \text{Unif}(1, \dots, N)$. By exploiting the true factor from the ith observation vector (i.e. $f_i(\Theta)$), an updated posterior $\hat{p}(\Theta)$ can be obtained by

$$\hat{p}(\Theta) = \frac{1}{Z_i} f_i(\Theta) q^{\backslash 1}(\Theta) \tag{23}$$

where Z_i is the normalization constant that is defined by

$$Z_i = \int f_i(\Theta) q^{\backslash 1}(\Theta) d\Theta = \sum_{j=1}^M \langle \pi_j \rangle \prod_{l=1}^D \left[\frac{a_i}{a_i + b_i} \int \text{IB}(X_{il}|\theta_{jl}) q^{\backslash 1}(\theta_{jl}) d\theta_{jl} \right.$$

$$\left. + \frac{b_i}{a_i + b_i} \int \text{IB}(X_{il}|\theta_l') q^{\backslash 1}(\theta_l') d\theta_l' \right] \tag{24}$$

As we may notice, the integrations in the above equation are intractable. To address this issue, we follow the idea as mentioned in [7,14] by approximating these integrands with Gaussian distributions through Laplace approximations.

Since the integrand $\mathrm{IB}(X_{il}|\theta_{jl})q^{\backslash 1}(\theta_{jl})$ is a product of an inverted Beta and Gaussian, a normalized distribution can be defined by

$$\mathcal{H}(\theta_{jl}) = \frac{h(\theta_{jl})}{\int h(\theta_{jl})d\theta_{jl}} \tag{25}$$

$$h(\theta_{jl}) = \mathrm{IB}(X_{il}|\theta_{jl})\mathcal{N}(\theta_{jl}|\boldsymbol{\mu}_{jl}^{\backslash 1}, A_{jl}^{\backslash 1}) \tag{26}$$

By using Laplace approximation, a Gaussian approximation to $h(\theta_{jl})$ which is centered on the mode $\breve{\theta}_{jl}$ of the distribution $\mathcal{H}(\theta_{jl})$ can be found as

$$h(\theta_{jl}) \simeq h(\breve{\theta}_{jl}) \exp\left(-\frac{1}{2}(\theta_{jl} - \breve{\theta}_{jl})\widehat{A}_{jl}(\theta_{jl} - \breve{\theta}_{jl})\right) \tag{27}$$

where $\widehat{A}_{jl} = -\frac{\partial^2 \ln h(\theta_{jl})}{\partial \theta_{jl}^2}\Big|_{\theta_{jl}=\breve{\theta}_{jl}}$, and the mode $\breve{\theta}_{jl}$ can be obtained numerically by setting the first derivative of $\ln h(\theta_{jl})$ equal to 0. Based on (27), we can approximate the integration of $h(\theta_{jl})$ as $\int h(\theta_{jl})d\theta_{jl} \simeq h(\breve{\theta}_{jl})\frac{2\pi}{|\widehat{A}_{jl}|^{1/2}}$. Using the same idea, an approximation to the integrand $\mathrm{IB}(X_{il}|\theta_l')q^{\backslash 1}(\theta_l')$ in (24) can be obtained with the corresponding mode $\breve{\theta}_l'$. Then, we can rewrite (24) as

$$Z_i = \sum_{j=1}^{M} \frac{c_{i,j}}{\sum_j c_{i,j}} \prod_{l=1}^{D} \left[\frac{a_i}{a_i + b_i}h(\breve{\theta}_{jl})\frac{2\pi}{|\widehat{A}_{jl}|^{1/2}} + \frac{b_i}{a_i + b_i}h(\breve{\theta}_l')\frac{2\pi}{|\widehat{A}_l'|^{1/2}}\right] \tag{28}$$

where $\widehat{A}_l'$ is computed in a similar fashion to $\widehat{A}_{jl}$.

In the following step, we revise the posterior $q^*(\Theta)$ by matching its sufficient statistics with the corresponding moments of $\widehat{p}(\Theta)$. More specifically, we can obtain the partial derivatives of $\ln Z_i$ with respect to each hyperparameters as

$$\nabla_a^{\backslash 1} \ln Z_i = E_{\widehat{p}}[\ln \epsilon_l] + \psi(a^{\backslash 1} + b^{\backslash 1}) - \psi(a^{\backslash 1}) \tag{29}$$

$$\nabla_b^{\backslash 1} \ln Z_i = E_{\widehat{p}}[\ln(1 - \epsilon_l)] + \psi(a^{\backslash 1} + b^{\backslash 1}) - \psi(b^{\backslash 1}) \tag{30}$$

$$\nabla_{c_j}^{\backslash 1} \ln Z_i = E_{\widehat{p}}[\ln \lambda_j] + \psi(c_j^{\backslash 1} + d_j^{\backslash 1}) - \psi(c_j^{\backslash i}) \tag{31}$$

$$\nabla_{d_j}^{\backslash 1} \ln Z_i = E_{\widehat{p}}[\ln(1 - \lambda_j)] + \psi(c_j^{\backslash 1} + d_j^{\backslash 1}) - \psi(d_j^{\backslash 1}) \tag{32}$$

$$\nabla_{\boldsymbol{\mu}_{jl}}^{\backslash 1} \ln Z_i = A_{jl}^{\backslash 1} E_{\widehat{p}}[\theta_{jl}] - A_{jl}^{\backslash 1}\boldsymbol{\mu}_{jl}^{\backslash 1} \tag{33}$$

$$\nabla_{A_{jl}}^{\backslash 1} \ln Z_i = \frac{1}{2}\left\{|(A_{jl}^{\backslash 1})^{-1}| - \left[\sum_{s=1}^{2} E_{\widehat{p}}[\theta_{jls}^2] + (\mu_{jls}^{\backslash 1})^2 - 2E_{\widehat{p}}[\theta_{jls}]\mu_{jls}^{\backslash 1}\right]\right\} \tag{34}$$

$$\nabla_{\boldsymbol{\mu}_l'}^{\backslash 1} \ln Z_i = A_l'^{\backslash 1} E_{\widehat{p}}[\theta_l'] - A_l'^{\backslash 1}\boldsymbol{\mu}_l'^{\backslash 1} \tag{35}$$

$$\nabla_{A'_l}^{\backslash 1} \ln Z_i = \frac{1}{2} \left\{ |(A_l^{\backslash 1})^{-1}| - \left[\sum_{s=1}^{2} E_{\widehat{p}}[\theta_{ls}'^2] + (\mu_{ls}'^{\backslash 1})^2 - 2E_{\widehat{p}}[\theta_{ls}']\mu_{ls}'^{\backslash 1} \right] \right\} \quad (36)$$

where $\psi(\cdot)$ is the digamma function and the right hand sides of above equations can be computed analytically based on (28). The expectations in above equations can be solved by moment matching. Then, we can update the hyperparameters of $q^*(\Theta)$ by substituting the expectations into the corresponding partial derivatives. Based on $q^*(\Theta)$ and $q^{\backslash 1}(\Theta)$, the revised hyperparameters for the factor $\widetilde{f}_i(\Theta)$ can be obtained. The last step in SEP learning is to update $\widetilde{f}(\Theta)$ as

$$\widetilde{f}(\Theta) = \widetilde{f}(\Theta)^{1-\frac{1}{N}} \widetilde{f}_i(\Theta) \quad (37)$$

The above procedure is repeated until the convergence (i.e., the stabilization of the hyperparameters). After the convergence, the expected value of the feature saliency in posterior distributions can be calculated as $E[\epsilon_l] = \frac{a^*}{a^*+b^*}$. The complete learning algorithm is summarized in Algorithm 1.

Algorithm 1

1: Initialize the truncation level M.
2: Initialize the approximating factor $\widetilde{f}(\Theta)$ by initializing hyperparameters $\{a, b, c_j, d_j, \boldsymbol{\mu}_{jl}, A_{jl}, \boldsymbol{\mu}'_l, A'_l, \}$.
3: Initialize the posterior approximation by setting $q^*(\Theta) \propto \widetilde{f}(\Theta)^N$ with hyperparameters that are calculated as shown in (12)~(15).
4: **repeat**
5:     Sample a data point $\boldsymbol{X}_i$ uniformly from the data set: $i \sim \text{Unif}(1, \ldots, N)$.
6:     Remove one factor from the posterior $q^*(\Theta)$: $q^{\backslash 1}(\Lambda) = q^*(\Theta)/\widetilde{f}(\Theta)$.
7:     Evaluate the new posterior by matching the sufficient statistics (moments) of $q^*(\Theta)$ with the corresponding moments of $\widehat{p}(\Theta)$.
8:     Update the factor $\widetilde{f}_i(\Theta)$ by updating the corresponding hyperparameters.
9:     Update the approximating factor $\widetilde{f}(\Theta)$ as in (37).
10: **until** Convergence criterion is reached.
11: Compute the estimated values of the features saliencies as in Eq. (32).

---

4   Experimental Results

We assess the performance of the proposed model that is learnt using SEP (InGFS-SEP) through both simulated and real data sets.

4.1   Simulated Data

The goal of this experiment is to verify the effectiveness of the developed SEP approach in learning the infinite GID mixture models. We conduct our experiment using two 10-dimensional simulated data sets with two relevant features and eight irrelevant features. As mentioned in Sect. 2, the geometric transformation is performed to generate data with independent features. Specifically, two relevant features are generated in the transformed space from a mixture of inverted Beta distributions using parameters as shown in Table 1. Eight irrelevant features are generated from a common inverted Beta distribution $IB(1, 6)$ and are appended to relevant features to form the simulated data sets. As illustrated in Table 1, the first simulated data set (D1) contains 5,000 data points with two clusters whereas the second data set (D2) includes 5,000 data points that are divided into three clusters. The average estimated parameters over 15 runs for each synthetic data set are illustrated in Table 2, using the proposed InGFS-SEP. As we can observe from this table, both the parameters of the model representing relevant features and the mixing coefficients can be efficiently learned by the proposed algorithm. The average features saliencies for the two synthetic data sets are shown in Figs. 1a and 1b, based on 15 runs. According to these results, it is obvious that high degree of relevance (greater than 0.9) has been obtained for features 1 and 2, which is consistent with the ground truth. Features 3~10 have been assigned low degree of relevance (lower than 0.1), thus are considered as irrelevant. For both data sets the algorithm converges within 200 iterations and was found robust to the initialization (i.e.

Table 1. Parameters of different generated data sets. N denotes the total number of data points, N_j denotes the number of data points in cluster j.

Data set	j	N_j	α_{j1}	α_{j2}	β_{j1}	β_{j2}	π_j
D1 ($N = 2000$)	1	1000	12	8	13	14	0.50
	2	1000	3	22	8	10	0.50
D2 ($N = 5000$)	1	1000	12	8	13	14	0.20
	2	1000	3	22	8	10	0.20
	3	3000	30	11	19	25	0.60

Table 2. Average estimated parameters of the synthetic data set in 15 runs by the proposed stochastic variational inference method.

Data set	j	$\widehat{\alpha}_{j1}$	$\widehat{\alpha}_{j2}$	$\widehat{\beta}_{j1}$	$\widehat{\beta}_{j2}$	$\widehat{\pi}_j$
D1	1	11.75	8.26	13.21	14.87	0.493
	2	3.17	23.08	7.67	10.52	0.507
D2	1	12.13	8.54	13.68	13.51	0.198
	2	3.22	21.63	8.33	9.82	0.204
	3	28.79	10.91	18.49	24.81	0.598

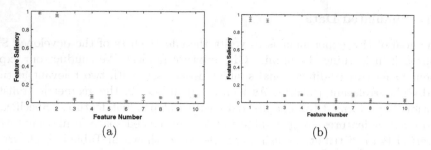

Fig. 1. Average saliences obtained by InGFS-SEP for data set (a) D1 and (b) D2.

Table 3. The four real-world data sets. N, D and M denote the number of instances, features and classes, respectively.

Data set	N	D	M
MPE	1080	77	8
IS	2310	19	7
HD	5620	64	10
LR	20000	16	26

Table 4. The average error rates (%) using different methods over 15 random runs. The numbers in parenthesis are the standard deviation of the corresponding quantities.

Method	MPE	IS	HD	LR
GMMFS-EM	12.49 (0.69)	19.31 (0.78)	17.28 (1.12)	34.56 (1.43)
GIDFS-EM	10.27 (0.75)	16.52 (1.03)	15.06 (0.91)	31.67 (1.73)
InGFS-VR	7.39 (1.13)	14.23 (0.85)	12.11 (0.97)	27.75 (2.02)
InGID-SEP	8.04 (0.82)	13.94 (0.44)	11.38 (1.26)	25.18 (1.81)
InGFS-SEP	5.93 (0.79)	11.17 (0.81)	9.13 (1.15)	23.04 (1.67)

different initial parameters values have been tested) which is mainly due to its Bayesian formulation. It is noteworthy also that an important feature of SEP is that it reduces the complexity of EP by a factor of N [13]. In the case of our model the complexity is $O(NMD)$.

4.2   Real Data

In this experiment, the proposed InGFS-SEP is tested on clustering four real-world data sets from the UCI Machine Learning Repository: the mice protein expression (MPE) data set, the image segmentation (IS) data set, the handwritten digits (HD) data set and the letter recognition (LR) data set. The details of these four data sets are demonstrated in Table 3. It is noteworthy that since we are performing clustering, class labels in the original data sets are not included in our experiment, but are used for evaluation of the clustering results. In a preprocessing step, all data sets are normalized into the range of [0,1]. We compare the proposed InGFS-SEP with three other mixture modeling approaches, which includes the finite Gaussian mixture model with feature selection (GMMFS-EM) as proposed in [12], the finite GID mixture model with feature selection that is learned using the expectation maximization (EM) approach together with the minimum message length (MML) criterion (GIDFS-EM) [15] and the infinite GID mixture model with feature selection that is learned by variational inference (InGFS-VR) [2]. In order to demonstrate the advantages of integrating feature selection into our model, we also implement the infinite GID mixture model without feature selection that is learned by SEP (InGID-SEP) on clustering the real-world data sets. The average clustering performance in terms of error rates over 15 runs are summarized in Table 4, in which the numbers in parenthesis are the standard deviation of the corresponding quantities. According to this table, it is clear that the proposed InGFS-SEP has provided the best clustering performance among all tested approaches in terms of the lowest error rates for all data sets. Particularly, the fact that InGFS-SEP outperforms InGID-SEP in terms of lower error rates has demonstrated the advantages of using feature selection technique for high-dimensional data sets. Since InGFS-SEP has obtained better clustering performance than InGFS-VR and GIDFS-EM, this shows the merits of using SEP learning algorithm than variational inference or EMM to learn GID mixture models. The features saliencies obtained by the proposed InGFS-SEP for each real-world data set are shown in Fig. 2. More specifically, for the MPE data set, 17 features (e.g., feature number 3, 6, 10, 12, 23, etc.) have saliencies lower than 0.5, and therefore contribute less to clustering. For the IS data set, we have obtained 5 features (feature number 3, 7, 14, 16, and 18) that have saliencies lower than 0.5. For the HD and the LR data sets, we have obtained 13 (feature number 2, 8, 9, 13, 15, etc.) and 4 irrelevant features (feature number 1, 9, 11 and 16), respectively, with feature saliencies lower than 0.5. Based on these results, it is obvious that different features do not contribute equally in the clustering analysis due to different associated relevance degrees, which demonstrates the significance of integrating feature selection.

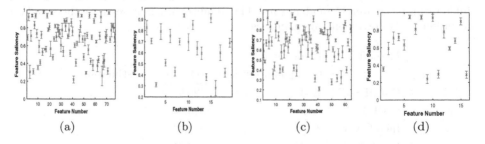

(a)   (b)   (c)   (d)

Fig. 2. Average saliences obtained by InGFS-SEP for data sets (a) MPE; (b) IS; (c) HD; (d) LR.

4.3   Occupancy Detection and Estimation in Smart Buildings

Building occupancy detection and estimation are important tasks to improve building operation with respect to energy management, security and indoor environment quality. These two tasks have been generally tackled using supervised machine learning techniques [1]. Unlike these previous efforts, the aforementioned tasks are carried out here automatically in unsupervised settings using our statistical framework. A recent unsupervised approach used specialized sensors to analyze different behaviours of essential components of many buildings including heating, ventilation, and air-conditioning [8]. It is noteworthy that this approach was based on the K-means algorithm. The dataset used in both experiments originates from [1], where the authors considered a network of sensors in an office of four people and frequent visitor guests with numerous meetings and presentations. The sensors collect motions, CO_2 concentration, temperature, relative humidity (RH), motions, door and window positions, power consumption, and acoustic pressure from microphone. Two cameras are used to record the true occupancy numbers as well as related activities. Many features can be extracted from the data collected through the presented sensors. The dataset has 717 instances from 5 classes including 0 occupant (503), 1 occupant (118), 2 occupants (60), 3 occupants (27), and 4 occupants (9). Various experiments were carried out including some preprocessing steps, information gain analysis, and building multiple classifiers with decision trees and random forest algorithms to validate the quality of the recorded data as well as the efficiency of applying machine learning techniques on this challenging problem. The imbalanced nature of the dataset has raised some significant challenges to the previous solutions [1] which were fully supervised. In the first experiment that concerns occupancy detection, our goal is similar to [8], which is to detect whether there is at least one occupant in the office or not. The main idea is that we could reduce the energy consumption of the room when there is no presence of any occupant. Due to the binary nature of the classes, the dataset now has two classes: 0 occupant (503) and at least one occupant (214). The results shown in Table 5 validate

Table 5. The average error rates (%) for occupancy detection and estimation using different methods over 15 random runs. The numbers in parenthesis are the standard deviation of the corresponding quantities.

Method	Error rates (%)	
	Occupancy detection	Occupancy estimation
GMMFS-EM	7.84	20.68
GIDFS-EM	3.79	15.34
InGFS-VR	3.77	15.33
InGID-SEP	4.87	16.75
InGFS-SEP	2.21	14.30
K-Means	9.91	37.10

the effectiveness of the proposed method as compared to K-means, for instance, which was used in a previous recent related research work [8] and as compared to the other approaches that we considered in Sect. 4.2. The drawback of previous experiment is ignoring the exact occupants number, which is rather important for building a flexible energy plan which dynamically alters the power consumption depending on the fluctuation of the occupants. This task offers possibilities for saving even more energy usage as compared to only two power consumption states in previous experiment. The results in Table 5 show that our model achieve the highest accuracy over other comparable models. It is noteworthy that the most important features in both experiments have been selected to be: the sum of four laptops power consumption, acoustic pressure, motion counter, and door/window position which confirms the conclusion reached in [1].

5   Conclusion

The clustering statistical framework developed in this article is an infinite generalized inverted Dirichlet mixture that integrates feature selection in a principled manner. The proposed approach is particularly useful for analyzing and clustering positive vectors. The proposed algorithm does not require the specification of the number of clusters in advance thanks to the nonparametric Bayesian nature of the model and the stochastic nature of the adopted learning approach. Through simulated, real-world datasets, and a challenging real application that concerns occupancy detection and estimation in smart buildings, the proposed approach appeared to be superior over other comparable algorithms. A natural extension of the proposed approach is to handle data of mixed types.

Acknowledgement. The completion of this research was made possible thanks to Natural Sciences and Engineering Research Council of Canada (NSERC), the "Nouveaux arrivants, Université Grenoble Alpes Grenoble INP - UGA /G-SCOP" program, and the National Natural Science Foundation of China (61876068).

References

1. Amayri, M., Arora, A., Ploix, S., Bandhyopadyay, S., Ngo, Q.D., Badarla, V.R.: Estimating occupancy in heterogeneous sensor environment. Energy Build. **129**, 46–58 (2016)
2. Bdiri, T., Bouguila, N., Ziou, D.: Variational Bayesian inference for infinite generalized inverted Dirichlet mixtures with feature selection and its application to clustering. Appl. Intell. **44**(3), 507–525 (2016)
3. Bishop, C.M.: Pattern Recognition and Machine Learning. Information science and statistics. Springer, Heidelberg (2006)
4. Bouguila, N., ElGuebaly, W.: Discrete data clustering using finite mixture models. Pattern Recogn. **42**(1), 33–42 (2009)
5. Bouguila, N., Ziou, D.: Using unsupervised learning of a finite Dirichlet mixture model to improve pattern recognition applications. Pattern Recogn. Lett. **26**(12), 1916–1925 (2005)

6. Fan, W., Bouguila, N.: Expectation propagation learning of a Dirichlet process mixture of Beta-Liouville distributions for proportional data clustering. Eng. Appl. Artif. Intell. **43**, 1–14 (2015)

7. Fan, W., Bouguila, N.: Face detection and facial expression recognition using simultaneous clustering and feature selection via an expectation propagation statistical learning framework. Multimedia Tools Appl. **74**(12), 4303–4327 (2013). https://doi.org/10.1007/s11042-013-1548-z

8. Habib, U., Zucker, G.: Automatic occupancy prediction using unsupervised learning in buildings data. In: 2017 IEEE 26th International Symposium on Industrial Electronics (ISIE), pp. 1471–1476 (2017)

9. Jiang, M.T., Hsu, W., Kuo, C., Yang, T.: Enhancement of unsupervised feature selection for conditional random fields learning in Chinese word segmentation. In: 7th International Conference on Natural Language Processing and Knowledge Engineering, NLPKE 2011, Tokushima, Japan, 27–29 November 2011, pp. 382–389 (2011)

10. Jiang, S.Y., Wang, L.X.: Efficient feature selection based on correlation measure between continuous and discrete features. Inf. Process. Lett. **116**(2), 203–215 (2016)

11. Korwar, R.M., Hollander, M.: Contributions to the theory of Dirichlet processes. Ann. Prob. **1**, 705–711 (1973)

12. Law, M.H.C., Figueiredo, M.A.T., Jain, A.K.: Simultaneous feature selection and clustering using mixture models. IEEE Trans. Pattern Anal. Mach. Intell. **26**(9), 1154–1166 (2004)

13. Li, Y., Hernández-Lobato, J.M., Turner, R.E.: Stochastic expectation propagation. In: Cortes, C., Lawrence, N.D., Lee, D.D., Sugiyama, M., Garnett, R. (eds.) Advances in Neural Information Processing Systems, vol. 28, pp. 2323–2331 (2015)

14. Ma, Z., Leijon, A.: Expectation propagation for estimating the parameters of the Beta distribution. In: Proceedings of the IEEE International Conference on Acoustics, Speech, and Signal Processing (ICASSP), pp. 2082–2085 (2010)

15. Mashrgy, M.A., Bdiri, T., Bouguila, N.: Robust simultaneous positive data clustering and unsupervised feature selection using generalized inverted Dirichlet mixture models. Knowl.-Based Syst. **59**, 182–195 (2014)

16. Maybeck, P.S.: Stochastic Models, Estimation and Control. Academic Press, Cambridge (1982)

17. Minka, T.: Expectation propagation for approximate Bayesian inference. In: Proceedings of the Conference on Uncertainty in Artificial Intelligence (UAI), pp. 362–369 (2001)

18. Minka, T., Lafferty, J.: Expectation-propagation for the generative aspect model. In: Proceedings of the Conference on Uncertainty in Artificial Intelligence (UAI), pp. 352–359 (2002)

19. Neal, R.M.: Markov Chain sampling methods for Dirichlet process mixture models. J. Comput. Graph. Stat. **9**(2), 249–265 (2000)

20. Panday, D., de Amorim, R.C., Lane, P.: Feature weighting as a tool for unsupervised feature selection. Inf. Process. Lett. **129**, 44–52 (2018)

21. Sethuraman, J.: A constructive definition of Dirichlet priors. Statistica Sinica **4**, 639–650 (1994)

22. Yang, T., Jiang, M.T., Kuo, C., Tsai, R.T., Hsu, W.: Unsupervised overlapping feature selection for conditional random fields learning in Chinese word segmentation. In: Proceedings of the 23rd Conference on Computational Linguistics and Speech Processing, ROCLING 2011, Taipei, Taiwan, 8–9 September 2011, pp. 109–122 (2011)

S-LDA: Documents Classification Enrichment for Information Retrieval

Amani Drissi[1]([⊠])(iD), Anis Tissaoui[2](iD), Salma Sassi[2](iD), Richard Chbeir[3](iD),
and Abderrazak Jemai[4](iD)

[1] FST, University of Manar, SERCOM, Tunis, Tunisia
drissiamani19@gmail.com
[2] VPNC Lab., FSJEGJ, University of Jendouba, 8189 Jendouba, Tunisia
{anis.tissaoui,salma.sassi}@fsjegj.rnu.tn
[3] E2S UPPA, LIUPPA, University Pau & Pays Adour, EA3000 Anglet, France
rchbeir@acm.org
[4] INSAT, University of Carthage, SERCOM, Tunis, Tunisia
Abderrazak.Jemai@insat.rnu.tn

Abstract. In recent years, the research on topic modeling techniques has become a hot topic among researchers thanks to their ability to classify and understand a large text corpora which has a beneficial effect on information retrieval performance, but recently user queries are more complicated because they need to know not only which documents are most helpful to them, but also which parts of documents are more or less related to their request. Also, they need to search by topic or document, not merely by keywords.

In this context, we propose a new approach of automated text classification based on LDA topic modeling algorithm and the rich semantic document structure which helps to semantically enrich the generated classes by indexing them in the documents sections according to their probabilities distribution and visualize them through a hyper-graph.

Experiments have been conducted to measure the effectiveness of our solution compared to topic modeling classification approaches based on text content only. The results show the superiority of our approach.

Keywords: Document classification · Machine learning · LDA topic model · Document structure · Hyper-graph · Information retrieval

1 Introduction

The text classification task has recently attracted significant attention from researchers as an important paradigm for understanding massive text corpora.

So, to better manage the large amount of textual documents, it seems crucial to use new techniques or tools that deals with automatically organizing, searching and indexing the large collection of documents in order to facilitate the information access [15].

C. Bădică et al. (Eds.): ICCCI 2022, CCIS 1653, pp. 687–699, 2022.
https://doi.org/10.1007/978-3-031-16210-7_56

Topic modeling for information retrieval has attracted significant attention and demonstrated good performance in a wide variety of tasks [22] because it provides a convenient way to analyze large textual corpus and find abstract topics. It can discover the mixture of hidden or "latent" topics that varies from one document to another. It is successfully used in many applications, such information retrieval, analyzing historical documents, multilingual data and machine translation and understanding scientific publications [11].

LDA-based approaches have proven to provide the best result in document classification [1,7,12], thanks to their ability to map a query to its relevant documents at the semantic level. In addition, these models address the problem of language discrepancy between Web documents and search queries by grouping different terms that occur in a similar context into the same semantic cluster [16].

The process of extracting information has evolved in response to change user requirements. Today, the queries used by the user to interrogate the system have evolved from a simple keyword or a list of words to an entire topic. In addition, they can go through the document topics to see which documents are the most or the least similar based on the probability distribution of the topics in each used document. Also, it can go much further to search for their desired topic by document section to see which sections are more or less similar to their asked topic by extracting the document sections most relevant to the user request.

As user needs change, managing them will become more complicated even with the use of a powerful technique such as LDA, which is very efficient at the level of classifying documents in an probabilistic way according to their related topics, but do not able to map a query to its relevant sections in a large collection of documents or to search the most or the least similar documents according to their topics densities. Additionally, this technique do not able to index the extracted topics in their document sections, as a result, the information retrieval system will be not able to map a topic query to most relevant sections in the given corpus.

In order to overcome these challenges, we propose a new automatic approach named S-LDA to classify a large text corpora and semantically enrich the generated classes by integrating the document structure in the classification process. Our approach was represented through a hyper-graph which helps to improve the classification accuracy and make the information retrieval model more accurate, scalable and efficient.

To achieve our objectives, two main challenges have been addressed in our study:

1. How to automatically classify a textual corpus in a probabilistic way?
2. How to semantically enrich the extracted classes in order to ameliorate the information retrieval process?

The rest of the paper is organized as follows. We study in Sect. 2 the related works and we illustrate a comparative study between existing approaches. Next, we explain in Sect. 3 the methodology of our approach which consists of classifying a text corpora collecting from many web pages according to their dominant topics using LDA and document structure. Section 4 describes the experiments conducted to validate our approach. Finally, Sect. 5 concludes the paper and discusses some future work.

2   Related Works

Text classification is an important task which could be used for information management applications by automatically allocating a specified document to one or more predefined classes. This technique aims to determine whether a given document belongs to the given category or not by looking at the words or terms of that category. Furthermore, text classification aids users' hold their fields of attention, specify them to be easily separated out texts that are not related to their attention by automatically grouping the texts according to their subjects [5, 18]. There are several works in the literature handling the text classification issue in order to facilitate the information retrieval task which help to make better decisions with more performance. [2,5] classify text documents according to a predefined class using supervised machine learning algorithms and based on the text contents. [8] explores the rich semantic structure in order to automatically classify Elsevier articles and facilitate the analysis of these papers after the submission stage which helps to accelerate the papers treatments and guarantee a better performance because the article that does not respect the requested structure will be rejected. After that, the accepted papers in the first stage will be classified according to their text contents using a supervised machine learning algorithm. The combination between the document structure and the text content improve the classification accuracy.

On the other hand, several approaches are dedicated to automatically classify text document based on probabilistic techniques such as [9,10,14,21], these approaches used unsupervised topic modeling algorithms, especially LDA [24] in order to model a given textual corpus in a probabilistic way which has a significant role and demonstrated good performance in the information retrieval task. These approaches treat the document as a probability distribution of topics which help to discover the mixture of hidden or "latent" topics that varies from document to document in a given corpus.

Table 1. Comparative study between existing studies

	Challenge 1			Challenge 2	
Criterion/Existing study	C1	C2	C3	C4	C5
Kadhim [5]	Unstructured	Non-probabilistic	Document	Predefined classes	No
Gong [9]	Unstructured	Probabilistic	Document	Topics	No
Bitew [8]	Unstructured	Non-Probabilistic	Document	Predefined classes	Yes
Luo [2]	Unstructured	Non-Probabilistic	Document	Predefined classes	Yes
Pavlinek [10]	Unstructured	Probabilistic	Document	Topics	No
Qiuxing [14]	Unstructured	Probabilistic	Document	Topics	No
Kim [21]	Unstructured	Probabilistic	Document	Topics	No
S-LDA	Unstructured	Probabilistic	Document + Section	Hyper-graph	Yes

In order to compare the existing approaches and to overcome the challenges described previously, we define here five criteria with respect to the defined challenges:

Challenge 1. How to automatically classify an heterogeneous corpus in a probabilistic way?

- **Criterion 1 (C1):** The Input data type which could be: (i) Structured, (ii) Semi-structured or (iii) Unstructured data.
- **Criterion 2 (C2):** The classification type, this criterion could be a Probabilistic classification or Non-probabilistic classification.
- **Criterion 3 (C3):** The level of classification, this criterion could be Document level or Section level.

Challenge 2. How to semantically enrich the extracted class in order to ameliorate the information retrieval process?

- **Criterion 4 (C4):** The output task which could be "Predefined classes", "Topics" or "Hyper-graph".
- **Criterion 5 (C5):** The document structure, it could be "Yes" if the approach explored the document structure or "No" if it did not.

Our comparison demonstrates that all existing works used unstructured data to classify their documents. Also, Table 1 illustrates that most of existing studies based on a probabilistic classification in order to model their textual corpus. In the other hand, these approaches neglected the rich semantic documents structure in their classification process, except [8] who combined a supervised machine learning technique with the documents structure in order to classify his textual corpus. However, none of the existing studies using probabilistic techniques integrate the document' structure to semantically enrich the output classes or topics in order improve the information retrieval process. We noticed that all the existing approaches tried to manage the large used corpus by classifying the semantically similar documents in the same cluster, for our proposed approach, the documents and the document's sections are classified based on their relevant topics. We observed also that the output task of all the existing studies was a predefined classes when the researchers used a supervised machine learning technique to classify their textual corpus or a set of topics when they used a topic modeling technique, for our approach, the output task was a hyper-graph. The main contribution of the paper consists of developing a new automatic method named S-LDA for automatically classifying a textual corpus based on document' structure and LDA probabilistic topic model. One strong aspect of our contribution is the combination of the topic model and the semantic extracted tree structure to semantically enrich the generated topics and improve the information retrieval task.

3   Methodology

The originality of S-LDA lies not only in the integration of document structure in the classification process, but also in the generation of a hyper-graph which helps to automatically classify a large textual corpus according to their topics as well as index the generated topics in document sections based on their probability distribution in order to explore more deeply the relationships between topics. The proposed technique extends LDA algorithm by taking into account the semantic structure of the input documents in the classification phase.

The S-LDA framework is summarized in Fig. 1 which consists of two modules: **(1)** Document structure analysis, **(2)** Document classification. We detail them below.

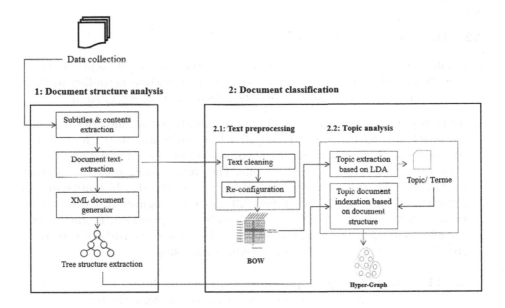

Fig. 1. S-LDA framework.

3.1   Document Structure Analysis

The Documents structure analysis aims to extract the semantic documents structure which helps to facilitate the classification of each document sections according to their relevant topics, this phase consists of three steps:

– **Subtitles and contents extraction:** this module consists of exploiting the document structure in the classification task. In this step, we extract the subtitles and the document contents in order to convert the used textual documents to a semantic tree structure and conserve the documents/word relationships which helps to better explore the relationships between the extracted topics based on their context root path.

– **Document text extraction:** this module consists of extracting the text from the collected data which will be restructured and used as an input in the Document classification phase in order to model the used corpus data according to their dominant topics.
– **XML document generation:** this module aims at representing the extracted text into an XML representation which provides semantic knowledge about the document where the HTML mark-up only indicates the structure and layout of documents, but not the document semantics [17]. As a result, we generate a tree structured document which facilitate the semantic process of the data by conserving the semantic context of each word. The idea is to produce a semantic tree structure to be consequently exploited in topics indexing and topics relationships extraction which makes the data access more easier.

3.2   Document Classification

This phase consists of cleaning data and extracting the corpus topics in order to classify each document as well as each document section according to their relevant topics which helps to improve the information retrieval systems.

1. **Text preprocessing:** preprocessing is an important task and critical step in Natural Language Processing (NLP), it acts a significant role [13] for transferring text from human language to machine-readable format and it affects substantially the results of the experiments. The preprocessing stage is important to structure the unstructured text and keep the keywords which are useful to represent the category of text topics [23]. Natural language text can contain many words with no specific meaning, such as prepositions, pronouns, etc. So, after obtaining the text, the preprocessing process consists of two steps: **(a)** Text cleaning step and **(b)** Re-configuration step:

   (a) **The text cleaning step** includes three sub-modules:
      – Normalization: this sub-module aims to transform the text into a single basic format or a more uniform sequence by converting the characters to lowercase, deleting all numbers, symbols, removing punctuation. This step is important in order to shrink the size of the vocabulary.
      – Tokenization: this sub-module aims to divide the given text into sentences and each sentence into smaller pieces called tokens (words).
      – Lemmatization: this sub-module aims to provide the Part-Of-Speech (POS).
      – Bi-grams extraction: this sub-module aims to extract the bi-grams for each tokenized document. This task consists of combining multi-word terms into single token, such as data-mining, web-page and machine-Learning.
   (b) **The Re-configuration step** aims to convert text data to an appropriate format, this task is necessary for an automated process. The used method

to establish this step is a Bag Of Words matrix representation where each document in our corpus represent a vector of tokens and the tokens represents the document terms. The output of this task is a BOW matrix where we have the corpus documents as well as the number of times of each term in the document.

2. **Topic analysis** The topic analysis module consists of two steps which are respectively: (a) Topics extraction based on LDA, (b) Topic document indexation based on document structure.

   (a) **Topics extraction based on LDA:** this sub-module consists of four steps which are respectively: The model parameters initialization, the model evaluation, the model execution and the documents cluster.

   – **The model parameters initialization**: this sub-module aims at stabilizing the LDA model. The stabilization process is based on **alpha** parameter representing a document topic density (Document concentration). (A high alpha value point to that every document is tend to contain a mixture of the most of the topics, and not any single topic especially. The lower value of alpha, means that the documents contain fewer topics [4].) and **beta** parameter representing a topic word density (Topic concentration). (It assumes that the topic is made of up most of the words and result in a more specific word distribution per topic. A high beta value means each topic is more likely to contain a specific word mix and in practice, that leads to topics being more alike in terms of what words they include and the lower value of beta, means they are composed of few word [4]) values as well as **the topics number**. So, to have a stable and efficient model, it is necessary to select the optimal combination of alpha and beta values by taking into consideration the optimal number of topics according to the used corpus, this step was explained in more details in our previous approach named Learn2Construct [3].

   – **The model evaluation:** this sub-module uses the coherence metrics to quantitatively evaluate the quality of the generated topics. It quantifies how much the words on one topic are, in fact, related to each other and are thus an attempt to capture human interpretability of topics [20].

   – **The model execution**: this sub-module executes the LDA algorithm using the optimal alpha, beta and topic numbers values according to the used corpus based on the coherence metric.

   – **The documents cluster**: this sub-module consists in generating and viewing the document/topic clusters as well as the topic/term clusters.

   (b) **Topic document indexation based on documents structure:** to index the document topics with high accuracy, we tacked the most semantically expressive terms for each topic. The input of this step was the semantic tree structure extracted in the first S-LDA framework phase. It is crucial to exploit not only the text content of a document, but also the rich semantic structure that organizes the document contents and their latent semantics, which involves reasoning under a probabilistic way. This sub-module, indexes the extracted topics using the extracted semantic tree structure which helps to explore more deeply the semantic relationships between the topics as well as their terms. However, each document is represented with the highest probability topics and each extracted topic is represented with the highest probability terms. In addition, the topic/document indexation based on document structure improves the classification accuracy and have beneficial effects on information retrieval performance. To achieve our goal and facilitate the topics sections indexation, we generated in this step three clusters: the first one indicates the probability distribution of each topic in each used document. The second one give us an idea about the probability distribution of each term in each generated topic. And we propose, in this paper, a third probability distribution which indicates the probability distribution of each topic in the document sections. To calculate this probability, we propose the above formula:

$$P(T_i/S) = \sum_{(t_i \in T),\ (S_j \in d)} \frac{P(t_i/S_j)}{P(t_i/d)} \tag{1}$$

where T is a set of the generated topics, t is a set of words describing the topic, S represent the document sections and d represent the document. The output of this step was a hyper-graph which guarantee a more expressive data structure that capture both the relations and the intersections of nodes because of its expressiveness, also, it can provide further insights regarding intersections and subsumption between nodes [6]. The integration of this hyper-graph in the information retrieval system makes it more efficient with the ability to answer to any complex user queries.

4 Experiments

Our experiments aim to evaluate the performance of our approach based on annotated and no-annotated documents structure using several metrics such as: the precision, recall and F-score.

4.1 Environment

As a programming language, we used Python. For the natural language processig we used NLTK[1] (Natural Language Toolkit), this library is used for tokenization, lemmatization and stop words removal. Regarding topic modeling, we used Gensim[2], a Python library for topic modelling, document indexing and similarity retrieval with large corpora. To train our models, we used laptop on Intel core (TM) i7-6500U 2.59 GHz of CPU with 8 GB of RAM and 64 GB of disk.

---

[1] https://www.nltk.org/.
[2] https://pypi.org/project/gensim/.

4.2   Evaluation Metrics

Topic Coherence measures scores a single topic by measuring the degree of semantic similarity between high scoring words in the topic [19]. The coherence of a topic calculated as the sum of pairwise distributional similarity scores over the set of topic words, V. We generalize this as

$$Coherence(V) = \sum_{(V_i,\ V_j) \in V} Score_{(V_i,\ V_j,\ e)} \qquad (2)$$

where V is a set of words describing the topic, Vi and Vj are topic words and e indicates a smoothing factor which guarantees that score returns real numbers. (We will be exploring the effect of the choice of e; the original authors used e = 1.)

Also, we evaluate our approach using conventional measures in information retrieval such as recall, precision, and F-score, denoted as R, P, and F-score respectively. The Recall R is defined as:

$$R = \frac{C_{Wp}}{K_{Wp}} \qquad (3)$$

where C_{Wp} defines the number of correct learned topic sections and K_{Wp} defines the number of correct topics document indexation.

The Precision P is defined as:

$$P = \frac{Cd_{Wp}}{Id_{Wp}} \qquad (4)$$

where Co_{sc} is the number of correct learned topic sections, Id_{sc} is the total number of learned topics documents indexation.

To assess the performance of our approach, we note that precision measure alone is not sufficient. The F-score measure (or F1) is defined as the harmonic mean of recall and precision:

$$F - score = \frac{2 \times P \times R}{P + R} \qquad (5)$$

4.3   Experimental Protocol

We have generated 350 Scientific papers from the web using Springer API[3] in PDF format for three domains which are: Ontology learning, Biological and Artificial Intelligence.

The objective of our study is to evaluate the performance of our approach using two documents types: "Annotated documents structures" where the document has an annotated sections and subsections which helps to better index the generated topics. And "No-annotated documents structures" where the document has no annotated section. In our experiments we used two textual corpus: the first one contains a set of annotated documents structures (represented

---

[3] https://dev.springernature.com/.

by the 350 scientific papers from springer) and the second one represented by 350 heterogeneous documents (50 annotated documents structures and 300 no-annotated ones) collected from the web arbitrarily and they are in different formats such as PDF, HTML and Words.

In the first step, we build our classification models by considering a sequence of topics values that starts with 2 up to 20, to guarantee a better classification we have chosen the smallest number of topics that has the highest coherence value. In our study, the optimal number of topics was 3.

Dominant_Topic	Topic_Perc_Contrib	Keywords	Document_Name
Topic1	1	paper, data, intelligence, Machine-learning, system, deep-learnin, information	Paper 1
Topic3	0.783599973	ontology, data, approach, process, system, technique, learning	Paper 2
Topic2	0.98180002	chemical, biology, concentration, paper, gene, system, result	Paper 3
Topic1	1	paper, data, intelligence, Machine-learning, system, deep-learnin, information	Paper 4
Topic3	1	ontology, data, approach, process, system, technique, learning	Paper 5
Topic2	1	chemical, biology, concentration, paper, gene, system, result	Paper 6
Topic2	1	chemical, biology, concentration, paper, gene, system, result	Paper 7
Topic1	1	paper, data, intelligence, Machine-learning, system, deep-learnin, information	Paper 8
Topic1	1	paper, data, intelligence, Machine-learning, system, deep-learnin, information	paper 9
Topic3	1	ontology, data, approach, process, system, technique, learning	paper 10
Topic1	0.999100029	paper, data, intelligence, Machine-learning, system, deep-learnin, information	paper 11
Topic2	0.917900026	chemical, biology, concentration, paper, gene, system, result	paper 12
Topic2	1	chemical, biology, concentration, paper, gene, system, result	paper 13
Topic1	1	paper, data, intelligence, Machine-learning, system, deep-learnin, information	paper 14
Topic2	1	chemical, biology, concentration, paper, gene, system, result	paper 15
Topic1	0.846000016	paper, data, intelligence, Machine-learning, system, deep-learnin, information	paper 16
Topic1	1	paper, data, intelligence, Machine-learning, system, deep-learnin, information	paper 17
Topic2	1	chemical, biology, concentration, paper, gene, system, result	paper 18
Topic3	1	ontology, data, approach, process, system, technique, learning	paper 19

Fig. 2. LDA classification output

The Fig. 2 shows the result of LDA based classification, which helps to discover the most relevant topic of each scientific paper as well as the most expressive terms of each topic. It is important to mention that if the probability distribution of the topic in the document less than 10% this probability will be ignored, that is why the most used articles are 100% related to one topic which is the most dominant.

Document	Topics	Outline	Topic-Section-Distribution
paper 2	['ontology', 'data', 'approach', 'process', 'system','technique','learning']	abstract	0.451325487
		1 introduction	0.582364781
		2 literature review	0.654782139
		2.1 background	0.758786123
		2.2 related work	0.854796358
		3 methodology	0.785946823
		3.1 preprocessing	0.387124569
		3.2 term extraction	0.252136942
		3.3 topic modeling	0.101200004
		3.4 concepts & relation extraction	0.821546987
		3.5 ontology visualization	0.654125879
		4 experiments	0.853694125
		4.1 experimental protocols	0.75692001
		4.2 evaluation	0.659800321
		5 conclusion	0.65842395

Fig. 3. LDA combined with document structure classification output

We integrated the document structure in the classification process in order to enrich the generated topics and give the user more details about their documents corpus which helps to interpret the data more deeply. The Fig. 3 shows the probability distribution of the third topic in each section in the second paper. In this reason, if two topics are related to the same section, or if one of these topics is more distributed in a section and the second one is more frequent in a subsection of this section, certainly, there is a semantic relationship between these two topics which designed through a hyper-graph model. So, the integration of topics relationships in the information retrieval system helps to improve the classification accuracy and have beneficial effects on this task.

Table 2. Model performance evaluation

Model	Precision (P)	Recall (R)	F-score (F-S)
Annotated documents	0.88	0.85	0.86
Non-annotated documents	0.21	0.15	0.175

The Table 2 resumes the results of the automatic evaluation of our approach using annotated and non-annotated documents. The obtained values are automatically calculated with reference to the classification and annotated sections given by Springer for each document. The discussed results in Table 2 shows that the existing of documents structures positively influences the performance of our approach. However, the annotated documents structures helps also to facilitate the topic sections indexation, but the use of non-annotated documents structure helps only to generate the most relevant topics of each used document.

5 Conclusion

In this paper, we have combined a machine learning approach which consists in the use of LDA -in order to generate the document/topic clusters, topic/section clusters, as well as the topics/term clusters- with the documents structure in order to semantically enrich the generated topics and index them in the documents sections based on their probabilities distribution which helps to improve the information retrieval task. We also evaluated the performance of our approach based on the precision, recall and F-score, which are the most recommended measures especially in information retrieval domain. In future work, we aim at extracting the semantic relationships between the generated topics based on the generated hyper-graph, and evaluating the performance of our approach with different user queries.

References

1. Slimane, B., Mounsif, M., Ghada, I.D.: Topic modeling: comparison of LSA and LDA on scientific publications. In: DSDE 2021, Barcelona, Spain, 18–20 February 2021 (2021)
2. Luo, X.: Efficient English text classification using selected machine learning techniques. Alexandria Eng. J. **60**, 3401–3409 (2021). https://doi.org/10.1016/j.aej.2021.02.009
3. Khemiri, A., Drissi, A., Tissaoui, A., Sassi, S., Chbier, R.: Learn2Construct: an automatic ontology construction based on LDA from texual data. In: MEDES 2021, Proceedings of the 13th International Conference on Management of Digital Ecosystems, November 2021, pp. 49–56 (2021)
4. Shaymaa, H.M., Al-augby, S.: LSA and LDA topic modeling classification: comparison study on E-books. Indones. J. Electr. Eng. Comput. Sci. **19**(1), 353–362 (2020)
5. Kadhim, A.I.: Survey on supervised machine learning techniques for automatic text classification. Artif. Intell. Rev. **52**(1), 273–292 (2019). https://doi.org/10.1007/s10462-018-09677-1
6. Devezas, J., Nunes, S.: Hypergraph-of-entity. Open Comput. Sci. **9**, 103–127 (2019)
7. Kherwa, P., Bansal, P.: Topic modeling: a comprehensive review. Researchgate (2018). https://www.researchgate.net/publication/334667298-Topic-Modeling-A-Comprehensive-Review
8. Bitew, S.K.: Logical structure extraction of electronic documents using contextual information. University of Twente (2018)
9. Gong, H., You, F., Guan, X., Cao, Y., Lai, S.: Application of LDA topic model in E-mail subject classification. In: International Conference on Transportation & Logistics, Information & Communication, Smart City (TLICSC 2018) (2018)
10. Pavlinek, M., Podgorelec, V.: Text classification method based on Self-Training and LDA topic models. Expert Syst. Appl. J. **80**, 83–93 (2017)
11. Boyd-Graber, J., Yuening, H., Mimno, D.: Applications of topic models. Found. Trends Inf. Retr. **11**(2–3), 143–296 (2017). https://doi.org/10.1561/1500000030
12. Rani, M., Dhar, A.K., Vyas, OP.: Semi-automatic terminology ontology learning based on topic modeling. Semantic scholar (2017). https://www.semanticscholar.org/paper/Semi-automatic-terminology-ontology-learning-based-Rani-Dhar/4948d5f16cd1f6733f2d989577119fdd18c83d02
13. Rajasundari, T., Subathra, P., Kumar, P.: Performance analysis of topic modeling algorithms for news articles. J. Adv. Res. Dyn. Control Syst. **11**, 175–183 (2017)
14. Chen, Q., Yao, L., Yang, J.: Short text classification based on LDA topic model. IEEE, ICALIP (2016)
15. Rubayyi, A., Khalid, A.: A survey of topic modeling in text mining. Int. J. Adv. Comput. Sci. Appl. **6**(1), 147–194 (2015)
16. Shen, Y., He, X., Gao, J., Deng, L., Mesnil, G.: A latent semantic model with convolutional-pooling structure for information retrieval. ACM (2014). https://doi.org/10.1145/2661829.2661935
17. Tyagi, N., Rishi, R., Agarwal, R.P.: Semantic structure representation of HTML document suitable for semantic document retrieval. Int. J. Comput. Appl. **46**(13), 0975–8887 (2012)
18. Bindra A.: SocialLDA: scalable topic modeling in social networks. Dissertation University of Washington (2012)

19. Keith, S., Philip, K., David, A., David, B.: Exploring topic coherence over many models and many topics. In: Proceedings of the 2012 Joint Conference on Empirical Methods in Natural Language Processing and Computational Natural Language Learning, pp. 952–961 (2012)
20. David, M., Hanna, M. W., Edmund, T., Miriam, L., Andrew, M.: Optimizing semantic coherence in topic models. In: Proceedings of the Conference on Empirical Methods in Natural Language Processing, Edinburgh, United Kingdom, pp. 262–272. Association for Computational Linguistics, USA (2011)
21. Kim, B.G., Park, S.I., Kim, H.J., Lee, S.H.: Automatic extraction of apparent semantic structure from text contents of a structural calculation document. J. Comput. Civ. Eng. **24**(3), 312–324 (2010)
22. Wu, D., Wang, H.L.: Role of ontology in information retrieval. J. Electron. Sci. Technol. China **4**(2), 148–154 (2006). https://www.researchgate.net/publication/301227711
23. Gonçalves, T., Quaresma, P.: Evaluating preprocessing techniques in a text classification problem. São Leopoldo, RS, Bras. SBC-Sociedade Brasilleira De Computacao, pp. 841–850 (2005)
24. Blei, D.M., Ng, A.Y., Jordan, M.I.: Latent dirichlet allocation. J. Mach. Learn. Res. **3**, 993–1022 (2003)

Distributed Anomalies Detection Using Isolation Forest and Spark

Maurras Ulbricht Togbe[1]([✉])(iD), Yousra Chabchoub[1](iD), Aliou Boly[2](iD), and Raja Chiky[3](iD)

[1] ISEP - Institut Supérieur d'Électronique de Paris, 10 rue de Vanves, 92130 Issy les Moulineaux, France
{maurras.togbe,yousra.chabchoub}@isep.fr
[2] Faculté des Sciences et Techniques (FST)/Département Mathématiques et Informatique, Université Cheikh Anta Diop de Dakar, BP5005 Dakar-Fann, Senegal
aliou.boly@ucad.edu.sn
[3] 3DS OUTSCALE, 1 Rue Royale, Saint Cloud, France
raja.chiky@outscale.com
http://www.isep.fr

Abstract. Anomaly detection is a major issue for several applications such as industrial failure detection, cybersecurity or transport. Several approaches, such as statistical methods, machine learning and sketch, have been explored by different research communities to detect anomalies in an increasingly challenging context. Indeed, facing the huge volume of data generated at an increasingly fast speed, the response time of the algorithms and their distributivity have become determining criteria, in addition to their accuracy in detecting anomalies. We focus in this paper on the unsupervised anomaly detection algorithm based on binary trees: Isolation Forest. It is a very powerful algorithm with an excellent accuracy and a very low execution time thanks to its linear complexity. In particular, we study the architecture of two distribution solutions of Isolation Forest based on the Apache Spark framework. We then compare the performance of these two solutions by testing them against 4 real commonly used datasets.

Keywords: Anomalies detection · Isolation Forest · Distribution · Apache Spark

1 Introduction

The emergence of different social networks, mobile applications, sensor networks, etc. contributes to the generation of large volumes of data at an ever increasing speed. Nowadays, the aggregation, correlation and analysis of these massive data streams is a source of very valuable information. Many application domains, such as anomalies detection, require a fast online analysis of all these information. In fact, real-time anomalies detection in data streams is useful for various application areas such as industrial production, cyber security, transportation or

C. Bădică et al. (Eds.): ICCCI 2022, CCIS 1653, pp. 700–712, 2022.
https://doi.org/10.1007/978-3-031-16210-7_57

pandemic prediction. Anomaly is often defined as a data with a large deviation from the normal behavior given by the majority of data [10].

Several techniques exist for anomaly detection such as those based on statistical methods, sketch, clustering, nearest neighbors [2,6], machine learning and deep learning [14,17]. Generally, these methods are based on computing the distance between the data items or on their density. Most of the existing methods build a model illustrating the normal behavior and define anomalies by the data that largely deviate from this model, by introducing a decision threshold. Isolation Forest (IForest), described in [12] and [13], is an unsupervised anomaly detection method that relies on binary trees to build its model during the learning phase. Anomalies are detected during the test phase by comparing their scores, generated from the trees, to a predefined threshold relatively to the normal scores. Compared to the other anomalies detection methods, IForest has several advantages: It has an excellent accuracy with a low false positive rate [22]. It also has a low memory consumption and a fast execution time thanks to its linear complexity.

Like most other anomaly detection methods, IForest has been designed to run on a single machine in a centralized manner. Such an architecture is quickly limited and does not scale up when we consider the huge volume of data generated by the various systems. Analysing big data in a single machine is quasi impossible in terms of storage and processing capacity. With the emergence of the cloud, distributed architectures, especially in the context of anomaly detection, have enabled better scalability, and have improved availability as well as response time through faster processing. Recently, researchers have been particularly interested by solutions based on distributed machine learning algorithms (see [7,26], and [18]). In 2016, Google introduced the idea of federated learning [16]. It consists of local learning at the level of each node. Each node sends its model to the server which aggregates the models to build a super model that will be shared with the different nodes. This technique is often used in the Internet of Things where each node builds its model on its local data [11]. Another technique, widely used in the literature, is distributed learning. Distribution consists in involving several nodes in the construction of a general model by sharing data and processing tasks between these nodes. Distribution requires communication between the different nodes to build the final result or to generate a collective decision, which induces an additional processing time compared to a centralized version. This communication time must be minimized compared to the time saved by the distribution of tasks. A comparison between the two data processing techniques mentioned above can be found in [3].

Anomaly detection is a research field where distributed machine learning algorithms are very relevant. Indeed, many adaptations of traditional anomaly detection methods to the distribution context can be found in the literature such as [21,24] and [4]. In particular, two Spark-based distributed IForest: LDIForest [1] and FDIForest [25] have been proposed. Since, during the learning phase, IForest builds independent binary trees based on different data samples, this algorithm is highly suitable to be distributed. In this paper, we are interested in studying and comparing these two distributed implementations of IForest.

The rest of the paper is structured as follows: In Sect. 2, we provide a detailed description of IForest. In Sect. 3, we first present the different components of the Spark distribution framework. Then we explain the two existing distributed IForest solutions that are based on Spark. And finally we compare experimentally these two solutions on different real datasets. The conclusion and future work are presented in Sect. 4.

2   Isolation Forest Algorithm

IForest is an unsupervised anomaly detection method proposed by Liu et al. in 2008 ([12,13]). It is based on isolation which consists in isolating a specific data in a mass of data. The isolation technique is based on two following characteristics of anomalous data :

- In a dataset, anomalies are very few, compared to normal data;
- Anomalies have a very different behavior compared to normal data.

With these characteristics, an anomaly can be isolated very quickly in a dataset. Let's consider a dataset $X(n, m)$ with n items and m dimensions. Like any machine learning method, IForest has a training phase and a scoring phase.

2.1   Training Phase

The main objective of the training phase is to build a forest of random and independent trees (itree). IForest randomly selects a subset of ψ data which constitutes the sample used to build a tree. The authors recommend to set $\psi = 256$ to have good results with small execution time and low memory requirement.

The isolation tree (itree) is a binary tree. The construction of the tree is realized as follows: Initially, the root node contains all of the sample data. When building the tree, every internal node is split into two subnodes (left and right) until a complete data isolation or reaching a maximal tree depth : $max\_depth = \lceil log_2(\psi) \rceil$. To split a node i, IForest randomly chooses a dimension d_i, called splitDimension. Then, the split value v_i (splitValue) is also randomly chosen among the values of the dimension d_i, in the addressed node. The splitValue is chosen between the minimum value ($\min(d_i)$) and the maximum value ($\max(d_i)$) of the considered node items. The elements of the node i are then divided into two groups (left and right) by comparing their values to v_i. The Fig. 1 shows an example of an itree *itree*.

To build the t trees of the forest, these two steps (sampling and building a tree) are repeated t times. Thus, each tree has its dedicated sample. For each itree, the sample is chosen from the entire X. The complexity of the training phase is given by $O(t\psi \log \psi)$ because each item of the ψ data items of the t trees must be isolated or quasi-isolated in the associated tree. The number of trees t is a key parameter for the performance of IForest. The authors recommend to set $t = 100$ trees for stable results.

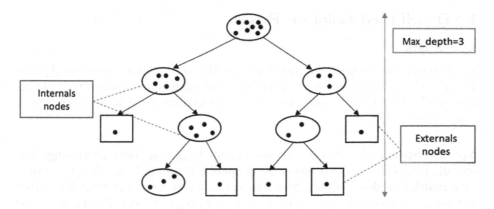

Fig. 1. Itree example (*itree*), $\psi = 8$.

2.2 Scoring Phase

During the scoring phase, the score for each item x of X is calculated. To calculate this score, the item x has to be treated by each tree of the forest. The number of nodes crossed by x from the root node to reach its external node is called the path length of x, denoted $h(x)$. A relatively short average path length implies that x is an anomaly. Once the data is processed by all the trees in the forest, IForest calculates the average length of the t paths of x denoted by $E(h(x))$. Using a well known result on Binary Search Tree (BST), the authors generate the score $s(x, n)$ of x with the following formula :

$$s(x,n) = 2^{-\frac{E(h(x))}{C(n)}} \tag{1}$$

$C(n) = 2H(n-1) - (2(n-1)/n)$ is the average length of the paths of an unsuccessful search in a Binary Search Tree. $H(i) = ln(i) + 0,5772156649$ (Euler constant) is a harmonic value. Note that $C(n)$ is simply used to obtain a normalized score $h(x)$.

The data x will therefore be classified by comparing its score with a threshold according to the following rule :

- If $E(h(x)) \rightarrow C(n)$, $s \rightarrow 0.5$. If all instances have a score of $s \approx 0.5$ then the dataset does not contain any identifiable anomaly;
- if $E(h(x)) \rightarrow 0$, $s \rightarrow 1$. If an item s has score very close to 1 then it is an anomaly;
- if $E(h(x)) \rightarrow n-1$, $s \rightarrow 0$. If an item has a score s much lower than 0.5 then it is normal data.

The complexity of the scoring phase is given by $O(nt \log \psi)$. Hence, IForest has a linear complexity, proportional to the size of the dataset (n).

3   Distributed Isolation Forest

3.1   Spark

The two solutions proposing a distributed version of IForest are based on Apache Spark[1]. The objective of this subsection is to explain the architecture of this framework. A more comprehensive survey on distributed machine learning tools is presented in [23].

Apache Spark. ([15, 20]) is a framework for large-scale data processing. The overall architecture of distribution using Spark is shown in Figure 2. Spark works with multiple nodes. For each Spark program, a spark context must be created to host and manage the program at the driver program level. The master node is the node that contains the spark context. The Master node works with a Cluster Manager that allows it to manage all the slave nodes in the cluster (Worker nodes). The cluster manager can manage different jobs and each job can be divided into several tasks that will be distributed to the slave node.

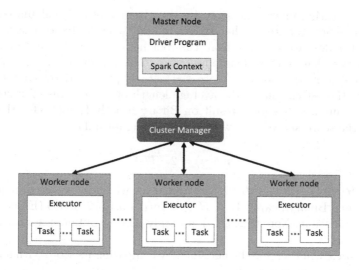

Fig. 2. Apache Spark architecture.

Figure 3 presents a simplified structure of the Spark' ecosystem. Apache Core is the core of Spark's power for large-scale parallel and distributed data processing. The Resilient Distributed Dataset (RDD) is the technology for data representation and distribution. Spark has powerful libraries for querying and processing structured data: Spark SQL. GraphX is the Spark module for graph processing. Spark Streaming is the module for managing data flows and incremental calculation. Machine learning is provided by the MLIB module. For the purpose of this paper, we will focus on RDD, Spark SQL and MLlib.

---

[1] https://spark.apache.org/.

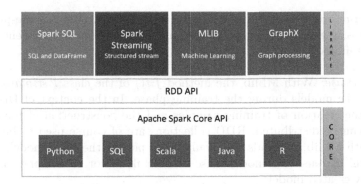

Fig. 3. The Apache Spark ecosystem.

Resilient Distributed Dataset (RDD). With Spark, data is represented in a particular structure that allows Spark to perform reliable distributed processing. This is the main innovation of Spark. It is a collection of fault-tolerant elements that can be managed in parallel. Recovery from a failure is possible thanks to the preservation of the RDD constitution history. It is therefore a resilient representation of a partitioned data collection that is distributable across multiple nodes in a single cluster. RDDs use memory and disk space as needed. Spark offers the ability to run RDDs in memory or persist them in cache for faster processing. Finally, in order to manage concurrent access to data, especially in a large-scale data context, RDDs are read-only accessible.

Spark SQL. Apache Spark allows through its Spark SQL library to query data using SQL. This library also allows the representation of datasets in the form of a dataframe. A dataframe is structured in columns containing the dimensions and in rows representing each data item. The representation in dataset format is also possible. The big difference between a dataframe and a dataset is that the dataset is highly typed and immutable. Coupled with the RDD, this allows a very fast execution of SQL queries.

MLlib. The Machine Learning library (MLlib) provides developers with several methods for processing data. The main functions are *fit()* for learning and *transform()* for the test phase (prediction). Different performance metrics are also available such as the air under the ROC curve (ROC AUC), the confusion matrix, the recall, etc. MLlib provides a complete environment to run a machine learning method while taking advantage of the power of Spark for distribution.

Based on Spark, the two distributed versions of IForest, LDIForest and FDIForest use the MLlib library. Figure 4 shows the general architecture of the machine learning algorithms in MLib:

Data Preparation Phase: Once the data are retrieved, they are pre-processed. Pre-processing generally consists of creating a vector from the different columns of the dataframe.

Training Phase: With MLlib, the method $fit()$ of the class *Estimator* is used to create the models during the training phase. In the context of Distributed IForest, the creation of training samples and the construction of binary trees (i-trees) can be distributed. RDD collections are of course used to build these trees. With MLlib, methods are available to persist the built model, which is very useful to reuse the model (case of data flows) or to compare or update previously created models.

Test Phase: During the test or scoring phase, the created model is used on the test data for a classification or a prediction. With MLlib, the $transform()$ method of the *Transformer* class is used at this stage. This phase is divided into two main operations: the first is the calculation of the scores of each test data, the second is the classification of the test data by comparison with the threshold. The decision threshold can be a predefined static parameter (the authors have proposed to set it to 0.5 in [12]), or calculated on the basis of the scores obtained. The latter way of dynamically generating the decision threshold is the one often preferred in the literature (see [25] and [1]).

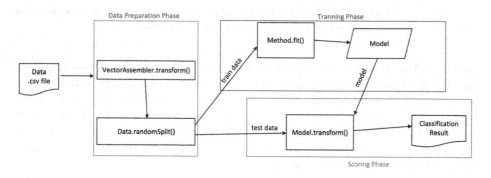

Fig. 4. General architecture of a machine learning algorithm with MLlib.

In this subsection, we give a general description of the Spark distribution framework and explained the common basis it provides for the two distributed versions of IForest: LDIForest and FDIForest. In the next subsection we will analyze these two implementations in depth to highlight their major differences. Then we will test them on different real datasets to compare their performances.

3.2 Description of LDIForest and FDIForest

LDIForest [1] and FDIForest [25]are two different implementations of distributed IForest using Spark. LDIForest is developed in Scala while FDIForest is available in Scala and Python. These two implementations are functionally identical. Figure 5 shows the general architecture of these two implementations.

First, during the data preparation phase, data are converted into a format adapted to MLlib: DataFrame or Dataset format. Then, during the training phase, t random samples of size ψ are generated. Each sample is transformed into an RDD to take advantage of the distribution under Spark and will be used for the construction of a tree. The trees will be distributed in the different nodes and represent the different models that will be used for the test phase. The test (or scoring) phase is also distributed and each item will be classified as anomaly or normal data according to its score compared to a unique decision threshold. The authors of IForest recommended to use a static score equal to 0.5. However LDIForest and FDIForest generate this decision threshold in a dynamic way based on the scores of the processed data items. Indeed, in order to have a decision threshold well adapted to the used dataset, this threshold is calculated from the statistical method *approxQuantile()* of the *DataFrameStatFunctions* class of Spark SQL. It is a variation of the Greenwald-Khanna algorithm. The idea is to configure this threshold according to the rate of anomalies in the dataset called contamination rate or contamination factor in several implementations of IForest like the scikit-learn project. This assumes that the rate of anomalies in the dataset is known in advance, which is not obvious in an unsupervised context. Moreover, we note that FDIForest computes this decision threshold from the scores of all the test data, while LDIForest uses only the training data to compute the threshold. This increases the execution time of the scoring phase of FDIForest and requires several passes over the dataset.

LDIForest is an industrial, open source implementation developed by LinkedIn. This implementation is regularly updated and upgraded. It is well structured and also includes an encryption module. However, the code of FDIForest is older and has not been updated recently.

3.3 Experimental Comparison Between LDIForest and FDIForest

In order to compare the performance of the two distributed implementations of IForest: LDIForest and FDIForest, we tested these two versions on 4 different real datasets. We set the number of trees, t, to 100, following the authors recommendations. For the choice of the sample size ψ, the authors recommend the value of 256 items for the construction of each tree. A more complete study on the impact of this parameter on the results and its dependence on the complexity of the data (size, dimensions, variability, anomalies rate,...) is proposed in [5]. We have therefore adapted this parameter to the considered dataset. The choice of ψ, as well as the characteristics of the 4 considered datasets are presented in the Table 1.

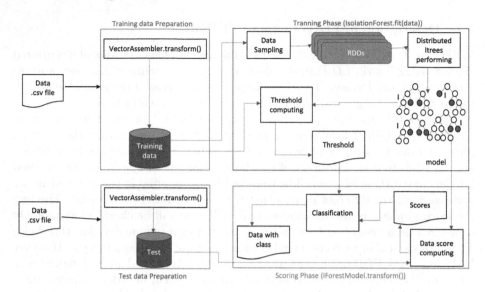

Fig. 5. General architecture of LDIForest and FDIForest.

Datasets. We performed our experiments on 4 datasets, widely used in the literature to evaluate the performance of anomaly detection methods. These datasets are available in [19] and [9]. A detailed overview of these datasets is provided in Table 1. Shuttle is a NASA dataset containing radar information. It contains 9 attributes and 7% of anomalies. SMTP is a dataset from the KDD Cup99 competition, it describes attacks. SMTP has 3 dimensions with 0.03% of anomalies. The original version of this dataset is presented in [9]. We used a pre-processed version to meet the requirements of anomalies detection. More details on the pre-processing performed are available in the following two studies: [19] and [8]. The ForestCover dataset has 10 attributes with 0.96% of anomalies. It contains information on trees present in 4 different locations in the Roosevelt National Forest in Colorado. Finally the Mammography dataset presents data for the classification of benign or malignant mammograms. It contains 6 attributes with 2.32% of anomalies. These 4 datasets are thus very varied and allow to cover a rather large panel concerning size, dimensions and rate of anomalies. They represent a good basis for comparison between the two implementations LDIForest and FDIForest. For these 4 datasets, during the training phase, $t \times \psi$ data were randomly selected from the whole dataset to build the models. During the testing phase, the scores of all datasets were computed to classify them into anomalies and normal data.

Table 1. Characteristics of considered public datasets.

Dataset	Size (n)	Dimensions	Anomalies	ψ
Mammography	11 183	6	2.32%	256
Shuttle	49 097	9	7.15%	256
SMTP	95 156	3	0.03%	2048
Forest cover	286 048	10	0.96%	4096

Metrics. In order to compare the performances of LDIForest and FDIForest, we tested them on the 4 datasets presented previously. More precisely, we evaluated the ROC AUC parameter and the execution time.

ROC AUC: The area under the ROC curve is a very common metric to evaluate the performance of a machine learning method. It is well adapted to the context of anomalies detection. It represents the relation between the rate of true positives and false positives of the algorithm. The closer the AUC value is to 1, the better the method is.

Execution Time: The main motivation for the distribution is to improve the speed of execution in order to handle data received at an increasingly high rate. Therefore, execution time is an important parameter to consider when comparing distributed versions of IForest. In particular, we addressed the impact of the number of distribution cores and the size of the data on the execution time of LDIForest and FDIForest.

Results and Interpretation. Table 2 shows the results of running LDIForest and FDIForest on the 4 datasets described above. The experiments were conducted on a mac OS computer with a 2.6 GHz Intel core i5 processor and 8 GB of memory. For the execution, we used Apache Zeppelin notebook as it is well adapted to run Spark and Scala code. Zeppelin is commonly used by Spark community. We ran Zeppelin 0.10.1 version with Spark 2.4.5, Scala 2.11.12 on Java 1.8. The source code is available on Github: https://github.com/Elmecio/Spark_Based_Distributed_Isolation_Forest.

This table shows that both distribution implementations perform well for anomaly detection with very similar values of ROC AUC, quite close to 1, for the 4 considered datasets. For each dataset, the total execution time of FDIForest and LDIForest is given by the average execution time of 10 successive runs. It is the sum of the execution time of both training and test phases. Table 2 shows that, for the 4 datasets, both methods are quite fast (with runtime less than 18s for the larger dataset). One can also notice that LDIForest is much faster than FDIForest. The execution time of LDIForest is about half that of FDIForest. This is due to the complexity of the process of generating the decision threshold in FDIForest: from the score of all the data items, while LDIForest relies only on the score of the samples to calculate the decision threshold.

Table 2. Comparison of LDIForest and FDIForest.

Dataset	ROC AUC		Execution time (ms)	
	LDIForest	FDIForest	LDIForest	FDIForest
Mammography	0.73	0.73	**1 655**	3 867
Shuttle	0.98	0.98	**2 843**	4 372
SMTP	0.83	0.83	**4 669**	7 929
Forest cover	0.84	**0.85**	**8 279**	17 316

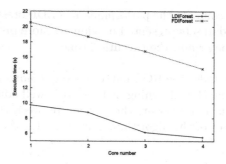

(a) Impact of cores number.

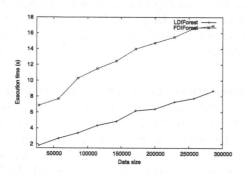

(b) Impact of data size.

Fig. 6. Impact of cores number and data size on the execution time of LDIForest and FDIForest, using the dataset ForestCover.

Figures. 6a and 6b show respectively the impact of the number of distribution cores and the size of the data on the execution time of LDIForest and FDIForest. For this experiment, we used the largest dataset, ForestCover. The number of trees constructed during the training phase is fixed to 100. Each tree uses a sample of $\psi = 4096$ random items chosen from the whole dataset. To vary the size of the data we truncated the dataset for each run.

The results confirm the speed of LDIForest compared to FDIForest. Moreover, we see that the execution time decreases significantly with the number of involved cores, thanks to the distribution implemented by Spark through the RDDs. Finally, the total execution time increases linearly with the size of the considered dataset, which is consistent with the complexity of the test phase given by $O(nt \log \psi)$. The complexity of the training phase is independent of the data size. It is only related to the number of trees to build (t) and the size of the sample that generates each tree (ψ).

4   Conclusion and Future Work

In this paper, we briefly introduced the distribution ecosystem: Apache Spark. We presented and compared two major distributed IForest implementations using Spark: FDIForest and LDIForest. Our experimental results show that both solutions perform well for anomaly detection with a noticeable advantage of LDIForest over FDIForest in terms of execution time. We also addressed the advantage of distribution by evaluating the impact of the number of cores and the size of the data on the execution time. Distributed anomaly detection in data streams is not enough explored in the literature. IForestASD is an evolution of IForest adapted to data streams context. In our next work we will design a distributed version of IForestASD with Spark, based on the study performed in this paper.

References

1. Ldiforest (2019). https://github.com/linkedin/isolation-forest
2. Aggarwal, C.C.: Outlier Analysis, 2nd edn. Springer, Cham (2017). https://doi.org/10.1007/978-3-319-47578-3
3. Asad, M., Moustafa, A., Ito, T.: Federated learning versus classical machine learning: a convergence comparison. arXiv:2107.10976 (2021)
4. Bogatinovski, J., Nedelkoski, S.: Multi-source anomaly detection in distributed IT systems. In: Hacid, H., et al. (eds.) ICSOC 2020. LNCS, vol. 12632, pp. 201–213. Springer, Cham (2021). https://doi.org/10.1007/978-3-030-76352-7_22
5. Chabchoub, Y., Togbe, M.U., Boly, A., Chiky, R.: An in-depth study and improvement of isolation forest. IEEE Access 10, 10219–10237 (2022)
6. Chandola, V., Banerjee, A., Kumar, V.: Anomaly detection: a survey. ACM Comput. Surv. (CSUR) 41(3), 1–58 (2009)
7. Das, K., Bhaduri, K., Votava, P.: Distributed anomaly detection using 1-class svm for vertically partitioned data. Stat. Anal. Data Min ASA Data Sci. J. 4(4), 393–406 (2011)
8. Ding, Z., Fei, M.: An anomaly detection approach based on isolation forest algorithm for streaming data using sliding window. IFAC Proc. 46(20), 12–17 (2013)
9. Dua, D., Graff, C.: Uci machine learning repository [https://archive.ics.uci.edu/ml/index.php]. School of Information and Computer Science, University of California, Irvine, CA, vol. 25, p. 27 (2019)
10. Hawkins, D.M.: Identification of Outliers, vol. 11. Springer, Heidelberg (1980). https://doi.org/10.1007/978-94-015-3994-4

11. Hussain, N., Rani, P., Chouhan, H., Gaur, U.S.: Cyber security and privacy of connected and automated vehicles (CAVs)-based federated learning: challenges, opportunities, and open issues. In: Federated Learning for IoT Applications. EICC, pp. 169–183. Springer, Cham (2022). https://doi.org/10.1007/978-3-030-85559-8_11

12. Liu, F.T., Ting, K.M., Zhou, Z.H.: Isolation forest. In: Eighth IEEE International Conference on Data Mining, pp. 413–422. IEEE (2008)

13. Liu, F.T., Ting, K.M., Zhou, Z.H.: Isolation-based anomaly detection. ACM Trans. Knowl. Disc. Data (TKDD) 6(1), 1–39 (2012)

14. Ma, X., et al.: A comprehensive survey on graph anomaly detection with deep learning. IEEE Trans. Knowl. Data Eng. (2021)

15. Meng, X., et al.: Mllib: machine learning in apache spark. J. Mach. Learn. Res. 17(1), 1235–1241 (2016)

16. Pandey, M., Pandey, S., Kumar, A.: Introduction to federated learning. In: Federated Learning for IoT Applications. EICC, pp. 1–17. Springer, Cham (2022). https://doi.org/10.1007/978-3-030-85559-8_1

17. Pang, G., Shen, C., Cao, L., Hengel, A.V.D.: Deep learning for anomaly detection: a review. ACM Comput. Surv. (CSUR) 54(2), 1–38 (2021)

18. Qasem, M.H., Hudaib, A., Obeid, N., Almaiah, M.A., Almomani, O., Al-Khasawneh, A.: Multi-agent systems for distributed data mining techniques: an overview. In: Baddi, Y., Gahi, Y., Maleh, Y., Alazab, M., Tawalbeh, L. (eds.) Big Data Intelligence for Smart Applications. SCI, vol. 994, pp. 57–92. Springer, Cham (2022). https://doi.org/10.1007/978-3-030-87954-9_3

19. Rayana, S.: ODDS Library. Stony Brook University, Department of Computer Sciences (2016). http://odds.cs.stonybrook.edu

20. Salloum, S., Dautov, R., Chen, X., Peng, P.X., Huang, J.Z.: Big data analytics on Apache Spark. Int. J. Data Sci. Anal. 1(3), 145–164 (2016). https://doi.org/10.1007/s41060-016-0027-9

21. Solaimani, M., Iftekhar, M., Khan, L., Thuraisingham, B., Ingram, J.B.: Spark-based anomaly detection over multi-source vmware performance data in real-time. In: IEEE Symposium on Computational Intelligence in Cyber Security (CICS), pp. 1–8. IEEE (2014)

22. Togbe, M., Chabchoub, Y., Boly, A., Chiky, R.: Etude comparative des méthodes de détection d'anomalies. Revue des Nouvelles Technologies de l'Information (2020)

23. Verbraeken, J., Wolting, M., Katzy, J., Kloppenburg, J., Verbelen, T., Rellermeyer, J.S.: A survey on distributed machine learning. ACM Comput. Surv. (CSUR) 53(2), 1–33 (2020)

24. Wang, C., Zhao, Z., Gong, L., Zhu, L., Liu, Z., Cheng, X.: A distributed anomaly detection system for in-vehicle network using HTM. IEEE Access 6, 9091–9098 (2018)

25. Yang, F.: Contributors: Fdiforest (2018). https://github.com/titicaca/spark-iforest

26. Zeng, L., et al.: Distributed data mining: a survey. Inf. Technol. Manag. 13(4), 403–409 (2012)

Defining and Extracting Singleton Design Pattern Information from Object-Oriented Software Program

Abir Nacef[1]($\boxtimes$), Adel Khalfallah[1], Sahbi Bahroun[2], and Samir Ben Ahmed[1]

[1] Faculty of Mathematical, Physical and Natural Sciences of Tunis (FST), Laboratoire d'Informatique pour les Systèmes Industriels, Tunis El Manar University, Tunis, Tunisia
nacefabir91@gmail.com, Adel.khalfallah@isi.utm.tn,
samir.benahmed@fst.utm.tn
[2] Institut Supérieur d'Informatique (ISI), Laboratoire Limtic,
Tunis El Manar University, Tunis, Tunisia
Sahbi.bahroun@isi.utm.tn

Abstract. In software engineering (SE), improving the quality of code and design by relying on pre-established restructuring (refactoring), such as detection and injection of a design pattern are still challenging problems. In this article, we focus on the Singleton design pattern, in which we indicate its variants implementation and define 33 features that can identify this pattern in its standard and non-standard form. Significant information can be extracted by applying the structural and semantic analysis of the source code. So use this information; it becomes easier to identify a pattern and inject it. We created specific data using 20,000 code snippets. This data is used to train deep learning models called RNN-LSTM classifiers to extract information from object-oriented software systems. The empirical result proves that our proposed LSTM-RNN Classifier can successfully extract proposed information with excellent results in terms of prediction recall and F1-score.

Keywords: Singleton design pattern · RNN-LSTM Classifier · Object-oriented program analyses

1 Introduction

In software engineering, the Singleton is a design pattern used for ensuring that a class has only one instance. That means restricting class instantiation to a single object (or even to a few objects only) in a system. This pattern is sometimes used for its efficiency when the system is faster or occupies less memory with few objects than with many similar objects. As well as being useful to facilitate the creation of quality designs, also Singleton design patterns aid to analyze existing systems, e.g. reconstructing the documentation from source code, i.e. reverse engineering. To be able to maintain and develop the legacy system, design patterns should be recognized, and properly detected. At this level, the recognition of instances of design patterns in source code is difficult, because the patterns are not formally defined and there are many representations of the code.

There are various studies on design pattern recognition to deal with the problem of informal representation of code. Based on different results; we found that using features at the pattern recognition level yielded better results (improved prediction rates) than using them in other forms such as graphs or other representations. Furthermore, using semantic information to recover features from source code will improve the accuracy of design pattern recognition. Based on these observations, we hypothesize that identifying features that define singleton design patterns and extracting these features from source code through semantic analysis will improve the accuracy of their detection.

There are many detection design pattern approaches based on features extraction, but a few of them are especially focusing on defining and identifying Singleton pattern variants. Stencel [1] has provided a tool D-Cubed, which can recover different Singleton variants from source code, but they use queries for defining every implementation. However, in our approach, we use lexical analysis based on the RNN-LSTM Classifier, which is more conducive to learning semantic features, patterns, and dependencies from source code.

Extracting semantic information from source code remains a challenging task due to its informal and diverse implementations. However, recent work has demonstrated the power of LSTMs in computer vision and natural language processing (NLP) [2]. Source code is a special structured natural language written by programmers [3], which can also be efficiently analyzed by LSTM models. Our approach aims to capture the intent of the singleton pattern and create detailed descriptions of different implementation variants. Based on this description and previous analysis, we define a subset of features that can be significantly identified:

- First, each variant of the Singleton design pattern (typical implementation)
- Second, analyze the structure of the program (recover necessary information) to make the developer able to inject the Singleton pattern.

The main contributions of this paper consist on:

- We present the Singleton intent in which we detailed the concept of every implementation variant. Based on a precise analysis, we propose 33 features dealing with every Singleton variant.
- We create a set of data named DTS whose total size is 20000 samples containing different implementations. The data is used to train the model to recover 33 information (features) from the source code.
- We create and label data extracted from DPD_f Corpus containing 200 java files. The DPD_f corpus is a corpus used in [4] and collected from the GitHub java corpus. The DPD_f Corpus is used to evaluate the Model.
- We build RNN-LSTM Classifiers. We train them by DTS and we evaluate them by the extracted DPDF Corpus. We prove by an empirical result that the proposed method makes full use of the context information of the sequence in the source code, and then can extract information directly from the source code text, with height performance.

The rest of this paper is organized as follows: In Sect. 2, we present the state of art proposed features to deal with Singleton design pattern detection. In Sect. 3, we define the Singleton intent and we indicate its different variants. Based on the established analysis, we propose a set of features defining each variant. Section 4 discusses the proposed approach process and techniques used. Section 5, represent empirical results obtained and a comparison with the state-of-the-art approach. In Sect. 6, we show the conclusion and future work.

2 Related Work

Reverse engineering is a field of research that started years ago and has steadily grown due to its important role in reducing the time and cost of maintenance and development of a legacy system. The Singleton pattern is the most popular pattern used in software systems. Due to its important use, many approaches have worked on its recognition. Therefore, the features highlighted to identify the Singleton pattern diversify from one to another, caused by the implementation worked on. This difference in focusing on implementation can unbalance results in the recovery process and can produce false-positive candidates. So that we should carefully analyze the concept of each implementation and extract only significant information that forty influence the definition of a true Singleton.

Many proposed detection approaches exist but not all of them are based on pre-established features. In this section, we focus on state-of-the-art features used to identify Singleton patterns.

Firstly, we begin with the structural relationships approaches. These approaches, which are solely based on structural relationships, cannot define correctly the Singleton pattern. FUJABA [5] for example, identifies a Singleton class as long as it matches only three constraints:

- Has class constructors
- Has a static reference to the Singleton class
- Has a public-static method returning the Singleton class type

The two first conditions are false regardless of accessibility. The dependence of only access modifiers (e.g. a Singleton constructor marked private) does not always guarantee a strict access control, it depend on a programming language (e.g. a Java inner class has access to the private attributes of the enclosing class). More than that, to control the number of instances, the constructor must not be always private, it can be declared as protected in the case of an abstract class (remember that a Singleton can be subclassed). The same with the reference of the class, we must restrict its accessibility to prevent external modification. Even if both conditions hold, it is still not enough because it has only prevented external instantiation and modification. It is still needed to control instantiation; the real Singleton pattern intent is embedded in the method instantiation's body (to control instantiation in the case if there are no instances created when loading class). As we see these criteria are based on only structural relationships and do not guarantee that a true Singleton class is reported, for example, FUJABA reports the class illustrated in Fig. 1 as a Singleton class (false positive).

As an advanced step in the analyzing process, PINOT [6] takes, in addition, the behavioral aspect. It addresses the behavior of the Singleton pattern, by searching for a code block representing lazy instantiation. However, it still produces a false negative result (case of Singleton class with an eager instantiation) because the tool verifies the existence of the static method with a lazy instantiation block and ignores the existence of the second static method producing new instances (case produced in Fig. 2).

```
public class Classe1 {
    private static Classe1 instance = new Classe1 ();
    Classe1 () {}
    public static Classe1 getInstance () {
            Return instance ; }
    }
public class Utilisation {
    public Utilisation (){
        Classe1 u1= new classe1(); }
}
```

Fig. 1. FUJABA reports Classe1 as false positive. Classe1 is not a Singleton

```
public class C2 {
    private static C2 instance;
    private C2 ( ) {}
    public static C2 getInstance1 ( ) {
            if (instance = = null) instance = new C2; }
    public static C2 getInstance2 ()
            { return new C2 ; }
}
```

Fig. 2. PINOT reports C2 as a false positive. C2 is not a Singleton

In [7] the Singleton pattern is identified using three variants:

– The first is based on the definition given in the literature [8], which required a final class, a private constructor, and a public static getter method.
– The second relax the specification by removing the final class constraints and private constraints from the constructor.
– the third variant, takes into consideration the management of the resource when the field instance is overridden to become a container

In [9] two signatures for the Singleton are presented. The features highlighted are:

– For first variant constraints: have a construction method of class Singleton that should not be public, have an Operation instance of OriginClass that not be private and

returns an instance of Singleton, have a private instance, have an instance operation with conditional statement body.
- For second variant constraints: have a construction method of class Singleton that should not be public, have a static and public Operation instance of OriginClass that returns an instance of Singleton, have a public static instance

These constraints respond to the pattern intent but do not recover all Singleton variants implementation. It can also make false-positive results like showing in Fig. 2, caused by non-considering the number of instance classes and the number of operation instances as conditions.

Zanoni [10], in MARPLE-DPD proposes a set of conditions in which we can consider a pattern as a true Singleton;

- The class is declared final.
- The class maintains a private control flag. A flag belongs to a simple type, typically Boolean; or a Boolean expression.
- Control instantiation; the instantiation must occur inside an if (or a switch) block, therefore under a condition.
- The class owns a private instance of the same class to restrict access.
- The class has a unique static instance of the same class inside the system.
- Unique instance of the same class is maintained, no matter if it is static or not.
- Private declaration of all constructors within a given class.
- The existence of throwing an exception inside a control block in a method of the class.

The final class modifier allows thread safety but makes it impossible to class inheritance. However, when we want to change the behavior of a Singleton, Subclasses are useful and needed. Singleton class can be subclassed, can be serialized, and can implement interfaces. That is why we should take into consideration that the constructor can be protected and the class should not be always final.

The previously discussed approaches do not take all information needed to define all Singleton variants. However, the study carried out by Stencel [1] is more detailed and proposes a specific definition for each implementation variant. Our work is an improvement of the method proposed by [1]. We base ourselves on the different constraints proposed in this approach to give a more detailed definition in which we propose other constraints and we take into consideration other variants. More than that, we propose a new efficient method to extract these constraints from source code other than Static analysis techniques and SQL queries proposed in [1].

3 Proposed Features for Singleton Implementation Variants

Based on different implementation variants existing in Gamma et al. [8], we represent in this section a study of the based concept of each one. It is worth noting that it can be other new variants created by combining these previous variants.

3.1 Singleton Variants

Singleton pattern can have many variants. The reported variants are:

- Eager Instantiation: Use an initialization block that is executed at the beginning of the program or when the class is loaded.
- Lazy Instantiation: Use an access method, in which the creation of an instance is controlled (the instance is created if and only if none exists).
- Different Placeholder based on the concept of using inner static in which the singleton instance is held as a static field. It is proposed to solve the problem produced by the prior version of java5.
- Replaceable Instance: Trait the case when a singleton instance is replaced at the runtime. The best way to symbolize this is to use a setter method to configure a different look-and-feel instance (GUI) as discussed by [8].
- Subclassed Singleton: There are cases where we need to subclass a singleton class, especially when we want to change the behavior of a singleton. So that constructor must be declared as protected.
- Delegated Construction: The use of delegation technique to create the sole instance of the Singleton. The Delegation concept is the passing to another object, the duty of a certain task (method call) to do it on the owner's behalf, that's why verification of the correct instance to be assigned must be carried out during dele-gated calls.
- Different Access Point: In some cases, the different classes can manage and access the Singleton class (create Singleton instance). In this whey, the Singleton class is considered an access point to the Singleton instance (static method).
- Limiton: There is a design concept similar to the Singleton in which, the number of instances of a class is limited. Its name is Limiton, which is considered an extended variant of the sole instance Singleton.
- Social Singleton: The idea of this variant is to implement Singleton classes. The use of social Singleton makes it possible to share static resources among Singleton objects that have a relationship (friends) with each other. Only authorized friend objects can have access to a resource owned by any other object.
- Generic Singleton using Reflection: The major motivation of this variant is the application of the reflection technique. The reflection technique is one of the powerful features provided by any modern programming language.

3.2 Proposed Features

The intent of the Singleton pattern seems straightforward when we just looked at its canonical implementation (what is simple). However, carefully analyzing structure can lead to defining more constraints. In the features identifying process, we have based on this analysis and identified 33 features as established in Table 1. These features reflect information that forty influence to preserve the Singleton intent.

Firstly, the only way to keep a Singleton instance for future reuse is to store it as a global static variable. So that we should verify this propriety in different variants and count the number of class attributes.

Second, as the intent of the Singleton pattern is to limit the number of objects to only one (exception Limiton variant), we must verify a set of properties like;

– Constructor modifier to restrict its accessibility for preventing external access.
– A global access point to get the instance of the class.
– Control object creation, the existence of conditions to limit the number of created instances or the existence of initialization block executed in loading class.
– Limit the number of class attributes, and the number of method-creating instances to only one, to make sure that one instance can be created.

Finally, extracting the signature of each variant:

– Make the Singleton thread-safe with a synchronized method, or double-check locking in the Lazy implementation variant.
– Use inner class to create a Singleton instance in placeholder implementation. In the inner class, a Singleton instance is held as a static attribute, and the static instantiation method is declared inside this class.
– In different access point variants, the Singleton instance is created within external classes. The Singleton class provides an access point (static method) to access that instance.
– Verify-in subclasses variant, that the Singleton class is declared abstract, with the non-private constructor, and a static accessor method which determines the particular subclass instance to instantiate (the subclasses constructors, in this case, should not be private since the Singleton class must be able to instantiate them.
– In a replaceable variant, we must make sure that a setter method of the Singleton class is correctly declared to assume changing of object configurations while keeping a single one.
– In Delegated Construction variant, we verify the existence of delegated method (a static access method that passes the duty of creating an instance to another method (method call). In this case, we must ensure that the correct instance is assigned during delegated calls.
– The most typical use of Generic Singleton is for creating new objects given the Singleton object class name. Therefore, to define Generic Singleton, we must ensure that a class is a variant of Singleton and this class is defined as a type for generic instantiation.
– Social Singleton intends to manage similar resources between multiple Singleton objects that have similar properties and behavior. So that objects need to maintain a friend list to register their friends and prevent global access; if an object wants to access resources from another, a checked list must be verified.
– The difference between the Limited variant and other implementation variants is that number of the instance created is more than one. Therefore, in the static instantiation method, there should be a control condition to limit the number of instantiations.

Table 1. Proposed features

No.	Abbreviation	Features	No.	Abbreviation	Features
1	IRE	Inheritance relationship (extends)	18	RINEC	Returning instance created by the external class
2	IRI	Inheritance relationship (implements)	19	CS	Control instantiation
3	CA	Class accessibility	20	HGM	Have one method to generate an instance
4	GOD	Global class attribute declaration	21	DC	Double check locking
5	AA	Class attribute accessibility	22	RR	Return reference of the Singleton instance
6	SR	Static class attribute	23	CNI	Use a variable to count the number of instances
7	ON	Have only one class attribute	24	CII	Create an internal static read-only instance
8	COA	Constructor accessibility	25	DM	Use delegated method
9	HC	Hidden constructor	26	GMS	Global accessor synchronized method
10	ILC	Instantiate when loading class	27	IGO	Initializing global class attribute
11	GAM	Global accessor method	28	LNI	Limit the number of instances
12	PSI	Public static accessor method	29	SCI	Use string to create an instance
13	GSM	Global setter method modifying instance in the runtime	30	SB	Static block
14	PST	Public static setter method	31	AFL	Allowed friend list
15	INC	Use of inner class	32	CAFB	Control access to friend behavior
16	EC	Use external class	33	GT	Type for generic instantiation
17	RINIC	Returning instance created by the inner class			

4   RNN-LSTM Classifier for Structural and Semantic Source Code Analysis

4.1   Program Analysis

Recently many researchers have proven that translating source code to text for generating source code summaries has carried out a high accuracy [11–13]. Code represents a language generated by developers. Similar to natural language [3], it has syntactic structures and semantic meaning. By using static analysis, it is relatively easy to obtain structural elements such as classes, attributes, methods, etc. However, Static analysis cannot capture the semantic dependencies inside code caused by various implementations, so a deep analysis (semantic) is required.

The sequence is the most often used form as input in most deep source code tasks. To deal with information and dependencies existing in these sequence forms we rely on a deep module whose objective is to capture the semantics and context of input for further processing. RNN [16] and its variants are sequential models, which are the most widely used, and her effectiveness for general-purpose software repository mining has been tested [2]. The LSTM [17] is an RNN variant used to deal with problems that can be encountered when training traditional RNN. His capacity makes learning long-term dependencies more easily with the LSTM network compared to the simple recurrent architectures.

In this paper, we propose to use structural and semantic analysis to extract all needed information from the source code. We model source code as text, and we apply RNN-LSTM Classifier to extract information.

4.2   RNN-LSTM Classifier for Features Extraction

The main steps of the proposed approach are illustrated in Fig. 3.

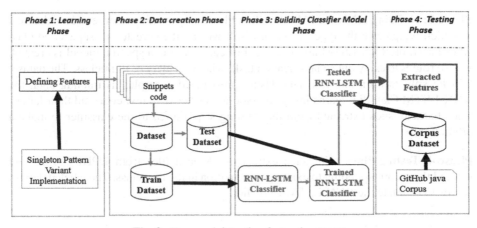

Fig. 3. Proposed detection feature's process

Phase 1: Learning Phase. To be able to recover each Singleton variant we should at first, analyze every implementation that makes the Singleton intent like showing in Sect. 2. Based on this large analysis, we extract involved information and its corresponding features.

Phase 2: Data creation Phase. To create the dataset we should identify firstly, the information needed to cover each feature. After that, we create snippets of code corresponding to extracting implementation from the analyses process (Learning Phase). Then we label these snippets of code depending on the corresponding output. These labeling snippets of code serve to create the dataset. We create 33 datasets corresponding to each information, the global size is 20000. The construction of a dataset is a very important task witch importantly influences the extraction process and the model performance. The data should contain a variety of implementations (including false implementation which can lead to predicted false-positive results). Figure 4 represents an example of an implementation that can be detected as a false positive in "Control instantiation".

```
private static C1 instance;
    private float ;
    private C1(){  }
    public static C1 getInstance(){
        if (C2.instance2 == null)
            {instance1 = new C1 ();}
            return instance1;}
}
```

Fig. 4. Example of snippets code that can be filtered as false positive in "control instantiation"

Phase 3: Building RNN-LSTM Classifier Phase. By creating an ensemble of datasets in which we precise the type of output result we can then create our supervised classifier based on RNN-LSTM architecture. For each feature, a specific model is created, whose role is to carry out a classification task; whether binary or multiclass. The dataset will be split to train and test data. Using pre-labeled examples as training data, the RNN-LSTM Classifier learns inherent associations between text code and their labels. The characteristics extracted from the training step are fed to the classifier to make a prediction.

Phase 4: Testing Phase. We have extracted 200 java files from DPDf Corpus and labeled them corresponding to existing information in the java class. The labeled dataset serves to evaluate the RNN-LSTM Classifier.

5   Experimental Setup

5.1   Evaluation Protocol

The performance evaluation is done using statistical measures like the prediction rate and the recall rate. The prediction rate indicates the proportion of identifications witch were correct. It is defined as follows (1):

$$Prediction = \frac{TP}{TP + FP} \tag{1}$$

The recall represents the proportion of actual positives witch was identified correctly. It is defined as follows (2):

$$Recall = \frac{TP}{TP + FN} \tag{2}$$

where true positive (TP) and true negative (TN) are respectively numbers of positive and negative classes, which are correctly predicted by the classifier. However, false-positive (FP) and false-negative (FN) are respectively numbers of positive and negative classes witch are incorrectly predicted.

To fully evaluate the effectiveness of a model, we must check both measures. Unfortunately, precision and recall are often in tension, which means, improved precision typically reduces recall and vice versa. Therefore, the F1-Score is a necessary measure because it is considered the harmonic mean of Precision and Recall. His formula is as follows (3):

$$F1 - Score = \frac{2 * (precision * recall)}{(precision + recall)} \tag{3}$$

In the case of multi-classes classification, it is the average of the score F1 of each class with a weighting according to the average parameter.

5.2   Experimental Results

Reported Results. Most results are slightly varied at each run, and there are no striking differences in the model's performance. Using our training dataset, the RNN-LSTM Classifier can predict most of the labels (features) accurately, reaching a Precision of more than 80+% and a Recall of 70+ %. Table 2 shows the results obtained from evaluating RNN-LSTM Classifier with the extracted DPD$_f$ Corpus. As is remarkable from the results most of the features are easily recognized by the LSTM classifier (Table 3).

Reported Variants. Our approach is an improvement of the approach D-cubed proposed by [1], therefore at this stage, we have chosen to compare our approach with this one. The comparison is based on the different reported variants.

Table 2. RNN-LSTM classifiers results in features extraction

Features	Measures			Features	Measures		
	Precision (%)	Recall (%)	F1-score (%)		Precision (%)	Recall (%)	F1-score (%)
IRE	100	100	100	RINEC	90.3	88.7	89.49
IRI	100	100	100	CS	93.26	89.78	91.48
CA	98	99	98.49	HGM	87.46	80.03	167.49
GOD	93,1	90.2	91.6	DC	91.25	95.87	93.5
AA	100	89	94.17	RR	96.4	94.28	95.32
SR	98	96	96.98	CNI	93.5	87.4	90.34
ON	86.35	82.96	84.62	CII	94.5	95.29	94.89
COA	95.36	96.87	96.1	DM	93.41	92.56	92.98
HC	89.6	90.45	90.02	GMS	83.52	87.6	85.51
ILC	94.8	92.4	93.58	IGO	93.42	88.69	90.99
GAM	82.65	84.07	83.35	LNI	82.6	85.95	84.24
PSI	81.79	82.36	82.07	SCI	84.34	80.3	82.27
GSM	85.9	80.05	82.87	SB	88.33	88.33	88.33
PST	88.96	81.23	84.91	AFL	87.32	80.01	83.5
INC	82.45	80.36	81.39	CAFB	89.5	72.8	80.29
EC	90.8	82.6	86.5	GT	88.69	92.48	90.54
RINIC	92.78	84.6	88.5				

Table 3. Compared D-cubed and proposed approach reported variants

Reported variants	D-cubed	Proposed approach
Eager instantiation	√	√
Lazy instantiation	√	√
Replaceable instance	√	√
Subclassed singleton	√	√
Different placeholder	√	√
Different access point	√	√
Limiton	√	√

(continued)

Table 3. (*continued*)

Reported variants	D-cubed	Proposed approach
Delegated construction	✓	✓
Uncontrolled usage (inner class)	✓	✓
Social Singleton	–	✓
Generic Singleton	–	✓

The D-cubed has proposed SQL queries to recover 9 Singleton variants. However, the 33 features proposed in our work make possible the definition of 11 variants.

6 Conclusion and Future Works

Deep Learning (DL) has been increasingly leveraged for source code treatment. RNN and its variations in particular was the most used DL architecture dealing with code sequence analysis. In our work and intending to identify Singleton's design patterns in his different implementation, we have defined a set of features that can effectively represent the aim of each various. Based on detailed features used in the literature along with detailed analyses we propose 33 features. To be able to create performed models we use a specific elaborated dataset in which we train the LSTM Classifier for each feature. The experimental result proves the technique's performance in extracting proposed features.

This work represents the first step to Singleton variant detection. In the next work, we proceed to use the proposed features and the detailed analysis to finish the detection process. On another side, we can use the same technique to identify other design patterns.

References

1. Stencel, K., Węgrzynowicz, P.: Implementation variants of the singleton design pattern. In: Meersman, R., Tari, Z., Herrero, P. (eds.) OTM 2008. LNCS, vol. 5333, pp. 396–406. Springer, Heidelberg (2008). https://doi.org/10.1007/978-3-540-88875-8_61
2. Goodfellow, I., Bengio, Y., Courville, A.: Deep Learning. Vol. 1. MIT Press Cambridge (2016)
3. Hindle, A., Barr, E.T., Su, Z., Gabel, M., Devanbu, P.: On the naturalness of software. In: Software Engineering (ICSE). 34th International Conference 2012, pp. 837–847. IEEE (2012)
4. Najam, N., Aldeida, A., Zhengc, Y.: Feature-based software design pattern detection (2021)
5. Fujaba. https://web.cs.upb.de/archive/fujaba. Accessed 12 Apr 2022
6. Paakki, J., Karhinen, A., Gustafsson, J., Nenonen, L., Verkamo, A.I.: Software metrics by architectural pattern mining. In: Proceedings of the International Conference on Software: Theory and Practice, pp. 325–332 (2000)
7. Bernardi, M.L., Cimitile, M., Di Lucca, G.: Design pattern detection using a DSL-driven graph matching approach. J. Softw. Evolut. Process **26**(12), 1233–1266 (2014)
8. Gamma, E., Helm, R., Johnson, R.E., Vlissides, J.M.: Design Patterns: Elements of Reusable Object-oriented Software. Addison-Wesley Longman Publishing Co., Inc., Boston (1995)
9. Mayvan, B.B., Rasoolzadegan, A.: Design pattern detection based on the graph theory. Knowl. Based Syst. **120**, 211–225 (2017)

10. Zanoni, M.: Data mining techniques for design pattern detection, Ph.D. thesis, Milano, Italy (2012)
11. Hu, X., Li, G., Xia, X., Lo, D., Jin, Z.: Deep code comment generation. In: 2018 IEEE/ACM 26th International Conference on Program Comprehension (ICPC), pp. 200–210. IEEE (2018)
12. McBurney, P.W., McMillan, C.: Automatic source code summarization of context for Java methods. IEEE Trans. Softw. Eng. **42**, 103–119 (2015)
13. McBurney, P.W., McMillan, C.: An empirical study of the textual similarity between source code and source code summaries. Empir. Softw. Eng. **21**(1), 17–42 (2014). https://doi.org/10.1007/s10664-014-9344-6
14. Nazar, N., Jiang, H., Gao, G., Zhang, T., Li, X., Ren, Z.: Source code fragment summarization with small-scale crowdsourcing based features. Front. Comp. Sci. **10**(3), 504–517 (2016). https://doi.org/10.1007/s11704-015-4409-2
15. Moreno, L., Marcus, A., Pollock, L., Vijay-Shanker, K.: Jsummarizer: an automatic generator of natural language summaries for java classes. In: 2013 21st International Conference on Program Comprehension (ICPC), pp. 230–232. IEEE (2013)
16. Sherstinsky. A.: Fundamentals of recurrent neural network (RNN) and long short-term memory (LSTM) network. J. Phys. D Nonlinear Phenom. **404**, 132306 (2020)
17. Chung, J., Gulcehre, C., Cho, K., Bengio, Y.: Empirical evaluation of gated recurrent neural networks on sequence modeling. arXiv: 1412.3555 (2014)

Correction to: Long Short-Term Memory Based Photoplethysmography Biometric Authentication

Khawla Ben Salah⬛, Mohamed Othmani⬛, and Monji Kherallah⬛

Correction to:
Chapter "Long Short-Term Memory Based
Photoplethysmography Biometric Authentication" in:
C. Bădică et al. (Eds.): *Advances in Computational Collective*
***Intelligence*, CCIS 1653,**
https://doi.org/10.1007/978-3-031-16210-7_45

The originally published version of chapter 45 contained the following errors: the Author's name was misspelled and wrong affiliation was erroneously provided. This has been corrected: Author's name has been changed to "Ben Salah" and the affiliation has been revised as "Technology, Energy, and Innovative Materials (TEMI), Gafsa, Tunisia".

The updated original version of this chapter can be found at
https://doi.org/10.1007/978-3-031-16210-7_45

Author Index

Printed in the United States
by Baker & Taylor Publisher Services